Gone
is the
Ancient
Glory

Gone
is the
Ancient
Glory

Spanish Town, Jamaica
1534–2000

James Robertson

Ian Randle Publishers
Kingston • Miami

First published in Jamaica, 2005 by
Ian Randle Publishers Ltd
Box 686, 11 Cunningham Avenue
Kingston 6
www.ianrandlepublishers.com

NATIONAL LIBRARY OF JAMAICA CATALOGUING IN PUBLICATION DATA

Robertson, James
'Gone is the Ancient glory!' : Spanish Town, Jamaica, 1534–2000 /
James Robertson

     p. ;   cm

Includes index

ISBN 976-637-197-0 (pbk)
ISBN 976-637-198-9

1. Spanish Town (Jamaica) – History   2. Jamaica – History   3. Jamaica – Social
conditions   4. Jamaica – Economic conditions 5. Jamaica – Politics and government
I.   Title

972.92   dc 21

Parts of chapter 1 of the present work were sketched in 'Location! Location! Location!
Placing Jamaica's New Urban Centre in 1534' *Archaeology Jamaica* n.s. 19 (forthcoming);
some of chapters 3 and 4 appeared in a slightly different version in 'Architectures of
Confidence? Spanish Town, Jamaica, 1655–1792' in Barbara Arciszewska and Elizabeth
McKellar eds. *Reconstructing British Classicism: New Approaches to Eighteenth-Century
Architecture*, Aldershot: Ashgate, 2004, 227–258 while arguments in the epilogue were
rehearsed in, 'Inherited cityscapes: Spanish Town, Jamaica', in Gunilla Malm, ed., *Towards
an Archaeology of Buildings: Contexts and Concepts* British Archaeological Reports,
International Series II86, Oxford: Archaeopress, 2003, 89–104.

Cover image: T. Picken, 'Scene in Jamaica, 1st August, 1838', cover from
*Quarterly Papers for the use of the Weekly and Monthly Contributors to the
Baptist Missionary Society* 77 (January, 1841), (Courtesy, National Library of Jamaica)

Cover and book design by Robert Harris

Set in Adobe Garamond 11/14.5 x 24
Printed and bound in the USA

for
L.L.S.

Contents

—

Illustrations

Acknowledgements

*T*HIS STUDY WOULD not have been undertaken without a two-year research fellowship from the University of the West Indies, Mona, which allowed me time to think, an opportunity to read beyond the late seventeenth century and, above all, the chance to write most of it. I am grateful to my then Dean, Joseph Pereira and to Lorna Murray, then at the University Research Office and to the committee of the University's Principal, Registrar and deans who supported my application. Grants from the University's Research and Publications fund have assisted with the costs of map making and in obtaining some illustrations.

Support for this project from the Jamaica National Heritage Trust, then under Ainsley Henriques's genial stewardship, provided an invaluable rod and staff. I am grateful to the Trust's Board for voting to provide research support for this project and for all the help I received from staff members as the work progressed including Kendry Jackson, Shirley Robertson, Lloyd Wright, Georgia Brown and Roderick Ebanks.

In Spanish Town the late Deryck Roberts and the late Trevor Goldson, two local residents and persistent advocates for the old capital, were both helpful in introducing me to their home town.

I am very grateful to the staff at the Jamaica Archives, to Sophia Moulton, Elizabeth Williams, and Raquel Stratchan. At the Island Records Office, now in Central Village, Joyce Brown and Peter Williams were always hospitable. In downtown Kingston thanks are due to John Aarons, then the National Librarian and to Eppy Edwards and their staff at the National Library of Jamaica, particularly Yvonne Clarke and Sharlene Blake and to Bernard Jankee and his team at the African Caribbean Institute of Jamaica. At the National Gallery of Jamaica Irina Leyva González, then of the Education Department, helped me to find my way, Karen Chung-Williams helped with obtaining photographs while David Boxer kindly showed me some remarkable early photographs from his own collection. In St Andrew Fr

Gerard McLaughlin made me welcome at the Roman Catholic Archives held at the Archbishop's Chancery. Last, but hardly least, the staff at the University of the West Indies Library, particularly Patricia Dunn, Joan Vacciana, Frances Salmon, Gracelyn Cassell and Paulette Kerr all provided invaluable assistance that extended far beyond 'going the extra mile'.

I am also grateful to the Baptist Missionary Society, David Buisseret, the William L. Clements Library at the University of Michigan, the Jamaica Archives, the John Carter Brown Library at Brown University, the National Gallery of Jamaica, the National Land Survey, the National Library of Jamaica, and the Victoria and Albert Museum for granting permission to reproduce images in their care.

This study also draws on material held in a fair number of libraries off the island. These include the library at Beloit College, in Beloit, Wisconsin, and at the University of Wisconsin, Madison. In the UK, Jamaican sources at the National Archives, then the Public Record Office, and the British Library; the Baptist Missionary Society's Collections held at the Angus Library at Regent's Park College, Oxford; the Bodleian Library, Friends' House Library; the Institute of Commonwealth Studies; the Institute of Historical Research; the London Metropolitan Archives; the Archives at the School of Oriental and African Studies Library; the National Army Museum Library; the National Library of Scotland, the National Maritime Museum's Caird Library; Rhodes House Library, the Royal Botanical Gardens Archives and the Wellcome Library for the History of Medicine all helped. In Richmond, Virginia, I was able to consult collections held in the Library of Virginia and at the Virginia Historical Society. In Williamsburg the Colonial Williamsburg Foundation's Library and Archives were very hospitable. In Chicago both the Newberry Library and the Chicago Historical Society held useful material, as did the Georgia Historical Society in Savannah.

A number of friends have looked at chapters at different stages: Lesley-Gail Atkinson, Fred Burwell, Piers Cain, Rollo Crookshank, Cathy Fisher, Ainsley Henriques, Janet Robertson, Bonnie Sturtz, John Sturtz, Linda Sturtz, Waibinte Wariboko and Gail Terry each found the time to comment on one or more. Roy Augier, Thera Edwards, Cecil Gutzmore, Beverly Hamilton, Norma Harrack, Kameika Murphy and Verene Shepherd all told me stories about Spanish Town. Philip Allsworth-Jones showed me a forthcoming summary of the excavations at the White Marl site, Patrick Bryan allowed me to consult his English translation of Morales Padrón's *Jamaica Española* and Veront Satchell let me see his article on Jamaica's railways prior to publication. Many more fellow workers in the field have generously provided references, including Philip Allsworth-Jones, Robert Barker, David Boxer, Erna Brodber, Trevor Burnard, Rollo Crookshank, Thera Edwards, Simone Gigliotti, John Gilmore, Juana Green, Ainsley Henriques, Jenny Jemmott, Mark Jenner, Alaric Josephs, Rupert Lewis, Paul Lovejoy, Shakira Maxwell, Sue Mills, Kathleen Monteith, Jacob Moore, Pat Mohammed, Christa Peatley, Steve Porter, April Shelford, Pauline Simmonds, Matthew Smith, Holly Snyder, Linda Sturtz and Swithin Wilmot. Thera Edwards also drafted the maps. April Shelford suggested I should quote Leslie Alexander's poem in my title. The team at Ian Randle Publishers remained helpful and patient, while Glory Robertson's copy-editing combed out obscurities. Whatever else such a long list of acknowledgements may demonstrate, with so many benevolent godparents and helping hands, all of this book's remaining flaws can only be mine.

Abbreviations

AKA	Archdiocese of Kingston Archives, Roman Catholic Chancery, Archbishop's House, Kingston
BL	British Library, London
Add Mss.	Additional Manuscripts
King's Mss.	King's Manuscripts
Sloane Mss.	Sloane Manuscripts
Bodl	Bodleian Library, Oxford
Rawl	Rawlinson Manuscripts
BMS	Baptist Missionary Society Papers, Angus Library, Regents Park College, Oxford
CLM	William L. Clements Library, University of Michigan, Ann Arbor
HEH	Henry E. Huntington Library and Art Gallery, San Marino
IRO	Island Records Office, Registrar General's Department, Spanish Town
JA	Jamaica Archives, Spanish Town
JNHT	Jamaica National Heritage Trust, Kingston
MMS	Wesleyan Methodist Missionary Society, Archives, School of Oriental and African Studies, University of London
NGJ	National Gallery of Jamaica, Kingston
NLJ	National Library of Jamaica, Kingston
HN	Historical Notes
NLS	National Library of Scotland, Edinburgh
NMM	Caird Library, National Maritime Museum, Greenwich
PRO	The National Archives, Public Records Office, London
ADM	Admiralty

C	Court of Chancery
CO	Colonial Office
HO	Home Office
MINT	Royal Mint
PRO	Public Records Office, Gifts and Deposits
WO	War Office
RHL	Rhodes House Library, Oxford
USPG	United Society for the Propagation of the Gospel
UCSD	Manderville Library, University of California, San Diego, La Jolla
UWI, Mona	West Indies Collection, University Library, University of the West Indies, Mona Campus, Kingston
UWI, St Augustine	Westindiana Collection, University Library, University of the West Indies, St Augustine Campus, St Augustine, Trinidad

Insertions into quotations are indicated by square brackets [ ], cuts are marked by . . .

'St. Jago de la Vega, the ancient city' [1]

Gone is the ancient glory!
    Oh, the blank that's left;
Dead are the lusty patriots!
    Oh, the remnant stock.
        Once there flapped a mighty flag:
        Never tongue or toil to lag;
        Now there droops a tattered rag:
        Only sloth and idle brag –
    Oh, the ancient City!

Gone is the golden sunshine!
    Oh, the gloom that reigns;
Hushed is the martial music!
    Oh, the dirge that lives.
        Once the Council-hall was filled:
        Never manly heart was dulled;
        In that Hall the swallows build:
        In those bosoms pride is stilled –
    Oh, the Ancient City!

Dwells there *still* the classic grandeur!
    Oh, the joy to see;
Live there *still* the old traditions!
    Oh, the pride to know.
        Pile and statue stand supreme;
        Deeds and heroes grandly gleam;
        Cobre, dear historic stream,
        Murmurs on 'neath Cynthia's beam –
    Ah, the ancient City!

Leslie Alexander
27.1.1895

Approaching Jamaica's Old Capital

A LARGE METAL sign that says 'Welcome to Spanish Town, founded 1534' greets drivers on the main road west from Kingston. This is often all they see as a bypass swings around the town. The lines of cars cross an agricultural landscape undergoing development, where new houses sprout from fields while shops and roadside warehouses stand among cow pasture and scrub. Despite the tentative face presented by its latest suburbs, Spanish Town remains a long-established city. Turn off the bypass and drive into its old centre, and there is far more to see.

This book offers an historical introduction to Spanish Town. It examines the development of a small settlement at a major crossroads beside a ford, tracing how residents and visitors have viewed a distinctive town whose streets and spaces have an important history disproportional to its size. As the long-term seat of government for the island, initially laid out by Spanish settlers in 1534 and then taken over by the English after they seized Jamaica in 1655, the town provided a political and social hub. This was where decisions were made. Money was spent here, too. As a result a fairly small town could support an impressive range of artisan craftsmen, while its market drew from a wide area. The seat of government was transferred to Kingston in 1871, but the old centre still retains the imprint of its former authority and prosperity. The survival of impressive public buildings along with distinctive streetscapes has earned it candidate status as a UNESCO World Heritage Site. It fully deserves that status. The town's past repays exploration and explanation.

1

Spanish Town's names are often the first unfamiliar item newcomers encounter, beginning with the choice of names. Two names remain current: Spanish Town, its English name and St Jago de la Vega, avowedly Spanish. Over a history of nearly five centuries the names assigned to the town have shifted to and fro. We do not know what the island's first Taino inhabitants called this ford, though we do know that they used it. For the town's initial Spanish and Portugese founders, it was the 'town in the fields' (Villa de la Vega) that provided their colony's principal settlement and administrative centre for 120 years. After the English conquest of Jamaica in 1655, it became the headquarters for the invaders' garrison; it then housed the administrative and legal hub of their colony for another 215 years. For a generation, the English settlers simply called it 'the Town' or else 'the Spainish Town'.[2] However, when taking over the Spaniards' town they also retained the name of St Iago, after St James, Spain's patron saint, as one of their names for the place. Under English rule the town's alternating names 'Spanish Town' and 'St Jago de la Vega' came to reflect the variety of its functions. St Jago (or Iago) de la Vega continued in legal documents, which were common in the seat of the colony's Assembly, law courts and archives.[3] The circulation of the weekly newspaper, the *St Iago de la Vega Gazette* among the island's planter class retained a wider currency for the more formal title during the nineteenth century, and the revival of the 'St Jago' title for Spanish Town's St Jago High School in 1959 helps to keep the older name alive. But, as an American journalist observed in the mid-nineteenth century, the town is 'now and for more than a hundred years called Spanishtown by the people'.[4]

It is a historic town – a town with old buildings, certainly, but also a town that provided a stage for historic events. This history examines how the material culture of Spanish Town, including these buildings, has shaped the history of the town that its residents knew. It offers a history of long-established urban spaces. We may now know how particular incidents played out here, but in what ways would local traditions shape the ways that these events were remembered? In making sense of Spanish Town's past, the advice that Ursula Le Guin recently offered to writers of fiction addresses the central issues:

> The way one does research into nonexistent history is to tell the story and find out what happened. I believe this isn't very different from what historians of the so-called real world do. Even if we are present at some historic event – do we comprehend it – can we even remember it – until we tell it as a story? And for

events in times or places outside our own experience, we have nothing to go on but the stories other people tell us. Past events exist, after all, only in memory, which is a form of imagination. The event is real *now*, but once it's *then*, its continuing reality is entirely up to us, dependent on our energy and honesty. If we let it drop from memory, only imagination can recall the least glimmer of it.[5]

This history of Spanish Town tries to recover long-past imaginations and in doing so, it retells stories. Because much of this book's narrative covers unfamiliar ground, very basic 'who', 'what', 'why' and 'how' questions all need to be addressed. This information can provide foundations for the broader 'so what' and 'how was this understood' questions, whose answers shaped the ways that people living in an old Jamaican town recognized its 'history'. We can then move on from identifying what happened there and when, to consider how some actions were understood.

Townspeople told stories about their town. We can hear echoes from their storytelling in the petitions presented to later governments by residents with an agenda to pursue. Two events remained particularly significant in shaping local identities. The individual petitioners seeking cathedral canonries or other grants from the Spanish Crown, who claimed that their kinsmen had rallied to Governor Don Fernando Melgarejo de Córdoba in 1603, when he and 60 musketeers held off an English attack, pinned their hopes for royal gratitude on a skirmish that (with or without the reported appearance of Spain's patron saint, St James) had become central in local self-definitions.[6] In a second instance, the repeated invocations of the 30 – or was it 70? – wagons used to carry the colony's archives back from Kingston in 1758 every time townspeople restated their case for maintaining the colony's 'Seat of Government' in Spanish Town, suggests that this story also continued to be told and retold in the town.[7] The colonial bureaucrats who received the townspeoples' petitions might not have found the number of carts particularly relevant. By contrast, when local residents drafted their petitions the association between the storytellers' details and the punch line of Spanish Town's restored status appeared inseparable. These were tales with strong local resonances.

Townspeople were right to be proud of their town's distinctive past. History was made in Spanish Town. Islandwide or imperial policies declared there had general consequences, while some local actions provoked wider repercussions. So how should we proceed with the recovery of this past? Some lines of investigation are closed to us. Much of its oral history is lost. We no longer know many of the tales that earlier residents told about their town, the ghost and duppy stories, the murders and scandals, the street cries and, with them, the associations that residents made between places and incidents in the past.[8] Similarly, while quantifying exactly who was living in the town at particular junctures might well offer valuable precision, this is rarely an option in a town that was administered as a part of the larger parish of St Catherine. Listings of townspeople or householders made for tax or militia service fail to consider Spanish Town as a distinct unit and instead consolidate their figures into totals for the parish. A list of the inhabitants from 1754 that described only the town is exceptional.[9] No others survive.

There may be significant silences, but we can still frame broader questions. For individuals understanding what it meant to live in Spanish Town was a matter of acquiring a familiarity with different parts of the town. Associations assigned to particular landmarks and urban spaces not only gave an old town character; they helped shape residents' recognition of the town – and this included a historical dimension. In Spanish Town the streets themselves helped organize residents' descriptions. This was hardly surprising when, well into the 1930s, passers-by on the north side of the town's principal square could see the foundations from the former Abbot of Jamaica's church looming out of the crushed limestone marl that made up the road surface.[10] For those who knew it, the townscape displayed traces from its long history.

If Spanish Town's old buildings and inherited street plan prompted memories and associations among residents, generations of newcomers received very different impressions. In judging the island's administrative centre – or from 1871 its former administrative centre – they generally employed comparisons and, when measured against what it was not, Spanish Town did badly. The resulting dismissals fed into a long tradition. New Seville, the settlement on the north coast of Jamaica that had served as the Spaniards' first town between 1509 and 1534, had been embellished with substantial stone buildings, and the masons appear to have kept working there until the town was abandoned.[11] In Spanish Town the best that could be said of its buildings during the Spanish period was that the 'houses were for the most part built of plaster, wood and tiles, but well constructed and designed; and there were some of brick . . .'.[12] Under English rule the town was never as grand as visitors expected for the seat of government of a thriving sugar colony. An army officer's comment in 1764 prefigured a host of subsequent criticisms when he judged it 'a confused poor Town'. His disapproval seemed particularly strong because the verdict followed close on the heels of positive first impressions of Kingston, which had appeared 'large and very well Inhabited, the Streets spacious, and regularly laid out, cutting one another at right angles . . .'.[13] Successive European travellers continued to compare Spanish Town's narrow streets unfavourably with Kingston's more symmetrical plan and broader streets. Anthony Trollope, the English author, offered a particularly scathing denunciation in 1859, when he found it a dilapidated, dull town with stray pigs the only living creatures in its streets.[14] These dismissals then helped shape metropolitan assumptions about a distant colonial centre. Meanwhile in-comers' incomprehension dictated initial responses towards the town's material past, be it in the 1530s, in laying out the town's plan, when the first Spanish settlers flattened burial mounds erected by their indigenous Taino predecessors; or, later, when settlers fresh from Britain dismissed the unfamiliar proportions of a foreign 'Spanish Town'. We do need to recognize the persisting edginess of successive outsiders towards this long-settled town in making sense of its past. For 300 years its streets and buildings have not fitted into the expectations that newcomers brought with them.

It did take time to get to know the place. Its residents then made alternative comparisons. Hence, when Edward Long, an eighteenth-century historian of Jamaica who had a house in Spanish Town, sought to describe the differences between Spanish Town and Kingston, he cited the surfaces of their roads. In Spanish Town these were 'repaired with pebbles brought in from the river-course, which prevents their being clogged with mud, as some other towns in the West Indies are, and answer the end of a regular pavement by not admitting the rain-water to stagnate'; Kingston's thoroughfares, in contrast, simply appeared a muddy slough.[15] The associations that townspeople made could extend further still, with the surfaces of its streets continuing to provide a distinctive element of later memories. Trying to describe Jamaica 'fifty years ago' in the late 1950s one Spanish Town resident chose to recall the difference between the town's early twentieth-century street sweepers using 'green bushes of branches of trees' as brooms with their successors' adoption of 'straw and other types of broom'.[16] This contrast highlighted a general transition over the mid-twentieth century, as tarmac superseded marl as the main road surface in urban Jamaica. However, what he recalled as distinctive about this development was neither the asphalt coating that motorists take for granted, nor even the all-pervading white dust that used to characterize driving in the island but, instead, the street sweeping on that new asphalt – and this through the changing materials and associated rustling of the brooms used. Recognizing which changes individuals look back on as distinctive is tricky, but can illuminate the specific experiences of living in a particular place at a particular time.

For people who do live in a town, the features they identify as characterizing its spaces or defining historical changes are not always the ones that people passing through may expect.[17] If sounds could jog one former resident's memories, then today tastes and smells define these urban spaces. A returning Jamaican who spent a summer in Spanish Town in 1995 recalls not only the crash course in current popular music that his neighbours' sound systems offered him, but also the foul taste of the local tap water. Today's undergraduates riding the evening buses back to Spanish Town can recognize when they reach their stop because of the smell of grease from a fried chicken shop beside it.[18] The particular sights, sounds, tastes and smells may change over time but they still matter. In discussing an old city this study attempts to identify and interpret what successive generations considered 'historical'. We need to acknowledge continuity yet contemporaries recognized change too. The challenge is to try and identify what changes townspeople noticed, while bearing in mind where continuities shaped their experiences.

Trying to appraise a town's past in a way that takes account of contemporaries' views – positive and negative – does offer many challenges but should provide fresh perspectives too. In researching this history we can draw on the scholarly efforts of several former residents of Spanish Town. Prominent among these are Edward Long the historian and William Augustus Feurtado, a long-term resident, who in 1890 gave a public lecture that crammed a host of local anecdotes into *A Forty-Five Years' Reminiscence* of the Spanish Town he knew.[19] In the twentieth century two public servants undertook further work rescuing and conserving the records this study depends on. Jacob Andrade was a long-serving parish clerk whose compilations on St Catherine's parish and Jamaica's Jewish community include a mass of useful material, while Clinton Black, the first Government Archivist of Jamaica, also wrote a pioneering guide to Spanish Town in 1960.[20] The information incorporated in each of their histories is valuable in its own right, while the choices that successive local authors made about what to include and exclude also illuminate wider assumptions about what appeared 'historical' in the societies where they wrote.

This study tracing the history of a West Indian town over nearly 500 years builds on the solid foundations laid by its local historians. It then sets the changes in the town and townscapes that they knew so well into broader Jamaican and imperial contexts. At different stages in the colony's past, actions in the capital both shaped and reflected developments islandwide. This prominence was despite the defining role of the island's rural economy in shaping Jamaican society, and despite too the competing importance of first Port Royal and later Kingston as the island's primary commercial ports. Much of the evidence is drawn from material held in Jamaican libraries and archives, as are most of the illustrations, though I have not hesitated to draw on visitors' descriptions which, because they were written by outsiders, can incorporate descriptions of things so familiar that local writers took them for granted.[21] As this book is written to introduce a general audience to Spanish Town's past the first or second endnote to each chapter lists existing studies of the periods and topics discussed. However, this study was not planned as a history of Jamaica. Readers already have several excellent overviews to hand.[22]

This book is an essay in Jamaican urban history. There is not yet a distinct tradition of writing urban histories in Jamaica or, indeed, in the English-speaking West Indies. However, valuable studies of late seventeenth-century Port Royal and of eighteenth- and nineteenth-century Kingston were completed in the 1970s.[23] Over the last few years a number of books and theses have addressed developments in Kingston, Martha Brae, Port Maria and the village of Woodside in the parish of St Mary, besides a useful collection of essays on 'Port Cities' – a focus that excludes Spanish Town – along with fresh work on Bridgetown in Barbados and perceptive studies on Basse-Terre in Guadeloupe and on Georgetown in Guyana.[24] In interpreting the wider social functions of towns the rationale offered for a recent study of towns in rural Ireland applies equally strongly in Jamaica: 'over much of its history, Ireland has been a relatively lightly urbanised society, and the bulk of its population has lived in the countryside.' This is certainly the case in Jamaica between the 1650s and, perhaps, the 1950s. In 1832 around 92 per cent of the island's slaves were living on rural properties. But, as the Irish analysis continues, 'towns and villages have provided vital economic and cultural hubs, profoundly influencing, as well as being influenced by their rural hinterlands'.[25] Or, as another historian argued in explaining his interest in the urban past in the American South, 'the daily life of southern history may have occurred mostly on farms and plantations, but the key stages for momentous change were the towns and cities that mobilized people and ideas'.[26] So too in Jamaica. All of which means that a history of Spanish Town examines a town whose experiences have lain near the centre of much of the island's past.

Contemporaries, visitors and residents alike, recognized Spanish Town's importance within Jamaican society. As the island's capital city – its 'Seat of Government' – Spanish Town housed the colony's Governor, its administration and its law courts. Under Spanish rule it also housed the principal cleric, the Abbot of Jamaica and the main friary too. The town was where much of the island's politics was played out, so that leading planters kept houses there for their attendance at Assembly Sessions or at the law courts. Free spending visitors and their households helped support not only the artisans who plied their crafts in workshops in the town, but also the market gardeners, many of them enslaved, who could find purchasers for their ground provisions and fruit in the town's Sunday markets. As the island's capital Spanish Town was a public stage furnished with public buildings, and as the capital of a rich colony some of those buildings were remarkably lavish. This splendour then outlasted its original settings. Much of the history of Spanish Town has not only been played out before impressive architectural backdrops, but often in front of architecture commissioned to embellish very different scenes. During the first English century in Jamaica buildings inherited from the Spanish colony remained resilient features in the town. Later, during the nineteenth century, when Jamaica's economy was in decline, Spanish Town retained a remarkable set of mid-eighteenth-century public and private buildings. Even after the seat of government was transferred to Kingston, many older buildings survived the transfer. Architectural continuity then testified to former functions and lost splendour rather than reflecting current business. Townspeople have grappled with the issues of 'heritage' almost from their town's foundation: the town's 'ancient glory' along with the fact that it has so often appeared to be 'gone', helped shape a very different identity for 'the ancient city' than that of its neighbour, the often-burnt, often-rebuilt Kingston.

Spanish Town is an old town that has been an urban centre for nearly 500 years – and well over twice that span if the indigenous Taino settlement, a mile to the east, is considered too. In examining this long urban past we encounter a whole sequence of overlapping towns. Spanish Town is therefore unlike many of the former seats of government established by various

European powers in their transatlantic empires, whose administrative centres were often relocated within a generation or two. Several North American states inherited a whole string of former capitals: St Mary's City in Maryland, Jamestown and Williamsburg in Virginia, New Bern in North Carolina, Charleston in South Carolina, or Savannah and Augusta in Georgia. In striking contrast, St Jago de la Vega was already a long-established centre when the English seized Jamaica. The town's administrative functions then survived the English conquest so that except for a hiatus in the mid-1750s, a town laid out by Spanish colonists served as Jamaica's capital for a further two centuries. Such continuity meant that old buildings were expanded and recased, new buildings were erected on old sites while further properties were divided and subdivided. Individual buildings generally follow the proportions of Anglo-American architecture, albeit adapted by local building traditions to accommodate a tropical climate and take advantage of local materials, but the earlier streets retain the widths of the preceding Spanish town plan.[27] The accumulation of rebuildings and subdivisions has produced a complicated series of urban landscapes with old, fairly old and new buildings all juxtaposed along still older streets.

This architectural legacy is distinctive in its own right. The physical fabric of the town consequently provides further evidence of the town's history. Spanish Town's streets and squares still hold an impressive array of eighteenth- and nineteenth-century buildings. A very rough estimate proposes pre-1920 dates for 142 structures, with 79, just over half, surviving from the period before 1830. As early elements in surviving domestic buildings are often concealed under subsequent alterations, the provisional looking-in-over-the-front-gate attributions offered in this survey may even understate how many older houses and shops survive.[28] The total remains high, although demolitions still occur. What is clear is that in Spanish Town's old buildings and inherited streets, in its property divisions and their subdivisions, we can trace the ways that successive generations of townspeople have made their impress, shaping and reshaping the island's former official urban centre.[29]

Reusing old buildings and boundaries shaped the town's streets after the English took over after they conquered the island in 1655. Similar processes continued when further streets and lot lines were laid out as the capital of a sugar-rich, mid- and late eighteenth-century colony expanded. At first, if tenants were scarce, a newly laid-out block might hold only one or two buildings and outhouses surrounded by a yard and trees. Over subsequent

FIGURE O.I An old house on Martin Street, Spanish Town. The block has changed around this structure, with a garage on one side and new shops rising behind it. (author's photograph).

generations, further structures were crammed into these open spaces. Modern construction is often wedged in beside existing buildings, so that old structures stand beside far more recent neighbours. This piecemeal infilling means that there are few blocks of houses all dating from a particular phase of rebuilding in the old town centre, as there are in many more recent cities where builders filled in fields or estates with new streets as a single speculation. During the twentieth century hurricane damage, petrol stations, parking slots and, indeed, the salvaging of old bricks for resale, all gnawed away at individual blocks, while new additions, new roofs and even new window frames transformed the appearance of other houses.[30] However, unlike all too many historic towns, later developments filled in Spanish Town's older streetscapes rather than simply erasing them.

The contrasts with other cities therefore go further: plain good luck has helped produce striking divergences between Spanish Town's past and the experiences of many other Caribbean towns. No single disaster defines its townspeople's understanding of their history, like the massive Jamaican earthquake that shook two-thirds of Port Royal into the sea in 1692, the hurricane that flattened Savanna la Mar in 1780, or the volcanic eruptions that buried St Pierre in Martinique in 1902 and, since 1995, have been covering Montserrat's Plymouth.[31] Spanish Town has also been spared the fires that punctuate the histories of Kingston and Montego Bay, of Barbados's Bridgetown and of Trinidad's Port of Spain. Nor, after the English invasion of Jamaica in 1655, has Spanish Town again endured the capture, looting and destruction which remained the experiences of so many towns across the Eastern Caribbean in the late seventeenth and eighteenth centuries. Fears of fires would still spark its residents' imaginations, with townspeople worrying that with a higher wind, the flames which destroyed the old King's House in 1925 could have ignited the rest of their town. Fifty years later a childrens' novel, *Escape to Last Man Peak* written by Jean D'Costa for the first generation born in an independent Jamaica, starts with a fire destroying Spanish Town's district hospital and then depicts another blaze 'lighting up the sky over the town'.[32] In reality the old capital was spared those fictitious catastrophes too. Together all these non-events add up to a remarkable run of good fortune. This book reads the material culture – the standing archaeology – that survives in Spanish Town as a foundation for writing a history of a distinctive place.

To comprehend this town's history we need to recognize its townspeople. From the start Spanish Town housed a mixture of ethnicities. The initial royal grant of privileges that established the Spanish township in 1534 was combined with further grants permitting the then treasurer of the island who had negotiated for the new town to import 30 African slaves and 20 families of Portuguese labourers to work on his sugar estate there.[33] Slavery remained a persistent presence, but so did freedom. Under Spanish rule the town housed people from a number of social groups: the Spanish-born governor and his household, certainly, along with island-born planters from a few intermarried Spanish families, but also families from Portugal and even a few secretly observing Jews. Up until the early seventeenth century some descendants of the island's original Tainos lived in its suburbs and worked in the town. It always housed a substantial African population; some free, many more enslaved. Under English rule the diversity of the social mix remained, although several of the component groups changed. The Europeans now included English and Irish with, from the early eighteenth century, increasing numbers of Scots. Jewish residents no longer needed to conceal their beliefs. From the 1690s they became a permanent presence in a town where most of the householders were seasonal. However, the principal continuity in residence from the Spanish period was among the town's free African and African Jamaican population. From the late 1650s this included some former members of the free *cimarrone* bands whose aid in the final stages of the protracted military conquest of Jamaica finally tipped the balance in favour of the English forces. An enslaved population was soon re-established. Along with all their other labours, the plots that the slaves cultivated provided most of the fruit and ground provisions offered for sale in the town market.

These resident African Jamaican populations shaped Spanish Town's longer term character. Their presence was conspicuous enough in the mid-eighteenth century, first through the individual free artisans, black and brown, who in the 1740s purchased plots on the newly developed streets to the west of the older Spanish-era town boundaries, then in the popular outbursts by such ordinary townspeople against the Governor who backed a 1750s project to shift the seat of the island's government to Kingston. The significance of these resident groups became even more apparent in the early nineteenth century, when Baptist and Wesleyan Methodist ministers led local churches which recruited townspeople. The English-born missionaries who came out to Jamaica after 1807 did sterling service – and provided very visible targets for the plantocracy's fury – in establishing congregations and then maintaining their vitality despite official disfavour. The local deacons and group leaders and, indeed, the ordinary members of these churches were essential too. After Emancipation the congregations remained influential forces within local society.

The town and its townspeople then underwent a further round of social transitions in the 1870s after the law courts, central administration and finally the Governor's own household were all relocated to Kingston. This move also transferred what remained of the colony's social junketing. The loss of long-established jobs, including renting out lodgings to litigants or feeding lawyers and their clients at taverns and cookhouses provoked wails of anguish from householders whose investments in leasehold property lost their value abruptly. However, the townspeople were still not sufficiently desperate to accept the Governor's proposed new University College inserted into the former public buildings. Lacking both students and local support it soon folded.

Despite all the bitter complaints that the government's move to Kingston provoked and then continued to generate for another 20 years, the old town does appear to have found some new roles. Once large brick houses proved un-leasable and were demolished, the sites did not lie idle. These spaces were reused for constructing small wooden 'cottages'. By the late nineteenth-century the town housed workers and their families from the nearby banana estates and remained the second largest urban centre in Jamaica. The social balance shifted too. By the late nineteenth century the remaining members of the town's local elite were able to enjoy a fairly self-contained social life. What seems even more significant, though it is more difficult to trace, is the parallel development of working-class social networks in Spanish Town. These proved particularly important as the town's economy faltered during the Great Depression of the late 1920s and '30s. In 1935 individuals affiliated with the town's pan-Africanist Universal Negro Improvement Association established a trade union.[34] Despite the unwilling-ness of the colonial Government to deal with such a body, the union's local leaders persisted in offering strategies and a voice for the town's working class and unemployed.

Post-Second World War policies aimed for development. Policymakers looked to build on different foundations, in part constructing factories on former banana fields lying empty across the Rio Cobre, but mostly using the road connections with Kingston upgraded by Depression-era and wartime public works schemes. A post-Second World War drift of householders across to Kingston's new suburbs abandoned Spanish Town's oldest town centre properties but then, in the 1970s and '80s, the tide turned, and a generation of Kingston commuters bought houses in new suburban developments outside Spanish Town. Clearly, being Kingston's near neighbour has shaped Spanish Town's modern economy. But, even as a dormitory town, Spanish Town still retains its own past, its own problems, and its own potential.

So where does this brisk summary leave us? Over the course of its history the town has combined three overlapping functions: first, providing a political and administrative centre for the colony and its dependent territories, second, offering a social hub for the island with a resident service population; and third, serving as a residential centre and market for the surrounding agricultural districts. Even as the first two roles have been transferred to Kingston, Spanish Town's Saturday market continues to provide a ready outlet for produce brought in from a wide hinterland. The recollections of a girl growing up in postwar Spanish Town, of her mother getting 'up at five in the morning to arrive at the market by six', along with the explanation that 'being early she got the pick of the fruits and vegetables and bought enough to last until the next market day', would have been as valid one, two, three and quite probably 400 years earlier.[35] Crafts and trades continue to survive, adapt and develop here. The public recognition offered in 1987 for the contribution to Jamaican culture made by another townswoman, 'Ma Lou', Mrs Louisa Jones, who continued to manufacture domestic pots using traditional African techniques, testified to both the high quality of the earthenware pottery that Mrs Jones and her family produced and to the continuing practice of much older traditions among some of the craftspeople who work in and around Spanish Town and sell in its markets.[36]

Spanish Town was always where the country met the town. During its nearly 500 years as an urban centre the town has offered a key site for the development of a specifically Jamaican culture. In the plantation economy the profits might indeed be generated in the cane pieces, cattle pens and coffee plantations of the countryside, but much of whatever was not immediately remitted to Europe was then spent in Jamaica's towns. The island's larger towns, in the late seventeenth century, Port Royal and Spanish Town, in the eighteenth, Kingston and Spanish Town, later joined by Montego Bay and Falmouth, all offered important 'centres of business activity, restless points of contact between classes and races', which, in turn, provided places where individual cultural overlaps and exchanges could blend into a distinct creole synthesis.[37] So how did this centre develop and how would the people who knew it, understand the past that still shapes its streets?

CHAPTER ONE

Location!
Location!
Location!

Establishing a Spanish City,
1534–1655

$\mathcal{E}$NGLISH VISITORS to Jamaica, be they Elizabethan pirates, conquering armies, eighteenth-century merchants, or nineteenth- and twentieth-century tourists, always found Spanish Town puzzling. They all asked why the 'Seat of Government' of what became the richest of Britain's eighteenth-century sugar islands should be located on a remote river crossing seven miles inland from a magnificent harbour. The question shows how deeply rooted their assumption was that the primary role for colonial towns was to provide centres for trade with England. St Jago de la Vega's location worked, but it was still a Spanish, not an English, choice.[1]

A Spanish Settlement

Over a century after Spanish Town's foundation a newcomer described its setting: 'The Town stands on almost plaine ground, but a little inclining towards the East, for the better fall of the Raines downe into the River, w[hi]ch is very shallow, & Runs a pretty distance below the Towne & Emptys it selfe into the Arme of the Sea.'[2] The site's location on a gradual slope

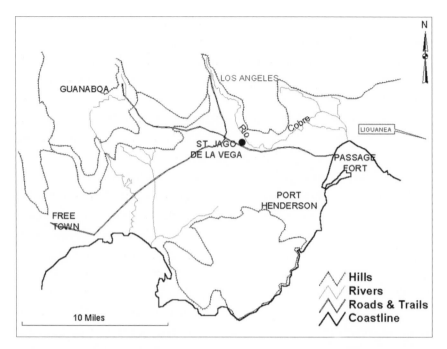

FIGURE 1.1 The local context for the town: the Rio Cobre Valley to the Ferry River and Old Harbour Bay.

towards the river appeared conspicuous, though it faced out towards the savanna to the west. The river provided the third key element, even if sailors who had just walked the seven miles up from the landing place at the river's mouth stressed the distance and that a shallow river was unnavigable. When the first Spanish settlers arrived to establish a town on the south side of the island the ford across the Rio Cobre here not only dictated the choice of this site but then shaped the town plan they laid out.

The town straddles a road junction rather than simply providing a convenient stopping place. Later residents could characterize its location as 'centrical with respect to the whole of the island', which made it 'extremely convenient for holding the chief courts of justice'.[3] In selecting a site on the south side of Jamaica for an administrative centre the resulting settlement benefited from its hub position in the network of routes across the island's central mountains as well as its proximity to what is now called Kingston Harbour. One track continued south along the west bank of the Rio Cobre and another extended the line of the main cross-island road south across the

savanna; both reached a sheltered landing place near where the river ran into
the harbour. Most east-west traffic along the south side of the island used this
ford, even though it was so far upstream and even though it remained liable
to closure by flash floods.[4] The going became far more difficult on the far
side of the Rio Cobre. Downstream from the crossing the swamps between
the Rio Cobre and the Ferry River and its tributaries to the east meant that
traffic between the Liguanea Plain and the St Catherine Plain would swing
inland here. There might be further fords nearer to the coast, but to find solid
going travellers were obliged to skirt the foot of the Red Hills.[5]

The Spanish settlers who laid out a town on the river's western bank were
encouraged to fix on this site by its position at the junction of a north-south
route with the principal east-west trail. To the north-west of the town runs
one of the two main routes through the island's central mountains. It uses the
gorge cut by the Rio Cobre, which the Spaniards called Boca del Agua,
literally Mouth of the Waters (and subsequently anglicised as the Bog Walk
Gorge). Early travellers coming across the island from the northern coastal
plain either left what is today the parish of St Mary where they followed the
Rio de Oro upstream to the inland valley of St Thomas in the Vale, or else
came east from today's parish of St Ann over the lower slopes of Mount
Diablo. Both routes then converged to follow the Rio Cobre south through
the Bog Walk Gorge, hugging the river's marginally less precipitous eastern
side along what would later be known as 'the River Road'. The river and trail
enter the southern coastal plain at Guanaboa, some ten and a half miles north
of the town. Southbound travellers would then cross to the west side of the
Rio Cobre, today using the Flat Bridge. This meant that they would not have
to ford the various tributaries of the Rio Cobre that enter the river's eastern
side further downstream. The route then cut south-east across country past
the settlement at Angels to join the main coastal trail just where it curved
inland to use this ford across the Rio Cobre. From its start the Spanish town
of Villa de la Vega or, literally, 'the town in the fields' was a crossroads town.

Geographical criteria explain the selection of this site in 1534. Some factors
were internal, determined by the few trails that cross the island's
mountainous topography and coastal plains. Others were external,
responding to the trade routes that began to traverse the Caribbean at that
juncture. In fixing on a site on the south side of the island to lay out the
colony's second capital the town's founders responded to wider shifts in
trading patterns within the Caribbean.

Villa de la Vega was not the settlers' first choice as a capital for Jamaica. Initially the Spaniards placed their administrative centre at New Seville, on the island's north coast at St Ann's Bay, the 'Santa Gloria' where Columbus spent a miserable year in his beached, waterlogged ships during 1503–04. The town was rebuilt after several fires, but its plan remained a fairly simple one with a single square in front of the church. Donations from the Spanish Court ensured that by the 1530s New Seville held not only a defensive turret built of stone but also an elaborate, if unfinished, chapel of worked cut-stone, a hospital and an aqueduct whose ruins would dominate the site.[6] The quantity of partially completed architectural stonework remaining in a Spanish-era stonemason's yard suggests that building projects remained in progress until the decision was made to abandon the town.[7] When New Seville was founded in 1509 its householders expected to establish a centre for assaying all the gold that they hoped would be mined in the mountains behind it. The settlement would also provide an *entrepôt*, offering a pivot point for the inter-island trade between the major Spanish territories concentrated in the West Indies. This had been the pattern followed for a new urban centre at Santiago de Cuba and, before that, in Hispaniola. By 1534, however, hopes that New Seville would become a centre for gold mining faded, because there was no gold to mine in Jamaica, and Spanish merchant ships were not anchoring there either. After a quarter century the ambitious port was a backwater, albeit a backwater graced with some splendid stone buildings. Several factors then combined to make the remaining Spanish settlers sufficiently dissatisfied with their existing settlement at New Seville to persuade them to abandon it and move to a new site on the south side of the island.

Shifting regional shipping patterns reduced New Seville's utility as a port. The arguments for remaining there appeared far less persuasive after the principal rationales that justified the original choice of the site failed to materialise. When it was founded, a port on the north shore of Jamaica faced the major artery of trade between the main Spanish settlement with relatively easy access from Santo Domingo and Puerto Rico to the east and to Santiago de Cuba to the north-east. The Spanish search for gold and land later shifted after Hernan Cortes sacked Mexico and after the news spread from the 1520s of Francisco Pizarro's achievements in subjugating the Inca civilization. By 1534 the reorganization of maritime trade patterns within a wider Caribbean, that included the mainland of Latin America and Mexico, would make a town sited on Jamaica's south coast appear far more appealing.

The West Indian islands ceased to be the primary destination for the fleets sailing from Spain to the transatlantic New World. In the new trading patterns that developed these fleets left Cadiz in two squadrons, one in spring for Mexico, the other in late July or August for the South American mainland. These convoys followed the same route across the Atlantic that Columbus pioneered on his second voyage: south-west for perhaps a week to the Canary Islands and then west for 25 days to Dominica or Guadeloupe.[8] From there the first squadron sailed west to Santo Domingo and the second south-west towards Cartagena. The Mexico-bound fleet left Santo Domingo and proceeded directly to Veracruz, to take aboard the accumulated wealth of New Spain in freshly minted gold and silver coins. Other island settlements were increasingly bypassed as the fleets were discouraged from making unscheduled stops. Rather than watching the ships passing along the north side of Jamaica en route to Mexico, townspeople looking for opportunities turned south where further westbound convoys now passed the south side of the island. The second squadron, the Tierra Firme Fleet, headed south-west for Cartagena and Porto Bello, where the ships loaded silver from the Peruvian mines which had been shipped up to Panama and portaged across to Porto Bello.[9] Both squadrons then sailed to Havana to rendezvous and refurbish. Initially the returning ships sailed east along the north coasts of Cuba and Hispaniola towards the Turks and Caicos islands and then out to the Atlantic. Later fleets sailed north from Havana towards the Gulf Stream which, if they left port prior to mid-August and the full onset of the hurricane season, would carry them through The Bahamas Channel and, if they avoided the shoals of The Bahamas and the Florida Keys, north along the coast of Florida to the Carolinas. There they turned east, hoping to catch a more favourable wind this far north than if they had altered course earlier, to sail towards Bermuda. Then south-east to the Azores and from there back to Seville.[10] This sixteenth-century wind- and current-driven itinerary through the West Indies then shaped European trade – besides piracy and salvage – with the Caribbean for the next 300 years. By the 1530s, the fleets' schedule was crystallising, as the royal authorisation of a permanent fort at San Juan in Puerto Rico in 1529, the foundation of Cartagena in 1533 and a first attack on Havana by French corsairs in 1536 all demonstrated.[11] The continued threat of further attacks led the Spanish Crown to require all westbound trading ships to sail in the annual convoys. All these developments decreased the utility of the optimistically-named trading settlement at New Seville on Jamaica's north coast. By the

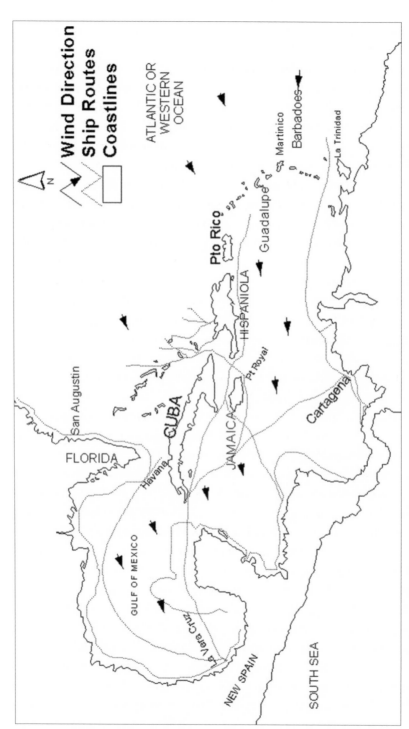

FIGURE 1.2 Sea routes: redrawn from 'A Map or Chart of the West Indies' in Charles Leslie *History* (2nd. ed. London: J. Hodges, 1740)

1530s the declining town was losing residents to the greener pastures of mainland New Spain.

The shift in schedule for transatlantic voyages contributed to the appeal of establishing a town on the south side of Jamaica and helped to persuade the remaining 20 householders of New Seville to leave. Prospective residents of the site that became St Jago de la Vega could hope that vessels from the Tierra Firme fleet might stop in Jamaica to take on provisions. They could also expect to sell Jamaican-grown produce to the new Spanish settlements on the South American mainland and receive payment in silver. In 1534 the householders who had remained at New Seville lived in a settlement that housed a sugar mill and provided a centre for raising cattle and horses. When they moved to Jamaica's southern plains they arrived at a ford on the Rio Cobre that – as at New Seville – was sited about a mile away from a major settlement established by the indigenous Taino. The site for the new town already held some Spanish buildings because it lay in the vicinity of a sugar estate and mill, while the surrounding savannas offered grazing for the townspeople's livestock.

A green field site on the south side of Jamaica

The area around this ford across the Rio Cobre was a major transit point even before Europeans arrived in Jamaica. When the townspeople began to lay out their town the gentle slope on the river's west side already held a few Taino burial mounds, though by 1534 these may already have been obscured by a crop of sugar or else would have simply appeared as so many hummocks in a cattle pasture. The largest pre-Columbian settlement identified on the island was at White Marl, which lay one mile to the east of the Spaniards' town. An archaeological section that cut through eight feet of deposits demonstrated prolonged residence there, perhaps dating back as early as 800 AD.[12] Shells and fragments of Taino pottery found mixed into early Spanish layers in sites in St Jago de la Vega suggest that when the Spaniards excavated and built, they dug through Taino middens and other features on the western side of the ford.[13] There were some continuities. The Spanish settlers used a Taino name, 'Cagway', for today's Rio Cobre. Their use of this name extended south to include the landing place at the river's mouth.[14] Archaeological research may yet identify more substantial Taino features underlying today's town. Though the English conquerors who later took over the town were convinced that the

Spaniards had employed Taino labour in its construction – current archaeological scholarship still suggests that the town the Spaniards established did not incorporate a pre-existing Taino settlement into its plan.[15]

In 1534 the slopes on the western side of the Rio Cobre ford faced potential competition as a capital city from at least two other settlements already established on the island's southern coast. The first of these, Oristán, was located at the western end of the island, in the vicinity of Bluefields Bay. It was probably too distant from most existing farms to be practical as an administrative hub.[16] The second, Port Esquivel, had been founded at the top of Old Harbour Bay by Juan de Esquivel, an early leader of the colony. The Spaniards would continue to use this haven for shipbuilding. However, the widely circulated later belief that Spanish fleets anchored offshore there in Galleon's Reach was probably false, as was the further claim that this was where Columbus first landed in Jamaica.[17] Seventeenth- and eighteenth-century pilots and French spies all claimed that the bay was not particularly easy to enter or, at any rate, not as easy as Kingston Harbour though today, with its approaches dredged and buoyed, Old Harbour Bay is used for loading cargoes of aluminum-rich bauxite ore.[18]

The more intractable problem with Port Esquivel's site was that it would not fit within the new official guidelines known as the Royal Laws of the Indies, framed in Spain for locating settlements in the New World. Would-be founders of towns within the Spanish Empire were expected to follow formal guidelines in establishing a new settlement. By the 1530s the growing threat created by seafarers from other European nations 'trespassing' in the Kingdom of Castile's West Indian territories led to the royal government declaring that in future new towns should be sited inland, distanced from the threat of pirate raids along with the temptation to indulge in unlicensed trading. These centres would then provide a focal point for agricultural settlement. The policy made sense in a European context, where attacks made by Muslim raiders from North Africa on Spanish shipping and coastal villages were on the increase and where the raiders were seizing around a fifth of their captives on shore.[19] Assailants landing in Spain would face more resistance if they ventured inland too far from their ships. In the sparsely populated West Indies, by contrast, moving the towns away from the coasts would provide less protection. As a contemporary observed, 'when the French [corsairs] heard where [the settlements] were, they did not fail to go; even eight miles from the sea-shore in Jamaica.'[20] Adopting these regulations meant that neither Port

Esquivel nor any settlement site nearer to the landing place on Kingston Harbour could fulfil the criteria for new towns. In contrast the site that became St Jago de la Vega fitted all these guidelines admirably.[21]

The Royal Laws were cited when St Jago de la Vega's merits were recommended to the King of Spain along with the case for abandoning New Seville.[22] The reports sent to the king claimed that the older settlement stood far too near to a swamp for its residents' health, a fact that caused the town's population to fall substantially. The reduction was true enough, although unlicensed emigration played a far bigger role. However, such comparisons took advantage of Jamaica's new capital standing 'in the fields' inland. The future St Jago de la Vega would then occupy a site that appeared far better than New Seville's – open to healthy breezes from the south-east and with an ample supply of fresh water.[23]

It certainly did not harm the cause of the future settlement that the island's treasurer, Pedro de Maçuelo, already owned a sugar mill there and recommended the site to benefit his own interests too. At the time the decision to establish the town was made he was in Spain to lobby for privileges for the new town and while he was there, secured further royal licences for his estate. Short of labour, he wanted permission to import 30 Portuguese labourers and their families, along with 30 African slaves. The King granted all these licences on the same day.[24] He also granted the new town fairly generous rights to hold common fields and to establish an urban government. These royal privileges, in addition to far rosier trading prospects for a site on the south side of the island, persuaded the remaining townspeople of New Seville to vote unanimously to remove to the new site.

The new town laid out on the southern side of the island was distinguished by its inland location and a more elaborate plan rather than by the magnificent buildings that New Seville had acquired. New Seville's first settlers appear to have envisioned another Santiago de Cuba, with a port and fortified stronghold where the newly mined gold could be assayed and stored, along with a hospital to accommodate sailors from passing merchant ships. In contrast St Jago de la Vega was laid out as a farmers' and administrators' centre, not as a merchants' or miners' base. It was unfortified. Its grid of streets and squares was ready to house ranchers' or planters' town houses, churches, chapels and some administrative buildings. This 'Villa de la Vega' was a city in the fields that was intended to provide an urban centre for an agricultural landscape.

When the island's Spanish settlers undertook the move from New Seville to St Jago de la Vega, Jamaica was a royal colony. This explains why the arguments shaping the decisions regarding the new town's location and for its layout were all phrased using the criteria set out in the Royal Laws of the Indies for founding new towns. In 1536, two years after the royal grants for the new town, a legal decision in Spain abruptly changed the local political groundrules. The Spanish Crown had never honoured the extravagant promises made to Christopher Columbus prior to his first transatlantic voyage. In 1536 the Crown granted his descendants the island of Jamaica as part of the settlement of a lawsuit they had undertaken.[25] This unexpected action effectively superseded all of Treasurer de Maçuelo's wheeler-dealing. Even though he had secured additional privileges that allowed him and his descendants to nominate the candidates for most of the posts in the new municipality's government, he enjoyed very little time to wield these powers. Instead, rather than the town's falling under the thumb of the de Maçuelo family, the court's decision in favour of the Columbus family meant that over the next 119 years the town and Jamaica would develop (or fail to develop) as a territory ruled by an absentee noble family who treated the island as a source of income without ploughing back much investment.

A Spanish Colonial Town

The layout of the new town offered spaces for all its intended functions. The Spaniards established their riverside town as a grid containing two distinct squares. Three north-south streets traversed by three or four east-west cross streets, divided the grid into nine blocks. Each of the two main squares focused on a church. The large open parade at the north-west corner of the town that has become today's Emancipation Square had the Abbot of Jamaica's church on its south side; while a second slightly smaller square, on the south-eastern side of the town, had the Dominican friars' church of Our Lady of Mercy on its east side.[26] This second square also housed the market. As with any Spanish colonial settlement, the town's streets also held other chapels and hermitages 'all very decent and venerable'.[27] Most of the original settlement lay to the east of White Church Street, in the bend of the river upstream from the church ford. The area running down to the river bank to the east of the grid held some light industry, including a brick kiln, as well as gardens and chapels.[28] Some tanneries stood further downstream. Successive

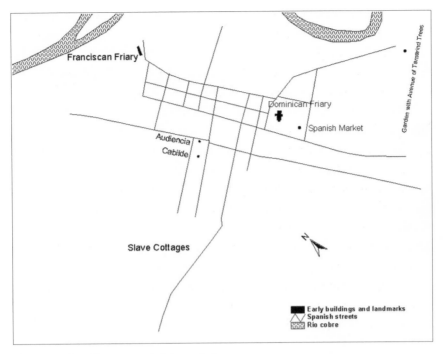

Figure 1.3 Spanish streets underlying today's townscape

complaints suggest that townspeople felt that these were not placed nearly far enough. With the prevailing wind from the south-east the same healthful sea breezes invoked when the town was receiving its original licences and privileges blew in the stench from any tannery established to the south to the town. Because influential colonists owned the tanneries these disputes were never resolved.[29] On the other side of the town, the eastern most of the town's north-south streets, today's Monk Street ran from the Dominican friary and out to the north beyond the grid, curving round towards another ford further upstream. Along this road stood some substantial country houses and a Franciscan friary dedicated to St John. The friary compound was surrounded by a wooden fence with a porter's lodge at the gate. It also held a gaol. These aspects of its layout were described in evidence given in 1649 after the then Governor and 20 armed supporters scaled the fence to free two men confined in the gaol – they did not call at the porter's lodge first.[30]

The town's riverside site was even more obvious in the east-west section of the grid plan. 'The Church Ford' across the Rio Cobre provided the starting

FIGURE 1.4 The resilience of the Spanish grid. Spanish Town from 5,000 feet in 1954, looking from the west with the Rio Cobre at the top. The approach road from the south paralleling the river can be seen curving round where it met the lane up from the Church Ford. The town's two squares, along with its basic grid, are clearly displayed. (Survey Department)

point for laying out the town's two squares and their surrounding streets. The lane down to the river is now grassed over, bypassed by bridges downstream. The original importance of the ford remains clear enough at the corner where Barrett Street – the urban end of the former north-south road running along the river bank towards the landing place – swings around in a near right-angle turn to join the old east-west road running up from the ford. This section of Barrett Street provides the backbone of the Spanish grid where it runs west for three blocks, some 300 yards. Three parallel north-bound roads join this spine at right angles: from east to west these are Monk Street, Red Church Street and White Church Street. The English names came later, but the streets themselves date from the city's foundation. The route up from the landing place was followed in 1608 when the Bishop of Havana visited the island for Lent and Easter. He was escorted to the town by a procession comprising 'all the population, clergy as well as laity'. As the crowd approached the settlement the space to the southeast that they reached first would have housed some tanneries. If work had begun on the stone-built Dominican friary, which was initiated during the term of the current governor, it had probably not got particularly far. As the procession swung round the corner where the road turned west after the ford even the footsore would know they were on the last lap to the Abbot's Church on the main square where the Bishop gave his blessing to the crowd.[31]

In getting to that square the western end of Barrett Street ended at a T-junction on the far side of Church Square. For most of this section it was bounded on its eastern side by the Dominicans' church before becoming the bottom of the town's second square. Today the open space is reduced by the block of nineteenth-century buildings around the church hall on the southern side, so that the west end of the Anglican Cathedral – the Dominican friars' successor – now faces the southern part of the plaza, rather than its centre. This square was later described as 'the old Spanish market place'. In the 1640s the houses there appeared more densely packed than anywhere else in the town.[32] One part of White Church Street, which makes the crossbar of the 'T' runs south. It originally cut across the open savanna in a more direct route down to the landing place at the mouth of the Rio Cobre. The other part of the cross-street runs north towards the town's main square.

To reach the town's second major square the Bishop's procession probably went to the T-junction before turning right into the northern part of White Church Street. After passing the churchyard of the town's other major church, the street then ran along the eastern side of a large square to the west, (for later townspeople 'the Parade,' or 'King's House Square,' today 'Emancipation Square'). Visitors up from the country would be impressed as architecturally this was the most striking section of the Spanish plan. Dominating the entrance to the square on its south side was the White Church, the church of the Abbot of Jamaica, (the senior clergyman on the island). The massive cement stubs of the White Church's stone gates remained a feature on this site well into the eighteenth century and, as we have seen, until the road on the south side of the square was paved over in the mid-twentieth century, the foundations of the old church could be made out through the gravel and marl

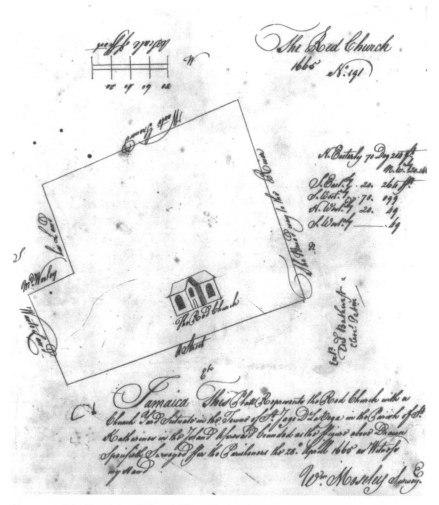

FIGURE 1.5 The Dominicans' church (the Red Church), 28 April 1665. The newly rebuilt brick building that the English took over in 1655. (Jamaica Archives)

road surface.[33] Over on the west side stood the *Casa Cabildo*, the municipal council chamber, along with the wooden-built *Audiencia* (court house) a large open hall. The buildings on the north side of the square included an old stable which was converted into a 'cook house', in the early 1660s. This battered structure remained facing the square into the 1780s, providing a social landmark for another 120 years. The town's prison was located on this side of the square too.[34] The road running from the north-western corner of the square past the prison joined the older route running north-west towards

Guanaboa, from there on to the Bog Walk Gorge and thence to the north side of the island. Behind these stables and probably also behind the *Cabildo* individual cross-streets may have run on out into the surrounding savanna.[35] The town was planned with space to expand logically from the original squares.

The original town plan was ambitious, the houses facing onto these streets and squares were less so. Visitors arriving from other Spanish colonies would remain unimpressed. These streets never held any of the large stone houses that the older Spanish settler families built in Santo Domingo, Havana and Santiago de Cuba in the early years of the sixteenth century.[36] Nor were there any public buildings of the scale of the stone-built chapel and fort that dominated the earlier settlement at New Seville, although the town's churches, chapels and public buildings were still creditable enough for a poor settlement in an earthquake- and- hurricane-prone area. Some incorporated skilfully worked stone pillars.[37] With only two or three exceptions all of St Jago de la Vega's houses were single-storey structures. The Spanish settlers had taken advantage of local materials in constructing their homes.[38] Sixteen-foot hardwood timber posts were set deep into the ground every two or three feet. These posts were subsequently enclosed within a brick wall. This frame gave the structure great resilience, particularly as the roof's wooden sill rested on

FIGURE 1.6 Spanish house, engraving published in Edward Long, *History of Jamaica*, (John Carter Brown Library, Brown University)

the top of these hardwood posts. The roof itself was thick, framed with hardwood rafters and a layer of bamboo or other canes, with a lining of approximately four inches of mortar between the rafters and a top layer of thick red tiles. The windows had wooden louvred blinds. These buildings not only withstood natural disasters but remained cool in the heat of the day and dry during heavy rain.[39] To the south of the town and probably also on its northern and western sides stood the smaller huts which housed the town's unfree African Jamaican population and, at least until the 1580s, a Taino community.[40]

The Inhabitants

St Jago de la Vega remained a small town throughout the sixteenth century. In the 1590s a clergyman's census of the number of Spanish colonists on the island gave a figure of 160 households.[41] Other estimates at this juncture ran from 'over one hundred' to 120 or else 130 Spanish households.[42] Deriving a total of individuals from such figures is difficult, as no estimates were offered for the amount of people an average household contained. What is clear is that the population had expanded from the 20 households who moved from New Seville in 1536 and the 30 Portuguese families whose immigration was licensed the same year, even if Jamaica was still not a particularly densely settled place. The town came to hold between 400 and 600 houses. The number of free settlers on the island rose slowly over the first half of the seventeenth century although a smallpox epidemic in 1650, which killed 100 slaves and 50 Spaniards, cut into a heavily concentrated population. Jamaica's inhabitants in 1655 totalled approximately 1,500 people, most of whom lived in St Jago.[43] During the Columbus family's rule the island's population became a distinctive cultural blend. By the mid-seventeenth century, very few new settlers migrated from Spain to Jamaica, indeed, in 1611 the Abbot of Jamaica claimed that 'all' the Spanish settlers on the island were descended from 'only three parentages' but, unlike most of the other Spanish islands, Portuguese immigration continued.[44] Meanwhile a trickle of slaves continued to arrive.

Different population groups expanded or contracted at different rates. From 1611 we have a breakdown of the various groups that made up the island's population. A particularly energetic new Abbot compiled figures from the numbers making confession that year, his estimate – which would exclude the very young, the housebound sick, runaways in the mountains and, perhaps, the most irreligious – provided a total of 1,510 people 'of all classes and conditions'. This broke down as 523 Spaniards, male and female; 173 children; 107 free negroes; 74 'indians, natives of the island'; 558 slaves and 75 'foreigners'.[45] The Spanish population gained numbers gradually while the Taino appear to have disappeared or died out after this estimate. Other groups grew faster. Both the Portuguese and the African populations in Jamaica continued to increase during the early seventeenth century as slave ships from the Portuguese settlement in Angola stopped *en route* to Cartagena and Porto Bello and landed sick slaves in Jamaica on their first landfall after crossing the Atlantic.[46] Many died; some lived. The survivors might include individuals from animist tribes in the interior. However, during the seventeenth century, protracted civil wars in Angola's neighbouring Christian kingdom of Kongo resulted in many of these newcomers being Roman Catholic refugees or prisoners from these wars. For what it was worth, Portuguese law required that all slaves be baptized before they were shipped out of Africa.[47] Although the island always remained short of clergy and chaplains, the goal of sustaining some of these slaves' existing Christian beliefs was not impossible.

Jamaican immigration therefore diverged from that of the other Spanish islands as it retained a significant Portugese component. When other Spanish governors followed royal orders by restricting immigration into the West Indies from Portugal during the early seventeenth century, Portugese were still permitted to settle in Jamaica. The Columbus family had married into the Portugese nobility, which may have influenced this policy, but the island also remained underpopulated, providing a welcome for any settlers. These immigrants included Christian families from Portugal who emigrated as labourers, together with other families of Portuguese stock who moved to the Caribbean from Portuguese settlements in West Africa.[48] The incomers also included some 'new-Christian' families whose Jewish ancestors had converted outwardly in the 1490s. While a very few of these converts did make free choices, many Spanish and Portuguese Jews were forced to adopt Christianity.[49] Some of them managed to retain Jewish beliefs and customs. Individuals of Jewish ancestry were officially forbidden to sail to the New World. However some did and, because Jamaica did not have an office of the Inquisition, it offered them a safer harbour.[50] Although all residents shared a common official religion, race divided Jamaica's population, while the island's principal population growth came from forced immigration.

Jamaica's vulnerability to attacks

In the late sixteenth century Jamaica continued to suffer attacks. French, Dutch and English raiding parties all turned their attention towards the smaller Spanish settlements around the Caribbean, including those in Jamaica.[51] A visit by such marauders could result in substantial damage. The former settlement at New Seville was attacked in 1554 by French pirates who destroyed its remaining 24 wooden houses.[52] The attackers were frequently disappointed in what they could find, but we can discover more about the island from descriptions included in accounts written after such raids. We often have to rely on self-justificatory reports as sea captains explained to sceptical investors how a voyage had only narrowly failed to secure sufficient booty to pay a dividend. Occasionally, we have some settlers' testimony too. One of the best documented encounters was the 1603 attack on St Jago de la Vega from an English flotilla under Captain Christopher Newport. The Spanish Governor Don Fernando Melgarejo de Córdoba successfully repelled that landing force and a whole group of local witnesses recalled this triumph.[53]

The reports described the following sequence of events. The ships approached from the east, travelling with the prevailing wind. At sunset a slave from the *hato* (estate) of Morante had observed eight sails off Morant Point, 12 leagues to windward of the town. When this ominous news reached the Governor an alarm was rung. Several townspeople described being awakened by the tolling of the church bell about an hour before daybreak. Roused early, the townspeople proceeded to the *Cabildo*, the city hall, to hear the news. They found the Governor forming up the militia and enrolling any other able-bodied residents for the defence. Drums were beaten and the militiamen formed up under their flags in the town square, which provided a rendezvous.[54] These preparations contrasted with the settlers' usual response to such news, when they would gather their possessions and make a dash for the mountains. The latest seaborne assailants had timed their approach to bring them into Kingston Harbour at daybreak, so there would be no warning from the watchmen in 'the Morro', the watchtower up in the hills facing the harbour. Captain Newport had not foreseen either the sharp-eyed observer at dusk or the speed with which the news could travel. A successful surprise attack at dawn might capture some townspeople who would pay ransom. Sighting of the approaching fleet the evening before meant that the townspeople received sufficient notice to remove their valuables. The Governor then attempted a defence. He appeared foredoomed to failure. Later that morning, once the English fleet had anchored off the mouth of the Rio Cobre, the attackers came ashore with a sizable force – afterwards the defenders claimed 1,500 men, probably at least a threefold exaggeration – and marched on the town.[55] It was still a far larger force than the townsfolk could rally, especially after some individuals slipped away from the ranks to flee to their farms with their families and their valuables. At this juncture a delegation of friars and clergymen begged the Governor to negociate.[56] As de Córdoba and the 60 militiamen he managed to recruit faced the enemy outside the town, order broke down and the Governor's own house was robbed; afterwards residents tried to assign the blame for this disorder to slaves.[57]

Generally, these seaborne raiders hoped for either loot or a ransom payment in return for not burning a town after they seized it. Often a military demonstration would persuade local officials to permit some mutually beneficial 'forced' trade, too.[58] The attackers wanted food, primarily beef and cassava flour and, like all sailing ships, they needed to refill their water casks and stock up on fire wood. In this instance Governor de Córdoba promised 'only supplies of [musket] balls' – out of the barrels of the militiamens' muskets.[59] What's more, the Governor then managed to chase off Captain Newport's sea dogs. Spanish sniping from the woods as the English assailants approached the town, marching up from the landing place, undercut their morale. When they reached a trench dug across the road 'where the road narrows' about 'a quarter of a league' outside the town, they were turned back.[60] A couple of volleys from the Jamaican militia men and a blast from the single cannon manhandled out from in front of the Governor's house, reinforced by a semi-directed stampede into the English ranks by some cattle, all combined to break the attackers' impetus. The sailors still made an orderly retreat back to their ships and then remained long enough to refill the ships' water casks. Afterwards settlers claimed that St James (Jago) of Santiago, the patron saint of Spain, himself appeared to rally the defenders and the town adopted its saintly protector's name.[61] With or without the saint's personal intervention this repulse was a remarkable performance, all the more so because the reports all highlight the absence of any defensive fortifications.

Clearly miracles could happen. With determined leadership, the inspiration of their patron saint and, indeed, with marvellous luck, the town's militia might beat off a substantial landing party. But by the 1590s an unfortified settlement was vulnerable to a seaborne assault. Despite the wake-up calls presented by several raiders' attacks during the next half century, neither the Columbus family nor the Spanish Crown succeeded in marshalling the resources necessary to fortify St Jago de la Vega. In 1655 the island's meagre defences remained much as they had been 60 years before. By this time Jamaica was the largest Spanish settlement in the West Indies where the colonists had yet to update defensive works already demonstrated insufficient to withstand attacks by the maritime predators of the late sixteenth century.

Legacies

Today the imprint from the Spanish phase in Spanish Town's past may well appear faint. It will take considerable extrapolation to blame modern traffic jams on Spanish decisions in 1534, although the Spanish ground plan still shapes the city centre. In any comparison between today's Spanish Town and the ford that the Taino knew for 700 years, the most pervasive legacy from the Spanish period is less in buildings or even building lines but, instead, in the ecological changes that accompanied the Spanish settlement. In the countryside these changes were imposed by the cattle and pigs that the Spaniards brought with them. The cattle's grazing kept the fields clear on the savannas that surrounded the town while the herds of feral pigs ranging the woods trod new paths through all of Jamaica's many forest types.

Within the town we can trace further ecological repercussions from 120 years of Spanish occupation at this site. Many of the species of fruit trees that the Spaniards imported from Europe, the East Indies and the mainland of South America continued to provide shade and refreshment for subsequent generations. Some proved remarkably long lived. A 'magnificent' avenue of tamarind trees remained a feature in the hospital gardens just beyond Monk Street well into the 1870s, when they were sufficiently spectacular to cause local tour guides to state that the Spanish Governor's House 'must' have stood there.[62] The tamarind trees were impressive. The last one survived until the 1951 hurricane. English rule only outlasted it by another 11 years.[63] In addition to these imported tamarinds, the period saw the forbears of the Panama Tall palm trees were brought across the Atlantic from Sao Tomé and the Cape Verde islands, where Portuguese ships returning from the Indian Ocean had carried an earlier generation of coconuts.[64] Coconuts remain a staple of Jamaican cooking, while the Panama Tall palms continued to grace the townspeople's horizons until blights in the late twentieth century afflicted their descendants. Latin American cocoa bushes flourished, too, with the Columbus family maintaining extensive plantations at 'Huanaboa' (Guanaboa).[65] In their houses the Spanish colonists had sipped chocolate – in the 1630s one of the few uses for Jamaican pimento suggested by a royal investigating committee was as an additive for chocolate.[66] Then, in the gardens of individual house lots, the limes, lemons and both sweet and bitter orange trees introduced to the island from Spain all flourished. Bananas brought west to the Caribbean from gardens in the Canary Islands provided a further lasting addition to residents' diet.[67] These Mediterranean and Atlantic legacies of Spanish rule still shade today's streets. They display the Spanish presence in terms that the Spaniards' Taino predecessors might well have acknowledged.

During the century and a half after Columbus's first arrival in Jamaica, Spanish domestic animals and the commercial trees that the Spaniards transplanted all spread across the island. In contrast, out-migration meant that the Spanish population remained small and a sparsely populated Spanish settlement could not continue to repel hostile invasions. The vulnerability of the Spanish colony had been apparent for half a century. The attack by Captain Newport in 1603, like earlier ones by Sir Anthony Shirley in 1597 and one a generation later by Captain William Jackson in 1643, which both succeeded in capturing the town and holding it to ransom, demonstrated that when hostile squadrons which could muster a sizable landing party ranged the Caribbean, occupying a site seven miles inland was no longer the sufficient defence that it had appeared in 1534. A Dutch force that seized and burnt San Juan, Puerto Rico, in 1625 and, even closer to home, persistent Dutch operations against Santiago de Cuba during the 1630s both offered ominous examples of the scale and the belligerence of the hostile fleets operating in the Caribbean.[68] Spanish colonists feared that Jamaica would be assaulted by a Dutch or a French force. However, the troops who disembarked in 1655 as the townspeople fled their town happened to be English. This landing was not only successful, but the invaders stayed. Thereafter Spanish rule ceased, but the town of St Jago de la Vega, with its Spanish street plan, its large numbers of Spanish-built houses and the imported trees in its gardens, would continue to appear a distinctively 'Spanish Town' to subsequent inhabitants.

CHAPTER TWO

—

'A Town Improving Every Day'

An English Town on Spanish Foundations, 1655–1692

*O*N MAY 10, 1655, an English fleet carrying an invasion force arrived in Kingston Harbour.[1] The English attacked Jamaica after they failed to capture Santo Domingo (in today's Dominican Republic), which they wanted as a base for assaults on the Spanish Empire and its treasure fleets.[2] The original plan, called 'the Western Design', was devised by England's then fiercely Protestant leaders and particularly its Lord Protector, Oliver Cromwell. Cromwell's prolonged run of military successes during Britain's Civil Wars provided the wider context for his West Indian adventure.[3] The competing need to maintain garrisons in Scotland and Ireland, along with limited funds, constrained the Western Design but its aims were expansive. It planned to re-centre the English presence in the West Indies moving west from its initial footholds in the eastern Caribbean into the heart of the Spanish Caribbean. The campaign succeeded in achieving this goal with the capture of Jamaica, although the island was not its original objective.

Jamaica had no place in Cromwell's initial agenda. The 'resolve' by the expedition's leaders 'to attempt Jamaica' was decided upon only after the army was repulsed at Santo Domingo. They 'consulted what was further to be done' and 'finding the soldiers so cowardly, and not to be trusted or confided in, except raised in their spirits by some smaller success' turned towards Jamaica, a largely undefended island.[4] It proved an easier target for an initial landing than Santo Domingo, even when dispirited and sickly troops undertook the assault. Despite all the recommendations made in official Spanish reports to erect more substantial fortifications after the raiders' attacks earlier in the century, nothing was built.[5] Afterwards, the Columbus family absolved itself, claiming that they never raised any defences because royal regulations forbade the construction of private fortifications.[6] There was blame enough to share.

The conquest itself was traumatic for Spanish Town, resulting in the flight of the town's Spanish residents and the destruction of many buildings. Afterwards the town underwent extensive changes during its first 40 years under English rule. Yet, although structural remains from this period are fragmentary, the modern town still bears the stamp of this half-century's changes and developments. Most significantly, during this period the choice was made to retain the old Spanish centre as the 'Seat of Government' for the new English colony, despite the emergence of Port Royal as an alternative urban centre.

The building undertaken at Spanish Town during this first generation of English settlement occurred in two distinct stages, reflecting the island's uneven development. The first of these phases spanned the period from May 1655 to 1661, when Spanish Town became the forward military base for an occupying army engaged in a long guerrilla campaign. This martial stage dictated the patterns of use within the town that the English colonists finally inherited, although there is little left of it today. The second phase began in 1661 when Britain's recently restored monarch, King Charles II, decided to retain Jamaica as an English colony instead of returning it to Spain and ended with the earthquake of 1692. Between 1655 and 1692 English settlers commissioned ambitious brick buildings as private residences across the island, most of which collapsed in the massive earthquake that most famously slid two-thirds of Port Royal into the harbour, but also *took* down buildings elsewhere across Jamaica.

An English Invasion: May 1655

The English landing of May 15, 1655, was not planned in advance and the invaders had very limited intelligence about Jamaica to draw on. The array of experts aboard the English fleet anchored in Kingston Harbour included one Thomas Gage, an English-born former Dominican friar, now a Protestant minister and one of the few Englishmen with first-hand experience in the Spanish settlements in central America. Gage, who had served as a parish priest in Guatemala, hoped that the Western Design would lead to 'the conversion of the poor Indians, who longeth to see the light of the gospel run yet more and more forwards, till it come to settle in the west among those poor, simple, and truly purblind Americans.'7 Protector Cromwell and his fellow councilors drew much of their knowledge of the New World from Gage's descriptions of Spanish rule in Mexico and Guatemala in *The English-American his Travail by Sea and Land: Or, A New Survey of the West India's*. This was first published in 1648 and reprinted in 1655, along with older re-tellings of Sir Francis Drake's exploits in the Caribbean during the 1580s and a new translation of Bartolomé de las Casas's descriptions of Spanish maltreatment of the Indians in the sixteenth-century.8 Yet even Father Gage's extensive wanderings had never taken him to Jamaica. He could act as an interpreter in the negotiations with Jamaica's Spanish Governor, but there would be no call here for his experience in dealing with the Indians of Guatemala and Honduras.9

If landing in Jamaica was not something that the English army had planned, the scale of the invasion also proved unexpected for the Spanish settlers. As the troops were rowing ashore someone on the beach called out to ask what they came for. The answer shouted back from the boats, 'fresh meat and pieces of eight' suggested that this was simply another, albeit far larger, raiding party that came 'to victual, plunder' and, most importantly, 'soe be gone.'10 This time, however, the newly arrived fleet carried far more fire-power than its predecessors in 1598, 1603 or 1643, with some 38 ships and 7,000 troops. The soldiers wanted to plunder, but delays between getting them ashore and marching on the town meant that the townspeople had ample time to remove their goods. When the English reached Spanish Town the population had already fled, leaving a trail of discarded furniture that stretched far out into the savanna.11 The soldiers were 'exceedingly hungry' for food, so they shot all the 'dogs, cats, colts or donkeys' that remained in the town and that evening slaughtered the sheep and goats that returned to their owners' corrals and sheds.12

The invaders remained destructive. Morale among the English troops was poor enough when they landed. Without any consoling loot the excitement of the conquest quickly wore off, particularly once the soldiers were obliged to plant crops or starve. Many starved. Some pulled down houses to provide fuel for their bivouac fires. Others hoped to make their position untenable so that the officers would abandon Jamaica and return the whole expedition home to England.[13] Hence, six months after the English landed, an incoming army commander's first impressions were of defeat: 'the soldiery many dead, their carcasses lying unburied in the high-ways, and amongst bushes.' Meanwhile, 'many of them that were alive, walked like ghosts or dead men, who, as I went through the town, lay groaning and crying out, bread for the Lord's sake. The truth is, when I set my foot first on land, I saw nothing but symptoms of necessity and desolation'.[14] Indeed, such was the misery of the English army's plight that by the beginning of 1656 the few former Spanish slaves who initially joined them 'are run from us' except some seven or eight who had to be kept shackled.[15] The invading army secured a bridgehead but their position was unstable and they remained very vulnerable for the next five or six years.

St Iago de la Vega became an English garrison. The ruin of the Abbot's Church on the main Parade that remained after the soldiers' treasure hunting was converted into a defensive strong point. Military officers 'requisitioned' buildings that had survived the soldiers' initial onslaught and the army commander took up lodgings in the former town hall. His officers obtained quarters in the town alongside a regiment of infantry and a troop of cavalry.[16] For the next 40 years the town's landmarks retained military echoes including 'the path to the troopers quarters' or 'the Troopers Ford' to the north east, out by the former Franciscan friary.[17] The imprint of these postings was long-lasting.

Once they were ashore the English faced disease, shortages of supplies and a protracted guerrilla campaign, particularly once the expedition's leaders offered harsh peace terms to the Spanish settlers and it became apparent that the English came 'not to pillage but to plant.'[18] The Spanish Governor was already very ill when the English landed and was unready to organize a resistance. He rode back into Spanish Town to negotiate. He and his party were greeted with the military honours befitting a Captain General: nine English infantry regiments with 66 banners stood in formation in the town square as the Governor was carried into town in a hammock.[19] He signed the surrender terms offered him. However, after the English had shipped him off to Cartagena, the remaining Spanish settlers felt free to ignore this capitulation. A handful of them organized a resistance – something that none of Cromwell's expert advisors foresaw.[20] The Spanish settlers' principal success lay in allying with the independent bands of African Jamaicans living on the south side of the island. We do not know how long-established these *cimarrone* settlements were. However, by the end of 1655 there were several autonomous communities, or *pelincos* (stockades). After the English invasion these ex-slaves and their descendants were joined by the slaves from the Spanish colonists' households and plantations. Invoking King Philip IV of Spain's name the Spanish settlers' promised them all legal freedom and land in return for aid in repulsing the English.[21] This appeared believable. The *cimarrones* were well aware that 'fine words butter no parsnips', so whatever counter-offer the English invaders made needed some real likelihood of fulfilment before it was worth considering. As things were, the *cimarrones* whose scouts observed the goings-on in the town, were not likely to put much faith in any long-term promises offered by such a demoralised force. For four years raids and ambushes by the *cimarrones* kept the English cooped up within the immediate vicinity of their encampments, while supplying the Spanish forces with a succession of English prisoners and deserters to interrogate.

The town's physical transformation was accomplished during the prolonged guerrilla campaign between 1655 and 1659, when it was both a major military base and a prime military target. Don Cristóbal de Ysassi, one of the Spanish settlers who led the initial resistance to the English, attacked the town in June 1656. He infiltrated the area under English control with 30 Spanish settlers and 15 African Jamaican *cimarrones*. He and his group first attacked an English watering party west of the town, then swung around to the south to inspect the English shipping in the harbour. After that they wiped out a mounted squad escorting supplies up from the landing place and entered the town after dark, killing some people in the streets and setting fire to two huts across from the former Governor's house. Ysassi reported, 'they were astonished and confused at two attacks at the same time, followed, at night by the burning of houses. Englishmen came out like bees.' Ysassi's confident dispatch describing his foray impressed Spain's King Philip IV, who then appointed this energetic local commander to the vacant Governorship of Jamaica.[22] Even as a desperate measure, this was still an unusual promotion within the Spanish empire where 'creoles' (locally-born settlers) were almost never appointed to senior commands, particularly in their home colonies.[23]

Ysassi concluded his dispatch with the news that the English commander had decided to burn the town and then retire to the stockade and trenches at the landing place. This rumour, like so many others in wartime, proved untrue. However, Ysassi's raid did lead to lasting changes in the invaders' occupation of Spanish Town. In the short term the English garrison demolished several huts, probably former slave cabins, at the edge of the town to deny future raiders a hiding place.[24] In the longer term they erected more elaborate fortifications to accommodate the garrison and defend the approaches to the town. The initial English strong point within the old White Church was presumably too small to offer a refuge for all the town's residents, civilian and military. It was now superseded by a stockade in the Parade. The bronze three pounder cannon that embellished this enclosure probably did more to boost the townspeople's confidence than deter further raiders.[25] Then, in a further response to the military weaknesses demonstrated by their openness to Ysassi's attack, the English constructed another new fort on the south side of the town. This fort was part of more substantial defensive works designed to protect both ends of the supply route running from the harbour to Spanish Town. However, despite these new fortifications, *cimarrone* raiders still snatched individuals off the town's streets for interrogation by Ysassi. An unlucky sailor was captured in this manner in 1658, just after he arrived in Spanish Town to enjoy some shore leave. This was a garrison centre – and it remained vulnerable.

The Conquest Concluded: 1658–1660

The Spanish settler holdouts and survivors from various companies of reinforcements sent over to assist their defence remained unwilling to abandon Jamaica. Only several defeats and shifting alliances in Jamaica would finally end their resistance. In early May 1658 the Governor of Santiago de Cuba chose to override Ysassi's advice to concentrate all the available forces at a secure landing spot on the south side of the island. As a former professional soldier Don Pedro Bayona Villanueva was convinced that he knew better: not only would a landing point on the north side of the island be easier when it came to shipping troops over from Cuba, but disembarking them there would leave the new recruits closer to St Jago de la Vega – whose capture provided the target for Spanish assaults. (Jamaica's rugged mountainous interior did not factor into these assertions).[26] Hence, when a further substantial reinforcement for the Spanish force in Jamaica arrived at Santiago de Cuba from Mexico, Bayona sent them and their supplies to the north shore of Jamaica. Once these reinforcements disembarked they erected a stockade at Rio Nuevo. Here Ysassi, who had been skirmishing on the south side of the island with his men, joined the newcomers and assumed command of their still unfinished fort 'Rio de la Concepcion'.[27]

This stockade lay on the far side of the mountains from the English army but it provided a fixed target for an English attack. Although outclassed in guerrilla warfare, when it came to over-running conventional fortifications the English senior officers were experienced military professionals. A combined naval and land force was shipped round from the south side of the island. On June 22 they attacked the stockade on its unfinished side.[28] Most of Ysassi's latest recruits were killed or captured, though Ysassi himself and over 100 of his most experienced men managed to get away along the shore and into the woods. At this juncture the campaign was hardly over. The Spaniards had lost their supplies, so Ysassi shipped most of the survivors from the Rio Nuevo debacle back to Cuba to reduce the number of mouths to be fed. He and his party then returned to the fray and continued to pick off stragglers and hunters who ventured into the woods beyond the English camps.[29] The Spanish Crown continued to support their efforts, sending out an experienced professional soldier to act as Ysassi's second-in-command.[30]

What began as a seaborne invasion was concluded by soldiers patrolling the bush. The English finally won the military campaign for Jamaica by maintaining patrols in the mountainous interior. At the beginning of 1660, through some hard-earned luck, they located the provision grounds of a *pelinco* in Lluidas Vale. The members of the *cimarrone* group did not have the choice that the Spanish colonists had enjoyed of fleeing across the mountains and over to Cuba because if they did so, they would be seized and re-enslaved as they stepped out of their canoes. They faced starvation without the crops from their provision grounds. Juan de Bolas, the group's leader, was left with few options. He negotiated a treaty with the English to secure freedom and land for his companions – similar terms to those the Spanish settlers had offered in the King of Spain's name. The English gained a valuable ally.[31] With de Bolas and his men participating in English patrols Jamaica's woods no longer offered Ysassi's forces a safe refuge.[32] The Spaniards' main camp was attacked and several senior officers killed, including the newly arrived second-in-command, or else captured.[33] Hard pressed and short of supplies Ysassi withdrew to Cuba.

The prolonged campaigning against the Spanish hold-outs helps to explain why the English troops maintained Spanish Town as a main base, even if they established forward settlements ten miles further inland at Guanaboa. The soldiers' extended occupation helped reshape the town. Any former Spanish resident who might have returned to it in late 1659 – perhaps among the captives from the fort at Rio Nuevo – would have found the changes striking. Now a stockade with artillery dominated the town's main square, while the Abbot's White Church, the mother church of the island under the Spaniards, lay in ruins. The former hermitage of Our Lady of Belén had become a sheep-pen; another former religious property was known as 'the Convent' but a local land surveyor would simply describe it as 'Two houses and a yard'.[34] The invaders had demolished many of the townspeople's older houses, casualties in searches for treasure, or fuel, or even building materials, while a fringe of new houses now filled the space between the White Church's walls and the south side of the square.[35]

Building priorities shifted: the Spaniards had built their town at a crossroads where the 'River Road' north across the island forked off from the east-west route that linked the coastal plains on the south side of the island. In contrast, most English visitors approached the town from the south, coming up the road from today's Kingston Harbour. On this side of the town many old landmarks changed as new priorities shaped the townscape. The English erected their second fort, Fort Henry, on the town's southern edge, out beyond the Red Church. It quickly became a hospital for sick soldiers. A bowling green, the latest accessory for English urban civility, was laid out beside it.[36] This new construction transferred the social centre of the town to the south, placing the Dominicans' former church and the market square it faced at the town's centre. Further south another small settlement developed by the landing place at the southern end of the road to the harbour. The troops quickly replaced the two small wooden piers and dilapidated stockade they found when they came ashore with a more substantial fort, several storehouses and a jetty stretching out through the surf.[37] The settlement called 'Passage Fort' acquired its name because this was where travellers from Spanish Town took passage across to the new Port Cagway or out to their ships. Looking out from this jetty anyone could see that the harbour now contained many more ships. For a long time the presence of several English warships provided the main guarantee of safety for the invading force.[38] However, in a change resulting in even greater consequences, these ships now used a different anchorage across the harbour over by the settlement of Cagway (the future Port Royal). This new haven quickly grew to be the largest urban centre in Jamaica.

Transitions: changing understandings of the town and its surroundings

The initial dealings between the Spanish and English settlers at the seizure of the island were shaped by the Spanish townspeople's initial hasty flight. The break quickly became complete. Spanish reports later claimed that the English brought a deadly fever with them from Santo Domingo which infected the refugees from St Iago de la Vega before these non-combatants trekked north across the mountains. When the Spanish colonists then sailed to Cuba, they brought the fever with them. This infection, however, is almost the only evidence that we have of contacts between the town's former residents and the English invaders.[39]

Further evidence that there was virtually no communication between the invaders and their predecessors lies in the fact that the English retained remarkably few Spanish names in the town and the area around it. This was an area that had lain at the centre of the Spanish settlement for over a century. We might well expect many more names to carry over if there had been many Spanish residents or renegades to interrogate. Instead there were few cultural holdovers. The army retained the earlier names for the administrative districts where troops were posted – Morant, Yallas and Liguanea to the east; Caymanas, 'the Angels' and Guanaboa to the north; and, at least into the early 1660s, 'Guardabocoa' for part of what became the parish of Clarendon, to the west.[40] More heavily anglicised versions of Spanish names were retained for the two major cross-island tracks: the 'Bog Walk Gorge' and perhaps 'Mount Diablo' on the River Road through to the north side of the island, along with the alternative route north, the Junction Road, that leaves the Liguanea Plain at Stony Hill and then follows the Wag Water valley, the latter name probably retaining an echo of an earlier Taino name 'Guaiguata' but received a popular etymology deriving it from Spanish, which invoked a former 'Agua Alta' or 'high water' anglicised into 'Wag Water'.[41]

Some surprising omissions occurred, even among these limited survivals. The Spaniards' name for today's Kingston Harbour, 'Guavayara', was quickly forgotten.[42] The initial terms offered by the English on 17 May 1655, stated that any Spanish settlers who wanted to take up the invaders' offer of a passage off the island were to gather in the savanna outside the 'Town of Caguaya', which from this context was the old landing place on the harbour. They would then embark from 'the Port of Caguaya', or the harbour itself.[43] In any event these treaty terms remained moot, as only the dying Governor and his household took up this opportunity to ship out. Afterwards the English dropped these usages. In their place the old Taino 'Cagway' river-name which formerly gave 'its name to the port' was transferred from the landing place at the mouth of the river, out across the harbour to the new haven established by the English naval commander at the Spaniards' former careening site, 'the Cayo de Carena', at the seaward end of the narrow peninsula that shelters Kingston Harbour from the sea.[44] On these sloping beaches wooden ships had been hauled ashore so that the growths of weeds below the waterline that slowed their speed could be burnt off, timbers that were either damaged or attacked by the *toredo navalis* wood-boring marine worms replaced and new protective coats of tar or grease slathered on. Spanish ships had required these precautions; so would their English successors. Just behind the tip of the peninsula, the 'long point', the English erected a battery to command the entrance to the harbour and later established a new settlement stretching back from the landing place there.[45] The subsequent success of this settlement of Cagway overwhelmed the earlier applications of the Cagway name to the mainland, though it would remain in use on maps of Jamaica for another generation to describe the entire sheltered harbour.[46] This reappropriation of the river's former name then left a gap: for 20 years the river running through Spanish Town was simply known as 'the Town River' before the optimistic 'Rio Cobre' (Copper River), which had come into use by at least the mid-1660s, was generally adopted.[47] These changes in the names current around Spanish Town also marked wider shifts in the town's social and economic functions: the old Spanish town beside the former Cagway River lost much of its trade and population to the seamens' newly established haven at 'Port Cagway.'

Less surprising is the fact that after a conquest by a self-consciously Protestant army the names and dedications of St Iago de la Vega's Catholic churches and chapels were not retained. Some of these buildings were demolished. However, the Spaniards' main churches and friaries continued to figure as landmarks in the names that the English assigned to the three main north-south streets in the town's grid. Monk Street (the easternmost) led to the former Franciscan friary, which the English described as 'the Monastery'.[48] Red Church Street (in the centre) ended at the 'red', brick-built Dominican friary that the English knew as 'the Red Church.' White Church Street linked the town's two plazas. It ran alongside the graveyard of the ruined 'White Church' (the former church of the Abbot of Jamaica) and was therefore occasionally described as 'the White Church Yard Street'.[49] These echoes from the Spanish religious presence were all the more conspicuous when the new townspeople did not assign specific street names to other streets in their town's inherited grid.

The very completeness of the transformation at the English conquest was in striking contrast to the expectations of previous raiders who, when the population was divided into different ethnic groups under the Spaniards, always expected to find local allies. Hence in 1598 Sir Anthony Shirley was able to find a Taino fisherman to pilot his invading fleet into harbour.[50] By 1655 there were no potential Taino allies left to recruit. Subsequent raiders generally assumed that if Jamaica were invaded the island's Portuguese population would rally to support the invaders, but this did not happen either.[51]

The absence of a carry-over of place names in the vicinity of Spanish Town also runs counter to the view that individual Jewish families who had passed as Christians under Spanish rule would immediately take the opportunity that the English conquest offered for their freedom of worship to provide a cultural transition for the English regime.[52] A Jewish community was established on the island after the English conquest. Some of these Jewish families arrived from England and the Dutch territories, and the community thrived after it recruited several families who had lived under Spanish and Portuguese rule elsewhere in the Caribbean.[53] The silences among the place names the English assigned to the landscape surrounding their principal settlement suggests that the settlers failed to listen to any earlier inhabitants who might remain.

Re-envisioning a Spanish City

Major changes occurred during the early years of English rule, though we do not know exactly when Cagway's population outstripped that of Spanish Town. The English settlers re-oriented the island's former self-contained, cattle-based economy towards export crops and maritime ventures, a shift which in practice fulfilled some of the initial hopes of St Iago de la Vega's original Spanish founders. Port Cagway, with its sea breezes discouraging mosquitoes promised its residents some relief from the fevers that continued to thin the army. Two of the commanders sent out from England to lead the invading army attempted to run the campaign from the great cabin of a warship anchored in the harbour. This strategy proved unsuccessful: neither General Robert Venables nor General Robert Sedgwick could win a guerrilla war this way and, while Venables abandoned his command to sail back to England; Sedgwick, his replacement, was still unable to avoid the island's fevers and died after eight months in Jamaica. Two further commanders sent out from England also died soon after they arrived. By default Edward D'Oyley, the senior surviving colonel in the invading army, took over command after each death and once further replacements ceased to be sent out finally became army commander. His military competence was demonstrated in the Rio Nuevo campaign.[54] During D'Oyley's command he settled much of the military administration at Port Cagway, erecting a substantial wooden mansion near to the harbour where he lived and the military council assembled for most of its discussions. The port became the administrative hub for the English invaders.[55] The new settlement might be rough-hewn, but it was laid out by English surveyors and its streets and building plots maintained familiar proportions.

Spanish Town retained much of its former plan. By 1660 any newcomers from England or from any of England's other transatlantic colonies who made their way from the harbour to 'Town' (Spanish Town), would be struck by how unfamiliar, indeed how 'Spanish', the older settlement still appeared. The town provided a centre for the officers and soldiers in the units that were not only engaging in 'planting' subsistence crops but, increasingly, aimed to harvest the cocoa groves established by the Spaniards. On its southern approach a Spanish shrine, the 'White Chapel', still served as a landmark, as did the old Red Church.[56]

Some contrasts between Spanish Town and Cagway appeared obvious. The basic proportions of their streets differed. As one visitor noted, in Spanish Town the roads ran straight and met at right angles, confirming the town's former grandeur.[57] These streets might be straight but they still appeared narrow to English eyes, because newcomers from northern Europe had yet to recognize the benefits in the tropics of the shade provided by adjacent buildings. Furthermore, many of the individual buildings lining these

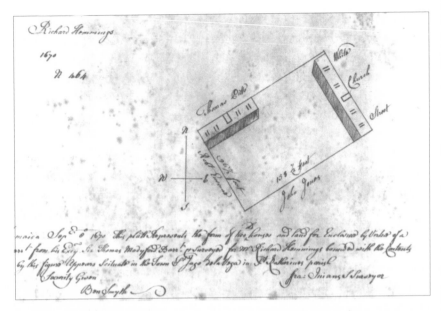

FIGURE 2.1 An English land surveyor's sketch of a Spanish-built compound. (Jamaica Archives)

cramped streets were not just unfamiliar; their underlying spatial organization followed an alien logic. Back in England frontage on a town's principal shopping streets was at a premium, so urban builders took full advantage of it, cramming tall houses onto the front of long narrow lots.[58] In contrast, the former Spanish settlers at Spanish Town had built compounds within a town block, where low-lying single-storey houses opened inward towards central gardens while presenting their backs to the surrounding streets and lanes. Newly arrived visitors continued to be struck by the large arched wooden gates that dominated the public facades of these compounds.[59] The gates that remained shut to such passers-by appeared Spanish, not English.

The town's Spanish houses looked thoroughly foreign too. There was more to this incomprehension than newcomers disparaging vernacular construction with local materials – though this certainly occurred too.[60] Metropolitan visitors would dismiss many of the wooden houses erected by first generation English settlers in both the Eastern Caribbean and the North American mainland as temporary structures, but those buildings retained English proportions and their nascent townships incorporated familiar urban alignments. Hence in Virginia, mid-seventeenth-century Jamestown had 'a street pattern focused on public buildings and lined with contiguous lots'.

Similar priorities oriented St Mary's City in Maryland.[61] The initial lay out in Bridgetown, Barbados, was less coherent, with house lots crammed into available spaces.[62] In contrast to all of these, Spanish Town's Spanish houses seemed 'scatteringly built'. In 1655 some newcomers who tried to apply their accustomed 'standards' to appraise the structures lining urban streets in a town whose buildings followed Spanish proportions could hardly tell where the streets ran.[63]

The designs of the surviving Spanish houses might be practical and sufficiently effective to withstand earthquakes and hurricanes yet remain cool and dry, but they still seemed alien. There was certainly much in these single-storey structures that should have looked familiar: wattle-and-daub construction, using panels of woven twigs with clay smeared over them, was widely used in England. Rural cottages and even some smaller town houses in Devon and the south west (where many vessels that sailed to the Caribbean originated or put in for final supplies) were still made of 'cob' with layers of clay, sometimes strengthened with chopped straw, built up between wooden shuttering.[64] But by the 1650s and '60s these mundane structures were not the urban building styles that up-to-date English townspeople chose. The differences remained decisive and here the proportions of the Spanish houses seemed jarringly unfamiliar too, with far lower ceilings than fashionable English builders had used for a century.[65] Visitors who arrived at Spanish Town by way of the aggressively 'English' Port Royal continued to find both the size and the scale of the older town a disappointment.

Despite all the wartime demolitions and rebuildings the townspeople continued to inhabit Spanish building lots on a Spanish ground plan. A returning Spaniard would have found the general continuity in the town's streets confirmed by the re-use of several public buildings. The White Church was now demolished; however, the brick-built Red Church of the Dominican friars by the market was retained by the army's Protestant chaplains. From the time of the town's initial capture the former city hall had become the military commander's house, though Colonel D'Oyley also built himself another wooden house over at Cagway, down by the quayside.[66] The wooden former *Audiencia* in Spanish Town's Parade remained standing, as did the old town prison and that cookshop established in an older Spanish stable.[67]

Any Spanish visitor who made more enquiries might find further continuities even among some of the town's most disconcerting new residents.

The incoming English settlers included a number of Quakers. In the late 1650s the Society of Friends was among the most radical of the godly sects then establishing followings in England; however, because the settlement in Jamaica remained desperate for recruits its leaders could not afford intolerance. The place of worship assigned to the Quakers out on the edge of the town was located either at, or very near, the site of the former Franciscan friary.[68] A generation later, in 1688, when changing politics in England allowed the town's Roman Catholic community to worship publicly for a year – before the pro-Catholic King James II was ousted – the Catholics also reused an older Spanish structure, taking over the old 'White Chapel' on the south side of the town.[69] Uniformity of religion was gone now and different congregations worshipped in former Spanish chapels. However, some of the chapels that shaped Spanish urban spaces were taken over. The English reused some old Spanish foundations, but in a very different fashion.

Spanish streets and structures continued to shape the town, but the African presence was always visible in these streets. In the early 1660s the status achieved by a few of the free African Jamaicans who lived in the town would appear remarkable to any newcomers arriving from other English West Indian colonies. The African Jamaican townspeople became the most significant group remaining from the island's pre-invasion population. The military alliance with Juan de Bolas was central to the final English defeat of Ysassi and the other Spanish holdouts, though generations of colonial histories of Jamaica would do their best to gloss over this fact. De Bolas, the Colonel of the 'Black Regiment' in the island's militia, was killed during an attempt to negotiate with the *cimarrone* band led by Juan de Serras based at the eastern (Leeward) end of the island. But, even after de Bolas's death, individual members of his group established themselves in Spanish Town, receiving grants of urban properties. In 1664 a neighbour's property boundary cited 'the Negro Mr De Camps House'. This deliberately assigned to de Camp the honorific 'Mr' that was not granted to all white males. If this is the same 'Major de Campo' whom the English military Governor gave 'a let pass for himself and other negroes' in 1660, then both de Camp's grant and another grant for one 'Anthony Rodrigues a Negro Soldier of the English Army', who received a house facing onto the Parade, suggests that one legacy of the military campaigns of the 1650s was continuing prominence in public spaces in the early 1660s.[70] Members of de Bolas's band also remained a distinct presence in the town's rural hinterland for at least the next generation. Besides holding land some chose different crops to grow in their fields. When they planted rice they produced a grain that English settlers did not know how to cultivate.[71]

The contrasts between Spanish continuities and English developments in Spanish Town's streets became more striking for planters who came into the town to do their marketing or participate in a lawsuit. Spanish Town provided an administrative and marketing centre for a rapidly developing agricultural hinterland and this hinterland soon bore the stamp of the sugar revolution that the English planters brought with them from the Eastern Caribbean. The English sought to transform the island's rural landscape. Across the settled parts of the island would-be planters rejoiced 'to see how bravely the canes grow' and how the slaves 'go tumbling down the trees'.[72] In the process surviving farm buildings from the Spanish period were demolished or swallowed up in the fast-growing bush. One legacy of the guerrilla war and the subsequent shift to sugar was that by the 1680s and '90s Spanish Town was the primary location in Jamaica where people could see Spanish buildings still in use. Further exceptions included the aqueduct and stone ruins at New Seville, a single two-storey Spanish farm house in Liguanea, an old tavern in Yallas and a few other scattered individual buildings, but only in Spanish Town was there such a concentration of 'Spanish' structures.[73]

The continuing Spanishness of the town was something that settlers stressed. Of course gullible visitors to the newly established English colony could hear wonderful tales of Spanish treasure. If they bought enough drinks at a tavern or punch house, they would be told of hoards hidden away in big pottery jars cached in remote caves up in the mountains, guarded with magic spells. Indeed, the same magic spells continued to conceal the Spaniards' gold and silver mines from the English. Because these mines remain lost to this day, our punch-sodden hearers would recognize how potent these enchantments were. However, many of the Spanish ghosts whose stories fuelled the Anglo-Jamaican imagination clustered in and around Spanish Town. One seventeenth-century story described how a thirsty townsman wandering down the streets to the river for a drink on one hot night, tripped over two heavy pottery jars that clinked. Unwisely deciding to leave them until he had slaked his thirst, he found that by the time he returned, they had gone, only leaving two telltale indentations in the dust. The tall tales continued as the bowls of ferocious rum punch circulated, assuring newcomers that ghostly Spanish cavaliers still galloped around the town's Parade after curfew, right in the very heart of the English colony.[74] Despite all the English colonists' efforts, in their imaginings St Iago de la Vega remained a Spanish town.

Criteria for selecting the island's capital

In 1662 this island colony conquered as a part of Oliver Cromwell's Western Design survived one of its biggest challenges. Jamaica was *not* returned to the Spaniards by Charles Stuart after he was restored to his father's thrones as King Charles II. Returning the island to Spain had appeared a likely option at the time – Colonel D'Oyley discouraged his soldiers from settling, assuming that the island would be given back by a monarch who was not only the heir of the king deposed and executed by Cromwell but had found refuge in Spain during Cromwell's regime.[75] Instead Charles II chose to retain Jamaica and the English would not leave for another 300 years.[76]

Establishing a civilian government raised new issues. If the town they called 'Spanish Town' remained so unfamiliar to English settlers while Cagway seemed so promising, why was the older inland centre retained as Jamaica's seat of government after the military campaigning was finally concluded? The primary urban centres of the earlier transatlantic English colonial settlements were at the principal port, such as Bridgetown in Barbados where in early 1655 the military council was established to lead the Western Design.[77] The previous half century had shown plenty of other examples of English port-capitals too: Virginia's Jamestown, Maryland's St Mary's City, Connecticut's Hartford and New Haven, Rhode Island's Newport, or Massachusetts' Boston.[78] Jamaica differs, not only in retaining a secondary urban centre located seven miles inland from the coast, but also in using this location for the seat of the colony's government. This was not where settlers from England expected to establish the administrative centre for a colony. What, then, was to prevent authority being relocated to a port in Jamaica, especially when English Jamaica quickly acquired a major port town of its own?

This question appears particularly relevant as the new port out in the harbour flourished. Ships sailing from Cagway/Port Royal enjoyed direct access to the Spanish ports of modern Colombia and Nicaragua. As we have seen too, it had provided the administrative centre of choice for Colonel D'Oyley, Protector Cromwell's final military governor. In contrast to Spanish

Town's inherited street grid and its surviving Spanish houses, the port's streets soon stretched back in a rough fan from the Chocolata Hole landing place filled with buildings that mimicked English architectural styles.

Initially the prospects looked favourable for settling the administration of Jamaica in Port Royal. In the royal colony of Jamaica the martial law that had regulated the settlement's first years was replaced by the introduction of the English common law and the calling of an Assembly. The first Assembly met at Cagway in January 1664. Recasting themselves as loyal royalists the settlers tactfully renamed the town Port Royal and replaced the name of its 'Fort Cromwell' with 'Fort Charles'. Yet, despite institutions' tendency to maintain an established pattern, the settlers' representatives who gathered in Port Royal in 1664 decided to return both the colony's subsequent assemblies and its new central law courts to St Iago de la Vega. The English colony did not simply retain the older Spanish town as its main administrative centre: instead, despite making a start at Port Royal the settlers' representatives made a deliberate choice to place Jamaica's legal and administrative business in the old Spanish site.

This decision leaves us with a further question: why? Negative reasons helped reinstate Spanish Town as Jamaica's seat of government. It was far more convenient than Port Royal; or, at least, not nearly as inconvenient. After holding one Assembly session out at Port Royal, the Assemblymen from the remainder of the island recognized this. What's more, the Assembly offered one forum where the mainland parishes could outvote Port Royal's merchants. The Spaniards' town stood 'in the heart of the country', it was far 'more easy for the planters to come at' as it was at the centre of the old Spanish road network.[79] Influential settlers had continued to seek property in Spanish Town even when the Council and Assembly were scheduled to meet in Port Royal. The incoming royal Deputy Governor secured a grant in 1661 for the former Fort Henry, which as 'the forthouse' became a prominent private residence on the south side of the town.[80] Similarly the old Spanish *Audiencia* building on the Parade was granted to Captain Richard Hemmings, a well-connected ex-army officer who had already succeeded in obtaining the site of the former Spanish settlement at New Seville as a plantation. However, after the Assembly decided to move the island's law courts to Spanish Town, the Council reconsidered the grant to Hemmings and reclaimed the old court house to be 'preserved for the use of the Publick'.[81] Undeterred, Hemmings soon acquired another house in Spanish Town.[82] This was, indeed, 'a Town improving every day' – even if it was not 'improving' nearly as fast as the colony's principal port.[83]

Certainly there were advantages to Port Royal. It offered seamen an excellent harbour: being 'every where good Anchorage', while the water alongside its moorings was 'so deep, that a Ship of a thousand tons may lay his sides to the Shore of the Point, and load and unload', simply walking their goods up and down the gangplank.[84] This was far easier than the lighterage required to get goods ashore at Passage Fort and other roadsteads. Port Royal provided a superb starting point for voyages either to break into the Spanish colonies' protected trade or to prey on their towns and shipping.[85] For this reason privateers and smugglers returned there, to drink and debauch their way through their cash in Port Royal's rum shops. But, while the port that developed at the Spaniards' former Careening Place offered mariners a sheltered anchorage and, indeed, soon housed extensive facilities for rest and recreation, the original reason for selecting this site as the English invading fleet's primary haven was so that the cannon mounted there could cover the entrance channel into Kingston Harbour. A location on a sand bank at the entrance to the harbour chosen because of the field of fire for its artillery not only offered a good anchorage but lay beyond the range of the mosquitoes and fevers that wiped out most of the English invading army. Colonel D'Oyley was prudent to move his administration out there.

Port Royal's advantages were still outweighed by major disadvantages. The town remained cut off from the mainland. Living expenses were always extraordinarily high as all its food came in by boat. Port Royal did not even have a local source of fresh water. Every day canoes rowed across the harbour to fill water barrels at a stream.[86] A question posed by the Royal Society in London to an outward-bound Governor of Jamaica demonstrated the extent of the problem: could hogs be sustained on the brackish water that the townspeople found whenever they dug pits?[87] They could not. Nor was this all. Even getting out to Port Royal proved a chore, involving long and expensive ferry rides. Assemblymen from the remainder of the island found Port Royal thoroughly inconvenient as a prospective administrative and legal centre for an agricultural colony. It was in these contexts that a petition delivered by the Assembly's first Speaker argued 'the said Town of St Iago de la Vega is in the heart of the Country and more easy for the Planters to come at, whereas the other is situate on a Point far out to sea, and is very chargeable for the Planters in general to come at it by Water.'[88]

Port Royal's merchants and their lawyers continued to publish critiques claiming that it was simply illogical to maintain the settlement at Spanish Town when Port Royal was available, 'because the trade of the Country consisteth wholly of Planters and Merchandising.' In such terms, planters should reside on their plantations while the merchants would carry out their business 'in the Seaport Towns', so that 'there is no occasion in the Inland parts for such a Community of Men to dwell together'.[89] Such clear-cut claims might appear reasonable enough when expounded in Port Royal's counting houses and taverns. Settlers who lived anywhere else in Jamaica would still be put off by the prospect of rowing out to Port Royal, to eat and drink at its inflated prices, while undertaking their legal business there, whether it be in the colony's government offices, at the Assembly, or in the law courts. Even farmers needed occasional town visits, and Port Royal remained a difficult town to reach from the mainland.

Back in London the claims made by the Port Royal merchants cut very little ice when set against King Charles II's statement that he intended to make Jamaica a colony of settlement and had no intention of simply establishing 'a Christian Algiers' where pirate ships could take on supplies and sell their plunder.[90] Similar priorities continued after King Charles' death. In 1687 King James II's Treasury officials recommended that Colonel D'Oyley's old wooden King's House from the 1650s standing in Port Royal be sold and the money used to pay for repairs to the dilapidated King's House in St Iago.[91] Both buildings' destruction during the 1692 earthquake rendered this recommendation moot. In the late seventeenth century courtiers and planters, both groups which valued the landed interest, placed the general accessibility of an administrative centre to the island's agricultural settlements well ahead of the concept of putting the Governor, administration and law courts out at the harbour mouth, convenient as the latter might be to the island's merchants and seamen.

Still an inland centre for a very different agricultural colony

In a further major shift, land settlement patterns were very different under English rule. The dispersed rural population in the English colony ran counter to Spanish social priorities. The Spanish always sought to establish towns in their rural landscapes rather than scattering households thinly across agrarian areas.[92] The inland town that developed as English Jamaica's administrative centre would undertake very different roles from its Spanish predecessor. In the town many households' residence were still determined by the seasons. Whether the island's sugar planters were Spanish or English, they were all eager to get back to their plantations during crop time. However, if under Spanish rule settlers expected to live in St Jago and go out to the country occasionally; under the English planters might own a house in Spanish Town, but their usual residence was out on their estates and they only came into town for a social 'season' during the law terms and for sessions of the Assembly.

The transition in the town's status proved more extensive. Spanish Town ceased to be the island's principal settlement – at least for most of the year. When the English disembarked in 1655, Jamaica's only town housed most of the island's total population of about 1,500 people.[93] Afterwards Port Cagway/Port Royal would win all subsequent population competitions hands down. By 1662, Spanish Town's population had declined to 207 men, 52 women, 42 children and 53 slaves, far fewer than under Spanish rule. Furthermore, this 354 was less than half of the 740 residents counted in Port Royal (and even the latter figures excluded the seamen on shore at any given time). However, the break from Spanish colonial priorities was broader still. Under English rule urban dwellers were a minority even among the island's free settlers. The combined total of 1,094 inhabitants of Port Royal and Spanish Town pretty well split between two sites the islandwide total under the Spaniards. In 1662, though, 1,094 was barely a quarter of the total 3,653 English and 552 slaves counted on the island.[94] Under this regime most of the free population as well as the slaves lived out in the countryside, dispersed across the island. Over the following 250 years the urban proportion of Jamaica's population – both free and enslaved – always remained a minority.

The process of dispersed agricultural settlement under the English still contributed to the continued utility of Spanish Town for people from the inland parishes. In the late seventeenth century the primary regions for new settlement were the Liguanea Plain, just north of today's Kingston Harbour and the St Catherine's plain. Outliers included the parishes of Vere and Clarendon just to the west, besides the parish of St Thomas in the Vale further north, with later expansion into the parish of St Elizabeth, farther west along the Spaniards' old coastal road. Spanish Town offered a convenient centre for many of the planters in English Jamaica. This would be particularly

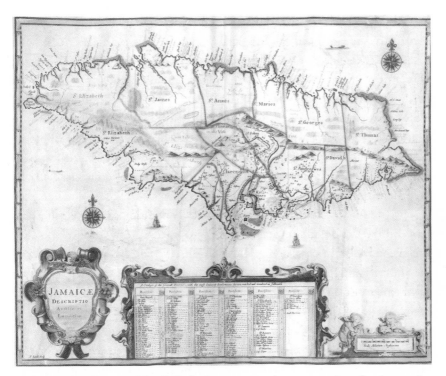

FIGURE 2.2 Jamaica, 1671, John Ogilvy's 1672 map: note the concentration of settlements in the parishes on the south side of the island. Spanish Town was accessible to many of the planters settled here. (John Carter Brown Library, Brown University).

significant in the Assembly, because even though Spanish Town and Port Royal each elected two Assemblymen, most of the members represented rural constituencies so the planter interest generally dominated the Assembly.

The site chosen by the Spanish settlers retained practical advantages in serving a scattered English rural population. A location at one of the principal crossroads on the island could provide practical services in addition to housing lawyers and litigants during law terms and assembly sessions. The sheer inconvenience of getting across to Port Royal also helped make the inland town's retail facilities more commercially viable. Planters could satisfy their day-to-day needs in Spanish Town. The blacksmith's shop that archaeologists have excavated on White Church Street would see a stream of local customers coming in to re-sharpen the axes, hoes and saws used in clearing fields. These customers might not be as freespending as the privateers and other seamen blowing their pay in Port Royal, but Spanish Town could still sustain a number of shopkeepers. Although retailers by the quayside could access a much wider range of luxury goods, they also carried higher overheads. The inland settlement offered further services. By 1672 a schoolmaster teaching in Spanish Town had managed to accumulate £18 sterling 'of lawful Coyned Money' to buy 162 acres in rural St Elizabeth, demonstrating that money could be made from teaching.[95] In the 1680s there may well have been a theatre.[96] For a different clientele, cheap intoxicants were on offer: the 'kill-devil' of freshly distilled rum, 'perino' made from fermented cassava bread, while 'rapp' and 'mobby,' the last 'a pleasant cold liquor', were both prepared from fermented potatoes.[97] When supplies of the white china clay tobacco pipes imported from Europe ran out, smokers could purchase serviceable pipes made locally from the island's red clay.

The opportunities for selling provisions from Spanish Town extended well beyond its immediate vicinity. Port Royal, with all its visiting ships, constituted a substantial market for island-grown foodstuffs.[98] In the early years of the English settlement slaves operated a Saturday market between the mouth of the Rio Cobre and Passage Fort where they sold the surpluses grown on their garden plots. In 1685, however, the local militia had broken up this unsupervised market after a 'disturbance' at Passage Fort.[99] Subsequently, this trade migrated to the markets held in the squares at Spanish Town, which were easier for local officials to police. The town already held charters for markets that ran 'every Day from 6 of the clock to eleven in the forenoon for fish, fruit and herbs' and on Tuesday, Thursday and Saturday 'for Flesh'.[100]

One further way that townspeople returned to Spanish practices, was as a part of the late seventeenth-century revival of a cross-island livestock trade in Jamaica. The vast herds of semi-wild cattle that formerly grazed the surrounding savannas soon dispersed as hungry soldiers began shooting them indiscriminately. By the 1670s only a few remained on the north side of the island. Some of these were herded through the Bog Walk Gorge and then around Spanish Town to Passage Fort. There they were slaughtered and the meat was taken across the harbour to Port Royal. Butchers from Passage Fort and Port Royal were involved in this trade, together with butchers and cattle hands from Spanish Town.[101] However, the leather trade and its associated tanneries never regained the importance it had held under the Spaniards.

Other innovations were far grimmer. From the mid-1660s, the transatlantic slave trade occupied a prominent place in Spanish Town, which housed the Jamaican headquarters of the Royal African Company, the merchant group that held the official monopoly on importing slaves from West Africa to the English settlements in the West Indies.[102] This company also maintained an office and clerks in Port Royal to note when ships arrived from Africa. It erected holding pens for newly arrived slaves within the old Cromwellian fort at Passage Fort, where the slaves waited to be purchased by planters in Jamaica or else trans-shipped to Cartagena and the Spanish settlements. However, these facilities remained sub-offices. The Royal Africa Company's local agent was well positioned to lobby the Governor and Council for policies that the company supported with his vantage point on the Church Parade in Spanish Town. He could also pursue the company's many planter debtors through the law courts.[103] Both slavery and the business of the transatlantic slave trade were well-established enterprises in Spanish Town.

The Seat of Government for a prospering colony

The scale of the planters' displays in Spanish Town during sessions of the law courts and Assembly was far more splendid than was attained in the English colonial capitals in mainland North America. Jamaica's newly wealthy planters spent lavishly on conspicuous consumption. In the evenings they would take their exercise by going for a ride in their carriages – just as though they were back in London's Hyde Park. While the Assemblymen dined and argued, visiting planters' carriages clogged the road out to the town's race course. In 1688 a political crisis arose when a member of the Assembly wanted to leave the House to race his horse. He objected when the Speaker refused to give him permission because even one more absentee would leave the day's session without a quorum and unable to conduct any business. The disappointed competitor's muttered 'salus populi suprema lex' (the safety of the people is the supreme law) or, maybe 'Populi est suprema lex' (the people are the supreme law), that marked his annoyance at missing a prime racing day, may not have been particularly appropriate. His unguarded phrase still appeared 'of dangerous Consequence'. Another Assemblyman, a former Royalist and 'ultra-prerogative man' reported this exchange to the Governor and for that breach of privilege, was expelled from the Assembly.[104] The subsequent controversy distracted the rest of the session even more than the racing. The episode not only illustrates a tactless Governor's nervousness about Jamaican politics, but also the assumption held by an Assemblyman from Clarendon that he could race his horse while he was in Spanish Town.

Judged by the standards of most English colonial centres in the late seventeenth century, Spanish Town provided a significant regional hub. It apparently supported more local trade than either Jamestown in Virginia or St Mary's in Maryland, the seats of government of larger and longer-established English colonies. Still, despite all its enterprises, the town never became as substantial a trading centre as Port Royal. Contemporaries (and, indeed, later historians) all emphasized this disparity, in part, certainly, because they could readily set Spanish Town's relatively modest achievements alongside Port Royal's remarkable growth. Such comparisons left Spanish Town looking disappointing, especially when contemporaries also measured the small inland settlement they found against the wildly over-optimistic descriptions sent back when the English first arrived in Jamaica. When set against the exaggerated claims for the size and wealth of the newly captured St Jago made by the leaders of the invading English army, the reality of late seventeenth-century Spanish Town was bound to be disappointing. Port Royal, of course, was hardly the easiest neighbour to match because it quickly outstripped most other English transatlantic ports, with traffic comparable to Boston, New York or Philadelphia.[105] Assessed on its own terms Spanish Town continued to prosper.

The seasonal nature of a social cycle tied to the law terms and Assembly sessions meant that most of the people in the streets were transients, albeit likely enough to return for another exchange of lawsuits or for a subsequent meeting of the Assembly. A resident population did develop within the town where shopkeepers and lodging-house keepers became conspicuous. In 1675 Spanish Town's shopkeepers, together with its tavern keepers and men who 'let houses to hire', appeared so prosperous that the Assembly proposed to recruit them for the Governor's bodyguard, an expensive and time-consuming honour. Urgent lobbying amended the bill, sparing the town's retailers the extra duty.[106] A proposal that only targeted the town's male businessmen can offer a skewed view of the make up of a resident population where female-owned establishments provided townspeople with long-lasting landmarks. By the 1680s and '90s two different surveys each report two streets identified by women's names: a 'Street by Anne Taylors' parallel to 'a street by Mrs. Keherne' in one survey and 'a Street by Mrs. Fleetwoods' and, running into it, 'A Street by Mrs. Cornwallis' in the second.[107] Lodging houses and 'ordinaries' (the restaurants of the day) were prominent components of townspeople's urban environment, hence the women who kept lodging houses and ordinaries were conspicuous in their own rights in a townscape with few permanent residents. Late seventeenth-century Spanish Town complemented Port Royal. While Port Royal became a rich port whose seamen forced their way into the trade between the Spanish settlements, the older settlement at Spanish Town increasingly offered a different urban synthesis. Retailers' displays in Port Royal outshone White Church Street's new shops, but Spanish Town's streets were quickly embellished with a number of new brick private houses erected on the old Spanish building lots. Although Port Royal's merchants out built them, these structures still remained impressive in their own right. From the early 1660s builders in the older city displayed their confidence in the long-term English presence on the island, erecting sturdy one- and two-storey brick buildings.[108] The trend began well before the 1670 Treaty of Madrid, where the Spanish Crown formally relinquished its claims to Jamaica.

All this changed when the 1692 earthquake not only shattered Port Royal, but also demolished builders' investments across the rest of the island. The over-rigid brick houses and sugar factories erected by the first generation of English settlers as monuments to their confidence collapsed.[109] In the process Spanish Town lost its splendid English brick private houses. Meanwhile, the older Spanish houses in the town, with their wall posts dug deep into the ground, absorbed the shock and remained standing, though the lots beside

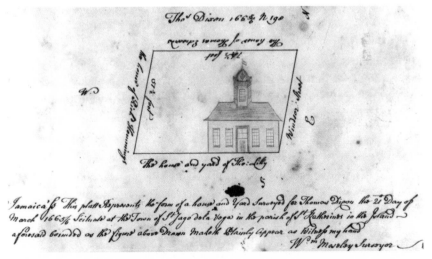

FIGURE 2.3 Brick Built Splendour, Spanish Town, a sketch of an ambitious house whose elaborate decoration would not have looked out of place on an English high street. The drawing was made just before the Great Fire of London, so that the rebuilding of London after the Fire could not have provided the impetus for these commissions. (Jamaica Archives)

them were filled with rubble.[110] After the earthquake, Spanish Town reverted from being an English town erected on older Spanish footings to a townscape where the most substantial surviving buildings – both public and private – were inherited from the earlier Spanish settlement.

Survivals

Little remains from the early periods of the town's history. Townspeople still called the square in front of the brick Red Church at the corner of White Church Street and Barrett Street, 'the Spanish Market Place'.[111] It remained the commercial centre of both the Spanish and the late seventeenth-century English towns. Properties facing onto what was also called 'the Church Parade' were more often subdivided, with the cookhouses sold to one purchaser and the houses themselves divided among other buyers.[112] Under the English the more densely packed retail area near the Red Church extended outward along the streets leading to the market. Properties on either side of the southern end of White Church Street and others backing up towards the river along today's Barrett Street were divided too. These subdivisions occasionally created such slivers of street frontage as the 'one Room belonging to a shade with the ground proportionable to it' (which stood just across the street from a surgeon's house at the top of White Church Street) or a single room in the house next door which then sold and re-sold over the space of two or three years, offering the hopeful purchasers sites for their shops, stalls and cookhouses.[113] Many of the buildings mentioned in these transactions were furnished with sizable 'shades' or proto-verandas. These added structures were not of either Spanish or English origins but appear to have developed in Barbados in the 1650s and had been then brought to Jamaica by the invading army.[114]

Today, the principal material remains surviving above ground from this key period of development are at the Anglican Cathedral. This is a thoroughly unexpected legacy from a society where not only would a visiting minister find 'sin very high and religion very low' but where an eighteenth-century rebuilding and Victorian 'restoration' replaced most of the seventeenth-century church.[115] The brick Church of the Dominican friars which was newly erected in 1655 was reused by the English who called it 'the Red Church'. The English did not recall its original dedication to Our Lady of Mercy and during the 1680s some claimed that it had been dedicated to St Paul, then during the eighteenth century, antiquarian whimsy filled the gap, claiming, with echoes of Edmund Spenser's Red Cross Knight in the *Fairy Queen*, that it was 'the Red-Cross Church'.[116] However, some of the first preachers in its newly rebuilt interior were English Protestants, including Thomas Gage, whom we met on the initial landing fleet. The basic space that Gage faced when he preached inside the nave of today's church remains, but only as an architectural fossil, because reused Spanish foundations dictated the current proportions of the body of the church. Today's windows, walls and roof are all later replacements.

The earliest material from the more confident English regime of the 1660s, '70s and '80s can be seen outside the Cathedral. These stone grave slabs commemorate leading early colonists. They now provide a supplementary drip course, sheltering the external foundations of the Cathedral choir. The Victorian rebuilding of the east end of the church in the 1840s dug up the chancel (the area around the altar) and the late seventeenth-century memorial slabs that surrounded the altar were pried up and placed outside. They were top quality imported carved stones and have withstood their removal and time outdoors remarkably well. On the north side of the Cathedral they include memorials to such successful early settler-governors as Sir Thomas Modyford and Sir Thomas Lynch, together with Modyford's wife and son-in-law, and to Thomas Duck, an early Attorney General for the colony whose wife was killed during a slave revolt at his plantation in 1678.[117] These dozen slabs outside and some additional worn slabs which remain inside lining the floor of the nave under the pews in front of the altar step are the most tangible remnants of the baroque splendour the first generation of English settlers in Spanish Town so admired.[118]

Gardens throughout the town constitute a further legacy of this initial period of English settlement.[119] Botanical notes made by a visiting English doctor in the 1670s show that the new residents had imported several popular English garden flowers, including marigolds, nasturtiums, lavender and red and white lilies.[120] Outside the town an ecological transformation of much wider extent got underway during this first generation of English settlement. Travellers on the road up from Passage Fort would see a landscape in the process of change as the island's hardwood forests were cut down. Then, behind newly planted hedges of limes, the process of development proceeded apace. At first the newly cleared land was planted with red peas, grown among the stumps. These were fed to the slaves. The next year potatoes were planted. Then, during the third year, after the hardwood stumps finally began to rot, they were pried up and burnt to clear fields for the sugar canes.[121] Stump by stump, hedge by hedge, these efforts created a new landscape as the practices of sugar growing developed in Barbados and the Leeward Islands in the 1640s were brought west to Jamaica, well ahead of the rest of the Greater Antilles. Spanish Town served as the centre for this planting society.

Jamaica may have been a Spanish agricultural colony for over 150 years, but after sugar cultivation reshaped the landscapes on the coastal plains on Jamaica's south side, then this former Spanish town increasingly appeared the most 'Spanish' place on the island. The transition from the Spanish St Jago de la Vega to the English Spanish Town in 1655 was abrupt. It involved an across-the-board transformation not just in the population but in the ways that the residents of the town then saw a town's place in a colonial settlement. The English settlers' choice of 'Spanish Town' as their name for the town, along with the fact that individual African Jamaican soldiers or members of Juan de Bolas's *pelinco* did have houses in the town, also testified to some continuities between the Spanish townscape and its English successor. Here the early grants of houses in Spanish Town to leading officers in the invading English army probably played a major role in ensuring continuity in the town's old streets and house lots, even under English governments that found Spanish spatial ratios very alien.

Once civil government replaced the military council, the crossroads site that Treasurer Pedro de Maçuelo recommended in 1534 continued to offer a convenient location for planters to gather to undertake their legal and administrative business. All the more so when the principal alternative offered to these planters was not only a highly expensive town out on the end of the Pallisados peninsula, but when Port Royal was dominated by merchant and seafaring interests whose priorities were not the same as those of the planters. Jamaica's English conquerors continued to use St Jago de la Vega despite themselves. They found it a Spanish Town, indeed.

—

CHAPTER THREE

'A mere scattered village'?

Spanish Town, 1692–1754

*T*HE 1692 EARTHQUAKE struck all the towns around today's Kingston Harbour.[1] Afterwards the rebuilt Spanish Town retained far greater continuity than its sister settlements, where few pre-quake structures survived. At this juncture each of the colony's three primary settlements – Spanish Town, Port Royal and, now, Kingston increasingly developed in distinctive fashions. This chapter examines how contemporaries understood distinctions in building styles and in urban roles and then explores the implications of these differences on the organization of the individual towns. Tracing the ways that the post-earthquake rebuilding reshaped all the towns around Kingston Harbour illuminates the growing divergence between the functions that they each performed. Over the 60 years between 1692 and 1754 competition for dominance, initially between Port Royal and partisans for the new Kingston, and then from the 1710s increasingly between Kingston and Spanish Town, would provide a central element in Jamaican affairs. The issues raised in these disputes offer useful insights into the roles that the island's principal urban centres performed in a colony where sugar planting and semi-legitimate trading with the Spanish mainland territories produced remarkable wealth in a brutal society.

The most extensive developments occurred at the newly built Kingston, a mainland port laid out on a site across the harbour from the destroyed Port Royal. Its ambitious design was intended to house the displaced residents of Port Royal, or at least those who survived the fevers that swept through the refugees. After the earthquake, the new Kingston replaced the former settlement of Liguanea, which had developed farther to the west on the north shore of what was then 'Port Royal Harbour' but would later become known as 'Kingston Harbour'. Initially the canoes that came over to the mainland from Port Royal to collect drinking water landed at Liguanea. The site lay on an old Spanish path. By 1665 some warehouses were built at the landing point, a Saturday market began and a settlement developed that by 1688 contained 'a new church, some twenty shops and houses and two or three taverns', which then provided the residents of Port Royal with a country retreat.[2] Despite these foundations, Liguanea never recovered from the earthquake that flattened it. Its successor, Kingston, lay at a junction in the local road network that the area's English settlers had developed over the previous 40 years. It was planned as an ambitious town from its start, laid out in a neat grid on a green field site – and, conveniently for power brokers, on a green field that belonged to the island's then Governor. From its beginning Kingston was expected to house the government and administration of the colony. However, while the plan was sketched briskly, persuading investors to erect buildings or anyone to settle there proved an uphill task.[3] It would take 60 years to transfer the seat of government, even briefly, away from Spanish Town.

Meanwhile, Port Royal was slated to become a secondary centre. This was not what its residents wanted. New building on its remaining streets left it looking very different and effectively constructed a creole town. The tall 'English' brick buildings that collapsed so spectacularly during the earthquake were replaced by one- or two-story wooden structures with shingled roofs and porches enclosed by wooden jalousie blinds.[4] Rebuilding commenced as soon as possible, regardless of the plans made by the island's Council that Kingston should supersede Port Royal. Merchants and mariners still preferred to return to Port Royal, which still offered an excellent harbour, even after it was reduced to a 25 acre island. The demand for building land there meant that the heirs of a leading official who died in the disaster faced several bidders for his former house lot, a 'piece of bare sand'.[5]

Spanish Town was also rebuilt fairly briskly after the earthquake. In contrast to the new layout of both the harbour towns, the rebuilt streets in the inland town appeared strikingly old-fashioned. This was mostly due to the sheer resilience of its inherited Spanish houses. Their deeply dug posts and thick roofs enabled them to withstand both the earthquake and the subsequent 1712 hurricane far better than either the brick buildings that the English settlers built before the earthquake or the shingle-roofed wooden houses they erected after it. The only Spanish houses to sustain any damage from the hurricane were those that stood too close to English buildings as they disintegrated.[6] With these buildings remaining in place the existing property boundaries were retained on those sites where English-built houses had collapsed, so that there was no opportunity to lay out broader streets. Yet, despite their proven resilience, these older houses still failed to impress. Travellers commended the town's charming location, but then disparaged its archaic Spanish houses along with its narrow streets. The contrast with Kingston remained all the stronger as the new houses lining Kingston's principal streets were all of a uniform height and displayed the brick facades and sash windows that demonstrated a properly up-to-date urbanity to visitors arriving from eighteenth-century Europe.[7]

The physical contrasts among Jamaica's principal towns remained prominent. To European eyes, Kingston appeared a more substantial place: being 'large and very well Inhabited' with wide regular streets. '[I]n the upper part of the Town [Kingston], called the Savannah, are many Sumptuous houses, with Gardens, and offices in proportion.' Spanish Town, in contrast, appeared far less active, 'supported alone by the concourse of people which the Government brings to it'.[8] Newcomers were unimpressed by the contrast between the low density of the single-storey buildings interspersed along Spanish Town's streets and the 'close built' blocks lining Kingston's thoroughfares. Some of Kingston's principal streets were faced with brick, but 'many of the Houses therein are of Deal [pine] and other North American Timber and are almost all of them Shingled with Deal' which, as their neighbours observed, 'are as ready to Catch fire almost as Tinder.' Comments from Spanish Town residents offered a far more positive spin on these differences arguing that, in contrast to Kingston, 'the town of St Jago is built in a very open and detached manner and most of the Houses stand separately and are built of Brick and Jamaican Timber and Tiled or Covered with Shingles of such Timber, which are not near so Subject to catch fire as Deal Shingles are.'[9] Long-term residents in the island might frame the contrast in terms of building materials: imported softwoods at the port, local hardwoods at Spanish Town, before citing Kingston's far greater fire risk. However, successive visitors from Europe, not only merchants, soldiers, sailors and French spies, but also royal governors, their guests and members of their households, were always far more favourably impressed by the familiarity of the brick houses and warehouses that lined Kingston's principal streets. So why wouldn't Jamaica's older-established settlers concur with all the newcomers' verdicts and acquiesce to abandoning Spanish Town for the thriving new port?

Considerably more was involved than contrasting building materials and styles. With the founding of Kingston in 1693 a further element was added to the earlier disputes among the colonists over where to locate Jamaica's 'Seat of Government'. Those arguments invoking the sheer inconvenience of Port Royal's site out at the end of a waterless peninsula that earlier planter Assemblymen invoked against using Jamaica's main trading centre as its capital would no longer appear valid once Kingston began to thrive. In practice Kingston's long-term success was hardly self-evident. Port Royal was rebuilt far more rapidly after the 1692 earthquake. It would then continue to be rebuilt after successive destructions: by a fire in January 1703, by a hurricane on August 28, 1712 and then by another hurricane and flood in 1722, which also struck on August 28th.[10] This decennial series of disasters provided repeated pushes, persuading merchants and seafarers to abandon Port Royal for the relative safety of Kingston, rather than Kingston's offering them any magnetic attraction.[11] However, after so many calamities, the result was the same: increasingly Kingston came to inherit the older port's trading functions. As a contemporary described Kingston in 1740, 'here the most considerable Merchants reside, which makes it a Place of vast Trade.'[12] The seafarers' transfer therefore had islandwide repercussions. Kingston stood on the mainland and could be reached by road from the remainder of the island. In the eyes of merchants based in Kingston, their bustling metropolis was surely the natural economic *and* political centre for the island.[13]

New Public Buildings in Spanish Town

Despite the growing competition from Kingston for pre-eminence, Spanish Town did not wither. To the contrary, official rebuilding efforts after the 1692 earthquake included several major commissions in the town, which remained the seat of the Governor, the Assembly and the Law Courts. Some of the fresh landmarks these provided still remain. Little is known of the fort constructed in a 'fairly regular square' that in 1706 stood 'behind' the church, but we do have evidence from an unlikely source: a French prisoner of war who took the opportunities offered by his captivity in Jamaica to compile notes on how the island might be seized, observed that the fort had 'four brick towers with very thick walls', each of which contained three cannons capable of firing 18 pound balls. However, the fort was still small so only the officers could be housed in it.[14]

Spanish Town's church, today's Anglican Cathedral, was also rebuilt at this juncture and remains the most substantial structure surviving today from the early eighteenth-century building campaigns. The Spanish-built Red Church had survived the 1692 earthquake but was destroyed in the hurricane in 1712.[15] Churchgoers would continue to be summoned to worship by the ringing of a small bell that hung on a free-standing wooden frame, which remained the case until a tower was built in 1760.[16] They would enter a brick Protestant church rebuilt on the foundations of the older Spanish church. This was in keeping with British usages. After London's 1666 'Great Fire' it was common practice for the Anglican churches erected in London in the 1670s, '80s and '90s to reuse medieval foundations and incorporate their floor plans – so in this, at any rate, the new building echoed fairly current English usages.[17] The eighteenth-century church inherited a traditional cross-shaped plan with north and south aisles, though its interior layout now focused on the pulpit in Protestant fashion. The rebuilt church was thus more 'English' in its ground plan than the rectangular wooden structures where many settlers worshipped in other British colonies on the North American mainland. Generally those churches did not have cross aisles.[18] Inside, however, the St Catherine parish church's mahogany and cedar panelled interior with its coved plastered ceiling, embellished with circles, ovals and lozenges, parallelled decorative features used in churches erected in early eighteenth-century Virginia.[19] The ceiling in Spanish Town remained less magnificent than one erected in Kingston's parish church in the 1750s, where drowsy members of the congregation could turn from the sermon to admire 'the gilded balls in the ceiling of the church'.[20] There were still massive brass chandeliers.[21] Until a hurricane in 1722 the altarpiece in Spanish Town included wooden statues of Moses and Aaron. Similar carved figures had flanked altars in London for nearly a century, but these would have a more immediate local impact with a synagogue standing only a few hundred yards

FIGURE 3:1 The Church of St Jago de la Vega. Costing £6,000, this was 'the finest and largest church in the English colonies in America', illustration from *Gentleman's Magazine*, December 1783, (John Carter Brown Library, Brown University).

to the north. After these figures fell and were damaged during the hurricane, the broken-nosed, broken-armed torsos were transferred to the vestry room and have subsequently disappeared as, by now, has all of the original internal wood and plasterwork from the 1712 structure.[22] We cannot therefore evaluate much of the craftsmanship lavished on this rebuilding, though the rich architectural carving on the ten mahogany columns that still support the organ loft suggests the elaboration of the 1712 woodwork that the mid-eighteenth-century carvers of these pillars aimed to match. A small area of alternating dark blue and white stone tiles from the eighteenth-century church's older floor lies under the crossing. These appear comparable to the 'six hundred blue and white Marble stones of a foot square' that the Kingston vestry ordered from Philadelphia for their own rebuilding in 1750.[23] The brick nave which survives from the early eighteenth-century rebuilding, does show that the parish vestry could recruit skilled bricklayers to carry out the work. These local craftsmen achieved work of the highest standard, producing a showpiece for the early eighteenth-century colony.

The principal new buildings that early eighteenth-century visitors to Spanish Town noticed were erected around the Parade, (the former main Spanish square). The new brick constructions were official commissions, emphasizing the town's continuing administrative roles. The old Spanish *cabildo* (city hall) on the western side of the Parade that the English Governors took over in 1655 was replaced. Even before the earthquake, by the 1680s the old 'King's House' (Governor's mansion) was proving too dilapidated to house the latest noblemen sent out to govern the island. As an expedient, incoming governors borrowed the mansion built by the Royal Africa Company's local agent, a favour that would do no harm to the Company's Jamaican interests.[24] After the earthquake the Council and Assembly voted for funds to build 'a very commodious House' that should be adequate to house a noble Governor. A range of new offices behind it was commissioned in 1711.[25] By the late-1720s further stone structures, some of which were two stories high, faced onto the Parade. A 'little court' stood alongside the Governor's 'great Dwelling-house' which held 'several handsome Apartments, now commonly used only for lodging his Excellency's Servants' and had 'a curious Garden towards the West'.[26] Subsequent hurricanes then enforced further rebuildings. A storm in 1726 left 'the King's house & other public Buildings in this Town . . . very much shattered', while another in 1744 that caused heavy damage in Kingston and Port Royal hit Spanish Town too.[27] Little survives from all this early eighteenth-century construction except for a brick platform which proved sufficiently resilient to provide a solid foundation for the still more magnificent King's House erected in the 1760s.[28]

The redevelopment of the Spanish Town Parade as a government centre inserted new structures into older sites. What changed in this round of rebuilding was who commissioned the work. In contrast to the 1660s, when the town's most prominent new brick buildings were private mansions, the construction projects undertaken in the 1690s led with public projects paid for out of the colony's tax revenues. The main buildings around the Parade addressed the administrative needs of both planters – and of the Kingston merchants' clerks – who rode in to check property titles, pursue lawsuits or, indeed, to petition his Excellency the Governor. Outside the law terms and sessions of the Assembly these areas saw less traffic, though the crowds who came in for the markets held in the Parade would generate plenty of noise and doubtless helped keep the 'ordinaries' (taverns) facing onto the Parade in business, even when there were no litigants needing to drown their sorrows.

The post-earthquake rebuilding around the main square also attempted to address visitors' spiritual needs, with a new Anglican chapel constructed on its south side as a permanent memorial to the earthquake. This was completed in 1697.[29] It stood just in front of the foundations of the former Spanish Abbot's White Church. This chapel was definitely an English structure, echoing the late medieval brick halls at the lawyers' Inns of Court in London.[30] Here preachers were to deliver memorial sermons urging their congregations to pray, repent and fast. Attendance proved sparse. Absentees included 'the *Tradesman* [who] even now (as it is his practice every Sunday too) enslaved in his mercenary gains, peeping thro' his half shut gates, in greedy expectation each passing hour will bring a customer', along with those 'who, even now, are close immured and in some house of vanity and riot, are deep engaged in *dice*, in *blasphemy* and *oaths!*' Meanwhile the planter remained out on his estate, taking the opportunity to inspect the 'hard-worked Slaves around their sultry fields' while his prodigal heir, even 'on this day of *direful memory* . . .' was barely waking 'from his horrid slumbers' while 'the *dark-hue'd* partner of his bed steals [away] thro' some private passage'.[31] As potential worshippers knew full well there were all too many alternative attractions. Preachers' recriminations could not fill the empty pews. So while fasting, repentance and prayer all remained necessary enough for the host of litigants, lawyers, assemblymen and socialites up for the season who flocked to Spanish Town during the law terms, within a generation the new chapel on the Parade was re-employed as a convenient fire-resistant storehouse for, first the parish militia's arms and ammunition and later for the arms held for the companies recruited among the town's 'free Negroes and Mulattoes'. A marble slab with an inscription that threatened anyone who dared put this building to any secular use proved insufficiently persuasive.[32]

Two less conspicuous buildings on and just behind the Parade's south-western corner brought further serious visitors into the town. One was a small brick office just beside the Governor's House – today its site lies under the southern end of the 1760s King's House ballroom. This housed the Island Secretary's Office, a place where key land and business transactions were registered.[33] Visitors to this building also included anyone wanting to leave the island who had secured a pass from the Governor: departing residents had to post their name at the Secretary's Office, to offer creditors and litigants due notice of their going.[34]

Of even more significance in a society where land underpinned wealth, the Island Secretary's Office processed and recorded property titles. Would-be settlers applied to the Governor for a grant of land in proportion to the number of people in their households. The claimant would employ a surveyor to make a measured sketch, or 'plat' of the particular piece of ground the new settler selected from the reserve of unclaimed Crown Land. To secure the grant, the new settler would then bring this plat, together with the grant from the Governor to the Island Secretary's Office for its official recording.[35] Subsequent mortgages would be noted in the margins of the ledger. Consequently, when neighbours took their quarrels over boundaries to court they would hire searchers to consult these records; if a landowner wanted to secure a further mortgage, or if a cautious merchant undertook a proto-credit check, similar searches took place.[36] Grants of land served to guarantee the merchant credits that underpinned the continuing development of the colony's plantations. Thus, the Island Secretary's Office in this small building remained a vital stop on many itineraries. The well-connected individual who held the royal patent to serve as Island Secretary remained in England, though he received a significant proportion of the fees collected by his local deputy's clerks when they registered the voluminous paperwork to confirm a title.[37]

Other visitors went another half block to the south-west, where the town's school stood behind the King's House and its stables complex. It backed onto the savanna. 'A street by the School House' and 'the school house land' continued to provide bearings that the townspeople used to describe where they stood in a town whose only three named streets were Monk Street, Red Church Street and White Church Street.[38] From the first it was an institution with influential patrons. Its trustees purchased a house there in 1677 for a schoolmaster 'ready to teach and instruct youth in the Latin Tongue and other learning necessary to be known'.[39] This was a pretty open-ended category. An Act of the Assembly in 1695 that aimed to establish a further Free School in the parish of St Andrew specified that its schoolmaster was to instruct the children of that parish 'in reading, writing, Latin, Greek, Hebrew, Arithmetic, Merchants Accounts and the Mathematics'.[40] This list would require a remarkably learned teacher for a programme which aimed to combine the traditional classical and religious training that English grammar schools promised with some more practical skills to equip pupils for commercial careers. These mixed ambitions were probably shared by the governors of Spanish Town's school too.

In practice the children of the richest settlers were sent off to England for their education, while the children of most of the free poor and of the unfree majority remained unschooled.[41] The St Andrew's school in consequence 'failed for want of means', while the enrollment in the grammar school in Spanish Town rarely rose above 14 boys.[42] The town also housed private school teachers who offered classes. The most famous of these was Francis Williams, an African Jamaican born to free parents in the town, who may – or may not – have been sent to Cambridge University, but who did study at the Inns of Court in London and then returned from England with a gentleman's education, able to compose creditable Latin verse.[43] Williams's portrait painted in Jamaica around 1734 showing off not just his gentleman's outfit and sizable library, but also the globe standing on the floor beside him and his copy of Sir Isaac Newton's *Principia* on the table, testifies to the range of his erudition.[44] The Jamaican plantocracy had difficulty accommodating his talents. However, educated visitors were impressed. Williams was probably the 'very agreeable Companion, though of an *African* Breed, a *Creole* of *Jamaica*, of *Negro* Parents', that one Scots physician recalled who had befriended him there in the mid-1740s: someone who 'had a superior Genius, a more liberal Education, and a better Understanding to improve it; which entitled him to keep better Company, . . . than any of the *Creoles* that ever I had the Honour of knowing in *Jamaica*'.[45] Few of the town's other teachers came up to Williams's standard while, as ever, writers describing Jamaica

Figure 3:2   Anonymous Portrait of Francis Williams, the Jamaican Scholar, c. 1734. In this portrait Williams is shown as a polymath among his books. (Victoria & Albert Museum)

continued to lament that 'Learning is here at the lowest Ebb', and would follow such dismal assertions with the general claim that 'there is no publick School in the whole Island'. Meanwhile good teachers proved hard to hire, particularly as they were 'looked upon as contemptible, and no Gentleman keeps Company with one of that Character'.[46] Yet, despite all the nay-saying, the town school continued to provide a landmark in townspeople's mental maps.

Other side streets held additional new buildings from the post-earthquake reconstruction. The Novéh Shalom (Dwelling Place of Peace) Synagogue on Monk Street provided another new landmark. Eighteenth-century Spanish Town housed a substantial Jewish community. Some of Port Royal's Jewish residents chose to move to Spanish Town rather than establishing a community and synagogue in Kingston. In November 1692, some six months after the earthquake, an 11-acre plot just to the south of the town was purchased by the 'Churchwardens of the Jewish Synagogue', part of which was then enclosed for use as a Jewish graveyard. A Prayer-Meeting Hall was erected by 1699. In 1703 what was then the island's principal synagogue transferred to Spanish Town shortly after the destruction of Port Royal's newly rebuilt Novéh Zedék (Dwelling Place of Righteousness) Synagogue in the fire that destroyed the whole town the previous January. The Novéh Shalom Synagogue was erected on a site in the older residential area on Monk Street, just at the northern end of the long-established Hospital Gardens.[47] The Jewish graveyard and synagogue remained a substantial presence in the town well into the twentieth century. Indeed, during the late seventeenth and early eighteenth centuries the Sephardim in Spanish Town became one of the most substantial Jewish communities anywhere in Britain's American empire.[48] The establishment of this thriving resident population in Spanish Town offered perhaps as substantial a vote of confidence in the town's future after the 1692 earthquake as the rebuilding work on the King's House or the continuing survival of the town's Free Grammar School.

During the first half of the eighteenth century Spanish Town already held a substantial number of public buildings: 'to wit, a very large and handsome Church; a Large and Convenient House and Outhouse belonging to His Majesty, in which the Governor of the Island has always resided, . . . a large Gaol, two Barracks for Soldiers, a Magazine for Powder, a Chapel Converted into a Magazine for Small Arms, [and] a Shed for Artillery.'[49] One of these Barracks stood between the Rio Cobre and the road south to Passage Fort.[50]

A contemporary's report described the gaol as 'excellently contrived; for the prisoners have the Liberty of a very large yard to walk in, which prevents the bad Consequences their close Confinement might produce in such a warm Climate' – although the author had probably not enjoyed its hospitality before commending it so highly.[51] Otherwise the Chapel faced onto the Parade while the other public buildings mostly stood nearby. All of them were erected after the great earthquake but, with the exception of the parish church, are now demolished. Private building commissions remain even more difficult to trace.

These post-earthquake building projects testified to continuing expectations for Spanish Town's viability, all the more so when a new brick bridge built over the Rio Cobre downriver from the town in 1699 should have helped tie the three towns of Kingston, Port Royal and Spanish Town together. Unfortunately a flood soon swept away this ambitious structure.[52] The scale of the public works projects undertaken to develop Spanish Town in the first half of the eighteenth century testify to its continuing importance. The Assemblymen who voted for them intended to improve the town that housed the Assembly. An ambitious plan to ease the town's connections with the sea by widening or re-digging the channel of the Rio Cobre found considerable support and the Assembly passed a bill allocating funds for this project in 1723. By opening Spanish Town's access for shipping the scheme looked to resolve the problems produced by the town's location several miles inland. Even with promises of financial backing from the Assembly the project still came to nought. Spanish Town would remain a seven-mile ride from the Harbour and 'as the river is not navigable, the town has but little trade'.[53]

An inland location would not cut off the town from the sea completely. Passage Fort, Spanish Town's harbour-side landing place, was rebuilt after the earthquake and continued to house a storehouse for the Royal Navy's victuallers.[54] During the 1730s Spanish Town's residents included the mother of Edward Teach, a notoriously bloodthirsty pirate who plagued the North Carolina coast and remains better known under his alias of 'Blackbeard'.[55] Not everyone in the crowds who gathered in the Parade to watch the executions of other Jamaica-based pirates attended out of ghoulish curiosity. Sailors continued to visit, particularly when the island's Governors objected to press gangs operating in Spanish Town and seizing seamen for service in the Royal Navy. In 1746 a naval party sent ashore to capture a number of deserters hiding there were themselves arrested by the local militia after 'being found armed in or about the town'. Merchant seamen seeking to avoid the press – and naval deserters too – might well decide to go inland to take their pleasures in Spanish Town's taverns. Another group of seamen arrested the same evening had come ashore to bring clothes to some messmates imprisoned there 'upon the information of a notorious strumpet', suggesting that once again 'Jack Tar ashore' had proved a rowdy guest.56 But, if such seafaring customers behaved themselves and paid for their pleasures, then in time of war any sailor who did not want to be dragged aboard one of His Majesty's warships would find it a safer refuge.

The town's privileges and its buildings both demonstrated that as the allocation of resources shifted around Kingston Harbour among Port Royal, Kingston and Spanish Town during the first 30 years of the eighteenth century, some substantial benefits came to the town that housed the colony's government. There were, indeed, solid reasons for individuals to settle in Spanish Town. From at least the 1740s its urban facilities included 'a Play-House, where they retain a set of Extraordinarily Good Actors' and, as one enthusiastic writer claimed, with 'frequent Balls' residents 'live as happily as if they were within the Verge of the British Court' – living so near to the royal palace as to be under the jurisdiction of its court.57 Two entries in an issue of the *Jamaica Courant* from June 1754 demonstrate the general range of Spanish Town's social facilities. On Saturday 22nd the Attorney General for the island lost his post to an individual who arrived with a more recent royal warrant. That evening 'the Gentlemen, Barristers and Attorneys of the said Supreme Court' offered the outgoing Attorney General an 'Entertainment prepared by them for that Purpose, at Mr Brown's Tavern, in the Town of St Iago de la Vega' where the guest of honour was 'cheerfully received' and enjoyed a speech in his praise. After which what remained of the evening was passed in 'Drinking his Majesty's and many Loyal Healths'. The same issue then noted another event the following Monday, when the 'Society of Free and Accepted Masons, met at Mr Curtis's in Spanish Town', – showing that this was not a one-tavern town. From there they processed to the parish church to sit through 'a learned Discourse suitable to the Day and Occasion' given by the Vicar, himself a Freemason, before returning to their Lodge to undertake 'the Ceremonies of the Day'. These were followed by 'a genteel Entertainment'.58 Even making allowances for what read like press releases, there was a fair choice of entertainment and an array of social venues on offer to any sojourners in the island's capital. Spanish Town provided a service town for seasonal visitors attending the Assembly and law courts. With these functions its permanent residents included a number of tradesmen in luxury crafts who employed skilled African Jamaican and African slaves in their workshops. There was also a fair number of landladies serving the same prosperous transient population who also constituted a prominent part of the town's year-round residents. The town still continued to recruit sufficient new residents to maintain its numbers and even to expand. The members of the synagogue management committee, who decided to move from Port Royal to Spanish Town, were not the only ones to relocate there. Its Spanish-chosen site proved fairly healthy – considerably more so than Kingston.

Kingston's opportunities

If Spanish Town prospered during the early eighteenth century; Kingston thrived. It became the primary landing place for slaves in the colony. Jamaica was a key transshipment point for slaves for the Western Caribbean, most – though never as many as the planters desired – would labour on Jamaican estates. Others were shipped on to the timber-cutting settlements on the Mosquito Coast (now part of Nicaragua) and Honduras (today's Belize) while, when politics permitted, larger numbers were shipped south to the Spanish mainland colonies, either to work on the farms there or in the silver mines of modern Peru. With all these markets to supply, increasing numbers of slave ships unloaded their cargoes at the dockside in Kingston. In 1708 the ending of the Royal African Company's monopoly over imports of slaves from West Africa into British territories offered Kingston's merchants an opportunity to move into this lucrative business. They seized it with both hands. During the first half of the eighteenth century Jamaica received 37 per cent of all the slave ships that sailed from West Africa to the British colonies in the West Indies and North America. Furthermore, the slave ships that sailed to Jamaica were usually the largest vessels.[59] This was a massive trade and it centred on Kingston. Among newly arrived slaves 'those who are not sold on board are sent to the factor's [local agent's] store to be disposed of there'. This latter group would include 'the weakly and sickly' slaves who were held in the pens and yards in the town belonging to the individual slave factors before they were auctioned.[60] If they lived – and after they had recovered somewhat from the voyage – the newly arrived slaves were then marched off to plantations inland, or shipped round to other ports in coasting vessels, or else held for re-export. The demand for labour on Jamaica's plantations provided the island's slave traders with an insatiable market.

Providing slaves and supplies of all sorts to Jamaica's planters was hardly the sum of Kingston's profits. The port's leading merchants made their fortunes from the ready access they enjoyed to the Spanish colonies on the South American mainland. The long-established Spanish convoy system never brought out enough consumer goods from Spain to supply the colonial markets. Small Jamaican schooners sailing out of Kingston filled the gap illegally, exchanging European cloth or African slaves for American silver and such tropical products as cocoa and indigo. Both the risks and the potential profits in these trades were high. Kingston's merchants could do very well for themselves, particularly when they acted as agents for British or North American merchant houses.[61]

Kingston's residents, however paid dearly for their prosperity. With swamps on both sides of its site the town was unhealthy from the first, and its death rates soared. Despite optimistic claims rejecting 'the objection' that Kingston was 'the most unhealthy part of the Island', as simply 'stale and worn out', reflecting the high death rates among the initial refugees from Port Royal, so that once the surrounding woods were felled the town would become healthy – this was never the case.[62] As a crossroads for international trade Kingston incubated tropical diseases that physicians, trained in medical schools in northern Europe, neither recognized nor knew how to treat. Mosquitoes bearing yellow fever or malaria or other fevers all found ready breeding grounds in the nearby marshland.[63] As a busy slaving centre Kingston became even more sickly. Frequent epidemics swept through the port, after the transfer of the slave trade to individual traders and partnerships, led to these traders abandoning the barracoon or holding pen over at the otherwise lightly populated Passage Fort that the Royal African Company had maintained, where its newly landed slaves had been concentrated. Afterwards, sick slaves were lodged in dealers' yards scattered across Kingston and the death rates among all of Kingston's populations remained dauntingly high.

Ambitious young merchants newly arrived from England or Scotland were always confident of their own ability to beat the odds and survive – and some lucky individuals then lived to accumulate handsome fortunes – but most 'Johnny Newcomes', white or black, free or enslaved, rich or poor, would not live long.[64] A resident's comment in 1747 on a recent attack of yellow fever was that 'we have lost above ⅓ of the Inhabitants of this town, and a great number of strangers.'[65] Precise statistics are scarce. However, successive visitors were appalled to note how few of the memorials in the town's churchyard commemorated anyone aged over 32.[66] Kingston prospered while its grave-yards filled. Spanish Town, in contrast, remained liable yellow fever, but its death rates were rarely as bad as those in Kingston.

The 1740s: an increased pace for urban development in Spanish Town

When viewed from mid-eighteenth-century Kingston, Spanish Town appeared a burden hindering the island's trade, due to the sheer trouble imposed on merchants and their clerks in travelling to carry out credit checks at the Island Secretary's Office, or to undertake lawsuits or even for jury service. Unfortunately for Kingston's partisans, this inland anachronism continued to secure impressive assets which then helped to reshape Spanish Town as an administrative and social centre, re-asserting its importance as a meeting point for the island's planters.

The most impressive testimony to Spanish Town's importance (and, perhaps, for its comparative healthiness too), was demonstrated in an islandwide collection to endow the free school in Spanish Town. The fund-raising built on a bequest to the parish of St Catherine by Peter Beckford, who at his death in 1735 was probably the richest planter on the island. His will left £1,000 to establish either a free school or a hospital in the parish, though only with the condition that within three years others would 'joyn in such an undertaking'; otherwise the money should 'be distributed to and amongst such house keepers as shall be the real objects of charity'.[67] Beckford's cash allowed Spanish Town's existing school to be re-established and endowed. It became popularly known as Beckford's School though legally it remained 'The Free Grammar School of Saint Jago de la Vega'. Of course, as with most gifts to academic institutions, even this generous bequest still proved insufficient until the Assembly intervened. In this instance, voting to allow Peter's widow, Bathshua Beckford, to transfer a further donation of £1,000 left to the poor of the parish over to the school. The Assembly followed this intervention by appointing the Speaker and a whole string of Assemblymen to sit on the re-endowed school's Board of Governors.[68] The group may have

FIGURE 3:3   The Archives Building. When it was first planned the property to its right, which now holds the northern end of the 1760s King's House, housed the old Spanish *Audiencia* building. (author's photograph).

proved unwieldy, but they included most of the influential figures in the colony.

New public buildings provided further tangible monuments to the town's status, reaffirming its place as an administrative centre. During the 1740s the Assembly was prepared to lavish funds underwriting the Archives building that still stands at the north-west corner of the Parade, where it replaced the old Spanish-era gaol that the English took over at the conquest. In 1744, when it was first proposed, Jamaica's new Archives building was among the largest and most ambitious civilian buildings erected anywhere in Britain's transatlantic empire.[69] We do not know who designed the building, though it remains an impressive structure.[70] The project's promoters promised their fellow Assemblymen a public building that would accommodate all the functions of the colonial government – sessions of the law courts, meetings of the Governor's Council, archival storage for the Island Secretary, holding the militia's arms and even housing future sessions of the Assembly.[71] Looking back it is difficult to imagine how even the most optimistic plans presented to a committee of Assemblymen could ever have allocated space for all of these activities within the two stories erected. However, the building's tall ground floor windows were part of the original plan: they would provide light to clerks consulting the crabbed handwriting in the official ledgers and, in case of fire, they were to offer a ready exit for any efforts to rescue the records. The planters also consoled themselves, in an unacknowledged echo of the original Spanish rationale for Spanish Town's inland site, that in case of an invasion there would still be time to load the essential records into carts and evacuate them before any attackers reached the town.[72] From the first, the building was to combine a Guard Room for the military guard that protected the Governor's residence with secure housing for the island's official records. Hence its separate outside stairs. Modern archivists might well have some qualms about locating a military guardhouse with its ammunition directly above their record store, but the Assemblymen who voted 'aye' to pay the growing building costs would have found the juxtaposition of soldiers and deed books reasonable enough. Together these guaranteed the planters' physical security and their property. The legalistic culture that the Assemblymen inhabited relied on written documents to support claims to land and other property. The security of these records therefore remained a very high priority.

Spending money does not necessarily buy architectural flair, particularly in official commissions; however, at a time when the town's other public buildings were appraised at valuations of between £800 and perhaps £1,500 each, the initial appropriation for this new building was £6,500. It soon absorbed £10,000 and, its critics feared, would still 'cost at least [another] ten thousand pounds to complete'.[73] When it was completed it would appear particularly striking as it stood alongside both the fairly mundane buildings erected after the 1692 earthquake and the archaic wooden structure that originally housed the Spanish *Audiencia*

The ambitious but slowly completed Archives Building was not the only evidence of public confidence undertaken during the 1740s. Spanish Town expanded during the decade, nearly doubling its size. This urban expansion coincided with the opening up of extensive lands in western Jamaica for new plantations after the conclusion of the Maroon Treaties in 1739. These treaties signed with the Windward and Leeward Maroons recognized their status, freedom and claims to mountain land. In return the Maroons ceased their campaigning, returned some recent runaway slaves who had joined them and committed themselves to track down future escapees.[74] Some escaped slaves continued to find refuge in Jamaica's mountainous interior, but these treaties shifted the balance in the planters' favour. They ceased to fear Maroon attacks on isolated settlements while the enslaved workforce who used to cut new fields out of the woods had fewer chances to make a break for freedom. The extension of land under cane that had stalled after the 1692 earthquake revived.[75] As a result there was sufficient confidence during the 1740s for the Assembly to sustain extensive development schemes. The new Archives building in Spanish Town provided a focus for this expansion.

The streets behind the King's House still show the extent of the townspeople's own investment in urban improvements. Legislation passed by the Assembly in 1747 opened the way for their construction.[76] Back in 1674 and 1687 well-connected churchwardens had secured grants for 1,235 acres of common fields surrounding most of the town for the parish of St Catherine's, thus effectively regaining most of the common fields granted in 1534 to the original townspeople by the Spanish Crown.[77] The race course known as 'the Horse Course' which was a prime social fixture during Assembly and Court meetings, was cleared out of these fields, but for 70 years most of the land remained open grazing. With no single tenant responsible for restraining the underbrush the fields became increasingly overgrown. In 1747 the Assembly gave the parish churchwardens authority to divide this savanna land into two parts, half of which would be preserved as commons for the town. Most of the second half was enclosed and leased out for agriculture.[78] The individual leaseholders would become responsible for keeping the encroaching brush under control.

The churchwardens used their newly augmented authority to accomplish considerably more than assigning grazing licences. They leased some of the newly enclosed savanna land for building sites, extending the inherited Spanish grid plan further west, out to the present market. The resulting strips of land, which townspeople called 'runs' for another century, were subdivided into building plots for shops and stalls. There was no master plan, and the grid of streets that extended west not only extended the original Spanish streets but also retained some older field paths as well. The area developed at this juncture lay behind the properties facing the street behind the King's House (still 'Western Street' on the 1786 map of the town). The military barracks south-west of the Parade provided a southern perimeter while today's Old Market street offered a northern boundary. A new market lay to the east. The process extended the built-up area by perhaps a third, though the initial development was mostly low density, so that the total population may not have risen nearly as much.

Speculations by local investors underwrote this expansion of Spanish Town. These included several vestrymen, the rector of the parish ('Parson Flemming'), local planters and office holders living in the town.[79] When the English heirs of two planter – investors sold out two or three years after the project began, the continuing development of their 'runs' was taken over by leading members of the town's Jewish community, including a Mr Martin, who is still commemorated by 'Martin Street'.[80] The individual plots that these intermediary developers sold off found ready buyers. Some enterprising individuals relocated to Spanish Town from Kingston, suggesting that the old capital appeared a promising commercial zone.[81]

Subdivision was often rapid. Purchasers moved in to take up such prime pitches as the one-third of a lot 'called or known by the name of number four' which lay 'next adjoining to a place called the barrack wall'. This was acquired by Richard Richards of St Catherine parish, 'free mulatto tailor', from Sir John Molesworth, Baronet, of Pencarrow, Cornwall, in 1749 and then resold by Richards within a year to Julia Tailor of the parish of Kingston, a 'free mulatto woman'.[82] Similarly, lot number five, amounting to an acre and a half was divided in half in 1750 and then the two halves were sold off in smaller parcels, one of the halves being divided into seven separate lots, some of which were then resold after further divisions.[83] Only active retail use could justify the resulting minuscule plots. After of the repeated sub-divisions and consolidations of individual properties over the ensuing 250 years it is difficult to date the various residential and commercial buildings erected in this area, though some may well date back to the mid-eighteenth century.

The result was Spanish Town's distinctive creolised urban layout. It might make sense for local residents. But its 'open' absence of defences, its dispersed layout, the narrow street widths inherited from the Spanish grid, its free black community with their shops and, indeed, its slave yards would all appear downright alien to visitors arriving from Europe. Of these the most foreign, the distinct residential districts for slaves, was already a long-established phenomenon in Jamaican townscapes, although both the houses and indeed the yards the slaves occupied remained so familiar that contemporaries left few descriptions.[84] Those early references we do have appear as asides to other stories. When the English first seized Spanish Town in 1655 the only saleable assets they found in their initial plundering were the untanned hides that had covered the floors of the slave cabins. The invaders pulled these hides up and shipped them north to New England.[85] Later the more fortunate European survivors of the 1692 earthquake in Port Royal crammed themselves into the slaves' houses there because these small wickerwork huts 'daubed with mortar and thatched, the eves hanging down to the ground', managed to ride out the quake far better than brick or stone houses. Similar huts continued to line the edge of Spanish Town's common fields.[86] Their eighteenth-century successor slave houses were mostly built of reused planks, with further pieces scrounged from the tops and sides of old wooden barrels. Small windows had wooden shutters that slid in groves. Then, in contrast to the thatched roofs on rural slave lines, the roofs on urban slaves' 'cottages' were shingled.[87] These spaces were very different from the arrangements in such mainland North American towns as late eighteenth century Charleston, South Carolina, where the enslaved were generally housed in rooms crammed into outhouses on the same lot as the owner's house.[88]

In Jamaican towns the existence of clusters of slave yards was taken for granted. Two linked bills enacted by the Assembly in 1749 acknowledged the town's sizable enslaved population and its separate neighbourhoods while at the same time attempting to control the streets throughout the whole of Spanish Town.[89] One act authorized the parish vestry to levy a tax on 'house negroes' to fund street cleaning.[90] The second, revising an earlier law passed in 1744, sought to regulate the buildings erected by slaves who lived away from their owners' households. The latter was more wide ranging because its provisions also covered Kingston and Port Royal.[91] This legislation recognized the existence of distinct urban areas inhabited by slaves. The letter of the act allowed these urban slave houses to have a door, which their residents might close on the slaveholders' town. The act also allowed their yards to be surrounded by tall fences which even mounted owners or overseers could not always peer over. It does remain difficult to determine exactly where Spanish Town's slave quarters were during this time. Archaeology may yet identify these spaces and help illuminate the lives they housed.[92] However, it is noticeable that the densely packed area of common land to the south and west of the Barracks (anti-clockwise, today's Melbourne Lane, Sherrier Lane, Bullock Lane, Condron Lane and Nugent Lane), with its small properties and curving lanes, was not invoked over the next century when property-owning townspeople recorded directions within the town. An area of amnesia among the town's white male voters seems likely territory for such networks of fenced-in yards.[93]

The building codes established for urban slave houses had nothing to say about either the quality of the materials employed or their vulnerability to fires. Instead, the law aimed at attaining some oversight of these yards, because 'such numbers of runaway negro and other slaves, from different parts of the island, daily resorting to and being harbored in the said huts or house, give an opportunity of forming cabals and conspiracies, dangerous to the public peace and security . . .'. The laws stated that if there were more than four huts in a yard they were each only to have one door and the individual compounds should have tall fences kept in good repair. The intentions were clear enough: as search parties hammered on the front door fugitives should not run out of a back door or vault over a fence to escape. The frequent re-passage of this legislation suggests that its clauses often went unenforced. In practice, fences tended to be patched up with whatever came to hand, while the slaves 'contrived to disperse their Huts in such a Manner as to leave several intricate windings, which favour escapes or sudden emergencies.'[94] The action by the St Catherine's vestry in 1760 in advertising in the *St Jago Intelligencer* that the act 'for regulating the Negro Hutts in and about the town' was to be enforced and then urging the justices of the peace to go on a tour of inspection, indicates that rigid social control required more constant efforts than the town's vestrymen were prepared to undertake.[95]

These laws demonstrate the relative autonomy that the people who lived in these yards might enjoy. The vestrymens' expedient of taking out a newspaper advertisement was very different from the experiences on rural plantations where the overseer would undertake regular searches of the slaves' huts for arms. In these yards African Jamaicans could 'find a respite from enforced labour' and, still more would be 'exclusively exposed to each other's company': they offered black spaces within the island's principal towns.[96] As the legislators recognized, urban slaves *could* harbour individual runaway slaves in these yards, while at the same time, husbands, wives or sweethearts, or, indeed, children, kin and friends might hope to secure time together. Not every yard would hold an escapee, a cache of weapons or a conspiracy, but there was still some room for neighbourhood entrepreneurship within the groups of huts standing behind the high fences that the law required. Furthermore, these yards lying on the edge of the town would offer an invaluable transition space for the rural slaves who relied on Spanish Town's market as an outlet to sell surplus produce from their provision grounds and raise some cash. Town-based higglers with the opportunity to store a stock in a fenced hut could either buy from loads as they were brought into town or else pick up bargains as time-constrained vendors needed to make a sale before their leave-pass expired. Later rural vendors would stay overnight on market days.[97]

Contemporaries acknowledged the importance of the vendors who supplied its markets. Spanish Town was recognized as the hub of an extensive economic catchment, with 440 farms in its neighbourhood and 'about twenty six thousand slaves [who] greatly depend on the Market of Saint Jago de la Vega for their comfortable substance in vending Fruits, Herbs, Ground Provisions, Plantains, Poultry and Eggs . . . '.[98] The town's Sunday market provided an outlet for the produce that these slaves grew on land assigned to them – so George II's officials were told – as a reward for loyalty.[99]

By the 1740s the town was increasingly redefined as a number of distinct neighbourhoods. If the Assembly's legislation was effective, the yards where many of the town's slaves lived would be enclosed behind tall hedges, fences or walls. Further streets and lanes were lined with the subdivided lots with the houses and yards that the town's substantial free black population occupied. The bricklayers, stonemasons and roofers who for a decade looked down over the town from the scaffolding surrounding the new Archives building during its protracted construction would have watched the laying out of the new development just to the west of them. The establishment of a new market out on the town's new western boundary led to the removal of the busy market that had hitherto met in the Parade. The old market had provided a noisy accompaniment to proceedings in the Courthouse, to the Assembly's deliberations and to the life of the Governor and his household at the King's House.[100] Anyone returning to the old capital after a prolonged absence would have recognized this relocation.

The resulting town was a creole town. Its architectural showpieces were impressive, comparable to the best work undertaken on either side of the Atlantic, but the streets that held them did not follow English patterns, while both the scale and the construction of its private buildings appeared unfamiliar to European visitors. A longer stay would reveal wider differences. During the early eighteenth century the range of plants to be seen in Spanish Town's streets altered. One resident's garden held two African baobab trees – which are a difficult species to germinate – grown from seeds brought over from 'Guiney' in West Africa and planted as specimens.[101] Travellers might well notice additional changes in the field boundaries lining the approaches to town and, indeed, on property lines within the town. Not only were the approach roads increasingly lined with houses and stalls, but the composition of the hedges beside these roads was supposed to change too. In 1748 'penguin hedges', of the prickly evergreen penguin bush, were banned because these banked hedges allegedly 'brought fevers', with mosquito larvae finding a ready harbour in puddles of water held within the clumps.[102] Householders were ordered to uproot them and replant their hedges with other plants. But, whatever the law said, some penguin plants remained and legislation against 'penguin hedges' would be repeated at intervals for another 150 years, outlasting both the Vestry and the Assembly. Meanwhile someone wandering these streets savouring the cooking smells emanating from the cookhouses that faced onto the Parade might occasionally detect the aroma of coffee. The coffee plant was introduced to Jamaica during the 1720s although its commercial cultivation did not take off until the late eighteenth century.[103] Jamaica's capital had not started as an English town; it became an increasingly Jamaican centre during the 60 years of building and expansion after the earthquake.

Actions 'done with ill-advising mind': removing the seat of Government to Kingston, 1754–1758.[104]

The simmering competition between Spanish Town and Kingston came to a head in 1754. Between 1754 and 1758 townspeople united in opposing schemes proposed by the then Governor, Admiral Charles Knowles, to relocate the 'Seat of Government' of the colony to Kingston. The Governor justified his decision by claims of greater efficiency. The residents of Kingston who jostled to sign a petition recommending the change could hope that the port which already dominated Jamaica's trade would dominate its politics too. The proposal proved highly controversial, provoking bitter complaints, political meetings, mass petitions and demonstrations that centred on Spanish Town but then spread across the island.

The passions that the dispute between Kingston and Spanish Town aroused extended widely. Class provided one line of argument with defenders of Spanish Town's rights claiming that the signatories of the Kingston petition included white men who had not worked off their indentures and consequently were not fully free, along with seamen from ships in harbour.[105]

On the other side the meetings held in Spanish Town to demonstrate support for its townspeople's cause, along with a subsequent proto-boycott of the Governor's household involved people of all social ranks.[106] The controversy remained a defining part of townspeople's traditions for another century.

There was plenty of support on the other side: 546 residents of Kingston signed the initial petition to the Governor[107] and 503 signed a similar petition from the parish of St Andrew, adjacent to Kingston.[108] Further supporting petitions reached the Board of Trade in London from parishes in Kingston's immediate economic hinterland. Interest in the issue then ranged beyond the island, as groups of merchants from Liverpool, Bristol and Glasgow along with New York and Philadelphia petitioned too, all testifying to Kingston's importance within intercolonial trade.[109] The petitioning strategy was perhaps a backhanded compliment to the scale of the developments in Spanish Town during the previous decade. To make their case Kingston's advocates were obliged to assert that the former Spanish capital was simply 'a mere straggling village' to compensate for the fact that the town was developing so strongly.

Later generations found both the local protests and the widespread political engagement disquieting. These were not the politics they saw practised in subsequent Jamaican Assemblies. Descriptions would therefore do their best to downplay the fierce passions this dispute aroused. Fifty years later a locally written history of Jamaica blandly summarized the proposed transfer as aiming to 'facilitate the dispatch of business' by relocating the island's public affairs to 'the centre of the commerce of the colony'. Colonists' recollections still stressed the moral counter-arguments offered in the dispute. Besides long usage, always a persuasive argument in a legalistic culture, Spanish Town appeared 'the most eligible spot for the administration of the affairs of the island' *because* 'being a place of comparative retirement, it was better fitted for the purpose of cool deliberation'. This effectively reversed the claims made in Kingston's petition that the move would be more convenient for everybody; stressing instead the practical disadvantages of transferring to Kingston. Furthermore, the Assemblymen and judges' 'removal to a populous town would not only render their attendance on the House of Assembly more expensive, but would introduce a taste of luxury, . . . which would be destructive of the morals of the members, and might eventually become the causes of their corruption'. How far the island's Assemblymen and judges remained immune from worldly temptations while they stayed in Spanish Town seems uncertain. However, these arguments appeared particularly persuasive within the wider analyses emphasizing metropolitan luxury and corruption that organized political debates in the mid-eighteenth century Anglo-American world.[110] Then, as the final argument against the move, Kingston appeared far 'more unhealthful than Spanish-town' because of its 'populousness and situation' – the very factors that Kingston's partisans asserted in claiming why their town should provide the natural centre for the colony. Consequently representatives 'might often be prevented by disease, or a fear of being exposed to it, from an attendance on their duty'. After invoking such a list of convincing justifications for the *status quo*, hindsight would hardly be surprised that once 'the planters' proceeded to 'urge' all these claims 'with great earnestness' then 'the Governor was necessitated to abandon the measure'.[111] In practice the contest proved far more bitter, while each side's arguments proved more passionate than reasonable.

We do not have hard figures to judge the claims that Kingston's and Spanish Town's advocates each produced. Kingston's 1745 tax roll listed some 700 white households. If each of Kingston's white households retained the same average of 4.11 people as in Port Royal in 1680 – and this assumption is debatable – this would put the town's white population in the order of 2,900 residents.[112] This is probably a high estimate. By contrast a survey of Spanish Town undertaken by the townspeople in 1754 produced the claim that their town held 500 houses, rentable at £20,000 (Jamaica currency) annually, with 'about' 800 white inhabitants and 'near 400 Negroes and Mulattoes of free Condition' who, together, contributed more than 300 militiamen of whom 90 were sufficiently prosperous to support the expense of appearing as cavalrymen.[113] Otherwise some rougher figures cited by an economic projector in 1750, allow us to set both sets of claims alongside current assumptions about Jamaica's urban settlements. Kingston was set down with 1,600 houses valued at an average of £600 each, for a total of £960,000. This was well ahead of Port Royal, which was assigned 100 houses averaging £200 in value, totalling £20,000. Spanish Town was put down as having 400 houses worth £400 each, amounting to a total of £160,000.[114] These estimates appraise Spanish Town's building inventory at a sixth of the value of Kingston's and eight times that of Port Royal. Kingston's size and wealth were recognizable enough, but Spanish Town was hardly a deserted village, and it was healthier.

The incumbent Governor backed the Kingston petitioners' proposal strongly, much to the chagrin of Spanish Town's supporters. In the event the Governor's advocacy would prove too strong. Meanwhile, Spanish Town's advocates included such notables as the Speaker of the Assembly and the Chief Justice, who had houses there, besides several local officials who had invested in new developments in the town. Together, they presented their counter-case very effectively. They started by claiming unfairness, because the original Kingston petition was sent to London before anyone it affected could see it or query its signatures.[115] Then, using the breathing space this procedural argument allowed them, they mounted an extensive legal campaign. Meanwhile, once the Governor appeared a strong supporter for the Kingston plan, he and his household became targets for widespread hostility in Spanish Town, to such an extent whereby he claimed that no one would sell meat to his servants and the town's doctors refused to attend to the governor's sick child.[116] The proto-boycott extended to the new marketplace where partisanship extended a long way down the social hierarchy, running across class and racial lines. Stallholders who had recently purchased their pitches were apparently prepared to forgo making sales to the King's House kitchens in the interest of making their point.

Once residing in Spanish Town became increasingly unpleasant, the Governor used his personal authority to transfer the island's law courts, the archives and his own residence to Kingston as a 'local reform' and then pushed a hand-picked House of Assembly to ratify the move.[117] His high-handed procedure generated a further storm of opposition, contested elections, accusations, counter-accusations and subsidiary lawsuits. In London the royal Privy Council passed the whole affair (along with all its accompanying petitions, counter-petitions, affidavits and statistics *pro* and *con*) on to the Board of Trade. These latter gentlemen listened to both sides' expensive witnesses and their still more expensive lawyers before deciding, based on a procedural point, that the whole dispute was moot; the bill should be vetoed and the town's former status restored.[118]

In vetoing the Jamaica Assembly's bill ratifying the move the Board did not address its merits. Instead, they decided on a technicality that Governor Knowles had overstepped his authority. He had allowed the Assembly to avoid the proper procedure for enacting colonial legislation. On a contentious issue the Assembly's bill should have included a clause suspending its operation until after the King and his English Privy Council had approved it. In this instance, because the aim was to authorize a fait accompli the clause was omitted. If nothing else, the parade of witnesses and lawyers in London demonstrated that this was a contentious proposal. Hence, when the Board of Trade returned the bill to the Privy Council and King George II for His Majesty's formal consideration, the Board recommended that the King should not approve it.[119] English monarchs may have ceased using their veto power over legislation in the Westminster Parliament in the early eighteenth century, but they – or the Board of Trade, the English Privy Council and the Board's and Council's legal council – had no qualms over disallowing legislation passed by colonial assemblies.[120] The Board's advice was followed. As a result, the bills became invalid so that the capital was to be returned to Spanish Town. Governor Knowles's thoroughly contentious removal laws appeared a prime case for a royal disallowance. Smarting from the royal refusal and, indeed, fearing further hostile questions in the English House of Commons, the Governor resigned.

Three years later the official news of the royal decision reached Spanish Town and celebrations followed. A convoy of 30 – the townspeople later remembered the number as 70 – carts rolled over from Kingston bringing back the colony's official archives.[121] The triumphant return of the archives provided an opportunity for massive public rejoicing, not so much for the preservation of a major historical data base as for the restoration that it marked of the town's administrative status and with it, the townspeoples' high rents and property values. The climax of all these celebrations occurred in the Parade, in front of the new Archives building and the King's House. Two enormous bonfires lit up the square: one was topped by an effigy of Admiral Knowles, the island's ex-Governor, the other by a model of his former flagship.[122]

CHAPTER FOUR

—

'The seat of the Government and the second town of the Island'

Spanish Town, 1758–c. 1780

*S*PANISH TOWN still bears the stamp of Jamaica's late eighteenth-century prosperity.[1] The public building campaign that commenced in 1760 reshaped the public spaces where townspeople had met during the 1750s to oppose the scheme to remove the island's seat of government to Kingston. The rebuilt town demonstrated the planters' renewed confidence in Spanish Town's continued role as the island's capital and in Jamaica's slave-based sugar economy as sugar prices entered a 30-year upswing. The initial decision to commit so much money to these projects then rode out a major slave uprising on the north side of the island in 1760. The colonial Assembly in an island that was 'not only the richest, but the most considerable colony at this time under the government of *Great Britain*' could continue to fund ambitious projects. Other impressive groups of mid- and late eighteenth-century buildings do remain in Jamaica, many of these are out on individual plantations.[2] By contrast, the buildings in Spanish Town now constitute one of the largest collections of late eighteenth-century structures still standing anywhere in the hemisphere. These buildings reflect the colonial administration they were commissioned to house. The public buildings among them were originally constructed using very high quality craftsmanship and materials. Some components were imported from Europe, but skilled local artisans undertook most of the surviving work. Many of the sub-contractors were based in and around Spanish Town and the buildings display the skills of the local people who erected them: black and white; enslaved and free.

The late eighteenth-century Assembly spent lavishly in Spanish Town. King Sugar may have provided the building funds, but the aftermath of Kingston's unsuccessful 1754–58 attempt to seize the seat of government provoked the political will. Commissioning these buildings helped to settle scores, but the Assemblymen's aims went far further than this. In 1758 the townspeople celebrated the legal victory that restored the capital and allowed them to retain the status quo. The Governor's residence, the Assembly, the law courts and the public records were all returned to St Jago de la Vega, but the Board of Trade's decision on the case remained narrowly written.[3] As a result Spanish Town's restored status only remained secured on a procedural technicality, not on any evaluation of the town's merits. This verdict left the way open for further legislation to remove the capital to Kingston.

To prevent this fate, the Jamaica Assembly went on a building campaign in an effort to anchor the capital there. The magnificent new buildings which housed the Governor, Assembly and law courts, provided arguments in their own right, so many 'facts on the ground', that offered solid justifications for retaining the island's public business in Spanish Town. The Assemblymen hoped that by pouring so much public money into splendid accommodation for the Governor and for the day-to-day business of legislation, administra-tion and law during the 1760s, their successors would never sanction any proposals to leave, because to do so would not only force a subsequent Assembly to admit that this choice was an error but also find the funds for another set of public works. The policy proved successful and Spanish Town enjoyed a public building binge. Meanwhile all attempts by Kingston's representatives to obtain Assembly cash for any new public buildings there were voted down. For 20 years the Assembly would not even find money to build a new customs house in the island's principal port.[4]

The opening lines of a contemporary poem show how some pro-Kingston colonists viewed the new buildings around the Parade in the context of the square's existing public buildings, even if it only circulated in manuscript. When an anonymous versifier ridiculed the 'knaves and fools' of the Jamaica Assembly during the 1760s, the hostile description begins in the centre of Spanish Town:

As I stroll ye Village of St I.
See a Building large and lofty
With Pediments & Columns graced
And near unto the Chapel placed
Making good my Grandam's Jest,
Near the Church, you know the rest,
Tell us what the Pile contains
Many heads that holds no Brains
These Demoniacks let me Dub
With the name of Legion Club
Such Assemblys you might Swear
Meet when Butchers bate a Bear . . .

After the poet reaches the honourable members of the Jamaica Assembly, the couplets roll on for another 275 lines, but we can already see a recognition of the Assembly's new architectural pretensions and the prominence of its site in this 'village'. Our would-be bard's attention focused on the Assembly building. In one flight of fancy the devil is imagined perched up on the roof with a red-hot poker to 'Crack the Bricks and melt the lead' to fall down upon the throng below, wiping out a nest of political vipers. Here our poet piously observes that God sometimes uses the devil to fulfil His divine plans. We are subsequently offered an extended comparison between the members of the Assembly and the patients chained up in a lunatic hospital.[5] These fantasies may say something about the continuing impact on local memories of the wooden cupola that initially crowned the Assembly building (through which any curious demons could peer in) or highlight recurrent schemes to found a lunatic hospital in Spanish Town.[6] At any rate, the Assembly's brick walls and lead roof appear readily identifiable by townspeople and visitors.

The poem's primary grievance with the gentlemen of the Assembly was their keeping the members from Kingston as a permanent minority. During any session the members 'Stare & Storm and frown/ At the Folks of Kingston Town'. The political split between Kingston's representatives and the Assembly's leaders shaped our poet's understanding of its debates, producing a bitterly negative appraisal. Near the end of the poem the Muse Clio (the classical demi-goddess responsible for history) bravely manifested herself and entered the Assembly to watch events there; however, she then fled in horror at the members' coarse ranting. The author stayed for just a little longer to scatter insults because, beyond keeping a long poem moving, there was no

FIGURE 4:1   A demi-goddess at the Jamaica Assembly. Printer's device used by Curtis Brett, a printer in Spanish Town, newly appointed to the post of Printer to the Assembly in 1756. This classical image provided filler in any space left at the end of issues of the daily *Votes of the Assembly of Jamaica*. (John Carter Brown Library, Brown University).

need for devils or demi-gods to manifest themselves. As this doggerel's original readers were well aware, the island's politicians who gathered under Speaker Price's direction, followed his line for the next generation.7

Despite such bitter verdicts on the Assemblymen's motives, the public buildings erected in the 1760s around the Parade would provide an architectural carapace for the island's government. These spaces housed the bureaucracy and administration of late eighteenth-century Jamaica. The choices made in laying out these buildings demonstrate mid-eighteenth-century judgements on how the colony and its government operated. A walk around the Parade offered an effective introduction to the planters' administrative priorities and to the 'civics' shaping their understanding of the colony.

The Parade became the centre for the Assembly's ambitious building policy. The proportions of the square changed as it was framed by substantial public buildings. Previously, private houses were not only interspersed among

FIGURE 4:2 'A View of the King's House and Public Offices at St Jago de la Vega' engraving dated 1 July 1774, published in Long, *History* 2, 1774, 10. The shadows stretching towards the square's western (right) side show that the original sketch was made fairly early in the morning. (The town clock on the church shows ten twenty-five). There is some passing traffic. The woman on the left in the foreground with a full basket on her head is probably returning from the market. The well-sprung coach with its magnificently liveried coachman and footman already has a passenger, who quite probably is someone getting their business done either before the full heat of the day or before the opening of any sessions of the Assembly and the Law Courts. (John Carter Brown Library, Brown University).

the public offices, but overshadowed many of them. In 1760 the private houses facing onto the square were demolished. In clearing room for the new building works, the old wooden *Audiencia* building inherited from the Spaniards, the brick Island Secretary's Office and most of the 1690s and 1720s King's House were all pulled down. The builders even removed the protruding stubs remaining from the gateway to the old White Church, a long-lasting reminder of the destruction that had accompanied the English conquest a century before.[8] Spanish Town looked towards the future, not the past. This was no preservationists' agenda.

The brick building that housed the Assembly took up the whole east side of the Parade. This ambitious and multifunctional 'Public Building' required extensive demolitions prior to its construction. Further new building work on the south side of the square later added to the expanse of new red brick. Fear of a partisan press encouraged the Assemblymen to build a new printing office on the square's south-west corner to publish the Assembly's *Laws*. This shop continued to compete for public business with the older established printer's shop in Kingston.[9] A guard house was built with public funds alongside the printer's to accommodate the company of regular troops posted on guard duty at the King's House.[10] Additionally, as an engraving of the Parade published in 1774 shows, £1,200 was laid out in enclosing the centre of the square with a very substantial brick wall 'intended as an ornament'; however, it did not prove popular because it bore too close a resemblance to a cemetery wall.[11] A subsequent published view that also looks towards the south side of the square suggests that by 1786 the expensive brick wall was already replaced by an enclosure of posts and chains.[12]

The massive new King's House also built during the 1760s on the west side of the square balanced, or sometimes threatened to overbalance, the Assembly building. Thomas Craskell, the island's military engineer, oversaw the construction of the King's House, which was 'designed for the usual place of residence of the [colony's] commander-in-chief'.[13] Previous houses for governors may have been built of stone and expensive, but they were simply crammed onto the site of the former Spanish *cabildo,* wedged in alongside the old *Audiencia*, with the governor's stables and household offices scattered around neighbouring blocks. Some cannons deposited outside the gate had

FIGURE 4:3 The Parade viewed from the north, detail from John Pitcairn's 1786 map of Spanish Town. After the demolition of the walls in the centre of the square we can now catch a glimpse of the lower sections of the 1690s chapel and the 1760s military guard room just to the west of it. However, the facade of the King's House, which excludes the venetian blinds added in 1771 and the 1770 portico that appeared in the earlier engraving, suggests that we cannot put too much trust in specific details – large or small – in this image. (National Library of Jamaica).

helped to indicate the Governor's military status.[14] This rebuilding reconfigured the site. The expanded King's House compound stretched across the whole western side of the Parade. It absorbed the former *Audiencia's* corner lot on the north end of the block where the Assembly and law courts formerly met. The reorganization also reshaped the southern end of the King's House block. The Assembly purchased the adjoining property, its buildings were demolished and the consolidated King's House lot then stretched across the neighbouring lane.[15] This addition provided space for the governor's stables, which had been tucked away across the street behind the King's House. Then, breaking up this section of the Spanish grid, the builders moved the original lane that used to run back to the former royal stables and the old schoolhouse south onto the next lot along. Tall wooden gates leading into the new out King's House stable yard closed off the former exit at the south-west corner of the square.[16] The King's House compound now extended from one end of the block to the other. These changes amounted to extensive – and, indeed expensive – revisions to the former town plan. Although traffic might find this re-jigging of the city grid inconvenient, the resulting 'King's House Square' became a showpiece that would figure in all subsequent visitors' itineraries.

The whole square was reoriented in these ambitious commissions. Public buildings now dominated Spanish Town's Parade in a manner not seen since the demolition of the old Abbot's Church at the English conquest in the 1650s. The new Assembly building replaced town houses facing onto the eastern end of the Parade that planter families had held since 1655. Some private buildings remained but they were far less substantial structures. The viewpoint looking south across the square that the artists chose for both the 1774 and 1786 engravings does downgrade the continuing retail presence in this public space. Both the artists and the passers-by they depicted would register the enticing aromas from the King's Arms, the cookhouse which continued to ply its trade from an old Spanish stable in the centre of the block on the north side of the square.[17] In making their preliminary sketches the artists adopted a vantage point immediately in front of this ramshackle hostelry to show off the Parade's refurbished public architecture.

The engraving published in 1774 appears to show the Parade near the end of 1770. This is a reasonable turn-around time for getting the sketches shipped back to England, engraved and then printed and bound with the rest of Edward Long's *History of Jamaica*. The portico on the King's House was only erected in 1770 after shipping over the stone pillars and massive lintel from

England. It was a costly structure in its own right. David Allen, the local stonemason in charge of erecting the component pieces, confirmed on oath that the workmanship was worth the £251 billed to the Assembly. Freight and insurance cost a further £570 pounds sterling, with over £300 more in Jamaican currency laid out 'for Boatage, Haulage and Wainage' in moving all the stone and lumber up to Spanish Town. Scaffolding and 'putting up' cost a further £100, as did shipping out and setting up 'the King's Arms'. All this building produced plenty of work for the Jamaican contractors. Local masons completed the 'dog tooth' carving around the edge of the portico adding up to 61 feet 'running measure' at £10 per foot. Additional work included 50 square yards of plastering for the ceiling, plus two-and-three-quarter 'rods' of brickwork. The project absorbed extensive supplies: 8,000 Carolina shingles, massive quantities of lime for the bedding mortar, £30 worth of nails, besides a final £50 for 'the Painting Bill and Painting the Whole six times over'. The whole sheaf of bills for the portico audited by the Assembly's Commissioners for Forts, Fortifications and Public Buildings amounted to £2,643 8s. 3d.[18] This constituted a very substantial sum when in the 1780s Montego Bay's 'small, but peculiarly elegant' Anglican church could be built for £1,200.[19]

The range of sources for these supplies highlights the fact that this was a colonial building from the start. We cannot put names to the designers for many of these commissions, but they aimed to accommodate a tropical climate. Further modifications to the King's House in the three years prior to the publication of the engraving continued to adapt to the harsh light and heavy rains of a tropical climate. The plain sash windows that the engraving shows on both the King's House and the Assembly were all provided with pairs of outside shutters (described as venetian blinds) in 1771. Large lanterns were placed on either side of the King's House doors in 1772.[20] These still survive. When the first Jamaican readers of Edward Long's *History* finally unwrapped their copies and examined the illustrations, their details were already out of date and buildings around this square already looked significantly different.

The extensive public building programme demonstrated confidence in Spanish Town's persistence as the colony's 'seat of government' and belief in Jamaica's own long-term prospects. The Assemblymens' optimism that sustained the building programme in Spanish Town may well have weathered the islandwide crisis of confidence provoked by Tacky's Rebellion in 1760 only because the then Governor did not call a session of the Assembly. By 1761 construction was under way. In any event, the timing for all this new building, dictated by local politics and funded by wealth from sugar, still ran well ahead of any comparable official projects in Britain and in North America. Only after the conclusion of the Seven Years War (which many mainland American colonists called the French and Indian War) in 1763, did other would-be builders find sufficient capital and confidence to undertake comparably extravagant architectural commissions.[21]

Local designs adapted classical orthodoxies to tropical realities. Jamaica's new public buildings were conspicuous in their massive scale and ambition. They appeared splendid projects from the start, designed to bolster the Assemblymen's own self-confidence and impress visitors to the island, including successive royal Governors. In describing the King's House townspeople could assert that 'there is no one of the colonies where the commander-in-chief is lodged in a manner more suitable to his convenience, and the dignity of his rank'.[22] As far as the then British transatlantic colonies were concerned, the boast may well have been justified; however, generations of visitors newly arrived from England would remain under-whelmed. An early nineteenth-century tourist's description elaborated widely shared opinions: the King's House's '*façade* of red brick, built completely *à l'Anglaise* – [was] an object on which the eyes of an Englishman delights to rest, as it presents to his view something more familiar than the low, piazzaed, and projecting-roofed houses, which compose the chief part of the town'.[23] It seemed commendable because it was more 'English' than its surroundings. In practice, colonial buildings could never win such visitors' approval: if the builders stuck to familiar patterns, they were derivative; if the plans were adapted to climate and materials, they were degenerate.[24] The would-be positive verdicts that the King's House would fit comfortably into an English market square forgot that the colony's public buildings were intended for specific sites in Spanish Town, Jamaica. The building's classical architectural style carried over many design elements that European visitors would recognize. Even so, anyone standing in the King's House Square who had actually *looked* at the town hall fronting their local English market square before they sailed for the West Indies should have recognized the fundamental differences between those buildings and the King's House and Assembly building now before them. The contrast was not just due to the palm trees on the horizon or the clear blue sky overhead.

Distinctive Jamaican building styles, particularly those 'low, piazzaed, and projecting-roofed houses' increasingly emerged during this period.[25] Setting the brickwork aside (and, in the case of the King's House, we now have very little remaining besides its brick carcass), many of the other materials used for the new buildings would appear startlingly incongruous to English visitors. A later resident's description of Jamaican buildings claimed that 'to a stranger, the roofs appear uncommonly neat, being covered with cedar, bullet tree, or broad leaf shingles, all of which soon assume a bluish cast, from the operation of the sun and heavy rains; thereby resembling the finest slates'.[26] Newcomers would recognize the contrast but not all would share this positive assessment. Spanish Town's mid-eighteenth century public buildings were roofed with wooden shingles imported from South Carolina. Whatever their origin, these weatherbeaten shingles were not the hard dark grey slates or even the bright red tiles used on comparable public buildings in Britain.

Moving down to the rest of the building, there were further adaptations. The Venetian blinds added to both the Assembly and the King's House in 1771 and painted green served to break up the facades so that they looked even less 'English', although the practical benefit of such additions was clear enough and the original Italian designs that northern European architects drew on featured shutters to break the force of the Mediterranean sun.[27] The interiors of both the King's House and the Assembly further demonstrated their tropical sites with the mahogany and cedar panelling that lined their walls. With these materials local craftsmen produced fashionably splendid interiors. Even the most magnificent buildings in England and in Britain's North American colonies would be panelled and floored in pine or perhaps oak. It has taken generations of grime and elbow grease to give these light woods a patina of age. Jamaican building contractors had ready access to prime quality hardwoods from stands of native mahogany and cedar, or even from mahogany logs felled in Honduras (today's Belize) that were transshipped from local schooners onto English-bound ships in Kingston. The width of the planks that still form the staircase up to the main floor in the Assembly building demonstrate the original size of the hardwood trees felled for these buildings. Local pride continued with the claim that most of the stone used for the corner stones and the window and door frames were quarried in Jamaica: 'a beautiful free-stone, dug out of the Hope river course, in St Andrew's parish'.[28]

The colony's Government Engineer supervised the construction of the King's House. The Assembly building may well have been a committee design from the start, as no one ever assigned blame to an individual for the numerous problems that arose.[29] This would help explain the combination of practical flaws in the building's design with the ingenious and effective organization of its floor plan. In the decade after they were 'completed' both buildings underwent an extended process of 'repair' and 'alterations' as their residents continued to adapt them to tropical realities.

The Assembly Building we see in the 1774 engraving had already undergone its first round of alterations. Its roof initially sported a central lantern, which meant that the building housing the Assembly which funded all these projects would stand taller than the Governor's mansion across the square. Subsequent rebuilding work on the Assembly then proved protracted and expensive. Removing the cupola because it leaked and fitting venetian blinds were only the start of the Building Committee's problems.[30] The first floor (or, in American usage, second floor) open gallery that was such a prominent feature of the original design remained ill-suited to Jamaican weather. Its pine plank floor soon shrank and warped in the tropical sun, allowing rain running off the roof to seep through to the plastered arches below. In early 1770, less than ten years after the building was 'finished', the initial planking was pulled out and replaced with better quality materials: local carpenters inserted new hardwood joists and treated the tongue-and-groove cedar planking with white lead squeezed into the joints. A further inspection determined that the colonnade underneath required re-plastering as well.[31] However, these elaborate and expensive refurbishments did not last long. The problem had been mis-diagnosed. It was not the use of shoddy materials that was at fault, but the original design.

The following November, just after the rainy season, the Assembly authorized a far more radical rebuilding. The Assembly committee members received a fresh proposal from the new Government Engineer, Captain Richard Jones, to resolve the problems with their own building. He recommended not only another re-flooring for the balcony but also 'covering the same with a flat Roof to be covered with Copper'. His solution left the windows on the Assembly's western side looking onto a covered porch while directing all the rainwater from the roof out to the street. The Assembly appropriated £900 and assigned further contracts, including one for new balcony railings to replace those which had rotted.[32] The execution of this round of revisions encountered further delays when the contractor submitting the lowest bid, a local man, faced ruin after the price of the copper sheathing

FIGURE 4:4 View of the Assembly, its balcony and the extended roof from the Archives.
(author's photograph)

rose unexpectedly. The Assembly committee allowed him an increase.³³ This
performed admirably, though it left the building looking even more ungainly.
The initial central portico, with its cupola above, broke up the tall vertical
lines of the ground floor arcade, while the wings protruding from each end
added additional variety and rhythm. Now, with the cupola lopped off and
the central roof line advanced to the front of the building, the end wings and
most of the central portico were submerged. The building became vulnerable
to nay-saying criticisms that it was 'cumbersome', 'too much extended' and
had 'too heavy an aspect to please the eye'.³⁴

Politics in brick and mortar: buildings to house a colonial administration

The complex of public buildings erected around the Parade was built to
provide the principal public stage for the island's affairs. The new Assembly
was functional despite all maintenance and aesthetic problems. It demonstrates the priorities framing the Jamaican Assemblymen's choice for the 'Public
Buildings' that located the Assembly as the centre of the island's government.
Initially the Archives building constructed in the 1740s on the north-west
corner of the square, promised to house all the various business of the colony's
government; the 1760s Public Building finally fulfilled that promise.

Property-holding colonists (the group entitled to a vote if they were white, free, male and Christian) arriving at this building could then proceed with other bureaucratic chores. A row of rooms on the ground floor, two on each side of the central staircase, housed the offices of the Island Secretary, the Provost Marshall, the Registrar for the Court of Chancery and the Clerks of the Crown and the Grand Court.[35] The crush was reduced because most of these key officials were actually local deputies for the heirs of the English courtiers who had secured royal grants to these lucrative Jamaican offices in the 1660s. They and their descendants viewed these offices as pieces of property to be leased out for annual rents. During the 1750s the numbers of absentee patent holders received further reinforcements when offices in Jamaica were used to pay off political debts accumulated during English elections. Sometimes lessees in Jamaica paid late or not at all, but by the late eighteenth century the remittances back to the patent holders and other intermediaries amounted to around £30,000 sterling a year. The local deputies and their clerks who did the actual work then tried to live off the remaining income that fees produced. Getting a piece of legal business done was rarely cheap. The Assembly did endeavour to establish scales for officials' fees, but these acts were always opposed by the patent holders in London as infringing their property rights.[36] However, from the 1760s on it was at least simpler to pursue such official business, because deputies no longer ran their offices out of their homes. Visitors could find and consult bureaucrats in Spanish Town far more easily than those in comparable English law courts or government offices.

Anyone entering the 'Public Building' through its central door encountered a broad staircase. Visitors had to pass a doorkeeper here, officials who made a mark in townspeople's recollections. If locals sometimes had trouble gaining admission, Assemblymen were received with ceremony. By at least the mid-nineteenth century, the doorkeeper was expected to rise from his seat and bow to each Member when he entered or left the House.[37] This staircase remains the only entry to the upper floor. The stairs fork half way up, leading left or right, north or south. The landing at the top is still light and airy (though that initial cupola would have made it lighter still) and, during the law terms or sessions of the Assembly, would have been packed with bystanders, litigants and everyone else who was attending either spectacle. The Assembly met in a chamber to the north and the island's law courts were held in a room to the south.

Much of the old Assembly chamber remains today. The mahogany-framed entrance from the landing is impressive, while a low mahogany rail divided the chamber from its entrance lobby. In the early nineteenth century when Michael Scott, a merchant apologist for the Jamaican colonial establishment, had his novel's narrator Tom Cringle delayed by rain in Spanish Town, Tom passed his time 'attending the debates in the House of Assembly, where everything was conducted with much greater decorum than I ever saw maintained in the House of Commons'. This was a fairly tendentious claim even though the Commons could certainly be disorderly. The novelist's description of the interior continued 'the Hall itself, fitted with polished mahogany benches, was handsome and well aired, and between it and the Grand Court, as it was called, occupying the other end of the building, which was then sitting, there is a large cool saloon, generally in term time well filled with wigless lawyers and their clients.'[38] This passage gives us some idea how the original layout operated. Notes recording several later visitors' impressions also comment on these public spaces, though most of these descriptions of the Assembly date from the 1840s and '50s, 80 or 90 years after the building's construction and after the completion of a separate building to house the law courts in 1819. Thus in 1849 an elderly Canadian legislator found 'no accommodation for strangers' attending the debates 'but the space below the bar', and this was 'without a seat'.[39] Inside the chamber an American visitor in 1850 described it as 'a plain, indeed homely sort of an apartment, competent to hold three or four hundred people, and divided in two by a bar, within which sat the members. The room was entirely without ornament of any kind, and resembled a country court room in the United States.'[40] A British Army Captain who attended the opening of a session of the Assembly as an aide de camp to the Governor in the early 1840s found the room crowded and hot, but still noticed that 'the Gallery was filled with well dressed and pretty women', suggesting a social dimension to these proceedings.[41] In the late 1850s another more critical visitor described a bar, where members and their guests 'take such refreshment as the warmth of the debate may render necessary' in 'a side room opening from the house', (presumably out on the balcony). This traveller's narrative also described how once speeches and arguments grew loud, passers-by in the surrounding streets could hear the Honourable Members' exchanges echoing around the square.[42]

The late eighteenth-century Assembly housed 41 members, two from most parishes and three from the three parishes that held the island's major towns

(Port Royal, St Catherine with Spanish Town itself and Kingston). Over time the membership increased to 47 as more parishes were added, (up to 43 with the separation of Trelawny as a parish in 1774, to 45 in 1816 when members sat for the new parish of Manchester, and then to 47 in 1842 when the parish of Metcalfe was established in what is today St Mary).[43] The Assemblymen elected a Speaker from among themselves. They retained a fairly wide discretion in initiating and framing legislation, although their bills then proceeded to the Council for a second reading and could be vetoed by the Governor, even before they were sent to England to receive the royal approval or disallowal. Numerous bills failed to surmount one or another of these hurdles. Governors and English bureaucrats tried devising alternative schemes, but the Assembly succeeded in retaining considerable power over the public purse, although at this juncture their refusing to vote funds could not bring the colony's administration to a complete halt.[44] Revenues from some local excise duties were permanently assigned as public revenues and these paid the Governor's basic salary. However, the funds allotted remained insufficient to cover the costs of even the island's peacetime garrison, never mind the 'additional' salaries customarily voted to the Governor and Lieutenant Governor on their arrival in Jamaica. Extra grants remained necessary to bridge the gap and as a result the Assembly still wielded considerable power over the Executive.

The chamber was built by a working legislature. Today it houses meetings of the St Catherine Parish Council. The magnificent silver Speaker's mace that formerly lay on the table during sessions of the Assembly – or was set on a rack when the House went into a Committee of the Whole – is now at Gordon House in Kingston, Jamaica's current Parliament building, where its presence offers a symbol of legislative continuity. There are modern partitions behind this speaking area, dividing off spaces for the Mayor of Spanish Town's 'parlour' and for a secretary's office. These spaces and functions effectively reconstruct the layout of the mid-eighteenth century, where the Speaker's room was 'furnished with proper conveniences for the private committees appointed to meet in it'.[45]

As a further carry-over from the original plan, the doors of the former Court Room and the Assembly Chamber remain directly across from each other. This was not just for the through breeze. Rather, it allowed the Speaker when seated in his official chair to have the option of looking up from the debate to glare across the whole building at the Chief Justice of the Island, seated at his court at the other end of the building. The aim was to remind the island's judges that they remained answerable to questions and even impeachment by the Assembly if they veered from 'a just dispensation of the law and their duty'.[46] This arrangement raised the Assemblymen's interpretation of justice and the common law tradition beyond not only the judges' own views but also beyond any input from the Governor and indeed, beyond shifting legal attitudes in England towards such contentious issues as slavery or, later, religious toleration. The colony's central appeals courts continued to pull in throngs of litigants from across the island to have their cases heard by a bench that held a significant representation of local planters whose decisions were uninhibited by any legal training in Britain.[47] The space that originally housed the courts has been reconfigured several times, so the initial layout is no longer clear, but when first built it was considered well designed and 'extremely commodious'.[48]

As we have seen, from 1760 the enlarged King's House stood across the square from the Assembly and law courts, rather than sharing the same lot as they formerly did. Legislators and lawyers gathering on that much-repaired balcony looked across the newly walled-in central garden at a building that housed both the Governor and his household, and the executive sections of the colony's government: the Governor and his Council. Gates to the enclosed centre to the Parade offered a direct path from the Assembly's main entrance to the King's House. The massive stone portico provided a splendid frame for the two front doors into the King's House: the door on the right opened onto a small hall with a set of stairs up to the Governor's private apartment. There were three large rooms on the ground floor on this side that led into each other. These, together with a long gallery above, could house public suppers during official balls or other public events. The left hand front door led into what its builders initially called the 'large room', and later described as the 'great saloon' or 'hall of audience'. This was a massive two-storey hall, panelled once again in mahogany. A row of pillars divided the space into a ballroom and a western side aisle. There was a second floor gallery and a small movable balcony to accommodate the orchestra for dancing.[49] This room was used when the Governor hosted balls, the social peak of an Assembly season. The superlative social facilities incorporated into the King's House reflected the priorities that the Assembly's building committee members assigned to the public roles of the King's House. Folding doors at the southern end of this room opened into a further bay which housed the Council Chamber. Here,

FIGURE 4:5   F.[Abraham] J[ames], 'A Grand Jamaican Ball! or the Creolian hop a la mustee; as exhibited in Spanish Town. Graciously dedicated to the Hon[oura]ble Mrs. R....n, Custodi Morum, etc, etc' (London: William Holland, 180-, National Library of Jamaica).

'with the Governor's permission', the Governor's official Council met.[50] Today's visitors to this space enter what remains of the old King's House through a side door, the Council's entrance.

The Governor's Council constituted the third component in the government of the colony. If the Governor died and there was no Lieutenant-Governor on the island, the Council's President, its most senior member, took over the government. Many of the Council's day-to-day functions were modelled on the English Privy Council. However, when it dealt with the Assembly, the Jamaican Council also adopted some of the roles of the English House of Lords, reconstituting itself to act as a second legislative chamber to vet and revise bills which had been passed by the House of Assembly. The Council consisted of a dozen members, several leading officials by right of their office (including the Chief Justice, the Solicitor General and the Attorney General, all Crown appointments). The other members were appointed individually by the Crown and were generally local landowners or rich merchants who had lived in Jamaica for decades. They were not necessarily either the largest resident landlords or Kingston's richest merchants, as these were as likely to be found in the Assembly.[51] The Council tended to represent the views of leading colonists, but there always would be problems in securing their presence at meetings – especially during crop time. This proved even more of a problem for Assembly sessions.

Prudent governors would not ignore the Council. Its members could sit far longer than individual governors remained in Jamaica. A Governor might well find advisors among his household, some of whom might even end up on the Council, but the Council remained a separate institution that expected to have a voice in decision making. Governors sent the names of potential Councillors back to the Board of Trade in London, who might also receive nominations via members of the English Cabinet and the Secretary of State for the Colonies. When vacancies occurred royal letters of appointment were sent directly to the chosen individuals.[52] This process could easily leave seats unfilled, given delays in the transatlantic mails. Governors could then suspend troublesome councillors. The extent of the Governor's power is apparent in a saying current in the mid-eighteenth century that asserted 'the Governor could turn out a Councilor and put in his Footman in his Stead'.[53] Individual Council members could obtain official permission to leave the island for the sake of health or business affairs. Otherwise illness, bad weather or bad roads might also prevent attendance. As a result there were times when it was difficult to convene the minimum number of Councillors to allow a meeting to make decisions. All of these variables could strengthen a Governor's hand. But while leaving seats empty or simply filling them up with cronies and office holders might allow day-to-day business to proceed, this also invited the further risk that the Council would just become an echo chamber for whatever His Excellency the Governor wanted to hear. In practice, the weaker the Governor and the more unpopular the policies that he might want to pursue, the greater his temptation to recruit pliant councillors, even if these were times when official policies would benefit most from well-established local supporters. It remained possible for the Council to have a distinct impact on policy making and in 1769, the Council intervened in the Assembly's building schemes, before either the portico or this wing of the King's House was completed. The Council vetoed a bill passed by the Assembly appropriating money to erect another house for the Governor to stay in when he was in the county of Surrey (the county that included Kingston, hence effectively authorizing the construction of a second King's House in Kingston).[54] In this instance the Councillors were taking no chances on re-establishing Kingston as an administrative centre.

The remainder of the King's House complex housed the Governor's household. There were several older structures at the back of the main King's House that dated from the 1690s rebuilding or intervening expansions. These included the suite of three offices where the Governor's private secretaries worked. The entire complex of offices, kitchens, pantries and servants' hall were linked with more permanent 'piazzas' – covered walkways – and there were gardens with orange and other fruit trees in the courtyards.[55] All of which meant that the Governor continued to work in a household where public and private roles overlapped, in contrast to the island's other officials in their offices underneath the Assembly. Indeed, leading colonists were quick to criticize should these roles fail to interact. Towards the end of one Governor's term, when he had just endured a bruising constitutional dispute with the Assembly and was not inviting many guests to his table, a hostile letter claimed that: 'His Royal Fatness slumbers over his Beef and Beer almost entirely with his own Family'.[56] This was not how things were meant to be.

The Assembly endeavoured to set its chamber in the centre of affairs, but as the King's representative and, indeed, as the island's commander-in-chief, the Governor always retained the power to override the civilian society the Assemblymen represented. Military threats, either external from the French or Spanish invasion fleets that populated settlers' nightmares or else internal from slave rebellions or rumours of rebellions, all justified the declaration of Martial Law. Such proclamations suspended the law terms and closed the law courts, sending the lawyers and their clients back to their plantations. Such declarations also mobilized the militia. All free male settlers between 16 and 60 were obliged to enroll in a militia company; thus, as a colonist observed on a proclamation of martial law due to white fears of slave plots, 'we are all Military men here at present'.[57]

The public building commissions of the 1760s and '70s in Spanish Town accommodated the military strand woven so closely into the fabric of colonial society. Housing the parish militia was the responsibility of the parish vestry. They paid for magazine built in brick just to the south of the Church Ford, later known locally as 'Gran Jan', which was erected in the aftermath of the 1760 slave revolt. It could hold 50 barrels of gunpowder.[58] These buildings came with their own risks. In 1703 a fire at the powder magazine in Port Royal had nearly flattened that town (with the townspeople seeking refuge standing up to their necks in the harbour before a drunken sailor went in and extinguished the blaze). Then in 1763 and, again, in 1782, lightning strikes blew up the magazine at Fort Augusta.⁵⁹ Prudence would dictate a site fairly distant from the rest of the town for the public magazine.

Spanish Town as a garrison centre

Spanish Town was never simply the seat of the Governor, Council, Assembly and law courts. In the mid-eighteenth century, it continued to house a sizable component of the island's garrison of regular troops. In 1760 the ready access to the north side of the island from the town proved a major advantage when Tacky's rebellion broke out among the island's 'Coromantee' slaves. The colonists were convinced that the Lieutenant-Governor's speedy dispatch of parties of regulars and mounted militia from Spanish Town to St Mary, where the rebellion had just started, was decisive in limiting its extension, even though its Akan-speaking organizers already had managed to coordinate plans for parallel uprisings in several north coast parishes, in Westmoreland and in Kingston.⁶⁰

We can catch some echoes of contemporary reactions to the state of affairs at this juncture by the name 'Tacky's Bridge' attached to a crossroads just to the north of the town. Tacky, the uprising's most prominent military leader, was killed in a skirmish with the Maroons. His head was subsequently 'brought to Spanish Town, and stuck on a pole in the highway'. But, demonstrating the views of the town's wider population, Tacky's head soon disappeared: 'stolen, as was supposed, by some of his countrymen'.⁶¹ The 'Tacky's Bridge' name was applied to this crossroads by at least the mid-1790s and remained in use into the twentieth century.⁶² The persistent currency of this name highlights the continuing fear of slave revolts, which reaffirmed older criticisms of Spanish Town's inland site that it was 'liable to be Surprised or Cut off in Case of an insurrection of the negroes'.⁶³ The persistence of such fears encouraged the Assembly to appropriate more funds for barracks.

In the early 1770s, with the Assembly and King's House standing complete, the Assembly funded a further extension of the existing barracks which stood to the south-west of the town. The town's expansion to the west in the 1740s had lapped against the existing barracks wall. In 1775 the Assembly paid a steep rate to acquire a neighbouring field, which increased the space around the barracks by a third.⁶⁴ An orderly room, 'old', 'new' and 'grenadier' barracks and a free-standing military hospital were all built around the enlarged compound in the mid-1770s.⁶⁵ A hurricane in 1784 levelled most of these structures, prompting complaints of insubstantial construction.[66] The military area now stretched west from Martin Street to Young Street. In peacetime, at least, these barracks allowed more of the British troops to be brought in from lodgings. The expansion also provided a vast parade ground with space enough for non-commissioned officers to manoeuver recruits under a hot sun – which presumably sent many over to the hospital. The brick wall around the compound constructed at a cost of £2,000 in 1779 still stands and continues to define traffic flows in and out of the western extension to the town.[67]

The regular troops stationed in Spanish Town provided a reserve against internal uprisings. After the King's House and the Assembly building the barracks for the garrison absorbed the largest sums extended on public works in the town. Unsurprisingly, the soldiers proved rough tenants, as the annual bills for repairs showed, so that the town's building craftsmen received regular employment replacing shingles and floorboards, whitewashing and re-glazing. Despite all this maintenance, the existing barracks remained insufficient. Successive commanding officers complained that there was not enough room to house the soldiers and their officers, so that the officers had to live in lodgings scattered around the town.[68]

Public building commissions and Spanish Town's building trade

During the 1760s and '70s the Assembly's funding for major public projects through its Commissioners for Forts, Fortifications and Public Buildings, was combined with public funding for further, smaller buildings in Spanish Town. Some, like the new structure to shelter the Island's Artillery Train commissioned in 1770, were clearly part of the committee's responsibilities.[69] However, the Commissioners included several representatives from Spanish Town and St Catherine parish and they could attend meetings far more easily than the other members. The committee's membership helps explain why the Assembly was persuaded to build a new gaol on one side of the new market on the western edge of the town. For any local representatives this project would appear particularly urgent after a prisoner being held for trial managed to make a hole in the roof of the prisoners' 'common room', crawl across the joists and then escape through the kitchens. In the short term the common room ceiling was lined with boards. Mr Engineer Jones then produced yet another plan for the Commissioners.[70] It absorbed £2,815.12.4 of public money.[71] The building was far more difficult to escape from (though escapes still occurred) but the unfortunate debtors incarcerated in the new thick-walled building as a result of eighteenth-century laws found it a miserable abode.[72] Today the brick-walled compound beside the market square still holds substantial elements of the 1776 'new' gaol, where a whole series of locally based contractors worked as masons, carpenters and blacksmiths. Further Assembly money was laid out in repairs to the parish Work House then located on the south-western corner of the Church Parade, in front of the parish church (today's Cathedral). A second substantial new brick structure was erected at this location replacing a wood framed structure with wattle-and-daub panels. The final bills for this structure were then paid by selling off the landed endowment of a local charity.[73] After these initiatives newly-refurbished houses of correction overlooked both of the market squares in the town where local slaves brought in surplus produce from their food plots to sell.

Additional public commissions were scattered around the town. Most years the parish vestry funded some rebuilding chores, some of which were substantial. In 1755, when the political debates over the town's future role were continuing, the vestry paid for a splendid new organ loft for the parish church, in part at least offering a gesture of local defiance against Governor Knowles's, moving the town's official functions to Kingston.[74] This loft still remains. The builders then returned five years later to erect brick buttresses ten foot high outside the church to help support the weight of the new organ.[75] They also refurbished the interior, painting the wooden pillars 'stone colour'.[76] The next year the parishioners built a new tower at the west end of the church.[77] Other vestry projects were far smaller, but we find in the accounts for the new gates and steps for the church erected in 1759 references to individuals like one Mrs Mary Brock, who sold the parish '4 hogsheads of Lime' for the project.[78]

The throng of official commissions offered opportunities for local artisans. There is certainly room for more research to identify the individual builders and contractors who erected these buildings. This would be particularly interesting because Spanish Town thereafter remained a centre for building trades. Some names recur in the public accounts. Thomas Perkins undertook a whole series of carpentry chores in and around the town, winning contracts for the Assembly balcony, the gaol and 'the Wall and railing round the Grass

Place at the End of the Kings House' but being outbid for the Venetian blind contract.[79] Later the 'carpenters yard' belonging to William Perkins who continued to receive regular contracts for carpentry work and lumber was substantial enough to be marked on the 1786 map, lying just to the west of the new market.[80] We have less information on the artisans who performed the skilled work at individual building sites. A payment made in June 1771 to a local carpenter for '1 day with 4 Negroes' to repair loose shingles at the barracks is unusual only in specifying the workforce.[81] The five shillings a day charged was usual for enslaved artisans or, as another account described them, 'Tradesmen negroes'.[82] These were mixed crews.

Some local contractors built up considerable expertise taking on a succession of public contracts. David Allen, 'Bricklayer', or, later, 'Mason', whom we met in 1770 swearing to the quality of the English stonemasons' work on the pillars for the King's House portico, continued to bid for and secure a succession of contracts in and around Spanish Town. He had completed the new gaol in 1776, despite the difficulty of securing 'Hard Timber & Northward Lumber at the Market Prices' due to the disruptions in shipments of building materials from North America during the American War of Independence.[83] In 1781, with the military crisis growing, Allen then went on to secure a contract for further bricklaying work at Fort Augusta, seven miles away, facing out into Kingston harbour.[84] Mr Allen extended his range still further later that year bidding for and winning a contract for carpenter's repairs to Rock Fort, over on the other side of Kingston.[85] The whole series of public building contracts in Spanish Town provided a foundation upon which more wide-ranging building concerns could be established.

Further substantial commissions then continued to fill local builders' order books. The rebuilding of the brick Novéh Shalom Synagogue in the 1760s was one such substantial project. The new rectangular building extended 32 feet in width, 52 feet in length and was 20 feet high. Inside it was panelled in cedar while some of its wooden pillars were painted to resemble marble.[86] For most of the year, when the Assembly and law courts were out of session and all the visitors had returned home, the synagogue provided the place of worship for a significant proportion of the resident white population. In 1774 there were about 300 Jews living in Spanish Town with another 50 living in the vicinity. At this juncture they amounted to about a third of the white families.[87] The building was also a landmark for the whole town. Over time the ford at the bottom of today's Adelaide Street, which ran past the synagogue, came to be known as 'the synagogue ford'.[88] Recent archaeological excavations reaffirm the parallels claimed between this building and the plan of the Bevis Marks synagogue erected by London's Spanish-Portuguese community in 1700. This Spanish Town building did aim to echo an existing metropolitan model, in contrast to the public buildings around the Parade – although its interior was lavishly panelled in tropical hardwoods. The building was damaged during the 1907 earthquake, but by then its congregation had moved away and without repairs, it crumbled. Today the most visible reminder of this former synagogue at the corner of Monk and Adelaide Streets is the overgrown mound left after it was finally demolished in the mid-1950s. The list of eighteenth-century commissions can go on, with the purpose-built theatre completed in 1776 – the year after one opened in Kingston – and paid for by public subscription. It put £2,471.16.1¼ into the pockets of the town's building workers.[89]

Local artisans erected these new public buildings, which then reshaped townspeople's landmarks. There were still very few street names anywhere in the town, except for the area to the west of the original Spanish town developed during the 1740s. But in giving directions residents took their bearings from the public buildings that adorned the town's streets. In practice, most streets were described by their destination, their origin, or what they ran past. Public buildings loomed large in townspeople's 'to,' 'from' and 'by' descriptions. People often cited the Free School and the King's House – particularly the street running behind the King's House – and frequently specified the barracks and the synagogue. Other descriptions invoked roads running into or out of town. Still other 'to' 'from' or 'by' clauses could cite prominent residents, following earlier naming patterns. For example, the splendid house at the bottom of Monk Street occupied by Sir Charles Price, Speaker of the Assembly, stalwart for the town's rights and, indeed, the namesake for a type of cane rat known as the 'Charley Price' rat, was mentioned particularly frequently. It looms large, too, in the 1786 map of the town.[90] The house of former President of the Council, Matthew Gregory, also figured prominently in townspeople's directions. Long after his will was proved in 1756, rents from this house continued to provide the principal endowment for 'Gregory's Trust', which provided for the 'maintenance and support of poor persons in or from any part of the Island and in and for the putting poor Boys and poor Girls apprentices in the said Island and for giving portions in marriage for any poor girls in the island'. Besides the Trust's general utility, which left more people as potential beneficiaries, a marble monument to Dr Gregory and a framed description of the bequest both hung in the nave of the parish church. The house therefore remained a local landmark – at least until 1792 Act of the Assembly permitted the trustee to sell the now dilapidated property and reinvest the proceeds.[91] Residents in a town that offered a centre for retailing and luxury trades mentioned some shops, too, even though their proprietors were not able to vote, as in the 'Henriques's Stores' owned by a Jew or 'a Store belonging to Mary Rennalls'.[92] If these name-based characterizations remained highly specific, some residents invoked more general areas of the town, of which 'the East End of Spanish Town' was the most general.[93] The most widely cited general areas, however, lay in the newer western area of the town, primarily 'the old Negro Market' but also the 'Negro New Market'. Individual householders could invoke a repertoire of landmarks to describe their properties and to orient themselves. Architectural and personal descriptions were blended in this repertoire.

The new public buildings and, indeed, townspeople's citing of them in their descriptions, still offer us only a partial view of the mid-eighteenth-century town. There was considerable expansion to the north in the generation between the town's western expansion in the 1740s and the January 1786 publication of John Pitcairn's map of the town. Houses lined the roads that now ran north extending older streets between 'Broad Street' (today's King Street) to the east and Young Street to the west. This process of extension occurred after the earlier western expansion was established. This second extension remains apparent where Nugent Street crosses Old Market Street (Western Street and Jew Street in the 1786 map), where the northbound street makes a short dog-leg. Before this street was extended northward a house had been built at the T-junction opposite from where the then Western Street ran into the commercial artery of 'Jew Street'. The new residential developments laid out in the Spanish Town expansion of the 1750s to 1780s proved far less coordinated, for all the splendid public buildings erected during the 1760s and '70s. It proved impossible to insert further cross-streets for the city grid once buildings were erected on prime commercial sites on T-junctions.

The town sprawled. Many of the suburban buildings erected at this stage were free-standing. As Edward Long, a resident himself, described the town's outskirts: the houses stood with 'a variety of trees in constant verditure, being scattered among the buildings, more especially in the skirts, it has the rural

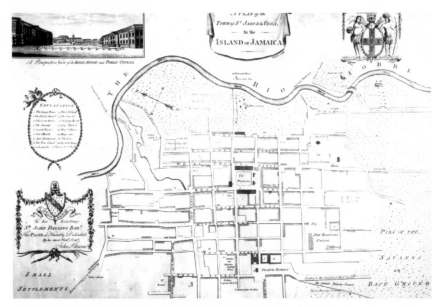

FIGURE 4:6   1786, John Pitcairn, 'A Plan of St Jago de la Vega in the Island of Jamaica', (London, W. Hinton, 3 January 1786), (National Library of Jamaica).

appearance of a village'.[94] The total area covered by the late eighteenth-century town extended remarkably, but while some early streets were built up compactly from the first, many of the new streets initially held only scattered buildings. Subsequent building has filled in the gaps subdividing these lots. The result of this protracted process is that a remarkable number of older retail and domestic buildings still remain on many of Spanish Town's streets, even though they have now become components of far more densely-packed streetscapes.

The Second City?

Despite all the period's magnificent buildings, public and private, townspeople continued to worry that Spanish Town was 'on the decline'. They also continued to hark back to the removal of the Governor, Assembly and law courts to Kingston between 1754 and 1758 as *the* cause why new private investment remained scarce.[95] Repeating these explanations helped to justify the residents' continued zeal in winning additional building commissions from the Assembly and in getting any proposed public works in Kingston voted down. These partisan activities both energized and embellished the town, but they could not resolve the broader problems that underlay the controversy between Spanish Town and Kingston in the 1750s. When most of the island's settlement clustered in the south coast parishes, Spanish Town offered an effective hub for Jamaica's government. The core of the colony remained in this area from the English conquest until the conclusion of the Maroon Wars in 1739. Indeed, if anything, the frontier of English settlement which had begun to advance inland during the 1680s in the north-east in the parish of St George, the hinterland of Buff Bay, and in the west inland from Montego Bay along the Great River, had retreated during the Maroon wars.[96] However persuasive the case offered by Kingston and its advocates, there were practical reasons for retaining Spanish Town as the seat of government during this period, even beyond Kingston's unhealthy site or its merchants' corrupting 'luxury'.

This changed after treaties were signed with the Maroons in 1739. Over the next generation there was extensive new settlement in Jamaica's western parishes. The highest rates of population growth occurred there from the 1740s.[97] Plantations increasingly ranged beyond the areas served by the network of roads centred on Spanish Town. For planters in the western sugar belt getting to Spanish Town was, at best, only marginally less inconvenient than travelling to Kingston – and, even once they arrived for a session of the Assembly, they were still obliged to make visits to Kingston to secure shipping space or deal with their agents.[98] The political coalition mobilized by Spanish Town's defenders in 1754–8 to oppose moving the seat of the island's government to Kingston succeeded in allying the inhabitants of Spanish Town and its rural hinterland with leading planters from the western parishes not because the latter were necessarily in favour of retaining the colony's administration in Spanish Town, but because they objected to the tactics used to ram the change through the Assembly. These partisan arguments were easier to make because the western parishes also suffered from Kingston's domination over the colony's imports and exports. As part of the political settlement after 1758 the ports serving the western parishes – Savanna-la-Mar and Montego Bay, along with Port Antonio on the north east coast – all acquired the status of free ports. The most immediate consequence of this privilege was that ships arriving from England could land there first, while ships departing for England could sail from these ports directly. Ships' captains could take care of all the necessary customs clearances without putting into Kingston. They therefore avoided beating back from the western end of the island against the prevailing winds. This was a considerable benefit in its own right, providing significant advantages of cost and time.

From the mid-1750s Spanish Town lost legal functions too. The effect was recognized in the restored capital. A further proposal to 'inquire into the effects of the law for dividing the Island into 3 Counties' in 1766 proved sufficient to unite 'all the small voters in Spanish Town' in opposition to any further adjustments.[99] As things were, assize courts which heard smaller cases were established in the county of Cornwall to cover the western end of the island and in the county of Surrey to cover the eastern end of Jamaica (cases from the central county of Middlesex continued to go to the courts in Spanish Town). These county-level courts spared the litigants from Cornwall and Surrey the costs in time and lodgings of pursuing minor cases through the island's central courts.[100] In practice Spanish Town and Kingston both lost out as a result of the customs and legal reorganization secured after 1756, though the island's growing prosperity compensated most of their losses. Even by the middle of the eighteenth century the economic balance was already shifting away from the older parishes on the southern side of the island towards the western parishes. In such terms the remarkable architectural commissions erected in Spanish Town during the 1760s and '70s provided impressive facilities anchoring the seat of government in a town that was increasingly inconvenient for not only the merchants in Kingston but, now, for the planters in the island's western sugarbelt parishes as well.

It still took a while for Montego Bay to overtake Spanish Town as the island's second city. The Reverend Thomas Coke, a Methodist missionary, landed in Montego Bay on 29 December 1790. His selection of a landing place after sailing from the Eastern Caribbean demonstrated the newer port's increasingly significant place in inter-island trade. Coke delivered sermons in Montego Bay before purchasing horses to ride across the island to Kingston, where some sparks from evangelical efforts were already taking hold. Coke stopped at Spanish Town on his way south; he described it as 'the seat of the Government and the second town of the Island'. Coke's choice of words to describe the town in his diary is significant and ironic. Significant because these were phrases that settlers on the island probably used and ironic because it was not long afterwards that the title 'second city' began to slip from Spanish Town and go to the 'flourishing and opulent town' of Montego Bay, which would hold it, off and on, for most of the nineteenth and twentieth centuries.[101]

CHAPTER FIVE

'The genteelest and handsomest town in the island'

Reorientations, 1780–1838

*T*HE 58 YEARS AFTER 1780 saw the transformation of the Jamaica of the plantocracy. The island's Governors, Council members and Assemblymen all continued to hold forth in the splendid settings constructed in Spanish Town during the 1760s, but within a single lifespan a succession of social, economic and political changes buffeted their hierarchical world and challenged most of their society's basic assumptions.[1] Some major social developments occurred in the 1780s and '90s in the aftermath of the American War of Independence and later during the French Revolution. During the late 1820s and 1830s an unwilling Assembly passed decisive changes. Wider definitions of 'Jamaican' came to be recognized in Spanish Town's streets, a process that culminated on August 1, 1838, when the Governor read a proclamation from the portico of the King's House that left all the former slaves fully free.

These successive transitions left their imprint on Spanish Town and this chapter investigates the physical and cultural reshaping of the capital in the generations before emancipation. The island's political and legal affairs were housed there, and the town remained both a social hub and regional market in its own right. Newcomers might assume that Kingston, with its 'immense trade' was 'the Capital of Jamaica', but they soon recognized that although Spanish Town was 'inferior in point of size', the older centre remained 'the seat of Government, and the place where the Courts of Jamaica are held'.[2] The protracted completion of a grandiose monument to a naval victory and then the outbreak of another war provided new backdrops for the major public events in Spanish Town and set the stage for a generation worried by impending military threats. The Industrial Revolution in England also presented further opportunities for spending public funds on important new public works and monuments, including purchasing the remarkable Iron Bridge that still spans the Rio Cobre. However, the construction of Baptist and Methodist chapels on the town's outer approaches showed some of the most significant social changes that transformed Jamaica over this period. These demonstrated wider cultural shifts from the plantocracy to 'free Jamaica', besides encouraging Jamaica's broader transformation from a profane to a God-fearing society. With the establishment of the chapels to rival the established Anglican places of worship an alternative urban geography developed that reorientated ttownspeoples' social patterns. Exploring these developments highlights the sheer range of the social and intellectual reorientations during this period.

Reappraising the Town: travelogues, cartoons and metropolitan views of Jamaican Society

Far fewer new public buildings were commissioned in the town during the 25 years after 1780 than during the previous 30 years but, even if they might appear shabbier, descriptions of Spanish Town's streets began to reach far wider audiences. Published accounts of West Indian life became increasingly plentiful in Britain during the French Revolutionary and Napoleonic Wars. Over the next 30 years the circulation of these images helped shape English views of Jamaican society.

Further direct lines of communication between Britain and the West Indies were opened by the host of soldiers and sailors posted to Jamaica during the prolonged wars with France between 1789 and 1815. Despite massive casualty lists, Britain maintained a strong military presence in the West Indies.[3] Some of the survivors endorsed the planters' point of view after they returned home. For a generation a succession of distinguished veterans who had enjoyed lavish West Indian hospitality would be marshalled as witnesses for the defence of

FIGURE 5:1   F.[Abraham] J[ames], 'Segar smoking society in Jamaica', (London: William Holland, 1802). Other artists' sketches of West Indian society also depicted this comfortable, but hardly polite, posture. (National Library of Jamaica).

the slaveholders' activities. Other visitors were more impressed by the growing differences between West Indian culture and English social norms. Between 1799-1801 the soldier-artist Abraham James served in the 67th Regiment while it was posted in Spanish Town. A set of cartoons by 'FJ 67 Regt' published in London from 1802, which satirized creole life in general and Spanish Town 'society' in particular, exemplified the latter attitude.4 His image of 'Segar smoking society in Jamaica!' probably depicts the town's Assembly Rooms, nominally a resort for genteel society. The white residents, male and female alike, are shown here smoking huge cigars (when this fashion was not widely established in 'polite' society in England) and lying back in chairs with their legs propped up against the wall.4 For general boorishness the individuals depicted in this cartoon outdo images of even the crassest *nouveau riches* thrown up by the Industrial Revolution. A second plate (illustration 4:5) depicted another Spanish Town scene: 'A Grand Jamaican Ball! or the Creolian hop a la Mustee; as exhibited in Spanish Town' and showed a ball in the Great Hall at the King's House with the dancers capering about to the music of an African-Jamaican band.5

The publication of Abraham Jones's cartoons of Jamaican life in London demonstrated a wide interest in West Indian scenes and highlighted the differences between creole lifestyles and English customs. They were published by a printseller whose publications generally had a radical slant. The markets in England for these and other late eighteenth- and early nineteenth-century prints depicting Jamaica was much greater than in the early and mid-eighteenth century, when authors who described the West Indies had a hard time finding publishers. As a result the 'Englishness' of Anglo-Jamaican society, a key element in its own self-definitions, became more open to metropolitan sneers and jeers. Just when the planters and their Assembly endeavoured to defend their slave-based society and tried to persecute the Protestant missionaries who challenged it, English readers of these publications were ready to buy – and increasingly believe – missionaries' descriptions of planter cruelty.

The Rodney Temple: celebrating Jamaica's avoiding a French and Spanish conquest

At first little appeared to have changed in Jamaican society after the American War of Independence, though both the island's merchants and planters soon complained against the British government's decision to close the West Indian colonies to trade with the new United States.[6] The continuity with earlier practices was displayed in the island's major civilian architectural commission of the 1780s which celebrated the colony's survival as a British colony. This followed the mid-century tradition by continuing to embellish the Parade in Spanish Town. The massive 'Rodney Temple' provided a monument to a hard fought naval victory that left Jamaica unplundered. On 12 April 1782, Admiral Sir George Brydges Rodney's fleet defeated the Count de Grasse's French fleet at the Battle of the Saints. In a dawn to dusk engagement in the Saints Channel between Dominica and Guadeloupe, Rodney succeeded in breaking the French fleets line of battle and then bludgeoning seven French ships of the line into surrendering, leaving 'the remainder of their Fleet . . . miserably shatter'd'.[7] Following on the heels of a long string of defeats in North America the British public 'with wonder heard the story,/ Of George's sway and Briton's glory,/ Which fame can ne'er subdue'.[8] This unexpected naval triumph occurred six months after the British army under Lord Cornwallis surrendered at Yorktown, a defeat that marked the end of any hopes for a British victory over the rebellious colonists on the North American mainland. However, the immediate effect of the Battle of the Saints was to prevent

Jamaica from falling into the hands of America's French and Spanish allies. While those of King George III's colonial subjects who remained under British rule would celebrate any military successes to be found, this victory marked a particularly important turning point in Jamaica's history. The island remained English, in contrast to all expectations in the months leading up to the battle.

During the war the Jamaica Assembly had poured out cash to repair forts and to erect artillery batteries across the island in anticipation of a French invasion.[9] 'Drums beat all day' but in one contemporary's nervous appraisal, disease cut into the garrison so that 'we have many Regiments on Paper but not 2,500 effective men', the doubts continued as the militia appeared 'disinclin'd to service' with 'as many men of American principles as loyalists amongst the principal gentlemen' who provided its officers.[10] The regular General in charge of the island's defences suggested some very radical measures to eke out a scanty garrison to resist the expected imminent attack. He proposed to 'double' the militia by freeing and arming large numbers of reliable slaves as skirmishers, then, should the enemy come ashore, the settlers were to burn everything that could not be hauled away and try to hold out in the mountainous interior.[11] Perhaps the planter officers in the local militia units would have obeyed such drastic orders; perhaps these desperate tactics could have worked – but it seems unlikely. Fortunately, they never had to find out. Even after the Assembly received the information that if Jamaica was captured it would be handed over to Spanish rule, fulfilling all of their worst nightmares, the Assemblymen still vetoed a proposal to recruit and free slave skirmishers as 'too dangerous'.[12] Meanwhile Spanish plans called for landing 20,000 men.[13] The French had still more troops. Short of a miracle or, perhaps, an outbreak of fever among the invaders, the soldiers and militiamen available in Jamaica could not have stopped the combined Franco-Spanish invasion once it got ashore. The French had already captured most of the British islands in the Eastern Caribbean.[14] Jamaica was next. As a contemporary ballad put it: 'For to besiege Jamaica [Admiral de Grasse] his course he straight did steer.' Desperate defensive strategies, or the alternative of French or Spanish conquest and rule, would certainly have transformed the colony. After Admiral Rodney's remarkable triumph at the Battle of the Saints, Jamaica remained unconquered. This success then enabled the British negotiators at the Peace of Paris of 1783 to regain all the Eastern Caribbean islands captured by the French.

The exhilaration in Jamaica about a 'great eminent and brilliant day' of naval victory rose higher still, in part because Rodney anchored his triumphant fleet in Port Royal Harbour. As the ballad proudly continued:

Now the lofty *Ville de Paris* is to Lewis no more,
Behold she trims her lofty sails to deck Britannia's shore,
With three more of their lofty ships to bear her company.[15]

After two weeks of parties and patching up Rodney sailed for England, but ran into an early hurricane on his way home. Several of the prizes, including de Grasse's flagship sank in the storm. The sightseers from across Jamaica who thronged Kingston 'to pay the tribute due to the deliverers of our Country' and 'see La Ville de Paris and the other Glorious Trophies of that day's Victory', were the only civilians to observe the full extent of Admiral Rodney's achievement.[16]

Thankful Assemblymen, recognizing the Royal Navy's achievement and the colony's amazing luck in avoiding invasion, voted £1,000 to commission a statue of Admiral – soon Lord – Rodney from John Bacon, the leading monumental sculptor in England.[17] This was an extravagant gesture. When the statue arrived in Jamaica in 1790 it provoked a further political tussle between Kingston and Spanish Town over where it should stand. The Kingston delegation's proposal would have their town raise subscriptions to set the newly arrived statue on a plinth in the Parade in Kingston, where it would be surrounded by 'a spacious basin' of water. A tied vote in the Assembly on which town should receive the statue was only resolved in Spanish Town's favour by the Speaker's single casting vote.[18] To provide a 'proper building' for the statue in Spanish Town the Assemblymen then voted to purchase the remaining private buildings on the north side of the Parade, filling in the square that already held the King's House and the Assembly. This cost £4,304. These public works proved expensive. The old Spanish-era King's Arms tavern and its commercial neighbours were finally demolished. Successive appropriations then paid for the erection of another block of public offices, using the Archives Building of the 1740s as a template, though the new building was twice as long. A neoclassical arcade joined the two buildings together. This focused on the elaborate 'Temple' in the centre to house Bacon's statue of Rodney.[19]

Spurred on by local rivalries the whole ambitious project continued, despite the onset of further warfare. A standing commission of Assemblymen

FIGURE 5:2 Statue of Admiral Rodney, 1790 (author's photograph) John Bacon's decision to
depict Lord Rodney in a toga reflected current artistic orthodoxy in London, which held
that changes in fashion meant that statues showing their subjects in civilian dress or military
uniform would soon become obsolete and seem ridiculous. Classical dress, in contrast, was
timeless.

was appointed in 1790 to oversee the 'additional offices . . . for the preservation of public records', while the masonry work on the 'Temple' was consigned to locally-based craftsmen.[20] The foundation stone was laid in 1790, just after the storming of the Bastille, when France and its West Indian colonies were already beginning to slide towards revolution. The statue of Lord Rodney was finally set up in 1792, in a ceremony that not only included a procession by the Governor, Council and Assemblymen but also the band of a newly raised regiment of Light Dragoons playing 'Rule Britannia'.[21] The building became one of the town's 'sights'. Five years later an otherwise grudging visitor commented that 'the portico and statue erected to the memory of Rodney are . . . magnificent, and an honour to the island'.[22] The Assembly continued to find money to complete the project, at a final cost of £8,200.[23] Public funds remained scarce in the island because of a whole series of natural disasters in the 1780s, a campaign against the Maroons in 1795–6, besides a greatly expanded garrison and reduced revenues during the French Revolutionary wars. Finishing was an achievement.

The colony celebrated the Battle of the Saints as a miraculous defence of the status quo, but even Admiral Rodney and the Royal Navy could not halt all the forces for change. In 1776 household slaves in the parish of Hanover, on the island's north shore, who had overheard Jamaican planters discussing North American assertions of 'liberty' planned an uprising of their own.[24] Their scheme failed, but several of the first stones in what was to become a social avalanche leading to Abolition for Jamaica and the other West Indian islands were nonetheless kicked over the edge during the American War of Independence and in its immediate aftermath.

The Arrival of Protestant Evangelists after the American War of Independence

After the war exiled loyalist refugees settled in Jamaica. In the process some of King George III's loyal North American subjects introduced fresh ideas to the island. Britain's remaining colonies all benefited from an influx of loyalist refugees uprooted by the war. In some, Ontario and The Bahamas in particular, the newcomers reshaped the subsequent development of hitherto marginal colonies. Their immediate impact was less obvious in Jamaica, but proved decisive all the same. Many of the incoming loyalists, white and black, came to Jamaica from the southern colonies of North America and, when they could, the slaveholders among them brought their slaves along too.[25] These enslaved African Americans introduced African Jamaicans to the first echoes of the evangelical revivals which had swept through North America in the 1750s and '60s. Among the migrants from Savannah, Georgia, was one George Liele, a freed slave originally from Virginia. Liele took on a contract as an indentured labourer in Jamaica to raise the passage money so that he and his family could escape from Savannah when the British army evacuated the town. It took Liele two years to work off this contract after he arrived in Kingston. There he worked for the former British military commander in Savannah, General Archibald Campbell, who had become the acting Governor of Jamaica. Before emigrating Liele had already served as the co-founder and pastor of the first black Baptist church in Georgia. In Kingston he began preaching before establishing a Baptist congregation there, which he described as 'Begun in America December 1777. In Jamaica, December 1783'.[26] Leile proceeded to baptize his converts both on the shore at Kingston Harbour and in Spanish Town's Rio Cobre. By 1792 a Jamaican sympathizer hoped that 'a way' was opening 'for another church in the capital, where the Methodists could not obtain any ground'. In January 1793, Liele wrote optimistically to Baptists in England that he had 'purchased a piece of land in Spanish Town, . . . for a burying ground, with a house upon it which serves for a Meeting-house'.[27] In the event, the purchase was not yet completed and the high tide for this initiative soon ebbed. As a result, although in early April, Liele and his wife signed bonds to purchase a corner property in Spanish Town between two roads leading to the hospital and another road leading to the barracks, the Lieles were obliged to break the contract by May 1.[28] Other immigrant preachers were active in this generation and Baptists in Spanish Town later claimed that the 'gospel [was] first introduced into this parish by Mr Gibbs a native of North America.' Little more is known of George Gibbs, 'a man of colour . . . from the southern states of North America' except that he carried on his evangelical labours 'with great diligence and zeal, in the midst of persecution and privitation' baptizing his converts under cover of darkness over a wide area until his death in 1826.[29] Liele's and Gibbs's efforts laid the foundations for many of the early nineteenth-century Baptist congregation's subsequent remarkable successes.[30]

Even with setbacks and disappointments the evangelical pulse began to reverberate through late eighteenth-century Jamaica. Late eighteenth-century

English society was increasingly reshaped by preaching and, given the openness of Anglo-Jamaican society to other metropolitan fashions, it could hardly evade this dynamic new social trend. In 1789 when Thomas Coke, an English Methodist preacher who had already helped establish a network of Methodist societies in the Eastern Caribbean islands, visited Jamaica, his diary entries for this and three subsequent visits when he roamed the island are dotted with references to his having received hospitality from individuals who had attended Methodist meetings in England.[31] By the 1790s Jamaica's hard-drinking, irreligious European population increasingly appeared different from the God-fearing, evangelical groups established in England where a rising tide of lay piety – a tide which rose higher and faster after the onset of the French Revolution – reaffirmed the social virtues of 'Church and King' as focuses for loyalty. The older, secular definitions of what it meant to be 'English' that remained current in Anglo-Jamaican society became increasingly out-of-step with mainstream metropolitan values.[32]

The island was indeed nominally Christian before the arrival of the missionaries, but potential evangelists viewed Jamaica as being in dire need of religion. Slaves traditionally had Sundays free from their masters' and mistresses' work, while Christmas and Easter were the colony's main public holidays. Public revenues paid generous stipends to the Anglican rectors, one per parish. These gentlemen were not necessarily idle. In the 1770s and '80s the Reverend Dr John Lindsay, rector in Spanish Town between 1773 and 1789, wrote to Principal William Robertson of Edinburgh University about demography, published two ingenious articles disagreeing with Benjamin Franklin's theories on the origins of waterspouts, compiled an impressive collection of natural history drawings and even drafted an elaborate (if completely unworkable) scheme to grant freedom to selected 'worthy' slaves.[33] These scientific and public policy interests were all eminently commendable and, as a fellow Anglican rector commented, projects to investigate the region's 'inexhaustible fund for philosophical & botanic Researches; and the various opportunities for getting Money as well as Knowledge, [were] perfectly compatible in the West Indies with the Character of a Clergyman & the Duty of a Missionary'.[34] In Dr Lindsay's case his scholarly exertions did not impede his carrying out the duties of his office. By contrast, under some of his successors Sunday services might not take place for three or four weeks in succession when the rector was ill and communion was only administered three times a year. Sunday services might also be interrupted should the

Governor and his household arrive late.[35] Attendance at church remained low. Indeed, one long-term resident recalled that 'Sunday forenoon was generally spent by the merchant in his counting-house, and was a favourite day for writing his packet letters'.[36] Residents of Spanish Town did continue to meet at the parish church to hear organ recitals. In 1800 the vestry inserted a new, larger, organ.[37] By then substantial churches stood in most of the island's towns and parishes, and the Anglican Church continued to oversee key rites of passage. Weddings and baptisms were private affairs, held at home, but funerals at the parish churches were well attended – and frequent.

But did this amount to Christianity as pious Englishmen and English-women increasingly came to understood it? Dr Lindsay might try to lay the blame for poor attendance on the bad examples given by recent Governors in not attending services, observing that 'Religion in Jamaica is In & Out of Fashion as its Governors shall be pleased to lead the way,' but few ministers from other denominations would rest satisfied with such a lame explanation for the lack of evangelical zeal among his fellow established clergy.[38] The criticism offered by an ex-Baptist missionary in the 1840s on the Anglican rectors' activities may have overstated when he claimed that the slaves dismissed their services as 'White man's Obeah' before arguing that, if anything, the religious state of the white community was actually far *worse* than that of the slaves.[39] The basic verdict remained valid. The island's established clergy hardly exerted themselves in preaching to their free parishioners and did even less to minister to the slaves.

It is difficult to generalize about the slaves' beliefs, as they drew on a range of West African religious traditions.[40] Slaves in Jamaica had dismally low reproduction rates throughout the eighteenth century, so a high proportion of them were 'salt water negroes', that is, individuals who had themselves been enslaved and transported from Africa to the Caribbean.[41] The rare Europeans who questioned individual slaves about their religious beliefs were likely to receive evasive answers because, after Tacky's Rebellion in 1760, the Assembly made the practice of African magic or 'obeah' a felony, punishable by death.[42] This put discussion of spirit possession off limits. Any queries about the slaves' 'notions of religion' were likely to produce bland comments invoking 'a good old man' above the clouds who 'would be kind to them if they did not tief' – no doubt a prudent reply to offer, but not necessarily a full answer.[43] Otherwise the legal ban on obeah was not particularly effective in constraining the slaves' belief systems. Another missionary recalled that during the 1820s in a slave burial ground 'at no great distance from . . . Spanish Town, there was scarcely a grave that did not exhibit from two to four rudely carved images'. Nor was this all; on some plantations slaves continued to place 'watchmen', described as 'pieces of wood-ants' nest, the roots of a particular grass, grave dirt, bunches of feathers, &c. either singly or together' by their provision grounds to deter thieves.[44] This emphasis on what Victorian readers would dismiss as 'heathen' superstitions hardly obscures the resilience of independent religious traditions among the enslaved.

A further religious alternative is demonstrated in a small paper notebook passed on from 'a young Mandingo negro' by a Baptist deacon to the Spanish Town congregation's first English minister in the early 1820s. It was misunderstood to be a passage from the Koran. However, its recent translation demonstrates that it was a text in which an African-born teacher, Muhammad Kaba, a slave in the parish of Manchester, well to the west of Spanish Town, summarized the tenets of his Muslim faith in his own West African language.[45] This document is a remarkable survival in its own right. Its composition hints at the potential continuation of Islamic belief among some African-born slaves. If the displays in graveyards and 'watchmen' remained anonymous public statements; the successes of the individual enslaved Muslims who sustained their faith were private achievements, unimaginable to most whites.

Over the next generation, Evangelism would transform these social and cultural beliefs. When Thomas Coke, the Methodist evangelist, preached in Spanish Town while en route from Montego Bay to Kingston in 1791, he borrowed a tavernkeeper's public room for his sermon. Rowdy whites heckled him. Coke's journal noted that he found attentive hearers all the same and was 'fully persuaded from the countenances and behaviour of the coloured people, that the Redeemer's kingdom might be enlarged by the preaching of the gospel in this place to them'. He therefore 'determined to move on the true gospel plan, "from the least to the greatest"' leasing a house on the outskirts of the town to house a new Methodist society and appointing a leader for the group.[46] Coke then left the island. Despite its promising beginnings this early group broke up. English Methodists remained hopeful about Jamaica's prospects as a mission field, so that in 1797, when 'the condition of Jamaica was such as' to encourage the London Missionary Society, an Anglican dominated group, 'to take active steps towards a mission station on that island' Coke protested, but received the answer that 'there was ample room in

Jamaica for all workers who could be sent'.[47] This was certainly true, but in the event neither the London Society nor the Methodists sent out any ministers for a decade. However, when a further generation of European nonconformist missionaries did reopen chapels in Spanish Town in the early years of the nineteenth century, they would duplicate the basic choices made in the 1790s: they, too, proceeded to rent suburban houses for preaching and to direct their missions towards groups who chose to listen to them.

1789–1815: the French Revolutionary and Napoleonic Wars and the Haitian Revolution put the Jamaican Assembly under siege

In the 1810s and 1820s, when a new generation of missionaries from England arrived to Jamaica and Spanish Town they found support among the local converts who remained from the evangelical efforts of the 1780s and 1790s. However, these new missionaries received a far cooler welcome from the colonial establishment. In the mid-1780s George Liele and his congregation had successfully petitioned the Assembly for permission to 'worship Almighty God according to the tenets of the Bible' and received the Assemblymen's sanction.[48] Once the West Indian planters felt increasingly threatened during the French Revolutionary and Napoleonic wars, white Assemblymen backed away from repeating such encouraging gestures.

Other responses to the period's events had appeared more daunting. In Spanish Town 'a body of negroes . . . who called themselves the Cat Club assembl[ed in 1791] to drink King Wilberforce's health out of a cat's skull by way of a cup, and swearing secrecy to each other'.[49] Whatever was going on at these meetings, which continued for several weeks, the participants were aware of the news from Europe. Such reports then reinforced slaveholders' fears. The Jamaican Assemblymen were already familiar with some potential assailants such as French invaders, Maroon risings, hurricanes and further bouts of yellow fever and the threat of escaped slaves gathering in bands and attacking outlying settlements.[50] After 1790 all West Indian slaveholders feared Haitian-type revolutions too. There, island-born slaves rather than newly imported Africans provided many of the rising's leaders. In looking for scapegoats, rather than admitting to the inherent brutalities of plantation slavery, Jamaica's planters laid the blame on the French General Assembly for introducing offers of emancipation into the debates in the French colony of

Saint-Domingue (today's Haiti).[51] In such contexts white Jamaicans would find all the more frightening the reports from England of increasing parliamentary support for not just the reform and regulation of the slave trade, but for William Wiberforce's motions in the House of Commons in 1789 and in 1792 calling for its abolition. As the Cat Club's toasts showed, this news quickly spread to the island's slaves.

Fear would dictate the Jamaican Assembly's policies for the next 30 to 40 years. While the external challenges were daunting enough, internal threats soon added to planters' nightmares. Waves of French refugees and their slaves arrived in Jamaica during the 1790s as the complicated political and military situation unravelled in Saint-Domingue, just upwind of Jamaica.[52] Some stayed, to the island's lasting advantage, but slaveholders in Jamaica worried that agitators concealed among all these newcomers could 'infect' their slaves with radical ideas. At least one would-be French agent arriving with the refugees did plan to stir up another Maroon rising, so these suspicions were not completely groundless.[53] Fear would erect vast superstructures on these foundations, especially when Jamaica's central place in British military efforts in the Caribbean led to Kingston Harbour holding a long row of prison ships crammed with prisoners of war.[54] In 1803, after the black triumph and French evacuation of Saint-Domingue, the Governor of Jamaica reported that 'we have 7,000 French Prisoners of War in Jamaica, including nearly 1,000 Officers of all Descriptions on their Parole on Shore'.[55] Assemblymen and their families frequently heard French spoken in Spanish Town as 'swarms' of captured officers paced its streets.[56] These sojourners would provide continuing grounds for apprehension, even before rumour added to the brew: in July 1803 two 'foreign negroes' were executed in Kingston for 'being concerned in a plot to fire the town', the fire being a signal that 'the negroes in the country were to rise', or so the story went.[57] Over the following Christmas holiday townspeople shared further 'unpleasant and alarming reports' of a prospective rising over the holiday from an alliance of domestic slaves, prisoners on parole and the ex-French POWs enrolled as British troops who were on duty in Spanish Town – all of which demonstrated to Jamaica's whites that no one else could be trusted.[58]

In such near-paranoid contexts any groups that encouraged slaves (or anyone else) to meet, even if only to hear sermons and discuss the Scriptures, would be viewed by whites with deep suspicion. Some of the Baptist and Methodist groups established in the 1780s had held together and were beginning to generate a cohort of local preachers. During the 1790s members of the Assembly and local justices of the peace increasingly saw these evangelistic efforts as hostile. By 1794 George Liele was obliged to swear that in a sermon on St Paul's *Epistle to the Romans*,

> he had not the least intention to offer or publish any words that had a Tendency to Stir up Sedition or raise any rebellious notions in the midst of the people of his own Colour or to give offence to the white Inhabitants of the Island nor had [he] any evil intent, whatsoever in delivering such discourse nor was he at the time sensible that the words he made use of were liable to be Construed as injurious to the peace and Quiet of the Inhabitants of this Island.[59]

The island's slaveholders were very nervous.

In this highly charged political environment the Assemblymen passed bills imposing fiercer and fiercer penalties on any agitator, white or black, who would encourage rebellion among the slaves or assist the prisoners of war in the prison hulks.[60] These bills then added 'Sectarian' (non-Anglican) ministers to their lists of dangerous persons.[61] This addition was plausible enough when looked at from the Assembly's own viewpoint. Despite repeated assertions by officials of the English Baptist and Methodist churches of their ministers' apolitical stance, the preachers' efforts to evangelize the slaves did strike at the foundation of the island elite's rationalizations of slavery and of the society and economy that slavery sustained. In the long term evangelism would overturn the slaveholders' world as effectively as any revolutionary agitators. This anti-preaching law aimed to stop 'the mouth of every black and dissenting minister and prohibits the poor people from meeting together to worship God'. A leading English Baptist could briskly dismiss the Assemblymen as 'mostly infidels and profligates', but nonconformist congregations were still slow to organize responses in London to the hostile actions by Assemblies across the British West Indies.[62]

Even though evangelical outrage only slowly focused on the new West Indian laws, public opinion in Britain would not stomach the persecution of Protestant ministers. Responding to requests from existing Jamaican congregations first the English Baptists and later the English Methodists began to send missionaries to Jamaica. These missionaries had been preceded by Moravian preachers and over the following 30 years would be joined by Presbyterians and Presbyterian Church of Scotland ministers, by Congregationalists and then by Anglicans, but, with the exception of the Anglican chaplaincy established in the 1830s, none of these later missions established stations in Spanish Town. The missionaries faced a whole series of legal hurdles when they arrived in Jamaica but, brandishing English preaching licences embellished with official seals and with their denominations ready to lobby on their behalf in London, they had a better chance at overcoming the legal obstacles that proved all too effective in silencing most 'local' preachers. Even then, foot-dragging by Jamaican magistrates remained an effective tactic in deterring evangelism and a number of newly arrived missionaries died of fevers before securing the necessary local licence to commence preaching.[63] Missionaries found that negotiating official obstructionism remained an uphill struggle.

In practice the Assembly's 'anti-sectarian' legal readings ran counter to the legal practice of tolerance to Protestant 'dissenters' (non-Anglicans) current in England since 1688.[64] When most of the persecuting laws and restrictive legal opinions produced by West Indian Assemblies and their lawyers reached England, they were vetoed or overturned. However, the offending law would remain in force during the lengthy time it took for its text to be evaluated and then for the news of the royal disallowance to arrive back in Jamaica and be formally published by the Governor.[65] Why, then, did successive royal Governors not use their own veto powers and refuse to approve such obnoxious laws? The war with France that pushed the Assemblymen towards paranoia and the same threats of invasion or local uprisings also constrained these Governors who, as we have seen, depended on funding from the planter-dominated Assemblies to pay for the garrisons of regular troops on the islands.

Local repercussions of the Revolutionary Wars: Re-deploying the Garrison to Kingston

The Governor's first priority was to maintain British rule in Jamaica. The island militia provided the island's initial line of defence. All able-bodied free males were obliged to enlist in their local militia regiment. By 1802 the force totalled 8,000 men. Their drills were intended to console civilian onlookers and overawe watching slaves. A regular army officer's sketch from 1800 shows a motley bunch of irredeemably civilian militiamen outside the King's House, though this cartoon understates the polish achieved by the island's free

FIGURE 5:3 F.[Abraham] J[ames], 'Proclaiming martial law in St Jago', from a set of cartoons, 'Martial law in Jamaica' (London, William Holland, nd. *c*. 1800), a regular officer's sketch of civilian soldiers in front of the King's House. (National Library of Jamaica).

coloured and black militia companies whose personnel had far less turn-over than the white companies.[66]

The local militiamen might drill diligently, but to withstand an invasion or subdue an uprising they would still need reinforcement by regular troops. By 1800 the Assembly was already maintaining 3,000 infantry regulars and funding a regiment of light dragoons, while governors schemed to transfer the cavalry unit over to the British army and use those funds to push the infantry total up to 5,000.[67] As the dragoons proved strikingly unsuccessful during the second Maroon War they had few local defenders.[68] But after ten years of war the Assemblymen told themselves that Jamaicans were more heavily taxed than the English and were loath to renew existing military taxes, still less, grant any new ones.[69] However 'diffuse' their calculations, the Assemblymen did have solid grounds for their complaints.[70] Even though the London price for sugar rose to unequalled heights, Jamaica still underwent prolonged economic hardships, in part because the island remained cut off from trade with North America and had to import its food and lumber from more expensive European suppliers. Wartime commerce raiders threatened transatlantic exports, raising insurance costs and shrinking the credit available from English merchant houses. In such politically charged contexts negotiations over paying for the garrison gave the Assembly plenty of opportunities to tack anti-missionary clauses onto other bills and then bluff governors into signing them. Subsequent peacetime governors, who found themselves financially stretched to maintain their households on their official stipend, became more conciliatory when the Assembly voted them supplementary salaries.

Conditions resulting from the French Revolutionary war gave the Assemblymen a strong hand in negotiating with governors, but it also forced the British Army to reconsider the relationship between Kingston and the island's capital. In practice the protracted wars with France led to Kingston's eclipsing Spanish Town's military functions. The immediate threats against which the regular garrison was to guard Jamaica against had shifted and this change transformed the role of the troops based in Spanish Town. The extensive barracks complex built in the 1760s, '70s and early '80s was designed to house soldiers who would take advantage of Spanish Town's excellent internal lines of communication to subdue slave uprisings on the plantations. The aim was to prevent a repeat of Tacky's Rebellion in 1760.[71] Such facilities appeared far less useful after 1790 when the primary threats to the colony came from offshore, or else lay among all the refugees and prisoners of war clustered in Kingston.

The garrison moved to Kingston in 1790 where a site was already available for their new barracks. In 1780, when the war with the rebellious American colonists and their French allies had reached a crisis point, the British government purchased Up Park Pen, 200 acres of land just outside Kingston. The deeds described it as the estate that Admiral Rodney had leased during his term of duty as naval commander in Jamaica. The Up Park property was not bought as a naval Commander's official residence because it was purchased seven years after the House of Assembly had acquired another estate just outside Kingston to house successive naval Commanders-in-Chief, which became known as Admiral's Penn.[72] Meanwhile the garrison's British regulars remained in Spanish Town. During the 1780s the Assembly rebuilt the old barracks there after extensive damage in a hurricane in 1784.[73] In 1790 as the political situations in France and its colony of Saint-Domingue worsened and a war appeared imminent, barracks were laid out at the British War Office's property at Up Park Camp and the main British regular garrison was transferred there. The Assembly offered no funds for this move.[74] Instead the Assemblymen tried to compensate for the garrison's relocation. It was at this juncture that the colony acquired 'a handsome pile of building' on White Church Street as a further official complex in Spanish Town to house the barracks, stables and riding school for the Jamaica Light Dragoons, a cavalry regiment raised in 1791 as a gesture of loyalty by the colony.[75] In the short term the old infantry barracks in Spanish Town remained full because the number of soldiers stationed on the island rose and barrack space proved so scarce that between 1792 and 1799 the town's playhouse was used as a barracks, but for the British army the move to Kingston was permanent. Spanish Town became a peripheral posting. In 1790 the British Government also purchased a large house on Kingston's Duke Street for the senior regular army officer, soon renamed Headquarters House. Other military properties in Spanish Town, such as the artillery yard whose freehold was held by the Office of Ordinance, were simply abandoned by 1792.[76] Henceforth not only would the island's senior military officers reside in Kingston but the King's artillery would be stored in Kingston in the new Ordinance Yard down by the harbour.

The tactical arguments for transferring the garrison to Kingston were plausible enough, but once the troops arrived military death rates immediately soared. A civilian observer soon observed that 'a mortality at present prevails among the soldiers' wives, which is new, as women do generally better than men – There is a cause for these Mortalities, yet unknown'.[77] The new military camp just outside Kingston, with its grid plan, houses for the troops and an aqueduct to supply water might indeed appear to newcomers 'the finest establishment to be seen in the colonies . . . where a great expenditure has been most usefully appointed', or else 'delightfully situated', but it was soon acknowledged to be 'very unhealthy'. By the 1820s a visiting officer would be told that 'the water about the Camp is excessively bad' and this 'together with [the camp's] low situation, is thought to be the cause of the great mortality that takes place amongst the Soldiery'. Such explanations found no space for the 'moschettas' (mosquitoes) that the same diarist described pestering him during his stay in Kingston.[78] Regiments posted in Spanish Town had certainly suffered from bouts of mosquito-borne yellow fever, but the overall death rates there remained far lower than those occurring at Up Park Camp. Acknowledging that a greater health problem existed in Kingston was not enough to bring the troops back to Spanish Town. Instead, the official response to growing death rates was to reassign the regular units to new barracks further from Kingston: first at Stony Hill in the hills above the Liguanea plain and then at a series of coastal sites that the Assembly granted to the Governor.[79] These subsequent removals and new buildings obliged governors to appeal to the Assembly for fresh funds, requests which then offered the Assemblymen further opportunities to push their own anti-missionary agendas.

It took half a century to resolve the army's problems with Kingston's fevers. A regimental commander who saw British garrisons posted in other ports in the Eastern Caribbean dwindle away summed up the problem: 'Commerce has already mournfully determined that situation to be the best for towns which appears most convenient for shipping and trade, namely, close to the sea; – regardless of the heat and the loss of health, which seem to be secondary considerations.'[80] In wartime the army was expected to defend those settlements. One ingenious proposal suggested 'an effective remedy' in 'the vast Resources of our Empire in the East' claiming that importing troops from India to guard the West Indies would reduce the number of British troops required in the West Indies, besides such recruits offering a 'speedy means of introducing *Civilisation* and *free Industry* into our Colonies'.[81] Even envisioning such a radical solution demonstrates the depth of the problem, though this scheme went no further. In 1841 an incoming garrison commander with experience in India, backed by a Governor who was a former acting Governor General of India, transferred most of the European troops stationed in Jamaica up to cantonments at Newcastle, 3,500 to 4,000 feet above sea level, which resembled the hill stations of Anglo-India. This proved an effective tactic because the troops were far less vulnerable to infection-bearing *Anopheles albimanus* mosquitoes there.[82] The base at Newcastle, which still houses the Jamaica Defence Forces, was 19 miles from Kingston on the road across the island to Buff Bay. At that time the British War Office also reassigned most of the Second Battalion of the West India Regiment, which had been housed in the Spanish Town Barracks to the barracks now vacated at Up Park Camp. A company remained but the 1841 transfer effectively concluded the process whereby Spanish Town lost one of its primary eighteenth-century roles as a garrison centre, first to Kingston in 1790 and then to Newcastle in 1841.

These answers to yellow fever lay well in the future. Meanwhile during the Revolutionary and Napoleonic wars preserving the troops' health in Jamaica remained a pressing problem. Enterprising governors resorted to recruiting among the miserable prisoners of war crammed into the hulks in Kingston Harbour, but besides the security risks, this expedient alone would not fill up the ranks of soldiers thinned by disease and desertion.[83] The British Army then turned to recruiting Africans, first buying newly landed slaves as recruits from the Kingston slave merchants and later purchasing recruits in West Africa. This appeared a dangerous move even though the colonists had always relied on slave trackers in campaigning against the Maroons.[84] Freed slaves were also enrolled in the former loyalist military units evacuated to the West Indies after the American War of Independence. In the 1790s Jamaica's free black population still included such individuals as Robert Carey, a blacksmith who was noted as 'American born' when he registered his free status. He resided near Tacky's Bridge, the crossroads just to the north of Spanish Town.[85] None of these precedents soothed the white settlers when, in response to the Haitian crisis, the British Army expanded the West India Regiment in the early 1790s, enrolling several new battalions of African soldiers who were still slaves. They provided effective military units that were not subject to the same death rates as the European regiments.[86] Jamaica's Assemblymen remained thoroughly nervous about these troops, so posting them near to Spanish Town provided Governors with a substantial bargaining chip when the Assembly tried to haggle.[87]

Hence, despite the Assembly's protests, the Second Battalion of the West India Regiment was transferred to Jamaica in 1801 after service in St Vincent, Trinidad and the Danish islands.[88] Initially the soldiers were housed at Fort Augusta on Kingston Harbour, one of the most unhealthy postings on the island, where they remained until 1809. On their return to Jamaica in 1816 after the end of the Napoleonic Wars companies of the Regiment were established in the old barracks in Spanish Town, where the regiment was based until 1841. Enslaved and free, the Regiment's soldiers proved a conspicuous presence in Spanish Town's streets, where a company remained to guard the King's House until 1866.[89] Governors and professional soldiers wished to retain them while the planters remained fearful of the presence of this force of armed Africans in their midst.

Further public commissions: the Iron Bridge and the 1819 Court House

Even after the garrison's transfers, Spanish Town remained the second largest settlement on the island. By 1807 it contained 'between five and six hundred houses, and nearly five thousand inhabitants, including Negroes and free people of colour'. These totals were certainly dwarfed by Kingston, which had 'about' 8,500 'white inhabitants' besides 'of free people of colour, three thousand five hundred; and of slaves, about eighteen thousand; amounting, in all, to thirty thousand souls.' But Spanish Town still compared well with the island's other secondary towns, including Port Royal, which even with the naval dockyards was still 'reduced to three streets, and a few lanes, and contains about two hundred houses' or even 'the very flourishing and opulent town' of Montego Bay, which had 'six hundred white inhabitants and consists of about two hundred and fifty houses, nearly fifty of which are capital stores or warehouses' or, indeed, of the island's other late eighteenth-century new town, Falmouth, which held 'about two hundred and fifty houses'.[90] Spanish Town provided the seat of government, 'here, too, are the public offices; so that this town, though not a large one, from its containing the government and assembly houses, and various other public buildings, may be considered as the genteelest and handsomest town in the island'.[91]

Neither comparative statistics nor even individual 'genteel' and 'handsome' public buildings would necessarily impress people passing through Spanish Town's streets. In 1797, a visiting army doctor who had already seen French, Dutch and English West Indian towns in Martinique, Barbados and Demerara, (today's Guyana) was favourably impressed by the road out from Kingston, but 'instead of handsome streets and magnificent buildings, the appearance of both was so humble, that when we arrived in the centre of Spanish Town we imagined ourselves to be only in the suburbs'. A 'very indifferent and badly served breakfast' did nothing to console him. Looking over the town 'the general view of the place was strongly calculated to confirm the opinion we had formed upon entering it': because the town resembled the suburbs 'of a more splendid city. The narrow confined streets look dark and gloomy, and the older houses are small, low, irregular, and of mean appearance, consisting of only a single story'. In this instance, after a local colleague 'conducted us to the different parts of the town and its environs, pointing out . . . all that was particularly worthy of the attention of strangers', a hitherto underwhelmed visitor was prepared to qualify his initial opinion slightly, acknowledging that 'although the general face of the metropolis be not prepossessing, handsome improvements are met with in various parts of it' while 'some of the houses, likewise, at the extremity of the town are

spacious, and of modern structure'.[92] His first impressions remained dismissive. The proportions that would suit a splendid urban centre were missing,
even though Spanish Town did house some impressive public buildings that
could receive grudging praise.

The war dragged on and the town's streets and thoroughfares had hardly
improved 20 years later, in 1816, when another weary visitor noted in his
journal that 'Spanish Town has no recommendations whatsoever; the houses
are mostly built of wood: the streets are very irregular and narrow; every
alternate building in a ruinous state, and the whole place wears an air of
gloom and melancholy'. Matthew 'Monk' Lewis, a prominent London
author, friend of Byron and Shelley and author of the early Romantic-era
'Gothic' best-seller *The Monk*, had inherited a Jamaican plantation and
compiled a journal during his visit to Jamaica with an eye to its subsequent
publication. At his arrival in Spanish Town Lewis had just ridden in from
Westmoreland and proved hard to please after a long journey.[93] His summary
omitted the most striking new construction undertaken in Spanish Town
during the French wars: because Mr Lewis drove his carriage into town from
the west, he would only traverse the impressive 1801 bridge as he left.

This bridge resulted from the need to improve communications between
Spanish Town and Kingston. Colonists persuaded the Assembly to arrange to
import a prefabricated cast iron bridge in an attempt to resolve a persistent
problem. This bridge was erected over the Rio Cobre just outside the town.
It succeeded a long string of wood, brick and stone bridges, which had all
been washed away. The most recent precursor, planned in 1797, relied on a
massively reinforced construction, with the foundations built around twenty-
inch-square hardwood pilings, shod with iron and then encased in thick
masonry buttresses, all standing behind cutwaters that would extend
upstream to break the force of the current. The design would be as reinforced
as contemporary technology allowed. With a contract for £26,000 two local
masons committed themselves to complete this project.[94] If this ambitious
structure was ever built it did not last for long. In 1801 a further £1,060 was
expended on importing 87 tons of cast iron for a prefabricated bridge from
England. In contrast to all of its predecessors, the 41 pieces, each two foot
wide, that comprised this structure were able to cross the river in one 80 foot
'rainbow' or span, thereby allowing it to avoid the floods that during the
previous century had torn away the piers for all earlier bridges across the Rio
Cobre.[95]

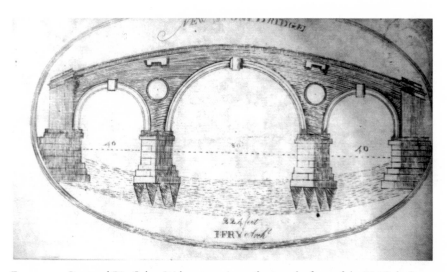

FIGURE 5:4   Proposed Rio Cobre Bridge, 1797. As a tribute to the force of the Rio Cobre's floods all the piers and abutments were elaborately reinforced: every other tier of stone would be bound together by iron rods and dollops of molten lead. The bridge's upper works would still be stone, curved in high arches over the floods below, but with holes left in the upper arches to allow flood water to pour through and diminish the structure's resistance. (*Columbian Magazine*, National Library of Jamaica).

In this purchase the Assembly drew on the most recent technology available in England to secure an elegant engineering answer to a hitherto unresolvable problem. Revenues produced by slave-grown sugar were applied towards purchasing a thoroughly modern industrial structure. An earlier prefabricated iron bridge erected over England's Severn River gorge at Colebrookdale in Shropshire in 1777–81 struck contemporary viewers as one of the most impressive engineering triumphs of the early Industrial Revolution.[96] The Spanish Town iron bridge imported by the Jamaican Assembly was among the first (if not the very first) of this type shipped across the Atlantic and today it is the oldest example still standing in this hemisphere. The new bridge helped ease civilian traffic and, together with a set of cast iron railings imported from England and erected around the Parade in 1802, these very current purchases provided impressive urban status symbols for Spanish Town. However, the immediate utility of the iron bridge was to expedite communications. The Rio Cobre's seasonal floods would no longer interfere with the dispatch riders and aides de camp who galloped between Headquarters House in Kingston and King's House in Spanish Town.

FIGURE 5:5 The Iron Bridge, 1801. The single span contrasted with its predecessors whose wood, brick or stone materials could only achieve shorter arches that all required intermediate piers, which then washed away. (photograph by J. Tyndale-Biscoe, 28 September 1984, Jamaica Archives, reproduced by permission).

The war years between 1789 and 1815 did not see many major building projects initiated in or around Spanish Town. Contemporaries certainly complained of the 'system of heavy taxation which prevails, and continues to prevail to discourage and distress enterprise and industry', and few proposals for civic improvements got very far, however plausible they might appear.[97] Townspeople continued to tell themselves that 'it is intended, too, that some considerable additions and improvements in the public buildings are to take place'.[98] There were indeed a handful of public commissions that included the completion of the Rodney Temple, the cavalry unit's barracks and riding school, the proposed new stone bridge over the Rio Cobre in 1797 and then, in 1801, its iron successor, along with those cast iron railings in the Parade the next year. Otherwise the completion in 1796 of the Ashkenazi synagogue, Mikvéh Yisroell (Hope of Israel) on the west side of Spanish Town, near to the market, was among the very few civilian commissions of the war years. It followed the establishment of an Ashkenazi synagogue in Kingston seven years before, in 1789.[99]

The schemes sketched for prospective improvements remained far more ambitious. During the 1790s, in an era when British and American investors underwrote canal-building booms, Jamaican would-be civil engineers proposed 'a great inland navigation on the South side', recommending an up-to-the-minute new canal to run from the mouth of the Bog Walk Gorge, alongside the Rio Cobre through St Catherine to Kingston Harbour. At a time when floods still closed the ford at Spanish Town and washed away any bridges, channelling this abundant flow seemed feasible. Readers were assured that the landscape 'would seem to invite to the undertaking, being a light mould, and presenting a smooth surface, with an easy and inconsiderable fall throughout its corresponding course of six or seven miles'. Of course the canal's promoters then promised general benefits, feeding irrigation ditches along the way and, as a supplementary essay claimed, offering remarkable savings for planters who could use it to send their hogsheads of sugar down to the harbour. Even with the further advantages claimed for extending the canal farther inland, by 'running an elevated canal on the margin of the road, or of traversing a new course in another direction,' which would have required massive blasting to achieve, and apparently some preliminary lobbying of the Assembly, the project made no progress.[100] So despite the tempting claim that with 'the success of this scheme a handsome interest is ensured to the gentlemen on the subscription list', the project died before it was even debated.[101] Investment capital remained scarce during wartime. Civilian projects would have to wait for the end of the war in 1815, and that proved a very long wait.

Visitors who did visit the parish church of St Jago (today's Cathedral) still came away impressed. Here the Assembly continued to commission leading London sculptors to execute some very impressive memorials to governors and their wives. Even Mr Lewis considered the church 'very handsome' commenting on 'the walls lined with fine mahogany, and ornamented with many monuments of white marble'.[102] Two of the largest were commissioned by the Assembly during the 1790s to commemorate a respected Governor, Lord Howard of Effingham (who died in office) and Anne Williamson, the wife of his Lieutenant-Governor, Sir Arthur Williamson, who died in Jamaica while her husband was endeavouring to conquer Saint-Domingue (Haiti) for

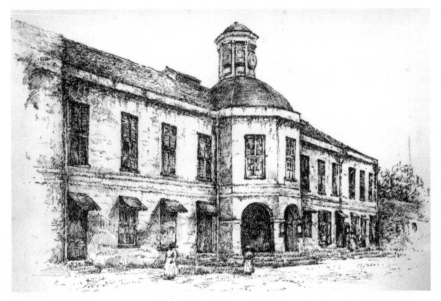

FIGURE 5:6   The 1820's Courthouse. Mrs Lionel Lee's sketch *c*. 1913. (National Library of Jamaica).

Britain. These marble shrines were both placed in the chancel, near the altar and close to the large pews reserved for the use of the Governor and his household and for members of the Council and Assembly, should any of these worthies decide to attend a service.[103]

When peacetime sugar exports resumed after the end of the war, the Assembly commissioned a further block of public buildings on the south side of the Parade to house the law courts and complete the square. The commission went to James Delancy, who had recently completed the Scots kirk in Kingston.[104] A decade later a fairly generous description characterized the complex as 'a handsome pile, of recent erection, and appropriated to government purposes'.[105] To find space for this block the 1680s chapel, the 1770s guard house and the printing office that had stood on the south side of the Parade were all demolished. The initial scheme was ambitious even if the 1818-19 building proved less elaborate than the Assembly building, and even less so than the exuberant Rodney Temple directly across the square. The Court House's protruding central tower held a large clock, taken over from the demolished chapel, where the parish vestry had paid someone for winding 'the Town Clock'.[106] The builder was dogged with problems in completing this structure within his £15,700 estimate. The town's antiquarians might be aware that the south side of the square once held the Roman Catholic Abbot of Jamaica's 'White Church', but the building specifications did not take into account the likely presence of a graveyard beside the former church. Once he discovered this fact the contractor was obliged to construct far deeper foundations because the subsoil was disturbed by graves. This additional outlay left no margin for a profit. Corners were cut, so that the building never received the stone facing that was supposed to conceal its brick construction. The stone cornice that tops the front wall, which was intended to make it appear complete (and for which the contractor was never repaid) hardly salvaged the overall effect.[107] The scrimping on this prominent public building demonstrated that peace had not brought a return of pre-war prosperity.

The new Law Courts replaced the court rooms at one end of the Assembly building constructed in the 1760s. With a growing case load, the judges received a purpose-built structure, with a number of offices located on the ground floor to house its administrators, while the floor above housed two large spaces for court rooms. A lock-up was built just behind the courthouse. Even though the judges ceased to sit directly under the eye of the Speaker of the Assembly, the majority of the magistrates, including those sitting on the island's Supreme Court, remained leading planters. Indeed, the Assembly worked hard to prevent outsiders taking the island's principal legal posts, doing their best to weigh the selection towards local candidates. Hence, whatever the common law tradition in England might say or do, the interpretation offered by this bench of planter-judges of the laws relating to slavery and to non-Anglican clergy remained shaped by planters' opinions. Any English-trained lawyers, Attorneys General or Chief Justices would be out-voted by their fellow judges should their decisions run too far counter to existing understandings of Jamaica's 'English' law.

Despite its construction problems, the Law Courts building was finally erected, completing the set of public buildings that still surround today's Emancipation Square. The King's House complex on the west side of the square also grew at this time. By the early 1840s a further building across the road to the north served as a dormitory for the Governor's bachelor guests. It was linked to the main King's House complex by a bridge across the road.[108] Finally a two-storey residence where the Duke of Manchester lived during his 19 years (1808-1827) as Governor was built farther down the street at the corner of today's Manchester Street.[109] The King's House was increasingly a working space. Earlier governors had left the King's House to stay in rural pens or mountain retreats; this new building provided a domestic refuge farther down King Street. Together, these immediately post-Napoleonic War building commissions reaffirmed Spanish Town's traditional functions as the colony's legal and administrative centre.

Missionaries return

At the end of the French Revolutionary and Napoleonic wars the missionary societies, maintained by several English and Scottish denominations, sent preachers out to assist the beleaguered evangelical congregations in Jamaica. The mission 'stations' that succeeded were those that managed to build local support groups, because to find audiences preachers entering a community needed to win the acceptance of established individuals, people whose example would encourage other residents to give a hearing to an outsider's contentious message.[110] Successful congregations then needed to recruit lay members ready and able to act as leaders, stewards, exhorters, catechizers, Bible class leaders and even substitute preachers. The long-term objective was to establish a God-fearing community. Here the missions aimed to fulfil this goal by reshaping the congregation members' lives along what they considered godly lines. Such endeavours ran counter to the established secular culture of late eighteenth-century Jamaica, characterized in one critic's list as including 'Vices of the very worst description such as Sabbath breaking, lying, drunkenness, slandering, profaneness, Adultery, Fornication, and Polygamy prevail . . . to a most deplorable extent'.[111] The ranking of these vices may surprise us, but not their number.

Over time both the Methodist and Baptist congregations in Spanish Town did develop into remarkably successful communities: recruiting loyal members, raising funds to construct substantial new buildings and providing the hubs for circuits of local chapels. But, although the town's ministers rode circuit to a number of chapels within a long half a day's ride, Spanish Town did not provide a primary centre for the networks of new stations that the missionary denominations established across the island. Both the Baptist Missionary Society, which began sending missionaries to Kingston in 1813 to assist the congregations established by Leile and his fellow pioneers in the 1780s, and the Wesleyan Methodist Society, which resumed its efforts to support the existing Methodist society in Kingston in 1815, then developed missions in Spanish Town. In time these achieved high profiles. The potential of attracting the town's influential population was itself a good reason for proselytizing because, as one early Methodist missionary observed, 'if we could once establish a decent Chapel in' the town, 'this Mission will ultimately flourish; whereas if we fail in this, we will be left to the Mercy of our Good Friends in this City [Kingston], whose tender mercies are bitterly cruel'. The public presence of these chapels also proved important when Spanish Town was 'the Seat of Government, and the residence of the successful lawyers and Gentry of the Island'.[112] Visitors from rural parishes, both enslaved and free, who came to attend the law terms or the Assembly might well encounter evangelical preaching there too. Several prominent converts, donors of further chapel sites or individuals willing to suffer martyrdom for their beliefs, initially arrived as transient visitors.

When they arrived in Spanish Town both the Baptists and the Methodists returned to Thomas Coke's earlier plan of leasing properties on the edge of the town. These locations were partially chosen by default: the new Baptist minister initially considered a house in the older section of the town, 'opposite the church', but lower rents on the outskirts appealed to groups operating with shoestring budgets.[113] The congregation's site on the corner of French Street and today's William Street on the north side of the town (where the Phillippo Chapel stands today) was found after another move. The location had the positive advantage of standing on a route into the market that slaves and smallholders traversed regularly. This brought potential converts past the chapel door and brought the mission into the midst of the society its preachers wished to change.

During the 1820s and '30s the Baptist and Methodist congregations both became increasingly visible institutions in the town. A Methodist missionary's report in 1823 still stressed that 'genuine religion has made as yet but a partial spread' in Spanish Town and its vicinity and that 'there are comparatively speaking but few who may be said to have even a form of Godliness'. He then continued in a more optimistic tone, demonstrating the ambivalent blend of experience and hope that underlay the whole missionary enterprise:

> We are happy however to state that there are in this Community those who form a pleasing contrast. A spirit of hearing the word of God has been excited to a tolerable extent, so that the places of divine worship are in general well attended.

In the Established Church there is a congregation of almost Six Hundred consisting of White, Coloured and Blacks who hear with great attention. In the Baptist Chapel from 200 to 250 regularly attend, the greater part of whom are Slaves: and in our own [Methodist] from 350 to 400 principally people of Free condition. It may with confidence be said of many composing these congregations that they have at least the form of Godliness and are seeking the power; whilst others rise to a degree of experience which must be highly gratifying to every lover of Christianity.

This was already a welcome change from the Spanish Town of 1790 where the Rev Thomas Coke was nearly booed down when he tried to preach. The missionaries knew that much remained to be done because, as the report continued, 'hundreds yea thousands are in the strictest sense living without God'.[114]

Achieving any initial foothold was hard. Maintaining a new station proved difficult too. In July 1819 the local Baptist congregation collected £200, a quarter of the asking price, towards the purchase of a property that although 'in a very dilapidated state, might be made convenient for a Meeting House, [and] dwelling for the Minister'. A grant from the Baptist Missionary Society in England then made up the difference.[115] However, just under a year later the mission faced a major set back with an arsonist's attack.[116] The stories that circulated afterwards vary in their details, though they mostly differ on what miserable end to assign to the arsonist. He was reported to be a jealous boyfriend, angry after his sweetheart left him to join the Baptists – or simply threatened to leave him for the church – so he set fire to a building in the compound. Shouts from the street woke the minister. The whole building burnt in minutes.[117] Successive retellings helped to fix the congregation's identity: its members would revive after crises, whatever miscreants might do. As unofficial groups with very limited financial resources, all the missionary congregations remained very vulnerable to mischances or disappointments.

The Baptist congregation found an alternative site in French Street at a former artillery yard and barracks, sold off after the garrison and its ordinance had moved to Kingston 30 years before. Refurbishments moved slowly. When a new minister, James Mursell Phillippo, arrived in Spanish Town in 1823 he recalled that this 'place of meeting . . . looked externally as if it had been a target to its former artillery possessors; Both the ceiling and the floor were so dilapidated as to be in a dangerous condition'. The primary legacy of his predecessors' efforts was a sizable community: it had 304 members in its books, though 'exclusion and death' then reduced that total to 250. These included two white people and three 'coloured', with the 'rest black and mostly slaves'.[118] The members provided the foundation on which a remarkably successful congregation would grow and thrive. As 'praying people' they lived under a strict discipline, one that not only excluded the island's all-too-prevalent sexual and alcoholic permissiveness, but 'attendance at dances, or merry-makings of any description, as well as at horse-races, were all sins which [were] visited with excision' from church membership.[119] Whatever its rigour, this was a discipline imposed and regulated on this primarily enslaved group by their fellow deacons and by frequent church meetings, rather than by their masters.

The Methodist congregation avoided arsonists' attacks and even survived a lightning strike to its chapel in 1829.[120] However, the Spanish Town Methodist Society's early development was also punctuated by relocations from one site to another. Initially, they had only a very gradual increase in membership and still numbered only 65 in 1816. In that year a gift of £500 in Jamaican currency from the Kingston congregation allowed them to move from one crumbling house to another somewhat larger site which faced onto White Church Street, a few hundred yards from the parish church. In time they purchased the property. The town's Wesleyan chapel remains at this site.[121] By 1821 growing numbers encouraged the society to erect a brick-walled, wood-shingled chapel that could seat 420 'comfortably'. The congregation had 'No income save the receipts of the society' at this time, though they also had 'No debt'.[122]

This building work testified to the increasing stability and substance of their community, though the wider society was still generally hostile towards evangelical congregations. The numbers attending services gradually increased and, as the Methodist congregation found out, cutting the existing seats narrower before cramming in still more pews and then wedging extra seats into every possible corner only offered a short-term solution.[123] The Spanish Town Methodists pulled down their manse in 1826 to erect an even larger brick chapel of 64 feet long by 49 feet wide and 26 feet high, with galleries on three sides. This was a gesture of confidence, even though it burdened the congregation with debts.[124] In the short term the congregation's resources were ominously overstretched, especially once the Kingston congregation could no longer spare money when other Jamaican congregations fell short, because it was itself over-committed to building the splendid brick Coke Chapel on the

Parade in Kingston. The ballooning building debt in Spanish Town provoked disapproval in London but also an interest free loan.[125] Whatever doubts and recriminations filled the ministers' correspondence, the new Methodist chapel appeared solid and impressive from the street. New chapels declared the strength of the evangelical congregations, albeit at a considerable financial cost.

Meanwhile, the Baptist congregation on the other side of town achieved remarkable successes as well, despite the continuing hostility from the St Catherine parish justices of the peace who remained convinced that all Baptist missionaries were agents of the anti-Slavery Society. In one particularly notable disturbance constables hauled the Rev James Phillippo away from his pulpit for militia duty during his first Sunday service. Scarcely a month passed without the local magistrates harassing the congregation by calling the new Baptist minister before them on one complaint or another.[126] In most Jamaican parishes the justices did their best to complicate the procedures for registering a Protestant minister's preaching licence – a simple pro-forma procedure in England. An earlier missionary described this attitude: 'nothing will be granted which they can possibly refuse' and it did not change.[127] Such official delaying tactics in Spanish Town left James Phillippo unable to preach for a year. He 'was not idle' however. He first established a sabbath school and Bible classes and then, in what he summed up in his autobiography in a remarkably understated phrase, in 1824 he 'also made arrangements for building a new chapel and the establishment of a high and common school' on the chapel premises.[128] The school thrived because Phillippo was a gifted teacher, while his wife and several other loyal workers contributed their efforts for negligible pay. Furthermore, he offered to educate children hitherto excluded by race and fees from the grammar school. Townspeople were impressed by the new school. Many local parents were eager for their children to learn. Later gossip claimed that the Governor, the Duke of Manchester, sent 'four or five' of his illegitimate children there for their education.[129] Phillippo's own reports made more of the pupils enrolled from the town's Jewish community, including a rabbi's children, alongside African Jamaican children, free and enslaved.[130]

The Baptists' new 'Lancastrian school' followed the procedures for mass education developed in England during the Industrial Revolution, with pupil-teachers passing on their lessons to the junior classes, thereby saving the costs of teachers for the younger pupils. This differed from the traditional Latin-based Grammar School curriculum which still shaped the teaching at the town's Free Grammar School. Although the new Baptist School's pupils would learn much of their information by rote and received their instruction via pupil-teachers, a succession of distinguished visitors still came away impressed by the range of information drilled into the children.[131] These pupils did not come to school to 'play dunce' – they wished to learn. Nor was Phillippo a professional schoolmaster who lived off his fees. As a result, tuition could remain low and then be channelled back into the school for other expenses. It still faced cash flow problems until Phillippo succeeded in raising external donations by appealing for funds in various missionary magazines published in England. Upbeat reports helped win support from English sources, both from the Baptist Missionary Society which provided another teaching assistant and from the Society of Friends (the Quakers) who made ongoing gifts to his school.[132]

The new school thrived; 150 pupils were enrolled early in 1825 with 250 later in the same year.[133] Meanwhile a new Sunday School at the Wesleyan Chapel enrolled 105 boys, 62 girls and 30 adults in June 1824. In contrast, the town's Free Grammar School a few hundred yards to the south at the other end of Young Street enrolled only 11 white pupils and 35 'of colour' in 1823, despite continuing to enjoy the interest from Peter Beckford's eighteenth-century endowment.[134] Perhaps the strongest testimony for the Baptist school's success was the rapid establishment of alternative church-based academies in and around Spanish Town. From 1826 the Anglican Vestry supported a 'School of Industry' that offered boys instruction 'in tailoring, basket making and wicker work, making straw hats, shoemaking, cabinet making, saddlery &c' and gave girls training 'in all species of needle-work, platting of straw, making of bonnets' together with orthodox religious instruction and the 3 'R's (reading, 'riting and 'rithmatic).[135] This was a very different curriculum, designed to maintain existing social roles rather than offering education as uplift. By 1828 the Anglican Vestry required that anyone receiving parish aid must send all their children aged over six to the School of Industry *and* that the children attend the Parish Church regularly with the schoolmaster. To enforce this edict the vestry declared that 'if the children be not sent to such school and do not attend the Church, that such aid be withheld'.[136] The Vestry's rivalry with Phillippo's school helped generate a further Anglican alternative. In 1830 Francis Smith, the then Custos of St Catherine, bequeathed £3,000 Jamaican currency to his successor as Custos, to the new Bishop of Jamaica and to the rector of the parish as trustees 'to be invested for some institution permanently for the instruction of the poorer classes of all colours, free and slave, in the doctrine of the Church of England and the Promotion of Industry'.[137] As with Peter Beckford's bequest a century earlier, the money had to be used within a year or it would go to one of Smith's many nieces. While the will ordered the money to be drawn 'out of any public certificates or other my readiest money of personal Estate', there were many other bequests too and Smith's executors could only pay just over half of this legacy. Custos Smith's donation still remained a remarkable testimony to the challenge that Rev Phillippo's schools offered to the Anglican status quo. The number of new Anglican foundations still did not translate into many classroom places. In 1837 Beckford's School, Smith's School and the Vestry's School of Industry were all under the same master and mistress and occupied the same building. The first two schools consisted of 30 children each while the School of Industry had 60 pupils.[138] By the 1830s attendance at the Baptist school had dropped back to 150, largely due to the presence of the Anglican and Methodist schools. Yet, despite all these efforts, numerous children in and around the town remained in need of schooling.

In addition to the crowds at the school house, attendance at Phillippo's Baptist chapel also increased. In May 1825, he claimed to pack in 1,000 hearers 'sometimes'. They were packed into a low room at the old Artillery Yard, where all the windows and doors would be crammed with overflow auditors. Even making allowances for statements originally made in what proved a successful begging letter, the numbers appeared substantial.[139] Fundraising within the congregation for a new building produced contributions from its free and enslaved members. One week's 'alms offering' exceeded £84. Further donations were raised around the town. Even those local justices of the peace who had earlier harassed Phillippo were persuaded to make a small gift for this cause. The congregation laid the foundation stone for the new chapel in 1825 and held the dedication service in 1827.[140] It was a sturdy brick affair that, if its congregation wished, could compare favourably with the Protestant chapels erected across Britain's industrial heartland over the previous generation. Unlike those British chapels, 'slaves were almost entirely employed in [the Spanish Town chapel's] erection', doing the building work and contributing their pennies and sixpences. It could hold 1,200 to 1,500 people.[141] While the old congregation had sheltered behind a brick wall, this new structure was only surrounded by iron railings so stood open to the

FIGURE 5:7   Baptist Chapel, Spanish Town, *c.* 1826, (Baptist Missionary Society, courtesy, BMS World Mission)

public gaze to shine 'forth as a beacon and a monument both of Philanthropy and of Prayer'[142] It quickly became a local landmark.

The Methodist and Baptist chapels erected in Spanish Town not only provided landmarks for local residents but also offered beacons for the growing numbers of church and chapel-goers in Britain who read missionary magazines. The individual denominations' publications regularly included woodcuts of new chapels constructed in one corner of the empire or another. With the rise of evangelical religion in Britain the question of preaching in the colonies became an issue in domestic politics. This development had several repercussions in Spanish Town. The opportunity for the individual missions to tap English funds, even if only in guaranteeing the local Methodists' debt repayments or through Baptist and Quaker support for the Baptist Chapel's school, probably helped embolden local chapel committees to undertake such ambitious building projects.[143] The English missionary press reports would support this view, though the missionary societies themselves always tried to use their donations to leverage matching local contributions.

Slaveholders on the island viewed these very public achievements with suspicion. Complaints about the new Baptist and Methodist chapels demonstrated how conspicuous the new structures appeared. A furious letter to the *St Iago Gazette* objected to the fact that rivals to the established church had secured the funds to build two chapels 'which appear to overawe both church and state'.[144] The members of the Assembly found local targets for their anger over these conspicuous projects by the upstart denominations. In 1828 the members of an Assembly Commission on the 'Sectarian' Missionaries blamed the preachers for persuading 'deluded' members of their flocks to hand over their trinkets and cash to the chapel building funds. The Assemblymen saw the missions as the cults of their day and tried to prevent slaves and free people of colour making such donations.[145] If nothing else, this mean-spirited proposal showed how much contemporaries who disapproved of the missions not only saw the newly erected chapels as a threat, but acknowledged the empowering role of individual members' gifts towards their construction. Competition from the established Anglican church then provided further back-handed confirmation of the local congregations' successes. In 1833 a petition from Anglican parishioners recommended the parish's newly appointed curate to the Governor and asked him to urge the Vestry to erect a new chapel. For what it was worth, the Governor forwarded their petition.[146] Chapel buildings and schools gave the dissenting congregations shape and purpose; by 1833 members of the town's Anglican congregation pushed to adopt similar institutions.

So how would these transformations change the ways in which the town was understood?

By the 1830s the landmarks that townspeople chose to cite when giving directions had altered. Urban improvements played their part. Now traffic coming south from Guanaboa and the Bog Walk Gorge to meet the east-west road to Kingston could bypass the town centre by following a 'new road leading from Tacky's Bridge to [the] Race Course' that ran around the western end of the town.[147] Within the town, there were several new public buildings that residents could use as reference points. These included the law courts erected in 1818–19 and the new chapels. Hence, a property might be identified as lying beside 'land . . . otherwise called the Old Chapel ground' in 1830; or else near 'a house now used as a Methodist Chapel' in 1831, or facing onto 'a Street leading to the Baptist Chapel' or, indeed, a site for a shop located 'opposite to the side of the Bishop's Office', both in 1832.[148] The currency of such descriptions already acknowledged how religious establishments reshaped the town for visitors and residents.

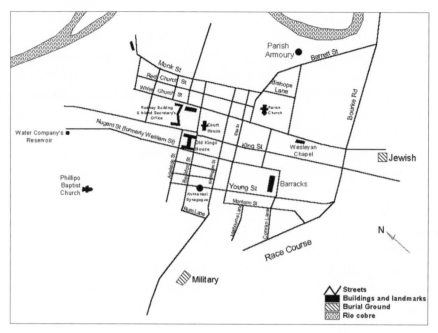

FIGURE 5:8 Spanish Town *c.*1830. Street names and chapels.

These new buildings were not the only indicators of wider changes. The names of the principal streets in the centre of Spanish Town still bear the imprint of the political struggles in Britain of the late 1820s and '30s over parliamentary reform. The bitter arguments leading up to the Great Reform Bill were reinforced by a wider process of grass roots social reform. The passage of the Whig government's 1832 Reform Bill enfranchised the townspeople in the new industrial towns whose residents read the missionary magazines and who also provided a key constituency in the evangelical and anti-slavery movements.[149] These towns' newly elected representatives then provided the reforming Whig government with sufficient majorities to vote through, first the funds for compensating the slaveholders which led to the ending of slavery in 1834 and subsequently to the end of apprenticeship and 'full free' in 1838. Spanish Town's streets commemorate champions of the Tory and pro-property side. Such names as 'Canning Street', 'Duke of Wellington Street' and 'Peel Lane' all honoured successive leaders of the conservative Tory party in the Westminster Parliament.[150] These were the politicians whose commitment to 'property' would, the island's plantocracy hoped, hold at bay radical proposals for change.

The group of high-Tory names given to the streets round the Assembly building testify to the Assembly's own partisan engagement with metropolitan politics. These streets were surrounded by others named to honour the political values that the beleaguered island elite thought that they shared with England: 'Constitution Street', of course, and 'King Street', along with the 'William' and 'Adelaide' streets which commemorate King William IV, who visited Spanish Town as a Royal Naval lieutenant in 1783 and 1788, and his consort, Queen Adelaide. Three more streets were named for long-term Governors: Nugent Street, which commemorated Major-General Sir George Nugent who governed Jamaica from 1801–06 during the Napoleonic Wars and who later sat as an MP in the House of Commons until 1832; Manchester Street, which ran alongside the house where the Duke of Manchester lived during his long governorship, and Belmore Lane a new street that commemorated the Northern Ireland peer who was Governor from 1829 to 1832. Further names had local echoes celebrating further notable residents and visitors: Beckford Street, running west from the King's House, applied the name of the Free Grammar School's principal benefactor to the townspeople's 'street in front of the Schoolhouse'; 'Barrett Street', the new name for the traditional approach road parallelling the Rio Cobre from the south, commemorated the then Speaker of the Assembly, who wielded all his considerable influence against changes imposed on the West Indies from outside by 'usurping Parliaments' and the Whigs' issue-driven 'straw catching Ministry'.[151] Other street names in the area developed on the north side of the town remained less contentious in re-echoing the patriotic monarchism of the first quarter of the nineteenth century, with 'Hanover', 'Brunswick' and 'Kent' streets, 'Cumberland Road' and, indeed, 'Waterloo Lane' commemorating royal dukes and a decisive British military victory respectively. These were generally pre-Emancipation names: assigned after King William and Queen Adelaide ascended the throne in 1830, but not long after. King William presided over the Reform Parliament and signed the 1834 Abolition act.

At that juncture, however, renaming streets after English politicians would appear a loyal gesture. During the 1820s some Jamaican slaveholders, bitter at the successes of the evangelical and anti-Slavery forces they considered 'the Anti-Colonial Faction', revived their grandparents' discussions of seceding from the British Empire and joining the pro-slavery United States.[152] Rabble-rousers organized a parallel militia, the Colonial Church Union, that targeted non-Anglican chapels, viewing them as nurseries for troublesome ideas.[153] In such contexts naming streets around the Assembly for leading British politicians invoked shared constitutional principles. Reasserting continuity was important during the late 1820s and early 1830s when although the public buildings lining the town's main streets did not change much, the social structures that framed the lives of the people using these streets changed considerably: the free coloured population received enhanced civil rights in 1826 and the island's Jewish community were finally enfranchised the same year. Notably, Jews could now hold any office on the island without swearing a Christian oath – an achievement secured 20 years before the Jewish community in England was enfranchised.[154] But the most significant change came when slavery was abolished in 1834 and, finally, with the end of the transition status of apprenticeship in 1838, the former slaves were made free – though the property threshold for voting remained prohibitively high.

The political landscape changed abruptly. A proposal made by the then Governor, the second Earl of Belmore, to the Assembly in 1830 to erect a lookout on the roof of the King's House demonstrates the underlying uncertainties of this period. The Assembly granted £500 towards the Governor's project, though no contractor would undertake it for that amount. Had it been constructed this vantage point would have allowed him to peer off to the south towards the Hellshire Hills, where he fretted that 'hoards of Negroes' were 'assembling'.[155] His fears were misplaced. The political crisis of his governorship broke out at the western end of the island, when slaveholders and abolitionists alike believed that with the imminent passage of the Reform Bill in England, slavery's days were numbered.

By December 1831 large numbers of slaves in western Jamaica were convinced that King William IV had granted emancipation already and sought to enact his royal grant. A proposed work stoppage at the start of the crop season organized by a slave and Baptist Deacon, Samuel Sharpe, escalated to arson and an armed uprising. This provoked not only an extensive campaign by the militia and regular garrison, but the locally organized reactionary Colonial Church Union then whipped up pro-planter mobs that targeted non-Anglican preachers and their chapels. Fear and an absence of leadership at the top helped turn a major crisis into a bloodbath. The Governor's presence in the capital offered no guarantee of security to the local 'dissenters'. During the emergency Spanish Town's Baptist and Methodist congregations guarded their chapels themselves: 'the women, especially, are determined to defend it to the last'.[156]

The immediate context appeared ominous. A policy of retaliating when an estate was burnt by targeting the slaves' own possessions, destroying their houses and killing their livestock may have appeared to make military sense. It quickly degenerated into frightened militia-men relying on martial law to justify their pilfering, whatever took their fancy from slave villages blazing away at anyone they could see and hanging their prisoners.[157] Angry Assemblymen condem-ned the missionaries during debates 'as instigators of "Rebellion and Bloodshed"' and the 'very pest of Society'. Two Assemblymen 'brought in Bills signed by some of the true members of the "Colonial Church Union", praying that the "Sectarian Ministers" may be banished from the Island'.[158] Once martial law was withdrawn, mobs of whites attacked missionary chapels across Jamaica. In the event, Spanish Town's Baptist and Methodist chapels were spared such assaults and several missionaries and their families found refuge in the town. Afterwards, though, the congregations told themselves this survival was only because the house of a prominent member of the Colonial Church Union stood close to the Baptist chapel and would have been threatened by a fire.[159] The story's circulation shows no trust in the Governor's ability – or wish – to restrain mob law, even on his doorstep.

An English tourist visiting the town in 1831, as the rising broke out, described the immediate impact of the news there. The spatial organization of the sixteenth-century Spanish town plan still continued to shape events during a crisis far more than King William IV's subjects would have liked to admit. Townspeople gathered in the Parade in search of news, with men nervously pacing up and down the arcade under the Assembly building, though now the militia rallied into the Parade to a drum beat rather than the ringing of the Abbey bell. Townspeople grew nervous when they observed an 'unusually large assemblage of persons' gathering around the Parade. This activity appeared particularly noticeable because the Assembly was in recess for Christmas. Military officers mingled with the civilians scurrying in and out of the King's House. Bystanders then recognized that 'the Council Chamber presented an animated scene; and it was apparent to all that something extraordinary had taken place'. These were indicators that townspeople used to recognize the political manoeuvring in their midst. After an hour the royal standard was hoisted in the Parade, symbolizing that the Governor would make an official announcement as the monarch's representative. Someone whom the tourist took to be 'a herald', then read the proclamation establishing Martial Law. A few nervous days later the St Catherine parish militia was marshalled in the Parade before they, too, marched off to the campaign against the rebels.[160] However, the white colonists' back lash went too far. Reports in England of not only pro-slavery mobs attacking Protestant chapels, but also of magistrates doing nothing to disperse the rioters helped turn the tide of British popular opinion against the slaveholders. The mobs' violence proved counter-productive to their goal of preserving slavery. The reformed Westminster Parliament passed the Abolition of Slavery Act in 1833 that authorized payments from the British Treasury to compensate slaveholders for the value of their slaves if they were emancipated; this then induced the individual colonial assemblies to pass acts to abolish slavery.[161]

Very different ceremonies occurred in the Parade. On 1 August 1834, a new Governor read King William's proclamation ending slavery. This declared the slaves free and immediately freed those aged six and under, but in a sop to the planter interest, left older slaves as 'apprentices' obliged to work for their former owners – domestic slaves for an additional four years, 'predial' (field) slaves for six years. Four years later, however, after further complaints documented the mistreatment of the ex-slaves under the 'apprenticeship' regime, the Whig government in Britain brought the whole scheme to an early close. Even the Jamaica Assembly was persuaded to pass the necessary legislation, with the main debate being whether to free Jamaica's slaves on Queen Victoria's Coronation Day (28 June 1838), or to wait another five weeks until the first of August, which was when the 1834 Law would free household slaves anyway. The advantage to the planters of the later date was that one last sugar crop would have been shipped out.[162] On 1 August 1838, Governor Sir Lionel Smith read a proclamation from Queen Victoria emancipating all the slaves. This ended the apprenticeship period. They were now 'full free'.

Special hymn-sheets were printed in 1834 for services to celebrate the emancipation of the slaves across the British Empire. The English congregations who purchased them and gathered for thanksgiving services sang of 1831 in Jamaica:

Satan, Satan heard and trembled,
And, upstarting from his throe,
Bands of Belial's sons assembled,
Fired with rancour all his own,
Madly swearing,
'Christ to slaves shall *not* be known'.

For what it was worth, the profits from the sale of these hymn-sheets went towards the 'Fund for rebuilding the thirteen Chapels in Jamaica, which were destroyed in the year 1832'. Moreover, the hymn's triumphant final verse then proclaimed:

Tidings, Tidings of salvation!
Britons rose with one accord,
Swept the plague-spot from our nation
Negroes to their rights restor'd;
Slaves no longer!
Free-men, free-men of the Lord.[163]

Fuller descriptions survive of the Spanish Town celebrations marking the 1838 'full free' proclamation. The official element of the ceremony was performed in the Parade. The royal standard flew again and the Governor, now accompanied by the Anglican Bishop and the Rev James Phillippo, read the royal proclamation from the King's House steps. It was an impressive occasion. However, the immediate beneficiaries of the proclamation started their own celebrations the evening before. 'Apprentices' filled 'the places of worship' across the island and, in some instances, remained there 'until the day of liberty dawned'. A missionary recalled that: 'Even the irreligious part of the community . . . seemed inspired with religious feeling, and flocked in crowds to the house of God.' Some 7,000 Spanish Town residents and 2,000 schoolchildren assembled at the Baptist Chapel and then walked in procession up to the Parade, carrying flags and banners with such mottos as (towards the front) 'Education, social order and religion'; 'Peace industry and commerce'; 'Freedom's bright light hath dawned at last'; 'Glory to God' and 'The slave is free', followed by 'Victoria', 'Sir Lionel Smith' and the names of several British abolitionists. Then came another dozen banners that included first the traditional abolitionists' motto, 'Am I not a man and a brother?' and the more immediate, 'The day of our freedom'; then came 'England, land of liberty, of light, of life' and 'Equal rights and privileges'. After stating this fundamental principle, further banners aimed to calm fears among the former slaveholders, 'Emancipation in peace, in harmony, in safety, in acquiescence, on all sides'; 'Truth, justice and right have at length prevailed' and, 'The first of August, 1838, never to be forgotten through all generations'. The final banner, not included in the main list, had in large capitals the message 'WE ARE FREE! WE ARE FREE! OUR WIVES AND CHILDREN ARE FREE!', which

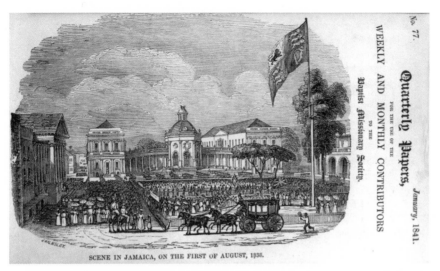

SCENE IN JAMAICA, ON THE FIRST OF AUGUST, 1838.

FIGURE 5:9   T. Picken, 'Scene in Jamaica, 1st August, 1838', cover for *Quarterly Papers for the use of the Weekly and Monthly Contributors to the Baptist Missionary Society* 77 (January, 1841). A view of the Parade from the south. The Governor stands on the steps in front of the King's House portico to the left; a massive royal standard is on the right. Here Baptist readers saw 'the Governor, the Bishop of Jamaica, and Mr Phillippo, as though testifying to the spectators the happy union of civil and religious feeling at this auspicious moment'. The perspective is compressed. The Rodney Temple on the north side of the square has ballooned, quadrupling in size, so that its cupola is higher than all the other buildings in the picture. To accommodate this enlarged structure, the arcade behind it stretches further back into a half circle. Its roof is depicted crammed with spectators. There are also pairs of sentry boxes shown in front of the Archives and the Island Secretary's Office. The woodcut shows everyone watching the parade marching off along the north side of the Parade and then turning down King Street en route to the Baptist Chapel. The audience is broken up by class. Those watching from inside the railings have plenty of parasols though the commentary emphasized that 'The children occupy the centre within the railings.' Otherwise while some parasols are sprinkled among the group in the street in front of the King's House many of the women are wearing bandannas. The image catches an event that reached across class boundaries. (National Library of Jamaica).

received loud cheers. The crowd arrived in the Parade and heard the Governor read the proclamation and give a good speech, which was also greeted with 'enthusiastic cheering'. After an hour the official ceremony closed with 'three cheers for Queen Victoria and another three for Sir Lionel'. The procession returned to the Baptist mission, whose entrances were embellished with triumphal arches, decorated with leaves and flowers and topped with flags bearing such messages as 'Freedom's come'; 'Slavery is no more' and 'Thy chains are broken, Africa is free'.[164]

At the time British subjects congratulated themselves on the achievement, convinced that:

> When a century shall have passed away – when statesmen are forgotten – when reason shall regain her influence over prejudice and interest, and other generations are wondering at the false estimates their forefathers formed of human glory – on the page of history one deed shall stand out in whole relief – one consenting voice pronounce that the greatest honour England ever attained was when, with her Sovereign at her head, she proclaimed THE SLAVE IS FREE.[165]

However, despite such very high hopes for history's verdict, emancipation's outcomes would remain laced with disappointments.

CHAPTER SIX

'Lively bright days are dawning on Our Island'

Early Victorian Spanish Town, 1838–1866

RITING IN the days just before the 1838 proclamation, the town's Methodist minister concluded hopefully 'Lively bright days are dawning on Our Island'.[1] With the end of apprenticeship the first 30 years of Queen Victoria's long reign opened at the apogee of British engagement with the former slaves in the West Indies.[2] The opportunities seemed splendid and, as one pamphleteer asserted, Jamaica would 'unquestionably' become a key site for instituting fresh imperial policies, as the largest 'colony in which the grand experiment of negro emancipation is to be tried'.[3] But, all too quickly, this favourable moment passed. The Queen's proclamation granting full freedom was succeeded by metropolitan lack of interest in the fate of the West Indian islands; other causes caught the public mind and later 'science' helped to make the revival of racism appear respectable.

Jamaica saw a period of rapid social transformation over this generation, when a society hitherto dominated by the sugar planting interest began to accommodate some of the hopes of the newly-freed slaves.[4] The period's substantive achievements would fall well short of some initial expectations of the island's becoming 'an Anglo-African Colony, where the descendants of negroes shall possess the chief share of property and power, . . . controlling and protecting their external relations, and exercising certain regulation and direction in their internal policy', while remaining a society 'where British capital shall find profitable employment, and the British adventurer, whether in agriculture or trade, a secure scene for action'.[5] The African Jamaican population still succeeded in developing some replacement social structures to the old plantations. Many of the most significant social changes on the island occurred – or else failed to occur – in the rural parishes.[6] Several of the central developments during this period were also reflected in the streets and the public buildings of the colony's seat of government.

Politicians meeting in Spanish Town continued to reach decisions whose significance was recognized by people across Jamaica. In 1838 1,796 voters, all male property holders, had chosen the Assembly's 45 members who were now to legislate for a third of a million of Queen Victoria's subjects. The Assembly had passed a law to emancipate slaves in Jamaica, but the Assemblymen still did not see themselves as answering to the island's newly freed population. As long as the franchise remained one of the key privileges tied to property holding, then not only the Assembly's policies (many of which were contentious in their own right) but also the elections that chose the Assembly's members would reflect the uneven progress of social change across the island. Among these changes was the phenomenon that a Canadian visitor to Jamaica's House of Assembly noted where, during a debate, the visitors' area was 'lined with black spectators'.[7] Ex-slaves' desire to secure voting rights led increasing numbers of them to scrape together sufficient cash to buy land and pay the fees to register as electors. Once they had done so, they altered the micropolitics of individual parishes when they rallied behind alternative candidates who might make these new voters' voices heard.[8] In such terms the voters of St Catherine parish achieved an early victory in 1847 when Edward Vickars, a Kingston landlord and shopkeeper, won one of the parish's seats in a by-election, becoming the Assembly's first black member. Black voters were decisive in his victory, where artisans in Spanish Town combined with 'mountain settlers', ex-slaves who had purchased land after emancipation in the mountainous areas to the north of the town. Assemblyman Vickars pushed for funds for education, for changes in the penal code and for a more equal taxation, though he swam against the tide in all these campaigns. He remained alone within the Assembly in supporting universal manhood suffrage. Vickars continued to hold his seat until 1860 when the Assembly's deliberate decision to restrict the voting population by imposing further fees on prospective voters hit his supporters disproportionately hard.[9]

Spanish Town's streets demonstrated further islandwide trends. Architecturally the most conspicuous change across the island just after emancipation was the erection of new churches. For a few years after 1838 the Assembly assisted congregations in erecting places of worship. Spanish Town not only saw the consecration of the Anglican Trinity Chapel in 1844, but also Assembly-subsidized repairs to the Sephardic synagogue after it was damaged by lightning, and a grant made to the town's Roman Catholics for their place of worship. The Assembly also supported a further round of rebuilding work on the former parish church when it was recast as the Anglican Cathedral of St Jago. These grants were part of a cross-island church building campaign. Even though pro-planter rioters after the 1831 rebellion had not destroyed Spanish Town's Baptist and Methodist chapels, the town still participated in the post-emancipation boom in publicly assisted church, chapel and synagogue building across Jamaica.[10]

This ecclesiastical building boom rode on an economic boomlet. During the decade after 1838 the town benefited from British investment in Jamaica where, for example, speculators ventured their money in companies to mine gold and copper in the Blue Mountains. More substantially, in 1843 at the height of the English railway boom, a newly founded Jamaica Railroad Company successfully raised funds in London to run a line from Kingston to Spanish Town and then a further two miles north-east to the Angels. The line opened in 1846. It even claimed to keep to schedule, receiving a qualified endorsement from an American visitor that 'slow as it is, however, it is the only punctual thing upon the island'.[11] These activities, besides several new government offices that the Assembly established in and around Spanish Town, all put a distinctive early Victorian stamp on the town.

Maintaining Momentum from 1834 to 1838

The islandwide jubilation of 1834 and 1838 would be difficult to equal, but the goal of sustaining freedom continued to provide considerable impetus for further projects. The most conspicuous of these was probably the establishment of new free villages in Jamaica. These were settlements where ex-slaves could purchase a house and a smallholding and move off the old estates. Planters were hostile to developments which challenged the social order, so even though the price of plantation land fell steeply they still refused to sell off peripheral land from their estates in small parcels which would have facilitated independent homesteading. In several instances missionaries, who could draw on funds and donations from Britain to meet the expense of purchasing sizable blocks of land, purchased the land for these settlements, subdivided the acreage into smaller parcels and then took the opportunity to frame God-fearing societies there. Sligoville in the mountainous areas north of the town, tactfully named in honour of the current Governor, the Marquis of Sligo, appeared the exemplar of these villages to successive visitors.[12] The links between Sligoville and Spanish Town were close. The settlement sprang from an earlier proposal by the Spanish Town Baptist Chapel to establish a satellite chapel and school there and, while that proposal suggests that prospective worshippers already lived in the vicinity, many of the initial settlers were members of the Spanish Town congregation.[13] Once established, Sligoville's smallholders worked on neighbouring estates, but took their surplus ground provisions down to sell in Spanish Town's market.

Further schemes continued to build on the hopes current in the aftermath of emancipation. Deliberately using the first anniversary of the end of apprenticeship, a special service at the Baptist Chapel in Spanish Town on August 1, 1839, established a Jamaican society to undertake missionary work in Africa, a project which would require a new missionary training college. The town provided early recruits for the mission. One of the first Baptist evangelists sent from Jamaica to Africa was Alexander Fuller, the son of 'a recently emancipated slave' and a former star pupil at Phillippo's school.[14] This project did not retain its initial base in Spanish Town for long. After supporters of a site near Spanish Town or Kingston were outvoted at the next islandwide Baptist Association meeting, the new training college was established near Falmouth, on the north side of the island.[15] August 1, 1839, was also employed for a well attended and enthusiastic meeting establishing a local branch of the new British and Foreign Antislavery Society, again held at the Spanish Town Baptist Chapel. This provided a forum for the continuing impulse to stem the slave trade and to extend the benefits of freedom out beyond the British Empire and particularly to Jamaica's major trading partner, the slaveholding United States: 'The vaunted land of liberty,/ Where lash and chain hold sway.'[16]

As long as the Governor resided in Spanish Town, public displays continued to be staged there. However, descriptions of large-scale demonstrations when Sir Lionel Smith, the Governor who oversaw the end of apprenticeship left the island in 1839, show how the participants in such rallies had changed. Sir Lionel was deservedly popular with the former slaves and, while he had scheduled his departure at daybreak to catch the morning's offshore wind, hundreds of people still assembled to line the way from the King's House and along the road to Port Henderson where he was to board his ship. As he exited the Parade and drove along White Church Street he passed under banners saying 'Sir Lionel Smith, the Poor Man's Friend and Protector' and 'We Mourn the Departure of our Governor'. More people lined the road south, while an even bigger crowd blocked the way at Port Henderson. It proved an emotional ceremony, leaving Sir Lionel and many members of the crowd in tears.[17] In practice the fact that such a show was staged demonstrated how far political awareness did extend in emancipated Jamaica's first years. The Parade, which had hitherto provided the site for some of the plantocracy's most self-confident public ceremonies, now saw a mass turnout reaffirming the end of apprenticeship that also demonstrated continuing popular respect for a Governor who had clashed with the Assembly.

The town in 1839: still a City in the Fields

When Sir Lionel's successor left Jamaica three years later he followed the same road but, after cultivating smoother relations with the Assembly, his carriage was escorted by both the military garrison and local militia units.[18] The route that both these parties followed across the savanna to a landing point on Kingston Harbour, where the ex-governors were rowed out to their waiting ships, retained many continuities with the geographical priorities that dictated the Spaniards' original choice of the town's site 300 years before. This remained a 'City in the Fields'.

By the 1830s the surrounding countryside had already been transformed over the previous two generations. The first change lay in the governors' immediate destination. In 1839 Sir Lionel's ship lay offshore from Port Henderson, a small settlement sheltered below the Healthshire Hills. This haven had developed from the 1750s, superseding the older Passage Fort of the Spanish and early English periods. By the late eighteenth century Port Henderson had also become a seaside resort.[19] A suitably healthy mineral spring was identified in 1776 and as 'New Brighton' it supported a substantial inn along with several elaborate cottages where the island's elite could socialise, drink the waters and indulge in the fashionable medical cure of sea bathing.[20] Governors, who transported all their household effects to and from the King's House in Spanish Town, were particularly likely to land at Port Henderson rather than Kingston, but the anchorage remained a significant outlet for produce from a hinterland that extended beyond the St Catherine plain.[21] Even though ocean-going vessels could not tie up alongside and it was not particularly sheltered, these factors hardly condemned it as a haven: lighterage was often needed in Kingston too, while sailing ships found beating the eight miles out to the open sea from the eastern end of Kingston Harbour difficult. Even the advent of steam power did not doom Port Henderson, as it became a terminus for a steam ferry service to and from Kingston.[22]

For a casual viewer the landscape along the road to Port Henderson might well appear much as it had in the 1750s, when pens between Spanish Town and Kingston supplied both towns 'with Grass, Wood &c – the inhabitants of the towns [sending] their horses there to pasture', while butchers from both towns sent 'Cattle & Mutton' to graze there too.[23] These uses continued. However, the gardens that surrounded roadside cottages were now shaded by the mango, ackee and breadfruit trees all introduced to Jamaica in the 1780s and '90s and, by the 1830s, 'now found in every part of the island'.[24] Within a few years, in areas where plenty of water was available, gardeners would add the *gros michel* banana transplanted from Martinique around 1835 and therefore known by its rural cultivators as *martnick*.[25] Not all agricultural experiments succeeded. Late eighteenth-century attempts to grow corn (maize) as an export crop in the land behind Port Henderson towards the great Salt Pond had failed when drought struck.[26] Instead, much of the former savanna land to the south and west of Spanish Town still remained predominantly grazing land for cattle, with some sugar grown alongside the Rio Cobre and in the coastal lands although some fields were reverting to brush. By the 1830s the resulting dense second-growth 'ruinate' scrub loomed large in descriptions of the St Catherine plains.[27] Near the town the former common fields were sub-divided and remained planted with grass and 'the valuable, always verdant Guinea-grass', an African grass, which provided fodder for the horses whose owners continued to throng the town during the law terms, Assembly seasons and the horse races in late November.[28]

To the north of the town coffee planting had altered older settlement patterns. Coffee began to be established in Jamaica in the mid-eighteenth century, but received a substantial boost when French refugees from the revolutions in Haiti introduced more effective production techniques. Jamaica was also able to move into the export markets for coffee because Haiti's prolonged civil wars and the flight of most planters marked the end of Saint-Domingue's former predominance in the European coffee trade.[29] In the long term the small coffee plantations established in the vicinity of Spanish Town might, or might not, prove financially viable (by the 1841 census no 'coffee plantations' were recorded in the parish).[30] Whatever their utility for growing coffee, these 'mountains' provided rustic retreats for local professionals – doctors, lawyers, even government clerks and, with the Governor's Pen located to the south of the town, for the Governor's own household too – who could then leave their families behind and ride or commute in to work in town by carriage.[31] After emancipation some unprofitable former coffee estates were sold, providing the sites for free villages.

The rural pens from which these professionals made their daily commutes into Spanish Town sustained a different residential pattern from the suburban 'pens' around Kingston. During the late eighteenth and early nineteenth centuries rich merchants bought and subdivided cattle pens around Kingston as rural retreats, though the need to keep abreast of shipping news meant that even leading merchants continued to maintain 'apartments or houses in town' and only retreated to their pens 'to exchange the comfort of fresh air for the suffocating atmosphere of Kingston' at weekends. 'In the vicinity or outskirts' of Kingston 'some genteel families . . . inhabit handsome houses surrounded by extensive gardens and shrubberies' but, as a visitor in 1831 continued, 'these are not numerous'. In Spanish Town, in contrast, if some professionals drove in to work, the regular social season during the law terms meant that many visitors stayed for a matter of weeks – the town provided 'the periodical or seasonal resort of those who may be termed the aristocracy of the island' – and when in residence, they continued to take lodgings in the town itself.[32] In Spanish Town elite houses along with the lodgings that the island's elite leased continued to occupy prime sites in the old centre of the town.

The continuing importance of this social season was clear enough just to the south of the town, where following seventeenth- and eighteenth-century practices, the race track continued to be cut out of the common fields. The Spanish Town races remained the island's principal sporting fixture, with a race run for the 'King's Purse', set at 'one hundred pistoles' in 1789 (£133 6s. 8d.) paid out of the island's revenues. By the 1830s the original requirement that the race occur on 'the first Tuesday in December' seems to have been waived, but the races continued to generate a 'concourse of fashionables'.[33]

Within the town, too, the daily routines followed by its residents at the start of Queen Victoria's reign had yet to alter much from those that had shaped townspeople's schedules over the preceding century. A description of ordinary morning activities in Spanish Town around 1838 is included in an undated fragment where a would-be humorist transported Charles Dickens's character Mr Pickwick to Jamaica. After bringing the central character from Dickens's first best-seller, *The Pickwick Papers* to Spanish Town and putting him through a long dinner, the author allowed him to wander off for an early morning stroll:

> A stranger to the town and its environs, chance brought him to the side of a river which skirts the Jamaican capital, and with him chance proved herself a lady of taste, for there was not near Spanish Town a prettier spot than the one he had wandered to. Seating himself on the root of a tree close to the stream, and resting his notebook on his knee, he selected from the scene and the objects before him, all he thought worthy to be recorded for instruction of the Pickwick Club. On his left stood about twenty black, brown and sambo girls, half immersed in water, washing linen, the [revealing] Næad style of whose dress rather offended his views of delicacy. [Nearby] some ebony coloured gentlemen were bathing; higher up a great number of grooms had brought their horses to work and water, and on either side of the stream, negroes of both sexes were filling their tubs, jars and pitchers for domestic purposes.[34]

Pickwick then hurries back to his lodgings for breakfast and our author returns to striving far too hard after every pun and wordplay. But in this passage we can see the crowd of servants – and there would be a crowd, with 2,104 enslaved residents recorded in the town in 1832 – starting on the household's daily errands in the cool of the early morning.[35] The various groups on the town side of the river were divided by gender, which was encouraged when different chores were undertaken in different spots. Horses brought down to be watered at the Synagogue Ford; cloths laundered further downstream – but with an earlier start – and all those buckets dipped into the river too. These tasks had brought household slaves and servants down to the riverside through the seventeenth and eighteenth centuries and they would continue to bring their successors there long after emancipation. Linens needed washing, horses had to drink and river water continued to fill most householders' pots and pans.

As free agents the ex-slave household servants described here would then deal with a town that was changing. From 1834 the new 'Sligo Water Company' drew its water from an intake just upstream of the town.[36] However, plenty of tubs, jars and pitchers would continue to be dipped into the river to supply the town's poorer residents and, indeed, when the new Company's water was only available to its subscribers six days a week from 5 a.m. to 9 p.m., then even the most prosperous households needed to top up their supplies with river side buckets or from the water cart.[37] Otherwise, in the late 1830s, contemporaries noticed that the island's main towns looked far less rundown. Many former slaveholding residents invested the compensation money they received at emancipation in building or rebuilding urban properties.[38] Local masons and carpenters raised their charges in response to the increased demand for their services.[39]

All these urban refurbishments only went so far, however, as while Kingston and Spanish Town both had active local governments, their oversight did not extend to providing sidewalks. Shoppers on Kingston's Harbour Street enjoyed a shaded 'piazza' or colonnade to shelter them from the direct sun and in Spanish Town visitors relished the shaded piazzas in front of the Assembly or beside the market. Elsewhere, individualism reigned. The complaint expressed 40 years later by a visiting American naval officer, that 'the sidewalks of Kingston are up hill and down hill – no regular pavement but each house has in front of it – its own level portion of brick pavement and it reminds one of walking up and down steep steps' described Spanish Town too.[40] In towns whose leading residents rarely walked if they could ride and, indeed, within an island culture where a 'walk-foot buccra', a white on foot, had lost all status, householders' property rights outweighed adding new taxes to assist pedestrians.[41] Eighteenth-century values still shaped townspeople's assumptions about their streets and spaces.

Spanish Town continued its administrative roles and its position as the marketing hub for the surrounding agricultural district while continuing to straddle one of the island's major cross-roads. In 1842, it could take four days to ride across the island from Kingston to Montego Bay and travellers were likely to stop at the old capital.[42] But by the early years of Queen Victoria's reign long-established residents may well have found it a quieter place, because some traffic had been diverted to an early bypass. From the beginning of the century a road swung round its southern edge (in the mid nineteenth century called Burke's Road, today Bourkes Road). This cut across the common fields from the western end of the 1801 iron bridge to the race track and then ran west to Old Harbour. With less need for through traffic to rattle through the town's 'dull streets . . . there were few moving objects'.[43] Townspeople probably took more notice of the end of the town's traditional Sunday markets, which moved to Saturdays – a measure successfully promoted by the missionaries in the immediate aftermath of Emancipation – changing the character of Spanish Town's Sundays even more.[44]

As Queen Victoria's reign progressed the proportion of the urban population attending religious services increased. The heckling during sermons which had remained a persistent nuisance for preachers of all denominations over the 40 years since Coke's visits in the 1790s through to the eve of emancipation, finally died down. With the ending of slavery preaching appeared less contentious, while broader shifts in social values chilled the support given to earlier rowdies. In this more sympathetic climate previously suspect religious groups could afford to adopt a more public profile. 'Old Duggan', William Duggan, an independent 'Native Baptist' preacher who had maintained his own clandestine following in Spanish Town and its vicinity during persecution now 'kept a Chapel on the Cumberland Road at a place called the Tamarind Tree'.[45] Then, in the mid-1850s, after persistent sickness ended Fr Joseph Bartolio's missionary work in British Honduras (today's Belize), his reassignment to preach to Spanish Town's Roman Catholics would help to structure another struggling local congregation. Twenty years later, Fr Bartolio still could 'not forget how [his parishioners] encouraged me at the very onset'.[46] In the first years of Queen Victoria's reign some social standards changed.

During the early 1840s the town gained several new churches, besides recognizing Duggan's Native Baptist chapel. The established church made the first move, in part because some members of the congregation had started pushing earlier in 1833. The Anglicans' Trinity Chapel, begun in 1842 and consecrated in 1844, is a solid building whose brick construction and rectangular plan appear far closer to the missionaries' chapels than to the splendid cut stone Anglican parish churches erected prior to 1800. Given the discrepancy after emancipation between the parish church's seating capacity of 1,200 and 17,000 potential worshippers, further 'Church room' appeared necessary. The new chapel would house a second Anglican congregation. A petition from several townspeople to the Vestry supporting the town's curate and recommending the building of a new chapel had gained the Governor's support in 1833, but this had not led to ground being broken.[47] Time was lost in resolving legal claims over the rector's rights to parishioners' fees and a disputed property title. An intercession by the Bishop of Jamaica in 1839 eased the first of these obstacles, while settling on an alternative site on the northern edge of the town (just across from the new Sligo Water Company's reservoir) meant that a proper title could be secured. A local appeal raised enough cash to buy the lot and clear it. In January 1842, a meeting of these subscribers agreed to build a chapel to hold 400. They elected a Building Committee who accepted a local contractor's bid. The Vestry and Assembly promised grants, and the Bishop and Governor offered individual pledges though, even with this lead, local donations paid for less than a quarter of the total raised. Two months later the Governor laid the first stone. Progress remained rapid. By December the walls and roof were up, while the doors, windows and ceiling were all ready, and the contractor needed paying.[48] The second Bishop of Jamaica consecrated the new chapel in 1844.[49] Even in Jamaica's established Anglican church local initiatives and enthusiasm were essential to push a building project through to completion. Other congregations commissioned cheaper structures while raising higher proportions of the cash.

The decade's next division of an existing congregation was far more bitter. A new Baptist church was erected on White Church Street in 1843, after a split led one of Phillippo's English assistant ministers, the Rev Thomas Dowson, along with nine of the older chapel's 13 deacons to establish a separate congregation which then joined the newly-established Native Baptist connection. This islandwide group emphasized their links to the congregations founded in the 1780s by George Liele and George Gibbs, 'long before the arrival of any Baptists from Europe'.[50] Initially Dowson preached in 'a booth' that could hold at least 200, while he and his followers sued the older Baptist congregation for the possession of the existing chapel and access to its burial ground. After this tactic failed the new congregation purchased 'a large dwelling' at the corner of White Church Street and Duke of Wellington Street, which they converted into 'a House of Worship', establishing themselves as the Ebenezer or Independent Baptist Chapel.[51] They would remain there for over a century, until the chapel was destroyed by a hurricane in 1951 after which, all the participants in the original dispute being dead, the congregation reunited with the Phillippo Chapel. In the early 1840s there were churchgoers enough to fill all the newly constructed chapels in Spanish Town.

Constructing a properly medieval Anglican Cathedral

The reorganization of the Anglican congregation broke from eighteenth-century patterns. First the Trinity Chapel was established, then the old parish church was reconfigured as a Cathedral. The rebuilding programme occurred in two stages. The first started in 1844, after royal Letters Patent arrived declaring the parish church of St Jago de la Vega the Cathedral Church of the diocese, (even if popular use was already calling it 'the Cathedral' from the first arrival of an Anglican Bishop in Jamaica 20 years earlier). The second phase began in 1848, when a new chancel was erected at the east end of the Cathedral.[52] These rebuildings both imposed extensive changes on the interior. In 1816, only 30 years earlier, Matthew 'Monk' Lewis noted in his diary how impressed he was at the mahogany-panelled brick church, with its walls lined with monuments to leading planters. The St Catherine parish church was one of the very few buildings that this leading exponent of 'Gothic' taste noted favourably during his visit to Spanish Town.[53] In 1824 another visitor characterized the parish church's interior as 'light and handsome'.[54] Only four years later verdicts shifted and it would appear 'like an old barn, without ornament or decoration' when set against the 'magnificence' of the town's new Baptist and Methodist chapels.[55]

By the early 1840s metropolitan tastes in church design had shifted. In 1841 an English worshipper simply dismissed the old parish church as 'poor' while its interior with its lavish eighteenth-century panelling was 'of no improving effect'.[56] Anglican clergy (and now some laity too) felt they knew what architectural forms were appropriate for divine worship. They would therefore do their best to reshape any church's interior to conform to the proper 'gothic' neo-medieval formulae then becoming the liturgical orthodoxy in Britain.[57] The first round of building work aimed to change the nave, where the congregation sat. The panelling Lewis so admired, along with the decorated plastered ceiling both became early casualties. Today's interior with its dark stained plank roof angling up into the shadows and capping painted plastered walls effectively reverses the colour scheme that earlier generations of worshippers saw. Originally the ceiling was lower, coved, plastered and painted white, 'graced with two magnificent chandeliers' of gilded brass. Only the bottom eight feet or so of the walls were panelled.[58] The refurbishers were remarkably thorough so very few traces remain of the original woodwork. The elaborately carved capitals on the pillars supporting the organ loft and perhaps part of the pulpit appear the only survivors. However, the bottoms of almost all of the eighteenth-century memorials on the walls of the nave are at least ten feet above the floor, suggesting that this was where the panelling originally stopped. Once the plaster ceiling was pulled down, the roof timbers were left exposed in a way that the building's eighteenth-century carpenters never intended.

For regular churchgoers all these elements in the reorganization of the nave remained secondary to the rearrangement of the seating. The church lost its old box pews, along with its benches at the back under the organ loft. The Vestry's restrictive assignment of the earlier pews, where only white families could rent the 'best' pews, had excluded potential worshippers, encouraging recruitment to the Methodist and Baptist missions.[59] The replacement pitch pine pews levelled the congregation in a new fashion. Pew rents continued to separate those families who could afford the fees from other worshippers who sat nearer the back, but those distinctions were defined by cash, not colour.[60] By 1844 the Cathedral was able to provide townspeople with an alternative to the chapels. This change became all the more apparent once the Cathedral had 'a new active stirring Bishop' and was 'open for public service not only on Sunday evenings, but on Wednesday and Friday evenings' too.[61]

The reorientation of the former parish church then continued. Extensive changes occurred in the chancel where the altar is situated. A design competition meant that on 1 January 1848, an advertisement was placed 'in the Colony's Newspapers offering £20 for the best design to rebuild the Chancel'. A month later, the prize was assigned to 'drawings and designs' by Mr John Calvert, the Cathedral organist. The commissioners made him 'Superintending Architect, receiving £5 per cent on all outlay & a sum not exceeding £50 Bonus on the completion of the work to the satisfaction of the Commissioners.' The five per cent was the standard fee claimed by professional architects in Britain.[62] However, the whole procedure and this scale of bonus still appears more appropriate for mundane repairs to the churchyard wall than commissioning such a major project. The choice had a fair whiff of an inside job as this would be a very quick turn-around if Calvert had no knowledge that the project was imminent. In 1849 an anonymous letter in the British professional journal *The Builder* complained that not only was the Spanish Town Cathedral design not made by a trained architect, but the estimate of £3,000 was far too high (though it would eventually cost £4,570). In addition the letter-writer claimed that the self-styled architect was demanding additional 'fees' of between five per cent and seven and a half per cent from the contractors. Calvert's rejoinder, that classical authorities recommended that architects be musicians and that he earned every penny of his official commission overseeing the building work in tropical heat was accompanied by further affidavits from the contractors. Hardly surprisingly, all involved denied paying kickbacks.[63] Prudently, Calvert's reply then avoided addressing the other charges made. Once the bills were all settled, the early Victorian chancel remained an ambitious building undertaken by a local designer employing local workmen. On Easter Monday 1848 the old brick chancel was pulled down.[64]

The new chancel was considerably larger, far wider, longer and higher than its predecessor and reversed traditional proportions by towering over the older nave. The rebuilding provoked further adjustments to the interior. By the late eighteenth century the chancel was primarily a mausoleum to former governors with the limited remaining space around the altar occupied by massive wooden pews reserved for the Governor, the Council, the Assembly and the Governor's household. The old Governor's pew even had an

FIGURE 6:1   Anglican Cathedral, Spanish Town, c. 1865. This photograph shows the 1848 chancel rising higher than the older nave. (National Library of Jamaica).

elaborately carved wooden canopy over it. Most of these structures were ousted in the first round of refurbishments. However, the enormous marble monument to Governor Lord Howard of Effingham which the Assembly had commissioned in 1792, after his lordship's death in office, continued to stand by one of the pillars beside the altar, and a mahogany chair for the Governor's use remained alongside it. In the far more radical 1848 reshaping of the chancel this arrangement changed, with the Effingham monument swung into a side aisle, where it could back on to the newly widened east wall. On the other side of the new building, where Governor Sir Brian Keith's monument used to edge forward into the space behind the communion rails on the north side of the former chancel, the rebuilding meant that this memorial too was pushed well back against the north side wall.[65] Then, in shifting the altar steps as the altar was moved further east in this longer building, the memorial slabs to the colony's seventeenth-century governors which previously lined the floor around and under the former altar were pried up and taken outside. Relaid, some would fulfill the mundane function of a drip course, preserving the foundations from the tropical rains running off the new roof, and others were broken in the move or else cracked after lying on soft soil.[66] Inside, the Governor's seat which had survived the 1844 refurbishment was finally removed. When future Governors and their households attended the Cathedral they too would be crammed into the nave with the rest of the congregation. Priorities were very different.

All these adjustments transformed the new chancel into a properly orthodox liturgical space. Instead of re-installing any of the old memorial floor slabs the whole floor was re-tiled with the latest English neo-medieval glazed tiles, whose designs copied fourteenth-century floor tiles then recently discovered at Westminster Abbey.[67] With at least ten different patterns of tiles employed, besides plain ones, the innovation appears a deliberate choice. On this authentically clerical surface the Cathedral authorities set up the Bishop's ecclesiastical throne. It backed on to the same pillar where, before the renovations, Governors had provided the focus for the congregation's attention in any services they attended.[68] A site for displaying the Governor's authority was recast as a clerical sanctuary with space enough not only for the Bishop of Jamaica, but for a full surplice-clad choir. Older values would remain embedded in the stained glass window erected over the altar, which incorporated the coat of arms of the Colony flanked by the arms of the then Governor and Chief Justice. The Colony and, indeed, the Chief Justice, were

FIGURE 6:2 The Cathedral chancel, interior, 1898. The photographer manages to omit the eighteenth-century tombs standing at the ends of the aisles to the left and right of the altar. As a result the chancel looks as though it could be in the English Home Counties. The banners hanging on either side of the altar belonged to the Second West India Regiment. They were presented in 1879. (National Library of Jamaica).

both generous donors to the rebuilding fund. Otherwise, the whole 'restoration' pushed the colonial authorities to the edge of what had become, for the first time since the English conquest in 1655, primarily an ecclesiastical sanctuary.[69]

The reconstruction of the Anglican Cathedral Chancel was a substantial (and very expensive) achievement in its own right. The reconfiguration marked a major transformation in the Cathedral's function, offering a suitable setting for a choral liturgy rather than 'a preaching box' and, alongside this, a further move away from the secular priorities of the eighteenth and early nineteenth-century colony. Among the items removed at this juncture was the wooden sounding box that had hung over the old pulpit. This decision seems particularly striking because as a piece of loot from some earlier naval raid on a Spanish cathedral, the heavy sounding board over the pulpit had been 'surmounted' by a bishop's mitre.[70] Even this did not save it, because, in the period's liturgical shift away from preaching and towards communion as the focus for worship, pulpits and their sounding boards were particularly vulnerable when they obstructed sight lines to the altar. This reconstruction adopted 1840s standards of taste, although the opinion, still current in 1943, that while 'the old portion is impressive in its simplicity and solidity, it is considered by many that the Chancel or new portion now constitutes the real beauty of this historical building', may no longer be so widely shared.[71] The builders might employ a neo-medieval vocabulary, but they viewed the building in functional not historical terms. To secure what they considered a satisfactory result they were quite prepared to destroy the church's original fabric. The design and work were carried out by Jamaican residents, but these priorities reflected changes in liturgical fashion sweeping across the Church of England.

The project did use local contractors and while much of the decoration carefully recreates English medieval usages, individual stone carvings – such as the two African busts interspersed among the kings, queens, bishops and martyrs whose sculptured heads decorate the outside bases of the window arches on the south side – suggest some recognition of the church's West Indian site. The congregation remained proud of its Cathedral. A new, even larger organ replacing that of 1800 was inserted in 1849 at a cost of £2,500. Imported from London it was to be 'one of the best in the West Indies'.[72] The numerous late Victorian memorials inserted below the older eighteenth-century monuments, where they now fill the bare walls exposed when the older panelling was removed, testify to local worshippers' continuing affection for the building.

The Trinity Chapel, Cathedral Chancel and the Native Baptists' Ebenezer Chapel were all new ecclesiastical buildings that passers-by would recognize and from which they would take their bearings. During the 1840s and '50s local builders also continued to work on the town's other places of worship. Such projects remained dependent on funds raised by the individual congregations. For the members of each congregation the struggle to maintain and, ideally, embellish their chapels provided a shared goal, feeding into their self-identification as Anglicans, Baptists, Independent Baptists or Methodists. A long list of work undertaken at the Methodist Chapel in 1855, when the town's economy was particularly impoverished, is primarily remarkable for its description of how the funds were raised. As the minister reported, 'we have been able to repair the shingling and put up a much needed Portico at the Front door, and to paint the doors and window sashes.' All this was funded by a 'Fancy bazaar' organized by the women of the congregation. Even if Queen Victoria's respectable subjects attended charity bazaars with the knowledge that the money they spent on tea, buns and handicrafts would go into the designated charity's coffers, the local Methodist ladies' ability to raise substantial sums this way remains a remarkable testimony to both the housewifely skills that produced such quantities of saleable goods and to the time they donated towards not just keeping a roof on their chapel, but paint on its doors and windows and a new porch to chat under too.[73] The island's social life had indeed changed: increasingly incorporating, alongside these tea meetings, 'Bible societies, school societies, anti-slavery societies, and various institutions of a similar kind, . . . [which] excited the sympathies and co-operation of the respectable female portion of the community'.[74] The capital's new and refurbished churches and chapels offered social and activist centres to a far wider section of the town's resident population.

The enlarged religious buildings that graced Spanish Town's streets testified to the optimism of at least the earlier years of the decade after emancipation. It was at this juncture that the Rev James Phillippo, while enjoying an active sick leave in England in 1842, set his sights higher still and tried to rally support to establish a university in Jamaica on the model of the then 20-year-old University of London. Other writers had already proposed similar projects. Correspondence in the *Kingston Chronicle* in 1830 recommended that a college of Physicians and Surgeons was needed in Jamaica and in 1835 the Assembly even passed a bill to establish such a college. A pamphlet that printed the Assembly's bill went so far as to list the by-laws for the college's library but, when it came to funding, the scheme went no further.[75] Phillippo's proposal followed a different track. In 1839 a friend of his had offered the Baptist Missionary Society a site for a new theological training college in the parish of Vere, but the Society baulked at terms attached to the gift, which would require them to erect buildings and 'form a missionary establishment thereon'.[76] Phillippo's university project looked to fulfill similar ambitions, but now aimed for wider support. He not only cited the numbers of schoolchildren currently enrolled and urged the economic and social benefits of a University to the island, but also urged the project as 'a monument to emancipation' and, indeed, as a gesture towards reparation for Jamaica's ex-slaves 'for compensation is still their due'.[77] Similarly wide-ranging ambitions inspired John Calvert, the designer of the Anglican Cathedral's new chancel, who apparently saw this commission as the first stage towards the construction of a new Cathedral and so left the edges of the chancel walls uneven to allow subsequent extensions to be keyed in. The height that the new chancel reaches above the eighteenth-century nave and the massive bases for crossing towers that were erected as part of the rebuilding, both demonstrate Calvert's ambitions. The Cathedral to match such a chancel would be a massive edifice. In the event Calvert was disappointed. He left Jamaica and eventually presented his 'beautiful working model of a cathedral erected in Jamaica' to the South African Museum in Cape Town. It was hardly appreciated there. By the late 1860s it stood between two cases of stuffed birds: a curiosity to be admired for its intricate workmanship.[78] What's more, by then any visitors to the South African Museum who knew Jamaica would find the idea of a vast Cathedral dominating the skyline of Spanish Town strange – indeed, perhaps almost as inconceivable as Phillippo's scheme for a Jamaican university.

Investments: 'a most gratifying instance of colonial enterprise'.[79]

One external reason why the early 1840s appeared comparatively optimistic was that commercial schemes in Jamaica attracted investments from London financiers. These speculators made no fortunes of the California gold rush type; instead, they received negligible returns on their outlays for prospecting for copper and gold in the hills of St Andrew.[80] Copper ore that might be marginally profitable if it came out of English mines (where an infrastructure of furnaces, coal mines and railways already existed) would not pay any dividends when excavated in Jamaica, where potential markets remained distant and refining equipment had to be built from scratch. Neither British investors nor members of the Assembly would find much consolation in the islandwide geological surveys funded by the Assembly to encourage further prospecting. These surveys were a remarkable achievement in their own right but did not help anyone to strike it rich.[81] Other Assembly-backed investments, like the new iron lighthouse erected at Port Morant in 1842, remained at the forefront of British technological innovation, while, in attempts to trim overheads, individual planters laid out their capital in the latest steam-driven sugar boiling machinery.[82] Importing technology and attracting investment capital appeared to offer a way forward.

In Spanish Town however, both the town and its relations with its traditional hinterlands were transformed for the worse by the arrival of what proved the most spectacular of this round of early Victorian investments in Jamaica – the railway.[83] In 1843 Victorian England was at the height of its 'railway boom', a share-buying frenzy that bears comparison with other periods of irrational financial exuberance, such as when investors were eager to buy into the South Sea Company, during the 1710s; the airlines during the 1920s, or into 'dot.coms' during the 1990s boom. Between April and October 1845 ten further would-be companies circulated prospectuses for schemes in Jamaica that, if they had all been completed, would have smothered the island under at least 300 miles of railway lines. Most proposals hardly moved beyond issuing advertisements in London.[84] In contrast the Jamaica Railway Company succeeded in making an early start. It was the among the first colonial railway companies to raise equity capital on the London Stock Exchange. The company had been incorporated in an Act of the Assembly in 1843 and by 1844 had succeeded in raising £150,000 in 30,000 shares of £5 each to undertake the first leg of its scheme: building a line from the Angels south to Spanish Town and then across the Rio Cobre and on to Kingston.[85]

In 1845 the railway bubble burst and as the boom turned to bust, provoking an economic depression in Britain, the Colonial Office intervened to prevent other colonies from tapping the London stock market to fund further railways. By then, however, the Jamaica Railway Company had already raised sufficient capital to build a 14-mile line, buy rolling stock and wood-burning locomotives, ship them out and open for business.

Laying 12 miles of line between Spanish Town and Kingston was an engineering feat in its own right. The course chosen ran well south of the older road. Several landowners held out for premium rates for their parcels of rough grazing land, but these purchase costs were dwarfed by the expense of constructing a stable track through flood plain and marsh. Even though the engineers tried to build on islands of firm land, plenty of soft ground needed stabilizing. This not only pushed the cost-per-mile well above the initial estimates, but explains the very low 20 mile an hour speed limit on the resulting track. Cost cutting led to the scaling down of the initial proposal's double line to a single track. The whole project still cost £222,250, rather than the prospectus' original estimate of £150,927, an overrun of almost 50 per cent. Construction expenses ran through the company's initial capital. Nothing was left for building either a further extension west to 'the Cherry Garden plantation . . . in St Dorothy's Parish' (today's western St Catherine), a rural site to the west of Old Harbour, which was authorized by another Act of the Assembly. Nor was there any money for a branch line south to Port Henderson, where the company had optimistically secured a lease to the township.[86] The railway company was always based in Kingston, where its principal terminus was built on the western side of the town to enjoy ready access to the docks. The townspeople in Spanish Town made considerable sacrifices to accommodate the railway even though, in the short term, the abandonment of the proposed branch lines meant that their new station would not become much of a junction, at least for a generation.

Spanish Town's railway station enjoyed a prime site just to the south of the town, with easy access to the main road running west to Old Harbour. The new line crossed the Rio Cobre well south of the Iron Bridge and then ran across the former savanna land south of the town, before swinging to the west of the town for the last couple of miles north to the Angels station. Guests visiting the Governor could travel in first-class carriages 'fitted up with armchairs', though they might complain that 'it was anything but smooth travelling' and that there were no view because the land was 'so thickly covered with "bush" a sort of jungle'.[87] Particularly fortunate visitors might be met by their host's carriage sent to the station, but public cabs and the town's horse-drawn omnibus all waited there too. A wide forecourt left plenty of turning space. Townspeople strolled over just to watch the passengers boarding and the train's departure. However, as even first class passengers recognized, the trains' 'passengers were chiefly marketing people travelling 3rd class'.[88]

The new railway proved popular. Clergymen in Spanish Town and Kingston soon agonized that Sunday travelling would undercut the good effects of the closing of Jamaica's Sunday markets. Despite all the admonitions issued from the pulpits against desecrating the Sabbath, people still flocked to ride on the trains: 'on one Sabbath it was reported to have conveyed eight hundred passengers'.[89] These early joyriders not only missed their ministers' sermons but enjoyed the journey. Legislation soon put a stop to Sunday travel. Even first-class passengers would need to borrow a fellow guest's carriage if they wanted to return to Kingston on a Sunday.[90] Nor would the line's regular passengers amount to the 800 a day figure that the clergymen cited. The

Jamaica Railway Company broke even but never returned high profits. Its construction costs ran well over budget, maintenance remained a drain and its revenues only offered a low return on the capital: initially the Company paid a fairly competitive 4½ per cent, but this rate tailed off.[91] This limited cash flow could not fund further expansions. Despite several passionate debates in the Assembly, no extensions were completed until 1867.[92]

Politics and economics in the 1840s

So why did the early Victorian optimism evaporate? The international economy hardly helped. Jamaica benefited as a site for speculative schemes during the boom of the early 1840s. It lost that access to British investment capital when the bubble burst. Changes in the British sugar duties then reshaped the market for West Indian sugar. The West Indian trade was hit particularly badly after the London price for sugar fell by a third. Thirteen London trading houses that dealt with the West Indies went bankrupt between August 1847 and August 1848, along with Kingston's Planters' Bank which collapsed in January 1848.[93] By the time the subsequent economic cycle turned upward again, the colony's troubled public finances made it appear a far more doubtful prospect for private investments. Risk money went elsewhere. Then there were countervailing forces on the island as well. A disastrous fire in 1843 destroyed much of downtown Kingston.[94] In itself, this wiped out many older householders' investment of their one-time windfall of slave compensation money.

Replacement capital remained hard to find. Businesses in Kingston already faced problems because, once the former Spanish territories in mainland Latin America won their independence, the old Spanish imperial restrictions on trading disappeared and with them, much of Kingston's utility as an entrepôt. There was no longer any need for merchants to break bulk in Kingston and consign their cargoes to smaller coasting vessels once British ships were welcome to sail directly into the new nations' harbours. The port's trade dropped off abruptly.[95] Few investors could be found to rebuild on its burnt-out sites. Furthermore, another fire in 1862 left still more blackened empty lots down by the docks.[96] For 30 years visitors would comment on the thoroughly depressing first impressions of Jamaica they received on landing in Kingston, where 'broken walls, charred beams, crumbling ruins meet one in all directions'.[97]

The Kingston merchants' gloom then combined with a dead weight of pessimism among what remained of the old planting elite. Even in the best economic time Jamaica's planters were not prepared to forget the 1831 uprising. The subsequent attacks undertaken by white settlers on the missionaries' chapels had helped to turn the tide of British public opinion against the slave-holding interest, but the former slaveholders hardly shared that spirit of revulsion. They may have pocketed the £6,161,927 compensation money from the British government which persuaded the Jamaica Assembly to pass an Emancipation Act, and their plantations then benefited from a further four years of underpaid labour during apprenticeship, but they remained deeply suspicious about social change.[98] In 1841 dinner-table conversations among planters who had gathered in Spanish Town for the races invoked fears 'that the country would in five years be entirely in the hands of the black population and that all white people would be driven off' combined with continued complaints against 'the harm the Baptist ministers are still doing in the country'.[99]

The ex-slaves had been quite right to regret Sir Lionel Smith's departure in 1839. As Governor, he had worked hard for a post-apprenticeship wage settlement incorporating 'civil treatment combined with cash wages regularly paid' and guarantees for the workers' continued opportunities to occupy their former cottages and provision grounds on the estates.[100] Smith's successors proved far less sympathetic towards the labourers and far more conciliatory towards the planting interest. The planters, unaccustomed to paying wages for labour, increasingly blamed all the inefficiencies of their estates on 'high' labour costs along with the difficulties of obtaining 'continuous labour'.[101] This diagnosis of the colony's problems shaped subsequent policy making.

In 1844 the political tide ran in the planters' favour when the then Governor called a snap election six months before the session's scheduled end. Electoral regulations required prospective voters to have registered their tenure of a property for a year before they were entitled to vote as property holders, so this action meant that throngs of owners of new smallholdings who would have been entitled to vote were effectively disenfranchised. In this instance the Governor acted to protect the island's established Anglican Church from a Baptist-led campaign for abolishing its subsidies from the colonial Treasury. In the process, however, he allowed the planter block to secure a majority in the last Assembly session before the island's economy fell into recession.[102]

Politics in the Assembly remained difficult. In the immediate aftermath of emancipation British abolitionists had drafted proposals for 'temporarily' suspending the Jamaica Assembly as 'an effectual preliminary towards the preparation of good and efficient laws for the balanced Government, of that Island', hence bypassing the plantocracy's entrenched influence and imposing a revised law code on the colony. This radical proposal was not adopted. Instead, the British Colonial Office's policy of accommodating the Assembly in order to cool the Assemblymen's heated tempers by permitting them considerable legislative independence – or, what the ex-slaves and their sympathizers saw as further legislative foot-dragging – appeared to be successful, if only because some tensions eased after the deaths of some of the most intransigent Assemblymen.[103] The Jamaica Assembly remained at the centre of the island's affairs. But could its members find solutions to the island's problems? To defenders of the status quo the Assembly's debates during the 1840s appeared exemplary, 'carried on with strict propriety' while 'the dignity of the chair [was] scrupulously attended to'.[104] The Assembly's 1843 legislation supporting the share issue for the Jamaica Railway Company did assist in floating the new company's initial public offering. This remained an isolated success. Procedural niceties alone were insufficient to resolve Jamaica's problems. Not only were the resources to be shared sparse and the island's problems extensive, but the absence of any consensus on what general policies to follow hamstrung the Assembly's effectiveness,'rendering' the legislative process 'peculiarly difficult and trying.'[105]

At an imperial level the planter-dominated Assembly did manage to pull off some successful coups. In 1839 the Assembly's stubborn intransigence provoked a constitutional crisis in Britain, when the Whig government's majority on a parliamentary vote to suspend the Jamaican constitution fell to five and the British Prime Minister offered his resignation.[106] These difficulties in London unseated Sir Lionel Smith from the Governorship. However, neither the Assemblymen's corporate obstinacy nor their personal readiness to accept the plentiful hospitality that Governors offered at the King's House could succeed in steering Jamaica through a prolonged economic crisis. Jamaica's social problems needed addressing too.

Domestically, the Assembly's planter majority undertook a partisan agenda. When the newly emancipated majority sought schools, school-teachers, access to land and a living wage, the Assembly instead raised taxes to employ policemen and prison warders while legislating to prevent squatting, penalize vagrancy and ease the collection of small debts, including rent from former slave cottages. The Assemblymen also endeavoured to encourage further immigration, allegedly to set an example of diligence to the ex-slaves, but in effect driving day labourers' wages down below subsistence costs.[107] Initially they recruited Europeans who proved expensive, objected to the conditions offered to them and – if they did not die before their terms were up – soon left. A further proposal to send out British convicts to labour in 'the sugar growing colonies' was not pursued.[108] In 1845 the Assembly committed colony funds to subsidize the recruitment of indentured labourers for Jamaica, primarily in the Indian subcontinent, but also in China and among Africans drawn from intercepted slave ships.[109] This programme parallelled policies undertaken in other British West Indian colonies after apprenticeship, particularly in Trinidad and Guiana, though there the planters' claims of labour shortages were more plausible. Meanwhile, to fund this agenda of recruiting 'steady' labour for the largest plantations, the Assembly constructed a tax structure that weighed heavily on the peasantry, taxing both their imported purchases and their exported products. Sugar plantations, the primary beneficiaries of the policy, their working stock and even their unused lands all remained lightly assessed.[110]

Whatever the alleged virtues within nineteenth-century social and economic orthodoxies of social policies designed to 'induce' the ex-slaves to labour for low wages; or for restraining the freed-peoples' 'desires . . . to what labourers in other countries are forced to be content with'; or even the claim that fertile areas of Jamaica were 'thrown out of the cultivation of the staple exports owing . . . to no other cause than the luxuriance of the provision grounds of the negroes', the Assemblymen's economic priorities remained backward-looking.[111] They aimed to maintain the sugar estates as the island's primary economic engine. As a social goal this had a certain logic: so long as Jamaica was viewed as a plantation colony, then planters could view themselves as its natural leaders. To guarantee this, the planter block in the Assembly reset suffrage regulations to ensure that they held the necessary votes. Despite these efforts, global economic trends undercut the planters' policies.

Sugar could no longer pay Jamaica's bills. By the late 1840s the island's sugar exports were in crisis. Even after importing indentured labourers to keep local wages low, laying out scarce capital on the latest steam-driven centrifugal boiling machines and vacuum condensers and setting up the new railway line, the costs of cutting the canes in Jamaica's fields and then getting the hogsheads of sugar down to the quayside remained high. Inefficient production and higher labour costs kept Jamaican sugar more expensive than comparable slave-grown Cuban or Brazilian sugar.[112] The final straw was the decision by the Westminster Parliament to remove all duties on sugars imported into Britain, which left West Indian sugar to compete for the home market against not just other British territories, but also against slave-produced sugar. Indeed, the opening of the British market to such suppliers encouraged an increase in the illegal slave trade to Brazil and Cuba.[113] Simultaneously, a rise in beet sugar production on European farms cut into the options for re-exporting West Indian sugar to continental Europe, which consequently pushed the prices offered for sugar in Britain even lower.[114] Desperate attempts to construct a new parliamentary alliance in Westminster between former abolitionists and the property-holding West India block to head off the 'free trade' challenge to the sugar duties failed – or, at best, only achieved a limited reprieve that expired in 1854. The well-intended hope that 'a joint appeal, supported as it obviously is by the common principles of justice, . . . could scarcely fail of being effectual', proved fallacious.[115] As Britain slid into economic recession in the late 1840s 'free trade' offered its politicians a unifying political slogan. The sugar duties and the protection they offered fragile West Indian economies were overwhelmed beneath the twin tidal waves of economic orthodoxy and the home electorate's desire for cheap food to feed the labourers crammed into Britain's industrial towns.

Weathering the 1850s

A decade after the end of apprenticeship the prospects for Jamaica looked far less promising than in 1838. The island's economy continued to drift in a prolonged slump. Enthusiastic claims that cotton would prove 'more profitable than sugar' never delivered, but testify to planters' desperation.[116] In a backhanded testimonial however, the arrival of cholera in 1850 did show Jamaica's increased incorporation in the world economy. During the previous European and North American cholera epidemic in 1832 the island had escaped infection. This time, with steam providing faster travel from port to port, the disease reached Jamaica from Panama, where it had arrived from the gold fields of California. The island suffered badly, enduring some of the highest death rates of areas the pandemic touched.[117] As the threat approached, a Board of Health was established in Spanish Town, enrolling local worthies including the Rev James Phillippo and the senior judge of the island's Chancery court. The Board did its best in 'perambulating every street, visiting every court, removing nuisances, and making arrangements for the immediate supply of medicine'.[118] They also established a hospital, where victims were brought to die. It stood at the old militia magazine on Barrett Street, just beside the Rio Cobre. A medical experiment undertaken during the early stages of the epidemic to test whether the air in Spanish Town was particularly 'putrid' was sending up a large kite with a piece of raw beef attached to it (which would then rot if 'corrupt air' was present to cause the disease), suggesting that some local doctors remained unpersuaded that cholera was water-borne.[119] In the meantime the townspeople continued to receive their water from the Rio Cobre, either through the Sligo Water Company, whose pumping station's intake was very near the town, or else from a water cart that filled up at the Church Ford, just up-stream of the cholera hospital.[120] For several weeks deaths in Spanish Town from cholera averaged 40 to 50 daily. Before the epidemic Spanish Town's population was about 7,000 people. Around 1,200 died. Proportionally these were heavier casualties than in Kingston, where 4–5,000 died out of a population of 40,000.[121] Such totals were comparable to an attack of the Black Death. Two years later a smallpox epidemic afflicted the island.

The epidemics did not persuade the island's politicians to pull together. If anything, shrinking resources led to policy making in the Assembly becoming increasingly contentious. The colony's Treasury was deep in debt. Newer policies fell victim early, (especially once planters recruiting further indentured labourers were obliged to pay more towards the overall costs). Despite the efforts by individual Assemblymen like Mr Vickars to defend education and equalize taxation, the planter block in the Assembly focused on budget-cutting 'retrenchment' as the prime remedy for all the island's ills. Programmes they did not care for, like mass education, certainly suffered but the Assembly's principal target was the high salaries assigned to public offices in better times. These economy measures therefore faced tenacious resistance from the same salaried officials who sat on the Governor's Council.[122] The result was a protracted legislative stalemate.

Assemblymen's cost-cutting efforts were combined with further attempts to assert their legislative independence. To this end the Assembly tried to claim control over the power of the purse. In 1853, as the last British sugar duties expired, it refused to authorize any revenue bills. The resulting crisis of confidence nearly brought down another British government. This time, however, the British cabinet was not to be bluffed into restoring the sugar duties. A prolonged deadlock followed. The Assembly's gamble did not pay off. Withdrawal of supply to secure redress of grievances is an ancient constitutional tactic. By the mid-nineteenth century its local repercussions would prove highly damaging when the government payroll comprised a considerable section of the colonial economy. This was particularly the case in Spanish Town, where 'most of the respectable inhabitants of the Town are government officials; and since they have been unable to secure their own salaries, they have been unable to pay their Merchants, Tradesmen and dependents'.[123] The whole community suffered.

The town became increasingly dilapidated during the 1850s. The loss of earlier optimism appeared particularly apparent just outside the town. When the railway line curved around the south and western sides of Spanish Town in the 1840s it sliced through the ring of pasture land that remained from the old common fields. The most immediate casualty was the former race course in the savanna south of the town. The northernmost end of the track was sacrificed to find space for the new railway's marshalling yards: 13 acres were transferred to the new railway company.[124] What remained of Spanish Town's race course later provided a site for an emergency burial ground for cholera victims. Racing in Spanish Town ended 'for years after'. By 1860 the allocations in the Island Treasurer's registers of funds for various Queen's Purses for the island's principal horse races no longer included any races in Spanish Town.[125] Meanwhile, when a survey was undertaken of the parish lands in 1867, 'The Old Race Course' was annotated 'Partly in bush and unoccupied', though the latter claim had not prevented some 'squatters' moving in.[126] The suspension of racing, a former highlight of the town's social season, may itself help to explain why Assemblymen tended to drift home early from contentious sessions. Without the races Spanish Town would be less likely to host the islandwide 'concourse of fashionables' that had encouraged aides-de-camp to gallop back from Kingston for race day.[127]

Effective political solutions proved hard to find. Defanging the Assembly so that it would no longer hamper government business deflected the colony's elected representatives from undertaking political oversight. But, rather than addressing Jamaica's economic woes, the Colonial Office found it far easier to introduce schemes reorganizing the legislature and shifting the constitutional balance in the executive's favour. A substantial 'loan' from the British Treasury could refloat the Island Treasury. Afterwards a political reshuffle, described as reform, reshaped the island's constitution. The Governor's Council, which had always had a role in vetting legislation, was elevated into a second chamber. Its 17 members would continue to be nominated by the Governor, now they sat for life. This had already become the norm on the former Governor's Council. In explaining this format to British readers the Councillors could be described as a 'quasi-peerage' and they were ready enough to invoke parallels with the British House of Lords.[128] Meanwhile the Assembly lost the power to initiate money bills. These were to come exclusively from the Executive Committee. The mid-century adjustments were intended to block any further attempts by the elected Assemblymen to close down the government of the colony. Attempts to exclude the Assembly from anything more than voting on the Governor's budget still failed, while the Assembly's leaders were successful in asserting a right to 'recommend' the introduction of individual money bills.[129] In the longer term these constitutional changes would mean that even if the plantocracy were to lose control of the Assembly the Council would provide another chamber to check popular initiatives.

Constitutional ingenuity could not resolve the fundamental problem that even after a British government loan, the island's economy continued to sink. The investments in new technology made during the 1840s were insufficient to maintain earlier export volumes, still less to allow Jamaica to win free from its economic doldrums. By the 1850s and early '60s, speculative capital proved even harder to tap while the island's situation seemed increasingly desperate. The various nostrums proposed in the Assembly – particularly trimming the costs of government and subsidizing further immigration by indentured labourers – provoked legislative log jams without delivering substantive results.

Ugly yellow buildings: an unprepossessing capital

Spanish Town left mid-Victorian visitors thoroughly underwhelmed. It was increasingly dilapidated, but the broader problem was that it remained a late eighteenth and early nineteenth-century creole town. Set against the brick-built centres of trade and industry in Victorian Britain, with their skylines dominated by tall factory chimneys, cramped smoke-stained tenements and

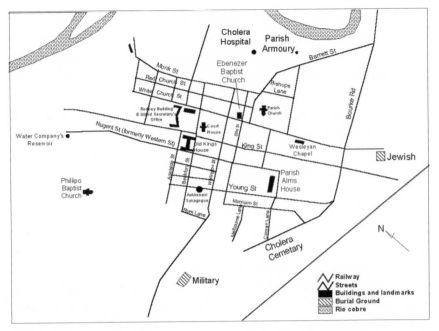

FIGURE 6:3   The town *c.* 1851.

shops glistening with brass, gas lights and plate glass windows, Spanish Town's array of one-and two-storey wooden buildings with their yellow plaster and green-painted woodwork appeared downright unprepossessing.[130] This was particularly the case for anyone who approached the Parade by a carriage from the railway station if the driver avoided traversing the town's main retail areas. The editor of the *New York Post* who visited Jamaica in 1851 commented that he 'did not see a store in the place'.[131] In a striking indicator of its limited development Spanish Town may well have been the only capital city within Queen Victoria's empire never to have had a 'Queen Victoria Street'. No new thoroughfare of a sufficient scale warranted receiving the Queen's name. Furthermore, once the Victorians learned to sneer at their parents' and grand-parents' neo-classical Georgian buildings, they devalued the architectural legacy of the late eighteenth-century sugar boom, even if it was admitted that the public buildings in Spanish Town were 'erected at considerable expense, and not without some pretence'.[132]

The most sweeping condemnation of the town was prompted after an unexpectedly short and punctual interview with the Governor in 1859 which left Anthony Trollope, the novelist, kicking his heels on the steps of the King's House waiting for his cab back to the railway station. He tried to fill the time as he would have in England, by going for a brisk walk. He started wandering around Spanish Town's streets and found himself even more disoriented than one of the rural clerics from his Barchester novels on a venture up to London. Very soon he wanted somewhere to sit and have a drink. He could not find anywhere and finally paid a passer-by sixpence – a massive tip – to show him to the Wellington Arms, just around the corner from where he was standing. By the time he reached that establishment he was too tired, or too hot or just too annoyed to note the old livery stables and shops that stood around the edge of the Church Parade by this hostelry, or even to catch what issues of local politics were under discussion in the tavern's more comfortable upper room. Instead he retained bitter recollections of hot empty streets whose 'yellow buildings' appeared 'ugly from their colour, ugly from the heat, and ugly from a certain heaviness which seems natural to them and that place'.[133] Deferred maintenance from the various crises of the 1850s had only compounded the archaic effect.

A short visit provoked ample copy. After leaving Jamaica Trollope roundly condemned both of the island's principal towns: 'Kingston as a town is the most deplorable that man ever visited, unless it be that Spanish Town is worse'.[134] Later, in a short story, he offered a further pessimistic assessment of Spanish Town claiming that:

> on the whole face of the inhabited globe there is perhaps no spot more dull to look at, more Lethean in its aspect, more corpse-like or more cadaverous than Spanish Town. It is the head-quarters of the government, the seat of the legislature, the residence of the Governor; – but nevertheless it is, as it were, a city of the very dead.[135]

His impatience was probably shaped by his agenda: in 1859, he visited Jamaica not as a respected novelist but as an official from the British Post Office whose mission was to persuade the colony to accept responsibility for the annual deficits in the island's postal revenues into its already straightened budget.[136] Mr Trollope brought news that nobody wanted to hear.[137] It is hardly surprising that he acquired a thoroughly pessimistic view of the Assembly and its procedures. He was most concerned with a bill which was highly unpopular and only squeaked through in the last days of the session – when Assemblymen who were also government officials stayed in town to provide a narrow majority in a thin house once the planter Assemblymen had slipped home for Christmas and the onset of the sugar crop.

Trollope remained underwhelmed by both of Jamaica's principal towns. The only solution he could suggest was to 'desert' Spanish Town, transfer all the government's business to Kingston and allow that desolate port to enjoy 'those advantages which would naturally attach to the metropolis of the island'.[138] This radical scheme probably sounded plausible when drafted on his voyage home. In practice, no Jamaican Assembly would vote the necessary funds to construct new government offices and law courts in Kingston – far less a new Assembly or King's House – when a full set of official buildings stood in Spanish Town already. It would hardly help that Trollope's brisk proposals also included abandoning Jamaica's representative government, 'this tinpot system of Queen, Lords and Commons', leaving the Governor and his officials unfettered, as their efforts 'might be a great deal better if their hands were not so closely tied' by the Assemblymen's speeches, amendments and adjournments.[139] When uttered these suggestions were only the pipe dreams of a transient civil servant.

In Jamaica townspeople and colonial administrators pinned their hopes on restoring Spanish Town's place as a communications centre. This was reasonable enough because the thrice weekly posts from the island's north side and from its south [west] side both came in to the Spanish Town post office at midnight before being sent on the last 13 miles to Kingston to arrive there by 3 a.m.[140] In 1861, proposals circulated for establishing a 'Great Interior Post Road' that would run from Linstead to Kingston via Spanish Town, extending an earlier 'Grand Interior Road' across the northern side of the island that already ran east from Falmouth to Brown's Town and Moneague before cutting across the mountains to Ewarton, just up the valley from Linstead.[141] This recommended road was a far cry from the dismal interior trails of earlier generations when, as late as the 1820s, at the end of an Assembly session governors needed to send for Maroon runners to carry the parcels containing the latest bills over the mountains to the north shore parishes.[142] Further hopes for improving internal communication were later repeated in 1862, when several of the then Governor's cronies effectively bypassed the Assembly, pushing a scheme through the island's autonomous Transport Board to develop a new 'tramway' that would have run west for 40 miles to Porus via Old Harbour. In the event, not only was the first stage of the proposed tramway poorly constructed, with its rails simply laid along the crown of the main road west to Old Harbour, obstructing the cart traffic on a major highway, it was unusable too. No tram ever rode the new line. Impatient road users finally broke up the eight miles of rickety track that were laid, pushing the fragments into the ditch. Local authorities turned a blind eye. One of the more candid justifications invoked by the contractor who produced the back-of-an-envelope estimates which underpinned this scandal-ridden project was 'the immense advantage it would be to our line', that is, to the Jamaica Railway Company.[143] Even though the whole scheme proved an expensive debacle, the unstinting support that two Governors gave to it demonstrates the continuing appeal of railway expansion as a prospective key to economic development, both for Spanish Town and for the interior parishes in general.

Such hopes had some foundations. The Jamaica Railway Company had already changed Spanish Town's traditional economy – if only negatively. The town's taverns and lodging-houses, long a backbone of the resident population's trade, suffered badly from the combination of easier access to Kingston and the rising tide of legal fees which cut into the numbers of litigants coming to pursue lawsuits. The immediate impact was felt lower down the social scale. If individual landladies hung on to their properties, hoping for better times, they still laid off their domestic servants and laundresses.

Meanwhile as a mere stop on the line between Kingston and Angels, the old town became less of a daily crossroads and its markets faced increasing competition from both ends of the line as outlets for farmers' crops. In this desperate context, local cattle thieves found some accommodating purchasers among Spanish Town's tradesmen, or so the sentencing of one Clarence Linden Dias indicated. This apparently respectable Spanish Town butcher had engaged in 'Cattle Larceny' on a grand scale. In August 1864 he lost his final appeal and was condemned to seven years penal servitude for buying a herd of '8 Cows, 4 heifers, 15 Oxen, 1 Bull, 2 Calves' from the original rustlers. Despite several petitions for mercy he ended up breaking rocks.[144] Whether hard times or easy money pushed a hitherto respectable resident into crime is nowhere stated, but Mr Dias and his fellow Spanish Town wholesalers were facing increasing competition for the produce of the town's traditional catchment area, whose farmers now enjoyed direct access to Kingston's markets. New challenges came from farther north where Linstead market, in particular, offered an alternative sales venue for the smallholders who had settled in the mountainous land nearby. A Governor who passed through Linstead in 1854 not only commented that the thriving township 'dates its origins from emancipation' but also noted that 'it boasts several large wholesale shops or "stores"'.[145] As a celebrated Jamaican song still assumes, would-be vendors who chose to 'Carry me Ackee Go-a Linstead Market' could expect to make a sale: even in dire times a failure to sell *anything* there would be surprising.

Crises compounded: the early 1860s

The American Civil War between 1861 and 1865 exacerbated all of Jamaica's existing economic problems. Confederate raids on commerce raiding along with the Union's wartime blockade of the Confederacy meant that the island lost its readiest sources for cheap cloth and corn.[146] Jamaica's difficulties were compounded when prolonged droughts in those years destroyed smallholders' provision crops and reduced opportunities for part-time work on sugar and coffee estates. The incumbent Governor's latest pet scheme for constructing an up-to-date mechanised dry dock in Kingston Harbour looked likely to mound up fresh public debt without finding any customers for its services.[147] A further proposal to import labourers from Barbados demonstrated the continuing currency of the planters' claim that 'steady' labour would resolve all of Jamaica's problems. This plan was finally rejected by the Barbadians' own Assembly.[148] Another scheme to recruit African-Canadians from Western Canada come to nothing. That initiative had itself followed close on the heels of redoubled attempts to ship more labourers from the Indian subcontinent, to take advantage of the social disruptions after the Indian Revolt ('the Mutiny') of 1857.[149] Meanwhile, as the Jamaica Assembly bickered and schemed, prices rose and the island's peasantry became increasingly impoverished, hungry and reduced to rags. A difficult situation was further compounded by a self-confident and stubborn Governor.

The political storm broke in 1865, a few months after the Confederacy's final defeat in North America. The November session of the Jamaica Assembly would have proved contentious anyway. Jamaican newspaper editorials had already commented on the possibilities for recruiting North American ex-slaves as indentured labourers, proposals that echoed the previous year's project for recruiting in Barbados. These schemes aimed to add more workers to an already glutted labour market and to drag down wages already desperately low. With the end of slavery in the United States vast numbers of immigrants might be expected. In August, writing to the newly appointed Governor of Virginia, the United States Consul in Kingston not only claimed to be 'acquainted personally' with 'every influential man in the Colony', but stated that 'there is an opening in Jamaica alone for one million' ex-slaves and asserted 'the Colonial Government is prepared to encourage their emigration hither by grants of money as well as by every other means at their disposal'.[150] In practice the Reconstruction Governor of a war-shattered Virginia had no time to pursue such proposals. By November 1865, when the Assemblymen the US Consul knew so well met again, the Jamaican political landscape had already changed drastically.[151]

After enduring a prolonged drought and import prices influenced by the wartime blockade, misery extended across the island. In Spanish Town, as elsewhere, this meant that many families were slipping down into abject poverty, with no resources left to cover illness or mischance. This was despite the Assembly's authorizing an extensive refurbishment of the King's House as a relief programme. Governor Edward Eyre saw this as a 'liberal' gesture 'for the comfort of myself and family' and, after getting some of the repairs carried out cheaply at the General Penitentiary's workshops in Kingston, he used the Assembly's grant to order further new furniture from England, forestalling any hopes of employment for local artisans.[152] Meanwhile townspeople's wages had fallen by a quarter over the previous two years. The results could be seen in such tangible terms as the poorer quality of people's clothing. Churchgoers who used to own draft animals, carts, cattle or 'small stock' – the resources of townspeople with a tie to the land – which they employed carrying produce to urban markets, had now sold them. The taxes imposed on their carts and livestock were far too high and the profits too low.[153]

In 1865 Spanish Town had a resident population of 5,261, which fell well short of the pre-cholera level of 15 years before. That total broke down as 422 white (195 male, 227 female); 2,193 'Brown' (854 male, 1,342 female) and 2,746 Black (1,016 male, 1,730 female). The population was therefore predominantly female, though among the male residents a disproportionately high figure – some 1,180, or just over half of the total adult male residents in 1864 – described themselves as tradesmen. Spanish Town continued to function as a service town. With such a population and, indeed, with a further 772 seamstresses who remained 'always poor, most of them only getting occasional work of the Country people before the August and Christmas holidays',

Spanish Town remained, as it had been since the 1660s, an urban centre for a much wider agricultural catchment area. By 1865, though, its agricultural hinterland had difficulty selling its crops and its urban craftspeople faced increased competition not only from Kingston's artisans or Linstead's shops, but also from cut-rate factory-made imports arriving from Britain and North America. These figures are drawn from returns compiled across the island to demonstrate the scale of the prolonged depression and the resulting impoverishment of the island's poorest residents. The Baptist ministers who collected this data suggested imposing new import duties on ready-made clothes. They also suggested importing some sewing machines so that Spanish Town's currently underemployed seamstresses could earn their keep, besides developing some light industry, like a dye-works or a paper mill.[154] For an island government which tinkered with tax rates to shelter the planters' livestock or wished to sponsor that drydock scheme, such proposals were neither particularly radical nor beyond the bounds of the possible; or so the compilers believed when they hoped that these dismal figures would prompt the British government to intervene, bypassing an obstinate Governor and an indecisive Assembly.

The Governor refused to consider any of these recommendations. The ministers presented their information and recommendations to Governor Eyre, but Eyre, the former Official Protector of Aboriginals in South Australia, studied the data with a closed mind. He even failed to acknowledge the contents of the very full returns relating to the 'pauper stricken' town just outside his office windows. Despite all the detailed information piled on his desk, Eyre remained convinced that these problems were primarily due 'to the faults or short-comings of the Peasantry themselves' while, even with all the evidence before him of destitution and misery islandwide, he was sure that the Jamaican 'Peasantry are relatively better off, and are in a position to do far better for themselves in their Station of life than the Planters in theirs'. From such a starting point, his comments accompanying the returns he sent back to the Secretary of State for the Colonies focused on peripheral details rather than the big picture. He marvelled at the suggestion that sewing machines be imported when the town's seamstresses were underemployed. As for all the other underemployed male artisans in the town, he thought they would be far better employed in unskilled labour (even if agricultural work was itself unavailable).[155] Then, in a fine example of blaming the messenger for bad news, he criticized the Baptist ministers who had compiled these returns as stirrers-up of disaffection. As purported trouble-makers, the ministers received torrents of criticism in the columns of most of the island's newspapers.[156] This response offered an easy substitute to analysing such miserable data.

The prolonged economic and social distress was not confined to Spanish Town. If the Governor would not look at problems outside his windows, neither would he listen to the succession of petitioners who knocked on his newly repainted front door. The continuing importance of Spanish Town and the King's House in popular visions of the island's political structure was demonstrated in the succession of delegations that made their way to the King's House to deliver sets of resolutions from local public meetings to the Governor in person. When a group arrived from Kingston Eyre did meet them, accepted their resolutions and said that he would forward them to London. But the Governor left his visitors in no doubt that he would not support their conclusions.[157] A further party led by one Paul Bogle, over from St Thomas in the East to Spanish Town to seek resolution for their grievances got a stonier answer and plodded the 45 miles home unheard.[158]

'One of the most horrible butcheries recorded in the annals of history': Morant Bay and its Constitutional Aftermath[159]

On 11 October 1865, the same Paul Bogle led an substantial party to Morant Bay, the chief town of the parish of St Thomas in the East to protest during a session of the vestry. Bogle had received a summons to attend after his participation in a shoving match in the court house at a trial there four days before. The subsequent 'notorious riot' proved a major turning point in West Indian history. The crowd was large, daunting and noisy. Some members had seized arms from the police station, though they could not fire them, others brandished sticks they had cut on the way. After the custos of the parish began reading the Riot Act people in the crowd started throwing stones. The parish's Volunteers, a company of uniformed local militiamen who were in attendance for a contentious court session, fired off a volley into the crowd that killed seven people. The crowd persisted, first burning the Volunteers and parish Vestrymen out of the court house and then burning down the house next door, the home of a black Justice of the Peace, where several had sought refuge. Eight were cut down, including the JP. The rioters then killed another

204 - GONE IS THE ANCIENT GLORY

ten in Morant Bay and across the parish.[160] Afterwards the 'rebellion' was suppressed violently: 350 were hanged, 600 flogged and over 1,000 houses burned or demolished. Trigger-happy troops shot at or slashed still more bystanders. The proclamation of martial law gave full discretion to the soldiers, which they seized, flogging 'people for looking sulky or for speaking a hasty word or for nothing at all'. Governor Eyre and the military officers he surrounded himself with reacted as though embroiled in a second Indian Mutiny.[161] Since 1857 'the Mutiny' had shaped the fears of British settlers and administrators across Queen Victoria's empire, while shouts of 'colour for colour' by the rioters fed into all the Anglo-Jamaican colonists' nightmares of a Haitian-type uprising. Fear shaped public responses across the island. Local newspapers praised the Governor's decisive actions for saving the colony. Uniformity was ensured when dissenting editors were arrested and their printing presses demolished by the police.[162] George William Gordon, a coloured politician who had often clashed with the Governor and who was an Assemblyman for the parish of St Thomas in the East where the riot occurred, surrendered himself in Kingston (which was never under martial law). By the Governor's orders, Gordon was then shipped to Morant Bay where on meagre evidence a court martial condemned the contentious Assemblyman to death as a ringleader. The executions of troublesome 'political prisoners' during Eyre's clampdown then extended to a black vestryman from St David, also arrested in Kingston, whose 'crimes' included teaching 'the people to be insolent and rude to their employers'.[163]

The November 1865 Assembly session met in Spanish Town after the uprising was subdued. It opened with a long speech from the Governor. Up to then the Assemblymen's confidence in their institution had remained high. Eyre, however, played his cards dramatically and, while boasting that the 'rebellion' was 'headed, checked, and hemmed in' within three days of the news reaching Kingston and 'fairly crushed' within a week, he still urged the Assemblymen to surrender Jamaica's ancient constitution which limited the Governor's power. He claimed 'there is scarcely a district or parish in the island where disloyalty, sedition and murderous intentions are not widely disseminated, and in many cases openly expressed,' so that according to Eyre the colony continued 'on the brink of a volcano'. Jamaica therefore needed a form of government 'in which union, co-operation, consistency, and promptness of action, may as far as possible be secured' – meaning that the Governor's executive power had to be unfettered.[164]

In Spanish Town, where the Assembly met, nervous residents continued to fear arson attacks igniting the shingles on their roofs, along with the prospect of further risings elsewhere in Jamaica. The Governor did nothing to calm these fears. Instead, the town's two companies of Volunteers were kept under arms for two months while, so urgent were the general fears, a third company was also enrolled.[165] Terrifying rumours circulated claiming that Gordon and other associates had visited Linstead Market and bought up all the cutlasses available. These had not been found. Would they now be used to murder people in their beds? Small wonder a bill was proposed to prohibit the importation, sale and use of cutlasses in Jamaica though, despite a closed-door debate, in this instance reality won out and that piece of legislation was not passed.[166] Yet to these nervous townspeople and indeed to a majority of the Assemblymen, the logical chain seemed plausible. If the government had executed Mr Gordon after a trial then clearly he must be guilty, and if he was guilty then the plot must extend wider still. The uncertainty continued. Townspeople feared there would be a second rising on Christmas morning, when church-going would offer a pretext for the assailants to gather for their would-be massacre. In Spanish Town an experienced missionary who had endured the Assembly's persecution of churchgoers before emancipation still wondered if it would be prudent for ministers to hold Christmas services that could allow would-be plotters such an opportunity.[167] Asserting that it was 'a rebellion' and not 'a riot', fearful people then heard all their worst fears repeated.[168]

In such contexts Eyre's scaremongering proved an effective political ploy. As he wrote to the Secretary of State for the Colonies, 'if we are to get a change of constitution thru the medium of the Assembly itself – now is the time to do it – when every body is in a state of the greatest alarm and apprehension and looking to the Government for every thing.'[169] Leading members of Eyre's Executive Council introduced a bill for changing the constitution to reduce the representative elements. As the Governor summarized the move, 'abolishing the existing Legislature & substituting a Legislative Council – half Nominees & half elected', would 'be a great boon for Jamaica'.[170] A contemporary's report noted that the plan would provide 'a Governor, Privy Council and one Legislative Chamber a fusion of Lords and Commons. The Chamber is to have twenty-one members. Nine are to be Nominated by the Crown. Twelve are to be elected. Four for the county of Middlesex, Three for the county of Surrey – one for the city and Parish of

Kingston and four for the county of Cornwall.'[171] Even in those extraordinary times, the proposal hardly enjoyed a smooth passage. It passed on a vote of 21 to four, nine assemblymen voted that it should be read a second time six months later, by which time the scare would have died down.[172]

As the session progressed the Governor's recommendations became more extreme as he aimed to seize 'the opportunity to try and get rid of the Assembly'.[173] The revised constitution the Assemblymen had spent a month discussing was already deliberately anti-democratic in abandoning the parishes as electoral units in an attempt to dilute the votes of black and coloured freeholders. Even so, a week after the Assembly finally passed the bill, the Governor rejected it. Apparently Her Majesty's Government would not accept a measure with so large an elective component. Instead Executive Council members introduced another bill in which the colony's entire constitutional future was surrendered so that 'it shall be lawful for Her Majesty the Queen to create and constitute a Government of this Island, in such a form, and with such powers, as Her Majesty may best see fitting.'[174] This offered the imperial government a blank cheque. The vote was far tighter: 13 to 15, but the Governor's majority just held.[175] By such desperate means 'a second Haiti' would be averted.

A local court reporter who saw the revised bill handed over by the Executive Council to the Governor for his approval recalled Eyre 'smiling away, while the countenances of the members were gloomy'.[176] Later, when Mr Eyre's selectivity with the truth was revealed during an extensive Commission of Enquiry in Jamaica and again during his subsequent public trial in England, the Colonial Office decided that they could not reinstate any of the former Governor's Executive Council and thereby excluded many of the colony's established political leaders from positions of influence under the successor regime.[177] Although several of the session's other emergency bills were disallowed by the Colonial Office, the bill abolishing the old Assembly was retained.[178] The Colonial Office would hardly consider reviving such an intractable institution as the Jamaican Assembly. The revised constitution assigned to Jamaica would not institute the 'local oligarchy' that the Assemblymen who voted for the second bill may well have expected 'would have the management of [the island's] affairs'.[179] Instead, if the Assembly majority had looked for a significant elected component in the island's decision making, then the promise offered in Eyre's opening speech to the Assembly that 'there is no reason why the new legislation to be called into existence in its place should not be organized and at work within a few months from the present date' would be long deferred.[180]

The 'Crown Colony' government instituted in Jamaica in 1866 was modelled on that of Trinidad – an island conquered by the British and left with limited political rights. Senior officials at the British Colonial Office increasingly viewed a system where the Governor retained a firm grip on the helm as suitable for a West Indian colony. Troublesome local elites were muffled and other groups, like Jamaica's free peasantry, who could have expected to win further representatives within the old Assembly, were effectively silenced. Subsequent administrators would no longer face embarrassing questions from local Commissions of Enquiry initiated by the Assembly or the hindrance of constitutional checks or balances. The Crown Colony constitution demonstrated that the sun had indeed set on those 'Lively bright days . . . dawning on Our Island' that the missionaries had predicted in 1838.

A new and very different day dawned for Jamaica. During the 1860s and '70s colonial approaches to democracy increasingly diverged from metropolitan politics. As political arguments in Britain focused on how far to extend the franchise, Queen Victoria's Jamaican subjects were obliged to justify anyone's eligibility to cast any sort of a vote.[181] The Crown Colony governments assigned to most of Britain's West Indian colonies not only shrank the electorates but, even more, these regimes drastically reduced the roles of any island-born officials, elected or appointed, in shaping policies at the colonial level or even in local government. The assumptions current in British and West Indian politics moved further and further apart.

Governor Eyre's successor did recall the Assembly on his arrival from England in January 1866, but only to pass the necessary bills to authorize a Commission of Enquiry into the rising. Meanwhile the 'Act to make provision for the Government of Jamaica' that the Westminster Parliament passed in February 1866 achieved not just bipartisan support but also 'the hearty concurrence' of both the governing Liberals and opposition Conservatives.[182] This British act of Parliament imposing a new government on Jamaica received the royal assent in June 1866. The island became a Crown Colony with no time for second thoughts. Instead, the urgent question facing the British Secretary of State for the colonies was who should accomplish 'the inauguration of the new Government'? After the Enquiry's findings, Edward Eyre appeared quite unsuitable for 'that arduous task'. Once the Commission of Enquiry ended the interim Governor also wanted to return home. Making a virtue of necessity, the Colonial Secretary considered the post should therefore go 'to some other person who may approach it free from all the difficulties inseparable from a participation in the questions raised by the recent troubles' and who, as a newcomer, could take 'the course best calculated to allay animosities, to conciliate general confidence, and to establish on firm and solid grounds the future welfare of Jamaica.'[183] The Colonial Secretary then appointed a new Governor, Sir John Peter Grant, whose previous experience as a civilian administrator had concluded with reorganizing Bengal after the Indian Mutiny.[184] In British India, Grant had never had to deal with elected local representatives. He would not deal with them in Jamaica either. In August 1866, when Jamaica's new Governor arrived bringing 'with him an Order in Council establishing a new form of Government', the colony's constitutional status had already changed.[185] Over the next decade Spanish Town would also be transformed.

—

CHAPTER SEVEN

'Oh, the Ancient City!'

Local Repercussions of Crown Colony Government, 1866–c. 1880

*I*N 1864, WHEN Lieutenant-Governor Edward Eyre was sworn in as Queen Victoria's Governor and Captain General of Jamaica, the pomp on display in Spanish Town's King's House Square was magnificent – even if running the royal standard up the flagpole reversed was later seen as an omen that under this Governor 'the Government was going to be turned "upside down"'.[1] The red coats of the local Volunteer Companies and the Second West India Regiment provided a backdrop for 'all the heads of departments and highest officials of the colony', along with the ecclesiastical pomp of the Anglican Bishop and three Archdeacons.[2] Ten years later, when Sir John Peter Grant's successor as Governor was sworn in at Kingston in 1874, the numbers of official guests from Jamaica had fallen. After the surrender of the old constitution there were no Assemblymen invited. Disestablishment pruned the number of Anglican Archdeacons. The Volunteer units were dissolved.[3] Crown Colony rule would change the way that government operated in Jamaica. These changes were extensive, rapid and imposed without consultation. The new system would hit the island's old capital city particularly hard.

This chapter examines local repercussions of the reorganization of the colony's administration, as an energetic Governor with a centralized bureaucracy replaced Jamaica's former uneasy constitutional balance between the Governor, the Assembly and the elected parish vestries.[4] Contemporaries had summed up the old Jamaican constitution in the phrase 'the Colonial Office might suggest, but could not enforce': under Crown Colony administration this was effectively reversed, with local opinion pushed out of the decision-making process while the Colonial Office and its Governor called the tune.[5] The Colonial Office officials who imposed this system on Jamaica hoped that freed from a deadlocked Assembly able governors could back worthwhile projects which would pull the colony out of its prolonged economic doldrums. During the early 1870s the former capital became subject to more intrusive official initiatives than almost any other place on the island while the decision to shift the seat of government away from Spanish Town exemplified the Crown Colony regime's willingness to break with long-established local traditions. Both the substantial achievements and, indeed, the very public failures of particular initiatives in and around the town show what 'pure' Crown Colony government could achieve in Jamaica, and what this meant for Jamaicans.

As far as the colony's incoming administrators saw things, when Jamaica's last Assemblymen surrendered the island's ancient constitution they voted to exchange self-government for good government: henceforth utility, as assessed by Colonial Service bureaucrats, would trump local opinions. The official justification for introducing a colonial government with only very limited local input remained Anthony Trollope's and Edward Eyre's goal of unshackling the island's executive. The new administration was meant to be active. The first Crown Colony Governor was certainly energetic and, as Sir John Peter Grant's private secretary concluded, 'he has left his mark in Jamaica. There is hardly a branch of the public service which did not feel the touch of his reforming spirit.'[6] This was well and good, but few Jamaicans expected variants of Crown Colony rule to continue for 80 years.

The Governor's decision to move first the central law courts and then the island's principal administrators to Kingston transformed the island's former centre. Once the move was made Spanish Town lost many of its traditional administrative roles, being demoted to 'an inland country town' while Kingston became 'the seat of Government of this Colony,' the 'present' or 'modern Capital' of Jamaica.[7] In 1874 the 2,000 plus residents of Spanish Town and its hinterland who signed a petition opposing the move to Kingston would have plenty to complain about.[8] Houses abruptly lost their values while many residents lost their livelihoods too. Meanwhile, locked gates denied townspeople entry to the King's House Square in its new guise as the quadrangle for a short-lived university, the Queen's College, though with only two professors, three students, a steward and some servants, the former public buildings appeared nearly empty. Yet, whatever their petition or its official rebuttals might say, Spanish Town continued to be an administrative centre: now, however, it provided a centre for the colonial government's secondary functions.

Townspeople feared their losses were permanent. The College did close and its gates were taken down, but the former public buildings around the Square remained underused. Visitors driving in through 'the deserted streets of the former capital' noted 'many half-closed stores', besides 'spacious houses in a state of dilapidation . . . their walls defaced with cracks, or their windows partly boarded up'.⁹ Fifteen of the houses that senior officials, judges and Jamaican visitors had leased for Governor Eyre's inauguration in 1864 were demolished within the next eight years.¹⁰ The process of change continued as the landlords, who were prepared to pull down residences for whom no tenants could be found, then leased the vacant plots for working class cottages. Such infilling extended an existing trend, as the houses lining Spanish Town's streets had long been 'of a miscellaneous character, ranging from mansions of the first class down to the most miserable sheds' that frequently stood 'side by side'.¹¹ During the late 1860s and early 1870s the social balance tilted away from the town's mansions. Anyone traversing these streets would recognize both the extent and the rapidity of Spanish Town's transformation.

A local poet's verses on 'St Jago de la Vega, the Ancient City' asserted that its 'Ancient glory' was 'gone', continuing,

Gone is the golden sunshine!
        Oh, the gloom that reigns;
Hushed is the martial music!
        Oh, the dirge that lives.
            Once the Council-hall was filled:
            Never manly heart was dulled;
            In that Hall the swallows build:
            In those bosoms pride is stilled –
        Oh, the Ancient City!¹²

Much more was involved here than a Governor's moving the 14 miles across to Kingston.

Recollections of the town's glory years soon translated into nostalgia and celebrations of 'ancient grandeur'. This might well appear a mixed blessing, 'those wicked old times when aides-de-camp used to ride alligators through the streets, when admirals used to give balls to the brown girls of the town, when vice in every shape was more reputable than it is at present' or else, among a slightly younger generation, hazy recollections of magnificent uniforms and gold lace.[13] Attributing all the changes in the town to a Governor's whim itself reflected the governor-driven priorities of the Crown Colony era. However, the elaborate social round that townspeople recalled so fondly had not appeared nearly so exciting to Governor Grant. When he looked out from the King's House in the late 1860s the place seemed empty, as his secretary recalled 'there was practically no resident society, and when the day's work was done, and the different officials had flitted away by train to their houses in the country or at Kingston, the desolation was complete, and Spanish Town became like a city of the dead.' Only the members of the Governor's immediate household, his private secretary, his military aide-de-camp and the Colonial Secretary dined together.[14] Viewed from such an isolated standpoint the decision to move to Kingston was another of the administrative rationalizations that characterized the first years of Crown Colony rule.

The townspeople were still wrong to attribute the move to Kingston solely to Governor Grant. He executed the transfer but the circulation of further schemes at this juncture shows that the idea of relocating the colonial capital was being discussed elsewhere in Jamaica – even if these alternatives got no official hearing. A proposal offered by an anonymous English pamphleteer 'A Fellow of the Royal Geographical Society' who had stayed in Jamaica, for transferring the island's administration from Spanish Town to Mandeville, highlighted the priorities that were reshaping the island's government. This 1871 plan aimed to take advantage of an ambitious proposal to extend the Jamaica Railway, which had already reached Old Harbour, ten miles west of Spanish Town and was meant to extend on to Porus, only eight or ten miles short of Mandeville. The new line would permit direct access to Kingston, 40 miles away. In this rosy depiction Mandeville not only stood 'nearly in the centre of the island', but its climate appeared 'not hotter than an English summer, and in winter not unlike some parts of the south of Italy', promising healthy tours of duty to civil servants from Europe. The argument could be elaborated. A lower official death rate would allow the colony to reduce its pension bill to widows and dependents. These savings, it was claimed, would pay for the added trouble in moving away from Spanish Town. The author then suggested that 'a lively town in a charming climate' would encourage planters to stay on the island and persuade English invalids to come out to Jamaica as a spa. In making this case the pamphleteer was quite correct in highlighting Kingston's 'unenviable reputation for unhealthiness' – yellow fever continued to afflict the port for another decade, in 1877 killing the Lieutenant Governor and members of the incoming Governor's household – though a further assumption that 'a Parliamentary season' in Mandeville would offer a social hub for the colony was misplaced.[15] The scheme went nowhere, but it does suggests how parallel arguments were being discussed over planters' dinner tables or out on their verandas. Meanwhile the Railway Company's hope-filled westward expansion ran out of steam at Old Harbour. Health tourism would not develop for another decade. But besides promoting a social centre for the island's planters well away from Kingston, the plan's primary aim was to ease conditions for the expatriate European bureaucrats recruited to govern Jamaica. Here the proposal did catch the new metropolitan priorities that shaped Crown Colony rule. Under this regime the island's old capital would no longer serve.

Moving to Kingston: a choice for the Governor of a Crown Colony

Crown Colony government aimed to break with the past. It was a radical expedient for a particular crisis and it did prove effective in resolving that crisis. Jamaica's new constitutional arrangements encouraged British investors to see the island as a better credit risk so that bonds for a wide assortment of projects could be sold on the London market. Here, too, a bumper sugar crop in 1866 – 'the largest known since the abolition of Slavery' – helped to pull the local economy out of its prolonged depression.[16] Business confidence was revived locally as well, buoyed up on the hope that 'the present Government seems to possess the confidence of the landed proprietors residing in England.'[17] The establishment of Crown Colony government both contribu-ted to and coincided with a window of opportunity for government-guaranteed develop-ments in Jamaica.

Under Grant's reforming governorship a long list of official initiatives attempted to transform Jamaican society. Some projects, like the reform of the island's school system, did win widespread support.[18] Establishing a Government Saving Bank after the collapse of several local savings banks and then injecting greater liquidity into local markets by placing in circulation £3,000 in new nickel pennies and halfpennies not only resolved immediately pressing issues but also helped to revive commercial confidence.[19] Reconstituting the Jamaica Constabulary, establishing local Boards of Health and instituting an Island Medical Service all echoed current British civil service reforms.[20] Consolidating the island's network of parishes was a more radical rationalization than British reformers could undertake.[21] Removing the Judiciary, the Executive and the Governor's household to Kingston pushed through another group of frequently proposed administrative initiatives. Buying out and then upgrading the inefficient Sligo Water Company in Spanish Town and later – once the Governor and his household moved to Kingston – purchasing the Kingston and Liguanea Water Works too, besides establishing fire brigade, gas and tram companies in Kingston, along with erecting a new market building there, all continued at a municipal and local level the same efforts to streamline inefficient services.[22] Guaranteeing a bond issue for the Jamaica Railroad Company followed similar priorities.[23] Reorganizing the court system around a new network of District Courts staffed by British judges where, it was hoped, peasants could find easier access to less partial justice, harked back to British administrative practices in Ireland.[24] Further projects, like the disendowment of the Anglican church and, the establishment of a new University College also echoed current Irish reforms, but effectively revived some of the most radical proposals floated in Jamaica during the 1840s and '50s.[25]

Overall, Grant extended his predecessors' efforts to transfer successful initiatives used elsewhere in the British Empire to revive the island's stalled economy. Since 1861, a project had been under way to naturalize seedlings of Peruvian *cinchona* trees brought from London's Royal Botanical Gardens at Kew to produce quinine, the most hopeful drug in the late nineteenth century's tropical pharmacopoeia. Grant then expanded existing projects to develop new staple crops, establishing further botanical gardens and formalizing exchanges with botanical gardens in India.[26] There was also an ambitious attempt to introduce the latest irrigation methods from India and make the St Catherine Plain around Spanish Town bloom. Together these programmes amounted to a tidal wave of innovation pushed through by a Governor who was not obliged either to answer to local opinion or even take it into account. In practice, his administration backed some duds too – so that in 1873 an imported English stage-coach was simply consigned to a shed after making its inaugural run from Kingston to Spanish Town because it was far too heavy for the island's marl-surfaced roads – but good sense, good luck and a more upbeat economy helped many of Grant's innovations to survive.[27] However, if official successes later appeared self-evident, public failures could no longer shelter behind preliminary debates and a majority vote in the Assembly. These were all the Governor's schemes – for good or ill.

Until April 1872 the government of the Crown Colony continued to operate out of Spanish Town. The town was particularly exposed to official initiatives at a time when government policies shifted rapidly. In 1866 the final paragraph in one of interim-Governor Storks's, last dispatches mentioned the dilapidation of much of the King's House and questioned whether further public money should be laid out on repairs, 'if the rest of Government were changed, as it ought to be, to Kingston' because in that case the King's House 'would be useless as a residence for the Governor'.[28] Despite its throwaway delivery the comment from Eyre's immediate successor found a sympathetic audience. Back in London a new Secretary of State for the Colonies invoked what he had 'heard' on the matter – presumably from Anthony Trollope's *West Indies and Spanish Main*, though earlier governors including the Marquees of Sligo in 1833 and, indeed, Admiral Knowles back in 1754 had offered the same recommendation – and ordered the newly appointed Governor Grant to supply fuller details on the *pros* and *cons* of such a move.[29] Mr Trollope's brisk opinions on West Indian affairs carried increasing weight in Britain as his literary fame grew, even while residents in Jamaica adopted the phrase 'going a-Trolloping' to describe superficial generalizing.[30] Once Grant arrived in Jamaica he soon concurred with the basic recommendation, but did 'not consider it practicable at present', advising 'postponement until some prospect of making good use of [the] present buildings' could be found. He was then obliged to defer executing the move for four years because of limited funds and lack of alternative accommodation in Kingston.[31]

In 1869 Grant formally decided to remove the seat of government of the colony from Spanish Town to Kingston. Local opinions had no bearing on his decision. The custos of the parish, several former Assemblymen besides the Rev James Phillippo of the Baptist Chapel 'as the representative of One Thousand Five Hundred small freeholders', presented a petition opposing a measure 'without due necessity and at an unnecessary expenditure of the Public Funds'. At this meeting and, indeed, at another 13 months later in 1870, the protestors had to make do with soothing comments.[32] Under the old constitution such a distinguished array of sponsors and signatures would have marshalled sufficient votes in the Assembly to stall the most self-assured Governor's proposal. In the Crown Colony of Jamaica the recommendation proceeded to the Governor's Executive Committee where it sailed through.

By 1872 the relocation of 'the Seat of Government' from Spanish Town to Kingston was completed. The transfer process reacted to opportunities rather than following a preset schedule. Each fortuitous opening that the administration seized then imposed further changes on the town and its residents. By 1868 office space began to open up in Spanish Town. The Postmaster moved into the Court House facing the King's House Square.[33] Within a few months the officials of the new municipal board of an expanded parish of St Catherine also took up residence in the Court House. In a symbolic shift the pace of the removals increased in 1869, when the statue of Sir Charles Metcalfe, a former Governor, was uprooted from the garden in the centre of the Square where a grateful Assembly had planted it in the 1840s. This statue had offered a focus for recollections of the old Assembly's free-spending ways, before the cutbacks and cheese-paring of the 1850s. Claims that the Assembly had spent £1,500 on it were highly exaggerated, but such boasts contributed to local pride. Now their prized statue was carted away to provide a suitable centrepiece for the new public gardens laid out in Kingston's Parade (today St William Grant Park). A comment offered by Governor Grant 'that he saw no objection to the removal' of the statue 'from Spanish Town to Kingston' prompted a formal request from Kingston's Municipal Board for its transfer.[34]

As far as moving the King's House, the Governor's own residence, was concerned an opportunity only opened in 1872 after Grant successfully initiated negotiations for the purchase of the Anglican Bishop's house from a cash-strapped and soon-to-be disestablished Jamaican Anglican church.[35] Securing this property just outside Kingston meant that the Governor's own household could abandon the old King's House in Spanish Town.[36] The moves then continued when the statue of Admiral Rodney was taken from its Temple on the north side of the Parade to a new plinth overlooking Kingston Harbour. A petition protesting this last removal was, again, unsuccessful, in part because it arrived too late.[37] Only half joking, newspaper editorials asked if the marble monuments were to be pried off the Cathedral walls and re-erected in Kingston's churches too.[38] As it was, exemplifying this regime's priorities, the former Assembly's clock was transferred to the newly built Government Audit Office in Kingston.[39] All these initiatives demonstrate that once the Governor made his decision to leave, the chronology was dictated by the availability of space in Kingston.

The last removals began when a new Customs House on Kingston's Harbour Street was sufficiently advanced to permit a succession of offices to relocate. Shifting the Customs staff allowed the General Post Office to take over the ground floor of the old Customs House, while the Colonial Secretary's staff could occupy its upper floor. This move led to the official transfer of government from Spanish Town to Kingston. The Colonial Secretary's office had replaced the more informal post of Governor's Secretary, with its suite of offices behind the old King's House. Within the Crown Colony regime the Colonial Secretary became a senior Colonial Office appointee and the effective head of the island's day-to-day administration. In 1870 his authority was increased again when his department took over the duties of the Financial Secretary, the colony's senior treasury post.[40] Once suitable office space for this department was secured in Kingston the Colonial Secretary's clerks could leave Spanish Town. After the Colonial Secretary's office had moved there was no reason to continue holding Legislative Council meetings in the old Executive Council's room in Spanish Town. In April 1872 the Council began meeting at Headquarters House, the former military commander's house in Kingston's Duke Street. One of the first matters under discussion was the final reading of a bill formalizing 'the removal to Kingston of the Supreme Court and Offices of the Clerk of Court and Offices, Clerk of the Courts and Crown'.[41] It passed. A notice published in the government *Gazette* for April 11, 1872, marked the formal transition. Correspondence for the Colonial Secretary's Office and the Legislative Council should be sent to their offices in Kingston.[42]

None of these decisions offered any opportunities for consultation. The decisive change under the 'Paternal Despotism' of Crown Colony government was that rather than governing with the assent of any segment of the island's population, the new regime governed as officials of the Queen and her Colonial Office.[43] Indeed, whatever chronology dictated the timing for moving particular offices to Kingston, in the new Crown Colony the imperial metropolis of London gained a far larger role within decision making in

Jamaica. The only constraints that Governor Grant acknowledged on implementing such a radical initiative were the limited public funds available at his arrival in 1866 and the need to find suitable uses for the existing public buildings in Spanish Town.

The changes went further still. There were few Jamaican voices in Grant's administration. In one of the more significant shifts in the way that the new Legislative Council operated and in contrast with the usages of all earlier Governors' councils, now the 'official' members (who included the Commander of the Garrison, the Colonial Secretary and the Attorney General) took precedence over the local Council members, now labelled the 'unofficial members'.[44] The Council to whom the Governor turned for advice was no longer a Jamaican group with some British officials foisted on to it. Instead it was a staff meeting for the colony's expatriate Heads of Department, with a finite number of local members attending the occasional full sessions and permitted to pose specific questions about current policies. In this transition, the bases for appraising public policies changed. Bureaucratic fiat rather than debates among the colonists' representatives defined which projects were undertaken. Once a policy was instituted further debate on its merits was moot, because reversing a major official decision would itself be bad policy.

Local Responses

Some people tried to object to the move from Spanish Town all the same. In 1874, when Grant's successor arrived, a memorial from St Catherine reaffirmed the argument traditional in Jamaican politics 'that in a Town devoted to official business the locality chosen should be detached from a place of commercial occupation'.[45] The parish's new Parochial Board was sufficiently aware of Colonial Office procedure and of the current decision-making process to present their printed petition in triplicate, to permit its forwarding to the Secretary of State for the Colonies in London. A further 500 printed copies were distributed locally.[46] If nothing else, the exercise demonstrated that in Spanish Town the abandonment of the old King's House and opening of the new Queen's College were lumped together as so many arbitrary projects of Governor Grant's. By 1874 he had left and his ambitious schemes were not working. The petitioners believed that affairs could return to their proper order. They were soon disabused of any residual dreams for a reversal of Grant's initiatives. The incoming Governor expressed his surprise 'that hopes of a retransfer of the Seat of Government to Spanish Town were still in some quarters entertained' and replied that 'to have taken steps to effect a retransfer . . . would have been a proceeding quite beyond the scope of the Governor's Authority'.[47] The decision to move the island's administration to Kingston had never been publicly discussed in Jamaica; by 1874 it was already far too late for any discussion.

For another generation individual townspeople continued to describe the move to Kingston as an 'act of vandalism'.[48] Their complaints had remained unheard, 'many' who 'would have petitioned against the Bill' did not, believing 'it would be to no purpose to do so, the Government being strong enough to put aside all opposition and to disregard their petition'. They were probably right. The one negative petition submitted to the Legislative Committee was simply left on the table and ignored.[49] People in Spanish Town held strong views all the same and reasserted their objections: Kingston did not have enough suitable office space; Spanish Town did. The colony had spent £3,000 to purchase the Anglican Bishop's Lodge (a 'miserable agglomeration of sheds, at an out-of-the-way place') as a new King's House and was spending a further £300 a year leasing Headquarters House in Kingston from the British government.[50] This wasted scarce resources. These passions were a very long way from the torpor that had characterized Anthony Trollope's impressions of Spanish Town and its residents.

Still a bureaucratic centre

Yet some changes would have occurred anyway. As the tide of Victorian moral reform swept in, the days were already numbered for urban lifestyles that an ex-missionary primly described as 'in the extreme of even Jamaican gaiety, frivolity, and sensual indulgence'.[51] However, the contrasts the townspeople drew between a golden past and a disappointing present also overshadowed their town's continuing role as an administrative centre. Jamaica's former capital continued to house some government officials. The local impact of the island's reorganization under Crown Colony rule was not simply the removal of Jamaican clerks pushing papers in Spanish Town and their replacement by expatriate civil servants circulating memos in Kingston, several major departments did go to Kingston, but others remained and some secondary offices were transferred to Spanish Town.

The move to Kingston was not the clean sweep that Anthony Trollope had proposed. The main exception to the bureaucratic dispersal from Spanish Town was one of the colony's oldest offices. A tight Kingston property market helped preserve the island's public records in Spanish Town. Individual government departments transferred plenty of official files to Kingston and, as the townspeople had feared, these papers fared badly there. However, the traditional 'public' records of the colony stayed in Spanish Town. Businessmen in late Victorian Kingston had far less call to check the status of any plantation's ownership. With the price of plantation land tumbling, records of property titles that once guaranteed the mortgages and loans from British merchants whose credit floated the late seventeenth and eighteenth-century sugar economies were no longer an important commercial asset.[52] These records could rest where they were. The Island Records Office continued to inhabit its late eighteenth-century quarters on the north side of the King's House Square until the 1990s. The continued presence of the Records Office in Spanish Town and the copying and record searching jobs it offered provided an institutional focus for a generation of local antiquarians in the 1880s and '90s.[53]

What did change was that few of the public officials who worked in the town had offices around the King's House Square, the colony's bureaucratic centre since the 1760s. From the mid-1870s the square housed the Island Records Office along with the local post office and a branch of the Government Savings Bank. These secondary institutions used some of the vacant offices beneath the old Assembly Building and their presence was noted by successive tourists.[54] The bureaucratic activities in Spanish Town remained far more substantial than this. During the 1840s and '50s the Assembly's pro-planter policies had established further administrative offices after the space around the Parade was full. Most of these departments stayed in Spanish Town after the Governor's 1872 move.

One significant addition was only established in White Church Street in 1860. The office of the Protector of Immigrants, whose presence reflected the reintroduction of an external labour supply after 1859 when shipments of indentured labourers from India recommenced. This official oversaw the Jamaican end of the indentured labour programmes that had run since the late 1830s. Arriving and departing Indian labourers were housed nearby in the parish 'Alms House' (the shelter offered to vagrants, the poor and the elderly) in the former Spanish Town Cavalry Barracks at the south end of White Church Street. These barracks had come into the parish's hands in 1815 and –

with a brief and unsuccessful exception in the 1830s when part was used as a theatre – served as the St Catherine Alms House.[55] Now the migrant labourers were crammed in as well. Under Crown Colony government the number of indentured labourers brought to Jamaica increased, although it would not be until 1873 that the colonial administration began offering time-expired indentured workers bounties in cash or land instead of the promised return passages to retain them as settlers in Jamaica.[56] This remained an active office.

A similar reuse of older buildings meant that when a training school for the Jamaica Constabulary was established in 1867 it was located in Spanish Town. In the aftermath of the Morant Bay crisis, where the island's former police force signally failed to maintain order, central facilities were set up even before the old parish police forces were fully replaced. The post-emancipation police system had been organized by parishes, with local men serving in their home parish. The reorganized constabulary received an islandwide remit with a central training facility.[57] The model used for the reorganized force was the Royal Irish Constabulary, which was far more a paramilitary *gendarmerie* than the deliberately civilian English 'bobbies'. Its officers were called Inspectors and Sub-Inspectors, but included a number of ex-army officers, while 'in the other ranks the purely military designations of corporal, sergeant and sergeant-major were adopted'. Ten or twelve months of drilling and instruction in Spanish Town provided the foundation for a recruit's training.[58] Spanish Town's 1780s infantry barracks provided the depot. At that juncture the last company of the Second West Indian Regiment had already been transferred to British Honduras (Belize), so those barracks stood empty.[59] They became 'the Constabulary Barracks' for nearly a century.

Other institutions also moved to Spanish Town. Jamaica's principal prison and its Leper Hospital were both transferred there. In the 1860s the old Middlesex county gaol became a prison for the whole colony while Jamaica's other two county gaols were closed.[60] In Kingston the Surrey County Gaol became the town's poor house. The Inspector of Prisons was ordered to transfer the remaining prisoners to Spanish Town which, along with Kingston's General Penitentiary, housed all the colony's convicts.[61] Spanish Town retained the island's gallows too.[62] The practice of establishing potentially contentious public institutions in or around Spanish Town continued in the 1890s, when the island's Leper Hospital, which was originally moved from Kingston under Governor Grant to an isolated site on the Hellshire coast, was moved again to a rural site a mile or so south of Spanish

Town. Patients could reach it from the railway station. The town remained a convenient location for colonial institutions, but under Crown Colony rule protests by townspeople could be ignored.

Communications with the colonial administration changed with the Crown Colony's shift from elected officials to civil servants. The second-tier bureaucrats in and around the town now loomed far larger in local affairs than officials from the old colonial administration ever had. In part access was likely to shift anyway, as Crown Colony rule saw the abolition of not only the Assembly, but of all the colony's elected institutions: Kingston's Mayor and Corporation, the parish vestries and even the local road boards. The appointed parochial boards which took over these duties no longer had independent mandates. In 1871 grand juries, with the opportunities that their presentations offered for representing local grievances, were also abolished.[63] Meanwhile the bureaucrats who ran the departments established in Spanish Town during the 1860s and '70s did have direct lines of communication with the Governor. A fire in 1873 demonstrated the shift. It would help, when the town's fire engines proved unable to deal with the blaze, that the Constabulary Training School was nearby with trainee policemen on hand to form a bucket line from the river. Afterwards a scathing report by the Inspector General of Police arrived on the Governor's desk, describing the disorganization of the local fire service whose engines not only arrived late but, when they finally turned up, had not brought the right connectors to attach their hoses to their pumps.[64] As the town fire service was now funded by the colony's budget the Governor could order the fire captain's immediate dismissal.[65] The presence of so many colonial bureaucrats meant that local failures would have public audiences. A subsequent decision by the St Catherine Parish Board granting a request by the Spanish Town Cricket Club for a municipal fire engine to water their pitch would demonstrate to local householders (as well as the Commandant at the Constabulary Barracks) that the reorganized town fire service *could* get its machines to pump water.[66] The gesture might even keep the local cricketers' pitch green too. The Parish Board was obliged to look to colonial officials more than local ratepayers.

Where did all these central initiatives leave local affairs?

Crown Colony government shifted the local Parochial Boards' role from initiating local policies to executing central policies locally. They were still made up of local men, many of whom had served as vestrymen for the pre-Crown Colony parishes, but now they were answerable to the Governor rather than to local electors. The St Catherine Board's successful deflection of even one official recommendation actually serves to demonstrate the constraints on local government. In 1874, after Grant's departure and just before his successor refused their proposal for restoring the seat of government to Spanish Town, the St Catherine Board managed to block an official suggestion that it should relocate its municipal Alms House from the old Cavalry Barracks complex to a strip of public land between Barrett Street and the Rio Cobre. Part of this plot held the former militia armoury but otherwise the ground lay empty.[67] In this instance the fact that the main outlet pipe for the municipal drains came out here provided the Board with an acceptable pretext for disagreeing. If this site were used, the new building would be erected over the pipe. Would this be healthy? After the improvidence of locating a hospital over sewage outfalls had been conspicuous among the items in Florence Nightingale's critiques of the British Army's hospital during the Crimean War, this would offer a particularly effective veto.[68] Government engineers and medical officers submitted positive reports – stating that the outlet pipe did not smell, was clear of obstructions and carried surface water rather than sewage – but by then the parish medical officer had submitted a dissenting report.[69] He felt that it would not be healthy. Because of bureaucratic arm-twisting he subsequently retracted this opinion, but his original report still offered a shield when the Board maintained its refusal. They may well have been right too. The site had housed a military hospital in the early eighteenth century and Edward Long had dismissed that institution's 'very ill-judged situation'.[70] Whatever the practical merits of their case, the Board's decision was motivated by local prestige. Their resolution concluded 'that a Poor House at the entrance of the town, would be most unseemly'.[71] Outflow pipes and health offered convenient pretexts.

The Immigration Office's acute shortage of space allowed the Board to strike a bargain. The 'coolie office' needed to erect new barracks to house the indentured labourers currently crammed into the old Cavalry Barracks. Once the parish handed over its former Alms House the building work could proceed at the Barracks. The impasse over the riverside site held everything up. The Parish Board proposed an alternative solution, successfully persuading the Governor to authorize £550 to purchase 13 acres on Monk Street to house a new parish Alms House and even wheedled a further £50 out of central government funds 'to make the place comfortable'.[72] The local Board could truthfully claim that the newly purchased site would be healthier. But even if a particularly contentious proposal could be deflected, a top-down administration still constrained the ability of the local Board-members to set limits on the Colonial Government's policies. The practice of parish government was transformed. The Colonial Secretary may have moved to Kingston but the parish clerk received a blizzard of official correspondence.[73] This might employ the language of suggestions and recommendations, but it effectively offered advice and consent.

Although Jamaica's new bureaucratic rulers were prone to write off local opinion, it remained a potent force. Even at the height of Crown Colony rule administrative fiat alone could not prevail against the dead weight of local hostility to a project. In 1870 St Catherine's leading citizens heard Governor Grant sketch his plans to revive their local economy by establishing a network of irrigation canals on an Indian model to 'Convert some part at least of the arid plain around [the] town into a fertile garden', while further ruminations considered developing educational projects beyond the secondary level 'and for any institution of the Class to which I now allude. I know of no place in Jamaica which it would be more conducive to the general good to select as the site, than in this town of St Jago-de-la-Vega'.[74] Both proposals echoed development schemes that colonial bureaucrats were fostering in India. In Jamaica, however, local residents remained unpersuaded. During the early 1870s, public disapproval proved a decisive factor in derailing the Governor's plan to establish a college in Spanish Town.

The Negative Impact of Jamaican Public Opinion: The Queen's College, 1872–1874

Sustained local disinterest could defeat the most ambitious efforts of the Crown Colony administration. For nearly two years Spanish Town housed the Queen's College, 'a grand College', intended to 'attract pupils from all the West Indian Islands'.[75] The institution was planned as 'a public central College, where education of the highest order for which a demand can be induced may be imparted' to offer 'a good education of a middle order . . . to all classes who require such an education' and could not afford to seek it off the island.[76] The scheme sounded commendable. Its execution proved contentious. In July 1873, the custos of St Catherine received a letter from the

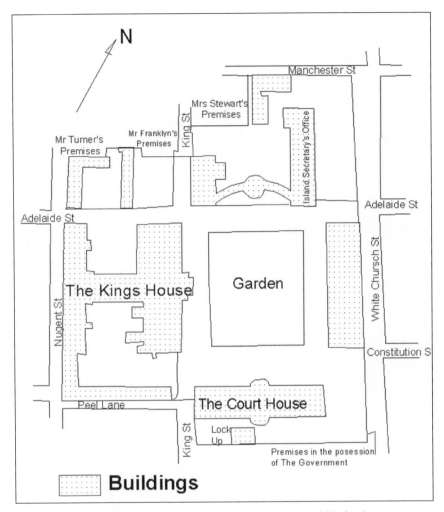

FIGURE 7:1 Spanish Town, Plan of the Parade, 1873. Properties available for the new Queen's College. Note how streets leading into the square are blocked off by railings. (Jamaica Archives) I am grateful to Thera Edwards for bringing this plan to my attention.

Colonial Secretary. The custos was requested to 'be so good as to give instructions' for the offices used by the Municipal Board in the eastern end of the old Court House to be 'vacated as soon as may be convenient'. The Board's clerks had to move because 'the Entire Eastern half of the Clock Tower Building', the turret in the centre of the former Law Courts, was now 'required for the College'.[77]

The plan aimed to reuse the space left by the departure of the island's

FIGURE 7:2   The most substantial relic of the Queen's College Project of 1872–4. A Mid-Victorian marble fountain in the centre of Emancipation Square. Photographed by J. Valentine in 1891 as a part of Jamaica's exhibit at the Columbian Exhibition in Chicago. This image shows elaborate cast iron fittings that have not survived. The view of the Rodney Temple in the background includes decorations on the balustrades which have also disappeared. (Matalon Collection, National Gallery of Jamaica)

administration and law courts by installing a university in their place. This would not only provide a capstone to the generally popular reforms of the island's primary and secondary education system, but would also offer a suitably ambitious use for the public buildings vacated by the government's removal to Kingston. Plenty of effort was put into transforming the King's House square into a college quadrangle, with iron fences to block traffic and a fountain inserted into the hole where Governor Metcalfe's statue formerly stood. Despite elaborate preparations, which included shipping in 200-plus sets of undergraduate caps and gowns, the Queen's College still failed. So what went wrong?

The Governor's project had had several local precursors. An 1830s plan for establishing a College of Physicians and Surgeons succeeded in getting a bill passed through the Assembly, though nothing followed. But the need was not forgotten. In 1843 the Rev James Phillippo had urged people of goodwill in England to found a university in Jamaica.[78] In the late 1840s some of the island's politicians recommended establishing a college to train students who could not afford to go to Britain for a medical or a legal education, while in

1864 a further scheme 'under which the youth of the country can be trained and qualified as medical men within the colony itself' was once again under consideration.[79] None of these projects got anywhere. When Governor Grant introduced his lavishly equipped scheme, Phillippo was 74 and on the verge of retiring.[80] Apparently the new college's bureaucratic sponsors did not take the precaution of seeking, either endorsements for the new project from Phillippo or from any of the former Assemblymen who had supported the other tertiary education schemes. With hindsight this appears a disastrous misjudgement, though typical of the Crown Colony's self-assured administrators.

Several issues contributed to the debacle. After the event taxpayers blamed the professors; at the time the institution itself was highly unpopular while, looking back on the whole affair, the College's basic failure after it opened its doors lay in its inability to recruit sufficient students to prove its local critics wrong. Here the island's secondary educational system needs to shoulder some of the blame. Even if there were many problems to surmount, the College's founding faculty hardly helped. In 1843 Phillippo had recommended a Jamaican university modelled on the Universities of London or Glasgow, he intended to recruit full-time academics rather than relying on local ministers as part-time teachers.[81] A little over a century later, in 1948, this policy proved effective when establishing the new University College of the West Indies.[82] In 1873, however, the Colonial Office's appointees reflected the assumptions of senior English bureaucrats. Rather than drawing its founding faculty from the non-denominational University of London, a pair of recent Oxford graduates were selected as the first professors. As a letter of recommendation for one of them confidently observed, the candidate would be 'perfectly competent to discharge . . . the duties of a colonial professor'.[83] This was not so certain. Even if their personal beliefs were liberal and Oxford University itself was on the verge of accommodating non-Anglicans, the founding faculty for Spanish Town's new Queen's College came to Jamaica from a solidly Anglican institution.[84] It would hardly help a college with such professors that the Church of England was no longer Jamaica's established church. A local Congregationalist minster later claimed that disestablishment provoked a 'degree of energy and vitality unknown in former days' among local Anglicans. Perhaps it did.[85] But this was hardly an optimal time for even a faculty recruited from Anglican Oxford to look to the former established church for assistance or support. Abandoning the funding for the Church of England which had long been among the largest single charges on the colony's peacetime budget had freed funds that could be employed for a new college; this would not win the college Anglican friends.

The college project was contentious well before it opened and became more so as events unfolded. In the short term the colony's general revenues underwrote it, but in the longer term Grant intended to reapply the revenues from the various endowed grammar schools scattered around the island to support his new tertiary institution.[86] Many Jamaican families could hope to benefit from the local grammar schools; few saw any need for 'the public central College' that was to replace them. Public opinion remained hostile. Hence Grant's observation that its prospective Principal 'must be a very sensible, *tacty* [tactful], pleasant, and above all, lucky man'.[87] Early in 1871, well before the St Catherine's parish bureaucrats were ousted from the old Court House or the first professors hired, the scheme was already under discussion – and already unpopular. A committee of Anglican clergy appointed to discuss establishing a theological training college in Jamaica considered taking advantage of this 'undenominational college of a superior class' that the Government was planning and therefore 'agreed that the most suitable place to locate [their] Institution will be Spanish Town, if the proposed government College should be established there'. The advantages seemed clear enough, especially as the Principal of the Anglican seminary would 'be able to exercise an influence over Church of England youths passing through the Government College, and to watch over their welfare'. Otherwise, the report continued, 'if the proposed Government College should not be established the committee are agreed that the place to locate this Institution will be . . . [in suburban] St Andrews.'[88] This statement proved controversial. Even qualified approval for the proposed Government College aroused 'strong objections' within the committee. The complaints then dominated discussions of the proposal in such an unlikely venue for venting opposition to a government-backed educational initiative as the island's Anglican diocesan synod, where it was argued that even 'if the Government should proceed with the scheme of establishing a College it is understood that the strongest objections will be urged by the public against its establishment in Spanish Town'.[89] The squalls that the proposed Anglican seminary faced once it became associated with the new college demonstrate that, whatever the possible merits of the Government's College might have been, local opposition was already widespread and deeply felt.

Three years later, after a last-stage meeting with Grant's successor in 1874 to discuss whether the College could be salvaged, a supporter of the scheme laid the blame on Grant having 'ignored . . . all the points deemed essential' by local sympathizers to push though his own vision of a college.[90] The Governor's image of a non-denominational undergraduate college had remained almost too persuasive. In India, where he had served before coming to Jamaica, undergraduate colleges founded by missionaries were well established, despite initial hostility from British governors.[91] But Jamaica's Queen's College reversed the trajectory followed by the Indian colleges: as 'the Government College' it received generous initial support from the colonial government, but then failed to institute any significant links with the various churches which continued to organize most of the island's primary and secondary education.

In the event, the Queen's College's short history was simply disappointing. The professors failed to win it a place in Jamaican society. The absence of local good will was then compounded by an absence of good local candidates. In 1872 the College advertised for students. When the first four would-be recruits arrived they were examined by the faculty, who accepted only one. Advertisements continued to run and two more students were enrolled; later a couple more boys arrived, but 'were both so ignorant' they too were turned away. The faculty kept hoping that 'a good number of fellows might have come at the New Year' or that 'if time were given to see how it turned out, people would begin sending sons by twos and threes' but all these hopes came to nothing.[92] Within a year, the 27-year-old principal died of dysentery. He was not replaced. The Vice-Principal continued teaching for another year but no new students matriculated. He and the English College steward were then shipped home, rather surprised that their employment had lasted as long as it had. If asked why no one had enrolled, the faculty blamed local snobbery, claiming that 'those who can afford to send their sons out of their islands for education would at once unhesitatingly send them to England for the *prestige* thereunto appertaining, although the education might be superior' at the lavishly equipped Queen's College.[93] Be that as it may, doing without that English steward and using the money saved for bursaries and scholarships might well have proved a more effective use of resources.

Afterwards the island's newspapers blamed the professors.[94] As outsiders, paid high salaries out of local taxes, they were easy scapegoats: the faculty upheld unrealistic matriculation standards and the College fell with them. They may well have gone too far in avoiding what the proposers of a later scheme for a West Indian university also feared, becoming 'less a centre of liberal education than a liberal source of second-rate degrees'.[95] Of course there were classes in latin translation. But the emphasis on scientific subjects at the Queen's College – its first Principal was a former Oxford University lecturer in mathematics, while the Vice-Principal occupied some of his copious leisure time as the Professor of mental and moral philosophy undertaking dissections and composing a book on *Physiological Æsthetics* – along with the new faculty's rigid insistence on accepting candidates for matriculation only after an examination, followed the best-practice recommendations of mid-nineteenth-century academic reformers.[96] Even so, the College's founding professors appear to have acted like fellows of Oxford or Cambridge colleges a generation earlier, when colleges could fulfill their academic functions by opening their doors during the University terms and offering the established courses of instruction to such young men who were competent to matriculate and prepared to stay in residence for the necessary years of instruction. As the richest country in the world mid-nineteenth century England could just about sustain such an educational anachronism. Even Oxford and Cambridge were obliged to reconsider their missions once English agricultural rents collapsed in the late 1870s, slashing colleges' incomes. The don's academic role would be transformed within a generation.[97] Meanwhile the opportunity for establishing a government-sponsored university in Jamaica slipped away. A decade later 'Lady Albion's Caribbean University' merely provided a setting for satire.[98] For another 75 years variations circulated on the arguments that the natural site for a West Indian University is 'in England' or 'that there is today no worth while university in the British Commonwealth but Oxford and Cambridge', and consequently 'no use for making any start with education here at all'. Suggestions that the islands should simply 'send the people home' to England for specialist training 'and, if possible, [send] fewer of them', were to be repeated – and, worse still, appeared plausible.[99]

The new Queen's College taught interesting subjects and the three students who studied there all did well. After its failure a further five generations of young West Indians would be cut off from local access to university educations. Sixty years later, in 1927, when plans to establish a West Indian university were raised again (only to be deferred by colonial administrators because of the expense), the planners recognized the practical costs of not having a regional university: when even the best of their young men and women can carry their education beyond the secondary stage only at the prohibitive price of a protracted and costly exile in a strange and frequently a foreign country. It would be hard to exaggerate the effects of such a disability. It amounts to an embargo on knowledge, a lowering of the general standard of efficiency and a bar upon the advancement of their collective statement on the world.[100]

Yet despite its embarrassing initial enrollment, the Queen's College still outlasted its first Principal's death and Governor Grant's departure. The colonial bureaucracy's support for the scheme was striking. If backing from the administration alone could have saved it, the College would have survived. But even with a second year's grace to turn things around no new students were recruited and the remaining professor failed to justify his retention.

Blaming faculty inflexibility is always easy – and may often be justified. But the failure of the Queen's College indicated deeper problems too. In 1872 the college was 30 years late. Its prospective pupils were the children of those pupils whose skills Phillippo had praised before Emancipation. The author of another pre-Emancipation appeal for funds expressed the fear 'that unless some system be organized and vigorously and promptly pursued, the effect of Educational exertion will soon disappear' and 'while the present generation may partially walk in its light posterity will lapse into gloom'.[101] That depressing prophecy appears all too accurate.

Providing splendid facilities and able faculty was not enough. The new Queen's College needed students too. The blunt axe of government 'retrenchment' wielded during the 1850s and early 1860s had sliced deeply into primary and secondary teaching across Jamaica.[102] During the 1850s even the Baptists' school in Spanish Town closed down for a period. When it reopened in 1859, 'amidst demonstrations of joy throughout the town', it still enrolled only 95 children. The town's endowed grammar school had remained open, but its poorly paid instructors taught shrunken classes while most of its revenue was creamed off for 'superintendence' by an absentee headmaster.[103] Such experiences extended islandwide. By 1864 there were about one quarter fewer children enrolled in Jamaica's schools than in 1837. *Even* Governor Eyre, who otherwise remained convinced of the Jamaican peasantry's general prosperity despite all evidence to the contrary, noted that the qualifications of the island's schoolteachers were 'very insufficient and unsatisfactory' and their 'salaries and emoluments' were 'for the most part too small to secure the service of efficient persons'.[104] The surviving professor had a point when he claimed 'years after' that the new Queen's College initially 'should have been run as a Board School'.[105]

The Crown Colony administration had already begun to address the problem. In 1867 the islandwide inspections of primary and secondary schools produced dismal results in the first year's assessment: of the nearly 300 schools evaluated, one was placed in the first rank, six in the second and another 89 in the third. The rest, nearly two-thirds of the total, failed. The local observer who recorded these totals rightly noted the improvements the following year when the number in the first and second classes doubled, but in the early 1870s Jamaica's schools were only improving when compared to a very poor initial benchmark. Even when schools achieved the new acceptable standards the government's grants remained miserably low: £54 and some shillings for a first rank school, £34 for the second and £24 for the third.[106] As a result, there was a great deal of recitation and rote learning. Argument and composition, be they in English or Latin, were far less prominent.[107] With such impoverished secondary schools, any attempt to transplant a college from Oxford to Spanish Town would face difficulties in finding prospective students who could pass its matriculation exam.

The more immediate problem, though, was that after 30 years many of the roles that a new university might take on to fill its classrooms were now provided elsewhere. In 1843 Phillippo had recommended that a new college should offer an educational foundation for would-be teachers and ministers. Governor Grant, too, expected that 'the bulk of the scholars will be young Browns and Blacks in training for the ministry of all denominations'.[108] By 1872 the new Queen's College which offered no theological training had no obvious niche, especially when the Anglicans, the only major denomination without a seminary on the island, remained cool about the scheme. Several churches had run their own teacher training for over 30 years, while most denominations had local training programmes for would-be ministers. By the 1870s Spanish Town already housed a private 'College or Normal School' for schoolmasters, where some of the leading African Jamaican intellectuals of the next generation studied. It would continue to train teachers for another decade.[109] In Kingston, the Mico College offered would-be teachers a locally respected training and a new Government Training School opened by Grant at the old Stony Hill Barracks, had already enrolled a further 20 students.[110]

Despite the very real problems endured by the island's secondary schools there were academically qualified candidates but they were enrolling elsewhere. The new professors' signal lack of success in winning recruits from among these groups doomed the college.

The Queen's College never set down local roots. Always viewed as 'the English Government's experimental college for the colony', it failed.[111] The list of ifs, buts and might-have-beens can be extended – an early decision to postpone establishing the college's legal and medical departments until later probably reduced whatever initial appeal the scheme might have found[112] – but a decisive issue that outweighed most of the others was that the local 'town' never came to the rescue of the transplanted 'gowns'. Spanish Town would not enjoy the future that Governor Grant had envisioned for it as Jamaica's college town. Instead, with the continued islandwide role of both the Mico men's teachers college and, from 1885, of the Shortwood women's teachers college, this function migrated to Kingston.[113]

Subsequent efforts to establish a university in the West Indies – proposed in the early 1920s, elaborated but then failing in 1927, reasserted in the political platform of Marcus Garvey's People's Party in 1929 and finally succeeding in the late 1940s – would all demonstrate that the Queen's College in Spanish Town had offered an irreplaceable opportunity.[114] Informed by hindsight, the townspeople's hostility seems an exercise in cutting off one's nose to spite one's face. Contemporaries did not view the matter in such terms. The new 'Experimental College' simply appeared an unasked for and unnecessary luxury. The Governor's high-handed decision to reuse the public buildings in Spanish Town made an unwanted college even more unpopular.

'A small work' to be 'easily, cheaply and profitably applied to the Rio Cobre'

Jamaica's taxpayers remained unhappy because while the new college did close, another of Grant's initiatives remained as an ever-growing drain on public funds. The Rio Cobre Irrigation Canal loomed large on contemporary horizons. There was anger enough over the expenditure of £6,000 on the Queen's College; in the canal's first four years it managed to run through 20 times as much public money. It would only be in the long term that the ambitious scheme helped to reshape the economy of St Catherine.

Floods continue to burst the Rio Cobre's banks, but the river generally remains a trickle at the bottom of its bed because three miles upstream from Spanish Town most of its water is retained by a dam where it is channelled into irrigation. Earlier it was far less tame and proposals for running canals across the St Catherine plain had elaborate precursors. In the 1790s, during England's canal age, the flat land around Spanish Town prompted suggestions for cutting a canal there, though those schemes also hoped to justify their expense by offering sugar planters cheap water transport down to Kingston Harbour along with water for irrigation.[115] Although the canal idea was hardly new, the fact that such an ambitious project could be undertaken in 1872 exemplified the opportunities for Crown Colony governors to institute major policies without so much consideration of the costs.

Governor Grant introduced the Rio Cobre Irrigation Canal as another personal initiative that harked back to his Indian experience. In a dispatch to the British Secretary of State for the Colonies in 1870, Grant claimed that 'the Rio Cobre, where it leaves its rocky bed in the hills, may be well described as an extremely minute miniature of the Ganges at Roarkee; and in such a venue the Spanish Town plain may well represent the Doab on the same scale' concluding 'that a small work upon the Indian principle could be easily, cheaply, and profitably applied to the Rio Cobre.'[116] Here too the first stage of Crown Colony rule offered an imperial solution to a Jamaican problem. A hydraulic engineer with experience in India was recruited to investigate the possibilities. Estimates for the cost of the project were then compiled while Grant was off the island, urging his scheme to English audiences.[117] In 1872 the Legislative Council authorized an issue of £60,000 in bonds (which, for comparison, was only twice the £30,000 issue authorized the next month to fund a new gas works in Kingston).[118] The initial proposal expected to generate sufficient revenue from sales of irrigation water to cover debt repayments and salaries. By 1876 the first canal was providing irrigation water while, over the next 50 years further canals fanned out across the St Catherine Plain and, by the 1920s, over towards the headwaters of the Ferry River too.[119]

The project still did not prove a good advertisement for Crown Colony government. The initial budget of £60,000 was massively overspent. It hardly helped that the original estimates omitted salaries and labour costs. By the time the first water flowed these added a further £32,581.[120] Floods destroyed some half-built sections of the works, which not only generated further reconstruction costs but once they were rebuilt to revised designs, added even higher bills. As a result, when a shorter stretch of canal than initially proposed finally came into service, the cost had doubled to £120,000. Its customers remained 'three sugar estates and a few pens'.[121] Income then fell well below the original projections. Rather than a reliable revenue stream paying off the government-guaranteed bonds, all the overruns had to be carried on the colony's general revenues. Little wonder that a local plantation owner described the whole project as 'this primarily ill-managed Government failure' battening onto 'the taxation of this uselessly burdened Island'.[122] The verdict summarized public opinion. Consequently, as a Jamaican member of the Governor's Legislative Council observed, 'the real matter of regret is, that the great cost of these Works, beyond what they were expected to cost, has thrown a damper on to public projects, and prevented the Government from undertaking other works of progress for the good of the Island'.[123] These two flawed projects cast long shadows.

New roles for an old town

So how had the town's roles changed over a decade? The St Catherine Parochial Board dealt with a town that was developing in the gaps left by the departure of the island's government and its social season. Instead of tackling the genteel decay that antiquarian hindsight emphasized, the Board focused on refurbishing market facilities across the parish, including those in Spanish Town.[124] Several requests to the Board suggest that considerable building activity was occurring in some quarters of the old capital. Thus the proprietor of a public house petitioned to throw 'a wooden bridge across Hanover Street' to link his tavern with a new building on the other side of the road.[125] The Board allowed it. There were enough thirsty labourers to support not only thriving rum shops, but to justify building a bridge between two of them.

The town's changed social functions and economy encouraged new foci. In identifying such centres a list of the establishments owned by one Spanish Town shopkeeper in 1878 is suggestive; these included his Tamarind Tree Shop, Monk Street Bazaar, Yellow Shop, Burke Road Shop and Cumberland Road Shop.[126] The Yellow Shop could be anywhere, while others like the shop on Burke Road, which looped south of the town and past the Railway Station, was already an established retail site. The Tamarind Tree area had housed Duggan's Native Baptist chapel in the 1840s. Other sites, though, like the predominantly residential Monk Street and the suburban Cumberland Road were less familiar retailing areas. In practice, the shoppers who frequented

FIGURE 7:3   A late nineteenth-century retail shop on Old Market Street, (author's photograph)

these venues were moving away from the old-established retail area west of the King's House Square. Visitors might well see more shops in this town, even if they appeared 'half-closed'.

Reuse of some vacant lots by local residents continued to change the face of the town. One unintended consequence of the falling price of building land in Spanish Town was that the town's Roman Catholic community could purchase a sizable lot on King Street. The plot the congregation obtained had formerly housed the establishment of the architectural carpenter and cabinet maker who had supplied the woodwork for the chancel when the Anglican Cathedral was rebuilt in the 1840s.[127] The town's Catholic congregation formerly worshipped in a 'house which serves as chapel' and while that property had included sufficient space to 'build a chapel', in 1864 the option still seemed unlikely as 'that could be done only in the case of a considerable increase in the number of Catholics'.[128] In 1872, with reduced land prices, the parishioners purchased a new site to erect a church, St Joseph's, along with a rectory and school. This brick church was not so lavish as either the Anglican Cathedral's rebuildings in the 1840s or the earlier 'dissenting' chapels of the 1820s and '30s, but it was a substantial building in its own right. The bulk of the money, £600, could be raised locally, so the number of worshippers may have risen.[129] Other lots remained vacant, though now these were fenced off behind wooden hoardings.[130]

Angry petitions to the Parochial Board show that the town's transformation left many householders unhappy. What processes did the complaints describe? Two petitions claimed that the houses at the southern end of White Church Street used to be in a respectable residential area. Now it was in decline. One petitioner claimed that the old Alms House was filled with time-expired Indian indentured labourers awaiting their voyage home, their 'disturbance of the neighbourhood night and day by their heathenish practice of yelling and drumming upon boxes and pans' not only scandalized the neighbours, but chased away their best tenants.[131] The number of homeward-bound Indian labourers crammed into the old barracks may have peaked in the early 1870s, just before the Jamaican government began offering cash bounties or land in lieu of a return passage; but given the practical difficulties in marshalling sufficient would-be returnees from Jamaica to justify hiring a ship back to India, their predecessors had waited there and no doubt some had danced and sung at the prospect of departing for home.[132] What drove this neighbourhood into 'disrepute' was a city-wide reduction in the demand for 'respectable' lodgings. Even if the petition had persuaded the Parish Board to act, placing the Indian labourers housed at the Alms House under more 'control,' would not have resolved the neighbourhood's plight. With the departure of so many of Spanish Town's government offices there was 'now little probability' of the petitioning landlady finding further good lodgers, even if 'the nuisance complained' of was 'removed'.[133] Yet what was novel here was not the decline in local property values, but the speed with which they fell.

Among disgruntled householders the single cause of Governor Grant's decision to shift the capital to Kingston was 'to gratify the mere whim and caprice, . . . of the "one man" rule of this island of Jamaica!' and this provided a straightforward explanation for their current plight.[134] In such terms, all of Spanish Town's problems appeared easily resolvable: just move everything back to their old settings. Well into the 1890s some local politicians continued banging the same drum, hoping 'that the day is not far distant when the united voice of the whole people in it, will demand its restoration to its former position'.[135] Such slogans appealed to householders facing rapid social change, but avoided the fact that Spanish Town was in decline well before the officials departed for Kingston. Only very selective hindsight could ignore the preceding 20 years of stagnation. Anthony Trollope may have been lost, hot, thirsty and increasingly annoyed while he wandered Spanish Town's streets in

1859, and so managed to miss the town's remaining shops, but he was underwhelmed by everything else he saw there during his visit. The 1850s, when cholera and smallpox epidemics were followed by the Assembly's stop on paying official wages, proved harsh for Spanish Town. The thoroughly miserable statistics for poverty and under-employment collected by the Baptist ministers in 1865 showed that its economy faced major problems.

The progressive abandonment of the town's synagogues demonstrates these broader changes. By the mid-nineteenth century, Spanish Town's Jewish population was already falling well below its late eighteenth-century highs. Alternating services between the town's Ashkenazi and Sephardic synagogues managed to keep them both open, but maintenance suffered as numbers shrank. At the end of Queen Victoria's reign only the Sephardic synagogue on Monk Street remained in use. It proved sufficiently solid to hold a service of thanksgiving for deliverance after the 1907 earthquake racked Kingston, but it had sustained some damage and without sufficient resources to undertake the necessary repairs, it closed. Some of its furniture was salvaged and reused in the United Congregation of the Israelites' synagogue erected in Kingston that replaced the Ashkenazi and Sephardic synagogues destroyed in the same earthquake.[136] Henceforth Jews living in St Catherine went to worship in Kingston's rebuilt synagogue. In such terms, the Crown Colony removal fitted into a longer trajectory of economic decline for mid- and late nineteenth-century Spanish Town.

Even if the new Governor did not cause all of Spanish Town's problems, the colonial government's actions clearly had an immediate impact on the town. The Crown Colony's administrators then failed to change things nearly as much as they had planned and so could not transform the old capital into a college town set in the midst of well-irrigated sugar fields. Their remedies did not work and the basic problems remained. The government's misjudgements in and around Spanish Town had proved very costly. Townspeople saw the negative consequences of the new regime. In 1883, when Dr James Phillippo, the Baptist missionary's physician son, drafted a pamphlet to urge the extension of both the franchise and of the role of elected representatives in the Government of Jamaica, he wrote and published in Kingston, but the two examples he cited as exemplifying the misconceived enterprises under Crown Colony rule were both from Spanish Town: the Queen's College and the Rio Cobre Irrigation Scheme. At best, these appeared 'ahead of their time' – and, implicitly, at worst a phenomenal waste of resources.[137]

The conspicuous mishandling of the administration's attempts to revive Spanish Town thus served to taint the whole notion of governor-driven social engineering that justified Crown Colony government. During the late 1860s Crown Colony administration was rapidly extended across the remaining self-governing islands of the British West Indies.[138] But by 1876, when recommendations reached the then Secretary of State for the Colonies to continue the trend by abolishing the Barbados Assembly to institute Crown Colony rule there too, he rejected the proposal. The unreformed West Indian assemblies may well have mishandled their affairs but, as the repeated complaints from Jamaica about the various official projects in and around Spanish Town demonstrated, Crown Colony schemes could also be spectacularly unsuccessful and mismanaged.[139] Crown Colony rule transformed Spanish Town, but the very public failures in and around Spanish Town then changed official views of Crown Colony administration.

Spanish Town still bears the imprint of this period. Contractors for the canal and railway extension projects on the edge of the town purchased the rubble of demolished splendid mansions that had earlier graced the town's streets when it was the seat of government, with the broken bricks going straight into the foundations. Otherwise it was not until 1879, when the town's water works began drawing their supply from the Rio Cobre Irrigation Canal and finally provided householders a constant flow of water, that this engineering project began to find much local appeal. By the 1890s 10,000 acres were being irrigated rather than the meagre 2,700 that initially benefited. Over the following decades Spanish Town and Lower St Catherine finally reaped a harvest from the irrigation works.[140] Meanwhile, the ambitious policy goals that characterized the initial Crown Colony government were abandoned. Later, as a further generation of Jamaican politicians pushed against the dead weight of a colonial bureaucracy that vetoed one public investment scheme after another, the image of Sir John Peter Grant's Crown Colony government as a development-oriented administration became far more attractive. Once the canal began to contribute profits to the public revenues, the acreage benefiting increased and the cost overruns were finally forgotten, another generation came to reappraise the value of official initiatives to encourage economic development. Under the highly risk-averse governments of the early and mid-twentieth century, the Rio Cobre Irrigation could be re-presented to a later generation of Jamaicans as exemplifying the positive achievements of Crown Colony rule.[141]

CHAPTER EIGHT

'Let that be your picture of heaven!'

Economic and social change in Spanish Town, c. 1880–1944

$\mathcal{B}$Y 1880 MUCH of the business of government was long gone, but Spanish Town remained far more than the mere 'inland country town' that the departing lawyers and administrators had expected to leave behind them. How would the town's economy adapt to further economic shifts and how would its earlier cityscape shape the society that developed over this period?[1] The townspeople retained some solid assets and the late Victorian town enjoyed a mild revival of its fortunes. The Rio Cobre Canal was in operation and with railways a central tool in promoting investment, the town retained the railway junction and station it had secured as the island's capital. Several plans for encouraging development in Jamaica promised benefits for Spanish Town and its hinterland – and some delivered – though many of these projects combined high initial ambitions with low follow-through. The area was well positioned to benefit from two of the new crops of the late nineteenth century – bananas and tourists – where international markets depended on the availability of reliable transport links. The economic balance established in the 1890s would continue to underpin the local economy into the late 1920s and early '30s, while the tourist itinerary established in the 1890s framed visitors' and official expectations of the old capital for the next century.

FIGURE 8:1   A late nineteenth-century or early twentieth-century 'Chattel House' on Hanover Street. These are not the houses of the elite, or even intended for leasing to the elite. (author's photograph)

Architecturally Spanish Town retains a firm imprint from the revival of prosperity in the late nineteenth and early twentieth century. With a population of over 7,000 in 1913 and lying at 'the centre of a banana and sugar parish' the town housed 'many who are employed on the plantations and estates' who either lived there or kept their families there.[2] Between the 1880s and the 1920s residents built the solidly constructed small houses that still line the town's older streets. The sizeable number of substantial working class houses erected in Spanish Town does suggest that some banana-era prosperity trickled down. The local carpenters who built these houses used imported lumber and employed fairly standard plans, but the ingenuity of the fretwork designs carved over the doors and verandas testify to the pride they took in their work.[3] Spanish Town's 'white-painted, green-shuttered villas in charming gardens and bright clean streets' also demonstrated the local impact of developments in Jamaica's economy.[4]

The social mix of residents included a handful of professionals who continued to live in the town, occupying larger houses on its eastern side. These included the canons at the Anglican Cathedral, the Resident Magistrate, doctors and schoolteachers, along with a few lawyers and bank managers.[5] In one instance, a gap on the town's prime residential White Church Street left by the demolitions after the government's move to Kingston was filled with a substantial upper-middle-class house of the sort that lined the 'best' streets in Jamaica's other late Victorian towns.[6] In contrast to its early and mid-nineteenth century brick neighbours, this house was constructed of imported timber. Passing Englishmen might dismiss Spanish Town's older streets of shops in the eighteenth-century grid behind the King's House, as 'a labyrinth of narrow streets, the most thriving institutions in which were grog shops and one or two stores,' but locals would recognize the fresh construction in the town's residential areas.[7]

The people who lived along these streets maintained resilient social networks. Some institutions, like the late eighteenth-century Freemasons' Lodge, remained as legacies from earlier prosperity. The town's cricket club dated back to at least the early 1870s.[8] Many more of the clubs and societies, the voluntary associations, church groups and benefit clubs that provided the warp and woof of working class socializing in late Victorian and interwar Britain and its other British colonies, were late nineteenth-century foundations. When a 'District' of the Ancient Order of Free Foresters was established in Jamaica in 1900, regularising a British benefit and benevolence society first introduced to the island in 1863, two of the society's 12 'Courts' were operating in Spanish Town. Similarly the Manchester Unity of the Independent Order of Odd Fellows, which reached Kingston in 1885, soon had two lodges in Spanish Town, one of which was among the first lodges established outside the island's capital, while the Grand United Order of Odd Fellows of England and America had one more. The list then continued with lodges of the Independent Order of Good Samaritans and Daughters of Samaria – a combined temperance and benevolence group whose 'Grand Chief' lived in Spanish Town in 1902. At the turn of the century several of the executive officers of another group, the Independent Order of Good Templars, were also from Spanish Town.[9] The social impulse continued in the years up to the First World War, with the establishment of further lodges of the Loyal Order of Ancient Shepherds (Aston Unity), the Independent United Order of English Mechanics and the Ancient and Illustrious Order of the Star of Bethlehem.[10] Of course the fortunes of individual societies ebbed and flowed with the membership and enthusiasm of their committees. The First World War then hit all clubs hard. By 1918 even cricket, so central to the rituals of British colonial socializing, in the shape of 'the veteran St Catherine

C[ricket] C[lub] had, under stress of war conditions, ceased to exist' while the town's other team, 'the St Catherine District Prison CC existed only in theory'. In this instance a vigorous 'Skipper' and committee could manage a successful amalgamation of the two clubs.[11] Other groups died out.

If anything, this long list of local branches of British social organizations active in pre-First World War Spanish Town overshadows the parallel, if unregistered, network of societies and mutual benefit clubs that operated within African Jamaican communities.[12] The most successful of these was probably the Jamaican Burial Scheme Society, founded in 1901 by Andrew Duffus Mowatt, then an employee at the West Indies Chemical Works in Spanish Town, which expanded across the island. By 1930 it had 124 branches.[13] But this society was hardly alone. In the mid-1920s the town housed a chapel of the Hamitic Church, an Afrocentric group originating in Kimberly, South Africa. They had their own sacred scripture and police detectives who attended a meeting found themselves singing hymns.[14] In such terms, an attempted dismissal of the old capital by an American visitor in 1912: claiming that 'Spanish Town . . . is very decidedly "Black Town" now,' recognized a significant social reality.[15]

The long-established influence of organized black groups in Spanish Town meant that 14 years later a parade of two lodges of an African Jamaican Benefit Society through the town centre was not particularly remarkable. Whatever the occasion, in late August 1929 the members of the town's 'Refugee Visiting Cottage Band' and 'Blue Ribbon Lodge' formed 'a long procession of men and women, . . . some of the women dressed as revellers, others bearing banners, and the men all rigged out in their best, with insignia of their Orders round their necks, like Masons'. They appeared a thoroughly respectable group. A police constable watched from a corner, but the marchers hardly merited his notice. The calm was only disturbed when a car coming through the town enroute from Kingston to Linstead endeavoured to pass the procession. The driver began passing alongside the procession, hooting all the while. Although the car's European passengers persuaded themselves that they were 'not troubling them at all', this opinion was not shared in the procession. According to a passenger, 'a man at the head evidently their leader and I suppose a sort of Grand Master – stepped out in front of the car with another man, and tried to bar our way with drawn swords which they brandished furiously, at the same time telling us to stop.' The driver did pause for a moment but, like motorists the world over when waiting for pedestrians, 'thinking we had as good a right to the street as they had, tried to go on'. He was halted again. The ceremonial swords were flourished a second time and a sword-bearing lodge member stayed by the car. The constable refused to be drawn into the argument (though he did note the names of the lodges' leaders) and the procession proceeded on its way. The car's passengers remained convinced of their own virtue.[16] What the incident reveals is that African Jamaican lodges, with their male and female membership along with their ceremonial swords and well-established hierarchies, were an established social fixture. They may have delayed traffic when they paraded on an August Saturday, but they met year-round.

This was a town with established social networks. The Lodges' leaders were sufficiently confident to step out of their line of march twice to halt an annoying vehicle, while a local police constable felt no obligation to intervene. Processions were customary and motorists were expected to wait their turn. What else was going on? These local lodge members marched through streets which successive early twentieth-century descriptions characterize as slow-paced, 'a silent funeral kind of place'.[17] This image remained in striking contrast with the tendency for recollections of turn-of-the-twentieth-century Kingston to emphasize the tramcar network that traversed the city.[18] A post card of 'a road in Spanish Town' in 1904 showed a quiet unsurfaced street lined with palm trees as a characteristic image.[19] Twenty years later a travel writer recalled it as looking 'more like a country village in England, or an old colonial town in New England . . . [with] grass-lined streets and lanes, neat gardens and a quiet sleepy air'.[20] Much effort went into maintaining this decorous pace as one young resident discovered. The young Norman Washington Manley, a future Premier of Jamaica, then a weekly boarder at Spanish Town's Beckford and Smith's School, had his first brush with the Jamaica Constabulary when they stopped him for galloping his horse through the town.[21] Later, the island's Legislative Council raised speed limits islandwide in 1917, allowing motorists to roar through towns at up to eight miles per hour, but Spanish Town believed this too fast. A Council member replied to a local correspondent who had lobbied for a six mph limit to assure him 'it is almost a walk' and agreeing that 'the furious driving through towns should be stopped'.[22] Residents' understandings of their town combined traversing its ancient streets at an old-fashioned rural pace with a readiness to take advantage of the practical benefits that new development could bring.

Promoting new schemes after reaping a harvest from earlier investments in infrastructure

Late nineteenth-century Spanish Town benefited when several of the early Crown Colony government's schemes from the 1870s began to bear fruit in the 1880s. These included expanding the railway across the southern plains along with the increased export crops that the Rio Cobre Irrigation scheme supported. Initially neither investment had paid off. A further round of ambitious public works begun in the 1880s and '90s under the second generation of Crown Colony government and demonstrated how far government participation continued to shape commercial opportunities across the island, with people in Spanish Town and its hinterland benefiting once again from these major public works. However, what had changed from Jamaica's pre-Crown Colony past was that leading townspeople were no longer active in the lobbying; now Spanish Town – like the rest of the island – received decisions made in Kingston or London. But as leading townspeople would also recognize, in a further contrast with the initial Crown Colony years of government projects and proposals, by the late 1880s and '90s Governors took few risks and promoted fewer initiatives. Persuading the colonial bureaucracy to act and undertake further development projects required sustained effort at the colonial level.

Spanish Town remained a railway town. Across the West Indies hopes for economic success remained tied to railways. In 1867 a consortium's ambitious plan had proposed making Spanish Town the starting point for a railway line extending 'round and through the island touching at the principal harbours and other Towns'. The project's organizer met Governor Grant and the Legislative Council and even drafted legislation to give extensive powers to a new railway company, but the scheme went no further.[23] Instead, official backing during the early Crown Colony years permitted the existing Jamaica Railway Company to undertake the first successful extension of its network since the 1840s. A government guarantee in 1867 helped the company to sell the bonds to build a new line west from Spanish Town to Old Harbour.[24] When it was opened two years later this ten mile extension finally made Spanish Town a railway junction. The new route was not a particularly successful investment. In 1873 the island's Postmaster offered a negative verdict, ending a contract for transporting mail to and from Old Harbour

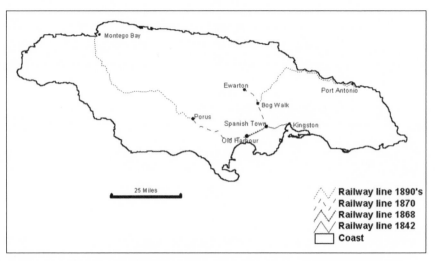

FIGURE 8:2   The railway, extensions in 1869 to Old Harbour; in the 1880s to Porus and Ewarton and in the 1890s through the mountains to Montego Bay and Port Antonio.

because mounted couriers were more reliable.[25] In 1879 the then Governor pushed through a bill that not only funded 200 miles of telegraph lines, but 'bought the railway for £90,000 with the view to restoring it and extending it' in a generally popular official initiative.[26] Between 1881 and 1885 further extensions north-west to Porus and north to the mouth of the Rio Cobre Gorge at Ewarton stretched the Jamaica Government Railway to 64 miles of track and effectively restored Spanish Town's older role as a crossroads for the south side of the island.[27]

Despite some public works projects, by the 1890s administrative inertia seemed to stifle Jamaica's economic development, effectively abandoning the original rationale for a top-down Crown Colony government. Jamaican merchants, accustomed to speculate in order to accumulate, complained that the Colonial Service's career bureaucrats lacked vision and shunned risk. Because the government payroll was the first charge on a colony's revenues these gentlemen would be paid regardless of the results, so had no incentive to foster development.[28] The colonial government, encouraged by increased revenues from the existing railway line and spurred on by such complaints, pledged Jamaica's credit on an ambitious scheme to reshape the island's infrastructure.[29] The project got some substantial public works completed, but only at the cost of doubling the island's accumulated debt. After the event the risks would appear all too obvious.

The Jamaican merchants' campaign to expand the island's railway network was prompted because Governor Grant's hunch that new crops offered a way out of the island's economic doldrums was finally proved correct. By the late 1880s the Rio Cobre Canal's irrigation channels increasingly watered a profitable export crop: bananas. Up until then the fruit was unfamiliar to northern palates. As a result in 1874 a disappointed English visitor briskly dismissed bananas as unpalatable exotics, combining 'the taste of butter, tallow-candles, and sleepy-pears'.[30] The island's planters and bureaucrats had not foreseen the subsequent development of bananas as an export. Government attempts to jump-start Jamaica's moribund agricultural economy had tried to establish new tropical crops, but not this one.[31] The island's large planters initially ignored the trade, dismissing it as a 'backwoods nigger business'.[32] Nevertheless, by the late-1880s bananas underpinned Jamaica's economic hopes.

In the 1880s and '90s the *gros michel* banana became known by peasant smallholders on the north side of the island as 'goyark' bananas, patois for an export fruit to 'go to New York'.[33] In 1870 several stems of green bananas provided deck cargo that one Captain Lorenzo Dow Baker, the owner of a Cape Cod schooner, picked up in Kingston. They weathered the voyage back to Boston and proved eminently saleable. Banana cultivation then drew on the skills of Jamaican peasant farmers who, in the aftermath of the American Civil War, found a new export outlet when Yankee sailing captains resumed trading in the Caribbean. Northbound ships took aboard stems of bananas, particularly the thick-skinned *gros michel* bananas established in Jamaica 40 years before and, by the late 1860s, a staple of peasant plots. The subsequent development of distribution networks for Caribbean bananas in the United States and later in Britain, particularly by Captain Baker and his 'Boston' then 'United' Fruit Company, was parallelled by the Company's development of supply networks first within Jamaica and then, after a merger in 1899 with a rival trading between Costa Rica and New Orleans, stretching across the wider Caribbean basin, to produce both a major new consumer demand in northern climates and a cash crop for Jamaican farmers.[34]

The banana boom was a remarkable commercial achievement in its own right and for two generations Jamaica remained at its hub. As one child of the 1890s recalled 60 years later: 'the United Fruit Company made Jamaica the biggest farm in the world'.[35] The practical expertise of Jamaican foremen remained essential in the establishment and cultivation of the Company's

Central American banana fields into the 1930s, while the Company's own sway in Jamaica was never complete.[36] In St Catherine, bananas watered by the Rio Cobre Irrigation Canal grew particularly well, so that the United Fruit Company paid St Catherine growers a three penny premium for their produce, besides purchasing the Twickenham Park estate, a former sugar plantation just across the Rio Cobre from Spanish Town, to lay out banana fields. All this fruit was shipped out via Port Henderson which, belatedly fulfilling the plans of the 1840's railway promoters, became the hub for a network of single line freight rails that transported bananas to the Company's wharf.[37] Profits from banana growing then encouraged further agricultural experiments and innovations. A former farm worker looked back to recall how his employer, a cattle rearer, 'first brought Cow peas in[to] St Catherine' as a subsidiary element of banana cultivation. Around 1897 he 'decided to try out Banana planting and secured a site on his property. Then he imported cow peas [and] planted it through the field to use as fertiliser'. As legumes, the new crop would help fix nitrogen in the soil. But there was an added benefit: 'the labourers found . . . that' cow peas were 'good to eat and used it as food, and thus it was established as food'.[38] The prospect of a profitable export crop encouraged agricultural investment and employment. Bananas paid for much of Spanish Town's revived prosperity.

The political and commercial repercussions of the spread of banana growing across the island then spread wider still. Kingston's merchants were tempted by proposals to improve contacts between Kingston and the main banana growing areas in the parishes of St Mary's and Portland on the island's north side. The new crop was already well established and increasing demand in North America and Europe continued to outpace supply. In these contexts colonial enthusiasm for extending the Jamaica Railway Company's tracks across the mountains could overwhelm the built-in caution of the Governor and the official members on the Legislative Council. In 1887 requests from newly elected members of the Legislative Council led to a survey to see whether the government railway could be extended from Bog Walk across the central mountain chain to Port Antonio on the northern coastal plain and from the current Porus terminus north-west to Montego Bay.[39] Both routes retained Spanish Town as the network's principal junction. The completion of these surveys was followed by an official Commission of Enquiry, which reached the eminently safe conclusion that the income from the new lines was unlikely to cover their massive construction costs. As a result, although the schemes appeared technically feasible, the Commission still recommended that nothing should be done.[40]

Jamaican enthusiasts for development were not persuaded by this bureaucratic naysaying and the colony's merchants threw their weight and London contacts behind further constitutional change. Their support was important because although the West India Department of the Colonial Office in London remained highly suspicious of any local initiatives to restore the influence of the sugar interest in island affairs – seeing it as a recipe for a return of 'the reign of jobbery, corruption and mismanagement' – the Colonial Office received petitions supported by the local trading interest with far more sympathy.[41] Elections for seats on the Legislative Council at this time ran on the issue of developing the railway link. After a pro-development slate won a majority a complicated series of constitutional and financial negotiations ensued, in which the Governor's veto was overridden and the colony sought funding for the extension on the New York Stock Exchange.

This preliminary stage of the pro-development campaign appeared an exemplary constitutional manoeuver to push at the political constraints of Crown Colony rule.[42] Given the continuing 'distrust of Government enterprise in development policy' after the Rio Cobre Canal *debacle*, selling the railway company to a North American consortium appeared 'less speculative' than the Colonial government's taking on a large loan to build the extensions itself.[43] The scheme would still prove a very expensive deal for the whole island. In 1889 the government sold its well-maintained and profitable railway to a New York syndicate which paid with secondary bonds secured on the railway. The bonds would receive a four per cent dividend *if* there was sufficient income after paying the primary bondholders. The newly founded West India Improvement Company then built the new lines across the island, receiving not only a fairly generous reimbursement of their costs but also one square mile of Crown Land for every mile of track laid. With the cash paid over by the Jamaican government, a first payment could be made to all bondholders. The company then raised further capital by issuing further primary bonds. These new bondholders all had priority over the secondary bonds that the colony held.[44] In the short term, solid achievements silenced fiscal qualms. One line reached Montego Bay in 1894; the second arrived at Port Antonio in 1896.

Building the new railway lines was an engineering feat. The route from Port Antonio involved 26 'tubes' or tunnels. Once completed Port Antonio became a three and a half hour ride from Spanish Town and a four hour trip from Kingston.[45] Passengers awed by these achievements would not register that the new tracks' gradients were often very steep and the routes included some very tight curves. In practice these serpentine lines pushed at the extremes that trains could negotiate. Such abrupt slopes and bends not only imposed unusually heavy wear on track and rolling stock, they also meant that individual locomotives could not pull much freight. The limitation meant that rather than tagging extra wagons on to regular services on days when banana boats were due, the railway had to schedule additional freight runs.[46] This was not only a logistical nightmare but such inefficiencies quickly ate into very limited profits. Unfortunately, the cautious – but ignored – preliminary estimates for incomes of the new lines' incomes remained far nearer to the mark than the more upbeat projections offered by the new syndicate and its local boosters.

Whatever anyone's calculations had promised, in 1898 the West India Improvement Company defaulted on its bond payments, with dire financial repercussions for the rest of the colony. Jamaica's Colonial Bank, a major source of credit for local enterprises, nearly collapsed too. Meanwhile several influential colonists had invested in railway bonds and not sold out in time. Rather than letting the company go bankrupt and then repurchasing the railway line afterwards, the Colonial government bought out all the other bondholders – and at face value too. The bondholders had purchased risky commercial paper. It was replaced with gilt-edged official bonds. Such fiscal rectitude proved highly expensive. In 1900 after a further round of constitutional and financial negotiations a loan of £88,000 from the British government enabled the colony to repurchase the Jamaica Railway Company, with a commitment to repay the other bondholders with three and a half per cent Jamaica Government bonds. The colony finally paid three and three quarter per cent for its loan, besides meeting the interest payments on the bonds.[47] It also needed to buy back the former Crown Lands assigned to the company and purchase rolling stock.

The result of all the legal appeals and constitutional wheeling and dealing was that Jamaica obtained 118¾ miles of new railway lines that linked Spanish Town and Kingston with the major ports on the island's north shore, albeit with lines that British engineers muttered were 'only' built to United States standards. Furthermore the London financiers whom the colony brought in to examine the books claimed that the original loan could have been floated more cheaply on the London market.[48] Meanwhile the colony's debt doubled after rescuing the railway. In 1900 the yearly charge for repaying the railway debt absorbed almost a sixth of the colony's total income.[49] Even aside from all the additional interest payments, maintaining the re-purchased Government Railway proved expensive. The tracks were three times longer and upkeep on the new routes cost far more per mile, so rather than the island's railway contributing an annual surplus into the Treasury as it had before its sale, the expanded system required annual subventions.

The scheme's supporters always recognized that any calculations of the project's costs and benefits should extend well beyond the railway's own balance sheet and promote further investments across Jamaica.[50] Spanish Town and other provincial centres expected to benefit in those estimates. Besides assisting the thriving banana industry, the scheme's local supporters hoped to jump-start the Jamaican sugar industry, which faced increasing competition from American investments in Cuba, the Dominican Republic and Puerto Rico. Some articulate 'boosters' for 'railway expansion' proposed a scheme to assist the island's sugar planters by building an up-to-date central sugar factory near Spanish Town, comparable to the latest rail-fed factories in Cuba or Trinidad, as the first item on their agenda. Promoters assured their audiences that 'plans, estimates and specifications' were all in hand, so if enough sugar planters in a wider region – not only St Catherine but also Vere, to the west and St Mary across the mountains to the north – would guarantee to provide 'the requisite quantities of Canes', then this project could advance.[51] It is not clear whether those particular blueprints were ever unrolled to build such a factory. The claim still suggests how far contemporaries expected the expanded railway network to widen Spanish Town's economic catchment area. More generally, this ambitious proposal for constructing a modern centralized sugar factory highlights the importance of secondary development in justifying the whole railway extension scheme. The expanded Jamaican railway might well make a loss as a commercial investment, but it would still pay off as 'social overhead capital' if it could increase peasants' and planters' access to international markets and enhance agricultural production islandwide.

The prospects appeared golden. Contemporary advocates would continue to claim that 'the increased shipping facilities and the opening up of the railroad naturally result[ed] in an era of increased prosperity'.[52] The actual economic benefits for Jamaica of extending the railway network remain less clear.⁵³ However, the marketing and cultivation of agricultural produce in St Catherine did benefit from both the railway extensions and the irrigation canal. Investment in the island's infrastructure offered an economic stimulus in Spanish Town and its vicinity. Proximity to the railway factored into the decision to establish a chemical factory just to the south of the town. It also served to reaffirm the government's decisions in the mid-1880s – before the routes were opened to the north shore but after the railway's lines were extended west and north – to undertake a massive extension of the St Catherine District Prison in 1884 and then to relocate the Leper Hospital to a site nearby. Over the next 20 years further buildings were added to the prison complex almost annually.⁵⁴ The railway was increasingly convenient not just for passengers, their parcels and their produce, but also for transporting patients and prisoners.

A Tourist Centre Again

The building in Spanish Town that exemplified the 1890s was not the District Prison, the Leper Hospital or even a new sugar factory, but the town's first modern hotel, the Rio Cobre Hotel, erected with the aid of tax breaks offered to newly constructed hotels in the Jamaica Hotels Law of 1890. This legislation aimed to encourage Jamaica's other new cash crop of the period – tourists. The Hotels Law was generated by a Governor-backed Jamaica Exhibition staged that year on the outskirts of Kingston.⁵⁵ Once the banana boats added passenger cabins and developed a luxury passenger trade to the West Indies, the first flows of North American and European tourists who were to occupy the new hotels arrived in Jamaica as a by-product of the banana trade.

How would the old capital appeal to these holidaymakers? Individually the tourists were transients and of course, as a historian of France commented on another set of foreign visitors: 'tourists, travelling in groups and staying in special hotels . . . are insulated from the inhabitants of the cities to which they are brief visitors, and they follow a fixed circuit that is unlikely to take them behind the scenes . . .' As a result 'there is no *intimacy* in their standardized circuits, nor any *memory* in the prestigious buildings that line them'.⁵⁶ Nevertheless, these tours had a lasting impact. Their schedules came to dictate what appeared 'historic' in Spanish Town. A turn of the twentieth century publication, *Side Trips in Jamaica* listed 'the special points of interest:

Rodney Temple, The Cathedral, Statuary by Bacon; King's House, Rio Cobre Hotel, with Native Cooking'. The pamphlet circulated widely with the third edition claiming '20,000 copies already published'.[57] It was composed for prospective tourists planning winter holiday breaks on the United Fruit Company's banana boats. While the ship loaded they could stay at the Company's lavish Titchfield Hotel in Port Antonio, the island's main banana port. If they wanted to stay longer they could catch another northbound steamer later. The idea of 'summering in winter' under Jamaica's tropical sun attracted people escaping from harsh northern winters. Vacationers enjoying a leisurely stay wanted some cultural and historical excursions too. Once the railway reached Port Antonio in 1896, passenger trains brought travellers south over the mountains to Spanish Town for side trips. During the 1870s Spanish Town had continued to provide a destination for some sightseeing visitors from Kingston and the neighbouring parishes.[58] From the 1880s, the growing numbers of North American and European tourists arriving in Jamaican ports also began to fit the old capital into their itineraries. Extending the railway increased the totals coming to Spanish Town.

They could enjoy a longer stay. After 1891 visitors could add the Rio Cobre Hotel to their schedule. This 'exceedingly comfortable and well-conducted hotel' stood 'just outside of the town' in the bend of the Rio Cobre to the north-east of the original Spanish grid of streets.[59] The hotel was 'clean and cool, with broad piazzas, upstairs sitting-room, general parlour, and reading room' and 'could accommodate between twenty-five and fifty guests'. Supporters soon boasted of its combining 'Creole comfort and good fare, with American management'.[60] The local police detectives dined there too, which suggests reliable quality. A tourist's journal recorded his party being 'regaled with "pumpkin soup" and other delicacies, including a shaddock nearly two feet in circumference'.[61] After an early start, a long train ride and a hot morning's touristing these culinary treats went down well. Yet even though the hotel stood in Spanish Town, the menu was not the 'jerked hog and black crab, . . . turtle-soup and old Madeira' invoked in earlier descriptions of 'the days when governors and bishops and judges held high festival' in the old capital, nor did the hotel revive the town's traditional specialties, like the 'famous pork chops' from Ramsey's Tavern that an elderly resident still recalled fondly in 1890. Townspeople, meanwhile, chose to tuck into the 'good meal consisting of soup, meat or fish, rice or rice and peas, salad, coffee, pudding or ice cream, bread and butter' at the St Albans Hotel

FIGURE 8:3 Rio Cobre Hotel, 1908, notice the buggies ready to transport guests either to and from the railway station or else off for an afternoon jaunt. (William L. Clements Library, University of Michigan).

on Adelaide Street.[62] In contrast to such solid Jamaican lunches, the Rio Cobre Hotel offered its guests well-presented Jamaican tourist fare – and they enjoyed it.

The new hotel provided a focus for the excursions that flourished once the railway extensions opened. Over a century later these 1890s itineraries continue to shape expectations for what a visit to Spanish Town *should* incorporate. Whether passengers arrived from the north shore or from Kingston, Jamaica's former capital was less a destination in its own right than a conveniently scenic stop on the line between Port Antonio and Kingston. Parties could break their journeys there en route to and from Kingston, or they could stay there before collecting ponies for a riding tour of the interior, or prior to taking a train up to Ewarton, and then make a leisurely two day drive to catch a returning banana boat at Montego Bay.[63] Train timetables dictated that tourists visit the town's historic buildings at a brisk pace. A 6:00 a.m. start at Port Antonio would get the punctual visitor to Spanish Town by late morning, just in time for a guided tour before the visitors caught either the 2:00 p.m. or the early evening trains on to Kingston. Otherwise Spanish Town provided a day trip for people staying in Kingston who if they left their hotel at six and took a trolley-bus down to the railway station, would catch the 7:30 a.m. train out to the old capital – and could breakfast at the Rio Cobre Hotel.[64] Once they arrived, visitors slotted their sightseeing in with lunch and an afternoon's excursion.

'The regulation sites' in a visit to Spanish Town became a stop at the Square in front of the old King's House, where 'you will see almost everything of interest there is in the place'.[65] The tourists plodded round, dutifully admiring John Bacon's classical statue of Admiral Rodney and listening to lectures on the valour of the Royal Navy. Late nineteenth-century and early twentieth-century school textbooks in the British West Indies incorporated sections on Admiral Rodney, in the same way that texts for Canadian schools foregrounded General Wolfe and children in Australia and New Zealand learned about Captain Cook. As a result, local tour guides were well primed to undertake speeches on Rodney, so that he might indeed appear 'the great popular hero of Jamaica'.[66] The parties of visitors received a short architectural promenade. The former public buildings facing on to the Square were not open for their inspection. In 1906 a correspondent writing to the *Daily Gleaner* claimed that 'tons of bat manure' could be found on the Assembly's, by now unused, upper floor. A proposal to make better use of the building by relocating the Jamaica Agricultural Society or some government office out from Kingston came to nothing.[67] Meanwhile tourists would note the presence of the Government Savings Bank on the ground floor, but guides rarely led their charges up the stairs to the former Assembly chamber.[68] The groups tended to focus their cameras on the exteriors of the old Assembly and the Rodney Memorial, in part, certainly, because any visitors wielding box-brownies who reached Spanish Town by mid-morning or later would find the facade of the old King's House on the west side of the Square already bathed in shadow. But, as local guides rarely got their charges inside the old King's House, late nineteenth-century and early twentieth-century guidebooks did not disappoint their prospective purchasers by lavishing long descriptions on the building's public rooms. This emphasis reversed earlier priorities, where the King's House had been the colony's principal showpiece.

Guides kept their parties moving and 'the Cathedral must not be forgotten'. Descriptions led with its former Spanish site and the succession of marble monuments inside: 'many' of which were, the guides confidently if vaguely asserted, 'full of interest'.[69] By 1900 one guide book recommended asking the Cathedral caretaker for a tour which might take two hours.[70] But even with their guidebooks in hand, late Victorian visitors were not likely to find much to admire in either what remained of the church's eighteenth-century nave or in the unfinished ambition of its mid-Victorian chancel expansion, though the battle standards of the Second West India Regiment, hung up by the altar, might receive a respectful glance.[71] Afterwards the tour groups were hurried on to the Rio Cobre Hotel 'for lunch, previously arranged for'.[72] This concluded their tour of Spanish Town, though there were other things to see – such as the visit that one enterprising individual undertook of the St Catherine District Prison, which he found 'admirably managed and scrupulously clean'.[73] Instead of scattering to wander through the town at a leisurely pace, the tourists were packed off for a prescheduled afternoon's trip up to the Rio Cobre Dam. They were assured that 'the drive . . . is the most beautiful on the island'.[74] Then they could enjoy a ride in a punt for a mile or so down the river. This gave passengers an opportunity to admire the lush riverside landscape before their transport (a buggy or later a motor vehicle) drove round to pick them up, just in time to catch the 5:52 to Kingston.[75] If this jaunt did not tempt them, tourists could undertake an alternative trip 'into the interior' south from Spanish Town, for a drive through fields of bananas, oranges and pineapples at the United Fruit Company's plantation at Great Salt Ponds.[76] Whatever option they selected, they would enjoy a properly delightful day trip.

Variations on this schedule later shaped visits when motor cars began bringing further parties of visitors through the Bog Walk Gorge to Kingston. These were on the final stage of a loop that first took them north from Kingston via the barracks at Newcastle and then, when they reached the island's north shore, west along the coast to one of the family hotels developing around Ocho Rios and Montego Bay. At the end of their stay the returning holidaymakers drove back through the Bog Walk Gorge to catch their ships 'home'.[77] The set place that King's House Square now held in all the island's guidebooks meant it would offer a suitable place to break their drive for a brisk, but worthy, 'historical' stroll. During the 1930s a contributor to the *Jamaica Standard* commented she could 'never get within view of the square during the tourist season without seeing one or more tourist cars stationed by this spot, while the occupants look over this historic relic'.[78] In 1936 when signs marking Jamaican historical landmarks were erected across the island one of the first batch went to the King's House Square.[79]

The official Spanish Town which visitors saw provided a complement to Kingston where, even before the 1907 earthquake and fire, 'there are really no fine buildings'.[80] After the earthquake, Spanish Town's status as an architecturally interesting counterpart became even more prominent as the rebuilt Kingston appeared 'the most disappointing town in the West Indies' so that, as another visitor concluded, 'if you would find houses of more solidarity you must go to Spanish Town.'[81] Nevertheless, some of the tourists who were brought out to the island's 'ancient' capital remained dissatisfied. A cruise ship passenger recalled that while he and his companions enjoyed their railway excursion to the Bog Walk Gorge and the 'delightful' scenic drive that followed, they 'were all sorry to reach Spanish Town' on their way back to Kingston, finding 'little of interest there, except the old government houses, now unoccupied, and some monuments'.[82]

The Rio Cobre Hotel apart, the 1890s tourist itinerary retained highlights from earlier visitors' explorations. Newcomers had always looked at the Square and, from the erection of John Bacon's statue of Admiral Rodney there, visitors had made a point of examining the statue. It remained the most expensive work of art in Jamaica, even if Bacon's stylized depiction of the Admiral in a breastplate and Roman cloak already appeared incongruous in 1817 and by the 1920s it simply looked 'miserable'.[83] In much the same way the town's parish church, the Anglican Cathedral of St Iago, had always attracted visitors. Earlier diarists sometimes dawdled longer than professional guides would permit, but the tourist parties of the 1890s were still escorted past buildings their predecessors had found striking. These, though, had not been the only historic buildings that the earlier travellers had noted.

What had changed was that the late Victorian tourist groups went no further into the town than the Square and the Cathedral. Why make these cuts? Fire and demolition had destroyed some former showpieces, like the mansion at the bottom of Monk Street built by Sir Charles Price, the mid-eighteenth-century Speaker of the Assembly, which burned in 1858.[84] In 1868, when another touring family took a carriage trip from Kingston they remembered a 'magnificent avenue of tamarind trees' they saw in Spanish Town which, so they were told, marked the site of the former Spanish Governor's house.[85] Their guide's assertion demonstrates mid-Victorian assumptions of what the gardens of a colonial governor should look like, which a glimpse into the stable yard at the old King's House would hardly satisfy. At that juncture the venerable Mulberry Garden on Monk Street belonged to the Anglican Rector and lay conveniently near to the Square and the Cathedral for tourists' strolls. In the 1870s the parochial board purchased this walled garden and proceeded to transfer the parish Alms House there. This act provided a very necessary facility but the paupers' presence effectively erased the gardens from all subsequent guidebooks.

The decision to skip another late eighteenth-century site, the Barracks, was striking. The complex remained in use as the Constabulary Training Depot. Ignoring the Barracks appears to demonstrate not just a Victorian lack of interest in Georgian architecture, but also suggests a tendency for tourist groups to bypass sites on the edge of the town. Other potential stops on the outskirts of the old capital were omitted too. Modern eyes will find the absence of the Iron Bridge particularly conspicuous, as it surely exemplified the technological triumphs that underpinned the period's rationales for Britain's imperial supremacy. In the 1820s and 1840s the bridge had appeared a suitable subject for sketching.[86] Any visitors coming to Spanish Town by road would still cross it but probably did not register it because their guidebooks no longer brought it to their attention; tourists packed into buggies at the railway station simply missed it. Yet the need to keep the tours moving will not explain everything. Broader shifts in European and North American visitors' recognition of what was 'noteworthy' factored into dropping the town's Baptist and Wesleyan chapels from tourists' itineraries and, indeed, from most of the period's guidebooks, though these chapels had loomed very large in pre- and post-Emancipation descriptions of Jamaica. Now they merely appeared to be 60- or 70-year old brick-built boxes.

Tourist guides shepherded their parties past a few public buildings. The major innovation of this generation of tours was their persistent lack of interest in Spanish Town's equally remarkable accumulation of eighteenth- and early nineteenth-century domestic buildings. These had caught earlier visitors' eyes. Even if the Spanish dates that passers-by tended to assign to 'the mahogany wainscotting, doors and carved cornichs' (cornices) decorating older buildings were way off in assuming that a primarily eighteenth- and early nineteenth-century housing stock was inherited from Diego Columbus, the storytellers were quite right to recognize that the town's older houses appeared characteristic of urban life in 'old Jamaica'.[87]

The tourists' focus on the new Rio Cobre Hotel added to their distance from the rest of the town. Spanish Town continued to have older hostelries open for business. The former 'Whittaker's Place' a hotel at the corner of Hanover, Martin and Manchester Streets and site of an Emancipation Day banquet remained open as the 'Marble Hall Hotel'. However, whatever its antiquity or associations, tourist parties did not come there. In part, certainly, because as a North American visitor dismissed it in the early 1920s, the place appeared 'a negro joint over-run with plate-licking cats and setting hens'[88] A lack of tourist customers helped to produce an absence of tourist-calibre facilities. In not taking their charges to a 'town' restaurant the guides avoided competing for tables with the hotel's regular clientele, even if the visitors lost an opportunity to mix with Jamaicans. The tourists received a narrowed experience while townspeople absorbed the message that the ancient capital's old shops and houses were not worth looking at.

This 1890s tourist itinerary was already breaking down before the outbreak of the First World War. Visitors' lunches, no matter how delicious, could not sustain a first class hotel in Spanish Town. The Government of Jamaica foreclosed on the Rio Cobre Hotel but found no other would-be hotelier to take it on. In July 1914 the Governors of the town's Beckford and Smith's School were lobbying to move there. They failed. The outbreak of war the next month meant that by September the hotel was used to house German prisoners of war and after four years' service as a POW camp it became a school for juvenile delinquents.[89] When holiday-makers returned to the island after the First World War, Spanish Town would fade as a sightseeing destination without those stops at the Rio Cobre Hotel as a focus for day trips.

The itineraries for cruise ship passengers' in the 1920s marginalised an inland railway junction. Prospective visitors planning to go ashore in Jamaica learned that 'the railway is now owned by the local government and is well cared for; but most people who can afford to do so prefer to travel by road'.[90] In the short term, while 'any party' going to Jamaica 'should certainly hire a car' they would still need to arrange to have their baggage sent on by rail to the hotels on their itineraries.[91] Visits changed. Rather than the leisurely exploration promised in the pre-First World War *A Happy Month in Jamaica*, when the United Fruit Company's schedule claimed that nine days was 'the briefest possible visit', or, in practice even a shorter run ashore while a ship loaded a cargo of bananas, offered 'three days in Jamaica', the stays for post-First World War ships' passengers were increasingly compressed into the tawdry excitement of '"Ship night" . . . any night when a large cruise liner is in port . . . and the only time when there's anything doing'.[92] In the schedules the United Fruit Company offered to potential tourists contemplating a Caribbean cruise on its 'Great White Fleet' in the early 1920s, Jamaica's Port Antonio would still be their first port of call, but now, such visitors were advised to drive south to Kingston while the ship stowed its cargo. The suggestion that they look at the Castleton Botanical Gardens en route implies they would be using the more direct Junction Road route along the Wag

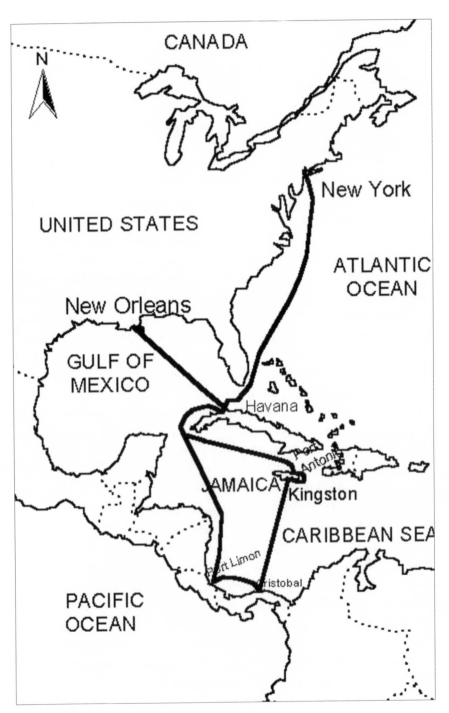

FIGURE 8:4 'A Great White Fleet Caribbean Cruise' United Fruit Company Cruise routes, 1922.

Water River, so would therefore bypass Spanish Town. When they reached Kingston, the guidebook encouraged passengers to do their curio shopping before re-boarding and sailing on to Panama.[93] This revised itinerary demonstrated Jamaica's continued place in the United Fruit Company's supply chain, but the holidays on offer had changed. Runs ashore at Port Antonio and Kingston remained part of pan-Caribbean cruises, but the time available for other excursions was trimmed.

The United Fruit Company had no monopoly on shipping tourists to Jamaica. Even so, the crowds who disembarked in Kingston from further 'big tourist steamers' in the 1920s were either quickly 'packed like sardines in motor-cars and rushed to the other American hotel at Port Antonio, and then rushed breathlessly back again, smothered in dust, just in time to re-embark', or else spent their brief stop-overs in Kingston itself, where 'four hundred Americans' would come ashore for 'a few hours, in which to examine the town, imbibe mint juleps through artificial straws, take photographs of each other with a Jamaican background, and bargain for curios'.[94] Prohibition in the United States certainly helped to fill Kingston's port-side bars, but such transients' stays were 'limited to a few hours' so they had 'no time to look at places of Historical interest'. Instead 'they usually just have a scheduled drive', and a visit to Spanish Town was no longer part of the schedule.[95] After all, it offered 'nowhere' to stop for lunch.[96] The numbers of passengers landing in Jamaica might increase but the old capital only received a limited exposure. There would never be enough new excursionists to break the mould for a 'proper' visit to the old capital set in the heyday of railway tourism.

Residents' understandings of an old town

Meanwhile, townspeople made increasing use of other public spaces in their town. In 1935 when the Governor visited the old capital to acquaint himself with its many problems, his official party sat down for their substantial luncheon in the old Assembly chamber which now housed Beckford and Smith's School.[97] Spruced up, it would probably interest tourists, if any should find their way there. Two years later, when the town celebrated the Coronation of King George VI in 1937, all the familiar public locations were employed: an Anglican 'State Thanksgiving Service' took place in the Cathedral and 'Music in the Square' was performed in the evening, but most of the communal celebrations occurred at the former parade ground in front of the Old Barracks – which, by then, had become a public Elementary School. In the morning this included the parish's Official Ceremony to celebrate the Coronation, attended by 4,000 school children. The early afternoon took the parish's custos and other local worthies on visits to the Poor House and the town's new Hospital. However, later in the evening, after a fireworks display, there was a public dance, again held at the Old Barracks.[98] Only guidebooks with their preset itineraries would omit such a central public space.

Townspeople continued to tell historical stories, attaching their own views of the community's past to particular places. Tour guides might discuss the same features, but their emphases remained very different. The tourists were always told to admire the heroic image of Admiral Rodney. Meanwhile, the 'temple' housing the statue became a focus for local pride once the Admiral returned to Spanish Town in 1889, after spending nearly 20 years standing at the dockside in Kingston. In the late 1880s townspeople described elaborate local protests against the statue's removal in 1871, including a mock funeral and an effigy in a coffin left in the empty 'temple'.[99] Rather than recalling otherwise unrecorded demonstrations against Governor Grant's arbitrary rule, these tales show local invention 20 years later, reimagining an official gesture to leave space for popular disapproval. Grant's decision to transfer the capital to Kingston was still resented. Similarly, the venerable tamarind trees in the Mulberry Garden on Monk Street also remained part of urban folklore, even if the tours deserted them. One of the ancient trees continued to be identified as the one where the leaders of a failed rebellion against Oliver Cromwell's last Governor were shot.[100] Another anecdote in circulation recalled how Mr Isaac Levy, a nineteenth-century custos of St Catherine, started his climb to wealth and political influence by running a small rum shop 'back of the barracks'.[101] Further tales accumulated after the vicissitudes of Marcus Garvey's political career led to the Jamaican-born orator and founder of the pan-Africanist Universal Negro Improvement Association being sentenced to three months at the St Catherine District Prison in 1929. These stories have Garvey putting a curse on his gaol cell, sealing the door so that no one would use that cell afterwards. Another variant has Garvey detecting a plan to kill him with a poisoned bath and refusing the offer.[102] In all these instances the 'histories' that townspeople told themselves undercut the authority of successive authoritarian governments.

Townspeople's storytelling recast and adapted recent history. They also retold older folk tales. These folk stories focused more on the older eastern side of the town and the river. In 1958 observant passers-by could see coins hammered into the bark of an old cotton tree that stood on the bank of the river, placed there as thank-offerings to the tree's spirit for wishes fulfilled.[103] A mermaid or 'fair maid' combing her long hair occasionally appeared at one of the fords across the river, which was an ominous sign because she would want blood.[104] Then in the Rio Cobre itself there were wonderful tales of a 'Gold Table', a splendid but daunting artifact that when it surfaced might be seen by children playing by the riverside. It would drown anyone foolhardy enough to grab it. This enchanted object lurked in a pool, 'the Broad Water', where the river makes its turn just above the town.[105] Mothers continue to invoke the Golden Table when warning their children against skinny dipping in the river. The Rio Cobre's Gold Table was sufficiently widely known to provide a subject for the annual Christmas pantomime in Kingston in 1986, 'River Mumma and the Golden Table'; though in further variants this or another 'Gold Table' also lurked just outside Kingston in a cattle pond lined with venerable tamarind trees.[106]

Themes of gold and danger extended more widely. The Rio Cobre's Golden Table floated alongside reports of a further hoard of treasure buried in the foundations of the old Iron Bridge. Perhaps this belief started with tales of surplus cannon from the French warships that Admiral Rodney captured being reused to stabilize the foundations for the bridge. If so, the story has a certain logic. Old iron cannon remain scattered around the historic town centre recycled as bollards to protect the corners of buildings, so it might seem feasible enough that cannons would provide pilings too. A cannons-in-the-foundation myth could then be extended back to the Assembly building where, a newspaper article claimed, 'many' old cannons were found under its staircase during repairs.[107] In 1930, when a new bridge was set across the river, straightening the road from Kingston and allowing heavier lorries across, a public-spirited citizen wrote to the Institute of Jamaica to urge that the cannons under the old Iron Bridge be sought for, photographed and salvaged when the now redundant bridge was demolished.[108] The story then seems to have undergone further modification, with the cannons transformed into treasure, now built into the Iron Bridge's foundations. Such a tale would encourage any hopeful individual with a pry bar to go and take a swing at the foundations. Hence, during the 1980s and '90s when limited funds postponed repairs, the action of the river's floods in scooping out the rubble fill from the bridge's piers was helped along by optimistic treasure hunters.[109] There is room enough for a sustained investigation of the townspeople's folk histories. What is already clear is that stories circulating in Spanish Town offered residents independent ways to understand the town's past.

Social boundaries and the social fabric

What was the society like in a town whose residents listened to such wonderful stories? A woman who grew up in Spanish Town before the First World War recalled a very circumscribed set of social interactions among her parents' circle. She remembered 'definite social strata', divided as follows: 'the so called Upper Ten – the Middle Class – the Lower Middle Class – Artisan – Domestic – and Peasant'.[110] Only a town person's ranking would set 'Domestics' ahead of 'Peasants'. Experiences still overlapped: even though the town's streets were lined with hedges and walls, some boundaries remained more porous. On weekdays residential streets in Spanish Town, as in most Jamaican towns, were cris-crossed by vendors calling out their wares, and a child could 'catch the tune, up and down in a kind of lilting refrain:

> Buy you bone dry Starch! Bone dry!
> Starch hey! Washerwoman Starch – Gwine Pass!

or,

> Buy you ripe Mango! Hairy Mango!
> Black Mango! Sweet No. 11! – Gwine Pass!'[111]

The intertwining barriers of class, gender and race were always far harder to overcome. Yet even these finely nuanced lines still left some boundaries where excluded groups could make some contacts. Another upper middle-class woman recalled that at the turn of the twentieth century 'no lady went to market' on weekdays; furthermore, her mother 'did not expect her domestics back till noon' from their marketing chores, because she recognized that they would meet friends and chat there while they undertook her errands. The town's markets were 'the clubs of the poor'.[112] However, other children from the local elite remembered the large open air market on Saturday and took haggling over the price of a purchase there for granted.[113] Churches, or at least the church porch, produced further crowded venues for some cross-class mingling, while, despite parents' warnings, children continued to play by the Rio Cobre.

On some evenings a fair cross section of townspeople went to the Town Hall (the former law courts on the south side of the Square) which could house all sorts of entertainments. The railway link to Kingston had made it a venue for a succession of visiting performers as well as home-grown shows. In the late 1840s events included acrobats dancing on a tightrope while, later, a local Amateur Dramatic and the Philharmonic Society offered performances – the latter group 'consisted of the big men of the town, not the young lads'.[114] In 1853 a newly formed Literary and Reading Society invited the Rev James Phillippo to lecture them on Cuba while in 1870 a visiting star offered audiences readings from Shakespeare, Dickens and Edgar Allen Poe.[115] In 1879, refurbished as the 'The Bijou Theatre', the courthouse venue even gained a positive review from Kingston's *Gleaner*. Some facilities would remain for staging ambitious performances. In 1885 'Slavin's Standard Opera Company' brought 25 singers, a violinist and a pianist, besides local musicians to crowded performances, later the town had a Choral Union too.[116] At the end of the nineteenth century the recreations on offer included a very early showing of a moving picture show. Seventy years after the event two different members of the audience that evening both recalled how people sitting in the front row jerked back when 'the water splashed'. Afterwards the local shopkeeper who brought this 'ProPectograph' machine to Spanish Town from Kingston then toured Jamaica and Haiti, before reselling 'the machine and equipment' to further entrepreneurs who took it to Venezuela.[117] An audience in Spanish Town's Town Hall had offered an early stop on a wider Jamaican and pan-Caribbean tour. Then, from 1925, the boys' grammar school was housed in the old Assembly building and used its upper floor to stage theatricals. The adolescent playgoers who slipped out for a cigarette during the intervals of these performances offered a strong reason why any empty store rooms in the building would be vulnerable to fire.[118]

Recollections compiled in the 1950s allow us to trace further turn-of-the-century social horizons. Amusements also included sport and here the venues ranged wider. Upper-class memories led with 'the inevitable' cricket and football for the boys, along with tennis for the young men and women. These pastimes differed from those of 50 and 60 years before, when leading townsmen joined the crowds at cockfights while, during the intransigent Assembly Sessions of the mid-1850s, Assemblymen's wives attended the archery matches that Lady Barkly, the Governor's wife, organized in a vain attempt to ease the political tensions.[119] The chance survival of a crowded schedule from the Spanish Town horse races in the 1880s alerts us to the revival of local racing at 'the always disorderly race course' there.[120] So far, in

FIGURE 8:5   Race card, Spanish Town races. (National Library of Jamaica)

many ways, so familiar. The memories from the 1890s of a shopkeeper's son invoked a very different set of sporting highlights, with Spanish Town holding the island's first cycle race at the Police Barracks, presumably sprinting around the old Parade Ground. Later the meetings were relocated to the parish Alms House on Monk Street, and later still the island's cycle races were transferred to Kingston.[121] Thus several of the older public spaces in the city provided sites for competing in a newly introduced sport. For townspeople the Barracks and the Mulberry Garden both continued to provide social spaces where residents could enjoy the latest competitive sports.

The town's secondary schools then provided a further focus for shaping distinct local identities. Facing on to the Square were two of the main educational institutions in the parish. Until 1925 the boys in Beckford and Smith's School were housed in a mid-Victorian brick structure inserted on the south side of the old Church Parade, just beside the Cathedral. After out growing its single schoolroom it moved into the former Assembly building. On the other side of the Square the Cathedral High School for girls had occupied the former servants' quarters behind the old King's House until 1924 – the school then moved to the town's then northern edge.[122] Both schools were for fee-paying middle-class children and taught towards the Cambridge Local Examinations, an anglo-centric syllabus, certainly, but providing qualifications recognized across the Empire. With its externally validated standards, this was the education that colonial employers and parents wanted, so these exams came to assume 'an importance out of all proportion to their value'.[123] Spanish Town's Beckford and Smith's School inherited the assets from Peter Beckford's 1735 donation to the St Iago Free School and from Custos Francis Smith's 1830 bequest of money to found a free Anglican school and as a result retained some 'foundation scholarships' open to boys from the parish of St Catherine – as it was expanded after 1866. One of the school's most famous students came from the Guanaboa Vale where a widow, Margaret Manley, had inherited a small estate in the uplands towards the mouth of the Bog Walk Gorge. Given her straightened circumstances, winning one of these scholarships offered her eldest son, Norman Washington Manley, his chance at getting on the first rung of the ladder up through the colony's exam-driven educational system. He seized it. At 13 the young Manley went on to win a half scholarship to Jamaica College which had recently relocated to suburban Kingston.[124] From there he went on to win a scholarship to Oxford and read law there.

Standards of instruction at the town school had improved from the scandalous mismanagement of the early 1860s.[125] The schoolmasters at the boys' grammar schools in Jamaica were expected to be university graduates, which effectively meant recruited in Britain and liable to go 'home' with little notice. At the beginning of 1914 Beckford and Smith's school was caught in a bind when both its teachers left and the Board of Governors turned to the Jamaican school leaver who had just secured the year's Jamaica Scholarship (awarded to the candidate with the year's best examination grades) to carry on the teaching. They also attempted to bring back their own old boy, 'Mr Manley – the Rhodes scholar', to help cover classes until a suitably qualified Anglican clergyman could be located to take over as headmaster.[126] These remained expedients. The school's governors usually recruited British graduates already teaching in Jamaica or else hired from England.

The girls at the Cathedral High School also had access to some remarkable opportunities, though not to the parish scholarships. The girls' school was not obliged to employ graduates and so recruited its teachers in Jamaica, placing a local social leader's daughter as Headmistress and then hiring back its own old girls as teachers. Because girls' schools had lower expectations for the professional qualifications of women teachers and, indeed, as these women had fewer alternative opportunities, the school was able to secure a more permanent staff who could sustain some challenging extracurricula

FIGURE 8:6 Sketches of 1st Jamaica Company, Girl Guides, on an early summer camp, 1931. Guides en route to camp, crammed into the back of a lorry and Guides under canvas at their camp. (Jamaica Archives).

activities. In 1915 during the First World War when the island's Boy Scouts 'were doing their bit and girls longed to be of service', a recent school leaver from the Cathedral High School 'copied my father's Scout Troop, . . . and organized a Company of "Girl Scouts" in Spanish Town'. She then wrote to invite her former head teacher to become Captain and 'Miss Daisy' then 'took over my little company and had it officially recognized'. It became the first troop of Girl Guides in Jamaica. By 1916 there were 272 Guides; in 1917, 301 were registered, along with 21 Brownies.[127] The Headmistress and her staff remained pillars of the Guide movement in Jamaica for the next 60 years, maintaining eager Guide and later Brownie troops in Spanish Town. Well into the 1970s Guides from across the island would come to visit 'Miss Daisy' in Spanish Town.[128] As a result several generations of young women were encouraged to become not only more self-reliant but also to sustain friendships outside their classrooms.

Other social patterns remained defined by class or race. The families in

Spanish Town's 'upper ten' organized their own social itinerary. Kingston was not their social hub. Looking back, one 1890's daughter recalled her mother and her friends moving in a self-sufficient social circle. On Sunday afternoons 'All the Families' drove down to Port Henderson after church 'to "take the air" and to exchange the gossip of the day'.[129] At that time the most socially exclusive tickets were to the balls held at either the Rio Cobre Hotel or at the old King's House, if well-connected charities or individuals could borrow the latter for an evening. 'There was no Public Ball – (at least here in Spanish Town) where Invitations could be bought – such a thing was unheard of'. An insider could still believe, however, that even for those without tickets, it would appear 'a beautiful sight to watch the carriages rolling up in the old square and to see the young girls alighting exquisitely dressed'.[130] Local committees in Spanish Town retained considerable authority even when the events they hosted attracted guests from Kingston.

What seems striking, beside the painstaking hierarchies that characterized British provincial society at this juncture wherever it became established, was that these turn-of-the-century events were dominated by families based in Spanish Town. This was new. In earlier generations Spanish Town provided the physical hub for the plantocracy's socializing, but until the Governor's departure in 1872 that hectic round of balls and banquets all occurred during the brief social seasons, when Jamaica's planters and merchants filled the town while they argued their legal cases or attended the Assembly. Looking out from the King's House earlier in the nineteenth century the press of guests cramming in at the official balls often seemed downright indiscriminate; but when it came to obtaining invitations, aspiring professionals living in Spanish Town could all-too-easily find themselves unsuccessful, elbowed aside by visiting planters, militia officers and Assemblymen.[131] With the removal of both the law courts and the Governor's household to Kingston in the 1860s and '70s these dynamics changed. In the short term Spanish Town's socializing did appear a shadow of its old self. The Rev James Phillippo, for example, 'sorely felt the loss of social intercourse which ensured' as 'many of his old friends were drawn off to the new capital'.[132] But by the 1890s the town's home-grown 'society' appeared far more self-confident. Once the governors and their households had departed, the town's remaining professional families could indulge in believing themselves 'an upper ten'.

Forty years later, in 1929, comparable self-reliance among the town's African Jamaican residents was particularly apparent. We have already encountered the town's Refugee Visiting Cottage Band and Blue Ribbon Lodge parading through town in August that year. In December, with Marcus Garvey's release imminent from the St Catherine District Prison after his three months detention there, the colony's senior officials were concerned about the ceremony that the Spanish Town division of the Garveyite Universal Negro Improvement Association was planning. The urgent bureaucratic paper shuffling offers hostile testimony, but it started from the assumption that when the movement's leader left the gaol on Christmas Eve, he would receive a hero's welcome organized by the Spanish Town UNIA, climaxing with 'a monster procession' to escort him back to Kingston. The British officials feared that the resulting publicity would give Garvey's People's Political Party a significant boost in the forthcoming Legislative Council elections. To prevent this possibility the Governor arranged for Garvey's release five days early at 4:30 p.m. on a Thursday – a full working day – rather than over the weekend. Then, to pry Mr Garvey away from his local supporters, he was to be offered an official car back to Kingston.[133] Here the Governor's own criteria for setting this release date effectively acknowledged the respectable working-class people who had joined the local Garveyite division: its members were likely to be employed, so that missing a half day's work mid-week would hinder their attendance. Even while Jamaica's Governor worked hard to keep the franchise tightly restricted, the organization and enthusiasm of Spanish Town's UNIA division demonstrated that self-help and politics remained persistent threads in the town's working class society.[134]

Maintaining an 1890s development model: 1900–1935

At the start of the twentieth century prospects for further development looked rosy. Even though the West Indian Improvement Company had collapsed, leaving the railway's 800 American staff members stranded in Jamaica, the immediate crisis was resolved.[135] The Colonial Bank survived the affair too.[136] The island now had an extensive railway network, though acquired at a very considerable cost. The island's peasantry remained burdened with heavy taxes while subsequent government cost-cutting in the shape of heavy cuts in the 1905 education budget embittered local politics.[137] Despite all these financial sacrifices, any hope for an economic upturn driven by investment in infrastructure was cut short as Jamaica weathered devastating hurricanes, the earthquake and fire that destroyed Kingston in 1907 and the First World War's prolonged adverse effect on the colony's trade.

After the war Spanish Town could expect to recover its prewar economic base. During the 1920s many households chose to subdivide older building lots in order to make room for new buildings, including the latest socially impressive bungalows that offered a very tangible gesture of confidence in the town's future.[138] Life in early twentieth-century Spanish Town might well appear good – even heavenly. During the early 1920s a Baptist preacher in the old free village of Sligoville urged his congregation to 'Picture to yourselves a nice, large room in Spanish Town, with a table beautifully decorated, and spread with tempting dishes, and gentle zephyrs wafting through the window' and then asked 'Would you like to be there, friends? . . . Let that be your picture of heaven!'[139] The ingredients for prosperity were all assembled: the railway network remained; some tourists still drove out from Kingston or broke their journeys in the King's House Square, and irrigation water from the Rio Cobre supported high-yielding *gros michel* bananas. By 1921, 21 per cent of the cultivated area of the parish was planted with bananas.[140] In September 1920 the opening of a thoroughly up-to-date sugar factory at the United Fruit Company's Bernard Lodge estate demonstrated that sugar also had revived locally as a major crop.[141]

Why, then, did the good times that formerly sustained the townspeople's respectable comfort not keep on rolling? The proposals for infrastructure development recommended by Jamaica's colonial administrators after the First World War all aimed to restore or extend the successful projects of the 1890s. In 1928, ten years after the end of the war, farmers using the Rio Cobre Irrigation network for large-scale operations requested still more irrigation water for their banana and sugar crops. Individual members of the island's Legislative Council might well be nervous about authorizing further outlays of public funds, but the projected returns appeared reasonable.[142] At this juncture hurricanes still appeared 'the greatest menace of the banana in Jamaica.[143] In the event, the Wall Street 'Crash' the next year and the deepening economic depression shrank export markets while investment withered. In the short term the new banana fields still offered year-round work.[144] However, because the government had not sought any alternative initiatives during the good years, finding new roles for the town or jobs for its residents during the subsequent lean years would prove very difficult.

For local residents three unexpected disasters in the late 1920s marked decisive breaks from their earlier prosperity. In October 1925 a fire destroyed the old King's House. Its shingled roof and 160-year-old timbers burnt fiercely and could be seen for miles.[145] The town's fire engines just managed to contain the blaze, though it was a close call with the Post Office across Adelaide Street suffering damage too. No lives were lost but the former governor's mansion was gutted.[146] Subsequent efforts to persuade the Colonial government to remove the rum stored in the old stables on the south side of the old King's House compound, the only buildings in the block to survive the fire, spotlighted townspeople's broader fears. They saw these rum barrels as a fire storm waiting to happen. If the wind on the night of the King's House fire had been any higher, embers blowing across the town could have ignited other wood-shingled roofs and the whole town would have burnt. The Governor was not sufficiently impressed by this argument to seek out a safer overflow store for bonded rum. The towns-people's further nervousness that these barrels would attract criminals from Kingston, driving fast cars, brandishing revolvers and aiming to smuggle all this unguarded booze into a teetotal USA illustrates rural anxieties about criminal elements in mid-1920s Kingston, but did not persuade the Governor to do anything about the rum.[147] Meanwhile, under the guise of removing debris after the fire, the Government's Public Works Department started to pull down the surviving interior walls, driving carts full of bricks away to reuse in construction or to fill potholes.[148]

The decade's next disaster, the arrival of 'Panama Disease' among the parish's banana fields in the late 1920s, took longer to come into full effect but had a far deeper impact. The disease caused by a soil fungus spread across the Caribbean killing *gros michel* banana plants. The United Fruit Company responded by carving new plantations out of the tropical forests on its Central American estates, which allowed the Company to keep ahead of the infection and continue growing the thick-skinned *gros michel* bananas that its highly mechanized distribution network was designed to process and that the Company's North American customers were accustomed to buying.[149] This option was hardly available in Jamaica.[150] Instead, the Imperial School of Tropical Agriculture in Trinidad and government botanists in Jamaica attempted to develop blight-resistant strains. The *lacatan* banana introduced into Jamaica in 1926 proved an effective substitute but its fruit has a much thinner skin which leaves it far more liable to bruising in transit and therefore less appetizing to purchasers. The switch had long-term consequences for

Jamaica because the United Fruit Company was less ready to purchase *lacatan* bananas. Banana estates on the north side of the island successfully made the transition to growing *lacatans*, held off further attacks of 'leaf spot', and then increasingly turned to supplying the British market, which was already geared to import this type of banana. Jamaican output would rebound to reach a new peak of 361,200 tons in 1937.[151] St Catherine, however, was not so fortunate. Its banana fields were not replanted with the new variety. The parish and its farmers lost both a cash crop and a major employer, despite all the sizeable public investments in the early 1920s on extensions to the Rio Cobre irrigation system.

Then, in 1930, a third pillar of the local economy tottered when the Jamaica Government Railway racked up massive debts that soon absorbed half the government's total allocations for capital investment. This too was unexpected. Only three years earlier the Colonial government had rejected out of hand any negotiations with a potential purchaser, sure that 'the Government has no intention of selling the Railway'.[152] However, after motor cars began transporting tourists around the island, lorries proved increasingly efficient in competing with the railway for freight. At this juncture the railway lines north of the mountains, which had never found sufficient customers to make up for their high maintenance costs over the short distances that freight was carried, began losing even more money.[153] A consultant recommended cutting services, consolidating staff and simplifying the fare structure to help the railway compete, as well as investing in replacement track and new locomotives.[154] These remedies were not enough to pull the line back into profitability. Although Spanish Town was not targeted for particular economies, trouble for the railway spelt further uncertainty for the city as a railway hub.

The Colonial government offered limited responses to Spanish Town's problems while discouraging local initiatives. In 1928, just as the latest scheme to resurvey the Irrigation Canal to benefit large scale banana growers was scheduled for the Legislative Council's agenda, the Superintendent of the island's public gardens was experimenting on Panama Disease-resistant bananas. He had planted his most promising seedlings in the garden of his house in suburban Kingston, where they seemed likely to die during a dry spell. He therefore requested permission to transplant them out to the farm just outside Spanish Town run by the St Catherine District Prison, a prime banana-growing plot. As his request wended its way from one government department to another, the colony's bureaucrats demonstrated their readiness to develop reasons *not* to do something unusual. With hindsight the annotation 'what's the urgency?' scribbled on the file by the Colonial Secretary, the number two in the colonial bureaucracy, seems downright blinkered given the potential social repercussions of the failure of the banana crop due to Panama Disease.[155] The experimental bananas were finally transplanted but the whole affair, with key botanical research being undertaken in the Superintendent's back garden and then the protracted bureaucratic foot-dragging, hardly showed an administration poised to react to crises in an energetic fashion.

When initiatives originated outside the bureaucracy, the disinclination of officials to hear alternative views became even more evident. There were many suggestions after the fire at the old King's House.[156] The St Catherine Parish Council urged the government to use the site for a new hospital but, primarily because of the expense, their proposal was rejected, leaving the charred walls to dominate the square for a decade. Visitors might ask 'why that burnt-out shell is left there' but 'no one seemed to know'.[157] When the Governor's official recommendation came, it was minimalist. The remaining walls were unstable, so demolish all the surviving ruins, remove the railings around the square and leave the pillars from the portico standing in the midst of a grassed-over void. Expatriate officials with a budget to balance considered this a realistic solution. It confirms a contemporary verdict on the then Governor as 'an excellent administrator' but 'a bore in all other respects'.[158] Whatever the Governor's views, some influential opinions on the island viewed the King's House Square as a distinctive symbol of Jamaica's former importance. They proposed a maximalist remedy: reconstruct the whole building. The Colonial government had smothered the parish politicians' hospital proposal. Jamaica's elite maintained their own influential contacts off the island and proved far more difficult to 'snub off'.[159] They invited a British historical architect out to Jamaica who composed elaborate plans showing that the building could be reconstructed.[160] After repeatedly asserting that nothing could be done, the Colonial government did not want to know.

The restoration project was coordinated by a committee led by the widow of a pre-First War Governor. Lady Mary Swettenham had lived in the old King's House after the 1907 Kingston earthquake destroyed the 'new' King's House and retained fond memories of the old building. She would not take an official 'no' for an answer. Her committee remained flexible about uses for the restored structure. Although they were vague about potential uses, the group agreed on the end they sought; the old King's House was a significant component in Jamaica's past and should not be erased. The committee was probably right that a restoration scheme could work; the colony's bureaucrats were correct that restoration would prove very expensive.

As Lady Swettenham's committee continued lobbying, the colonial bureaucracy became even more stubborn in its refusal to consider anything to do with the old King's House.[161] Administrators became so defensive that in 1927 after a proposal from the well-connected West India Committee in London urging official support towards recording or preserving old buildings in Jamaica initially gained a sympathetic reception, senior colonial officials then reread it far more suspiciously, as 'probably an attempt to get the Gov[ernmen]t to rebuild King's House Spanish Town'. It therefore only received a deliberately noncommittal reply.[162] Even before the 1928 Stock Market crash, bureaucrats' fiscal prudence veered towards blinkered intransigence. Attempts to raise rebuilding funds off the island proved unsuccessful. Money became tight as the Depression set in, but the rebuilding committee managed to collect some cash in Jamaica and while this could not fund a full restoration, it was enough to stabilize the remaining walls facing the Square. This was an achievement. A longer delay and these unsupported walls would have fallen down while, as Jamaican journalists recognized, the limited restoration 'gave back to that old square a completeness' which would otherwise have been lost.[163]

During the Depression years local projects sank or swam on their own. In the 1930s, when the Cathedral needed extensive repairs, its clergy tried to tap fresh donors, as neither the colony nor the Anglican Church in Jamaica had money to spare for fresh paint, shingles and drainpipes. The Cathedral Chapter attempted to mobilize 'Friends' to donate money because, as their fundraising flyer admitted, 'the town is suffering keenly from loss of trade, [and] from the closing down of operations of the banana companies'.[164] As a fund raising device their proposal appears a generation ahead of its time, but the times were unpropitious and the Friends' scheme was unsuccessful. The Cathedral's roofs and gutters continued to leak. The clerks in the Colonial Secretary's office who looked over a copy of this appeal commented 'if only Lady Swettenham would turn her attention to this instead of K[ing's] H[ouse] something might be done'.[165] Even once the Colonial government began to search for projects to use for public work relief schemes, it would not pay any of the local unemployed to paint or re-roof 'the oldest [Anglican Cathedral] in the British dominions'.[166] Instead, the Governor and his officials continued to rely on the public bureaucracy – primarily the Public Works Department and the parishs' road maintenance sections – to find unskilled 'rough labour' jobs for a day or so per week, rather than supporting the island's voluntary sector or assisting projects that would employ skilled or semi-skilled workers.[167] There would be no 'New Deal' schemes in 1930s Jamaica.

'... it is for us to tell the government of this country when we approve, and not for us to wait for their permission to think and form our own opinions.'[168]
The end of Crown Colony Rule.

Spanish Town's dealings with the colonial bureaucracy before the Depression already demonstrated the difficulties in applying to the Colonial government for solutions to local problems. The Colonial Service administrators who dismissed prospective candidates for the island's Legislative Council in the 1920s, claiming that they were 'confused about the major issues facing the colony' and 'lacked constructive ability in formulating useful alternatives' – while the bureaucrats' own pet schemes did – were not just complacent, but unwilling to take 'the natives' opinions seriously.[169] Neither the parish's banana planters and their impoverished employees nor even ex-Governor Swettenham's widow and her committee's well-connected members could initiate programmes that required these bureaucrats to *do* something. Then, once the world economy entered the Great Depression, more problems swept in, producing dire poverty as 'the prices of the principal West Indian exports were on the average almost halved between 1928 and 1933 and workers were forced to submit to drastic wage cuts, increased taxation and unemployment'.[170]

Over the 1930s, when Jamaica endured many problems, potential solutions pushed against administrative inertia. The currency of mutually contradictory views on how the colony's government should operate meant that any practical attempts to solve Jamaica's all-too-real social and economic problems or to raise questions about recruitment to the civil service could all-too-quickly be recast as constitutional clashes. Crown Colony status assigned the executive a decisive role and there was no fallback option to official inaction. Yet, faced with a massive crisis, the colony's centralized administrative structure proved slow and inflexible. The First World War had bled far too much talent from the cohort of imperial bureaucrats who ran the island in the '20s and '30s. In a system when schoolboy service as a house prefect *and* captain of the cricket eleven provided key qualifications for recruitment into the interwar Colonial Service, these administrators would have character and self-confidence in abundance, but very little knowledge of commerce or, indeed, readiness to compromise or even listen.[171] Meanwhile, Jamaican residents suspected the motives of the local advisors Governors chose, a group primarily drawn from the island's planter establishment. A correspondent from St Catherine who wrote urging a newly arrived Governor not to 'regard the subject that the rich man's put before you in the Previl Council' and, instead 'take your eyes and see', optimistically hoped that his letter could persuade His Excellency to 'make time and visit the old Spanish Town and consider the fact[s]', but the underlying distrust for the motives of that aptly misnamed privileged 'Previl Council', rather than 'privy council', was widely shared.[172]

Even before the First World War Jamaicans complained that 'the Government has been steadily encroaching upon the powers of the elected members, while the people of the colony are becoming less and less disposed to be ruled entirely by officials'.[173] After 1918, objections against government with only limited representation continued. During the relatively prosperous 1920s, descriptions of the island generally emphasized the elaborate checks and counter-balances built into its administration. An American writer remained unimpressed by the resulting system, judging it 'both backward and clumsy', producing 'a division of responsibility from power and frequent deadlocks that make the apparent autonomy of the island a constant process of "standing pat"'. To compound these constitutional difficulties, the American also considered 'the few white officials . . . slow, antiquated, [and] precedent-ridden'.[174]

Unsurprisingly, expatriate officials judged the colony's administrative structures differently. They would probably admit that 'the present Constitution of Jamaica is chaotic [and] almost certainly destined to break down in some period of excitement or financial strain', before concluding that 'the problems of Jamaica, (within the narrow sphere of matters that are considered government business,) are not inherent; they have been foisted on the place as a result of a very stupid piece of constitution-building'. Much of this diagnosis might well receive wider local agreement, even including its late Victorian conviction that negligible government intervention was the best government policy. However, the subsequent recommendation of a further reduction of the electorate, in order to free British civil servants from bullying by elected local officials and help persuade 'better class whites' to stand for elective office, would be far more contentious.[175] Analyses of this sort retained their appeal within the expatriate-dominated colonial bureaucracy. As late as 1939 the incoming Governor's pet scheme for reform would have introduced even more civil servants into local government, by replacing the volunteer parish custos and the locally appointed parochial board secretary with officials who had passed the civil service exams.[176] These would be outsiders and probably expatriates. Professional public servants would doubtless prove honest, avoiding the scandals that tainted the Kingston and St Andrew Corporation. They might well balance the books and process all the right paperwork on time, but they would have little knowledge of local landscapes or local people's ambitions. This last scheme did not occur. However, under Crown Colony rule a consensus on possible policies for Jamaica, or even the mutual respect on which such a consensus could be built, remained sorely absent.

Something needed to be done all the same. During the 1930s the economic projects initiated before the First World War collapsed across Jamaica and, indeed, across the West Indies. Spanish Town suffered with the rest of the island as the centralized Crown Colony administration failed to respond to the region's multiple economic challenges. Money was tight; remedies scarce. The 1860s ideal of a small and efficient colonial administration able to initiate whatever policies were necessary, now merely appeared a closed group of expatriates working to keep things ticking over as they were. Public confidence ebbed as the inherited structure of Colonial government failed to deliver solutions. The notes that a police detective made at a trades union meeting in St Catherine in 1937 concluded with a fiery speaker from Kingston, Alexander Bustamante, offering a comment and posing a question, 'while Governor Denham is here he will get us in the poor house. What does he care when he is gone back to England?'[177]

Hard Times: '. . . Many morning plenty people cannot even drink tea.'[178]

By the early 1930s, three of the main props for Spanish Town's local economy – bananas, tourism and the railway – had already crumbled. The Great Depression shrank the number of tourists taking West Indian vacations;

Panama Disease wiped out plantations of *gros michel* bananas across the Caribbean and, perhaps as seriously, killed the banana plants growing in the labourers' own gardens whose fruit had provided them with food and supplementary cash, and cutbacks in the Jamaica Government Railway slowed the economy of the whole island. The resulting misery was widely spread. But the destruction of the old King's House in 1925 and the infection of the hitherto prime banana lands irrigated by the Rio Cobre still meant that Spanish Town suffered twin economic blows before the rest of the island. Little else remained from the development schemes of the Crown Colony era – except, perhaps, for the District Prison and the Constabulary Training Depot. Employers continued to assert that work was available. Indeed, four local sugar factories operated in the vicinity, but much of the work they offered remained highly seasonal. What had changed from the 1920s was that the banana estates no longer offered jobs that could even out the cyclical unemployment on the sugar estates. Meanwhile, although the figures cited for people unemployed in and around the town fluctuated, the number of individuals seeking work increased. Spanish Town was well on the way to the damning verdict offered by the author of a 1937 guide book who considered the town 'rather horrid – hot and dusty, and quite unlovely – the most unattractive place on the whole island'.[179]

Figures compiled by local officials showed the extent of the problem. A 1936 report by the local Police Inspector had no doubt 'that there is a fair amount of unemployment, particularly in Spanish Town' and gave an estimate of 'about 750 (men and women)' unemployed. Even this figure had to be qualified because 'a fair proportion of these people manage to obtain occasionally about two days work a week on the local properties'. Still, they only received low pay while 'there are probably several thousands in the parish who have no permanent or semi-permanent work'.[180] The Parish Board collected more specific figures later that year which gave a sharper focus to the overall misery in the lean months before the sugar harvest. The Board reported a population of approximately 12,000 workers living in the town and its immediate vicinity. Of these, 'about 3,000 are tradesmen and persons of independent means', a further 500 had jobs as clerks 'in offices, stores, shops *etcetera*', perhaps 1,500 more residents had full time jobs as labourers on the neighbouring estates, and a further 200 worked for the Public Works and Parochial Board. A total of 5,200 people were employed. So, in all, less than 50 per cent of the local labour force enjoyed an income or a steady job. The remaining 6,000 'of the labouring class' besides another 1,000 'of the women and men need employment'. The Parochial Board concluded its letter with the comment that 'this Board cannot impress too strongly on Government the great necessity of relieving unemployment in this area'.[181] Protest at these conditions grew more widespread. By early May 1938 a mass union meeting in Spanish Town drew up a 'unanimous' resolution requesting government intervention to find money to create jobs, because 'thousands of unemployed men, women and children' in the town and its vicinity were reduced to sleeping rough under trees or in old buildings, while 'starvation is also rampant among them . . .', reaffirming that the Depression's poverty bit very hard.[182]

Faced with such intractable problems in the island's second largest town something should be done – and, by default, the Colonial government should be doing it. So what was being recommended? The Governor laid out his own assumptions in March 1937 in a memorandum to Britain's Secretary of State for the Colonies where he attempted to justify his administration's limited responses to the dire state of affairs in Kingston:

> The problem of unemployment today is widespread and as has been found elsewhere is by no means easy of solution. A lesson can, however, be learned from experience elsewhere which has shown that unemployment is far more prevalent in industrial than in agricultural countries, and this indicates the desirability of this Government developing its available resources to the employment and development of agricultural rather than development projects.[183]

With such pessimistic assessments the government might indeed undertake reforms of the island's forestry policy, but there were few lifelines to throw to townspeople living in 'a dusty, dry, decayed and squalid town'; even if Spanish Town was 'inhabited chiefly by labourers working on the banana plantations . . .' in an area where Panama disease had now wiped out the leading cash crop.[184]

As times grew worse, who would speak out on the townspeople's behalf? Members of the town's middle class formed themselves into a self-appointed Spanish Town Citizens' Association, which aimed to alert the Colonial government to current concerns. By the 1930s a number of local citizens' associations had been formed across the island.[185] However, in 1932 the Governor 'made a rule of not "recognising" a Citizens' Association as representing the Parish or any part thereof' and declined 'to receive an address from them'. Officials were to acknowledge letters from the Associations' Secretaries, but he did not welcome their input. The Governor recognized his frosty policy 'gave considerable umbrage in some quarters', but claimed that this response 'was applauded by the Custos and most reasonable people'.[186] By default, then, the parish custos or the elected member of the Legislative Council (both of whom were large-scale planters based in northern St Catherine) remained the only 'proper' route for anyone to communicate public disquiet in Spanish Town to the island's government.[187] The Governor's snubs proved effective in silencing groups self-defined as 'respectable'. He could not wish away the town's problems so easily.

The views that the parish's local representatives (the Parish Board, Legislative Council member and Custos) did express contrasted with the Governor's do-nothing verdict. A formal visit that Governor Denham made to Spanish Town in April 1935 offered local officials opportunities to describe problems, even if fewer solutions resulted from the visit than townspeople had hoped. A long speech by the custos offered a wish list. Few others in this audience would worry about the lack of a shed by the Court House for visiting officials to park their cars. He then raised the question of restoring the King's House, praising Lady Swettenham's fund-raising efforts. The Governor's response on this point was particularly evasive. After these preliminaries the speech permitted some more widely-felt local grievances to be aired. The unfair competition that the St Catherine's District Prison was offering to nearby farmers was among the main issues. The Prison Farm should keep to 'useful' export crops and not ruin the 'small settler's' market for 'yams, cocoes and such provisions'. Before the Panama Disease struck, bananas from the Prison Farm provided a useful contribution to the Prison's budget; after the bananas died the Prison had turned to growing ground provisions and then consigned its surpluses for sale. The custos objected strongly. His complaint went further, illuminating the desperate straits to which unemployed men and women were driven in order to earn any cash. The Prison's quarries were selling rubble too and such sales undercut the local market for individuals who were breaking stones for sale. For the custos and his local audience these appeared resolvable instances of unfair official competition.

The rest of the speech addressed existing government projects in the area. Here plans for an enlarged hospital for the town came first. Then the Governor was asked what the government was going to do about the Leper Hospital just to the south of the town? In a passage that was not in his preliminary draft the custos described being jostled and threatened by patients at the Leper Hospital the previous day, before going on to express widely shared worries about lepers shopping in town and fears that vegetables from their plots were being offered for public sale. The lepers needed controlling and the institution should probably be moved.[188] When the official speeches and replies were finally over the official party toured a number of the public 'places of interest' that were proving contentious, particularly the Lepers' Home, the town's hospital and the Prison Farm.[189] The speech and tour both urged the Governor to adjust existing policies and projects. Such a survey of the town's problems sought to adjust officials' assumptions, not to challenge them. There were no requests for the Colonial government to undertake any fresh initiatives.

Other townspeople also tried to gain a hearing during the Governor's official visit, particularly a group that would increasingly speak for the town's unemployed and underemployed. During the preliminary planning for the visit the Governor ignored an alternative invitation from the local division of the Universal Negro Improvement Association (UNIA) to take him on a tour of Spanish Town's slums 'to see for himself the true conditions that exist' there.[190] The first response by the colonial bureaucrats to this invitation was to check whether the Garveyite movement was still active and, having decided that 'the movement is practically dead', there were no further replies, even when the local UNIA wrote again to 'request His Excellency be kind enough to visit the slum areas of the town' and then a third time, 'to refresh' his 'mind to visiting the Slum areas'.[191] However, the Governor's silence here was not nearly as effective in deterring the leadership of the local UNIA division as such official snubs proved when dealing with middle-class citizens' associations. In not taking up this offer the administrators bypassed a street-by-street itinerary through the western side of the town, besides the local UNIA's supplementary suggestions that the visit should include inspecting not only the hospital 'as conditions isn't of a healthy nature', but 'also the Poor House and Market' too. These alternative recommendations demon-strated that when the opportunity of hosting a visit from the Governor occurred six years into the Depression, townspeople agreed some public institutions like the hospital and, perhaps, the Leper Hospital deserved his attention. The basic difference being that the working-class group wanted the Governor to see – and then respond to – the townspeople's daily misery, while the parish's established politicians held far more limited expectations for official action that would then work through the existing public institutions.

Three years later, in August 1939, a further opportunity for comments expressing local opinions occurred when the island's next Governor came to Spanish Town to meet with the Parochial Board. Local officials' views still varied, but they now expected more from the island's government than minor adjustments to existing policies. Some of the issues from 1935 remained current, including a plea for extensions to the town's hospital, this time with the suggestion that it should include an isolation ward for tuberculosis patients. The Leper Hospital again appeared a local grievance, though with fewer specific concerns. The afternoon's discussions had two foci. One was general, on the necessity of obtaining land near to town to allow local families to settle somewhere, because there was currently very little smallholding land near to the town. The other was specific, debating where these settlements should be located. Land settlement schemes where estates were purchased by the government and broken up into smallholdings were not new in Jamaican politics. Individual projects had been proposed elsewhere in the island after the Land Settlement Law of 1920. During the early 1930s the north of St Catherine housed one of these schemes established for First World War veterans from the British West India Regiment, while by 1934 another completely unofficial settlement-cum-commune was established at Pinnacle, three miles from the town on the road to Sligoville by Lawrence Howell and the new Rastafarian movement.[192] Now the St Catherine Parochial Board urged the Governor to apply this remedy to Spanish Town's problems.

Two more years of misery and agitation passed before an expanded local political agenda opened. In the meantime the trade union that started in Spanish Town and then spread across St Catherine articulated most of the new issues. In trade unionists' eyes the link between land settlement and easing unemployment locally was direct: 'we must have Land Settlement Schemes, etc., to relive the unemployment . . . [so] we are asking that Government may give strict attention to Land Settlement to make permanent employment.' In August 1938 the Secretary of what had become the local branch of the Bustamante Industrial Trade Union (BITU) wrote to the acting Governor to suggest several possible properties in the vicinity as candidates for official purchase and subdivision.[193] The United Fruit Company wanted to sell some 8,000 acres of its former banana estate at Twickenham Park, but government 'experts' – and some parochial board members too – refused to accept this offer. Likewise, efforts to acquire another estate to the south called

'Portmore', sited beside the old Passage Fort settlement, where 'the people could be settled on higher and more productive ground', failed in the Legislative Council. Only the St Catherine representative voted for adopting them.[194] These initiatives presented practical strategies to introduce broader social changes for the town and its surroundings.

1938: 'The alarming arrogance which has arisen among the labourers.'

In 1938 the riots and political demonstrations that reshaped Jamaican politics flared up elsewhere. The Kingston dockyards with their unionized labour force and the western sugar belt with its disappointment and misery provided the first recruits for angry crowds, 'disturbances' and riots. In April, a section on 'labour relations' in a report on St Catherine made by the Police Inspector in Spanish Town observed that there had 'been no unrest amongst the labourers' during the sugar harvest and pointed to 'the failure of the Labour Union formed in several parts of this section to impress labourers' as the cause for what he considered 'this satisfactory state'.[195] The calm did not last. Just over a month later, at the end of May, as labour protests spread out beyond Kingston, St Catherine was among the first locations to which the strikes extended. Starting initially among workers employed by the Parochial Board in Spanish Town, the protests were quickly taken up on neighbouring sugar estates too.[196] In these troubling times workers challenged the status quo across the island. By the middle of May the custos of St Catherine wrote to the Colonial Secretary on behalf of the owners of farms and local officials of the United Fruit Company requesting authorization to enroll them into 'a Special Reserve Platoon of the armed Special Constables' to protect their families and to preserve 'order on their properties'. Such precautions appeared necessary with 'the general unsettlement of conditions . . . and in particular the alarming arrogance which has arisen among the labourers'.[197] Employers found the scale of the labour organization in Spanish Town and in St Catherine's daunting.

The townspeople's engagement with wider politics in 1938 had deeper roots. Workers formed a locally based labour union, the St Catherine Labour and Workers Union, in April 1935, two weeks before the Governor's inconclusive visit to Spanish Town.[198] As workers' lives became increasingly desperate and the Colonial government's conventional solutions did little

FIGURE 8:7   The aftermath of trouble, 23 May 1938, a wrecked shop. The main crowd has gone by and a police constable is moving people along. (Jamaica Archives)

good, the union increasingly offered proposals. Over time their suggestions for local land settlement and a local land bank eventually shaped official agendas for reviving the regional economy.

The union's first demonstration in September 1936 was deliberately orderly. The Corresponding Secretary notified the Governor in a preliminary telegram: 'Hungry march situation serious.'[199] Three hundred men then marched through the town to the local Public Works Department office. The union's leaders addressed them and the crowd sang the National Anthem before dispersing. As the watching police observed, the marchers were careful not to lay themselves open to arrest for blocking traffic.[200] The new union began with experienced officials. Lawrence Washington Rose, a 30-year-old shoemaker from rural Manchester was the 'principal mover' and Corresponding Secretary. Until 1931 he was the Garveyite movement's organizer for the Kingston Corporate Area, and had been behind the attempts by the Spanish Town UNIA division to show the Governor the miserable state of the old capital's slums during his 1935 visit. During 1938–39 Rose served as Chairman of the Spanish Town UNIA division. Initially the union used the same address as the Spanish Town UNIA and its early official correspondence, which invokes 'resolutions' from 'mass meetings', echoes public declarations made by the UNIA.[201] Meanwhile the union grew to become a parishwide institution. How far the new union's recommendations extended Garveyite analyses to the current crises remains an open question, but by 1938 the parish custos would describe the union's 'authority' as being 'directed by racial influence', rather than depending on a formally enrolled and subscribing membership.[202] It did not break from its UNIA origins.

The leaders of St Catherine's trade union movement built on substantial local foundations and then added further muscle to their members' claims by affiliating with islandwide unions. In 1936, a month after its first demonstration, a further 'very orderly' procession occurred when a crowd marched 'to the Parochial Board Offices to interview the Parochial Authorities regarding the Unemployment Situation'. This exchange was followed by speeches from the union's local leadership, who now described themselves as the Labouring Class Political Party, suggesting that they intended broader social aims. The next day, however, the union officers abandoned their prospective party to affiliate with an islandwide labour union led by Allan George St Claver Coombs, a trade union stalwart who had established his Jamaica Workers and Tradesmen Union earlier that year.[203] The prescriptions for social change offered at the new branch's mass meeting held in Spanish Town's market square ranged well beyond immediate employment. The workers demanded 'the development of native industries in the island, the putting into operation of a land settlement scheme at once, and the setting up of an Agricultural Loan Bank to assist the settler to work the lands'.[204] The links to Coombs would remain solid. As late as 8 June 1938, the local union leadership continued to reaffirm that he was the leader of their union, while Alexander Bustamante remained 'just a mediator' from Kingston, 'a general labour leader' rather than any 'sort of President with Mr Coombs'.[205] Later that month, however, as union politics in Kingston grew especially tense, the St Catherine union transferred its affiliation to the newly established Bustamante Industrial Trades Union.[206] This shift would prove a pivotal move that allowed the hitherto Kingston-based BITU to expand from the capital, setting it on its way to becoming a decisive force in Jamaican politics.

In the meantime, the government still had little work to offer to Spanish Town's unemployed workers. Seizing on any available expedient the colonial administration was even obliged to turn to the old King's House restoration project. Stabilizing the fire-damaged walls would provide some immediate jobs. Lady Swettenham's committee had accumulated £3,500. So, in an unexpected reversal of earlier official policies, cleaning and strengthening the ruins at the old King's House became a public relief project. In December 1936, in the hungry pre-Christmas weeks before the sugar cane was harvested, the Divisional Secretary of A.G.S. Coombs' Jamaican Workers and Tradesmen Union wrote to complain at the protracted start of the project. Two days later the Colonial Secretary sent an official letter to Mr Rose reporting that the work had begun.[207] Meanwhile the Governor urged the Public Works Department to locate further relief schemes. Poverty remained deeply rooted in Spanish Town and its surrounding area, despite the repairs to the old King's House and projects for regrading local roads. What slowly shifted after the union intervened were the official responses to such poverty.

After the 1938 riots almost all sides proposed radical remedies to address the area's intransigent social problems – though as a group the elected members of the island's Legislative Council proved conspicuously inactive. Even the Colonial government offered some initiatives. Thus in 1940 the Governor steamrollered the Legislative Council into authorizing a new administration for the troubled Leper Hospital, although this meant accepting the introduction of sisters from the Marist order of Roman Catholic nuns into Jamaica.[208] The colony's persistent economic problems demonstrated the need for broader political reform. Locally, individual developments in Spanish Town and its vicinity began to deliver some of the remedies proposed by the union movement in 1936. Liquidity expanded after Spanish Town finally housed the 'Lower St Catherine's People's Co-operative Bank' in 1939, which offered short-term loans to smallholders on the security of their land. Many of the bank's early loans were for sums of between £5 and £20 and ran for from two to six months. In 1940 further credit became available when townspeople who purchased shares in the 'St Catherine Mutual Building Society' could raise money through mortgaging freeholds in Spanish Town itself.[209] These were solid achievements, though they still left the town's economy with a long way to go.

By the end of the politically charged central months of 1938 the local situation might look better: 'conditions commenced to revert to normal . . . as the majority of the people are employed and receive higher wages.'[210] But this upbeat state of affairs did not last. Unemployment remained stubbornly high across the parish and in 1942 the parish poor rate, which had fallen in 1937 and 1938, jumped higher – well ahead of increases in other parishes. The assumption organizing the subsequent official investigation of this phenomenon was that there must be some administrative 'laxity' to be identified.[211] The parish's problems remained deeply rooted. Instituting improvements was going to be hard under any system of government.

However, the island's government did change. The 1938 riots led to an official acknowledgement that the island's Legislative Council provided too limited an outlet for local opinion. Constitutional reform became part of the overall solution. In 1938 the Legislative Council proposed re-establishing a two-house legislature in a variant of the 1865 constitution that the Assembly had passed after Morant Bay, before their bill was replaced at Governor Eyre's insistence by the complete surrender of the Assembly's powers. The British Colonial Office first derailed this recommendation and then put it on hold during a wartime political truce. Not until 1942 did the Legislative Council again advise reinstituting a two-house elected legislature. This was finally accepted in London, effectively offering the death knell for Crown Colony government. Sixteen years after the Depression demolished the economic achievements of Crown Colony rule in Jamaica, the island's central administration also underwent reconstruction. Among the speeches made in the Legislative Council in 1942 when the recommendation finally went through, one harked back to a petition in 1865 from residents of St Catherine protesting the Assembly's decision to surrender its authority.[212] The clock would not be turned back completely. The new legislature continued to meet in Kingston and none of the offers sent in by optimistic realtors and estate agents, proposing buildings available for lease to house the new representative body were in Spanish Town.[213]

In 1944, Jamaica finally made the bold leap of faith of instituting universal adult suffrage.[214] In the meantime the local economy in St Catherine only grew very slowly. The treatment offered to the unemployed – or the responses to public officials who treated unemployed job applicants brusquely – demonstrated the broadest shifts in approaching the island's problems. In 1946, when the Superintendent at the Spanish Town Public Works Department faced another crowd of men demanding work and refused to find anything for them, the island's Majority Leader and Minister of Communications, the Honourable Alexander Bustamante, rose in the House of Representatives to support a parliamentary motion made by Leonard Washington Rose, now the Jamaica Labour Party's Representative for South East St Catherine, calling for an official investigation of the incident.[215] In 1944 both men had been elected to Jamaica's House of Representatives on the colony's new universal franchise. The political landscape had changed. Subsequent developments for Spanish Town and its surrounding area would continue to build on the social and political initiatives proposed during the Depression era.

Views from the Air, 1942–2000

$\mathcal{I}$N THE OPENING chapters of her 1966 novel, *Wide Sargasso Sea*, Jean Rhys, the mid-twentieth-century Dominican author, offered impressionistic descriptions of Spanish Town, where it appeared as a crumbling backdrop for a decaying creole society. Somewhere for her heroine to be married, perhaps, but also somewhere to leave.[1] Jamaica's former capital city proved even harder to accommodate to Anglo-American assumptions about urban functions. For Jamaica's post-Second World War policy makers, who increasingly looked to industrialization and modernization to deliver the jobs that the island's population so sorely needed, this urban centre with its persistent high unemployment posed a signally intractable problem.[2] Would post war opportunities allow the town to escape from the dismissive verdict offered by Governor Stubes in 1930, that it was only 'a decaying town, too far from Kingston to share its prosperity and too near to have an independent prosperity of its own'?[3]

Despite persistent concerns about decay the old town remains a distinctive presence in today's Jamaica. The legacies of its former roles are conspicuous, making its town centre a potential UNESCO World Heritage site. Meanwhile the town still sits astride a major cross roads, though now proximity to Kingston dictates a growing proportion of residents' employment opportunities. The population of the town has grown too, though not as fast as Kingston or Portmore, the new dormitory town to the south. A succession of aerial photographs indicate some of the transitions the town and its residents have undergone, showing how Spanish Town has adapted between

1942, when it was incorporated in a photographic mapping of the island undertaken by the US Army Air Corps, to the end of the twentieth century.

The economic base for mid-twentieth century Spanish Town remained weak. It would not be easy to restore the pillars of its late nineteenth-century economy that had disintegrated by the 1930s. It gained no new government offices. In the short term, wartime petrol and tyre rationing helped the Jamaica Government Railway to compete with road traffic more effectively, but otherwise neither bananas nor tourism enjoyed any rebound.[4] The fungal infection of Panama Disease continued to linger in the soil, precluding the replanting of banana plantations in St Catherine, particularly as the war in the Atlantic cut off exports of fruit from Jamaica to Britain. The war stopped most recreational travelling too. In 1941 the latest Caribbean travel guide published in New York did recommend making a stop in Spanish Town while driving north across the island to get to hotels in Ocho Rios and Montego Bay after landing at the flying boat depot in Kingston harbour.[5] The writer's chosen route across the island raised the prospect of the old capital enjoying a more prominent role as a stopping point as another transport revolution began to reshape foreign visitors' itineraries. Air travel would not only dictate how they reached Jamaica, but then where they travelled within the island to get from the new airports to their hotels. However, Pearl Harbor and the United States' entry into the war later in 1941 meant that for the next few years this particular guidebook would not inspire further carloads of tourists to pause in Spanish Town.

The war did bring US servicemen to Jamaica. Spanish Town featured on some of their horizons. Training exercises in 1942 between the US and Canadian troops had the American force defending the old capital, while some GIs dated Spanish Town women too.[6] However the Colonial government's expectation that Spanish Town's unemployed would find jobs constructing the Americans' new bases went unfulfilled.[7] A donation made to the town's Roman Catholic Church in 1944 of office equipment from the US naval air base established at Goat Island in Old Harbour Bay fell well short of these hopes.[8]

The US Army Air Corps photographed the town in the first days of 1942.[9] Pilots stationed at Fort Simonds on the lend-lease Vernam Field base in Clarendon were just beginning to navigate Jamaica's airspace. The old capital with its nodal position on the island's main road and rail routes offered them a ready landmark. Details are hard to make out as a cloud casts its shadow

FIGURE 9:1 Spanish Town in December 1941 or January 1942. The railway line is to the south of the town. Detail from a US Army Air Corps Map of Jamaica, derived from aerial photograph taken between 20 December 1941 and 14 January 1942. (Jamaica Archives)

across the town and the consolidation of the prints into an islandwide map blurred whatever definition the original photographic plates had achieved.

Several features still remain clear. We can make out something of this agricultural town whose economy had yet to emerge from the Depression. To twenty-first-century eyes, Jamaica's second largest urban settlement appears a small place with tightly defined boundaries, lying amidst open fields. The 1890s Leper Hospital remains isolated, off to the south of the town. The cutting for the railway line frames the town's southern and western boundaries – indeed, to the west, houses have not stretched all the way out to the railway, though a single bulge of houses just south of the railway indicates the boundaries of the old race course and the edge of the subsequent late nineteenth-century squatting and rebuilding on those municipal lands. To the north and east, the Rio Cobre defines the city, though the older streets of the Spanish-era grid are hidden by the trees that lined this select residential area. The bright white lines traversing the surrounding fields mark roads, surfaced with white limestone marl.

The roads appear pristine because government-funded road repair provided a standby for job creation schemes. Twelve years into the Depression, many nearby roads had already been worked on. The pay was miserably low, but the road gangs' culminative efforts are apparent.[10] Over the next three years, however, the road-building projects undertaken around Spanish Town changed, increasingly concentrating on upgrading 'the lovely white road west from Kingston' running out to Spanish Town and then on to May Pen and the American base.[11] Jamaican politicians might well object when road repair jobs on this main road moved beyond a reasonable walking distance from Spanish Town, reducing their utility as relief projects. Alexander Bustamante weighed in with a characteristically forceful recommendation that 'in spending money for unemployment one wants to spend it on works of necessity, work that must be done, if not today – tomorrow; and there is plenty of such work in St Catherine, somewhat near to Spanish Town where unemployment is highest'.[12] His objections were in vain. The Colonial government employed its discretionary power to channel job creation projects towards a major infrastructure project.

The main road from Kingston to Spanish Town which the unemployed laboured on during the war would ease peacetime communications. In practice the most ambitious hopes for elaborate internal 'Island Motor Highways' across post war Jamaica, perhaps funded by tolls, did not come to pass. The highways project was prominent in a semi-official appraisal of the opportunities for reviving the island's tourist industry to take advantage of 'the expected large-scale travel movement of people from the northern countries as soon as wartime travel regulations are lifted'. This was compiled in April 1945, prior to VE-day (8 May 1945, marking victory in Europe), so before the fighting was over and, indeed, before anyone sketching plans for postwar development foresaw the restraints that sterling's post war crises would impose on British tourism. In these ambitious schemes airline passengers could follow that 1941 guidebook's path to drive across the island from Kingston to their hotels on the north shore. The new motor highways, the island's tourism advocates claimed, would provide 'an attraction unsurpassed in the Caribbean Area'.[13] In the event post war tourists would drive across Jamaica, but after reaching Spanish Town they used existing roads. In time these might be asphalted but they fell well short of the planners' magnificent *autobahns*.

Post-war development plans for Spanish Town looked to the newly upgraded road. Assumptions about the numbers who would be driving to and through the post-war town remained high and, if anything, this traffic was expected to increase. A Kingston tour company offered bold estimates for the numbers of passing tourists: 8,000 in 1956 rising to 10,000 in 1957 and 1958. Then, as these totals only reflected tourists on organized tours, further multipliers were proposed, first to round up the initial numbers by a further 25 per cent 'to include visitors transported through Spanish Town by independent taxi operators and then by a further 25 per cent, representing private individuals either driven across the island in drive-yourself cars or taken by friends'.[14] The roundness of these estimates may well reduce our confidence in their reliability, but such hopeful calculations demonstrate the optimistic assumptions that underpinned official plans through the 1960s. Because Spanish Town lay on the route that the tourists' buses and taxi-cabs followed, then with so many transients the town's historic centre could expect to catch some lucrative crumbs. The hope was tempting – and not necessarily unreasonable.[15] The difficulty remained that all too few of these passing tourists chose to make a stop and, even if they did, very few pounds or dollars were spent while they lingered. The former tourist infrastructure from the railway-era tourism of 60 years before was long gone: the Rio Cobre Hotel now held troubled adolescents while the punt trips on the Rio Cobre that had so enchanted an earlier generation of visitors never restarted. So what was there to stop for? For most of these drivers the town's narrow streets appeared a bottleneck rather than a destination. Its old brick buildings were glimpsed, not viewed. All those tourist-crammed buses and cabs simply roared on through the old town en route to the north shore hotels, with their beaches and their bars.

Moving east across the Rio Cobre

Broader changes began to reshape the old capital and its surroundings after the war. Turning back to the aerial photograph, the next newest element in this image is that by December 1941 all the banana trees to the east of the town have disappeared, leaving what appears to be rough grazing in their stead, even while local farmers were benefiting from 'ideal weather'.[16] These fields of bananas had provided a conspicuous part of the surrounding landscape from the start of the twentieth century, when successive visitors commented on the neat lines of banana trees they saw out of the train windows as they travelled between Kingston and Spanish Town.[17] The sale by the United Fruit Company of its Twickenham Park estate to the Government of Jamaica in 1946 marked the Company's final retreat from banana growing on the south side of the island, while bringing a broad swathe of land to the east of the Rio Cobre into public hands.

How to put this land to use? The main change in post-war Jamaican society was not so much a change in available opportunities – though there were some – but the far more engaged approach towards developing any available opportunities taken by the island's governments.[18] When the colony's officials aimed to nurture industrial employment, the space once occupied by those former banana-filled fields lay wide open. Developing substitutes for imports during the war had provided a spur for subsequent attempts to encourage Jamaican production in the post war period. Spanish Town was not the primary centre for these ambitious industrializing policies – the introduction and encouragement of the aluminum-extracting bauxite industry during the 1950s, along with the development of a manufacturing sector in and around Kingston loomed far larger – but it was a beneficiary all the same. A line of new factories laid out during the late 1950s on former Twickenham Park estate land beside the approach road from Kingston were part of the same endeavour. Prospective investors could be attracted by the claim that the road from Kingston to Spanish Town was 'the island's major highway'.[19]

Among the initial tenants was the Island Worcester Company that planned to use raw materials from Jamaica and locally recruited and trained painters to produce fine porcelain for the regional and North American export markets. The company planned to manufacture 'three-quarters of a million pounds worth of pottery for sale on the world market per year' in their pottery factory, still a substantial sum in 1962. After the colony's wartime good fortune in discovering that the fine red clay of St Elizabeth and St Ann was aluminum-rich bauxite ore, the prospects for further geological discoveries seemed highly promising. In 1955 the arrival of a Canadian 'oil expert' to Prospect, raised further hopes though he found nothing.[20] In such optimistic contexts it seemed that Jamaica most have clay beds suitable for all sorts of pottery which only needed to be looked for. The subsequent government investment in the new pottery factory then exemplified the development programmes undertaken in the last years of colonial rule when Jamaica enjoyed 'a decade of rising production and rapidly accelerating economic advance.'[21] The Royal Worcester Company, an old established British firm,

FIGURE 9:2 'Island Worcester' pottery. From the first the manufacturers aimed 'to produce something with a Jamaican image that is hand decorated in Jamaica by Jamaican women and girls'. (Photograph, David Buisseret)

setup a West Indian branch: the managing director's holiday in Jamaica in 1956 helped, as did rumours that an American rival might enter the regional market, along with sunny promises from the official geological surveys. Central planners in Britain and Jamaica helped ship in equipment and some training staff. The British Colonial Development Corporation and the Jamaica Industrial Development Corporation both provided funds to assist the project.[22]

The newly established Island Worcester Company secured its first contract from the future independent nation's Governor General early in 1962, (just before he doffed his official cocked hat as the last British Governor). The company produced the 4,000 pieces required to make up 500 table settings which then received their first use at the 'Royal Independence Banquet'.[23] It aimed for far larger markets two years later in 1964, when sets of hand-painted Jamaican-manufactured porcelain went on sale in New York department stores. They were well made, well designed and priced at seven pounds for a 62 piece dinner set, a remarkably good buy.[24] However, a fundamental problem remained. An extended search by the company's own geologists for

FIGURE 9:3 'Carerras Cigarette Factory', today the Jamaica Cigarette Company Ltd, with a statue of its signature black cat trademark standing out in front. Looking from the south. A purpose-built factory in former farmland facing the road from Kingston. (Jamaica Archives, photograph by Jack Tyndale-Biscoe, 15 December 1964, by permission).

suitable white kaolin clay proved unsuccessful: all the clay beds they found contained far too high an iron content which stained the clay, blotching the translucent effect desired in fine porcelain.[25] By default the factory continued shipping its primary raw material in from England. Island Worcester's skilled workmanship and striking designs could not make up for such a basic flaw in its business plan. After a couple of years of operation the pottery was unable to pay its utility bills and closed.[26] Next door, though, the Carerras cigarette factory was another early tenant in this row of factories that proved far more successful in producing goods for the domestic market. The Carerras factory housed a venture undertaken by an old Kingston firm which already knew its market. As the Jamaica Cigarette Company the factory remains in operation, successfully competing with imported brands and still providing a very effective exercise in import substitution and job creation. Outside funding for proposals to bring new firms to Jamaica and widen the range of manufactures undertaken on the island was a major change from the 1920s and '30s. These outlays could encourage innovative proposals, but the civil servants who administered this bounty in Kingston and in London still needed to evaluate the ideas before the aid money was wasted. In the competition for manufacturing jobs promised by new factories, Spanish Town's Twickenham Park site offered ready access to transport routes.

A 'curiouʃ combination of beauty and ʃqualor':[27] planʃ for the old town centre.

The industrial developments on 'green fields', the former Twickenham Park estate during the late 1950s and early '60s demonstrated government optimism and sustained attempts to move beyond Jamaica's traditional agricultural economy. Spanish Town's original centre declined over the same period. Hurricane Charley hit the town hard in August 1951 – as it also hit the island's south coast between Morant Bay and St Catherine. Not only did the hurricane kill the last of the ancient Spanish-era tamarind trees in the Alms House gardens, but it damaged the 1820s Wesleyan Methodist Chapel on White Church Street and, farther along the same street, the 1840s Ebenezer Native Baptist Chapel so badly that the congregations closed the buildings permanently. The Wesleyan chapel was demolished and a replacement erected.[28] The ruins of the Ebenezer Chapel remained standing into the 1980s, when they were pulled down as a safety risk.[29] Fifty years after the hurricane the site remains empty. The remaining ruins of the Novéh Shalom synagogue were finally pulled down in the mid-'50s too, before the site was handed over to the parish council as a park or to hold a library.[30] Further architectural casualties included two more small Roman Catholic chapels associated with Spanish Town's St Joseph's Church, the 1900 St Wilfred's in Port Henderson and a 1908 wooden chapel at Gregory Park. Both were demolished and replaced with larger concrete structures after sustaining damage during the hurricane.[31] The 1950s were a dangerous time for any buildings deemed 'obsolete' and in need of repairs. 'Modern' tastes reacted against Victorianism and appeared particularly hostile towards the wood and brick chapels that enshrined the cultural values of their Victorian grandparents. At a time when 'planners' in England and the United States confidently flattened nineteenth-century townscapes to build a properly rational society, few Jamaican voices were raised to recommend reconstruct-ing roofless and badly battered chapels. Insufficient insurance provision may well have factored in too, but the persistent omission over the preceding 80 years of any of the town's historic chapels from the guidebooks sitting on administrator and academic shelves probably sealed the fate of the two brick chapels on White Church Street.

After the hurricane residents continued to leave the town's former principal streets in the old Spanish grid between the Square and the Rio Cobre. More widespread car ownership and a good road allowed senior professionals to commute from Kingston's new suburbs to Spanish Town because 'even those who work there prefer to live elsewhere'. An outbreak of yellow fever in Spanish Town – but not in Kingston – in 1955 offered one more push. In a remarkable reversal of eighteenth- and nineteenth-century experiences suburban Kingston became a healthier place to live than Spanish Town. Visitors from Kingston's new suburbs commented on the mosquito netting they noticed on the windows of 'the better off houses' as 'a thing one never sees in St Andrew'.[32] Sales of substantial former residential properties in the older sections of the town provided remarkable opportunities for several of the town's schools to expand and relocate to larger premises in the 1950s. Low prices benefited institutions which remained based in the town, but the overall social mix shifted.

Declining property values provided one impetus for continued change in the old town centre, but hardly the only one. Spanish Town still housed many homeowners who were proud of their properties and eager to adapt them to accommodate their current needs. Here the establishing of a cement factory just to the east of Kingston, another of the island's postwar import-substitute initiatives, meant that from the 1950s householders and their contractors had access to a wider range of materials for building additions and repairs.[33] Rather than being constrained to use the brick, lumber, shingles and lime wash that Jamaican builders had relied on for 300 years, cinder blocks, steel construction rods and corrugated zinc sheets all permitted far more drastic 'improvements'. Locally made prefabricated metal windows succeeded older wooden jalouseie blinds or the projecting wood-framed 'coolers' that had offered a distinctive visual rhythm to the one- and two-storey houses that still made up the bulk of Spanish Town's housing stock. So, while demolition and decay certainly played their parts in transforming older streetscapes, many of the town's older houses were camouflaged under homeowners' alterations. These included new roof lines, cinder block additions and new steel windows which then combined to transform the facades facing on to the old capital's streets.[34] The accumulated actions by active householders proved as much of a break from the past as their neighbours' dilapidation. Much of the old town might remain standing, but it was increasingly coated in new facades.

FIGURE 9:4 Spanish Town Square before independence. Viewed from the north east. The new Archives building is on the right hand side. The old King's House stables by now housing the Folk Museum, are at the top. (Jamaica Archives, photograph by Jack Tyndale-Biscoe, 5 October 1960, by permission).

A stage for public ceremonies during the last years of the empire

Despite fundamental changes in local residence patterns, the town's central public spaces continued to provide sites for major public events. During the 1950s Jamaica's elite drove out from Kingston to the old capital to stage many of the colony's most impressive civilian displays. In 1950 even such a Kingston-based institution as the new University College of the West Indies, with its campus already established just to the north of Kingston at Mona, sought to marshal its most formal academic pageantry in Spanish Town, when it held a religious service to install Princess Alice, Countess of Athlone, a grand-daughter of Queen Victoria, as the College's first Chancellor. The Anglican Cathedral of St Jago provided an appropriate site for staging a ceremony to stamp the new College as 'respectable' – and deserving regional respect.[35] So too, three years later, when the newly crowned Queen Elizabeth II visited the colony just after her coronation, Spanish Town's main Square provided a site for her to make a public appearance: a resident's dialect poem recalled not just that 'The sun was hot and a thirsty', but the large crowds:

> An a good ting a did go early
> For de people jam de park
> From de early hours of de morning:
> Dem mus' a bin stan'up from dark . . .

It was worth the wait too:

> . . . 'She da come, she da come' dey is crying
> An a rustle like breeze da blow
> An de people bowing and cheering
> An de car go pass dead slow.[36]

Then, two years later, when the three hundredth anniversary of the English Conquest of Jamaica presented an occasion for another official visit, the Queen's younger sister Princess Margaret came to Spanish Town to attend a special 'State Service' at the Cathedral.[37] In each instance the old capital offered appropriate backdrops for imperial pomp.

Other speakers also found it a suitable venue. In July 1961, when the clock was running down fast on British rule, the King's House square in Spanish Town appeared 'mysterious' in the lights from a truck during an evening rally. A very different set of orators addressed crowds there, as they would again in Morant Bay, in Brown's Town and at Montego Bay's Charles Square (now Sam Sharpe Square).[38] These speakers were West Indians and this time the speeches looked to the future, urging townspeople to support the Federation of the West Indies in an imminent referendum where Jamaica's vote to withdraw from the Federation demolished the whole organization. Looking back, the decision to address crowds at Spanish Town and Morant Bay appears to invoke central sites in Jamaican history.[39] At the time, however, these venues offered convenient places where speakers based in Kingston could find sizeable audiences, while the principal speeches in the campaign were offered at the Brown's Town meeting and then at the tightly packed Charles Square, which may have provided less 'historic' sites, but drew far bigger crowds.[40]

Neither hosting royal visits nor public meetings generated much further public expenditure in the historic town centre. In 1961 a building to house the Jamaica Archives was erected just behind the Rodney Temple and beside the late eighteenth-century Secretary's Office, but official investments went no further.[41] In the absence of significant gestures of public confidence the whole town centre continued to crumble. This despite persistent lobbying efforts by Jamaican preservationists and far more support for restoration projects from senior colonial administrators than their Depression-era predecessors had ever offered. Even with encouragement from Donald Sangster, the Minister of Finance and a future Prime Minister, persuading the colony's government to underwrite major restoration work was not easy as the costs remained dauntingly high.[42] With the tantalizing prospect of securing funding for such a major project imminent, the campaigners left smaller-scale repairs until later. After the big fish got away, they had nothing. In the early 1950s, as the three hundredth anniversary of the English conquest approached, surviving members of the committee that had worked to preserve the burnt-out King's House in the 1920s and '30s revived their efforts to restore this brick shell to its former glory. They urged the construction of a museum in Spanish Town to describe the period up to 1872 and the government's move to Kingston. In pressing for immediate action they pushed the claim that a campaign to restore the old King's House would provide a suitable gesture to mark the royal visit that the anniversary would produce.[43] Playing the royal card appeared plausible as loyalty and royalty were both powerful forces to invoke in Jamaica then. Fund-raising committees were established. Corporate sponsors began to express interest. But all these bandwagons rolled elsewhere after Princess Alice, as the Chancellor of the University College of the West Indies, threw her personal support behind an alternative project to mark the anniversary by transporting an eighteenth-century cut stone rum store across the island from Trelawny to the campus and re-erecting it as the college chapel. This was not just an imaginative project in its own right; it had a bona fide princess pushing behind it. The island's corporate cheque books opened for the Princess Alice Appeal Fund.[44] Fundraising for the proposed museum in Spanish Town was 'put aside . . . it being realised that two large scale Public Appeals could not be successfully pursued simultaneously'.[45]

Regaining momentum proved difficult. The island's last British Governor chaired meetings of the central King's House restoration committee. He had earlier served in the Leeward Islands, where the restoration of Nelson's Dockyard in Antigua already provided a valuable tourism asset. By the late

1950s though, this was as far as his support could go, because constitutional reforms prior to Independence meant that 'the Governor of Jamaica has no responsibility for the government of Jamaica'.[46] Comparable support from his predecessors would have been far more valuable. The pre-1955 proposal to build a museum within the old King's House ruins to display Jamaican furniture and other artifacts from the Institute of Jamaica's collections appeared prohibitively expensive: initial estimates quoted a daunting £100,000 'somewhat less than half of which, it was thought, might be raised by Public Appeal'.[47] This plan also incorporated a scheme to convert the former stable block and government rum store as supplementary exhibit space. After the three hundredth anniversary opportunity was lost, the former secondary proposal was revived with an appeal for private donations to establish a Folk Museum (today's People's Museum). It proved an attainable goal. Over the last five years of British rule sufficient money could be raised to stabilize the stables, set up the new museum and gather some exhibits although, regrettably, neither the hoped for donations of an old railway carriage from the Jamaica Railway Company nor an old tramcar from Kingston Omnibus Company, either of which would also have served as an innovative museum office, proved forthcoming.[48] Over the subsequent 40 years school parties have trailed through the former stable block, peering at an accumulation of earthenware yabbas, basketry and old tools. Housing the Folk Museum in the King's House stables offered another lease of life to the whole complex. The Museum proved a worthwhile project, one whose success lay in appealing to Jamaican visitors rather than pursuing the will-o'-the-wisp of international tourist traffic.

The Folk Museum was only the tip of an iceberg of plans and proposals. Rather than breaking the problems of refurbishing Spanish Town's town centre into achievable component parts, veranda chatter invoked sweeping proposals for 'rehabilitating' the old town as 'a show place', one holding a larger number of 'authentic buildings than Williamsburg!' Impressive buildings were certainly standing there, but the slogans avoided grappling with the current householders' eagerness to sell their residences in the historic town centre and use the proceeds to move to Kingston's latest suburban developments. Unfocused plans for urban renewal were also hampered by basic incomprehension about what such efforts should involve. Tourists of the 1950s expected historical architecture to appear properly pretty, something that would look nice printed on the lid of a box of chocolates. Spanish Town hardly fitted into such glossy preconceptions. Opinionated commentators lamented that its 'gracious houses' were 'swamped' among 'awful shacks'.49 As another travel writer summed up the veranda consensus: before Spanish Town 'can hold any real attraction for the ordinary tourist, more than the King's House will need to be restored'.50 Overambitious expectations therefore got in the way of practical efforts to establish any sort of a tourist destination. Williamsburg has its historic public buildings and eighteenth-century houses and shops, but visitors dig most deeply into their pockets when they ease their thirst at its old taverns or dine as its 'period' restaurants. In the 1950s and '60s Spanish Town still had an authentic pre-emancipation inn, the 'Marble Hall Hotel' that 1920's tourists had disparaged, but nothing was done to redevelop this solid and authentic building. Instead, the restoration efforts led with scrubbing off the old lime wash on the structures facing the Square in order to reveal the underlying brickwork. Providing something as useful as a restaurant for transients does not seem to have featured in the decade's much-ballyhooed schemes.

The general failure of these 1950's projects for developing Spanish Town to capture contemporary imaginations was further demonstrated in the persistent absence of any roles for Spanish Town in the thrillers that Ian Fleming was currently churning out in Oracabessa, on Jamaica's north shore. Several of his wildly popular James Bond novels employed Jamaican settings. When it came to finding striking island venues for cold war combats with communists and their criminal stooges, Spanish Town never figured.

Development, education and heritage in an independent Jamaica

The 1960s and '70s saw the pace of change in the city centre increase. During the 1970s Jamaica's Rastafarians would attribute a prophecy to Marcus Garvey: 'that when you see Kingston and Spanish Town joined together into one, then you will know that your redemption is at hand'.51 As Kingston's suburbs increasingly stretch across the Liguanea Plain towards the borders of St Catherine redemption seems imminent. The explosive growth of Kingston's population was a key factor in both shaping modern Jamaican society and in Spanish Town's own development during these decades, as the currency of this millenarian prophecy highlighted.

Residential patterns altered. Ground breaking at the end of 1961 for a new housing scheme at Portmore, to the south of Spanish Town, stretching from the harbour to the old Gregory Park railway station, produced longer-term consequences. In 1938 the St Catherine Branch of the Bustamante Industrial Trades Union had proposed the Portmore estate as suitable for a smallholders' settlement.[52] Twenty years later the development of the site followed a single plan. During the late 1960s and '70s developers constructed flood walls and then extended a grid of new streets south from the old Gregory Park railway station and over the remnants of the former settlement of Passage Fort to Port Henderson, erasing old streets, farm tracks and field boundaries as it went. The new town provided homes for Kingston's latest upwardly mobile employees who could now purchase a house. It echoed the checkerboard layouts of new suburbs sprawling across European and North American landscapes over the same years. Portmore's householders mostly looked east to Kingston, commuting to work in the capital by buses, cabs or, more recently, private cars. Indeed, by contrast with its new neighbour's avenues, Spanish Town's streets still appear too narrow to persuade shoppers from Portmore to use the shopping centres that now cluster on the older town's south side and, instead, they go to Kingston to shop. Portmore showed the opportunities to distinguish home and work for a culture of commuting into Kingston. After this demonstration, the mortgages began flowing and new suburbs around Spanish Town increasingly housed commuters too.

Jamaican Independence and the departure of British Colonial government in 1962 provided few immediate opportunities for the old capital. The new public buildings commissioned to house the independent nation's public business were concentrated in Kingston, though as an outlier from these public commissions the road to Spanish Town gained the Arawak (now Taino) Museum, completed in 1965. This striking modern building at White Marl was constructed at the island's largest Taino site.[53] Some of the earliest prehistoric excavations in Jamaica had been undertaken there in the 1890s, though these did not prevent road works during the 1940s slicing through the deepest accumulations of Taino material to remove a sharp curve on the road to Kingston. After further postwar excavations the landowner recognized the importance of the site and donated the White Marl quarry to the then Jamaica National Trust Commission.[54] Shortly after Independence the Trust commissioned a building to house the accumulated finds and provide a base for subsequent fieldwork.

Heritage policy changed and these changes were felt in Spanish Town. The issuing of a Town and County Planning Order for the town in 1964 addressed the old buildings remaining in the old town centre. The order attempted to put a brake on building and demolition by requiring planning permission in a 'Development Area' in doing so Jamaica adopted the best-practice recommendations of the day. This proto-Heritage zone also endeavoured to 'make provision for the orderly and progressive development of Spanish Town and adjacent areas' by encouraging population growth away from the main roads in and out of the town and towards the poorer, but better drained, limestone soil to the north of the town. Within the development area the measure primarily aimed to protect the main Square along with the area round the Cathedral and such outliers as the Phillippo Chapel and the Iron Bridge. It was a significant advance as it formally recognized the importance of the wider townscape. The scheme's stated goal of maintaining the town centre's 'peaceful and unspoilt atmosphere' characterized the town's older buildings as imparting 'a peculiar sense of tradition' that was 'an important part of the island's heritage'.[55] Clearly several important buildings have gone since it was passed, but we should not underestimate the continued effectiveness of such public orders in persuading responsible property holders to adopt preservationist strategies.[56] Without this order and its successors, far less would remain along these streets.

Archaeological excavations in the centre of Spanish Town marked the continuing potential for ambitious developments in the old town centre. During the late 1960s the Jamaican government dusted off and revised the 1950's proposal to construct a museum on the old King's House block, this time aiming to tap international development grants to fund the scheme. Architects at the Jamaica National Heritage Commission recopied plans of the interior of the old King's House and commissioned further plans from consulting engineers to reuse the space within the surviving exterior walls for a museum.[57] The preliminary archaeological excavations started in July 1971. The diggers completed two seasons' work.[58] But, after national elections swept the People's National Party into power in 1972, political backing for the scheme waned. Some skepticism about the economic rationales justifying the project may well have been reasonable enough, as the numbers of tourists visiting Kingston were shrinking with the refocusing of the island's hotels and cruise ship traffic to the north side of the island. The political climate seemed unpropitious. The archaeological director left Jamaica.[59] The engineers' proposals were returned to the plan chests. Yet although the government

FIGURE 9:5 'The Cuban School' in the process of building. Looking south, with the Rio Cobre behind the school. (Jamaica Archives, photograph by Jack Tyndale-Biscoe, 2 December 1976, by permission).

abandoned the project, efforts to conserve the fabric of the town slowed rather than stopped during the 1970s. Jamaican heritage groups and local enthusiasts would continue to record Spanish Town's architectural heritage.[60] Without government support for conservation, though, local passion was insufficient to halt the pace of demolition. It was at this juncture that the old Marble Hall Hotel was pulled down.

Then, counterpoised to Spanish Town's increasingly dilapidated colonial-era streets, a strikingly different architectural commission began to rise out of the fields just to the east of the 1950's Twickenham Park factories. Early in 1976 a team arrived from Cuba to construct the Jose Marti School. They erected a complex designed to house five hundred boarders with another 200 semi-boarding pupils, employing Euro-Cuban blueprints to build a modernist school that could as easily have stood in a sugar beet field in Poland or Prussia as in this former banana field.[61] At the time the school exemplified the Jamaican government's independent diplomatic line. The new school was a 'fraternal gift' to the people of Jamaica from their revolutionary comrades in Cuba. What would accepting such a gift mean for the status of Jamaica's ongoing socialist transformation or, indeed, for any subsequent dealings with Richard Nixon's USA?[62] Many Jamaicans were nervous about the project's implication, even if a contrarian *Daily Gleaner* commentator offered a less alarmist assessment: 'if someone wants to give us a school and to send chaps down to build it for us, I can't for the life of me see what's wrong with that . . .'.[63]

What would the project mean? A functionary from the Ministry of Education told the crowds who had waited for the ground breaking ceremony that the 'Cuban gift school . . . would introduce to Jamaica the Cuban discipline of work'. With considerably more flair Prime Minister Michael Manley used the occasion to argue that 'the real significance of the friendship between Cuba and Jamaica was not the result of the gift school but that the school was the result of the friendship', which 'was a friendship of two countries . . . that had its roots in the nature of the struggle they faced in today's world'. He continued by urging his audience to dedicate themselves 'to the struggle to build not only a Jamaica of opportunity and justice and equality for the masses, but to continue the struggle for a world of opportunity and justice for the poor of mankind'. This was all stirring stuff and only the Cuban Ambassador's speech was tactless enough to mention any 'resistance' to the project.[64] It was probably well worth braving the afternoon's drizzle to listen. Yet doubts remained. Townspeople worried whether the Cuban building crew would leave once the job was over and then feared that the new school's pupils would become socialist *brigadistas*, indoctrinated to undertake a class war.

Academic historians' 20:20 hindsight can all too easily obscure the immediate reality of people's hopes and fears for what the future *might* bring, views which shaped contemporaries' understandings of this project and its significance. In 1976, while the Jose Marti School was being built, uncertainties about where the nation was going extended widely. When townspeople worried about the building workers' encampment, or what prospective students might be taught there, the current use of the Jose Marti Technical High School's buildings as a polling centre during elections was not necessarily the future they could expect.

For today's residents the Jose Marti school appears important as just one among a number of high schools established in the town between the 1950s and the 1970s. Perhaps more than any public buildings – even those Kingston

Ministries – the island's new high schools represent the principal institutions marking the opportunities open to Jamaica's post-independence generations. When the Cuban team broke ground for the new school there were already several new or expanded high schools in the town. The former Beckford and Smith's School, whose governing board had lobbied to move into the Rio Cobre Hotel in 1914, did leave its cramped accommodation in the old Assembly building for a purpose-built site just to the south of the hotel property in 1959.[65] This move also combined the town's boys' grammar school with the Cathedral girls' school, which then led to the revival of the former St Iago Grammar School's name for the combined school as the 'St Jago High School'. Alongwith this consolidation and expansion of Spanish Town's former government-supported Anglican schools, the postwar period also saw rapid extensions to the town's Roman Catholic schools. The presence of the Marist sisters between 1944 and 1994, who undertook teaching at the Catholic Primary School may well have achieved a more lasting local impact than the mission to oversee the Leper Hospital that initially brought them to Spanish Town.[66] The town's Catholic High School started on a property purchased during the war that lay between the Roman Catholic Rectory on King Street and the Cathedral square. It initially offered places to students from the existing Catholic Middle School. Enrolments continued to increase, so that the high school was obliged to shift to a house in Brunswick Street and then seek purpose-built new premises. Low property prices in the late 1950s helped this effort, allowing what had become the St Catherine's High School to purchase a former rice field on the edge of the town. Building efforts just prior to Independence provided a further boost.[67] Then in the 1970s consultations between the school's Board of Management and the Ministry of Education facilitated the development of the existing school into a far larger Comprehensive High School teaching 2,500 students.[68] New buildings and Ministry support of local schools were invaluable but, the donated Jose Marti School aside, all these projects developed and expanded pre-existing institutions. During this period Spanish Town's experiences demonstrated the difficulties in coordinating urban development, educational policy and heritage policy in a developing nation. In several instances urban heritage projects lost out, but Jamaican heritage policies were articulated systematically and, particularly when heritage projects could be aligned with education – as in the Folk Museum and the Taino Museum – they received a sympathetic hearing.

Where are we now?

Today, if gaps in the clouds permit, airline passengers who look down on Spanish Town as jets make their approach into Kingston's Norman Manley airport, or else turn inland just after take-off to fly north across the island, see the old town centre surrounded by extensive new building. Each year a widening radius of former cane and banana fields, pasture and steep slopes are scissored into narrowly bounded house plots. On both sides of the Rio Cobre a dense network of roads slice through the landscape. Those around the town are lined with house plots, reaffirming that, like most Jamaican towns since Independence, the area of the town and its population are growing rapidly. Many of the people they house commute into Kingston, reversing the removals to Kingston that transformed the town's older elite residential streets in the 1950s and '60s.

The bird's eye view of the town offered in an aerial photograph from the mid-1980s demonstrates processes that continue to shape Spanish Town's development. (Illustration, 9:6) The total size of the town has increased since the US Army Air Corps took its photograph 40 years before. In shaping this expansion, the transport system that organized the town in 1941 has altered. After 40 years a ring road swings south of the town while the railway looms far less large. The line of the track is still a feature, but in the early 1990s the marshalling yards to the south of the town were sold for development. The land now houses a shopping centre. Extensions to the road network shaped urban development. In 1989 when Jean D'Costa, a Jamaican novelist, sought instances to highlight the differences between the 1950s and her current adolescent readers' experiences, she would cite the way 'the main road from Kingston to the north coast [went] through the middle of Spanish Town with no bypass . . .'[69] The repercussions of constructing a bypass extended well beyond the flow of traffic. By 1983 ribbon development along the ring road had already encouraged some new housing developments that stretch farther south from the main road. Even if Spanish Town has yet to join hands with Kingston, the prospect of the older town's southern housing estates colliding with the northward expansion of Portmore does seem imminent.

The greatest continuity with older patterns is shown in the open spaces in the city centre. Even though the railway closed to passenger traffic in 1992, the area in front of the old station is still filled with passengers – now waiting for

FIGURE 9:6 Spanish Town in 1983 East at the top, north to the left. The ring road running to the south of the town and the tree-lined course of the Rio Cobre, snaking through the town centre, offer bearings. (Jamaica Archives, photograph by Jack Tyndale-Biscoe, 5 November 1983, by permission).

or alighting from the buses and cabs that pick up and disgorge their passengers there. The taxi men have reversed a nineteenth-century trend. At the end of Queen Victoria's reign local antiquarians remarked that Spanish Town's long-established livery stables finally closed because travellers arriving in the town no longer needed to rent horses and buggies to get them home after the extension of the railway network in the 1880s.[70] Once the railway's passenger services ceased, taxi drivers operating from Spanish Town have become central in filling the resulting gap in the island's transport network. Today people who may find 'a trip into Kingston on a minibus/a little too adventurous' or who seek rides from Kingston to the northern side of the island and cannot wait for a bus to set off, take a route cab to Spanish Town, find a second driver to take them across the island to Ocho Rios, where a third driver from a local taxi rank drives them to their destinations.[71] The town now provides a hub for the island's route taxi network, reverting to its status before the railway opened as the cross-roads at the south end of the 'River Road'.

So what has changed? Entering Spanish Town from this south-western corner is convenient for anyone planning to buy to sell at the market, as it was for their predecessors disembarking at the railway station. However, the bustling area where the taxi-men and minibuses load and unload looks and sounds very different from earlier streetscapes. Different building materials produce facades that are far taller than their predecessors with more glass; a new generation of exterior paints provide shopkeepers and stallholders with a far more exuberant palette to decorate their premises while, of course, in blaring out dancehall beats, improved technology allows the resonance of sound systems to replace the tinny squawk of transistors. More cars and minibuses are creeping through the crowds and, while some intrepid goats continue to forage the rubbish in the gutters there are few pigs and, the proportion of livestock to humans and cars has diminished.

The newer houses on the estates surrounding Spanish Town can appear uniform to anyone driving past, though residents have personalized the building contractors' basic boxes with gates, gardens and extensions. And yet older patterns underlie even these mass-produced developments. Despite all the demolitions of old buildings and infilling of original lots, the older gridded ground plans of the sixteenth-century settlement and its 1740s expansion still organize the heart of the town. Inherited patterns extend further still. When we look down from our bird's eye view, it is clear that there is not the same all-pervading planner's grid that shapes Portmore's successive expansions. Instead, the individual schemes that comprise Spanish Town's growing suburbs are organized within an older tenurial landscape, so that developments retain the boundaries of far earlier fields and estates.[72] Even with the increasing pace of 'development' and 'suburbanisation', today's Spanish Town remains shaped by the area's older past.

Heritage zones and heritage policies – Recognizing a distinct urban past in Spanish Town

Uncertainty about what to make of Spanish Town's inherited buildings has helped define the town's identity. How this uncertainty manifested itself varied. Shortly after the Second World War, a visiting author characterized Spanish Town's empty streets as 'full of sunlight and heavy with that late-afternoon atmosphere which is peculiar to towns that have lost their importance.' Winds of change were gusting through Europe's imperial possessions and a description of Spanish Town's dusty eighteenth-century splendour provided a suitably elegiac finale for a tour of the Caribbean.[73] After another half century Spanish Town still retains the stamp of its 'Ancient Glory'. The most elaborate buildings that shape the town were commissioned when it was the Seat of Government and it was at this juncture, too, that a local building tradition developed. Then alongside, and indeed interwoven with, the town's distinctive built legacy is the affection that townspeople hold for the place.

Buildings in Spanish Town have lain near the centre of the continuing debates on the evaluation of Jamaica's material heritage since the 1920s, when Lady Mary Swettenham and her committee tried to make a case for the old King's House's significance and why it should be restored. Not all of the arguments they presented then would appear persuasive today, but they were asking interesting questions. In the 1950s too, the ambitious proposals for Spanish Town to emulate Williamsburg, the colonial capital of Virginia, did not get particularly far, but these planners still engaged with the contribution that inherited buildings and monuments could offer to tourism in Jamaica. The People's Museum remains a valuable legacy from this period. After independence, Governors retreated from these efforts and the Jamaica National Trust Commission now the Jamaica National Heritage Trust received the responsibility for setting general policies. With hindsight we will regret buildings lost, but the Trust's 1964 Heritage Zone policy helped preserve many more. Furthermore, the Trust remains respected. A very rough poll undertaken in 1994 suggested that local residents might be sympathetic to a proposal floated in the *Daily Gleaner* to declare central Spanish Town a National Monument, even if this would constrain householders' and businesses' alterations and rebuildings.[74]

The remarkable potential for urban conservation and heritage tourism projects in the town's old centre is clear.[75] Wider questions will continue to play out on these streets relating to the development of heritage policies in Jamaica and what criteria should shape official priorities. All attempts to explain why the town's material heritage is so impressive still have had to work against the tide of neatly packaged descriptions told and re-told in shelves of guide books. Would-be preservationists must first deal with the long-standing fallacy that if something is not included in the guide book it can not matter. Next comes the up-hill push to present alternative arguments demonstrating why a place or a building should repay consideration. It is not that the justifications proposed by long-dead tour guides are necessarily 'wrong', but the basic scripts these books repeat were composed in a very different era. They were not written to dictate cultural policies for modern Jamaica. An earlier generation of visitors may well have been cheered to be told that some buildings appeared 'English', but in making sense of the distinct creole architecture developed in eighteenth- and nineteenth-century Jamaica, invoking the relative 'English-ness' of a structure is not particularly helpful. Instead when appraising the old buildings that still line Spanish Town's streets the issues to consider include the buildings' construction, perhaps any borrowings from the African techniques that fellow artisans used, or the local materials employed, or else engaging with the expectations about forms and functions that builders and buyers brought to them. Turning away from our guide books to look up and down these ancient streets may mean foregoing easy answers – but there will be far more to see.[76]

Recognizing the distinctive architectural syntheses developed by artisans working in Jamaica can replace the earlier dismissals of so many buildings in Spanish Town as either 'un-English' or mere 'shacks'. The wider significance of this architectural legacy was acknowledged in 1987 when Jamaica made a submission to UNESCO's World Heritage Committee for the inclusion of three sites on the new World Heritage List: Port Royal, the seaport mostly submerged in the 1692 earthquake; New Seville, the island's first Spanish capital; and Spanish Town.[77] Only the proposal for Spanish Town won conditional acceptance. Before UNESCO could grant full approval, it required the local government to fill potholes, lay sidewalks and make infrastructure improvements. Funding these projects has remained beyond the reach of the parish's over-stretched budget. However, the prospect of achieving full acceptance as a World Heritage Site does encourage local efforts at preservation. International grants have paid for a recent stabilization of the Iron Bridge, and a project funded by a European Community grant successfully refurbished the complex of late eighteenth-century administrative buildings on the north side of the main square. Further plans include continuing the archeological excavations on the site of the former Novéh Shalom synagogue and refurbishing the shell of the late eighteenth-century barracks as storage and conservation facilities for the Jamaica National Heritage Trust's Archaeology Division. The brick shells facing onto Spanish Town's Square offer a challenge for imaginative re-use.[78]

New political initiatives may yet signal new opportunities. The Government of Jamaica recently decided to rename Spanish Town's main square 'Emancipation Square' because the royal proclamation ending slavery in Jamaica was read from the steps of the old King's House on 1 August 1834. Across the Caribbean monuments are proving catalysts for debates over the meaning of Emancipation and the place of slavery in nations' pasts.[79] These discussions may yet transform popular views of Spanish Town and its Emancipation Square. When it comes to declaring national monuments, understandings of what the 'heritage' of a nation consists of continue to adapt and are likely to keep adapting.[80] The commemorative plaque could simply stay on the King's House wall, but the decision to erect it and, indeed, the public subscription that paid for it, do suggest that another generation of Jamaicans will re-examine their island's former capital. Here continuing research by historians and archaeologists should help to re-grind and polish the lenses in the spectacles through which the nation's past is viewed.

Rather than Spanish Town remaining a dusty focus for long-departed colonial splendours, the town centre can be re-appraised in its own right as a remarkable architectural legacy. The town fully deserves its candidate status as a World Heritage site. Its Historic Area retains one of the most extensive surviving collections of Jamaican building craftsmen's work from the late eighteenth and early nineteenth century. Spanish Town also houses an impressive corpus of the work of local masons and carpenters during the town's 35 years as the capital for a post-emancipation Jamaica and then from the development-driven economy of the Crown Colony generations. There is room enough for further research on both the 'who' of the people who built these shops, houses and public buildings and on the 'what' of understanding how the people who inhabited these buildings knew and used them.

The former capital's 'Ancient glory' may well have departed, as glories have so often departed in Spanish Town's long past, but an impressive inheritance survives today. The town retains the potential to figure in modern Jamaicans' comprehension of their nation's development and their heritage, where its streets and squares can offer standpoints for examining the island's past and a destination for Jamaican visitors. Preserving Spanish Town – St Jago de la Vega will maintain a legacy for future Jamaicans.

Notes
—

Acknowledgements

1. K.E. Ingram, *Manuscript Sources for the History of the West Indies, with Special Reference to Jamaica in the National Library of Jamaica and Supplementary Sources in the West Indies, North America, the United Kingdom and Elsewhere* (Kingston: the UWI Press, 2000), extending the project begun in his *Manuscripts Relating to the Commonwealth Caribbean Countries in US and Canadian Repositories* (Barbados: Caribbean University Press, 1975), idem. *Sources of Jamaican History, 1655–1838: A Bibliographical Survey with Particular Reference to Manuscript Sources*, 2 vols. (Zug: Inter-Documentation, 1976), idem. *Sources for West Indian Studies: A Supplementary Listing with particular reference to manuscript sources* (Zug: Inter-Documentation, 1983), which all incorporate collections relating to Jamaica in their lists.

Introduction

1. NLJ Ms 91, Leslie Alexander, 'Poems, vol. 2', ff. 158–59. This is the version Alexander transcribed into his notebook. He subsequently added two further revisions, substituting 'that stays heart-true' for 'that's left' in line two and replacing 'on' with 'still' in the penultimate line. Cynthia is a poeticism for the moon.

2. The 'road to town' or 'The Town Road', JA 1B/11/1/9, [ff. 216–216v], 14 January 1683/4, patent to Samuel Bernaid; 'the Spanish Town as they call it' phrase, NLS Ms. 9250, f. 18, Dunlop Papers, 24 November 1685, 'from your friends and acquaintances' to Principal William Dunlop, Glasgow University.

3. The translated form, 'St James in the plain', was not used in Jamaica. It appears as a London legal draftsman's coinage, IRO Deeds, o.s. 1, ff. 164v–165, 1 April 1661, Mortgage, Stanley Stephenson to Mary Bower. The phrase is also used by Sir Hans Sloane, as a translation of 'St Jago de la Vega', *A Voyage to the Islands of Madeira, Barbados, Nieves, S. Christopher and Jamaica. . . .* 2 vols. (London: BM for author, 1707, 1725), lxiv. Sloane uses the 'Spanish Town' name too, ibid. vi. A further early coinage 'town of Saint Angelo Delvega' appears a transcription of an unfamiliar name misheard, George Wilson Bridges, *The Annals of Jamaica* 2 vols.

(London: John Murray, 1827–8), 1,427, and also 28 October, 1662, Arthur P. Watts, *Une Histoire des Colonies Anglaises aux Antilles (de 1649 á 1660)* (Paris: Presses Universitaires de France, 1924), 483.

4. John Bigelow, *Jamaica in 1850: or, the effects of sixteen years of freedom on a slave colony* (New York & London: George E. Putnam, 1851), 30.

5. Ursula K. Le Guin, *Tales from Earthsea* (New York: Harcourt, 2001), xiv.

6. Citing his uncle's participation in the defense when applying for the next vacant canonry in Mexico or Tlaxaca, NLJ Ms 291, Pieretz Bequest, 2nd ser, Seville Transcripts, translations, unfoliated. 1642, petition to King of Dr don Alonso de Espinosa Centeno.

7. The 70 wagons claim, JA 1B/5/75/3, 'A Copy of a Memorial presented to Sir John Peter Grant on the 18th or 19th November, 1869, against the removal, from Spanish Town, of the Seat of Government, Superior Courts of Law and Equity, and the Records. . . .' However, a history of Jamaica composed only a few years before gave the lower figure. BMS Langton Collection, 6, 'History of Jamaica by Rev John Clarke', (nd. *c.* 1864), f. 52. Clarke had formerly served as a Baptist missionary in Spanish Town.

8. Discussing the relations between the stories people told and how they understood the island's past, James Robertson, '"Stories" and "Histories" in Late Seventeenth-Century Jamaica', in Kathleen E.A. Monteith and Glen Richards, eds., *Jamaica in Slavery and Freedom. History, Heritage and Culture* (Kingston: University of the West Indies Press, 2002), 25–51; see also Kenneth M. Bilby, '"Two Sister Pikni": A Historical Tradition of Dual Ethnogenesis in Eastern Jamaica', *Caribbean Quarterly* 30 (1984): 10–25.

9. See Linda Sturtz, 'Proprietors and Tenants: People of Free Condition, Spanish Town, 1754', paper delivered to the Text & Testimony Collective Conference, City Life in Caribbean History: Celebrating Bridgetown, University of the West Indies, Cave Hill, Barbados, (2003).

10. JA 1B/5/77/981, 'Tourist Trade Development Board, Erection of Notice Boards and Sign Posts'.

11. Robyn Woodward, 'Sevilla La Nueva Archaeological Project, 2002', *Archaeology Jamaica* n.s. 14 (2002): 9.

12. Don Pedro Colon de Portugal y Castro, Duke of Veregua and La Vega, Marquis of Jamaica, *The Columbus Petition Document for the Island of Jamaica, 1672* (trans.) Jeremy Lawrence (Kingston: Mill Press, 1992), H.

13. B.L. King's Ms 213, 'Journal of an Officer . . . to North America 1764–1765,' f. 9, June, 1764.

14. Anthony Trollope, *The West Indies and the Spanish Main* (2nd ed. London: Chapman & Hall, 1860), 119.

15. Edward Long, *History of Jamaica* 3 vols (London: T. Lowndes, 1774), 2, 26. He registered a right to vote in elections in the parish because of this house, JA

2/2/27, St Catherine, List of Freeholders, 1757–1840, (pencil foliation), 34, 27 October 1763, Edward Long.

16. JA 7/12/198, 31 October 1959, recollections of John R.V. Massias.

17. For a suggestive discussion of some of these issues, Joseph A. Amato, 'Writing History through the Senses: Sounds', in his *Rethinking Home: A Case for Writing Local History* (Berkeley: University of California Press, 2002), 60–76.

18. I am grateful to Cecil Gutzmore and Kameika Murphy for these observations.

19. Walter Augustus Feurtado, *A Forty-Five Years' Reminiscence of the Characteristics and Characters of Spanish Town* (Kingston: W. Alexander Feurtado, 1890).

20. NLJ Ms 62a. Jacob A.P.M. Andrade, 'Parochial Handbook'; idem. *A Record of the Jews in Jamaica From the English Conquest to the Present Time* (Kingston: Jamaica Times, 1941); Clinton V. Black, *Spanish Town: The Old Capital* (Spanish Town: St Catherine's Parish Council, 1960, 2nd edn. 1974). Black's annotated copy is at the Jamaica Archives.

21. On Jamaica's remarkably full surviving manuscript records, James Robertson, 'Jamaican Archival Resources for Seventeenth and Eighteenth Century Atlantic History', *Slavery and Abolition* 14 (2001): 109–40. On outsiders' insights, Peter Burke, 'The Sources: Outsiders and Insiders', in *The Historical Anthropology of Early Modern Italy: Essays on Perception and Communication* (Cambridge: Cambridge University Press, 1987), 15–24.

22. Discussing earlier published histories, Elsa V. Goveia, *A Study on the Historiography of the British West Indies to the End of the Nineteenth Century* (Tacubaya Mexico: Instituto Panamericano de Geografa e Historia, 1956, reprint Washington, DC: Howard University Press, 1980); for their successors up to 1991, Howard Johnson, 'Historiography of Jamaica', in B.W. Higman, ed., *Methodology and Historiography of the Caribbean* (General History of the Caribbean, 6. Basingstoke: Macmillan for UNESCO, 1999), 478–530. Subsequent overviews include David Buisseret, *Historic Jamaica from the Air* (Barbados, 1969, 2nd rev edn. Kingston: Ian Randle Publishers, 1996); Philip Sherlock and Hazel Bennett, *The Story of the Jamaican People* (Kingston: Ian Randle Publishers, 1998), and Patrick Bryan, *Inside Out and Outside In: Factors in the Creation of Contemporary Jamaica* (Grace Kennedy Foundation Lecture, Kingston: the Foundation, 2000).

23. Michael Pawson and David Buisseret, *Port Royal, Jamaica* (Oxford, 1974, reprint Kingston: University of the West Indies Press, 2000), and on Kingston, Wilma R. Bailey, 'Kingston 1692–1843: A Colonial City' (PhD thesis, UWI Mona, 1974), idem. 'Social control in the pre-Emancipation society of Kingston, Jamaica', *Boletín de estudios latinamericanos y del Caribe* 24 (1978): 97–110, and Colin G. Clarke, *Kingston, Jamaica, Urban Development and Social Change, 1692–1962* (Berkeley: University of California Press, 1975).

24. These include Trevor Burnard, '"The Grand Mart of the Island": The Economic Function of Kingston, Jamaica in the Mid-Eighteenth Century', in Monteith and

Glent Richards, *Jamaica in Slavery and Freedom*, 225–41; Lorna Simmonds, 'The Afro-Jamaican and the Internal Marketing System: Kingston, 1780–1834' in ibid. 274–90, and Swithin R. Wilmot, 'The Politics of Protest in Free Jamaica – The Kingston John Canoe Riots, 1840 and 1841', *Caribbean Quarterly* 36: 3&4 (1990): 65–75. Anthony S. Johnson, *City of Kingston Souvenir: Commemoration of the Bicentennial of the City Charter* (Kingston: ISKAMOL, 2002); Jean Besson, *Martha Brae's Two Histories: European Expansion and Culture Building in Jamaica* (Chapel Hill, NC/Kingston: University of North Carolina Press and Ian Randle Publishers, 2002); Michelle Eaton, '"The Shaping of a Town:" The Historical Development of Port Maria, 1821–1921', (MA thesis, UWI, Mona, 2003); Erna Brodber, *The People of My Jamaican Village, 1817–1948* (Woodside: blackspace, 1999). Regional studies include Franklin W. Knight and Peggy K. Liss, eds. *Atlantic Port Cities: Economy, Culture, and Society in the Atlantic World, 1650–1850* (Knoxville, Tenn: University of Tennessee Press, 1991); Pedro L.V. Welch, *Slave Society in the City: Bridgetown, Barbados 1680–1834* (Kingston: Ian Randle Publishers, 2003): along with Martyn Bowden, 'The Three Centuries of Bridgetown: An Historical Geography', *Journal of the Barbados Museum and Historical Society* 49 (2003), 1–137; Anne Pérotin-Dumon, *La Ville aux Îles, la ville dans l'île: Basse-Terre et Pointe-à-Pitre, Guadeloupe, 1650–1820* (Paris: Éditions Karthala, 2000); Juanita De Burros, *Order and Place in a Colonial City: Patterns of Struggle and Resistance in Georgetown, British Guiana, 1889–1924* (Kingston: McGill-Queen's University Press, 2002). A pioneering earlier volume did not lead to further work, W. Adolphe Roberts, ed., *The Capitals of Jamaica* (Kingston: Pioneer Press, 1955). The wide-ranging Text & Testimony Collective Conference, 'City Life in Caribbean History: Celebrating Bridgetown', University of the West Indies, Cave Hill, Barbados, (2003), demonstrated the extent of urban-related research underway across the Caribbean.

25. Kevin Whelan, 'Towns and Villages', in F.A.H. Aalen, Kevin Whelan and Matthew Stout, eds., *Atlas of the Irish Rural landscape* (Cork: Cork University Press, 1997), 180. The eight per cent living in towns figure, Barry Higman, *Slave Population and Economy in Jamaica, 1807–1834* (Cambridge: Cambridge University Press, 1976), 57.

26. David Goldfield, *Region, Race and Cities: Interpreting the Urban South* (Baton Rouge, La: Louisiana State University Press, 1997), 13.

27. For clear introductions, Edward E. Crain, *Historic Architecture of the Caribbean Islands* (Gainesville, Fla.: University Press of Florida, 1994); Pamela Gosner, *Caribbean Georgian: The Great and Small Houses of the West Indies* (Washington, DC: Three Continents, 1982), and David Buisseret, *Historic Architecture of the Caribbean* (London: Heinemann, 1980); on stylistic adaptations, see John E. Crowley, *The Invention of Comfort: Sensibilities and Design in Early Modern Britain and Early America* (Baltimore, Md: Johns Hopkins, 2001), 235–41 and,

independently, Douglas Blain 'Georgian Jamaica: A New Way of Looking at a Unique Heritage', *Georgian Jamaica: Newsletter of the Friends of the Georgian Society of Jamaica* 3:3 (September, 1995): 3; idem. 'The Frantic Search for Shade', ibid. 3:4 (December, 1995): 3–4, and idem. 'Towards a Tropical Georgian Style', ibid. 4:1 (March, 1996): 3–4. The earlier transitions are discussed in James Robertson, 'Jamaican Architectures before Georgian', *Winterthur Portfolio* 36 (2001): 73–95.

28.   Figures derived from Patricia E. Green, *Proposal for the Preparation of a Preservation Scheme Master Plan for the Spanish Town Historic District, Final Draft.* (UNDP/UNESCO/GoJ Project, JAM/91/008, typescript, 25 January 1995). I used a copy at the Jamaica National Heritage Trust. An earlier survey also records many buildings, some of which have since been demolished; Georgian Society of Jamaica, *Spanish Town: a Photographic Record* ([Kingston: the Society, 1973]).

29.   I address some of these questions at greater length in 'Inherited Cityscapes: Spanish Town, Jamaica', in Gunilla Malm, ed., *Towards an Archaeology of Buildings: contexts and concepts* (British Archaeological Reports, International Series, 1186, Oxford, Archaeopress, 2003), 89–104.

30.   T.A.L. Concannon, 'Our Architectural Heritage: Houses of the 18th and 19th Century with Special Reference to Spanish Town', *Jamaica Journal* 4 (1970): 23–8, shows the ease with which householders' 'improvements' can conceal older structures.

31.   Larry Gragg, 'The Port Royal Earthquake', *History Today* 50:9 (September, 2000): 28–34. On the aftermath of the 1780 hurricane, Linda L. Sturtz, 'The 1780 Hurricane Donation: "Insult offered instead of relief"', *Jamaican Historical Review* 21 (1999): 38–46; assessing the immediate social impacts of disasters and subsequent recollections, see Howard A. Fergus, ed., *Eruption: Montserrat Versus Volcano* (Montserrat: University of the West Indies, School of Continuing Studies, Montserrat, 1996) and idem. and E.A. Markham, eds., *Hugo versus Montserrat* (Coleraine and Boston, Mass: Linda Lee Books, 1989).

32.   Annette Constance Brown, 'Old King's House destroyed by fire', *Jamaican Historical Society Bulletin* 11:6 (2000): 153–57. For the townspeople's fears after the 1925 fire, below 272. Jean D'Costa, *Escape to Last Man Peak* (Harlow: Longman, 1975), 18.

33.   Irene Wright, 'The Early History of Jamaica, 1511–1536', *English Historical Review*, 36 (1921): 76–95.

34.   JA 1B/5/77/859, Unemployment, St. Catherine, (1935), item 7, 23 April 1935, Report from Inspector General of Police to Colonial Secretary.

35.   Norma Benghiat, *Traditional Jamaican Cookery* (London: Penguin, 1985), 13.

36.   In 1987 Mrs Jones was awarded a medal by the Institute of Jamaica. Describing her work see Suzanne Francis-Brown, 'Mama Lou', (1983), reprinted in Linda Gambrill, ed., *A Tapestry of Jamaica: The Best of Skywritings* (Oxford: Macmillan

Caribbean, 2002), 272, and Doreen Morgan, 'Ma Lou: Profile of a Potter', ([Kingston]: Petroleum Corporation of Jamaica, nd [post 1989]), copy in NLJ HN 'Pottery'. Cecil Baugh, the distinguished Jamaican potter, offered a fellow craftsman's appraisal of her work in a presentation made during the 1985 Heritage Week. His comments are on record at the African-Caribbean Institute of Jamaica, Video Vi10. For a careful record of her procedures, Roderick Ebanks, 'Ma Lou and the African-Jamaican Pottery Tradition', *Jamaica Journal* 17:3 (1984): 31–7.

37.   Lucille Mathurin, 'Creole Authenticity', *Savacou* 5 (1971): 117.

Chapter 1

1.   The standard introduction remains Francisco Morales Padrón's 1952 *Spanish Jamaica*, now translated by Patrick Bryan (Kingston: Ian Randle Publishers, 2003). Patrick Bryan, 'Spanish Jamaica' *Caribbean Quarterly* 38 (1992): 21-31 offers a further useful survey. For the rationales justifying the societies that the *conquistadors* established, Luis N. Rivera-Pagán, 'Freedom and servitude: indigenous slavery and the Spanish Conquest of the Caribbean', in Jalil Sued-Badillo, ed., *Autochthonous Societies* (General History of the Caribbean, 1, Basingstoke: Macmillan for UNESCO, 2003), 316–362, Comparative studies of Spanish urban settlements include Alfred Castillero-Calvo, 'The city in the Hispanic Caribbean, 1492–1650', in Pieter C. Emmer and German Carrera Damas, eds., *New Societies: The Caribbean in the long sixteenth century* (General History of the Caribbean, 2, Basingstoke: Macmillan for UNESCO, 1999), 201–246 and Richard M. Morse, 'Urban development', in Leslie Bethell, ed., *Colonial Spanish America* (Cambridge: Cambridge University Press, 1987), 165–202. Aida R. Caro Costas, 'The Organization of Institutional and Social Life', in Arturo Morales Carrión, ed., *Puerto Rico: A Political and Cultural History* (New York: Norton, 1983), 25–40, is also useful for its description of the administration of another peripheral royal colony.

2.   NMM WYN 10/2, W[illiam] B[urrows], 'A journal of every dayes proceedings in the expedition of the Fleet sent into the West indies under the command of General William Penn' 20 December 1654–4 September, 1655, unfoliated, 15 May, 1655.

3.   Long, *History* 2, 39.

4.   Thus in 1749 a planter then in Spanish Town described, 'the River so High & Damaged the ford so much that It is Impossible to ford it.' UCSD Ms. 220, Barnett/Hall Collection, Box 1, folder 27, 3 June, 1749, William Hall to Thomas Hall.

5.   After the Rio Cobre dam was completed in 1876 the water level of the modern river changed. For a 'Roses Ford' downstream from the eighteenth-century town,

JA 2/2/27, St Catherine, List of Freeholders, 1757–1840, pencil foliation, 4, 18 August 1757, Ballard Beckford.

6. G.A. Aarons, 'Sevilla la Nueva: Microcosm of Spain in Jamaica', 2 parts *Jamaica Journal* '1: the Historical Background', 16:4 (1983): 37–46, and '2: Unearthing the Past', 17:7 (1984): 28–37; Sylvia Wynter, *New Seville: Major Facts, Major Questions* (Kingston: Jamaica National Heritage Commission, 1984), also idem. *New Seville, Major Dates: 1509–1536, with an aftermath 1537–1655* (Kingston: Jamaica National Trust Commission, 1984); Charles S. Cotter, 'Sevilla Nueva: The Story of an Excavation', *Jamaica Journal* 4 (1970): 15–22 and, re-investigating the surviving records from these excavations, Robyn Patricia Woodward, 'The Charles Cotter Collection: A study of ceramic and faunal remains', Texas A&M University, MA thesis, (1988). Ms Woodward's current excavations at Seville should shape future discussions of this important site.

7. Woodward, '*Sevilla La Nueva* Archaeological Project, 2002', 9.

8. S.E. Morrison, *The Second Voyage of Christopher Columbus from Cadiz to Hispaniola and the Discovery of the Lesser Antilles* (Oxford: Oxford University Press, 1939), 29–41. For the route of the first voyage see Robin Knox-Johnson, *The Columbus Venture* (London: BBC, 1992).

9. Battista Agnese's partolan atlas shows the fleet's route from Spain to Porto Bello, running south of Jamaica, along with the connecting route of the silver fleet from lima to Panama. It is reproduced in Samuel J. Hough, *The Italians in the Creation of America: An Exhibition at the John Carter Brown Library* (Providence, RI: John Carter Brown Library, 1980), plate II. Cf Alan K. Craig, *Spanish Colonial Silver Coins in the Florida Collection* (Gainesville, Fla: Florida Bureau of Archaeological Research and University Press of Florida, 2000).

10. For these routes, see Pablo E. Pérez-Mallaína, *Spain's Men of the Sea: Daily Life on the Indies Fleets in the Indies Fleets in the Sixteenth Century* (Seville, 1992, Eng trans, Baltimore, Md: Johns Hopkins, 1998), 8–15; Carla Rahn Phillips, 'The growth and composition of trade in the Iberian empires, 1450–1750', in James D. Tracy, ed., *The Rise of Merchant Empires: Long-Distance Trade in the Early Modern World, 1350–1750* (Cambridge: Cambridge University Press, 1990), 76–78, and 29 May, 1675, Captain James Jenifer to Samuel Pepys, Bodl. Ms. Rawl. A. 175, f. 316. Inertia. Studies of individual Spanish wrecks provide useful examples of the misfortunes that these vessels suffered. On the loss of the Nuestra Señora de la Merced in 1595, Fr Andrés de Segura, *An Early Florida Adventure Story* ed/trans, John H. Hann, (Gainesville, Fla: University Press of Florida, 2000); the sinking of the Nuestra Señora de Atocha in 1622, Eugene Lyon, *The Search for the Atocha* (New York, 1979, 2nd ed Port Salerno, Fla: Florida Classics Library, 1989); for the Nuestra Señora de la pura y limia Concepción lost in 1641, Peter Earle, *The Wreck of the Almiranta: Sir William Phips and the Hispaniola Treasure* (London: Macmillan, 1979), 15–58; and on the Nuestra Señora de las Maravillas, sunk in

1655/6, Dave Horner, *Shipwreck: A Saga of the Sea, Tragedy and Sunken Treasure* (Stroud: Sutton, 1999).

11. Albert Manucy and Ricardo Torres-Reyes, *Puerto Rico and the Forts of Old San Juan* (Riverside, Conn: Chatham Press, 1973), 29; Castillero-Calvo, 'The city in the Hispanic Caribbean,' 233; Girolamo Benzoni, *History of the New World* (1565), ed/trans., W.H. Smyth, (Hakluyt Society, 21, London: the Society, 1857), 102.

12. Allsworth-Jones, 'Site Summary: White Marl' in *The Lee Collection: CD Rom* (in preparation); J.S. Tyndale-Biscoe, 'Arawak Specimens from some middens of Jamaica', *Jamaican Historical Society Bulletin* 1:10 (1954): 124; Robert Howard *et al* 'Arawak Findings at White Marl', *Jamaican Historical Society, Bulletin* 3:4 (1961): 61; 'Part 2', *Bulletin* 3:5 (1962): 79–82.

13. R. Duncan Mathewson, 'History from the Earth: Archaeological Excavations at Old King's House', *Jamaica Journal* 6:1 (1972): 4. I am grateful to Philip Allsworth-Jones for this reference.

14. On the Taino origin of the name, Frederic G. Cassidy, 'The Earliest Placenames in Jamaica', *Names* 26 (1988): 154.

15. The Taino 'assistance,' B.L. Sloane Ms. 1394, f. 14. [Thomas Lynch], Description of Jamaica, *c.* 1660.

16. The locations given for this settlement vary, with early descriptions apparently placing it in the vicinity of Savanna la Mar while later reports and Spanish maps place it in Blewfields Bay. Wilma Bailey proposed that the townspeople may well have moved from the initial site, especially as marshes near present-day Savanna la Mar would have made the original site unhealthy. Wilma Williams [Bailey], 'A note on the Spanish Towns of Jamaica', (nd.), typescript, UWI Mona, 1–2.

17. These stories continued to circulate in the nineteenth century, eg NLJ Ms. 1900, Letterbook of William Jowett Titford, 1802–1807 (transcript), 14 January, 1802, 'Dear Richard' and Philip Henry Gosse, *A Naturalist's Sojourn in Jamaica* (London: Longman, 1851), 299.

18. For the French spy's appraisal, Frank Cundall, ed., 'What a French Traveler in Jamaica saw in 1765', *Jamaica Times* 24 (1 April, 1922): 2–3; the eighteenth-century pilots, PRO CO 137/28, f. 143v. 21 November 1754, Humble Answer of the Town of St Jago de la Vega to Board of Trade.

19. Ellen G. Friedman, *Spanish Captives in North Africa in the Early Modern Age* (Madison, Wis: University of Wisconsin Press, 1983), 4.

20. Benzoni, *History of the New World*, 106.

21. The townspeople who relocated from New Seville *may* have had a further pre-existing settlement site available to consider for adoption. Traces of a Taino settlement site to the south of the landing place that the Spaniards would use (and presumably more convenient for the landing site in that vicinity where the English raider, Sir Anthony Shirley, brought his troops ashore in 1597, see Irene A. Wright ed., 'The Spanish Version of Sir Anthony Shirley's Raid on Jamaica, 1597',

Hispanic American Historical Review 5 (1922): 227–248), are reported as the 'Port Henderson Hill Site' in G.A. Aarons, 'Archaeological Sites in the Hellshire Area', *Jamaica Journal* 16:1 (1983): 78. Aarons invokes the adoption of some European forms in the otherwise traditional Taino pottery excavated there in assigning a post-Columbian date to this otherwise undated settlement. I am grateful to Philip Allsworth-Jones for discussing the ambivalence of the available evidence for dating this settlement.

22. For a comparison between the wording of the 1525 laws and the description of the new town site sent back from Jamaica, Bailey, 'Kingston 1692–1843', 71–72; translating the 1573 text of the Ordinances, Dora P. Crouch, Daniel J. Garr and Axel I. Mundigo, *Spanish City Planing in North America* (Cambridge, Mass: MIT Press, 1982) 8–9, ordinances 35 and 41.

23. NLJ Ms 291, Pietersz Bequest, 2nd series 'Translations, Seville'. These are English translations of transcripts from Seville held at the National Library. Pietersz's manuscript and typescript translations do not give volume or folio references to identify the transcript he translated. They are themselves unsorted and unfoliated. The criteria quoted here are all cited in the royal grants made on 19 July 1534.

24. Wright, 'Early History of Jamaica,' 76–95.

25. Padrón, *Spanish Jamaica*, 62–65; urging the King not to hand over Jamaica, NLJ Ms 291, 10 November 1536, Pedro de Maçuelo to King.

26. The dedication, Padrón, *Spanish Jamaica*, 119.

27. *Columbus Petition Document*, H.

28. Buisseret, *Historic Jamaica from the Air*, 36–37.

29. Frank Cundall and Joseph Pietersz, *Jamaica under the Spaniards* (Kingston: Institute of Jamaica, 1919), 47.

30. NLJ Ms 291, [1649], testimony of Fr Pedro de Balbena.

31. NLJ Ms 291, Diego de Ayala, the Bishop's secretary, enclosed in 23 August 1608, Bishop of Havana to King. Attributing the foundation of the Dominican friary to Governor Alonso de Miranda, Padrón, *Spanish Jamaica*, 119.

32. The phrase, JA 1B/11/1/3, Patents, 3. 1668–1670, ff. 206v–207, Grant to Lt-Col John Cope, 3 March 1663/4. The square's earlier southern boundary is shown in John Pitcairn's 1786 map of the town. 'A Plan of St Jago de la Vega in the Island of Jamaica' (London: W. Hinton, 3 January 1786), NLJ Map. 727.35edc. The density, Vincent T. Harlow ed., 'The Voyages of Captain William Jackson (1642–1645)', *Camden Miscellany XIII* (Camden 3rd ser 34, London: the Society, 1924), 19.

33. Long, *History* 2, 3; G.F. J[udah], *Old Saint Jago* (Kingston, W.A. Feurtado's Sons, 1896), 24.

34. JA 1B/11/2/5, Platt Book, St. Catherine, 1, A–G, 1663–1707, f. 55, 25 July 1664, Survey for Mr Hemmings.

35. Later English property boundaries cited old Spanish lanes: eg 'an old ruined street' in 1B/11/1/1A, Patents, 1661–65, ff. 118–118v, 12 September 1665, Grant to

Samuell Sage, while John Taylor, an English would-be settler who visited Jamaica in 1688 assumed that the Spanish city must have been much larger because 'the Streets being about four Miles long', which would only be possible if they ran on out into the surrounding savanna. NLJ Ms 105, John Taylor, 'Multum in Parvo or Taylor's History of his Life and Travells in America . . .' 3 vols 2. f. 249.

36. On these buildings see Pamela Gosner, *Caribbean Baroque: Historic Architecture of the Spanish Antilles* (Pueblo, Colo: Passeggiata Press, 1996), 36–38, 149–53, and Erwin Walter Palm, 'Plateresque and Renaissance Monuments of the Island of Hispaniola', *Journal of the Society of Architectural Historians* 5 (1946): 3–6.

37. Long, *History* 2, 3.

38. NMM WYN 10/2, Burrows, 'A Journal,' 15 May 1655.

39. Long, *History* 2, 19–21.

40. NLJ Ms 291, 26 December, 1598, Fernando Melgarejo de Córdoba [to King]. At this juncture Governor de Córdoba proposed establishing a separate town for the island's surviving 'indians'.

41. NLJ Ms 291, [1597], testimony of Pedro del Cuna, notary of Santo Domingo, (formerly a notary in Jamaica). The priest's census is cited in *ibid.* [1597], testimony of Francisco Hernandez, priest and canon of Jamaica, 'at present residing in the city of Santo Domingo'. This total was quoted when the colony requested tax relief after an English attack and may well have been pitched fairly low.

42. NLJ Ms 291, 1597, testimony of Antonio Hernandes, inhabitant of Santo Domingo, 'over one hundred'; ibid. 15 August, 1597, Governor de Córdoba to Council, 120; ibid. 12 July 1597, Garceia del Valle Alvarado to King, 130.

43. Padrón, *Spanish Jamaica*, 35.

44. NLJ Ms 291, 14 July 1611, Bernardo de Balbuoa, Abbot of Jamaica, Description of the Island.

45. Padrón, *Spanish Jamaica*, 35.

46. NLJ Ms 291, 15 September 1638, Report, Bitrian de Biamond [to King and Council].

47. On the background for one group of slaves shipped from Angola, John K. Thornton, 'The African Experiences of the "20. and odd negroes" Arriving in Virginia in 1619', *William & Mary Quarterly* 3rd ser 55 (1998): 421–434.

48. 'The greater part of the inhabitants are Portuguese and have come by way of Angola.' NLJ Ms. 291, 24 September, 1650, report by Governor Jacinto Sedeño Albornoz to Admiral of the Indies, [Duke of Veragua].

49. Bernard Lewis, *Cultures in Conflict: Christians, Muslims and Jews in the Age of Discovery* (New York: Oxford University Press, 1995), 36–37.

50. Seymour B. Lieberman, 'The Secret-Jewery in the Spanish New World Colonies, 1500-1820', in R.D. Barnett and W.M. Schwab, eds., *The Sephardi Heritage: Essays on the History and cultural contribution of the Jews of Spain and Portugal, 2, The Western Sephardim* (Grendon, Northants: Gibraltar Books, 1989), 474–496;

Mordechai Arbell, *The Portuguese Jews of Jamaica* (Kingston: UWI Press, 2000), 7–8.

51.   Padrón, *Spanish Jamaica*.

52.   Benzoni, *History of the New World*, 106; Bridges, *Annals of Jamaica*, 1, 169.

53.   Translations of several of the witnesses' depositions have been published, [Francis J. Osborne, ed.], 'A Spanish Account of the Attack by Christopher Newport on Jamaica in January, 1603', *Jamaican Historical Society Bulletin*, 3:12 (1963): 188–190.

54.   NLJ Ms 291, 6 February 1603, testimony of Juan de Palencia Carrillo, Serjeant Major of the militia and Alcalde of the town, also, [1608], testimony of Juan Gomez Grota, a Portuguese pilot.

55.   NLJ Ms 291, 26 January 1603, Balthasaro Diaz Devilla, Sergeant of the Company of Captain Pedro Lopez.

56.   NLJ Ms 291, 26 January 1603, Balthasaro Diaz Davilla.

57.   NLJ Ms 291, [1608], testimony of Sub-Lieutenant Francisco Cartagena de Leyva.

58.   Amy Turner Bushnell, 'How to Fight a Pirate: Provincials, Royalists and the Defence of Minor Ports during the Age of Bureaucracy', *Gulf Coast Historical Review*, 5 (1990): 18–35.

59.   NLJ Ms 291, 26 January 1603, Balthasaro Diaz Davilla.

60.   NLJ Ms 291, [1603], testimony of Juan de Proenca, Sub-Lieutenant of the Company of Captain Pedo Lopez.

61.   Because Newport's attack did not occur on the saint's day Padrón suggests that Governor de Córdoba fought off two assaults, with a second occurring on July 24, the eve of the feast of St James, *Spanish Jamaica*, 143. This may be the case, but as saints are not constrained to come to the assistance of their devotees only on their saint's day, one successful skirmish may have been quite enough to stretch the settlers' luck.

62.   Charles Joseph Galliari Rampini, *Letters from Jamaica: The Land of Streams and Woods* (Edinburgh: Edmonston and Douglas, 1873), 46.

63.   Black, *Spanish Town*, 24.

64.   H.C. Harris, 'The Cape Verde region (1499 to 1549): the key to coconut cultivation in the Western hemisphere?' *Turrialba*, 27 (1977): 227–231.

65.   *Columbus Petition*, H2v.

66.   NLJ Ms. 291, 28 November, 1638, Bitram de Biamond to Council, the point was repeated in a 1644 survey, Padrón, *Spanish Jamaica*, 263.

67.   John Rashford, 'Arawak, Spanish and African Contributions to Jamaica's Settlement Vegetation', *Jamaica Journal* 24:3 (1993): 17–23.

68.   Manucy and Torres-Reyes, *Puerto Rico and the Forts of Old San Juan*, 54–8; Irene Wright, *Santiago de Cuba and its District (1607–1940)* (Madrid: Felipe Pena Cruz, 1918), 50–8.

Chapter 2

1. On the early English settlements see Richard S. Dunn, *Sugar and Slaves: The Rise of the Planter Class in the English West Indies, 1624–1713* (Chapel Hill, NC: University of North Carolina Press, 1972), Carl and Roberta Bridenbaugh, *No Peace Beyond the Line: The English in the Caribbean, 1624–1690* (New York: Oxford University Press, 1972), Hilary McD. Beckles, 'The "Hub of the Empire": The Caribbean and Britain in the Seventeenth Century', in Nicholas Canny, ed., *The Origins of Empire: British Overseas Enterprise to the Close of the Seventeenth Century* (Oxford History of the British Empire, I, Oxford: Oxford University Press, 1998), 218–40, and David Barry Gaspar, '"Rigid and Inclement": Origins of the Jamaican Slave Laws of the Seventeenth Century' in Christopher L. Tomlins and Bruce H. Mann, eds., *The Many Legalities of Early Modern America* (Chapel Hill, NC: University of North Carolina Press, 2001), 78–96. Michael Pawson and David Buisseret, *Port Royal, Jamaica* (Oxford, 1974, 2nd edn. Kingston: the University of the West Indies Press, 2000), offers an excellent introduction to Jamaica's other urban centre.

    The best account of the English attack on Jamaica and the Spanish resistance remains Irene A. Wright, 'The Spanish Resistance to the English Occupation of Jamaica, 1655–1660', *Transactions of the Royal Historical Society* 4th ser 13 (1930), 117–47. This can be supplemented by Arthur P. Watts, *Une Histoire des Colonies Anglaises aux Antilles (de 1649 à 1660)* (Paris: Presses Universitaires de France, 1924), by Padrón, *Spanish Jamaica*, and, reflecting a close familiarity with the Jamaican landscape, by S.A.G. Taylor, *The Western Design: An Account of Cromwell's Expedition to the Caribbean* (Kingston: Institute of Jamaica and Jamaica Historical Society, 1965). Julian de Castilla, 'The English Conquest of Jamaica (1655–1656)', ed/trans., Irene A. Wright, *Camden Miscellany XIII* (Camden Society, 3rd ser 34. London: Royal Historical Society, 1923), v–32, is a contemporary description of the first year of the Spanish resistance. There are numerous studies of Oliver Cromwell and of Britain during the 1650s. Starting points for appraising the Western Design include John Morrill, 'Postlude: Between War and Peace 1651–1660', in John Kenyon and Jane Ohelmeyer, eds., *The Civil Wars: A Military History of England, Scotland and Ireland 1638–1660* (Oxford: Oxford University Press, 1998), 306–28, 342–44, and Roger Hainsworth, *The Swordsmen in Power: War and Politics under the English Republic 1649–1660* (Thrupp: Sutton, 1997). On urban developments in England, Peter Borsay, 'The Restoration Town' in Lionel K.J. Glassey, ed., *The Reigns of Charles II and James VII and II* (New York: St Martin's, 1997), 171–90, 247–8, 278–88.

2. On the Santo Domingo debacle, Irene A. Wright, 'Narratives of the English Attack on St Domingo (1655)', *Camden Miscellany XIV* (Camden, 3rd ser 37, London: the Royal Historical Society, 1926), i–80.

3. David Armitage, 'The Cromwellian Protectorate and the Language of Empire', *Historical Journal* 35 (1992): 531–55; Timothy Venning, *Cromwellian Foreign Policy* (Basingstoke: Macmillan, 1995), 71–90.

4. C.H. Firth, ed., *The Narrative of General Venables* (Camden Society, n.s. 40, London: Longmans for the Society, 1900), 34.

5. NLJ Ms 291, 28 November 1638. Bitram de Biamond to royal council.

6. *Columbus Petition*, F.

7. Thomas Gage, 'Some briefe and true observations concerning the West Indies, humbly presented to His Highness, Oliver, Lord Protector of the Commonwealth of England, Scotland, and Ireland', in Thomas Birch, ed. *A Collection of the State Papers of John Thurloe, Esq:* . . . 7 vols. (London: Executor of Fletcher Gyles, 1742), 3. *December 1654–September 1655*, 59.

8. J. Eric S. Thompson, 'Editor's Introduction', to *idem* ed., *Thomas Gage's Travels in the New World* (Norman, Okl: University of Oklahoma Press, 1958, 2nd ed 1969), xvii–xix, also, Norman Newton, *Thomas Gage in Spanish America* (London: Faber, 1969), 184–95; William S. Maltby, *The Black Legend in England: The Development of anti-Spanish Sentiment* (Durham, NC: Duke University Press, 1971), 13.

9. Gage as interpreter, Castilla, 'English Conquest of Jamaica', 5–6.

10. Francis Barrington to [ ], 14 July 1655, *Historical Manuscripts Commission 7*, (London, HMSO, 1879), 573; 3 June 1655, J. Daniell, 'A letter from Jamaica', *Thurloe State Papers*, 3. 507.

11. 'Letters Concerning the English Expedition into the Spanish West Indies in 1655', Appendix D in *The Narrative of General Venables*, 138.

12. Castilla, 'English Conquest of Jamaica', 5.

13. *Thurloe State Papers 4. September 1655–May 1655*, 390–1, Petition delivered by Samuel Barry, John Filkins, Robert Smith, William Smith, Henry Jones, J. Humphrey to Colonel Edward D'Oyley, Commander in Chief of the Army, 4 January 1655/6.

14. *Thurloe State Papers 4*, 153, 5 November 1655, Major Robert Sedgwicke to Oliver Cromwell.

15. *Thurloe State Papers 4*, 456, 24 January 1655/6, Vice-Admiral Goodson and Major Sedgwicke to Oliver Cromwell.

16. Castilla, 'English Conquest of Jamaica', 3.

17. 'the path', JA 1B/11/1/1A, Patents 1, 1660–1665, ff. 50–50v, 17 August 1664, grant to George Newell; 'troopers ford', 1B/11/2/7, f. 26, 6 August 1690, survey for Thomas Brookes.

18. *The Narrative of General Venables*, 36.

19. Padrón, *Spanish Jamaica*, 190.

20. For example, Gage, 'Some briefe and true observations', *Thurloe State Papers* 3, 60.

21. Cundall and Pietersz, *Jamaica under the Spaniards*, 62, 29 August 1657, Ysassi to Duke of Alburquerque, Viceroy in Mexico.

22. J.L. Pietersz and H.P. Jacobs, trans., S.A.G. Taylor, intro, 'Two Spanish Documents of 1656', *Jamaican Historical Review* 2. (1948): 11–35, for another Spanish description of this raid, Castilla, 'English Conquest of Jamaica', 24–6.

23. Joseph Pietersz, 'The Last Spanish Governor of Jamaica', *Jamaican Historical Review* 1 (1945): 24–30.

24. F.J. Osborne and S.A.G. Taylor, eds., 'Edward D'Oyley's Journal, part 1', *Jamaican Historical Review* 10 (1973), 45, 5 February 1655/6.

25. Cundall and Pietersz, *Jamaica under the Spaniards*, 58, 24 July 1657, Domengo Rodriguez de Vera to Alburquerque.

26. Cundall and Pietersz, *Jamaica under the Spaniards*, 73–8, 88, also, NLJ Ms 291, 19 July 1658, Don Christoval Ysassi Arnoldo, to King; 11 August 1657, Don Pedro Bayona Villanueva, to [Don Pedro de Zapata], and 16 November 1657, Don Pedro de Bayona Villanueva to King.

27. The Mexicans were sufficiently proud of their fort to send a watercolour painting of it back to the Viceroy, who then sent it on to Spain, Wright, 'Spanish Resistance', 141, n. 5.

28. [Edward D'Oyley], *A Brief Relation of a Victory, Obtained by the Forces under the Command of Gen. Edward Doyley, Commander in chief of his Highness's FORCES in the Island of JAMAICA, against The Forces of the King of SPAIN, Commanded by Don Christopher Arnoldo Sasi, Commander in chief of the Spanish Forces there* (Edinburgh, Christopher Higgins, 1659).

29. James Robertson, 'The Last Cromwellian Victory: Rio Nuevo, 15–17 June, 1658', *Jamaican Historical Society Bulletin* 11:10 (2002): 285–94. The standard authorities remain Wright, 'Spanish Resistance,' 135–7, and Taylor, *The Western Design*, 165–80.

30. Padrón, *Spanish Jamaica*, 211–12.

31. NLJ Ms 383, no. 2, 24 January 1659/60, Edward D'Oyley to Commissioners of the Admiralty. David Buisseret and S.A.G. Taylor, 'Juan de Bolas and His Pelinco', *Caribbean Quarterly* 24 (1978), 1–7, offer a more negative reading of de Bolas's actions.

32. BL Add. Ms 18986, f. 346, 10 April 1660, Edward D'Oyley to Commissioners of the Admiralty.

33. Padrón, *Spanish Jamaica*, 214–5.

34. Padrón, *Spanish Jamaica*, 252; IRO Deeds o.s. 4, np. 2 June 1671, Bill of Sale, Thomas Lyon to Thomas Swayne.

35. For plots backing on to 'the foundations of the White Church', see JA 1B/11/2/5, f. 11, 8 March, 1668/9, plat for Matthew Grimes; 1B/11/2/7, f. 6, 4 August 1669, plat for John Applin; ibid. f. 9, 21 May 1668, plat for Gabriell Adkins; ibid. f. 22, 18 February 1664/5, plat for Susannah Barker, also, 1B/11/1/1A, f. 55v, [ ] March, 1664, patent for Thomas Evans.

36. As 'Fort Henry', 'Edward D'Oyley's Journal: part 2', *Jamaican Historical Review* 11 (1978): 105, 26 May 1658; a warrant assigning rations for 'the sick at Fort Henry',

UWI Mona, 'D'Oyley's Journal: part 3', f. 68v, 21 January, 1658/8; 'The Bowling Green', JA 1B/11/2/5, f. 122, 28 June 1683, survey for Hender Molesworth and Samuel Bernars.

37. The initial jetties, NMM WYN 10/2, 15 May 1655.

38. Castilla, 'English Conquest of Jamaica', 24.

39. Castilla, 'English Conquest of Jamaica', 19–20.

40. Cassidy, 'Earliest Place Names in Jamaica', 160–1; 'Guardabocoa', JA 1B/11/2/8, Plat Book, Clarendon, 1. f. 126, 20 May 1663, survey for Robert Downes and Philip Roberts, ibid. f. 151, 25 June 1665, survey for Richard Gray.

41. Cassidy, 'Earliest Place Names in Jamaica', 154; the 'Agua Alta' derivation circulated by at least the 1760s, BL King's Ms 'Journal of an Officer', f. 9v.

42. *Columbus Petition*, H. The 'Guavayera' name was included in the first published description of the English conquest, 'A brief Description of the Island of Jamaica, and a Relation of possessing the Town of *St Jago de la Vega*, with the Routing of the Enemies from their Forts and Ordinance, and taking the Island, May 10. 1655', *A Book of the Continuation of Foreign Passages* (London: M.S. for Thomas Jenner, 1657), 43.

43. The treaty, *The Narrative of General Venables*, 36–9; 'Port of Caguaya' at 38. This 'Caguaya' usage is also incorporated in the description in *A Book of the Continuation of Foreign Passages*, 42.

44. For a Spanish settler's description of 'the Caguaya river, which gives its name to the port' and description of the new English fort erected 'on Careen Key'. Castilla, 'English Conquest of Jamaica', 3 24. Wright's editorial footnote suggests that the Careen Key site was the mudbank to the east of the river mouth that in the mid-eighteenth century became the site of Fort Augusta. There are, however, no other references to any seventeenth-century entrenchments in this area, while the ships that accompanied the expedition started careening, apparently out at the Spanish careening point, the day after the initial English landing, John F. Battick, ed., 'Richard Rooth's Sea Journal of the Western Design, 1654–55', *Jamaica Journal* 5:4 (1971): 16, 11 May 1655. It seems more likely that Castilla's 'Careen Key' was the future Port Cagway, today's Port Royal.

45. Pawson and Buisseret, *Port Royal, Jamaica*, 7–24.

46. Eg 'Cagway harb:[or]', NLJ 727fa 1671, 'A New and Exact Map of the Isle of Jamaica as it was lately surveyed by order of Sir Thomas Modyford', published in Richard Blome, *A Description of the Island of Jamaica, with the other isles and Territories in America, to which the English are Related ... Taken from the Notes of Sir Thomas Linch* (London: I. Milbourn, 1672). Frederic Cassidy traces earlier Spanish uses of the name, but assumes that it referred to the cay that became Port Royal, Cassidy, 'Earliest Place Names in Jamaica', 153–4, 159.

47. The 'Town River' phrase is from JA 1B/11/2/5, 138, 17 March 1665, patent to Nathanial Newberry. It continued to be used in some grants into the mid-1670s.

The Rio Cobre name was current as early as 1665, ibid. 133, survey for 'The Negroes', 19 March 1665/6.

48. 'The Monastery', JA 1B/11/1/3, ff. 22v–23, 4 July 1668, grant to Humphry Freeman.

49. 'D'Oyley's Journal, 1,' 46, 13 February 1655/6, 'the Redd Church'; JA 1B/11/1/7, f. 114, 28 September 1663, patent for John Jones.

50. NLJ Ms 291, 15 August 1597, Governor Fernando Melgarejo de Córdoba [to Council]. Current archaeological work is investigating when the Tainos' destruction was completed. Excavations found classic Taino pottery at Nanny Town, the early Maroon centre, but whether this shows that Maroon bands occupied a former Taino settlement, or that there were overlaps between Taino survivors and the first Maroons awaits the dig's final publication. For an interim statement, E. Kofi Agorsah, 'Archaeology of Maroon Settlements in Jamaica', in *idem.* ed., *Maroon Heritage: Archaeological, Ethnographic and Historical Perspectives* (Kingston: The UWI Press 1994), 178–82.

51. Offers of assistance from 'divers Portugals' besides 'some discourse with their Negro Slaves' are both cited in 'The Voyages of Captain William Jackson', 19.

52. Although for the early, well-informed and enthusiastic suggestions on the opportunities that the conquest of Jamaica offered which one Simon de Castres sent to Oliver Cromwell in September 1655, see, *Thurloe State Papers* 4, 61–3.

53. Arbell, *Portuguese Jews of Jamaica*, 9–12.

54. David Buisseret, 'Edward D'Oyley 1617–1675', *Jamaica Journal* 5:1 (1971): 6–10.

55. Pawson and Buisseret, *Port Royal*, 12–16.

56. For the White Chapel, see, for example JA 1B/11/2/6, f. 56, September 10, 1670, Survey of the Town Savanna.

57. Sloane, *A Voyage* 1, lxv.

58. Michael Laithwaite, 'Totnes houses 1500–1800', in Peter Clark, ed., *The Transformation of English Provincial Towns* (London: Hutchinson, 1984), 62–98, now revised and expanded in idem. 'Town Houses up to 1660', in Peter Beacham, ed., *Devon building an introduction to local traditions* (Exeter: Devon Books, 1990, 3rd ed 2001), 95–115, 152, and John Thorp, 'Town Houses of the Late Seventeenth and Early Eighteenth Centuries', in ibid. 116–27, 152. More generally, John Schofield, 'Urban Housing in England 1400–1600', in David Gaimster and Paul Stamper, eds., *The Age of Transition: The Archaeology of English Culture 1400–1600* (Oxford: Oxbow, 1997), 127–44.

59. For a sympathetic analysis of such creole urban layouts, Albert Manucy, *Sixteenth-Century St Augustine: The People and their Homes* (Gainesville, Fla: University Press of Florida, 1997); for an uncomprehending English visitor dismissing the gates as an indication of Spanish 'pride', NLJ Ms 105, Taylor, 'Multum in Parvo', 2. f. 509.

60. Crowley, *Invention of Comfort*, 60–2.

61. On temporary buildings erected in the initial stage of English settlement in Virginia, Alain Charles Outlaw, *Governor's Land: Archaeology of Early Seventeenth-*

Century Virginia Settlements (Charlottesville, Va: University Press of Virginia, 1990); for the persistence of 'impermanent' elements in buildings constructed in the Chesapeake in the mid- and late seventeenth-century, Cary Carson, Norman F. Barka, William M. Kelso, Garry Wheeler Stone and Dell Upton, 'Impermanent Architecture in the Southern American Colonies', *Winterthur Portfolio* 16 (1981): 135–96. Describing the proportions organizing early English settlements, Kathleen Bragden, Edward Chappell and William Graham, 'A Scant Urbanity: Jamestown in the Seventeenth Century', in Theodore R. Reinhart and Dennis J. Pogue, eds., *The Archaeology of 17th Century Virginia* (Richmond, Va: Archaeological Society of Virginia, 1993), 227. The initial orientations of buildings in St Mary's, Maryland, Henry C. Miller, 'Archaeology and Town Planning', in Geoff Egan and R.L. Michael, eds., *Old and New Worlds* (Oxford: Oxbow, 1999), 72–83 and idem. 'The Country House Site: An Archaeological Study of a Seventeenth-Century Domestic Landscape', in Paul A. Shackel and Barbara J. Little, eds., *Historical Archaeology of the Chesapeake* (Washington, DC: Smithsonian Institution, 1994), 79–80.

62. Bowden, 'Three Centuries of Bridgetown', 8–9, 13–31.
63. NMM WYN 10/2, 'A journal of every dayes proceedings', 15 May 1655.
64. Alex Clifton-Taylor, *The Pattern of English Buildings* (London, 1962, 2nd ed 1965), 42–47; J.R. Harrison, 'The Mud Wall in England at the Close of the Vernacular Era', *Transactions of the Ancient Monuments Society* n.s. 28 (1984), 154–74, and Peter Beacham, 'Local Building Materials and Methods', in idem. ed., *Devon Building*, 18–22.
65. Maurice Howard suggests that for gentry houses the transition occurred in the mid-sixteenth century. By the seventeenth and eighteenth century the proportions of older, lower ceilinged, English rooms would be criticised as 'low and dark'. *The Early English Country House: Architecture and Politics 1490–1550* (London: George Philip, 1987), 106–07.
66. This was the 'old Timberwork House . . . called the Kinges House' seen by John Taylor in 1688. NLJ Ms 105, Taylor, 'Multum in Parvo', 2. f. 493.
67. Long, *History*, 2. 13.
68. NLJ Ms 24, Leslie Alexander to Frank Cundall, 2 April 1897.
69. F.J. Osborne, *The History of the Catholic Church in Jamaica* (1977, 2nd ed Chicago, Ill: Loyola University Press, 1988), 125–30. IRO Deeds, o.s. 20, 2–2v, 21 March 1687/8, Joseph and Mary Smallwood to Father Thomas Churchill and, for the Convent name, JA 1B/11/1/2, Patents, 2. 1666–69, 4, 23 March 1665/6, patent to Katherine Smith.
70. JA 1B/11/1/1A, f. 60v, 16 August 1664, patent to George Newell; UWI Mona, 'D'Oyley's Journal: part 3', f. 84v, 26 March 1660; JA 1B/11/2/6, f. 37, 1 June 1664, survey for Anthony Rodrigues.
71. Sloane, *A Voyage* 1, xix.
72. William Whaley to William Helyar, 20 January 1672, quoted in J. Harry Bennett,

'William Whaley, Planter of Seventeenth-Century Jamaica', *Agricultural History* 40 (1966): 114.

73. David Buisseret, 'Fresh Light on Spanish Jamaica', *Jamaica Journal* 16:1 (1983): 72–3; also, Steven Panning, 'Spanish Ruins at Orange Valley', *Jamaican Historical Society Bulletin* 10:12 (1995): 134–6.

74. I discuss these stories at greater length in 'Re-inventing the English Conquest of Jamaica in the Late Seventeenth Century', *English Historical Review* 117 (2002): 813–39.

75. William Beeston, 'A Journal Kept by Col. William Beeston from his first coming to Jamaica', in *Interesting Tracts Relating to Jamaica* (St Iago: Lewis, Luna and Jones, 1800), 272.

76. A.P. Thornton, *West-India Policy under the Restoration* (Oxford: Clarendon, 1956), 66–123.

77. NMM WYN 10/2, 31 January 1654/5.

78. James Robertson, 'Stuart London and the idea of a royal Capital City', *Renaissance Studies* 15 (2001): 37–58.

79. *Journals of the Assembly of Jamaica, 1. January 20th. 1663–4 . . . to April 20th. 1709* (Spanish Town: Alexander Aikman, 1811), 2, 20 October 1664.

80. JA 1B/11/1/1A, f. 3, 25 October 1662, grant to Sir Charles Lyttleton.

81. JA 1B/5/3/1, Council Minutes 1661–1678, f. 103, 12 October 1664.

82. JA 1B/11/1/1A, f. 113, 12 September 1665, grant to Richard Hemmings. This property faced onto White Church Street.

83. Sloane, *A Voyage* 1, lxiv–lxv.

84. John Ogilby, *America: Being the Latest and Most Accurate Description of the New World* (London: by the author, 1671), 343.

85. Nuala Zahedieh, 'The Capture of the Blue Dove, 1664: Policy, Profits and Protection in Early English Jamaica', in Roderick A. McDonald, ed., *West Indies Accounts: Essays on the History of the British Caribbean and the Atlantic Economy* (Kingston: The UWI Press, 1996), 29–47 and idem. 'A Frugal, Prudential and Hopeful Trade: Privateering in Jamaica, 1655–89', *Journal of Imperial and Commonwealth History* 18 (1990): 145–68.

86. NLJ Ms 105, Taylor, 'Multum in Parvo', 2. 513.

87. BL Sloane Ms 3984, ff. 194–195v at f. 194, 16 December 1670, Royal Society, 'Inquiries Recommended to Colonel Linch going to Jamaica', number 5.

88. JA 1B/5/3/1, 91, 20 October 1664.

89. F[rancis] H[eeson], 'To the Reader', *The Laws of Jamaica, Passed by the Assembly and Confirmed by His Majesty in Council, February 23, 1683* (London: H. Hills for Charles Harper, 1683), 6bv.

90. Thornton, *West-India Policy under the Restoration*, 220. Citing Secretary Coventry to Lord Vaughan, 8 June 1676.

91. JA 1B/5/3/3B, 16 October [1687], unfoliated.

92. Helen Nader, *Liberty in Absolute Spain: The Habsburg Sale of Towns, 1516–1700* (Baltimore, Md: Johns Hopkins University Press, 1990), 17–45, also Duvon C. Corbitt, '*Mercedes* and *Realengos* a Survey of the Public Land System in Cuba', *Hispanic American Historical Review* 19 (1939), 262–85.

93. Padrón, *Spanish Jamaica*, 35.

94. 'Population de la Jamaïque au 28 octobre 1662', Watts, *Histoire des Colonies Anglaises aux Antilles*, 483. Padrón, *Spanish Jamaica* 35, estimates a total population of 1,500 in 1655.

95. I am grateful to Dorrick Gray and Audene Brooks for discussing the material from the JNHT's White Church Street excavation with me. IRO Deeds, o.s. 5, ff. 163v–164v, 21 March 1672/3, George Wildrush to Isaac Wells.

96. Richardson Wright, *Revels in Jamaica, 1682–1838* (New York, 1937, reprint Kingston: Bolivar, 1986), 6.

97. NLJ Ms. 105, Taylor, 'Multum in Parvo', 1. ff. 502, 471.

98. Nuala Zahedieh argues for the importance of Port Royal's appetite for locally grown foodstuffs in promoting the development of seventeenth-century Jamaica, '"The wickedest city in the world": Port Royal, commercial hub of the seventeenth-century Caribbean', in Verene Shepherd, ed., *Working Slavery, Pricing Freedom: Perspectives from the Caribbean, Africa and the African Diaspora* (Kingston: Ian Randle Publishers, 2002), 3–20.

99. JA 1B/5/3/3A, ff. 193–194, 11 May 1685.

100. JA 1B/5/3/2, f. 159v, 8 August 1678, Grant.

101. For such a cattle drive, JA 1A/3/1, Earliest Chancery Record, 1676–8 and 1684, ff. 155–164, Lewis *v*. Mann, 7 July 1684.

102. K.G. Davies, *The Royal African Company* (London: Longman, 1957), 307–310. On their sales, Trevor Burnard, 'Who Bought Slaves in Early America? Purchases of Slaves from the Royal African Company in Early Jamaica, 1674–1708', *Slavery & Abolition* 17 (1996): 68–92.

103. The Company's office stood near the modern Cathedral. JA 1B/11/2/7, f. 88, June 20 1667, survey for 'The Royal Company' and 1B/11/1/1a, f. 169v, 1 August 1667, patent to Duke of York and Royal Company. The relationship between this property and the Red Church can be located through, 1B/11/2/6, f. 32, April 1, 1669, survey for William Rignall.

104. *Journals of the Assembly of Jamaica* 1, 114, 6 April 1688. The 'ultra-prerogative' phrase is from John Roby, *The History of the Parish of St James, in Jamaica, to the Year 1740* . . . (Kingston: R.J. De Cordova, 1849), 18, footnote.

105. Dunn, *Sugar and Slaves*, 179, 182, 271–2.

106. JA 1B/5/3/2, f. 44, 11 May 1675.

107. JA 1B/11/2/7, f. 65, 11 May 1695, survey for William Brodrick; 1B/11/2/5, f. 100, 30 October 1688, survey for Abell Meacham.

108. Discussed in Robertson, 'Jamaican Architectures before Georgian', 73–95.

109. Ibid. 76.

110. Sloane, *Voyage* 1, xlcii.

111. JA 1B/11/1/3, ff. 206v–207, 3 March 1664, Grant to Lieutenant-Colonel John Cope.

112. Thus the 'Church Parade' name is used in the 1786 John Pitcairn Map of Spanish Town; selling a cook room, IRO Deeds, o.s. 8. 41v, 26 September 1676, Edward Blackman to Elizabeth Inglett; ibid. 95v, 14 December 1676, Thomas and Anne Westfield to Mabel Langfield.

113. IRO Deeds, o.s. i. ff 10–10v, 26 November 1664, Bill of Sale, William Bently to Francis Papworth.

114. Robertson, 'Architectures before Georgian', 75–6.

115. Henry J. Cadbury, 'Conditions in Jamaica in 1687', *Jamaican Historical Review* 3 (1957): 53.

116. Padrón, *Spanish Jamaica*, 119; as St Paul's, NLJ Ms. 105, Taylor, 'Multum in Parvo', 1. 191; the Red Cross Church, Long, *History* 2, 2.

117. John Roby, *Monuments of the Cathedral-Church and Parish of St Catherine* (Montego-Bay: Alex: Holmes, 1831), 15–19. In 1824, when Roby made his notes, these slabs were 'within the Communion rails', or else lay under the rails themselves.

118. Philip Wright, ed., *Monumental Inscriptions of Jamaica* (London: Society of Genealogists, 1966), outside, 118–20, still inside, 106–14, *passim*.

119. John Rashford, 'Arawak, Spanish and African Contributions to Jamaica's Settlement Vegetation', *Jamaica Journal* 24:3 (1993): 17–23.

120. Boston, Boston Public Library, Ms. Eng.179. Dr Smallwood's Memoranda.

121. NLJ Ms 105, Taylor, 'Multum in Parvo', 2. 535, 'The manner of clearing woody ground, in order to make it fitt to plant, according to the custom of Jamaica.'

Chapter 3

1. Wilma R. Bailey, 'Kingston 1692–1843: a colonial city', PhD thesis, University of the West Indies, Mona, (1974), offers the best starting point for the island's urban history in this period, as, on the planters, does the chapter 'Debtors and Creditors' in Richard Pares, *Merchants and Planters* (Economic History Review, Supplement, 4, Cambridge: for the Economic History Society, 1960), 38–50. The guerilla campaigns by the Jamaican Maroons which shaped colonial politics between 1692 and 1738 are described in Mavis C. Campbell, *The Maroons of Jamaica 1655–1796: A History of Resistance, Collaboration and Betrayal* (Trenton, NJ: Africa World Press, 1990). A great deal of information is also accumulated in Frank Cundall, *The Governors of Jamaica in the First Half of the Eighteenth Century* (London: West India Committee, 1937). Carl Bridenbaugh's discussion of the

eighteenth-century capital of colonial Virginia offers useful comparisons, *Seat of Empire: The Political Role of Eighteenth-Century Williamsburg* (1950, new edition Williamsburg: Colonial Williamsburg Foundation, 1958). Wider contexts are offered in Richard S. Dunn, *Sugar and Slaves, the Rise of the Plantation Class in the English West Indies 1624–1713* (Chapel Hill, NC: University of North Carolina Press, 1972), Richard B. Sheridan, 'The Formation of Caribbean Plantation Society, 1689–1748', in P.J. Marshall, ed., *The Eighteenth Century* (Oxford History of the British Empire, 2, Oxford: Oxford University Press, 1998), 394–414, and Jack P. Greene, *Pursuits of Happiness: The Social Development of Early Modern British Colonies and the Formation of American Culture* (Chapel Hill, NC: University of North Carolina Press, 1988). For a helpful discussion of the difficulties involved in fitting another inland market centre into the categories that academics use to appraise English towns at this juncture, I.L. Williams, 'The Urbanity of Marlborough: a Wiltshire Town in the Seventeenth Century', *Wiltshire Studies: Wiltshire Archaeological and Natural History Magazine* 94 (2001): 139–47.

2.   On early grants in the nascent settlement, UWI Mona, 'D'Oyley's Journal: part 3', f. 93v, 1 August 1660. Property grants 'on Store house Bay' include JA 1B/11/2/1, St Andrew's Plat Book, I, A–H, 1661–1712, f. 7, 23 December 1665, surveys for Colonel Henry Archibald and Captain Charles Whitfield, and 1B/11/1/2, f. 9, 23 March 1665/6, patent to William Long and the inhabitants of Liguanea. The confirmation of the Saturday market, 1B/5/3/1, ff. 32–33, 27 August 1661. For its development by the 1680s, William A. Claypole, 'The Settlement of the Liguanea Plain between 1655 and 1673', *Jamaican Historical Review* 10 (1973): 7–16, and NLJ Ms 105, Taylor, 'Multum in Parvo', 2. ff. 512–14. Citing an 'Old Spanish Path' there in 1742, Duncan Crewe, *Yellow Jack and the Worm: British Naval Administration in the West Indies, 1739–1748* (Liverpool Historical Studies, 9, Liverpool: Liverpool University Press, 1993), 111.

3.   J.G. Young, 'The Founding of Kingston', in W. Adolphe Roberts, ed., *The Capitals of Jamaica*, 38–47, also idem 'Who Planned Kingston?' *Jamaican Historical Review* 1 (1946): 144–53. Kingston was established near where the 'Old Hope Road' that ran south parallel to Long Mountain met 'the Windward Road', the main track running along the coast to the eastern end of the island.

4.   Francis Rogers, 'The Diary of Francis Rogers', in Bruce S. Ingram, ed., *Three Sea Journals of Stuart Times* (London: Constable, 1936), 226–7. 30 November 1705, also, Anthony Priddy, 'The 17th and 18th Century Settlement Pattern of Port Royal', *Jamaica Journal* 9:2–3 (1975): 8–10, 17.

5.   The shrunken site, Pawson and Buisseret, *Port Royal*, 169; UWI Mona, Papers relating to the Wilson Family of Bromhead, Yorkshire, *c.* 1694–1768, unfoliated, [1699], [Josiah and George Heathcote to Charles Wilson].

6.   BL Sloane Ms 3918, Henry Barham, 'Account of Jamaica', (1722), f. 266.

7. David Buisseret, ed./trans., 'A Frenchman looks at Jamaica in 1706', *Jamaica Journal* 2:3 (1968): 7–8. Exploring English aspects of this wider transformation in European taste, Peter Borsay, *The English Urban Renaissance: Culture and Society in the Provincial Town, 1660–1770* (Oxford: Oxford University Press, 1989).

8. BL King's Ms 213, 'Journal of an Officer . . . 1764–1765', f. 9.

9. PRO CO 137/28, ff. 145–46, 21 November 1754, Answer of the Town of St Iago de la Vega to Board of Trade.

10. 'An Act for establishing a perpetual anniversary fast on the twenty-eighth of August', (16 November 1722) *The Laws of Jamaica: Comprehending All the Acts in Force Passed between the Thirty-Second Year of the Reign of King Charles the Second, and the Thirty-Third Year of the Reign of King George III* (St Iago de la Vega: Alexander Aikman, 1792), 1., 241–2; Pawson and Buisseret, *Port Royal*, 170–71.

11. In 1729 the Royal Navy started developing Port Antonio, on the north side of the island, as an alternative dockyard to the disaster-prone Port Royal. The proposal was supported by a pushing naval officer, a then Commander RN, Charles Knowles. Elaborate facilities were constructed but it proved inconvenient to send ships in need of refit there from Port Royal and the new base rotted. By the late 1740s, when Knowles returned to Port Royal as Admiral, even he made little use of it. Crewe, *Yellow Jack and the Worm*, 219–25.

12. Charles Leslie, *A New History of Jamaica from the Earliest Accounts to the Taking of Porto Bello by Vice Admiral Vernon in Thirteen Letters from a Gentleman to a Friend* (2nd ed London: J. Hodges, 1740), 15.

13. BL Add. Ms 22676, ff. 6-14, '*c.* 1694' (but after 1703), 'Reasons offered for removing the Seat of Government from Spanish Town to Kingston'.

14. Buisseret, 'A Frenchman', 7.

15. BL Sloane Ms 3918, Barham, 'Account of Jamaica', f. 240.

16. Long, *History* 2, 5.

17. On the reuse of older stonework shaping the rebuilding of London's St Mary at Hill church after London's Great Fire of 1666, Gustav Milne, *The Great Fire of London* (New Barnet: Historical Publications, 1986), 106–08, similarly at St Mary Aldermary, Howard Colvin, 'The Rebuilding of the Church of St Mary Aldermary after the Great Fire of London', (1981), in idem. *Essays in English Architectural History* (New Haven, Con: Yale University Press, 1999), 195–205, and, more generally, Margaret Whinney, *Wren* (London: Thames & Hudson, 1971), 45–80.

18. The structural components in the rebuilding are discussed at greater length in Lewis Nelson, 'Building "Cross-wise": Reconstructing Jamaica's Eighteenth-Century Anglican Churches', *Jamaican Historical Review* 22 (2003): 11–39, 70–76.

19. Roby, *Monuments*, 7. On church-building in late seventeenth- and eighteenth-century Virginia, see Dell Upton, *Holy Things and Profane: Anglican Parish Churches in Colonial Virginia* (1986, reprint New Haven, Conn: Yale University Press, 1997).

20. JA 2/6/2, Kingston Vestry Minutes, 1750–1752, f. 136, 30 July 1750.

21. Roby, *Monuments*, 8.

22. Discussing statues of Moses and Aaron in seventeenth-century London churches, Stephen Porter and Adam White, 'John Colt and the Charterhouse Chapel', *Architectural History* 44 (2001): 228–36; the subsequent relegation of the Spanish Town carvings to the vestry, R.A. Minter, *Episcopacy without Episcopate: The Church of England in Jamaica before 1824* (Upton-upon-Severn: Self Publishing Association, 1990), 242, citing Lambeth Palace, Fulham Papers, 18. The interior woodwork fell casualty to Victorian zeal to create a properly neo-medieval interior, see below 178–99.

23. JA 2/6/2, f. 131, 25 June 1750.

24. For an attempt to trace the property known as 'the Eagle House' or, more commonly, 'the John Crow House,' Cundall, *Historic Jamaica*, 108–10. This stresses ownership rather than tenancies. See also H.V. Ormsby Marshall, 'Eagle House', *Jamaican Historical Society Bulletin* 3:16 (1964): 260–3, for recollections of the house's twentieth-century decay and final demolition.

25. Bodl. Ms Rawl A 312, f. 8, 28 July 1711, Council Order, also f. 17, 15 August 1711; f. 28, 11 October 1711; f. 61, 22 November 1711. Under Queen Anne the Governor's house was known as 'the Queen's House'.

26. Leslie, *New History of Jamaica*, 29.

27. JA 1B/5/18/1/2, Dispatches, Jamaica to England, 1 November 1726, John Ayscough, President of Council to Duke of Newcastle; I am grateful to Robert Barker for discussions of the damage done by the 1744 hurricane.

28. On the reused foundations, Mathewson, 'History from the Earth', 3–11.

29. BL Sloane Ms 3918, Barham, 'Account of Jamaica', f. 210. It was built at Governor Beeston's own cost.

30. Long, *History*, 2, 6.

31. John Lindsay, 'Sermon for Annual Fast for Earthquake, 1760', *Columbian Magazine* 2 (1797): 501–02.

32. Long, *History*, 2, 6.

33. In Virginia an equivalent Secretary's Office was constructed a generation later in 1747 and survives as 'the Public Records Office'. It is described in Marcus Whiffen, *The Public Buildings of Williamsburg, Colonial Capital of Virginia: An Architectural History* (Williamsburg Architectural Studies, 1, Williamsburg, Va: Colonial Williamsburg, 1958), 130–34.

34. Describing this procedure, James Houstoun, 'Dr Houstoun's Memoirs of His Own Life-Time', in *The Works of James Houstoun MD* (London: S. Bladon, 1753), 402.

35. *Laws of Jamaica*, 1, 124–6, 11 Anne .IV. 'An act for preserving the public records of this island'.

36. Eg. UWI Mona, Wilson Papers, June 7, 1755, Edward Lewis to Mr Wilson, and 29 March 1758, George Lewis to John Wilson.

37. J.H. Parry, 'The Patent Offices in the British West Indies', *English Historical Review* 69 (1954): 200–25; W.K. Hackman, 'William Beckford's Profits from Three Jamaican Offices', *Historical Research* 63 (1990): 107–109.
38. 'A street by the school house', JA 1B/11/2/6, f. 24, plat for John Paris, 28 April 1692; 'the school house land', 1B/11/2/7, f. 22, plat for Anne O'Bryan, 20 October 1698.
39. IRO Deeds o.s. 8, f. 89, 17 February 1676/7, John Barkley to Sir Thomas Modyford *et al.* This date was nearer to the schools which some Barbados planters founded than to any other in Jamaica. Thus for a Barbados planter's bequest in 1671 to establish a 'free school' in Christ Church parish, Henry Drax's 1682 bequest of £2000 for 'a Free School or College in Bridgetown' which may have initiated today's Combermere School and a donation in 1686 to finance the construction of a charity school in St George's parish. Woodville Marshall, 'Charity for the Undeserving? The Carpenter Trust and the Creation of the Parish Land Tenantry in St Philip', *Journal of the Barbados Museum and Historical Society* 49 (2003): 168.
40. IRO Laws of Jamaica, 1st series, 1. f. 58, 26 December 1695, 'An Act for the Erecting and Establishing a Free School in the Parish of St Andrew'.
41. Andrew Jackson O'Shaughnessy, *An Empire Divided: The American Revolution and the British Caribbean* (Philadelphia, Penn: University of Pennsylvania Press, 2000), 19–21.
42. Cundall, *Governors . . . First Half of the Eighteenth Century*, 75, describes the failure of the school in St Andrew. On the enrollment in Spanish Town, Long, *History* 2, 257. This still compares well with the figures Long cites for Wolmer's School in Kingston and two rural endowed schools, Vere School and Manning's, which enrolled perhaps six apiece, though their endowments were over double those of the school in Spanish Town. However, Long cited these numbers as part of a case for pooling all the schools' assets and forming a new islandwide school. His estimated enrolments may well tend towards the low side.
43. Edward Long printed Williams's verses and an English translation in his *History of Jamaica*. They are reprinted in Thomas Krise, ed., *Caribbeana: An Anthology of English Literature of the West Indies, 1657–1777* (Chicago, Ill: University of Chicago Press, 1999), 319–324. In a still unpublished paper John Gilmore argues that Long's translation does not do justice to Williams's latin. Vincent Caretta, 'Who Was Francis Williams?' *Early American Literature* 38:2 (2003): 213–25, discusses the evidence for Williams's education and career. An unpublished paper by Linda Sturtz sheds further light on Williams's family.
44. Rosalie Smith-McCrea, 'Fiction, Personality and Property: A Jamaican Colonial Representation in Miniature', *In Tribute to David Boxer: Twenty Years at the National Gallery of Jamaica, 1975–1995* (Kingston: Institute of Jamaica, 1995), 4–9.
45. This individual was also 'educated in *England*', Houstoun, 'Houstoun's Memoirs', 346. Houstoun left Jamaica in 1747.

46. Leslie, *New History*, 35. Long, *History* 2, 246–59, is nearly as pessimistic.
47. Jacob A.P.M. Andrade, *A Record of the Jews in Jamaica: From the English Conquest to the Present Time* (Kingston: Jamaica Times, 1941), 259–60 (the purchasers were Jacob Nunes, Jacob daCosta Alvarenga and Jacob Correa, 'Merchants and Churchwardens . . .'), 39–40, translations of synagogue names from ibid. 38. The 1699 Prayer-Meeting hall received a bequest in the will of Jacob daCosta Alvarenga 'of St Jago de la Vega,' translated in ibid. 179. Richard D. Barnett and Philip Wright, *The Jews of Jamaica: Tombstone Inscriptions 1663–1880* ed., Oron Yoffe (Jerusalem: Ben Zvi Institute, 1997), 83–114, offer a fuller description of the graveyards and memorial stones surviving into the early 1960s. Andrade op. cit. 261, cites an earlier tombstone from 1694 which apparently did not survive to be incorporated in Barnett and Wright's compilation.
48. Eli Faber, 'The Jews and their Role in Slaves and Slavery', *Jamaican Historical Society Bulletin* 11:2 (1998): 27.
49. PRO CO 137/28, f. 140, 21 November 1754, Humble Answer of Town of St Iago de la Vega to Board of Trade.
50. Long, *History* 2, 17. These Barracks stood next door to a wheelwright's yard which became the subject of a later dispute in the Grand Court. The yard also abutted on the Rio Cobre to the Northwest and 'Southwest on the Road leading to the Passage Fort'. JA 1A/11/1, Writs of Extents, 1755–1769, ff. 62–63, February Grand Court, 1764, V. R.Y. Topley *v.* Richard Bone.
51. Leslie, *New History*, 2, 29–30.
52. Long, *History* 2, 25.
53. 10 George II, c. 7, 'An Act for Clearing the Rio Cobre', 12 November 1723, *Laws of Jamaica*, 1, 152–55. There was plenty to re-engineer. A massive storm in 1722 shifted the channel of the Rio Cobre downstream of the town, moving it away from the former Taino settlement at White Marl and wiping out the Passage Fort settlement at the old Spanish landing place. Cundall, *Governors . . . First Half of the Eighteenth Century*, 97. Robert Renny, *An History of Jamaica* (London: J. Cawthorn, 1807), 101.
54. For several reports condemning stores held at 'the Victualing Office at Passage Fort', Bodl. Ms. Rawl. A. 232, Orders from naval commanders in the West Indies to Joseph Gyde, victualing agent in Jamaica, 1706–1710, [42v], 10 June 1709, [53v], 15 October 1709, [62v], 5 September 1710.
55. Leslie, *New History*, 275.
56. Crewe, *Yellow Jack and the Worm*, 124–25. These incidents both occurred in 1746.
57. Leslie, *New History* 27, discussed in Errol Hill, *The Jamaican Stage 1655–1900: Profile of a Colonial Theatre* (Amhurst, Mass: University of Massachusetts Press, 1992), 20–21, 76.
58. *The Jamaica Courant* 5 no. 295, (Saturday June 22, to Saturday June 29 1754). I consulted a copy in PRO CO137/28, ff. 37–38v.

59. Trevor Burnard and Kenneth Morgan, 'The Dynamics of the Slave Market and Slave Purchasing Patterns in Jamaica, 1655–1788', *William & Mary Quarterly* 3rd ser 58 (2001): 206.

60. 'Characteristic traits of the Creolian and African Negroes in this Island', *Columbian Magazine* 2 (April, 1797): 701; Trevor Burnard, 'E Pluribus Plures: African Ethnicities in Seventeenth and Eighteenth Century Jamaica', *Jamaican Historical Review* 21 (2001): 8-22, 56–59.

61. Trevor Burnard, '"Prodigious riches": the Wealth of Jamaica before the American Revolution', *Economic History Review* 2nd ser 54 (2001): 510–12.

62. BL Add. Ms 22676, 'Reasons offered', f. 11v.

63. Trevor Burnard, '"The Countrie Continues Sicklie": White Mortality in Jamaica, 1655–1780', *Social History of Medicine* 12 (1999): 45–72, also, Crewe, *Yellow Jack and the Worm*, 41–51, and Wilma Bailey, 'The geography of fevers in early Jamaica', *Jamaican Historical Review* 10 (1973): 23–31.

64. For the phrase, see the early nineteenth-century engravings, NLJ P/102/VIII Ja. F.J., [Abraham James] 'Johnny New-Come in the Island of Jamaica', (London: William Holland, 1800), and P/221/VIII, F.J., [Abraham James] 'Johnny Newcome in Love in the West Indies', (London: William Holland, nd. c. 1808).

65. NLJ Ms 1579/4, Papers of Captain David Hamilton, 1744–1747, 4 May 1747, J. Tyler to David Hamilton.

66. NLJ Ms 2006, Bruce E. Burgoyne, trans., 'As they Saw us: Hessian Views of America During the Revolutionary War', Philipp Waldeck's 'Journal', December 13 1776; ibid. Carl Philip Steuernagel, quartermaster sergeant in Captain Pentzel's Company of the Regiment, 'A Brief description of the . . . Expedition of the Prince of Waldeck's Third Regiment in America from 20 May 1776 until the return from America in the year of 1783', 2 December 1776. A similar observation was made by another German visitor a decade later, 'Through European Eyes: Jamaica 200 Years Ago', *Jamaica Journal* 17:4 (1985): 41.

67. Will of Peter Beckford, witnessed 3 February 1730, entered 6 October 1735. IRO Wills, o.s. Liber 26, where the original was recorded is now lost. A late nineteenth-century transcript survives among the papers of a subsequent governor of the school, JA 7/32/568, copies of the wills of Francis Smith and Peter Beckford. To put this bequest in context, Beckford owned personal property in Jamaica valued at £159,933 sterling in addition to extensive estates.

68. 17 George II c. 10, 'An act for vesting the sum of one thousand pounds, devised by the last will and testament of Peter Beckford, esquire, deceased, to the poor of the parish of St Catherine, in a free-school in the town of St Jago de la Vega; and for erecting a corporation for the better government thereof', 9 June 1744, *Laws of Jamaica*, 1. 307–312; BL Add. Ms 22676, f. 145, 9 February 1743, Justices and Vestry of St Catherine to Mrs Bathshua Beckford.

69. Indicating the scale of civilian public architectural commissions undertaken in

Charleston, South Carolina in the 1750s, Carl R. Loundsbury, *From Statehouse to Courthouse: An Architectural History of South Carolina's Colonial Capitol and Charleston County Courthouse* (Columbia, SC: University of South Carolina Press, 2001), and more generally, in the British North American colonies during the 1740s, '50s and '60s, see Carl Bridenbaugh, *Peter Harrison, First American Architect* (Chapel Hill, NC: University of North Carolina Press, 1949), 45–67, 98–117.

70.　Gosner, *Caribbean Georgian*, 126, provides clear sketches of this structure.

71.　*Laws of Jamaica*, I. 304–7, 1744, 'An Act for erecting a house or edifice for the use of the council and assembly, and for the better preserving of the public records, and for the reception of the small arms'.

72.　Long, *History* 2, 39.

73.　For successive Assembly grants of £2,000 (in 1753 of £2,500) towards building 'the Public Edifice,' PRO CO 137/27, ff. 49–50. Deficiency Tax, 1751–1753. The quotation, ibid. 176, 20 January 1754, Governor Knowles to the Merchants of Kingston.

74.　Long, *History* 2, 344–8. Three acts of the Assembly ratified the various treaties: 20 George II, c. v, 'An act for confirming the articles executed by colonel John Guthrie, lieutenant Francis Sadler, and Cudjoe, the commander of the rebels; for paying rewards for taking up and restoring runaway slaves; and making provision for four white persons, to reside at Trelawny Town; . . .' 12 May 1739; 23 George II, c. 8, 'An act for confirming the articles executed by colonel Robert Bennett, and Quao the commander of the rebels; for paying rewards for taking up and restoring runaway slaves; and making provision for four white persons to reside at Crawford's Town and New Nanny Town; . . . ' 27 May 1740; 24 George II, c 7, 'An act to encourage colonel Cudjoe and captain Quao, and the several negroes under their command in Trelawny and Crawford Towns, and all other towns of rebellious negroes who submitted to terms, to pursue and take up runaway slaves, and such negroes as continue in rebellion . . .' 8 May 1741. Campbell, *The Maroons*, 126–41, offers a close reading of these texts.

75.　Campbell, *The Maroons*, 141–7, also Higman, *Monpelier*, 12–18.

76.　*Laws of Jamaica*, I. 324–7, 1747, 'An Act to enable the justices and vestry of the parish of St Catherine to keep clean part of the savanna land, to be a common for the said parish, and to make leases of the remainder for the benefit of the parish . . . '.

77.　JA 1B/11/1/6, 152–153, 8 January 1674/5, patent to inhabitants of St Iago de la Vega; 1B/11/1/11, 116–116v, 13 June, 1687, patent to Parish of St Katherine.

78.　20 George II c. 10, 'An Act to enable the justices and vestry of the parish of St Catherine to keep clean part of the savanna land, to be a common for the said parish, and to make leases of the remainder for the benefit of the parish . . . .' 28 May 1747.

79.　'Land formerly in possession of parson Flemming deceased,' IRO, Deeds, o.s. 142,

30–30v, [pencil foliation, 37b–38], 4 January 1750/1, Sale, William Morris of St Catherine, a free negro man by trade of carpenter, to Christopher Hooke, Jeweler.

80. NLJ StC.154, 1748/9, 'Lots of Footland in St Jago de la Vega'.

81. Eg. an advertisement by 'William Foster, of Kingston Merchant, being removed to Spanish-Town', *Jamaica Courant* 5 no. 295, (1754): 2v.

82. IRO Deeds, o.s. 142, 3v–4, [pencil foliation, 11-11b], 31 July 1750, Sale, Richard Richards to Julia Taylor. The text cites Richards' purchase of the plot on 27 June 1749.

83. IRO Deeds o.s. 142, ff. 126–v. 24 March 1750/1, John Flaherty of St John's and John Burke of St John's. This deed includes a plat.

84. In 1743 Kingston's tax collectors noted over a hundred 'yards' in the town, some were recorded as 'negro yards' and others where 'houses and hutts are let out to hire' which were leased out and if some slaveholders leased space for their slaves here, they were also leased to some free colored families. Bailey, 'Kingston, 1692–1843', 251–6.

85. Taylor, *Western Design*, 56.

86. John Pike to 'Loving Brother', 18 June 1692, reprinted in Cadbury, 'Quakers and the Earthquake at Port Royal', 20.

87. BL Add. Ms 12405, f. 229v. Long Ms. Arleen Pabón takes the case for privacy further, arguing that 'the desire for privacy and interior autonomy from the exterior' encouraged slaves to construct small windows and doors to their huts. '*Por la encendida calle antillana*: Africanisms and Puerto Rican Architecture', *CRM: The Journal of Heritage Stewardship* 1:1 (2003): 21.

88. Bernard L. Herman, 'Slave and Servant Housing in Charleston, 1770–1820', *Historical Archaeology* 33 (1999): 88–101.

89. Both bills were presented to the Assembly on the same day, although one was brought in by a member of the Governor's Council and the second by the island's Attorney General, *Journals of the Assembly of Jamaica*, 4. *1745/6–1756*, 118, 28 April 1748.

90. *Laws of Jamaica*, 1. 345, 1749, 'An Act for amending and rendering more effectual an act entitled "an act for causing the streets, ways and avenues leading into the town of St Jago de la Vega"'.

91. *Laws of Jamaica*, 1. 312, 1744, 'An Act for remedying the inconveniences which may arise from the number of negro huts and houses built in and about the towns of St Jago de la Vega, Port Royal and Kingston'.

92. Barry W. Higman's studies of the slave lines at the Montpelier plantation show how far archaeology can illuminate these questions, *Montpelier*, 136–45, 171–2, 211–57.

93. Discussing the comparable 'mysterious space' of the Jewish quarter within the medieval topography of Marseilles, Daniel Lord Smail, 'The Linguistic Cartography of Property and Power in Late Medieval Marseille', in Barbara A.

Hanawalt and Michael Kobialka, eds., *Medieval Practices of Space* (Medieval Cultures, 23, Minneapolis, Minn: University of Minnesota Press, 2000), 44.

94. 'An Act for remedying the inconveniences which may arise from the number of negro huts . . .'; BL Add. Ms 12405, f. 229v.

95. JA 2/2/4, St Catherine, Vestry Minutes, 1759–1768, f. 23, 4 February 1760 and 1 March 1760.

96. Phrases from Erna Brodber, *A Study of Yards in the City of Kingston* (Working Papers, 9, Kingston: Institute of Social and Economic Research, University of the West Indies, Mona, 1975), 5.

97. Brodber, *Yards*, 16–7.

98. PRO CO 137/28, f. 145; Charles White, survey of Spanish Town, 1754, cited in Sturtz, 'Proprietors and Tenants: People of Free Condition, Spanish Town, 1754'. The elaborate surveys and figures generated by both sides in this dispute are to be published by Jack Greene. In the meantime, see David Ryden, '"One of the fertilest, pleasantest Spotts": an analysis of the slave economy in Jamaica's St Andrew parish', *Slavery & Abolition* 21 (2000): 32–55, and Sturtz, 'Proprietors and Tenants'.

99. BL Add. Ms 33,029, Newcastle Papers, cccxliv, Papers relating to the affairs of the American and West Indian Colonies, 2. 1744–1758, ff. 182–192, Minutes of Evidence re. Removal of Seat of Government from Spanish Town to Kingston, May 8, 1755 – June 5, 1755, f. 192, (final day).

100. PRO CO 137/27, f. 190, 15 February 1754, Knowles to Lords of Trade.

101. Long, *History* 2, 41. Discussing other specimens in Jamaica, John Rashford, 'The Search for Africa's Baobab Tree in Jamaica', *Jamaica Journal* 20:2 (1987): 1–7.

102. *Laws of Jamaica* 1, 341–4, 1748, 'An Act for causing the streets, ways and avenues leading into and out of the town of St Jago de la Vega to be cleansed'. The mosquito larvae explanation, Winifred Mary Cousins, 'The Emancipation of Slaves in Jamaica and its Results', London University, PhD thesis, (1927), 171. I consulted a copy, NLJ Ms. 168.

103. Cundall, *Governors . . . First Half of the Eighteenth Century*, 98. Michelle Craig's forthcoming Michigan University PhD thesis 'From Cultivation to Cup: A History of Coffee in the British Atlantic World, 1765–1807', should shed light on early exports of Jamaican coffee to North America.

104. Quotation from Francis Williams's Latin ode welcoming George Haldane as Governor of Jamaica. Edward Long suggested that this phrase alluded to Governor Knowles's move to Kingston. I have used the English translation by Judith Hallett in Carretta, 'Who Was Francis Williams?' 234. Long's note is reprinted, ibid. 234.

105. PRO CO 137/27, f. 210, [April, 1754], Petition of Justices and Vestrymen of Clarendon and others the Freeholders & Inhabitants of the said Parish.

106. In dismissing the petition from Spanish Town, Governor Knowles claimed 'that

out of the Number of Persons who have signed this Petition not one twentieth Part are Proprietors of Land'. PRO CO 137/27, f. 190v, 15 February 1754, Knowles to Lords of Trade.

107. PRO CO 137/27, ff. 153–156v, [1754], Petition of the Merchants Factors and Agents residing in the Island of Jamaica.

108. PRO CO 137/27, ff. 157–158, [1754], Petition of the Justices and Vestry and the rest of the Planters and Inhabitants of St Andrew. Also, CO 137/60, ff. 73–79, a further copy.

109. PRO CO 137/27, f. 152, 14 June, 1754, Council to Board of Trade; CO 137/28, f. 59, [1754, received, 4 December 1754], The Memorial of the Merchants of Liverpool; ibid. f. 66, 2 September 1754, Remembrance of the Master, Wardens, Assistants and Commonality of the Society of Merchants Venturers within the City of Bristol; CO 5/1066, July 30, 1754, Memorial of the Merchants Residing in New York; CO 5/1274, ff. 13–13v, August 1754, Memorials of the Merchants residing in the City of Philadelphia.

110. See J.G.A. Pocock, *The Machiavellian Moment: Florentine Political Thought and the Atlantic Republican Tradition* (Princeton, NJ: Princeton University Press, 1975), 462–552.

111. Renny, *History of Jamaica*, 64–5.

112. Bailey, 'Social control in the pre-Emancipation society of Kingston,' 98.

113. Sturtz, 'Proprietors and Tenants: People of Free Condition, Spanish Town 1754'.

114. [Charles White], *An Inquiry Concerning the Trade, Commerce, and Policy of Jamaica: Relative to the Scarcity of Money*, . . . (1st published, Jamaica, *c.* 1751, reprinted, London: for T. Kinnersly and G. Woodfal, 1759), 86.

115. PRO CO 137/27, ff. 184–187, [1754], The Humble Petition of the Inhabitants of the town of St Iago de la Vega, and of the Planters and other Proprietors and Occupiers of lands and settlements, in the Neighborhood of the same.

116. PRO CO 137/27, f. 197v, 7 May 1754, Knowles to Lords Commissioners of Trade and Plantations.

117. Knowles's own version, BL Add. Ms 32855, 21 May 1755, Knowles to Duke of Newcastle and, expressed at greater length, George Metcalf, *Royal Government and Political Conflict in Jamaica, 1729–1783* (London: Longmans for Royal Commonwealth Society, 1965).

118. Notes on these hearings are in BL Add. Ms 33,029, ff. 182–192, Minutes of Evidence re. Removal of Seat of Government from Spanish Town to Kingston, May 8, 1755 – June 5, 1755.

119. I consulted a copy of the Board's letter in the papers of William Hall, one of the Assemblymen for Westmoreland parish. UCSD Ms 220, Barrett/Hall Papers, Box 3, folder 50, 3 July 1755, Board of Trade to Privy Council Committee.

120. When looked at from the Privy Council table, the actions were different. In exercising the royal veto on an Act of Parliament the monarch acted as a

constituent member of the Westminster Parliament; while in recommending that colonial acts be disallowed, the Privy Council was reining-in assemblies who owed all their legislative powers to charters and rights granted by the Crown. Charles M. Andrews, 'The Royal Disallowance', *Proceedings, American Antiquarian Society* 24 (1914): 343–44.

121. The seventy wagons claim, JA 1B/5/75/3, 'A Copy of a Memorial presented to Sir John Peter Grant on the 18th or 19th November, 1869, against the removal, from Spanish Town, of the Seat of Government, Superior Courts of Law and Equity, and the Records . . .'.

122. Bridges, *Annals of Jamaica* 2, 87.

Chapter 4

1. This chapter's assessment of the late eighteenth-century town and its buildings builds on Edward Long's *History of Jamaica* 3 vols. (London: T. Edwards, 1774). T.A.L. Concannon, 'Our Architectural Heritage: Houses of the 18th and 19th Century with Special Reference to Spanish Town', *Jamaica Journal* 4 (1970): 23–28, is also perceptive. On the constitutional and administrative contexts, useful studies include Jack P. Greene, 'The Jamaica Privilege Controversy, 1764–66: An Episode in the Process of Constitutional Definition in the Early Modern British Empire', *Negotiated Authorities: Essays in Colonial Political and Constitutional History* (Charlottesville Va: University of Virginia Press, 1994), 350–393; Neville Hall, 'Public Office and Private Gain: A Note on Administration in Late Eighteenth Jamaica', *Caribbean Studies* 13:3 (1972): 5–20, and Frederick G. Spurdle, *Early West Indian Government: Showing the Progress of Government in Barbados, Jamaica and the Leeward Islands 1660–1783* (Palmerston North, New Zealand: self-published, 1963). News from the Assembly punctuates the correspondence between a leading Jamaican politician and an absentee landholder, Betty Wood *et al.* eds. 'The Letters of Simon Taylor of Jamaica to Chaloner Arcedekne, 1765–1775', *Travel Trade and Power in the Atlantic, 1765–1884: Camden Miscellany XXXV* (Camden 5th ser 19, Cambridge: Cambridge University Press, 2002), 5–155. Developments in Kingston are set out in Trevor Burnard, ' "The Grand Mart of the Island": The Economic Function of Kingston, Jamaica in the Mid-Eighteenth Century', in Kathleen E.A. Monteith and Glen Richards, eds., *Jamaica in Slavery and Freedom: History, Heritage and Culture* (Kingston: UWI Press, 2002), 225–241.

2. T.A.L. Concannon, 'The Great Houses of Jamaica', in Morris Cargill, ed., *Ian Fleming introduces Jamaica* (London: André Deutsch, 1965), 117–26, also Gosner, *Caribbean Georgian*, 133–47.

3. UCSD Ms 220, Barnett/Hall Collection, Box 3, folder 50, 3 July 1755, Halifax *et al.* to Council.

4. Long, *History* 2, 116–17.

5. UCSD Ms. 220, Box 3, folder 56, nd. 'What of his knaves & fools of D_ did write Applied to ours will fitt them just as right'.

6. A public hospital stood near the market on the west side of the town, but it primarily served as a refuge for wayfarers. Long, *History* 2, 17.

7. See Michael Craton, 'The Real Sir Charles Price', *Jamaica Journal* 4:4 (1970): 10–4.

8. Long, *History* 2, 13, 3.

9. JA 7/15/1, 'Summary of and extracts from letters written by Curtis Brett to his son Curtis, 1775–1780', 17–9; Long, *History* 2, 40–1.

10. JA 2/2/4, St Catherine, Vestry Minutes, 1759–1768, f. 2, 16 January 1759.

11. Long, *History* 2, 13.

12. NLJ Map. 727.35edc, John Pitcairn, 'A Plan of St Jago de la Vega in the Island of Jamaica', (London, W. Hinton, 3 January 1786).

13. Long, *History* 2, 6–7.

14. NLJ Ms 105, Taylor, 'Multum in Parvo', 2. f. 508, for the King's House 'having four pieces of Ordinance Mounted before the gate thereof' in 1688; Cundall, *Governors . . . in the First Half of the Eighteenth Century*, 5, after the military officer who, as Governor, ordered the import of a battery of field artillery died, the unused guns stood 'before the Governor's door in the Spanish towne'.

15. JA 1B/5/15/1, Commissioners for Forts, Fortifications and Public Buildings, Minute Book, 1769–1771, f. 62, 3 December 1770.

16. JA 1B/5/15/1, f. 73. 4 April 1771, adding 'pulleys & weights to the Gate in ye Stable yard' included in extra carpenter's work on the King's House.

17. Long, *History* 2, 13.

18. JA 1B/5/15/1, ff. 64–65, 3 December 1770. The payments for the bricklayers, like the stone masons, were calculated in linear units, with each rod amounting to 5½ yards squared, that is 30¼ square yards.

19. Thomas Coke, *Extracts from the Journals of the Rev Dr Coke's Five Visits to America* (London: G. Paramore, 1793), 130.

20. JA 1B/5/15/1, f. 113, 27 February 1772.

21. Giles Worsley, *Classical Architecture in Britain: The Heroic Age* (New Haven, Con: Yale University Press, 1995), 226, 278–87.

22. Long, *History* 2, 9.

23. Theodore Foulks, *Eighteen Months in Jamaica with Recollections of the Late Rebellion* (London: Whittaker, Treacher and Arnott, 1833), 55.

24. Thomas R. Metcalf, 'Architecture in the British Empire', in *Historiography* eds., Robin W. Winks and Alaine Low, (Oxford History of the British Empire, 5, Oxford: Oxford University Press, 1999), 589–590.

25. Quotation, Foulks, *Eighteen Months*, 55. These domestic developments, Crowley, *Invention of Comfort*, 235–241; also Blain, 'Georgian Jamaica', 3; idem. 'The

Frantic Search for Shade', 3–4, and idem. 'Towards a Tropical Georgian Style', 3–4.

26. [Bernard Martin Senior], 'A retired military officer', *Jamaica, as it was, as it is and as it may be: Comprising Interesting Topics for Absent Proprietors, Merchants &c. and Valuable Hints to persons intending to emigrate to the Island* (London: T. Hurst, 1835), 21.

27. Thus, for example, Palladio's Villa Cornaro, illustrated in Joseph Rykwert, *The Palladian Ideal* (New York: Rizzoli, 1999), 90–1.

28. Long, *History* 2, 7.

29. For a discussion of comparable committees and their oversight of the South Carolina capitol in Charleston, Loundsbury, *From Statehouse to Courthouse*, 23–5.

30. Long, *History* 2, 10.

31. JA 1B/5/15/1, f. 28, 18 January, 1770; f. 29, 16 May 1770.

32. JA 1B/5/15/1, f. 61, 21 November 1771; ff. 75–76, 4 April 1774.

33. JA 1B/5/15/2, Minute Book, Commissioners for Forts, Fortifications and Public Buildings, 1773–1783, unfoliated, 24 February 1773.

34. Long, *History* 2, 11; Matthew Gregory Lewis, *Journal of a West India Proprietor Kept During a Residence in the Island of Jamaica* (London: John Murray, 1834), 161.

35. Long, *History* 2, 9–10.

36. Hall, 'Public Office and Private Gain', 5–20, also James A. Henretta, *"Salutary Neglect": Colonial Administration under the Duke of Newcastle* (Princeton, NJ: Princeton University Press, 1972), 37, 110, 236–46; and disentangling a particularly blatant case, J.H. Parry, 'American Independence: The View from the West Indies', *Proceedings of the Massachusetts Historical Society* 87 (1975): 25–9; payments from deputies in arrears, NLJ Ms. 1646, 'Jamaica Papers 1768 Council, St Iago', (ex-Phillipps Ms. 17100), no. 1, 9 April 1750, Mr Leech's Case as Vendue Master of the Island of Jamaica; the total remitted, Parry, 'The Patent Officers', 200–225.

37. Feurtado, *Forty-Five Years' Reminiscence*, 10.

38. Michael Scott, *Tom Cringle's Log* (1833, citation from Everyman edition, London: Dent, 1915, rpt. 1969), 513.

39. [William Morris], 'Twilight in Jamaica', *Douglas Library Notes* 14:2 (1965): 4.

40. Bigelow, *Jamaica in 1850*, 35.

41. NLJ Ms. 112, E.R. Wingfield Yates, Journal, 3 vols. 1, f. 148, 26 October 1841.

42. Trollop, *West Indies and the Spanish Main*, 121.

43. Edward Kamau Braithwaite, *The Development of Creole Society in Jamaica, 1770–1820* (Oxford: Oxford University Press, 1971), 43–44.

44. Greene, 'Jamaica Privilege Controversy', 250–294.

45. Long, *History* 2, 10.

46. Long, *History* 2, 10.

47. Mindie Lazarus-Black, 'John Grant's Jamaica: Notes Towards a Reassessment of Courts in the Slave Era', *Journal of Caribbean History* 27 (1993): 144–159.

48. Long, *History* 2, 10.
49. Long, *History* 2, 7.
50. Long, *History* 2, 8.
51. Braithwaite, *Development of Creole Society*, 40–2.
52. For example, HEH ST 14, Roger Hope Elletson, Letters to and from Jamaica, 1769–1776, 2 parts, 1. unfoliated, 10 June 1770, Richard Welch to Roger Hope Elletson.
53. NLJ Ms 1646, (ex-Phillipps. Ms 17100), no. 4, 14 November 1756, Sir Charles Price to John Sharpe, Agent for Jamaica.
54. HEH ST 14, 23 December 1769, unfoliated, Dr Duncan Macglashan to Elletson.
55. For work on these piazzas, JA 1B/5/15/1, f. 27, 10 January 1770; f. 54, 7 April 1770; f. 55, 14 July 1770; ff. 71, 72, 4 April 1771; 1B/5/15/2, November 2 1781. The orange trees, Long, *History* 2, 9.
56. Greene, 'Jamaica Privilege Controversy', 350–393. The quotation, HEH ST. 1425, unfoliated, July, 1769, Macglashan to Elletson.
57. HEH ST 14, unfoliated, 23 December 1769, Macglashan to Elletson.
58. Long, *History* 2, 17, 464; the name, Feurtado, *Forty-Five Years' Reminiscence*, 30.
59. BL Sloane Ms 3918, f. 226; BL King's Ms 205, f. 408v. Copy of Answers of William Henry Lyttleton, Esq., Governor of Jamaica to the Questions proposed by the Lords of Trade, 4 April 1764; the second explosion at Fort Augusta, Frank Cundall, *Historic Jamaica* (London: West India Committee for Institute of Jamaica: 1915), 145–46.
60. Long, *History* 2, 450–464.
61. Long, *History* 2, 457.
62. JA 2/2/28A, St Catherine, Register of Free Persons, 1789–1840, 19 June 1796, Robert Carey; twentieth-century uses include an order transferring several roads through Spanish Town from the schedule of main roads to the Parish Council's oversight, 25 November 1915 in NLJ Ms 62a, Jacob Andrade, 'Parochial Handbook', unfoliated.
63. BL Add. Ms 22676, 'Reasons offered', f. 8v.
64. Assessing the value of the land, JA 1B/5/15/1, ff. 152–153, 25 November 1772; the Assembly's allocation of £3000 in the Rum Bill for its purchase and for construction, 1B/5/15/2, unfoliated, 22 December 1775.
65. JA 1B/5/15/2, unfoliated, 29 August 1776.
66. *Journals of the Assembly*, 8, 24, 24 November 1784.
67. JA 1B/5/15/2, unfoliated, 24 February 1779.
68. JA 1B/5/15/1, f. 114, 27 February 1772.
69. JA 1B/5/15/1, f. 28, 18 January 1770.
70. JA 1B/5/15/1, ff. 115, 129–131, 27 February 1772.
71. BL Add. Ms 12405, f. 14.
72. Another gaol break, *The Daily Advertiser*, 2 August 1793; Edward Long makes a

parallel between the old gaol and the Black Hole of Calcutta, *History* 2, 14–5.

73. JA 2/2/4, f. 27, 2[9] September 1760, also, f. 34, 29 June 1761. Afterwards George Fletcher's 1714 charity for pensions for three poor widows of the parish became an annual charge of £90.16 on the parish's tax revenue. This transaction was retroactively legalised in 1847, 10 Victoria, c. 45, 'An Act to enable the Justices and Vestry of the Parish of Saint Catherine to raise, by an annual tax on the inhabitants thereof, a sum of money sufficient to pay the Annuities given under the Will of the late George Fletcher, deceased'.

74. John W. Fonseca, 'The Cathedral of St Jago de la Vega', in *Centenary of Granting of Royal Letters Patent to the Cathedral of St Jago de la Vega, 1843–1943* ([Spanish Town? 1943]), 13.

75. Paying to 'raise the Organ loft', JA 2/2/4, f. 28, 5 February 1761;'building a brick wall on each side of the Church to support the Organ', ibid. f. 35, 29 June 1761.

76. JA 2/2/4, f. 19v, 10 January 1760.

77. Roby, *Monuments*, 7. The bell was inscribed 'St Catherine's, 1818.' ibid. 6.

78. JA 2/2/4, f. 18v, 9 January 1761.

79. JA 1B/5/15/2, unfoliated, the balcony roof, 30 September 1773 and 11 August 1772; the gaol, 8 December 1774; the grass place by the King's House, 8 December 1774; those blinds, 23 February 1774.

80. Several contracts simply went to 'Perkins'. A William Perkins, carpenter, shared a contract for work on the King's House in 1770, JA 1B/5/15/1, f. 27, 18 January 1770.

81. JA 1B/5/15/1, f. 106, 23 July 1771.

82. JA 1B/5/15/2, unfoliated, 20 December 1780.

83. JA 1B/5/15/2, unfoliated, 29 August 1776.

84. JA 1B/5/15/2, unfoliated, 2 November 1781.

85. JA 1B/5/15/2, unfoliated, 2 November 1781.

86. Andrade, *Jews in Jamaica*, 41.

87. Long, *History* 2, 18, discussed in Aubrey N. Newman, 'The Sephardim of the Caribbean', in Barnett and Schwab, *Sephardi Heritage*, 2, *The Western Sephardim*, 456–457.

88. Feurtado, *Forty-Five Years' Reminiscence*, 38.

89. Philip Allsworth-Jones, D. Gray and S. Walters 'The Noveh Shalom synagogue' site in Spanish Town, Jamaica in Malm ed., *Towards an Archaeology of Buildings*, 77–88. Some of the interior fittings, including the five large brass chandeliers, were also similar to those at Bevis Marks and may have been made by the same copper smith. Andrade, *Jews of Jamaica*, 200. The surviving sections of the substantial purplish- red brick perimeter wall on Adelaide Street incorporate the pillars for a blocked entrance gate and provide an excellent example of the high quality of the brickwork in eighteenth-century Spanish Town. Hill, *Jamaican Stage*, 21.

90. JA 2/2/27, f. 1. [1757], no name, also Pitcairn's map. For the claim that Price introduced a breed of rat 'into the colony . . . with the object of keeping down the smaller vermin' and that 'it is commonly spoken of as the Charley Price-Rat', Gosse, *Naturalist's Sojourn*, 445.

91. On Gregory's Trust I have relied on the notes collected by Jacob Andrade, in NLJ Ms 62a. 'Parochial Handbook' unfoliated. On Gregory's monument, Roby, *Monuments*, 44–45; the text on the painted wooden board, Wright, ed., *Monumental Inscriptions*, 100; the 1792 law, *Laws*, 27–30, 'An Act for vesting a certain . . . dwelling house, . . . granted by the late Matthew Gregory, esquire, . . . to a trustee'.

92. JA 2/2/27, f. 26, 6 February 1761, John Thompson; f. 20, 5 April 1759, Joseph Rennalls.

93. JA 2/2/27, f. 27, 5 October 1761, Thomas Edwards.

94. Long, *History*, 2. 37. He also observed that 'Spanish Town covers a large extent of ground, many of the houses having great areas, and several lots being vacant or unbuilt'.

95. Long, *History* 2, 37–39.

96. Campbell, *The Maroons*, 58–61, 65–7, 74, 79–85.

97. Long, *History* 2, 218; Higman, *Montpelier*, 12–8.

98. Thus, for a representative from Westmorland, in western Jamaica, describing his repeated visits to Kingston during a single Assembly session in successive letters home written in Spanish Town: UCSD Ms 220, Barnett/Hall Collection, Box 1, folder 16, 1 May 1747, William Hall to Thomas Hall; folder 26, 21 May 1748, same to same; folder 27, 3 June 1749, same to same; folder 28, 21 June 1748, same to same.

99. 29 November 1766, Simon Taylor to Chaloner Arcedekne, 'The Letters', 33.

100. The business of these courts is surveyed in Jonathan Dalby, *Crime and Punishment in Jamaica, 1756–1856* (Kingston: Social History Project, 2000), 29–91.

101. Coke, *Extracts from the Journals*, 133.

Chapter 5

1. Michael Duffy, 'Contested Empires, 1756–1815', in Paul Langford, ed., *The Eighteenth Century, 1688–1815* (Oxford: Oxford University Press, 2002), 213–242, provides an overview of the wider imperial context. Maria, Lady Nugent, *Lady Nugent's Journal of Her Residence in Jamaica from 1801 to 1805*, ed., Philip Wright, (Kingston, 1966, n.e. Kingston: University of the West Indies Press, 2002), is a record by a Governor's perceptive wife of life at the King's House. On the wider developments in Jamaican society during this period see Edward Kamau Brathwaite, *The Development of Creole Society in Jamaica, 1770–1820* (Oxford:

Oxford University Press, 1971); M.J. Steel, 'A Philosophy of Fear: The World View
of the Jamaican Plantocracy in a Comparative Perspective', *Journal of Caribbean
History* 27 (1993): 1–20; Clare Taylor, 'Planter Attitudes to the American and
French Revolutions', *National Library of Wales Journal* 21 (1979): 113-130, and,
Barry W. Higman, *Slave Population and Economy in Jamaica, 1807–1834*
(Cambridge: Cambridge University Press, 1976). The missionary enterprise in
Jamaica, which was probably the most radical of the period's challenges to the
established order, is analysed in Mary Turner, *Slaves and Missionaries: The
Disintegration of Jamaica's Slave Society, 1787–1834* (Urbana, Ill., 1982, reprint.
Kingston: The University of the West Indies Press, 1998). For the changing
economic contexts of these developments, see several of the essays in Heather
Cateau and S.H.H. Carrington, eds., *Capitalism and Slavery Fifty Years Later –
Eric Eustice Williams, A Reassessment of the Man and his Work* (New York: Peter
Lang, 2000), along with J.R. Ward, *British West Indian Slavery, 1750–1834: The
Process of Amelioration* (Oxford: Oxford University Press, 1988). Gad Heuman,
Between Black and White: Race, Politics, and the Free Coloreds in Jamaica, 1792–1865
(Westport, Conn: Greenwood, 1981), offers reappraisals of several key arguments
heard before the Assembly, while James Spedding, 'Bill for the Suppression of the
Jamaica Constitution, 1839', (1839), reprinted in his *Reviews and Discussions:
Literary, Political and Historical, Not Relating to Bacon* (London: Kegan Paul,
1879), 87–120, presents a critical report on the Jamaican Assembly's successive
political evasions during the period this chapter covers.

2. A potential immigrant's first impressions, NLS Ms 17956, Journal of a visit to
Jamaica by [   ] of Loanhead near Ruthven, Banffshire, 1823-4, f. 15, 19
December 1823; ff. 17–17v. 27 December 1823.

3. On the British military campaigns in the West Indies during the 1790s, see Roger
Norman Buckley, *The British Army in the West Indies: Society and the Military in
the Revolutionary Age* (Gainesville, Fla: University Press of Florida, 1998), also
Michael Duffy, *Soldiers, Sugar and Seapower: The British Expeditions to the West
Indies and the War against Revolutionary France* (Oxford: Clarendon Press, 1987),
and David Patrick Geggus, *Slavery, War and Revolution: The British Occupation of
Saint Domingue 1793–1798* (Oxford: Clarendon Press, 1982).

4. Roger Norman Buckley, 'The Frontier in Jamaican Caricatures', *Yale University
Library Gazette* 58 (1984): 152–62, and idem. *British Army in the West Indies*,
180–182. H. Bullock, 'Major Abraham James, 67th Foot, Military Author and
Artist', *Journal of the Society for Army Historical Research* 39 (1961): 42–9, only
discusses James's military publications dating from his regiment's subsequent
service in India.

5. NLJ P/940 Ja, F[Abraham] J[ames], 'Segar smoking society in Jamaica.' This was
not simply caricature, another wartime watercolorist's sketch entitled 'Custom of
the West Indies' also shows a girl sitting on a porch with her feet propped up on

the front rail. NLJ P/699, Quizem, [Robert Hawkins], 'Book of watercolours,' [1810-1811], these sketches are mostly in the Eastern Caribbean. NLJ P/939 Ja. 'A Grand Jamaican Ball! or the Creolian hop a la mustee; as exhibited in Spanish Town. Graciously dedicated to the Honble Mrs. R . . . n, Custodi Morum, ect, ect', F.[Abraham] J[ames], (London, William Holland, 1803).

6.   Parry, 'American Independence: The View from the West Indies', 30–1 and, on an unsuccessful attempt to fill the gap, S. Basdeo and H. Robertson, 'The Nova Scotia-British West Indies Commercial Experiment in the Aftermath of the American Revolution, 1783–1802', *Dalhousie Review* 61:1 (1981): 53–69.

7.   *Annual Register* 25 (1782): 208–14; 14 April 1782, G.B. Rodney to Brigadier General Archibald Campbell, in George Brydges Rodney, Lord Rodney, *Letter-Books and Order-Book of George, Lord Rodney, Admiral of the White Squadron 1780–1782* 2 vols. (Publications of the Naval Historical Society, 12, 13, New York: New York Historical Society for Naval Historical Society, 1932), 1. *Letter-Books, July 6, 1780–February 4, 1781; December 10, 1781–September 21, 1782*, 357. On the battle itself, Charles Lee Lewis, *Admiral de Grasse and American Independence* (Annapolis, Md: United States Naval Institute, 1945), 230–50.

8.   Stephen Conway, ' "A Joy unknown for Years Past": The American War, Britishness and the Celebration of Rodney's Victory at the Saints', *History* 86 (2001): 180–199; 'The Watery Grave', Bodl. Firth c.12(23), (London: J. Pitts, [1819–1844]).

9.   These outlays can be followed in JA 1B/5/15/2, Minute Book, Commissioners for Forts, Fortifications and Public Buildings, 1773–1783 unfoliated. For ex-Governor John Dalling's criticisms of the Assembly's procedures for commissioning and assessing military projects, see CLM Shelbourne Papers, v. 87, 101–108v, 'Observations Respecting the Island of Jamaica'.

10. PRO C 110/141, Chancery Exhibits, Douglas *v.* Harrison, no. 33, John Jackson, Advocate General for Jamaica to Henry Jackson, 19 December 1781. I am grateful to Linda Sturtz for a copy of this letter.

11. NLJ Ms 16, Major General Archibald Campbell, 'Memoir Relative to the Island of Jamaica, 1782'.

12. *Journals of the Assembly of Jamaica*, 7, 461, 3 March 1782. The figures for the size of the Franco-Spanish invasion forces were daunting, see 27 February 1782, 'Intelligence receiv'd from the Prisoners taken in the Schooner Maria Louisa', Rodney, *Letter-Books . . . 1780–1782*, 1, 312–314, enclosure in 20 March 1782, Campbell to Rodney.

13. Padrón, *Spanish Jamaica*, 226.

14. O'Shaughnessy, *An Empire Divided*, 232–37.

15. 'Hood's Conquest over the Count de Grasse', in C.H. Firth, ed., *Naval Songs and Ballads* (Navy Records Society, 33, London: the Society, 1908), 263–64. 'Rodney's Glory', a further ballad that placed the battle, 'Not far from Old Port Royal', was

wrong geographically but quite right in linking it to Jamaica. Bodl. Firth c.12(24), (London: J. Pitts, [1819–1844]).

16. NLS Ms 10925, Airth Ms f. 3, 23 December 1782, James Henry to William Graham. I am grateful to Linda Sturtz for bringing this reference to my attention.

17. Joan Coutu, 'The Rodney Monument in Jamaica and an Empire Coming of Age', *Sculpture Journal* 2 (1998): 46–57.

18. James Hakewill, *A Picturesque Tour of the Island of Jamaica, from Drawings made in the Years 1820 and 1821* (London: Hurst & Robinson and E. Lloyd, 1825), (unpaginated), 'King's Square, St Jago de la Vega'; Brathwaite, *Creole Society in Jamaica*, 107–08.

19. Lesley Lewis, 'English commemorative sculpture in Jamaica', *Jamaican Historical Review* 9 (1972): 21, 20–3.

20. 31 George III c. 21, 'An act for appointing commissioners for purchasing a sufficient quantity of land, on the north side of the public parade in the town of St Jago de la Vaga, whereon to fix the statue of Lord Rodney, and to erect one or more offices for holding and better preserving the public records', 30 March 1790; on three Welsh-born brothers who came to Jamaica in the early 1780s as indentured craftsmen and had worked off their time before winning the contract, Clare Taylor, 'The Williams Brothers: Welsh Stone Masons in Jamaica', *Jamaican Historical Society Bulletin* 8:1 (1981): 10–12. By this time they had established families in Jamaica.

21. Coutu, 'Rodney Monument', 49, also, L.B. Oatts, *Emperor's Chambermaids: The story of the 14th/20th King's Hussars* (London: Ward Lock, 1973), 45–6.

22. George Pinckard, *Notes on the West Indies . . . with additional letters from Martinique, Jamaica and St Domingo* 2 vols (1806, 2nd expanded, ed. London: Baldwin, Craddock & Joy, 1816), 2. 376. This was in 1797.

23. The statue alone accounted for 3,000 Guineas or £3,150.

24. Richard B. Sheridan, 'The Jamaican Slave Insurrection Scare of 1776 and the American Revolution', *Journal of Negro History* 61 (1976): 290–308.

25. Wallace Brown, 'The American Loyalists in Jamaica', *Journal of Caribbean History* 26:2 (1992): 121–46.

26. Clement Gayle, *George Liele: Pioneer Missionary in Jamaica* (Kingston: Jamaica Baptist Union, [1982]); Robert Scott Davis, Jr. 'George Liele', in Kenneth Coleman and Charles Stephen Gurr, eds., *Dictionary of Georgia Biography* 2 vols. (Athens, Ga: University of Georgia Press, 1983), 2. 620–21, idem. 'The Other Side of the Coin: Georgia Baptists who fought for the King', *Viewpoints: Georgia Baptist History* 7 (1980): 47–57. The phrase is the subtitle to *The Covenant of the Anabaptist Church* ([Kingston], 1796).

27. 'Letters showing the Rise and Progress of the early Negro Churches of Georgia and the West Indies', *Journal of Negro History* 1 (1916): 84, 12 January 1793. Some of these letters by and about Liele, excerpted in the *Baptist Annual Register* and

then reprinted in the *Journal of Negro History* were initially collected for and quoted in Alexander Pringle, *Prayers for the revival of religion in all the Protestant churches* (Edinburgh: Schaw and Pillans, 1796), 101–116, these include a letter of 16 November 1792, from Stephen Cooke, an evangelical sympathizer in Kingston, which mentions Liele's plans for Spanish Town.

28. IRO Deeds, o.s. 408, ff. 205v–206, 13 April 1793, George Liele to Mary and Martha Clifford both of Kingston and, breaking the contact, Deeds, o.s. 417, ff. 135–135v, 1 May 1793, Bond, George and Hannah Liele to Mary and Martha Clifford.

29. James M. Phillippo, *Jamaica: Its Past and Present State* (London: John Snow, 1843), 358-59; John Clarke, *Memorials of the Baptist Missionaries in Jamaica* (London and Kingston: Yates & Alexander and McCartney and Wood, 1869), 15–8, also BMS Langton 6, idem. 'History of Jamaica', f. 77. He was presumably the George Gibbs who was one of the trustees for the newly established Kingston 'Anabaptist' chapel in 1790, IRO Deeds, o.s. 384, 1790, ff. 161v–162, James Whitfield Smith to George Liele *et al.*

30. In 1829 John Clarke's first missionary station incorporated areas in St Thomas where Gibbs had ministered. Clarke made a point of emphasizing the solid grounding in the tenets of their faith received by those of Gibbs's converts he knew. As not only their pastor but as a British-trained minister and a Baptist minister's son, Clarke's assessment should not be dismissed lightly. BMS Langton 6, Clarke, 'History of Jamaica', f. 78.

31. For example, Coke, *Extracts from the Journals*, 102, 184, 191, 192–93.

32. On the establishment and resilience of this older set of values, see, Paul Langford, *Englishness Identified: Manners and Character, 1650–1850* (Oxford: Oxford University Press, 2000). The growing importance of religion in the concoction, particularly after the irreligious French Revolution, is brought out in Linda Colley, *Britons: Forging the Nation, 1707–1837* (New Haven, Conn: Yale University Press, 1992), 43–48, 367–369, also 353–360.

33. NLS Ms 3942, Robertson-Macdonald papers, ff. 216–18, Rev John Lindsay to Rev Dr William Robertson, May 3, 1776. Lindsay, 'An Examination of the Hypothetical Doctrine of Water-Spouts in Opposition to the ingenious Speculation of Dr B. Franklin of Philadelphia', *Gentleman's Magazine* 51 (1781): 559–60, (with diagram), 615–16, and idem. 'Continuation of Dr Lindsay's Ingenious and original Hypothesis on Waterspouts', *Gentleman's Magazine* 53 (1783): 1025–28. *Journal of the Assembly of Jamaica* 6, 313, 11 December 1770 and idem. 317, 13 December 1770; Bristol Museum and Art Gallery, John Lindsay, 'Eligancies of Jamaica', 4 vols. (1758–1771). (I have not seen these last volumes which are described in Ingram, *Manuscript Sources for the History of the West Indies*, 345–6); BL Add. Ms 12439, John Lindsay, 'A Few Conjectural considerations upon the creation of the Humane Race, occasioned by the present British Quixottical rage of setting the slaves from Africa at liberty, by a

inhabitant'. Some of this material is summarized in Minter, *Episcopacy Without Episcopate*, 177–79.

34. RHL, USPG, C/WIN/GUI f. 2, 17 July 1775, Rev Thomas Warren to the Secretary of the Society for the Propagation of the Gospel. Warren was urging the Society to appoint a successor as an Anglican missionary to the Mosquito Coast, today part of Nicaragua, but at that juncture a British outpost. The passage is from a letter written from the King's House in Spanish Town after he had accepted an appointment as Rector of St Elisabeth parish in Jamaica.

35. NLJ Ms 1900, Titford Letterbook, Letter 15, 2 July 1803, 'Dear Richard'; *Lady Nugent's Journal*, 17, 23 August 1801. For the arrival of the Governor's party, 'just in time not to keep the Service waiting', ibid. 44, 6 December 1801.

36. James Kelly, *Jamaica in 1831: Being a Narrative of Seventeen Years' Residence in that Island* (Belfast: James Wilson, 1838), 38. Describing the state of affairs in 1814.

37. NLJ Ms 1900, Titford Letterbook, Letter 10, March 1803, to William Gadesby; Fonseca, 'The Cathedral', 13.

38. BL Add. Ms 12439, Lindsay, 'A Few Conjectural considerations', f. 193.

39. E. Woolley, *The Land of the Free, or, A Brief View of Emancipation in the West Indies* (Cincinnati, Oh: Caleb Clark, 1847), 10.

40. Mary Turner, 'Religious beliefs', in Franklin W. Knight, ed., *The Slave Societies of the Caribbean* (General History of the Caribbean, 3. Basingstoke: Macmillan for UNESCO, 1997), 287–321.

41. Herbert S. Klein, 'The English Slave Trade in Jamaica, 1782–1808', *Economic History Review* 2nd ser 31 (1978): 25–45; for the phrase, Long, *History* 2, 410.

42. Long, *History* 2, 451–52, 463; also, Jerome S. Handler and Kenneth M. Bilby, 'On the Early Use and Origin of the Term "Obeah" in Barbados and the Anglophone Caribbean', *Slavery & Abolition* 22:2 (2001): 87–100; 1 George III, c. 22, 'An act to remedy the evils arising from irregular assembles of slaves, and to prevent their possessing arms and ammunition, and going from place to place without tickets; and for preventing the practice of obeah . . .', 18 December 1760. While this particular act was later repealed, laws against obeah remained current well into the twentieth century, Anthony Harriott, 'Captured Shadows, Tongue-Tied Witnesses, "Compellants" and the Courts: *Obya* and Social Control', in Monteith and Richards, *Jamaica in Slavery and Freedom*, 115-43.

43. NLS Ms 17956, 1823–4, Journal of a visit to Jamaica, f. 26, 18 January 1824.

44. Phillippo, *Jamaica*, 283, also discussed in Elizabeth Pigou, 'A Note on Afro-Jamaican Beliefs and Rituals', *Jamaica Journal* 20:2 (1987): 26; the 'watchmen', H.T. de la Beche, *Notes on the Present Condition of the Negroes in Jamaica* (London: T. Cadell, 1825), 30, footnote. His examples drawn from Halse Hall in Clarendon.

45. BMS WI/5, James Coultart Correspondence. See Yacine Daddi Addoun and Paul Lovejoy, 'The Arabic Manuscript of Muhammad Kaba Saghanughu of Jamaica,

c. 1823', Second Conference on Caribbean Culture, UWI, Mona, January 2002. It has still to be determined whether this text of Kaba's is in his own hand or is a recopied version. I am grateful to Paul Lovejoy for discussing these points with me.

46. Coke, *Extracts from the Journals*, 137–9.
47. Richard Lovett, *The History of the London Missionary Society, 1795–1895* 2 vols (London: Henry Frowde, 1899), I. 103.
48. 'Letters showing the Rise and Progress of the early Negro Churches', 71–2.
49. Olwyn M. Blouet, 'Bryan Edwards and the Haitian Revolution', in David P. Geggus, ed., *The Impact of the Haitian Revolution in the Atlantic World* (Columbia, SC: University of South Carolina Press, 2001), 46, quoting Thomas Barritt to Nathaniel Phillips, 8 December 1791 also in Taylor, 'Planter Attitudes', 124.
50. Most of these fears are expressed in NLJ Ms 624, [20 May], 1798, Simon Taylor to William Taylor, copy inclosed in 6 July 1798, William Taylor to Dundas.
51. Blouet, 'Bryan Edwards', 49–51.
52. Jacques de Cauna-Ladevie, 'La Diaspora des colons de Saint-Domingue et le monde créole: le cas de la Jamaïque', *Revue Française d'Histoire d'Outre-Mer* 81 (1994): 333–59, also Philip Wright and Gabriel Debien, 'Les colons de Saint-Domingue passés à la Jamaïque (1792–1835)', *Bulletin de la société d'histoire de la Guadeloupe* 26 (1975), and Patrick Bryan, 'Émigés, Conflict and Reconciliation: French Émigrés in Nineteenth Century Jamaica', *Jamaica Journal* 7:3 (1973): 13–19.
53. Gabriel Debien and Piere Pluchon, 'Un plan d'invasion de la Jamaïque en 1799 et la politique anglo-américaine de Toussaint-Louverture', *Revue de la Société d'histoire de geographie et de géologie* 36 (Notes d'Historie Coloniale, no. 186, Port-au-Prince, 1978): 3–72 and, on the same scheme, Zvi Loker, 'An Eighteenth-century plan to invade Jamaica – Isaac Yeshurun Sasportas – French patriot or Jewish radical idealist', *Transactions of the Jewish Historical Society of England* 28 (1984): 132–44. For earlier fears of French 'emissaries' among the Maroons, NLJ Ms 1681, 24 September 1796, Captain Robert Rollo Gillespie to Earl Balcarres, and on the execution of other alleged agents, Bryan, 'Émigés', 14.
54. PRO ADM 98/284, ff. 66–66v, 4 August 1793, [Admiralty] to Edward Gibbons; ibid. f. 108, 8 May 1800, same to Edward Gibbons; ibid. ff. 115v–116, 17 January 1801, same to Vice Admiral Lord Hugh Seymour. On the arguments for keeping these prisoners and particularly the crewmen off privateering vessels, languishing in these hulks, Richard Pares, 'Prisoners of War in the West Indies in the Eighteenth Century', *Journal of the Barbados Museum and Historical Society* 5 (1937): 12–7.
55. HEH STG Box 44, Grenville Correspondence, personal and political. George Grenville, 1st Marquis of Buckingham, Letters to him, N-Sp, No. 8, 21 December 1803, Sir George Nugent to Marquis of Buckingham.

56. The 'swarms' metaphor, NLJ Ms 1900, Titford Letterbook, Letter No 19, 19 December 1803, 'Dear Father'.
57. NLJ Ms 1900, Titford Letterbook, Letter 15, 2 July 1803, 'Dear Richard'.
58. *Lady Nugent's Journal*, 187, 13 December 1803.
59. IRO Deeds, o.s. 450, f. 172, 8 September 1794, deposition, King against George Liele. His text was Paul's *Epistle to the Romans*, 10:1–3, 'Brethren, my heart's desire and prayer to God for Israel is, that they might be saved. For I bear them record that they have a zeal for God, but not according to knowledge. For they being ignorant of God's righteousness, and going about to establish their own righteousness, have not submitted themselves unto the righteousness of God.' (*King James Version*).
60. Governor Balcarres appears to have tried to deal with all the perceived security risks at once, so in 1796 during the second Maroon war French prisoners of war on parole were sent to Fort Augusta. NLJ Ms 1682, 12 December 1799, Admiral Parker to Earl Balcarres.
61. For a copy, MMS Box 663, Various Papers, 'Government Publications and General Papers: West Indies', file, 'Jamaica Missionaries: licensing for preaching, etc 1804 (*recte* 1800)–12', *Supplement to the Royal Gazette* 15 February to 22 February 1812, 12, 'A Bill entitled 'An Act for the prevention and punishment of seditious practices, and attempts to excite insurrection and rebellion, in this island; and for other purposes'. Clause 13; item 2, 43 George III, c. 30, 'An Act to prevent preaching by Persons not duly qualified by Law' 18 December 1802. The Jamaican Assembly appears to have based its act on a law recently passed in St Vincent.
62. Andrew Fuller to William Carey, [1804?], quoted in Gordon A. Catherall, 'British Baptist Involvement in Jamaica 1783–1865', Keele University, PhD (1970), 18.
63. Turner, *Slaves and Missionaries*, 15–8, 21–5, 108, 122–6.
64. Although, demonstrating the ambivalent statutory basis for religious toleration in England, see Hugh Trevor-Roper, 'Religious Toleration in England after 1688', in idem, *From Counter-Reformation to Glorious Revolution* (London: Secker and Warburg, 1992), 267–285. The island Assemblies would not pass the regular Acts of Indemnity which allowed the English system to work. The planters might persuade themselves of the legality of their practices, but they still ran against established English custom.
65. MMS West Indies, General, Box 111, File 1805–1806, no. 2, 8 February 1805, William Fish to General Secretary.
66. NLJ P/98/IIJa, F.[Abraham] J[ames] 'Martial law in Jamaica', (London: William Holland, nd.).
67. HEH STG Box 44 (3) f. iv, 25 May 1802, Sir George Nugent to Marquis of Buckingham.
68. Maroons killed the Regiment's Colonel and 14 troopers in an ambush in the early stages of the campaign. Oatts, *Emperor's Chambermaids*, 55.

69. NLJ Ms 72, Nugent Correspondence, Box 3, 1805–6, Earl Camden to General Nugent, 9 February 1805. Here hushed-up scandals over the embezzlement of government funds by some of the Admiralty's local agents would not help. HEH STG Box 152 (3), 15 January 1807, J[ohn] Halkett, to Henry Petty-Fitzmaurice, 3rd. Marquis of Lansdowne.

70. Governor Nugent's verdict on calculations offered by a leading Assemblyman, 20 August 1802, Nugent to Colonial Secretary, cited in *Lady Nugent's Journal*, 131, footnote.

71. On the importance of the peacetime garrison, David Patrick Geggus, 'The Enigma of Jamaica in the 1790s: New Light on the Causes of Slave Rebellions', *William & Mary Quarterly* 3rd. ser 44 (1987): 274–99.

72. IRO Deeds o.s. 327, 32v–37, 25 August 1780, Sir Ludovick Grant, Bart., *et al.*, trustees of Sir Alexander Grant, Bart., deceased, to George III. The property is distinguished as 'Sir George B. Rodney's Park' in a 1772 manuscript map in the German Papers: CLM 7-F-4, George Gauld, 'A General Plan of the Harbours of Port Royal and Kingston, Jamaica . . .'. The Admiral's Pen purchase, *Lady Nugent's Journal*, 30, footnote 1. Both properties may well have been bought at Admiral Rodney's insistence, but after the purchase of Admiral's Pen there was no urgent need to buy Up Park Pen to house future Admirals commanding in Jamaica.

73. *Journals of the Assembly* 8, 57, 14 December 1784.

74. JA 1B/5/75/1, Colonial Secretary's Office Correspondence, General, 1867–1869, unfoliated, 'Up Park Camp', 3 February 1869, Thomas Harrison, Government Surveyor, to Lieutenant-Colonel J.R. Main, Superintendent of Public Works. It is difficult to prove a negative: but, besides examining the *Journals* and *Votes* of the Assembly, Harrison was also able to consult Barrack Masters' and Island Engineers' 'reports and accounts' that were subsequently destroyed in the 1907 Earthquake. He could 'not find that the Colonial Government ever found one shilling towards the erection of any of the works at the Camp'.

75. 32 George III, c. 25, 1792, 'An act for appointing commissioners for purchasing a sufficient quantity of land for enlarging the barrack in the town of St Jago de la Vega'. The remaining members of this unit were subsequently transferred to the British service in the 20th Hussars. The phrase, Pinckard, *Notes on the West Indies*, 2. 376.

76. Hill, *Jamaican Stage*, 21; PRO HO 50/366, f. 59, 13 January 1791, Secretary Board of Ordinance to Evan Nepean; WO 55/1620/6, Jamaica Rents, December, 1826, unfoliated, 10 January 1831, Office of Ordinance, 'Spanish Town'.

77. London, Royal Botanic Gardens, Kew, Library and Archives, Forsyth Correspondence, Foreign Letters, ff. 60-63v at f. 61v. 15 January 1793, Thomas Beath to William Forsyth.

78. Édouard de Montuelé, *A Voyage to North America, the West Indies and the Mediterranean*, (New Voyages and Travels, 3rd ser 9:2, London, Sir Richard

Phillips, 1821), 35, 15 March 1817; NLS Ms 17956, Journal of a visit to Jamaica, f. 15v. 22 December 1823; the 'moschettoes,' ibid. f. 15v. 19 December 1823, and ff. 16–16v, 24 December 1824.

79. These developments can be followed in Governor Nugent's correspondence with the Marquis of Buckingham. HEH STG. Box 44 (3), Grenville Correspondence; also, David Buisseret, 'The Stonyhill Barracks', *Jamaica Journal* 7:1–2 (1973): 22–4.

80. NLJ Ms 284, Lieut-Col A. Light, *Sketch for Improving the Condition of our Troops in the West Indies* (1816, author's annotated proof of an unpublished volume), 22.

81. NLJ Ms 617, 1796, 'Plan for the Defense of the West India islands by natives from the East Indies', iv.

82. Philip Curtin, *Death by Migration: Europe's Encounter with the Tropical World in the Nineteenth Century* (Cambridge: Cambridge University Press, 1989), 43–4, 47–50.

83. HEH STG Box 44, N-Sp. no. 8, f. 1. 21 December 1803, Nugent to Buckingham.

84. The Jamaican planters' earlier foot-dragging on recruiting slaves for British expeditions in 1741 and 1762 is described in Daniel E. Walker, 'Colony versus Crown: Raising Black Troops for the British Siege of Havana, 1762', *Journal of Caribbean History* 33 (1999): 74–83.

85. JA 2/2/28A, Register of Free Persons, no. 5, Robert Carey, 19 June 1796.

86. Buckley, *British Army in the West Indies*, 117–24.

87. Buckley, *British Army in the West Indies*, 193–4.

88. James E.W.S. Caulfeild, *One Hundred Years' History of the 2nd Battalion West India Regiment* (London: Foster Groom, 1899), 5–24.

89. In 1867 there were 'no troops in Spanish Town, the Guard having been withdrawn for service in British Honduras'. PRO CO 137/423, f. 279v, 23 March 1867, Sir John Peter Grant to Lord Carnarvon.

90. Renny, *History of Jamaica*, 101–5.

91. [John Stewart], *An Account of Jamaica and its Inhabitants, by a Gentleman, long Resident in the West Indies* (London: Longman, 1808), 12–13.

92. Pinckard, *Notes on the West Indies*, 2. 374–6.

93. Lewis, *Journal of a West India Proprietor*, 160. On Lewis's best-seller, see Howard Anderson, 'Introduction', Matthew Lewis, *The Monk*, ed., Howard Anderson, (Oxford: Oxford University Press, 1973), vii–xix, also André Parreaux, *The Publication of The Monk: A Literary Event 1796–1798* (Paris: Didier, 1960).

94. 'The Rio Cobre Bridge', *Columbian Magazine* 2 (May, 1797): 263–4.

95. Details on the Iron Bridge's shipping and components from *Royal Gazette* (29–31 January 1801), 10, cited *Jamaican Historical Society Bulletin* 4:9 (1967): 182; new commissioners were appointed to oversee its completion, 43 George III, c. 23, 'An act for rendering more effectual the several laws of the island, relating to the public road from the church, in the town of Saint Jago de la Vega, to the church

in Kingston,' 9 December 1802; also, discussing its construction, David Buisseret, 'The Iron Bridge of Spanish Town', *Jamaica Journal* 44 (1980): 106–8.

96. Neil Cossons and Barrie Trinder, *The Iron Bridge: Symbol of the Industrial Revolution* (Bradford-on-Avon: Moonraker Press, 1979), 35, 53–66.

97. A.B. 'Further observations on the projected Canal from St Thomas in the Vale', *Columbian Magazine* 2:4 (April, 1797): 749.

98. [Stewart], *An Account of Jamaica*, 13.

99. 'New Synagogue, Spanish Town', *Columbian Magazine* 1:3 (September, 1796): 256–7. Translation from Andrade, *Jews in Jamaica*, 38.

100. XY 'Proposal for an Inland Navigation on the South-side Jamaica; and on the fertilising the land for Irrigation', *Columbian Magazine* 2:2 (February, 1797): 570–77; 'Further observations on the projected Canal from St Thomas in the Vale', ibid. 2:4 (April, 1797): 747–751.

101. HF of Port Royal, 'To the Printer of this Magazine', *Columbian Magazine* 2:5 (May, 1797): 827.

102. Lewis, *Journal of a West India Proprietor*, 161. On the West Indian planters' general practice of importing splendid funeral monuments, Joan Coutu, 'Carving Histories: British Sculpture in the West Indies', *Church Monuments* 12 (1997): 77–85.

103. Roby, *Monuments*; also Lewis, 'English commemorative sculpture', 57–61. There were further private monuments imported from the same London sculptors, ibid. 41–67, *passim*.

104. Lewis, 'English commemorative sculpture', 24.

105. [Senior], *Jamaica, as it was, as it is, and as it may be*, 17.

106. For example, JA 2/2/4, St Catherine, Vestry Minutes, 1759–768, f. 26, 16 February 1760, to Richard Poore; 2/2/45, St Catherine, Accounts Current, 1810–1824, 22 May 1812, to Archibald Congreve.

107. Black, *Spanish Town*, 48–50; Lewis, 'English commemorative sculpture', 24.

108. NLJ Ms 122, Yates Journal, 1. f. 161, 24 November 1841.

109. Sketched in Gosner, *Caribbean Georgian*, 123.

110. For some examples, Phillippo, *Jamaica*, 399–400.

111. JA 5/6/1, Methodist District Meeting Minutes, (Jamaica Synod), 5/6/1/1, District Minutes, 1817–27, unfoliated, 8 January 1823.

112. MMS West Indies, General, Box 112, File 1814, no. 25, 22 April 1814, J. Wiggins to General Secretary.

113. NLJ Ms 703, 26 June 1819, Rev Thomas Godden to Rev C. Kitchen.

114. JA 5/6/1/1, unfoliated, 8 January 1823.

115. BMS Minute Book A, 1819–1823, f. 8, 7 October 1819, citing a letter from Spanish Town dated 26 July 1819. The figures are in Jamaican pounds, not sterling.

116. Edward Bean Underhill, *Life of James Mursell Phillippo: Missionary in Jamaica* (London: Yates & Alexander, 1881), 37, gives the date and time, 'the evening of 17th July 1820'.

117. For various versions see, Godden to Ryland, 7 August 1820, *Missionary Herald* (23 November, 1820), 88; Underhill, *Life of Phillippo*, 37; Clarke, *Memorials of the Baptist Missionaries* 81–2; contemporary jokes about the fire that circulated in Spanish Town are in NLJ Ms 60, 'Jack-Jingle', f. 283.

118. BMS James Phillippo, autobiography, 'Rough Sketch or an Outline only to be completely revised', ff. 78–9. Stressing the chapel's dilapidation allowed Phillippo to borrow £200 sterling towards repairing the premises. BMS Committee Minute Book, B, 1823–1827, ff. 80–81, 1 July 1824.

119. Phillippo, *Jamaica*, 337, 334.

120. JA 5/6/13/6, Spanish Town [Methodist] Circuit Accounts, 1829-49, 9 December 1829, 'Carpenter's Bill for repairing damage done by lightening'.

121. Franklin A. Roberts, *The Origin and Development of Methodism in Spanish Town and its Environs, 1791–1841* (William Fish Lecture, Kingston: Methodist Book Centre, 1977).

122. JA 5/6/1/1, unfoliated, 6 February 1821.

123. Peter Samuel, *The Wesleyan-Methodist Missions, in Jamaica and Honduras, Delineated* (London: Partridge & Oakey, 1850), 120.

124. Samuel, *Wesleyan-Methodist Missions*, 121.

125. JA 5/6/10, Extracts and Copies of Letters from the Wesleyan Missionary Committee, London, unfoliated, Extracts from the Minutes of a Meeting of the Committee, 7 September 1831. On the extravagant chapel in Kingston, Turner, *Slaves and Missionaries*, 28–9.

126. BMS Phillippo, 'Rough Sketch', ff. 86, 93.

127. MMS West Indies, General, Box 111, File, 1803–1804, no. 17, William Fish to General Secretary, 9 March 1804.

128. BMS Phillippo, 'Rough Sketch', f. 83.

129. Joseph Sturge and Thomas Harvey, *The West Indies in 1837: Being the Journal of a Visit to Antigua, Montserrat, Dominica, St Lucia, Barbados and Jamaica, Undertaken for the Purpose of Ascertaining the Actual Conditions of the Negro Population of those Islands* (London: Hamilton, Adams & Co., 1838), 182

130. Underhill, *Life of Phillippo*, 42, 45, 50.

131. Phillippo, *Jamaica*, 193–8. For a useful survey of the scholarly literature on education in both Jamaica and Barbados prior to emancipation, Olwyn Blouet, 'Thirst for Knowledge: Education in Barbados, 1823–1838', *Journal of the Barbados Museum and Historical Society* 47 (2001): 185–93.

132. BMS Phillippo, 'Rough Sketch', f. 94.

133. BMS Phillippo, 'Rough Sketch', f. 95.

134. Sheila Duncker, 'The Free Coloured and their Fight for Civil Rights in Jamaica, 1800–1830', MA thesis, London University, (1960), 64.

135. BMS Phillippo, 'Rough Sketch', f. 124b.

136. Duncker, 'The Free Coloured', 150.

137. 30 April 1832, Last Will of the late Francis Smith, Esq., made 20 August 1830, original, IRO Wills o.s. 112, f. 160. I have used a transcript in JA 7/32/568. The English office of 'Custos' of a county – or, in Jamaica, of a parish – still remains a prominent feature in Jamaican public life. It was a Crown appointment. The original post of *custos rotulorum* was a medieval creation for the justice responsible for the records of the county court. The holder became the senior member and chairman of a county's justices of the peace. In Jamaica's first century as an English colony more legal cases were held in the main courts in Spanish Town, but the custodes were important local figures, all the more so as during martial law they often doubled as General of the parish's militia. Discussing the status of the post in early seventeenth-century England, just prior to the office's transatlantic transfer, Thomas G. Barnes, *The Clerk of the Peace in Caroline Somerset* (Department of English Local History, Occasional Papers, 14, Leicester: Leicester University Press, 1961), 14–9.

138. Sturge and Harvey, *West Indies in 1837*, 187. 9 February 1837.

139. BMS Phillippo, 'Rough Sketch', f. 94a.

140. BMS Phillippo, 'Rough Sketch', f. 94, also Black, *Spanish Town*, 65.

141. BMS Phillippo, 'Rough Sketch', f. 95. I have found no contemporaries describing Spanish Town Baptist Chapel as a copy of any particular British chapel, but its various components do echo the chapels erected in England over the previous generation. Cf. *An Inventory of Nonconformist Chapels and Meeting-Houses in Central England* (London, HMSO, 1986). When Phillippo republished his early attendance figures in his *Jamaica* they appeared simple untruths to his Methodist colleagues, MMS Jamaica Correspondence, Box 48, file 1844, no. 56A, 23 July 1844, H.B. Britton to General Secretary, f. iv. 'The dimensions of his chapel in the *outside* are precisely what ours are on the *inside*. 1500 slaves would fill our chapel nearly to suffocation, & yet he has an *average* congregation in his of 2000 slaves!!'

142. BMS Phillippo, 'Rough Sketch', f. 95.

143. Further benefits from these metropolitan contacts were demonstrated when the Baptists purchased a house in the vicinity of their chapel. The absentee owner received payment in Scotland via a bill of exchange drawn on the Baptist Missionary Society in London. In this transaction the Jamaican congregation benefited by deducting from the purchase price the usual 12 per cent premium on obtaining a sterling bill of exchange. JA 1B/5/83/1, Attorney's Letter Book, J.G. V[idal] for Messers Michell, 21 November 1831–25 April 1838, f. 113 (foliation from the rear of volume), 27 May 1834, Vidal to Lady Clare.

144. Clipping in BMS Phillippo, 'Rough Sketch', f. 109b, letter to the editor from 'Quarantotti', 1827? Underhill, *Life of Phillippo*, 58, assigns it an 1827 date.

145. Brian Stanley, *A History of the Baptist Missionary Society 1792–1992* (Edinburgh: T&T Clark, 1992), 73. Witnesses describing a collection taken at the Methodist

chapel in Spanish Town, *Votes of Assembly, 1828*, 456–457; Duncker, 'Free Coloured', III; Underhill, *Life of Phillippo*, 58.

146. Duncker, 'Free Coloured', 116.

147. JA 2/2/27, f. 158, 19 July 1831, Robert Sayers Barrow.

148. For 'the Street leading aback of the Court house', JA 2/2/27, f. 164, 25 June 1832, John William Byles, Nathaniel Byles and Benjamin Lyon; ibid. f. 151, 17 December 1830, Adam Warren; ibid. f. 153, 8 January 1831, John Sadler; ibid. f. 163, 21 May 1832, William Morgan; ibid. f. 166, 5 September 1832, Anthony Austin.

149. Michael Brock, *The Great Reform Act* (London: Hutchinson, 1973), 80–1.

150. Canning Street was later submerged under the expansion of the District Prison in the 1890s.

151. Citing the street 'in front of the schoolhouse', JA 2/2/27, f. IV. [1757?]; ibid. 3V. 17 August 1757; ibid. 21, 13 February 1760, Joseph Curtis; ibid. 32, 16 May 1763, Henry Lord; ibid. Francis Wright; NLJ Ms. 321j. (3), Beldam Papers, 27 February 1839, J. Sturges to J. Beldam. The quotations are both from Speaker Richard Barrett's Election Address in 1839. To be fair, as editor and proprietor of the relatively liberal *Jamaica Journal and Kingston Chronicle* and as Custos of the parish of St James, Barrett had earlier proved the missionaries' 'most important single ally', Turner, *Slaves and Missionaries*, 19–20, 23, 164.

152. The phrase, Foulks, *Eighteen Months in Jamaica*, 103.

153. Turner, *Slaves and Missionaries*, 166–8, 179–89.

154. Duncker, 'Free Coloured', 239; Newman, 'Sephardim in the Caribbean', 458.

155. JA 1B/5/81/2, Island Letter Book, 8 May 1827–26 December 1831, on the lookout, f. 181, 11 May 1830 to Captain Tapp; for 'the Hoards of Negroes Which have again Assembled in Healthshire Hills . . .', ibid. f. 100, 10 May 1830, Governor to Major General Manshally(?). The belief had circulated more widely. During James Hakewill's visit to Jamaica in 1820 and 1821 he also heard that 'the Healthshire Hills, in the parish of St Catherine, are the favorite haunts of the runaways on that side of the island, . . .' Hakewill, *Picturesque Tour of the Island of Jamaica*, 6.

156. Clarke, *Memorials of Baptist Missionaries in Jamaica*, 135–6, also Rev H.C. Taylor to Phillippo, [11 August 1832], quoted in Phillippo, *Jamaica*, 167.

157. The policy, Higman, *Slave Population . . . in Jamaica*, 230; the militiamen's depredations, Benjamin M'Mahan, *Jamaica Plantership* (London: E. Wilson, 1839), 89–107.

158. MMS West Indies, Box 132, no. 139, 26 May 1832, Charles Wilcox to General Secretary; Turner, *Slaves and Missionaries*, 166–7.

159. Clarke, *Memorials of Baptist Missionaries in Jamaica*, 135–6.

160. Foulks, *Eighteen Months in Jamaica*, 57, 62–3.

161. 4 William IV, c. 41, 'An act for the abolition of slavery in the island, in consideration of compensation, and in promoting the industry of the manumitted slaves . . .' 12 December 1833.

162. Underhill, *Life of Phillippo*, 158; one Assemblyman at least, freed his slaves on the earlier date, Wilmot, 'The Politics of Protest in Free Jamaica', 67.

163. 1 August 1834, *Hymns adopted for the Celebration of the Negro's Jubilee* (Finsbury: J. Haddon, 1834), verso, Hymn V. I consulted the copy in MMS Box 662, Various Papers, Anti-Slavery Papers, no. 21.

164. Phillippo, *Jamaica*, 175–9.

165. Phillippo, *Jamaica*, 175.

Chapter 6

1. MMS Jamaica, Correspondence, Box 47, File, 1838, no. 66, 28 July 1838, J. Randerson to Secretary, f. 2v.

2. Four wide-ranging studies each offer perceptive introductions to this period. Philip Curtin, *Two Jamaicas: The Role of Ideas in a Tropical Colony, 1830–1865* (Cambridge, Mass: Harvard University Press, 1955); Douglas Hall, *Free Jamaica 1838–1865: An Economic History* (New Haven, Conn: Yale University Press, 1959); Thomas C. Holt, *The Problem of Freedom: Race, Labor, and Politics in Jamaica and Britain, 1832–1938* (Baltimore and Kingston: Johns Hopkins University Press and Ian Randle Publishers, 1992), and Catherine Hall, *Civilising Subjects: Metropole and Colony in the English Imagination, 1830–1867* (Cambridge: Polity, 2002). Three academic round tables discuss the last of these: *Journal of British Studies* 42:4 (2003): 505–38, *Small Axe* 14 (2003): 127–178 and *Victorian Studies* 45:4 (2003): 699–728. Otherwise Demetrius L. Eudell's comparative study, *The Political Languages of Emancipation in the British Caribbean and the US South* (Chapel Hill, NC: University of North Carolina Press, 2002), and Gad Herman's *Between Black and White* suggest why some issues proved particularly contentious within the colony's political debates. Anton V. Long, *Jamaica and the New Order 1827–1847* (Special Series, 1, Kingston: Institute of Social and Economic Research, UCWI, 1956), incorporates a great deal of useful information on administrative topics. A bibliographical essay by Carl Campbell, 'Early Post-Emancipation Jamaica: The Historiography of Plantation Culture 1834–1865', in Montieth and Richards, *Jamaica in Slavery and Freedom*, 52–69, surveys a generation's scholarly controversies.

   What remains clear is the extent to which economic factors shaped contemporary responses to the island's newly opened political and social opportunities. The vicissitudes of the Jamaican economy are delineated in Gisela Eisner, *Jamaica, 1830–1930: A Study in Economic Growth* (Manchester: Manchester University Press, 1961). The first two chapters of Philippe Chalmin, *The making of a sugar giant: Tate and Lyle 1859–1989* (Paris, 1983, Eng. trans, London: Harwood, 1990), offer a brisk summary of the changing markets for sugar in nineteenth-century Europe. The shifting economic orthodoxies that then redefined Jamaica's place in British trade are surveyed in P.J. Cain and A.G. Hopkins, *British Imperialism: Innovation and Expansion, 1688–1914* (Harlow: Longman, 1993), while in '"An Empire of the Mind": Emancipation, Race and Ideology in the British West Indies and the American South', in J. Morgan Kousser and James M. McPherson, eds., *Region, Race, and Reconstruction: Essays in Honor of C. Vann Woodward* (New York: Oxford University Press, 1982), 283–313, Thomas C. Holt explored the economic components in the different understandings of 'freedom' that abolitionists, ex-slaves and ex-slaveholders each held.

In examining the social and political crisis in 1865 that marked the end of 'Free Jamaica', Gad Heuman, *'The Killing Time': The Morant Bay Rebellion in Jamaica* (Basingstoke: Macmillan Caribbean, 1994), offers a clear survey. Rhoda Cobham, 'Fictions of Gender, Fictions of Race: Retelling Morant Bay in Jamaican Literature', *Small Axe* 8 (2000): 1–30, demonstrates the passions these events continue to generate. There are numerous other studies. Readers new to the field will find that Sidney Haldane Olivier, Lord Olivier, *The Myth of Governor Eyre* (London: Hogarth Press, 1933), still provides a forcefully written introduction to both the immediate crisis in Jamaica and the wider issues behind it.

3. T.H. Milner, *The Present and Future State of Jamaica Considered* (London: H. Hooper, 1839), 21–2.

4. Woodville K. Marshall, ' "We be wise in many tings": Blacks' Hopes and Expectations of Emancipation', in FR Augier, ed., *The University of the West Indies: 40th Anniversary Lectures* (Kingston: University of the West Indies, 1990), 31–46.

5. Milner, *Present and Future State of Jamaica*, 28.

6. See Swithin R. Wilmot, 'Black Space/Room to Manoeuver: Land and Politics in Trelawny in the Immediate Post-Emancipation Period', in Claus Stolberg and Swithin R. Wilmot, eds., *Plantation Economy, Land Reform and the Peasantry in a Historical Perspective: Jamaica 1838–1980* (Kingston: Friedrich Ebert Stiftung, 1992), 15–24.

7. [Morris], 'Twilight in Jamaica', 4. This was in 1849.

8. Swithin R. Wilmot, 'Politics at the "Grassroots" in Free Jamaica: St James, 1838–1865', in Shepherd, *Working Slavery, Pricing Freedom*, 449–66, also, dealing with St Mary and Vere parishes, idem. 'Politics and Labour Conflicts in Jamaica: 1838–1865', in Kari Levitt and Michael Witter, eds., *The Critical Tradition of Caribbean Political Economy: The Legacy of George Beckford* (Kingston: Ian Randle Publishers, 1996), 101–17; idem. ' "The Old Order Changeth": Vestry Politics in two of Jamaica's Parishes, Portland and Metcalfe, 1838–65', in Brian L. Moore and Swithin R. Wilmot, eds, *Before and After 1865: Education, Politics and Regionalism in the Caribbean* (Kingston: Ian Randle Publishers, 1998), 101–11, 384–87; idem. 'From Bondage to Political Office: Blacks and Vestry Politics in Two Jamaican

Parishes, Kingston and St David, 1831–1865', in Monteith and Richards, *Jamaica in Slavery and Freedom*, 307–323, idem. 'The Politics of Protest in Free Jamaica: the Kingston John Canoe Riots, 1840 and 1841', *Caribbean Quarterly* 36:3/4 (1990): 65–75, and idem. '"A Stake in the Soil": Land and Creole Politics in Free Jamaica, the 1849 Elections', in Alvin O. Thompson, ed., *In the Shadow of the Plantation: Caribbean History and Legacy* (Kingston: Ian Randle Publishers, 2002), 314–33.

9.   Swithin R. Wilmot, 'The Growth of Black Political Activity in Post-Emancipation Jamaica', in Rupert Lewis and Patrick Bryan, eds., *Garvey: His Work and Impact* (Trenton, NJ: Africa World Press, 1991), 39–46, also idem. *Freedom in Jamaica: Challenges and Opportunities, 1838–1865* (Kingston: Jamaica Information Service, 1997), 16–7. As a candidate in 1844 Vickars had campaigned with the slogan 'Vote for Vickars the Black Man.' Heuman, *Between Black and White*, 121.

10. On the Assembly's building grants see, Phillippo, *Jamaica*, 105; MMS 16 April 1840, Jamaica, Correspondence, Box 48, 1840–42, File 1840, number 27, J. Randerson to General Secretary, for grants voted to Methodist chapels in Kingston and St Thomas in the Vale, and Carl Campbell, 'Social and economic obstacles to the development of popular education in post-emancipation Jamaica, 1834–68', *Journal of Caribbean History* 1 (1970): 67–73, where votes of money for new church buildings competed with applications for educational funds. Voting money to complete the Trinity Chapel, *Votes of the Assembly, part 1, 1844*, 423, 20 February 1844. The Novéh Shalom synagogue's success in 1844, ibid. 143–4, 392–3, 7 November and 13 December 1844; Andrade, *Jews of Jamaica*, 42. The Catholic Chapel's grant, *Votes, 1844*, 497, 21 December 1844.

11. Bigelow, *Jamaica in 1850*, 30.

12. Hall, *Civilising Subjects*, 115–17.

13. In 1838, 218 members of the Spanish Town congregation transferred to the new Sligoville chapel. Underhill, *Life of Phillippo*, 176.

14. Phillippo, *Jamaica*, 197.

15. BMS West Indies Missionary Letters, 1840–1846, f. 27, 20 January 1842, J.M. Phillippo to Secretary. Since then the instituion has become the Calibar College which, after another move, remains a leading secondary school in Kingston, while its theological teaching tradition is integrated into the United Theological College at Mona.

16. *Speech of the Rev J.M. Phillippo delivered at the Baptist Chapel, Spanish Town . . . 1839* (Kingston: np. 1839). (I used the copy from Phillippo's papers, NLJ, Pamph. 264.061 Ja. Ser no. 5). Also, two visitors' descriptions: Joseph John Gurney, *A Winter in the West Indies: Described in Familiar Letters to Henry Clay, of Kentucky* (London: John Murray, 1840), 112–13, and John Candler, *West Indies Extracts from the Journals of John Candler whilst traveling in Jamaica* (London: Harvey and Darton, 1840), 30. The final phrase is from an English antislavery ballad, 'The Slave', Bodl. Firth.b.25(279), (Pocklington: J. Firth, nd).

368 — Notes to pages 171–172

17. Phillippo, *Jamaica*, 254–56.
18. Appraising the successes of Metcalfe's rule, Douglas Hall, 'Sir Charles Metcalfe', *Caribbean Quarterly* 3:2 (1953): 90-100. The rapprochement with the planters undertaken by Lord Metcalf was recommended by the British Colonial Office, Long, *Jamaica and the New Order*, 45. On the procession at his departure, Feurtado, *Forty-Five Years' Reminiscence*, 3. Edward Thompson, *The Life of Charles, Lord Metcalfe* (London: Faber, 1937), 354, reports that people 'knelt as their Governor went through their streets for the last time', but as he was known to be afflicted with cancer this was also a demonstration of respect for a dying man.
19. Long, *History* 2, 42.
20. On the development of Port Henderson I have relied on the material in NLJ Ms 62a, Andrade, 'Parochial Handbook', unfoliated, and Buisseret, *Historic Jamaica From the Air*, (1996 ed), 91. In 1803 the then Governor's new-born son was brought down to Port Henderson to be bathed there. *Lady Nugent's Journal*, 140–2, 174, January, and 30 August 1803.
21. General Nugent and his household landed at Port Henderson, *Lady Nugent's Journal*, 10, 29 July 1801. For exports, JA 1A/5/2/29, Port Henderson Journal, May 1803 – January 1805. Each shipment lists the originating estate, most were in St Catherine but the lists also included Worthy Park in St Thomas in the Vale.
22. The steamer, Feurtado, *Forty-Five Years' Reminiscence*, 31.
23. NLS Ms 9253, Dunlop Correspondence, f. 105, 10 February 1792, John Blackburn Jr to Robert Dunmore, extolling a farm near Spanish Town as 'perhaps the most valuable rent on the Southside of Jamaica'.
24. Sturge and Harvey, *West Indies in 1837*, 179.
25. Theodore Sealy and Herbert Hart, *Jamaica's Banana Industry: A History of the Banana Industry with particular reference to the part played by the Jamaica Banana Producers' Association Ltd*, ed. Clinton V. Black, (Kingston: Jamaica Banana Producers Association, 1984), 7. On the *martinick* name, Clinton V. Black, *The History of Jamaica* (London, 1958, 2nd ed Harlow and Kingston: Longman Caribbean, 1983), 141.
26. XY 'Proposal for an Inland Navigation', 574.
27. A botanist briskly dismissed the brush-choked area near the town as 'far from being interesting', while in assessing Spanish Town's strategic setting another pamphleteer saw the thickets of 'cashaw (a prickly and tough hard-wood scrub)' that filled the plains surrounding the town as a potential obstacle to any attackers. NLJ Ms 1983, James McFayden, 'Sketch of a short botanical excursion in Jamaica', recording a trip on 22 December 1829; the military appraisal, 'An Anglo-Indian', *A Letter to the Colonial Secretary on the Precarious Tenure of the Island of Jamaica and the other West-Indian Possessions* (London: Effingham Wilson, 1839), 14.

28. The phrase, Gosse, *A Naturalist's Sojourn in Jamaica*, 91.
29. Kathleen Montieth, 'Planting and Processing Techniques on Jamaican Coffee Plantations during Slavery', in Shepherd, ed., *Working Slavery, Pricing Freedom*, 112–29.
30. Barry Higman, ed., *The Jamaican Censuses of 1844 and 1861* (Kingston: Social History Project, 1980), 1; the difficulties of one small and unprofitable coffee walk in the Red Hills, owned by a Spanish Town physician, can be followed in the letter book compiled by Dr Titford's son, NLJ Ms. 1900, Titford Letterbook, 1802–07.
31. NLJ Ms 1900, Titford Letterbook, letter 14, 19 June 1803, 'Dear Mother'; Pinckard, *Notes on the West Indies*, 2. 377; J.E. Alexander, *Transatlantic Sketches, Comprising Visits to the Most Interesting Scenes in North and South America and the West Indies* (Philadelphia, Penn: Key and Biddle, 1833), 171.
32. Samuel, *Wesleyan-Methodist Missions*,113.
33. 30 George III c.12, 'An act to encourage the importation of horses from Great Britain, by granting a purse to be run for in each country; . . .: 19 December 1789; the amount and dates the race was run, JA T1018, General Ledger, 1828–1832, ff.122–23, 'King's purse', paid 31 December 1828, won Spanish Town, 25 November 1828; meeting acquaintances there, NLS Ms 10924, Airth Ms, f.164, 30 December 1820, David Finlay to Thomas Graham. I am grateful to Linda Sturtz for this reference.
34. NLJ Ms 31, W.G. Freeman. 'Pickwick Jamaica', (nd, set pre-1838; written on paper watermarked 1862; acquired in 1891), 40–41.
35. Higman, *Slave Population . . . in Jamaica*, 58, table 7.
36. 4 William IV, c. 38, 'An Act to constitute certain persons into a corporation or body politic for better supplying the town of St Jago de la Vega with water', 20 December 1834; in the early 1950s a property described as 'the Old Engine House Premises' remained at the end of Waterloo Lane, suggesting how close to the town the water company's pumping station was. Kingston, Titles Office, Liber 405, f. 46, 12 June 1953.
37. On the Sligo Water Company's service, NLJ Ms 62a. Andrade 'Parochial Handbook', unfoliated, 'Spanish Town Water Works'.
38. Gurney, *A Winter in the West Indies*, 112; Kathleen Mary Butler, *The Economics of Emancipation: Jamaica and Barbados, 1823–1843* (Chapel Hill, NC: University of North Carolina Press, 1995).
39. MMS Jamaica Correspondence, Box 47, File, 1837, no. 52, 14 November 1837, J. Edmondson to General Secretary.
40. UCSD Ms 171, Hill Collection, Hugh H. Cline, Diary, 1872–1876, ff. 53–54, August, 1873.
41. The phrase, Turner, *Slaves and Missionaries*, 26.
42. NLS Ms 9266, f. 22, Alexander Graham Dunlop, fragment of a journal of a visit

to Jamaica, (1842). The nights en route were spent at Spanish Town, Moneague and Rio Bueno.

43. Alexander, *Transatlantic Sketches*, 171.
44. Phillippo, *Jamaica*, 284.
45. Feurtado, *Forty-Five Years' Reminiscence*, 24, see also, Clark, *Memorials of the Baptist Missionaries*, 223.
46. Osborne, *History of the Catholic Church in Jamaica*, 114–16; AKA Reply by Reverend J.M. Bartolio, SJ to an Address Presented by the Congregation of St Joseph's Church, Spanish Town, 8 May 1870.
47. Duncker, 'Free Coloured', 116.
48. The estimated cost was £2,869 12/-. Several petitions describe the project's uneven progress. RHL USPG C/WIN/JAM2, f. 469, May, 1843, Memorial of Certain Inhabitants of the Parish of St Catherine, Committee . . . to Superintend the erection of Trinity Chapel to Society for Propagation of the Gospel; ibid. f. 500, 21 November 1842, James Gayland to Bishop of Jamaica; ibid. f. 502, 22 November 1842, Building Committee's Report to Bishop.
49. Feurtado, *Forty-Five Years' Reminiscence*, 23.
50. *The First Annual Report of the Jamaica Native Baptist Missionary Society* (Kingston? nd. 1841? 'second to be published in 1842'), 1.
51. BMS WI/1, 24 March 1845, William Young, Edwin Palmer to 'Reverend Sir' [Joseph Angus?]; Underhill, *Life of Phillippo*, 226–36; Robert J. Stewart, *Religion and Society in Post-Emancipation Jamaica* (Knoxville, Tenn: University of Tennessee Press, 1992), 83–94.
52. The Letters Patent of 28 November 1843, are reprinted in a celebratory pamphlet, *Centenary of Granting of Royal Letters Patent to the Cathedral of St Jago de la Vega, 1843–1943* ([Spanish Town, the Cathedral, 1943]), 7–9. Roby, *Monuments*, in both his title and text consistently describes it as 'the Cathedral'.
53. Lewis, *Journal of a West India Proprietor*, 161.
54. Roby, *Monuments*, 7. Roby made his notes on a visit on 25 August 1824.
55. 'Quarantotti', *St Jago Gazette*, (1827?) clipping in BMS Phillippo, 'Rough Sketch', 109b.
56. NLJ Ms 112, Yates, Journal, 1. 12 December 1841.
57. For surveys of these trends, Nikolaus Pevesner, 'Scrape and Anti-scrape', in Jane Fawcett, ed., *The Future of the Past: Attitudes to Conservation, 1174–1974* (London: Thames & Hudson, 1976), 35–53, and Stefan Muthesius, *The High Victorian Movement in Architecture, 1850–1870* (London: Routledge, 1972), 1–10.
58. Long, *History* 2, 5, also Roby, *Monuments*, 8.
59. Analysing a 1822 Anglican vestry resolution on seating, Duncker, 'The Free Coloured', 117–19. At the Methodist chapel anybody could purchase a 'good pew'.
60. Recalling pew rents around 1900, JA 7/12/262, Daisy E. Jeffrey-Smith, 'Jamaican memories', f. 2.

61. MMS Jamaica Correspondence, Box 48, File 1844, no. 56A, 23 July 1844, H.B. Britton to General Secretary.

62. JA 1B/11/8/3/18, St Catherine, Burials, 1848–55, (unfoliated, at back of volume), I.N. Garland, 'Memorandum respecting the taking down of the old Chancel of the Cathedral Church of St Iago de la Vega, Jamaica, and the rebuilding the same', 15 November 1848. Calvert's post as Cathedral organist, Feurtado, *Forty-Five Years' Reminiscence*, 21. On the five per cent commission, Howard Colvin, 'Architect and Client in Georgian England', (1991), in idem. *Essays in English architectural history*, 270–72.

63. The letters in *The Builder* of 11 August and 11 November, 1849, are summarized in Lewis, 'English commemorative sculpture in Jamaica', 27–8. The £4,570 figure is from O.C. Plant, 'The Architecture of the Cathedral', *Centenary . . . Granting Royal Letters Patent*, 20.

64. The preliminary demolitions not only removed the whole of the eighteenth-century brick structure and a number of family tombs just to the east of the original chancel, it also called for the excavation of substantial foundations. JA 1B/11/8/3/18, Garland, 'Memorandum'.

65. For the Effingham and Keith monuments' original locations on either side of the altar, Roby, *Monuments*, 9, 11–12, 15. The Effingham monument's interim position beside a pillar is noted in J.A. 1B/11/8/3/18, Garland, 'Memorandum'.

66. Wright, *Monumental Inscriptions of Jamaica*, 118–121.

67. Cf. *Victorian Church Art* (London: HMSO, 1971), 170–4.

68. JA 1B/11/8/3/18, Garland, 'Memorandum'.

69. The 'restored' phrase was used, with no apparent irony, in Cundall, *Historic Jamaica*, 91.

70. Roby, *Monuments*, 7.

71. Plant, 'Architecture of the Cathedral', 20.

72. Fonseca, 'Cathedral of St Jago de la Vega', 13.

73. MMS Jamaica, Correspondence, Box 49, File 1855–56, no. 11, 23 October 1855, W. Tyson to General Secretary, f. 2r.

74. Hill, *Jamaican Stage*, 257–61; Phillippo, *Jamaica*, 141.

75. *Letter on the Necessity of Establishing a College of Physicians and Surgeons in Jamaica, Addressed to the Editor of the Kingston Chronicle and Originally Published in that Paper, with Additional Notes and Observations* ([Kingston: Kingston Chronicle], 1830); *Act of the Legislature of 3rd. William IV c.7 Establishing a College of Physicians and Surgeons in Jamaica* ([Spanish Town]: Aitken, 1835). This included the would-be College's by-laws, regulations for its Library and a list of Fellows.

76. Horace O. Russell, *The Missionary Outreach of the West Indian Church: Jamaican Baptist Missions to West Africa in the Nineteenth Century* (New York: Peter Lang, 2000), 95.

77. Phillippo, *Jamaica*, 477–85, 212–13.

78. R.F.K. Summers, *A History of the South African Museum, 1825–1975* (Cape Town: A.A. Balkema for the Trustees, 1975), 33. I am grateful to Charles Strauss for hunting for this model in Cape Town. It is no longer in the Museum and no drawings or photographs can be found.

79. Quotation from the report in the *Illustrated London News* describing the opening of the Jamaica Railway. I am grateful to Simone Gigliotti for this reference.

80. Hall, *Free Jamaica*, 138–40.

81. Hall, *Free Jamaica*, 145–51.

82. On the engineer who constructed the lighthouse, Jan Bouws, 'Sir George Grove', in Stanley Sadie, ed., *The New Grove Dictionary of Music and Musicians* 20 vols (Basingstoke: Macmillan, 1980), 7. *Fuchs-Gyuzelu*, 752; the new boilers, Hall. *Free Jamaica*, 69–75. These purchases extended pre-emancipation trends when Jamaican planters had invested in the latest steam-driven equipment as it became available. Veront Satchell, 'Early Use of Steam Power in the Jamaican Sugar Industry, 1768–1810', *Transactions of the Newcomen Society* 67 (1996): 221–231, idem. 'Steam for Sugar-Cane Milling: The Diffusion of the Boulton and Watt Stationary Steam Engine to the Jamaican Sugar Industry, 1809–1830', in Monteith and Richards, *Jamaica in Slavery and Freedom*, 242–58.

83. See, generally, Michael Freeman, *Railways and the Victorian Imagination* (New Haven, Con: Yale University Press, 1999).

84. A. John Dickenson, 'Appendix A: The railway "Mania" Spreads to Jamaica: Projected Railways 1845–46', in idem. 'The Jamaica Railway, 1845 to 1915: An Economic History', MSc thesis, UWI, Mona, (1969), 136–63. In late 1845, just as the English boom reached its climax, the Jamaica Southern, Eastern and Northern Railway published advertisements in Jamaica listing its proposed routes and its principal shareholders, but this line never broke any ground. JA 4/97/1, Gunter Papers, Sir Geoffrey Gunter, 'Centenary History of the Jamaica Government Railway', (30 May 1945), 2, citing *Falmouth Post*, 21 October 1845.

85. 7 Victoria, c. 25, (1843), 'An Act for making and maintaining a Railway from Kingston to Spanish Town, with liberty to continue the same to the Angel's pen or plantation situate in the Parish of St Catherine, and for other purposes', and 8 Victoria, c. 12, (1844), 'An Act for the protection of the Public by amending an Act of Legislature passed in the Seventh Year of Queen Victoria, Chapter 25 . . .'; JA 4/97/1, Gunter, 'Centenary History of the Jamaica Government Railway', 1–5.

86. 9 Victoria, c. 30, (1845), 'An Act for amending the acts relating to the Jamaica Railway, and for raising additional capital for the purposes thereof.' JA 4/97/1, Gunter, 'Centenary History of the Jamaica Government Railway', 4.

87. London, London Metropolitan Archives, Ms F/LEG/897, Diary of Lt Col Edward H. Legg, Coldstream Guards, 1. 1859, ff. 134–135, 4 February 1859.

88. Feurtado, *Forty-Five Years' Reminiscence*, 31, 37–8, for the strolls and the omnibus;

in 1859 Anthony Trollope took 'a public vehicle' from the station, Trollope, *West Indies and the Spanish Main*, 119; Legg Diary, 1.f. 134. 5 February 1859, for both the Governor's carriage and the third class passengers.

89. MMS Jamaica Correspondence, Box 48, File 1846, no. 9, 19 January 1846, T.M. Tylder to General Secretary.

90. Legg Diary, 1. f. 137, 6 February 1859.

91. Dickenson, 'Jamaica Railway', 59. Figures for expenses between the railway's first 18 months and 1879 are not available, idem, 'Appendix D: The Jamaica Railway Financial Results, 1845–1914', 167.

92. A proposed extension of the railway was under debate in the Assembly session Anthony Trollope attended in 1859, *West Indies and the Spanish Main*, 121–4.

93. C.W. Guillebaud, 'The Crown Colonies, 1845–1870', in J. Holland Rose, A.P. Newton and E.A. Benians, eds., *The Growth of the New Empire, 1783–1870* (Cambridge History of the British Empire, 2, Cambridge: Cambridge University Press, 1940), 706.

94. PRO CO 137/275, f.153, Elgin to Stanley, 6 September 1843. I am grateful to Jenny Jemmott for this reference. Henry E. Vendryes, 'Great Fires of Kingston: the James the Founder Fire of 1843', *Jamaican Historical Society Bulletin* 6:15 (1976): 277–82.

95. Richard Hill, *Lights and Shadows of Jamaican History: Being Three Lectures* (Kingston: Ford and Gall, 1859), 65; Clarke, *Kingston, Jamaica*, 36–7.

96. Harry E. Vendryes, 'Great Fires of Kingston: the Fisher Fire of 1862', *Jamaican Historical Society Bulletin* 3:1 (1961): 26–8.

97. Rampini, *Letters from Jamaica*, 19.

98. Butler, *Economics of Emancipation*, 28, 30–3.

99. NLJ Ms. 112, Yates, Journal, 1.f. 164, 25 November 1841.

100. Charles Darling (a planter and the Governor's Secretary) to Sir Lionel Smith, 13 May 1839, cited in Swithin R. Wilmot, 'Emancipation in Action: Workers and Wage Conflict in Jamaica, 1838–1840', *Jamaica Journal* 19:3 (1986): 58.

101. Curtin, *Two Jamaicas*, 141–4, 127. On the development of comparable attitudes among absentee proprietors, B.W. Higman, '"To Begin the World Again": Responses to Emancipation at Friendship and Greenwich Estate, Jamaica', in Monteith and Richards, *Jamaica in Slavery and Freedom*, 291–306.

102. Swithin R. Wilmot, 'Baptist Missionaries and Jamaican Politics, 1838–54', in Keith Laurence ed., *A Selection of Papers Presented at the Twelfth Conference of the Association of Caribbean Historians (1980)* ([St Augustine, Trinidad]: Association of Caribbean Historians, 1986), 49–54, also idem. 'Politics and Labour Conflicts', 102–17. On the Governor's motives, Sydney Checkland, *The Elgins, 1766–1917: A Tale of Aristocrats, Proconsuls and Their Wives* (Aberdeen: Aberdeen University Press, 1988), 112.

103. Spedding, 'Bill for the Suppression of the Jamaica Constitution', 104–120; Long, *Jamaica and the New Order*, 44–5.
104. NLJ Ms 112, Yates, Journal, 1. f. 163, 25 November, 1841.
105. The phrase is from the tombstone of a member of Council who died in 1850, before the 'shut downs' and constitutional reorganizations of the 1850s. Duncan Robertson, 9 May 1850, St Elizabeth Parish Church, Black River, Wright, *Monumental Inscriptions*, 169. Highlighting 'the primacy of local autonomy' as a further key issue in these Assembly controversies, Eudell, *Political Languages of Emancipation*, 46.
106. Long, *Jamaica and the New Order*, 34–43.
107. Hall, *Free Jamaica*, 55, 57–8, also, Eudell, *Political Languages of Emancipation*, 56–61.
108. On one group of European immigrants who did not all die or leave immediately, Carl H. Senior, 'German Immigrants to Jamaica, 1834–8', *Journal of Caribbean History* 10 & 11 (1978): 25–53. For a contemporary's critique of the early scheme for European immigration, M'Mahan, *Jamaican Plantership*, 264–80. UWI St Augustine, West India Committee Papers, 16, Minutes, 4 January 1845–July 1851, f. 175, 26 January 1847, notes a letter and pamphlet from a Mr James Window on the employment of convicts submitted to the West India Committee. These recommendations went no further, being 'left on the table'.
109. On changes in the indenture process, Verene Shepherd, 'The Politics of Migration: Government Policy towards Indians in Jamaica, 1845–1945', in Moore and Wilmot, *Before and After 1865*, 177–189, 394–5; Monica Schuler, *'Alas, Alas, Kongo' A Social History of Indentured African Immigrants into Jamaica, 1841–1865* (Baltimore, Md: John Hopkins, 1980).
110. Heuman, *Between Black and White*, 157.
111. Swithin R. Wilmot, ed., *Adjustments to Emancipation in Jamaica* (Kingston: Social History Project, 1988), 10, 8, 28.
112. Philip D. Curtin, 'The British Sugar Duties and West Indian Prosperity', *Journal of Economic History* 14 (1954): 157–64.
113. Arguing that removing the sugar duties boosted slave exports, Pierre Verger, *Bahia and the West Coast Trade (1549–1851)* (Ibadan: Ibadan University Press, 1964), 36; while a witness before a House of Commons select committee claimed that the price of slaves in Havana rose by 15 per cent on the news of the 1846 Sugar Act, David Murray. *Odious Commerce: Britain, Spain and the abolition of the Cuban Slave Trade* (Cambridge: Cambridge University Press, 1980), 215. David Eltis suggests that imports of African slaves may have actually dropped at this juncture, but points out that contemporaries had expected the new British policy to lead to an increase. *Economic Growth and the Ending of the Transatlantic Slave Trade* (New York: Oxford University Press, 1987), 201.
114. On the parallel increase in sugar beet production in Europe as grain prices fell

due to increased imports from Russia, Chalmin, *Making of a Sugar Giant*, 6–8.

115. Murray, *Odious Commerce*, 210. The rational hope, Joseph John Gurney, *Reconciliation Respectfully Recommended to all parties in the Colony of Jamaica Addressed to the Planters* (London and Kingston: George Eightman and Cathcart and Sherlock, 1840), 8; and, a decade later, the fears shaping 'the unanimous opinion of all the people of all classes in the community that unless something is done and speedily done to prohibit slave produce from entering the British markets as it now does, this island will soon return altogether into its native wilderness'. BMS H14/2, Letters to Edward Underhill about Jamaica, 1852–1866, 21 April 1852, Annotto Bay, Samuel Jones to Revs Frederick Trestrail or Edward B. Underhill; for a pessimistic summary by a delegation from the Jamaica Assembly in London, [Edward Thompson, William Smith, William Girod], *Statement of Facts Relative to the Island of Jamaica* (London: Noseworthy and Lewis, 1852).

116. 'Cotton Cultivation More Profitable than Sugar', [1851], reprinted from *Cornwall Chronicle,* and Edward McGeachy, 'Real Sea Island Cotton Seed', *Jamaica Dispatch* (20 March 1851). Clippings in NLJ Ms 227, J.E. Pietersz, Scrapbook, 1826–1944, f. 28.

117. Carl H. Senior, 'Asiatic Cholera in Jamaica (1850–1855)', *Jamaica Journal* 26:2 (1997): 25–42, and Brian T. Higgins and Kenneth F. Kipple, 'Cholera in Mid-Nineteenth-Century Jamaica', *Jamaican Historical Review* 17 (1991): 31–47.

118. Underhill, *Life of Phillippo*, 255–6.

119. Feurtado, *Forty-Five Years' Reminiscence*, 30, 29.

120. Feurtado, *Forty-Five Years' Reminiscence*, 39.

121. MMS Jamaica Correspondence, Box 49, File 1850, no. 42, 12 December 1850, Robert A. Johnson to General Secretary. Underhill, *Life of Phillippo*, 257, gives different figures: 2,500 'in the parish of Spanish Town' (presumably the whole of St Catherine) and 10,000 'stated to have perished' in Kingston. These figures slice even further into Spanish Town's population, though suggest that Kingston suffered dire losses too.

122. For a contemporary summary, Bigelow, *Jamaica in 1850*, 46–52. Modern analyses include Swithin R. Wilmot, 'Race, Electoral Violence and Constitutional Reform in Jamaica, 1830–54', *Journal of Caribbean History* 17 (1982): 8–13, Heuman, *Between Black and White*, 141–4 and Mona C.M. Macmillan, *Sir Henry Barkly: Mediator and Moderator, 1815–1898* (Cape Town: AA Balkema, 1970), 61–93.

123. MMS Jamaica Correspondence, Box 49, File 1853, no. 33, 25 November 1853, William Tyson to General Secretary.

124. NLJ St.C. 140, 1846, 'Plan of 13 acres 3 roods and 37 perches of land . . . occupied as a terminus of the Jamaica Railway Company', surveyor, John M. Smith.

125. Feurtado, *Forty-Five Years' Reminiscence*, 29; JA T1000, Treasury, General Ledger, 1859–60, f. 228, Queen's Purses. The intervening volumes of these ledgers are missing.

126. NLJ St.C.143, 1867, 'Rough Plan of the St Catherine parish lands around Spanish Town showing the names of the persons in possession', surveyor, Thomas Harrison.

127. NLJ Ms 112, Yates, Journal, 1. f. 167, 30 November 1841.

128. On the bicameral government, C.V. Gocking, 'Early Constitutional History of Jamaica: with special reference to the period 1838–1866', *Caribbean Quarterly* 6 (1960): 121–33, also, Heuman, *Between Black and White*, 153–6, and H.L. daCosta, 'The Constitutional Experiment in the Twelve Years Before the Morant Bay Rebellion', *Jamaican Historical Society Bulletin* 4:6 (1966): 109–21; invoking the House of Lords, Trollope, *West Indies and Spanish Main*, 114. As late as 1865 a committee of the Legislative Council was considering the merits of 'a stricter adherence . . . to the rules and practice which govern the House of Lords' for procedure. JA 1B/5/5/11, Legislative Council Journals, 1864–1865, f. 86, 21 February 1865.

129. The efforts here of the then Speaker, Charles Hamilton Jackson, are summarized in NLJ Ms 62a, Andrade, 'Parochial Handbook', unfoliated.

130. Asa Briggs, *Victorian Cities* (1963, 2nd. rev. ed. Harmondsworth: Penguin, 1968); exemplifying this industrial-era aesthetic, Mark Girouard, *Victorian Pubs* (New Haven, Conn: Yale University Press, 1984), 33–60; for the Jamaican paint schemes, [Senior], *Jamaica as it was*, 21.

131. Bigelow, *Jamaica in 1850*, 31.

132. Trollope, *West Indies and Spanish Main*, 120.

133. Trollope, *West Indies and Spanish Main*, 20–23, 120.

134. Trollope, *West Indies and Spanish Main*, 119.

135. Anthony Trollope, 'Miss Sarah Jack of Spanish Town, Jamaica', (1860) *Tourists and Colonials* (Anthony Trollope: The Complete Short Stories, 3. London: William Pickering, 1991), 5. In Greek mythology the Lethe was the river that ran through Hades. Drinking its waters led souls to forget their pasts.

136. N. John Hall, *Trollope: A Biography* (Oxford, Clarendon, 1991), 172, also C.S. Morris, 'The Transference of the Control of the Post Office', in G.W. Collett *et al.* eds., *Jamaica: Its Postal History, Postage Stamps and Postmarks* (London: Stanley Gibbons, 1928), 39–42.

137. Trollope saw himself as reforming local mismanagement and saving the British Post Office '£1300 a year'. Anthony Trollope, *An Autobiography* ed., David Skilton, (Harmondsworth: Penguin, 1998), 85; the savings, Anthony Trollope to Mrs Francis Trollope, 27 January 1859, N. John Hall, ed., *The Letters of Anthony Trollope: I, 1835–1870* (Stanford, Cal: Stanford University Press, 1983), 81.

138. Trollope, *West Indies and Spanish Main*, 17.

139. Trollope, *West Indies and Spanish Main*, 124.

140. Collett, *et al. Jamaica: Its Postal History*, 15.

141. MMS Jamaica Correspondence, Box 199, File 1861, no. 23, 23 April 1861, William

Tyson to General Secretary, (from Brown's Town). The track of the northside road can be followed in 'Ford and Gall's New Map of Jamaica, 1858'. This is published in Hill's *Lights and Shadows*, The map adds the further proud boast to that route, 'never used for military purposes'.

142. JA 1B/5/81/2, Island Letter Book, 8 May 1827 – 26 December 1831, f. 50, 26 January 1828, to Superintendent, Accompong Maroons, St Elizabeth and ibid, 26 January 1828, to Superintendent, Charlestown Maroons.

143. Olivier, *Myth of Governor Eyre*, 62–3, quotation at 63; also, Ronald V. Sires. 'Governmental Crisis in Jamaica, 1860–1866', *Jamaican Historical Review* 2:2 (1953): 5–6.

144. JA Supreme Court, 1856–1865, Shelf AB, no 1. ff. 337–338v. The Queen against Clarence Linden Dias, Larceny of Cattle, 1 August 1864. Dias petitioned for a reprieve, claiming that former Governors had permitted other white malefactors to leave the island rather than serving what he and his family saw as a prospective death sentence. PRO CO 137/391, ff. 473–473v. petition of Clarence Linden Dias (nd received, 13 June 1865), also ibid. ff. 490–91, 14 June 1865, Hugh W Austin to C.H. Jackson, E. Jordon, S.W. Mais and others; 'The Convict Dias', *Colonial Standard* (22 June 1865): 2. I am grateful to Steve Porter for locating this and several other *Colonial Standard* references to this case.

145. Barkly to Newcastle, 26 May 1854, in Wilmot, ed., *Adjustments to Emancipation*, 18.

146. Mary E. Thomas, 'Jamaica and the US Civil War', *Americas* 24 (1972): 25–32.

147. PRO CO 137/390, ff. 64–71, 24 March 1865, George William Gordon to Edward Cardwell, MP Secretary of State for the Colonies. Though, as with many of Edward Eyre's schemes it was not *completely* unreasonable. The docking facilities *might* have helped to win the local base for transatlantic mail runs away from St Thomas in the then Danish Virgin Islands to Kingston, a possibility that Trollope and his reviewer in the *Times* had both recommended. The proposal remained an expensive gamble while there were far more immediate problems to face.

148. The Barbados scheme, George W. Roberts, *The Population of Jamaica* (Cambridge: Cambridge University Press, 1957), 102–103.

149. Robin W. Winks, *Canadian-West Indian Union: A Forty-Year Minuet* (Institute of Commonwealth Studies, Commonwealth Paper, II, London: Athlone, 1968), 13; Brimsley Samaroo, 'The Caribbean Consequences of the Indian Revolt of 1857', in Serge Mam Lam Fouch *et al.* eds., *Regards sur l'histoire de la Caraïbe, des Guyane aux Grandes Antilles: Les actes de la 32e Conférence de l'Association des Historiens de la Caraïbe. Cayenne, avril 2000* (Petit-Bourg, Guadeloupe: Ibis Rouge, 2001), 445.

150. Richmond, Virginia, Library of Virginia, Record Group 3, Governor's Papers – Executive Papers, Francis H. Pierpont, (Accession #37024), Box 2, Folder 4, 7 August 1865, John N. Camp, from United States Consulate, Kingston, Jamaica.

151. Further petitions for the colonial government 'to act and facilitate the passing of

such measures as would introduce Immigrants into the Colony from the
Southern States of America' were presented in 1867, but the proposal went no
further. JA 1B/5/9/1, Legislative Council Minutes. October 1866–January 1869,
unfoliated, 27 August 1867.

152. JA 1B/5/5/11, f. 2, 1 November 1864. Eyre's decision to have some of the new
furniture made in the prison workshops may have shown admirable frugality, but
ran directly counter to the intentions of a job-creation scheme. JA 1B/5/8/1,
Finance Letter Book 2, 21 May 1864 – 27 April 1865, f. 345, 31 December 1864, to
John Clarke, Clark of Works, General Penitentiary, also f. 356, 6 January 1865.
Eyre's self-justifying summary of the dealings that led to his ordering new
furniture without going to the Assembly put the blame on 'party politics . . .
running high'. He even succeeded in getting his unauthorized expenditure of
£351.8.4 refunded. PRO CO 137/406, ff. 216–217, 13 July 1866, Edward Eyre to Sir
Henry Storks. The controversies were remembered locally, with stories of a
munificent Assembly grant and subsequent disputes after Eyre imported a piano
from England, Feurtado, *Forty-Five Years' Reminiscence*, 7.

153. PRO CO 137/391, ff. 128–190, Baptist 'Underhill' Survey (manuscript returns).
The quotations are from Schedule B, 'Poverty and Distress', ff. 147–52 at f. 150,
J.M. Phillippo, Spanish Town, Sligoville. These figures were subsequently
published, Edward Bean Underhill, *A Letter Addressed to the Rt Honourable E.
Cardwell, with illustrative documents on the condition of Jamaica and an explanatory
statement* (London: Arthur Miall, nd. [1865]). Some of Phillippo's comments were
also reprinted in Underhill, *Life of Phillippo*, 328–29.

154. PRO CO 137/391, f. 189, Schedule H, 'Special as to large Towns'. Comparable
figures circulated in 1864, including an estimate of the town's adult population as
3,124, a suspiciously round total of 800 for servants and a breakdown of the crafts
total as 'nearly 150 carpenters, 60 masons, 91 shoemakers, 127 tailors'. These were
incorporated in the resolutions of a public meeting held in Spanish Town, 18 May
1864, published in Edward B. Underhill, *The Tragedy of Morant Bay* (London:
Alexander & Shepheard, 1895), 20.

155. PRO CO 137/391, ff. 94–122v. 6 May 1865, Eyre to Cardwell. On the
unavailability of agricultural employment locally, ibid. f. 162. Eyre's imperial
career and changing attitudes are sketched in Hall, *Civilising Subjects*, 23–65.

156. Heuman, '*The Killing Time*', 48; for criticisms from a fellow missionary, MMS
Jamaica Correspondence, Box 199, File 1865, no. 14, 23 March 1865, J. Corlett to
General Secretary; also, no. 25, 24 April 1865, same to same.

157. Heuman, '*The Killing Time*', 54.

158. Olivier, *Myth of Governor Eyre* 165; considering the implications of this failure to
offer Bogle and his group a hearing, Eudell, *Political Languages of Emancipation*,
150.

159. RH *The Insurrection in Jamaica* (London: Richard Barrett, 1866), 11.

160. Heuman, *'The Killing Time'*, 3–14. The recollection of an elderly resident of Stony Gut, whose father took part: 'is stick them cut and is stick them carry', is cited in Edna Manley, *The Diaries*, ed., Rachel Manley, (Kingston: Heinemann Caribbean, 1989), 68, 19 November 1964.

161. Clinton Hutton, 'The Defeat of the Morant Bay Rebellion', *Jamaican Historical Review* 19 (1996): 30–8, 65–6. For slash wounds, see PRO ADM 101/230, Log, Septimus Terry, Assistant Surgeon, HMS Wolverine, 1 June 1865 – 22 December 1865, 14 October 1865; describing martial law, PRO 30/48/42, Cardwell Papers, Jamaica, August to December, 1865, 20 October 1865, Louis Mackinnon to Mr Shedon, 'copy'.

162. JA 1B/5/18, Dispatches, Jamaica to England, 1871–1873, f. 3, 8 May 1871, Grant to Lord Kimberly. This forwarded a renewed petition for recompense from William Kelly Smith and Isaac Moses Vaz whose printing press was destroyed in 1865. They were unsuccessful as an Act of Indemnity passed by the Assembly in 1865 excluded their claim.

163. Olivier, *Myth of Governor Eyre*, 324–32; Swithin R. Wilmot, 'The Politics of Samuel Clarke: Black Creole Politician in Free Jamaica, 1851–1868', in Verene A. Shepherd and Glen L. Richards, eds., *Questioning Creole: Creolisation Discourses in Caribbean Culture* (Kingston: Ian Randle Publishers, 2002), 227–42.

164. *Votes of the Assembly* . . . *7 November, 1865 to 22 December, 1865* (St Jago de la Vega: George Henderson, 1866), 5–6, 7 November 1865.

165. Feurtado, *Forty-Five Years' Reminiscence*, 34–5.

166. MMS Jamaica Correspondence, Box 199, File 1865, no. 90, f. 3v. 9 December 1865, J. Corlett to General Secretary; William James Gardner, *A History of Jamaica* (London: Elliot Stock, 1873), 492.

167. MMS Jamaica Correspondence, Box 199, File 1865, no. 90, f. 4v. 9 December 1865, J. Corlett to General Secretary.

168. Noting the continued insistence on the 'rebellion' phrase a year later, John Douglas Sutherland Campbell, Marquis of Lorne (later 9th Duke of Argyle), *A Trip to the Tropics and Home through America* (London: Hurst & Blackett, 1867), 90.

169. PRO PRO 30/48/42, f. 17v. 23 October 1863, Eyre to Cardwell. This comment was made in a postscript to the first letter Eyre wrote to the Secretary of State for the Colonies after the riot.

170. PRO PRO 30/48/42, f. 20, 26 October 1863, Eyre to Cardewll.

171. MMS Jamaica Correspondence, Box 199, File 1865, no. 87, f. 3v. 24 November 1865, J. Corlett to General Secretary.

172. Gardner, *History of Jamaica*, 491; *Votes of the Assembly, November–December 1865*, 120, 5 December 1865.

173. PRO PRO 30/48/42, f. 32v. 7 November 1865, Eyre to Cardwell.

174. 29 Victoria, c. 11 'An Act to alter and amend the Political Constitution of this Island', and its subsequent revision, c. 24 'An Act to amend . . . act to alter . . . '.

175. Glory Robertson, 'Death of a Constitution', *Jamaican Historical Society Bulletin* 5:13 (1972): 175–81; *Votes of the Assembly, November – December, 1865,* 180, 19 December 1865.

176. Feurtado, *Forty-Five Years' Reminiscence*, 8.

177. Gardner, *History of Jamaica*, 492.

178. Acts of 29 Victoria, Session 1. The vetoed bills included one offering the Governor and his officers indemnity for their actions during the crisis, besides others allowing people arrested under martial law to remain under arrest once martial law was over, or continuing the military tribunals after martial law or, with echoes of medieval rebellions, confiscating the assets of people condemned for treason or felony during the rebellion.

179. James Cecil Phillippo, *Jamaica Its Government and its People* (Kingston: R. Jordon, 1883), 9.

180. *Votes of the Assembly, November-December 1865*, 7, 7 November 1865.

181. On the ways that public opinion in Britain changed over the generation after abolition and how the controversy over Governor Eyre provoked further shifts in British attitudes towards Jamaica and the West Indies, see Catherine Hall, Keith McClelland and Jane Rendall, *Defining the Victorian Nation: Class, Race, Gender and the Reform Act of 1867* (Cambridge: Cambridge University Press, 2000), 192–204.

182. Underhill, *Tragedy of Morant Bay*, 81.

183. JA 1B/5/19/1, Dispatches (Draft) Jamaica to England, 1866–1867, (in this instance, England-Jamaica), 18 June 1866, Cardwell to Storks.

184. Walter Scott Seton-Karr, *Grant of Rothiemurchus: A Memoir of the Service of Sir John Peter Grant, GC, MG, KCB* (London: John Murray, 1899), 42–74, 78–86.

185. Alfred Chichele Plowden, *Grain or Chaff? The Autobiography of a Police Magistrate* (London: Thomas Nelson, [1908]), 81. Plowden was Grant's Private Secretary.

Chapter 7

1. Feurtado, *Forty-Five Years' Reminiscence*, 7.

2. Judah, *Old Saint Jago*, 46–7.

3. The racist fears that shaped the successor units organized after the 1879 Volunteer Militia Law are discussed in Patrick Bryan, *The Jamaican People 1880–1902: Race, Class and Social Control* (Basingstoke: MacMillan, 1991), 78–80.

4. There is little written on the transition to Crown Colony Government. Roy Augier, 'Before and After 1865', *New World Quarterly* 2 (1966): 21–40, remains an academic classic and locates the wider transformations after the Morant Bay uprising in the development of post-Emancipation Jamaica. In a case study from rural St Ann, K.E. Ingram, *The QC and the Middleman* (Bishop Auckland:

Pentland Press, 1997), demonstrates the ambivalent local impact of the new regime and its administrative innovations. Otherwise, on the processes of instituting Crown Colony government in Jamaica, Vincent John Marsala, *Sir John Peter Grant, Governor of Jamaica, 1866–1874: An Administrative Study* (Cultural Heritage Series, 3, Kingston: Institute of Jamaica, 1972), provides a starting point. A pamphlet by an anonymous English visitor, 'A Fellow of the Royal Geographical Society', *Jamaica and its Governor During the Last Six Years* (London: Edward Stanford, 1871), offers another favorable appraisal.

5. The phrase, Underhill, *Tragedy of Morant Bay*, 38.

6. Plowden, *Grain or Chaff?* 84.

7. These phrases were all used by Governor John Peter Grant: his draft of a reply to an address from Spanish Town first simply described Kingston as 'the capital' then inserted 'present' before having second thoughts, striking his first addition through and replacing it with 'modern'. JA 1B/5/75/2, [1872], Grant's draft reply, ff. 1, 3v. The 'country town' phrase, idem. 'Memorandum', 12 June 1873, *Trelawny & Public Advertiser* (21 July, 1873): 2. I am grateful to Jenny Jemmot for showing me this article.

8. For the number of signatories, JA 2/2/30, f. 66, 17 October 1874, J.M. Phillippo to Parish Board, postscript. Entered under Board meeting of 30 October 1874.

9. Sir Sibbald David Scott, Bart., *To Jamaica and Back* (London: Chapman & Hall, 1876), 238–9.

10. JA 1B/5/75/3/3776, *Memorial of the Municipal Board of the Parish of St Catherine* (1874), 2v.

11. Samuel, *Wesleyan-Methodist Missions*, 113.

12. NLJ Ms. 91, Alexander, 'Poems, vol. 2', ff. 158–159, 21 January 1895, 'St Jago de la Vega, the Ancient City'.

13. Rampini, *Letters from Jamaica*, 45; Judah, *Old Saint Jago*, 46–8.

14. Plowden, *Grain or Chaff?* 84–5.

15. *Jamaica and its Governor*, 23–6; describing the yellow fever at Governor Musgrave's arrival and the deaths of Lieutenant Governor Bosworth and of Musgrave's valet, Adelaide, Public Library of South Australia, Archives Department, SA Archives, R.G. 58, September 1877, Sir Anthony Musgrave to Sir Henry Ayers.

16. PRO CO 137/406, f. 208, 11 July 1866, Sir Henry Storks to Cardwell. On the more positive economic prospects for all the West Indian colonies during the 1860s, Guillebaud, 'Crown Colonies', 729–31.

17. MMS Jamaica Correspondence, Box 200, File 1869, no. 3, 22 January 1869, T. Raspass to General Secretary.

18. On the island's reorganized secondary education, Underhill, *Life of Phillippo*, 359–61.

19. The Government Savings Bank, Marsala, *Sir John Peter Grant*, 68, 81. The

collapse of the Trelawny Savings Bank, Jacqueline Welds, 'The Bank Secretary Embezzled the Money', *Jamaican Historical Society Bulletin* 5:8 (1970): 110–13. By 1873 there were further problems with the new coins after a rise in the price of nickel brought the cost of the metal above the face value of a prospective issue of the coins, PRO MINT 13/54, 8 August 1873, [Deputy Master of Mint] to Secretary of Treasury, draft.

20. Marsala, *Sir John Peter Grant*, 39–42, 48, 58–9.

21. As part of a cost-cutting consolidation of the island's former 22 parishes St Catherine now incorporated the former parishes of St Dorothy (to the west, around Old Harbour), St John (to the north, around Linstead) and St Thomas in the Vale, (to the north, in the centre of the island).

22. Marsala, *Sir John Peter Grant*, 75–8, 83–4, 86, 105; 66.

23. For these schemes, see below, 245–6.

24. See Ingram, *QC and the Middleman*, 51–61, which unravels the doings of a particularly intemperate and self-righteous expatriate judge on his arrival in Jamaica.

25. Underhill, *Life of Phillippo*, 361–8, offers a partisan's view of disestablishment. On the Government College, see below 224–33.

26. When the Government Botanist made his report to the Jamaica Assembly in November 1865 the *chinchona succiribra* seedlings were already 'three years and six months old', so would have been planted after June 1861. *Votes of the Assembly, November-December, 1865*, 135–136. The government botanic gardens at Castleton were established 29 November 1862, well before Crown Colony Government, but the Cinchona experimental plantation in the Blue Mountains was initiated in 1868. Alan Eyre, *The Botanical Gardens of Jamaica* (London: André Deutsch, 1966), 28, 71. On the broader scope of Grant's initiatives, Richard A. Howard and Dulcie A. Powell, 'The Indian Botanic Garden, Calcutta and the Gardens of the West Indies', *Bulletin of the Botanical Survey of India* 7 (1965): 1–7; Marsala, *Sir John Peter Grant*, 61–2.

27. Morton, 'The Jamaica Post Office', in Corlett *et al. Jamaica Its Postal History*, 17–8, citing the *Morning Journal*, (15 August 1873). The next year an English visitor found it 'curious that there should be no public horse conveyances on the roads' particularly 'stage-coaches', suggesting this scheme reflected then-current English usages. Scott, *To Jamaica and Back*, 228.

28. PRO CO 137/406, f. 214v. 14 July 1866, Storks to Cardwell.

29. PRO CO 137/406, f. 215, 31 August 1866, [Earl of] C[arnarvon]'s annotation to Storks's dispatch of 14 July 1866. Governor Sligo's suggestion was included in Howe Peter Browne, 2nd Marquess of Sligo, *A Letter to the Marquess of Normanby Relative to the Present State of Jamaica and the Measures which are rendered necessary by the refusal of the House of Assembly to Transact Business* (London: John Andrews, 1839), 49.

30. Olivier, *Myth of Governor Eyre*, 44, footnote.

31. I have been unable to locate a copy of Governor Grant's dispatch number 13, dated 11 January 1867, which included his report and concurrence with the proposal. An abstract is in PRO CO 351/7, 'received 26 February 1872', unfoliated. He summarized his earlier arguments in JA 1B/5/18, ff. 275–276, [7 February 1872], Grant to Lord Kimberly, Secretary of State for the Colonies.

32. For the texts of these petitions, JA 1B/5/75/1, unfoliated, 19 November 1869, (annotated, 'received 5 December'), The Humble Memorial of the Undersigned Inhabitants and Owners of Property in the Town of St Iago de la Vega or Spanish Town and the Parish of St Catherine; Addressed to Sir John Peter Grant [1 November 1870]. Their reception was described in the *Humble Memorial of the Municipal Board of the Parish of St Catherine* (nd. 'received 8 June, 1874'), i–iv.

33. Morton, 'The Jamaica Post Office', in Corlett *et al. Jamaica: Its Postal History*. 15.

34. Treasury officials in Grant's administration were diligent in trying to nail down what was spent on this over-budget commission, which had required a public subscription to complete, but could not settle on a total. It was not £1,500. JA 1B/5/75/1, unfoliated, [nd. 1869], Memo on money expended on Metcalfe statue. The official correspondence between May and August 1869 preparatory to this removal can be followed in the same bundle. Quotation from 27 April 1869, Dr Louis Bowerbank, Custos of Kingston, to Edward Rushworth, Acting Colonial Secretary.

35. J.B. Ellis, *The Diocese of Jamaica: A Short Account of its History, Growth and Organisation* (London: SPCK, 1913), 105–12; for disputes over the Bishop and Synod's authority and over the distribution of the denomination's remaining funds, James Walvin, *The Life and Times of Henry Clarke of Jamaica, 1828–1907* (London: Frank Cass, 1994), 62–7.

36. JA 1B/5/18, ff. 277–282, [7 February 1872], Grant to Kimberly, also ibid. ff. 293–8, 24 February 1872, same to same.

37. The town's tardy memorial, Marsala, *Sir John Peter Grant*, 85.

38. *Morning Journal*, (15 April 1872). I owe this reference to Beverley Davis, 'The effects of the removal of the capital on Spanish Town, 1872–1900', UWI Mona, Caribbean Study, 1976/27, 13.

39. Feurtado, *Forty-Five Years' Reminiscence*, 12.

40. Law 7 of 1870, 'A Law to Abolish the Office of Financial Secretary, and Transfer the Duties of that Office to the Colonial Secretary', 17 February 1870, *Statutes of Jamaica*, v. *1866–1873* (Kingston: Government Printing Establishment, 1889, rpt. 1912).

41. Law 2 of 1871, 'A Law for the Removal to Kingston of the Supreme Court, and the Offices of the Registrar and Clerk of the Courts and Crown', 27 January 1871.

42. *Jamaica Gazette*, (11 April 1872). Quoted in Davis, 'The effects', 11.

43. The 'Paternal Despotism' phrase, Marsala, *Sir John Peter Grant*, 51–2, *et passim*.

44. *Regulations of the Legislative Council of Jamaica* (Spanish Town: George

Henderson, 1867), 1, copy in PRO CO 137/422, ff. 272–7v.

45. JA 2/2/30, f. 53, Municipal Board, St Catherine, Minutes, 1873–1879, 5 June 1874.
This was the occasion that generated the parish's official memorial now in JA
1B/5/75/3/3776.

46. JA 2/2/30, f. 53v, 20 October 1874, also, ibid. 53–53v. 5 June 1874, cover letter from
Hon L.J. Mackinnon (Custos) to Governor; ibid. f. 54, the 500 copies.

47. JA 2/2/30, f. 54, 9 July 1874, Colonial Secretary to Custos.

48. Feurtado, *Forty-Five Years' Reminiscence*, 2.

49. *Memorial of the Municipal Board of St Catherine*, 1874, IV–2, including the 1872
Petition of Elizabeth Stewart of Spanish Town, to Legislative Council, printed
from the petitioner's copy.

50. Judah, *Old Saint Jago*, 25. Grant, in contrast, characterized the site of the Lodge as
'a convenient distance from the town of Kingston; and it is healthily situated
upon high lying ground' while claiming that 'there could not, I think, be a better
selection . . .' JA 1B/5/18, Grant to Kimberly, [7 February 1872], ff. 278, 277.

51. Samuel, *Wesleyan-Methodist Missions*, 115.

52. *Memorial of the Municipal Board of the Parish of St Catherine*, 2. On the
unsatisfactory housing of the records in Kingston prior to the 1907 Kingston
earthquake and fire and their subsequent disorganization and destruction, H.C.
Bell, D.W. Parker *et al.* eds., *Guide to British West Indian Archive Materials, in
London and in the Islands, for the History of the United States* (Washington, DC:
Carnegie Institution, 1926), 362–3, 370. Regulations imposed on colonial banks
after the bank failures of the 1840s limited their accepting land or houses as
security for loans, which downgraded mortgages as assets in banks' portfolios.
Kathleen Monteith, 'Regulation of the Commercial Banking Sector in the British
West Indies, 1837–1961', *Journal of Caribbean History* 37:2 (2003) 210–30.

53. Thus Walter Augustus Feurtado had a post as a 'Searcher' at the Records Office
for over a decade, as did Leslie Alexander, whose project to write a history of the
Anglican Cathedral was never completed. Feurtado, *Forty-Five Years' Reminiscence*,
28, also JM King, 'Walter Augustus Feurtado and His Manuscripts', *Jamaica
Journal* 3 (1969): 13–15; NLJ Ms 254, Leslie Alexander, 'List of Plans in the Record
Office'. The notes for Alexander's unfinished history were later used in S. Purcell
Hendricks, *History of the Cathedral Church of St Jago de la Vega, Spanish Town*
(Kingston: Jamaica Times, 1911).

54. For example, in 1902 by an American banker, E. Quincy Smith, *Travels at Home
and Abroad* 2 vols (New York: Neale, 1911), 1: 47.

55. The sale of the cavalry barracks complex was authorized by the Assembly in 1812.
It was then sold to the Parish of St Catherine in 1815, 56 George III c. 22, 'An Act
for vesting certain land and buildings belonging to the public, in the town of St
Jago de la Vega, in the justices and vestrymen of the parish of St Catherine, for
the purpose of establishing a parochial poor-house thereon', 22 December 1815. A

theatre operated from 1831 to 1835. I owe this information to NLJ 62a, Andrade, 'Parochial Handbook', unfoliated.

56. Sherlock and Bennett, *Story of the Jamaican People*, 322.

57. Law 8 of 1867, 'A Law to Organize a Constabulary Force', 19 March 1867; RHL Ms WI s.22, Clive A. Crosbie-Smith, *History of Jamaica Constabulary*, nd.

58. Herbert T. Thomas, *The Story of a West Indian Policeman, or Forty-Seven Years in the Jamaican Constabulary* (Kingston: Gleaner Company, 1927), 35, 350, also Claude McKay, 'Flat-Foot Drill', *Constab Ballads*, reprinted in Winston James, *A Fierce Hatred of Injustice: Claude McKay's Jamaica and his Poetry of Rebellion* (Kingston: Ian Randle Publishers, 2001), 189–90, and discussed, *ibid.* 78–80.

59. PRO CO137/423, ff. 278–282v, 23 March 1867, Grant to Carnarvon.

60. The move did develop existing practices. In the eighteenth century representatives from St Catherine had argued that the Assembly should pay for rebuilding the county gaol in Spanish Town because it received prisoners from across the island. Long, *History*, 2. 15–16.

61. Law No 5 of 1867, 'A Law to Abolish the Surrey County Gaol', 26 February 1867.

62. Marsala, *Sir John Peter Grant*, 85.

63. Marsala, *Sir John Peter Grant*, 80.

64. JA 2/2/30, ff. 7v–8, 2 July 1873, J.N. Prenderville, Inspector General of Police to Colonial Secretary.

65. JA 2/2/30, f. 7, 23 July 1873, Colonial Secretary, William A.G. Young, to Clerk to the Parochial Board.

66. Letter read and permission granted. JA 2/2/30, f. 10v. 21 August 1873.

67. JA 2/2/30, f. 55, 3 July 1874, Colonial Secretary to Municipal Board.

68. Colleen A. Hobbs, *Florence Nightingale* (New York: Twayne, 1997), 53–4.

69. JA 2/2/30, f. 55v, [July, 1874], District Engineer's Report, which criticizes the local Medical Officer's views and the Board's subsequent resolution: 'the Board does not approve the site near the Magazine, for the erection of the Alms House'.

70. Long, *History*, 2. 17.

71. JA 2/2/30, f. 59v. 7 August 1874, Colonial Secretary to Board, enclosing the medical superintendent's retraction, along with the Board's resolution, 28 September 1874, 'adhering to the opinions expressed by the medical Officer of the Parish'.

72. JA 2/2/30, f. 69, 14 January 1875, Colonial Secretary to Board.

73. The sheer volume of this correspondence led to the original letters from the Colonial Secretary's Office being filed in 'Guard Books', rather than transcribed into the Board's Minute Books. Now lost, these files provided a separate series in the parochial records listed by the parish clerk. 'List of records in the care of the Parish Clark' (nd. *c.* 1916), NLJ Ms 62a, Andrade, 'Parochial Handbook', unfoliated. St Catherine was not unique in either receiving or accumulating such missives. A similar series running from 1866 comprising 'Letters from the

Colonial Secretary, Financial Secretary and the Audit Office' survives among the Hanover parish records, JA 2/4/7/1–16.

74. JA 1B/5/75/1, unfoliated, 1 November 1870, Grant's draft reply, ff. 2v–3, 3v–4.

75. Scott, *To Jamaica and Back*, 247. The author visited the College and had lunch with its faculty, so his comments probably reflect their understanding of its potential role.

76. PRO CO 137/464, ff. 180–180v, 8 July 1872, Grant to Kimberly.

77. JA 2/2/30, f. 9v, 21 August 1873, 14 July 1873, J. Macglachan, Colonial Secretary, to Custos of St Catherine.

78. Above, 184, and Phillippo, *Jamaica*, 477–85. He gave Grant a copy of this book, Underhill, *Life of Phillippo*, 359.

79. Wilmot, 'Race, Electoral Violence and Constitutional Reform', 32; JA 1B/5/5/11, f. 3, 1 November 1864.

80. Underhill, *Life of Phillippo*, 378–81.

81. Phillippo, *Jamaica*, 481.

82. Philip Sherlock and Rex Nettleford, *The University of the West Indies: A Caribbean Response to the Challenge of Change* (Basingstoke: Macmillan Caribbean, 1990), 17–9.

83. PRO CO 137/464, f. 227, 18 March 1873, Robert Williams to 'Sir Henry', recommending Grant Allen.

84. In 1871 Parliament repealed the Test Acts, which had precluded non-Anglicans matriculating at Oxford or Cambridge. A.J. Engel, *From Clergyman to Don: The Rise of the Academic Profession in Nineteenth-Century Oxford* (Oxford: Clarendon, 1983), 77–81. Grant Allen the Vice Principal was an 1871 Oxford graduate. After graduating he had been a tutor to the sons of Lord Huntly and was recruited from part-time teaching at the Brighton College, the Cheltenham Ladies' College and Reading Grammar School. Edward Clodd, *Grant Allen: A Memoir* (London: Grant Richards, 1900), 37; Paul Matthew St. Pierre, 'Grant Allen (*24 February 1848–28 October 1899*)', in W.H. New ed., *Canadian Writers, 1890–1920* (Dictionary of Literary Biography, 92, Detroit, Mich: Gale Research, 1990), 6.

85. Gardner, *History of Jamaica*, 501. The subsequent decision by the Baptist minister at the Phillippo Chapel in Spanish Town to 'sever my connection' in order to 'enter the ministry' of 'the *disestablished*, Voluntary Church of England in Jamaica' does demonstrate the potential appeal of this legal transition. BMS Sub-Committee Reports, 1878–79, unfoliated, 9 April 1877, Thomas Lea to the Secretaries of the Baptist Missionary Society.

86. Grant outlined his plans for securing these funds in his dispatch proposing the establishment of the College, PRO, CO 137/464, ff. 181–182v, 8 July 1872, Grant to Kimberley.

87. Seton-Karr, *Grant of Rothiemurchus*, 108.

88. *Proposals for a Church Training Institution in Jamaica, February 1871*. I used a copy

inserted in JA 5/1/5/1, Jamaican Church Theological College (St Peter's), Minutes of the Committee of the Training Institute, 1871-1876, unfoliated.

89. *Proceedings of Synod*, 12 August 1871, 'Report of Training Institution Committee', copy in JA 5/1/5/1.

90. Frank Cundall, *The Life of Enos Nuttall: Archbishop of the West Indies* (London: SPCK, 1922), 31. This was in August 1874.

91. E. Daniel Potts, *British Baptist Missionaries in India, 1793–1837: The History of Serampore and its Missions* (Cambridge: Cambridge University Press, 1967), 129–31, 183–204.

92. Marsala, *Sir John Peter Grant*, 96–7; Clodd, *Grant Allen*, 42–3.

93. Scott, *To Jamaica and Back*, 248. The claim was plausible enough. The rival appeal of Oxford and Cambridge, along with administrative inefficiency, would contribute to the collapse of the contemporary Catholic University College in London. Tom Horwood, 'The Rise and Fall of the Catholic University College, Kensington, 1868–1882', *Journal of Ecclesiastical History* 54 (2003): 302–18.

94. Clodd, *Grant Allen*, 41.

95. Sir James Currie and R.R. Sedgwick *West Indian University, Resolution of the First West Indian Conference* (1927), 4, copy included in JA 1B/5/77/109, (1927), 'Proposals for the Establishment of a West Indian University, 1927–31'.

96. Clodd, *Grant Allen*, 57–9; outlining the changes in one Oxford college during the 1850s and '60s, Alan Ryan, 'Transformation, 1850–1914', in John Buxton and Penry Williams, eds., *New College, Oxford, 1379–1979* (Oxford: New College, 1979), 72–87.

97. Sheldon Rothblatt, *The Revolution of the Dons: Cambridge and Society in Victorian England* (New York: Basic Books, 1968).

98. RHL Ms Brit Emp s. 23, British and Foreign Anti-Slavery and Aboriginal Protection Society, G. 49, 'Lady Albion's Caribbean University', nd. This skit seems to address nepotism in the administration of the Leeward Islands in the 1870s.

99. Editorial, 'Is the University Issue Decided?' *Jamaica Daily Express* (6 April 1944): 2, clipping included in UWI, Mona, R.E. Priestley, 'West Indian Journey, 1944', 2 vols., 1. 6 April 1944; ibid. 12 April 1944, summarizing 'a perfectly appalling' presentation to the Irvine Commission on West Indian Higher Education by the then Director of Medical Services in Jamaica. The second passage is quoted in Sherlock and Nettleford, *University of the West Indies*, 4.

100. Currie and Sedgwick, *West Indian University*, 7. Invoking the expense in vetoing the proposal, 7 November 1930, R.E. Stubbs annotations to JA 1B/5/77/109, (1927).

101. [James Phillippo?], *Report of the Schools composed of the Negro and Free Population of Spanish Town, Jamaica, for the year ending May, 1831* (Leicester: R. Tebbutt, 1831), 9.

102. On the Assembly's rejection of two education acts in 1856, Macmillan, *Sir Henry Barkly*, 84–5. Because Phillippo and his Baptist colleagues feared these bills were 'calculated to jeopardise mission schools, and give an undue prominence and control over public instruction' to Anglican clergy, they had joined in opposing 'the "monstrous bill"'. Underhill, *Life of Phillippo*, 277. For the thoroughly disappointing schooling that government economies bought, Shirley Gordon, 'Schools of the Free', in Moore and Wilmot, *Before and After 1865*, 1–12, 375–6.

103. Underhill, *Life of Phillippo*, 296–7; Eisner, *Jamaica, 1830–1930*, 332.

104. Curtin, *Two Jamaicas*, 159; Eyre to Newcastle, in Wilmot, ed., *Adjustments to Emancipation*, 38.

105. Clodd, *Grant Allen*, 42.

106. Gardner, *History*, 502–03.

107. For several comments on official inspections of individual schools in the 1880s, see RHL Ms W. Ind. s.51. Journal of Thomas Capper, Inspector of Schools, Jamaica, January – July, 1881.

108. Seton-Karr, *Grant of Rothiermurchus*, 108.

109. On these early teacher training colleges, see Carl Campbell, 'Teachers and the Training of Teachers in the first Primary Schools', 2 parts, *Torch: Journal of the Ministry of Education, Jamaica* 24 (1975): 51–8, 25 (1976): 64–72. On the graduates from the Normal School in Spanish Town, Bryan, *Jamaican People*, 239, 242. It stood near the railway line and burnt down in the 1880s. Feurtado, *Forty-Five Years' Reminiscence*, 26–7. By the time this accident occurred retrenchment had reduced the number of places for schoolteachers so it did not reopen.

110. Frank J. Klingberg, 'The Lady Mico Charity Schools in the British West Indies, 1835–1844', *Journal of Negro History* 29 (1939): 304–05, and Frank Cundall, *The Mico College, Jamaica* (Kingston: for the Directors of the College, 1914), 45; Marsala, *Sir John Peter Grant*, 88–9.

111. The phrase is from the memorial in the Cathedral erected to Principal William Chadwick, died 27 June 1574, Wright, *Monumental Inscriptions of Jamaica*, 99.

112. PRO CO 137/464, f. 187v, 8 July 1872, Grant to Kimberley.

113. John F. Gartshore, *Outline History of Shortwood College, 1885–1935* (Kingston: Gleaner, [1935]).

114. For the arguments set out earlier in the 1920s, R.J. Campbell, 'Education in Jamaica: moral sense needs purifying', one of a series of Jamaican articles in *The Church Family Newspaper* (9 January – 26 March 1920). I consulted a bound set of clippings at the National Library of Jamaica. The 1927 proposals, Currie and Sedgwick, *West Indian University*. From the opposite end of the political spectrum Marcus Garvey recognized the same problem by including the establishment of 'a Jamaican University and Poly-technic' as plank number eight in the People's Party's political platform, as 'there is no reason why people here should strain to send their sons and daughters to far away England when they could have a

University here to give them similar training.' Marcus Garvey, *The Marcus Garvey and Universal Negro Improvement Association Papers* ed., Robert A. Hill *et al.* (Berkeley, Cal: University of California Press, 1983–), 7. *November 1927–August 1940*, 329, 336, 9 September 1929.

115. For the earlier schemes see above, 147.

116. 29 October 1870, Grant to Kimberly, published in *Papers Relating to the Proposed Irrigation Canal for the Rio Cobre* (Kingston: Government Printing Establishment, [1876?]), 1, copy included in JA 1B/5/76/3/7, 'The Proposed Irrigation Canal from the Rio Cobre'.

117. UWI St Augustine, West India Committee Papers, 39, Letters and Memoranda, 1866–1870, f. 32, 22 June 1870, Minutes of a Meeting of Gentlemen interested in Jamaica held in Walbrook House [London] to . . . confer with Sir John Peter Grant.

118. Gardner, *History of Jamaica*, 505; Law 27 of 1872, 'A Law to Provide for the Construction and Maintenance of Works of Irrigation by Water taken from the Rio Cobre', 27 June 1872, also Law 31 of 1872, 'A Law for the Erection and Management of Gas Works for the City of Kingston', 4 July 1872.

119. These developments can be followed in the successive maps and plans produced by the Rio Cobre Irrigation Canal now in the custody of the Jamaica Archives, JA 1B/56/1. They should be illuminated by Phillipa DaCosta's research on 'The Industrial Archaeology of the Rio Cobre Irrigation Canal System', UWI, Mona, MPhil thesis (in progress).

120. *Report on the Rio Cobre Irrigation Works. From their First Construction to the Present Time, with the Opinion of the Director of Roads and Surveyor-General as to their Future Prospect* ([Kingston: np.], 1876), 6.

121. *Jamaica Gazette*, 18 (13 July 1876): 219, Speech to Legislative Council by Henry Westmorland.

122. JA 1B/5/76/3/7, 15 April 1882, W.G. Dawkins to J.R. Main.

123. *Jamaica Gazette* 18 (13 July 1876): 220, Westmorland to Legislative Council. He was an 'unofficial' member of the Council, nominated by a Governor but not on the Government payroll.

124. JA 2/2/30, f. 62 July 1874, a Committee 'to consider ... what alterations and additions are required to be made to the present Buildings, now used as a Market in Spanish Town'. These repairs followed Governor Grant's example in establishing clean and convenient markets for Kingston, where the Victoria Market was opened in 1872. Marsala, *Sir John Peter Grant*, 83–84 and, describing that now demolished building, Gosner, *Caribbean Georgian*, 57. 130.

125. JA 2/2/30, f. 3v, 12 June 1873, petition W.H. Lyon.

126. JA 1A/5/32, Journal, Estate of D.P. Mendes, December 1876–November 1878.

127. Feurtado, *Forty-Five Years' Reminiscene*, 21–2.

128. AKH 23–7 October 1864, Fr J. Dupeyron to Cardinal Prefect of Propaganda,

(draft). The second passage is crossed out. This item is in Dupeyron II 1863–1864. I used a typescript calendar, 'Summary of Documents Contained in Chancery Office, Kingston, Jamaica.'

129. 'History of St Joseph's Church, Spanish Town', in *Centenary Celebrations 1872 to 1972: St Joseph's Church, Spanish Town, November 29, 1972* ([Spanish Town: St Joseph's Church], 1972). A building fund was established in Kingston while another £200 was contributed by the then Vicar Apostolic from a recent legacy.

130. JA 2/2/30, f. 17v. n.d. (discussed, 22 October 1873), A. Herber, to Chair and Members, Municipal Board.

131. JA 2/2/30, f. 40, 21 April 1874, Petition of Elizabeth Hamilton; also ibid. 14–14v. 20 August 1874, W.D. Bylis to Chair and Members, Municipal Board.

132. Marsala, *Sir John Peter Grant*, 64; on the problems in scheduling earlier ships, Verene Shepherd, *Transients to Settlers: The Experience of Indians in Jamaica, 1845–1950* (Leeds: Peepal Tree, 1993), 97.

133. JA 2/2/30, f. 40, 21 April 1871, Elizabeth Hamilton.

134. Judah, *Old Saint Jago*, 24.

135. Judah, *Old Saint Jago*, 13.

136. Andrade, *Jews of Jamaica*, 42-3.

137. Phillippo, *Jamaica: Its Government and its People*, 17.

138. Dominica in 1865. Antigua, St Kitts and Nevis in 1866. St Vincent in 1868, Guillebaud, 'Crown Colonies', 737.

139. I am grateful to Roy Augier for this point.

140. 'Notes in the Returns of the Revenue and Expenditure of the Government of Jamaica for the financial year 31st March 1901', *Jamaica Gazette* (25 July 1901). Clipping included in NLJ Ms 62a. Andrade, 'Parochial Handbook', unfoliated; H.S. Burns, 'Rio Cobre Canal – Dream That Came True and Made Money', *Daily Gleaner* (2 June 1951): 6.

141. For example, Black, *History of Jamaica*, 141; Burns, 'Rio Cobre Canal', 6. I owe this observation to Swithin Wilmot.

Chapter 8

1. Three complementary studies provide introductions to this period. Patrick Bryan, *The Jamaican People 1880–1902: Race, Class and Social Control* (Basingstoke: Macmillan, 1991), Erna Brodber, 'The Second Generation of Freemen in Jamaica, 1907–1914', PhD thesis, University of the West Indies, Mona, (1984), and Winston James, *A Fierce Hatred of Injustice: Claude McKay's Jamaica and his Poetry of Rebellion* (Kingston: Ian Randle Publishers, 2001), all investigate what Jamaicans of this generation saw as distinctive about Jamaican society during this phase of Crown Colony rule. A further sympathetic study by a former Governor,

Sydney Haldane Olivier, Lord Olivier, *Jamaica: The Blessed Island* (London: Faber, 1936), is also helpful. Gisela Eisner, *Jamaica, 1830–1930,* is again invaluable on the statistics that shaped the island's affairs. Trevor A. Turner's discussions of the policies shaping educational goals in late nineteenth-century Jamaica extend well beyond the classroom, 'The Socialisation Intent in Colonial Jamaican Education, 1867–1911', (1977), reprint in Ruby Hope King, ed., *Education in the Caribbean: Historical Perspectives* (*Caribbean Journal of Education* 14:1&2, Kingston: Faculty of Education, University of the West Indies, 1987), 54–87. Turner's tables demonstrate the costs of the crumbling of the island's export revenues in the late 1890s. On the railway, the most expensive of the public investments of the early 1890s, see Veront M. Satchell and Cezley Sampson, 'The rise and fall of railways in Jamaica, 1845–1975', *Journal of Transport History* 24 (2003): 1–21, while David Rollinson, *Railways of the Caribbean* (Basingstoke: Macmillan Caribbean, 2001), illustrates the wider appeal of this investment.

There are few discussions of the 1918–38 period. James Carnegie, *Some Aspects of Jamaica's Politics: 1918–1938* (Cultural Heritage Series, 4, Kingston: Institute of Jamaica, 1973), collects a great deal of valuable material. Howard Johnson, 'The British Caribbean from Demobilisation to Constitutional Decolonisation', in Judith M. Brown and W. Roger Louis, eds., *The Twentieth Century* (Oxford History of the British Empire, 4, Oxford: Oxford University Press, 1999), 597–622, offers comparative perspectives, as does William Macmillan's contemporary polemic, *Warning from the West Indies: A Tract for Africa and the Empire* (London: Faber, 1936). For the late 1930s the introductory chapter in Trevor Munroe's *The Politics of Constitutional Decolonisation: Jamaica, 1944–62* (Kingston: Institute of Social and Economic Research, 1972), 1–35, along with his 'The Bustamante Letters 1935', *Jamaica Journal* 8:1 (1974): 2–15, are both suggestive. Don Robotham, 'Nineteen Thirty Eight', in Levitt and Witter, eds., *The Critical Tradition of Caribbean Political Economy,* 119–28, discusses academic writing on the demonstrations and strikes of 1938. Ken Post's massive, *Arise ye Starvelings: The Jamaican Labour Rebellion of 1938 and its Aftermath* (The Hague: Nijhoff, 1978), helps to contextualise the roles played by the Spanish Town-based trade union in the political crises of 1938; crises which then spelt the end for the Crown Colony political system.

2. H.G. de Lisser, *Twentieth Century Jamaica* (Kingston, Jamaica Times, 1913), 83–84.

3. The quantity is suggested is Patricia E. Green, *Proposal for the Preparation of a Preservation Scheme Master Plan for the Spanish Town Historical District* (1995). Analyzing the construction of comparable buildings, Joan D. Van Andel, *Caribbean Traditional Architecture: The Traditional Architecture of Philipsburg, St Martin (N.A.)* (Antillen Working Papers, 10, Leiden: Caraibische Afdeling Koninklijl Instituut voor Taal-, Land- en Volkenkunde, 1986), 23–31. For

tantalizing discussions of these carvings, Elizabeth Pigou-Dennis, 'Traditional Ornament: Fretwork', *Axis: Journal of the Caribbean School of Architecture* 2 (1998): 55, and Patricia Bryan, 'The African Aesthetic in Jamaican Intuitive Art', *ACIJ Research Review* 1 (1984): 4–5.

4. H. Hyatt Verrill, *The Book of the West Indies* (New York: Dutton, 1917), 268. The passage dates from before 1914. He apparently found this image striking, repeating the 'white-painted, green shuttered' phrase again in two later books. In these he substituted 'houses' for 'villas,' idem. *In the Wake of the Buccaneers* (New York: Century, 1923), 278, and *Jamaica of Today* (New York: Dodd, Mead & Co., 1931), 47.

5. The Bank of Nova Scotia opened a branch in Spanish Town in 1916, 26 years after its first arrival in Kingston and ten years after the bank's first branch offices in Montego Bay and Port Antonio. Neil C. Quigley, 'The Bank of Nova Scotia in the Caribbean, 1889–1940', *Business History Review* 63 (1989): 809, table 4.

6. David Harrison, '19 White Church Street', *Jamaican Historical Society Bulletin* 8:7 (1982): 167–78. The Roman Catholic rectory on King Street is another substantial wooden residential building from the late nineteenth century. For further descriptions of socially ambitious Jamaican buildings of this period, Geoffrey de Sola Pinto and Anghelen Arrington Phillips, *Jamaican Houses: a Vanishing Legacy* (Montego Bay: de Sola Pinto Printers, 1982).

7. Villiers Stuart, *Adventures Amidst the Equatorial Forest and Rivers of South America, also in the West Indies and the Wilds of Florida, to which is added 'Jamaica Revisited'* (London: John Murray, 1891), 206.

8. See above, 222.

9. On British usages R.J. Morris, 'Clubs, societies and associations', in F.M.L. Thompson, ed., *Social agencies and institutions* (Cambridge Social History of Britain, 1750–1950, 3. Cambridge: Cambridge University Press, 1990), 395–443; the Jamaican groups, *Handbook of Jamaica for 1902* (Kingston: Government Printing Office, 1902), 447–53. Discussing the path breaking black Jamaican politicians of this generation, Joy Lumsden notes the prominence of freemasonry in several of their careers, including those of Joseph Milward Gordon and Dr J.J. Edwards from St Catherine. 'A Forgotten Generation: Black Politicians in Jamaica, 1884–1914', in Moore and Wilmot, *Before & After 1865*, 117, 120.

10. *Handbook of Jamaica for 1930* (Kingston: Government Printing Office, 1930), 471–3.

11. JA 7/108/6, Mrs Owen F. Wright, 14 June 1920, Farewell Address of Saint Catherine Prison CC to Owen F. Wright. As an indication of the more inclusive social catchment of the club's leadership, none of the eight signatories of this address are listed in *Who's Who in Jamaica 1916* (Kingston: the Gleaner for Stephen A. Hill, 1916).

12. On African American societies, see Elsa Barkley Brown, 'Womanist

Consciousness: Maggie Lena Walker and the Independent Order of Saint Luke',
Signs 14:3 (1989): 610–33. In the Eastern Caribbean, Glen Richards, 'Friendly
Societies and Labour Organisations in the Leeward Islands, 1912–19', in Moore
and Wilmot, *Before & After 1865*, 136–49, 390–1, and Aviston C. Downes, 'Sailing
from Colonial into National Waters: A History of the Barbados Landship',
Journal of the Barbados Museum and Historical Society 46 (2000): 93–122.

13.   Clinton V. Black, 'Andrew Duffus Mowatt', in *idem. Living Names in Jamaica's
History* (Kingston: Jamaica Welfare, 1946), 34–7; *Handbook of Jamaica for 1930*,
444. The society was initially established in the village of Banbury, outside
Linstead. Its third branch was in Linstead, the fourth in Spanish Town.

14.   JA 1B/5/79/41, 1926, 'Hamatic (sic) Church', 16 February 1926, E.G. Orrett to
Inspector General, (verso).

15.   Chicago Historical Society, Sterling Morton Papers, Box 1, folder '1908–1914',
Sterling Morton, 'On the Spanish Main: Account of a Trip from New York City
to the West Indies, Panama, Columbia and Venezuela, January 17 – February 20
1912', 26.

16.   This description draws on a letter that the mother of one of the passengers passed
on 'in confidence' to the Colonial Secretary's Office and an ensuing official
dossier. JA 1B/5/79/347, Colonial Secretariat, Confidential Correspondence,
Interference with traffic of a UNIA procession in Spanish Town, 1929. The
incident only received this much attention because the colonial administration
were nervous about the United Negro Improvement Association's activities. The
file closes with a bureaucrat's annotation, 'Not the UNIA after all!'

17.   de Lisser, *Twentieth Century Jamaica*, 83.

18.   The remarkable collection of essays describing Jamaica 'fifty years ago' submitted
to *The Gleaner* in November 1959, includes many descriptions of Kingston's tram-
cars from men and women who were teenagers at the turn of the century. For
example JA 7/12,/233, [1959], G.V. Barton. See also R. Pullen-Burry. *Jamaica as it
is, 1903* (London: Fisher Unwin, 1903), 41; John Henderson, *Jamaica* (London:
Black, 1906), 13, 26–7, and Carol Mae Morrissey, '"Ol' Time Tram" and the
Tramway Era, 1876–1948', *Jamaica Journal* 16:4 (1983): 12–21.

19.   I am grateful to John Gilmore for sending me a copy of this postcard from his
personal collection. It was apparently made from an amateur snapshot. This
example bears a 1904 postmark. For introductions to early West Indian postcards
and the information they can incorporate, see John Gilmore, *Glimpses of Our
Past: A Social History of the Caribbean in Postcards* (Kingston: Ian Randle
Publishers, 1995), and Glory Robertson, 'Some Early Jamaican Postcards: their
Photographers and Publishers', *Jamaica Journal* 18:1 (1985): 13–22.

20.   Verrill, *In the Wake of the Buccaneers*, 278.

21.   NLJ Ms 2035, f.6, 1st Autobiography of Norman Washington Manley, 16 April–30
May 1969.

22. JA 7/32/488, 14 September 1917, [ ] to Canon S. Purcell Hendricks.
23. NLJ Ms 1839, 'Draft Railway Bill', f. 2, 9 March 1867. Simone Gigliotti drew this manuscript to my attention.
24. JA 4/97/1, Gunter, 'Centenary History of the Jamaica Government Railway', 8.
25. Collett, et al. *Jamaica: Its Postal History*, 16.
26. Adelaide, Public Library of South Australia, S.A. Archives 58, 25 December 1879, Sir Anthony Musgrave to Sir Henry Ayers. He concluded 'just at this moment I think I am the most popular man in Jamaica'.
27. JA 4/97/1, Gunter, 'Centenary History of the Jamaica Government Railway', 10–13.
28. This criticism was hardly fair as the colony was undertaking extensive road and bridge building programmes across the island, Eisner, *Jamaica, 1830–1930*, 177–8. Up to the 1890s most of these roads were intended to benefit the sugar industry, ibid. 224. For a visitor's positive verdict on the 'splendid macademized road' he saw in 1890, Villiers Stuart, *Adventures*, 192.
29. Discussing the parallel increases in government expenditure on education at this juncture, Turner, 'Socialising Intent', 72–4.
30. Scott, *To Jamaica and Back*, 264. This traveler's taste in fruit did not adjust during his stay: he disliked avocados, mangoes appeared 'sickly things', shaddocks simply bitter oranges, while the even best Jamaican pineapples were 'not equal to English hot-house pines'. Clearly travel will not broaden some palates, or some minds.
31. 'Abyssinian' bananas were among the new species introduced to the government's Cinchona Research Station in 1869, but this import did not provide the base for Jamaica's late nineteenth-century banana industry. Sealy and Hart, *Jamaica's Banana Industry*, 7.
32. Phrase from Lord Olivier, *Jamaica, the Blessed Island*, quoted in George Beckford and Michael Witter, *Small Garden . . . Bitter Weed: Struggle and Change in Jamaica* (Kingston: Institute of Social and Economic Research, 1980), 50.
33. Sealy and Hart, *Jamaica's Banana Industry*, 7.
34. Frederick Upham Adams, *Conquest of the Tropics: The Story of the Creative Enterprise conducted by the United Fruit Company* (New York: Doubleday, 1914), 38–39. Two recent retellings emphasize different aspects of the same story: Peter N. Davies, *Fyffes and the Banana: Musa Sapientum, A Centenary History, 1888–1988* (London: Athlone, 1990), 23–35, and Virginia Scott Jenkins, *Bananas: An American History* (Washington, DC: Smithsonian Institution, 2000), 17–27, 42–51. For a different perspective, Sealy and Hart, *Jamaica's Banana Industry* 11–15.
35. JA 7/12/265, f. 2, [November, 1959], Una Wilson, 'Life in Jamaica over fifty years ago'.
36. Steve Marquardt, '"Green Havoc": Panama Disease, Environmental Change, and Labor Process in the Central American Banana Industry', *American Historical Review* 106 (2001): 49–80.
37. Sealy and Hart, *Jamaica's Banana Industry*, 15. For a passenger's record of a fruit

ship's itinerary in 1902, sailing round from Port Antonio to Port Morant and then to Port Henderson, Smith, *Travels at Home and Abroad* 1, 57; the local railway network, JA 1B/5/104/12, Ordinance Survey Maps of Jamaica, (1920), Kingston District, sheet 3. This map and sheet 2 show the extent of banana growing in the Spanish Town area. I am grateful to Thera Edwards for this reference.

38. JA 7/12/147, ff. 7–8, [November, 1959], Lawrence P. Peters. The chronology described here fits with the decision by the revenue department in 1898 to allow the import of cow peas duty free as a foodstuff, 1B/8/3, Collector General's Department, Letter Book, April 1900–February 1904, f. 2, 28 May 1900.

39. JA 4/97/1, Gunter, 'Centenary History of the Jamaica Government Railway', 14.

40. On these Legislative Council debates, Satchell and Sampson, 'Rise and fall of railways in Jamaica', 7.

41. The phrase was used in 1883 by E. Wingfield, then Head of the Colonial Service's West Indies Department. It is quoted in H.A. Will, 'Problems of Constitutional Reform in Jamaica, Mauritius and Trinidad, 1880–1895', *English Historical Review* 81 (1966): 694.

42. The campaigning behind the recent reorganization of the Legislative Council to incorporate a minority of elected members is described in Ronald V. Sires, 'The Jamaican Constitution of 1884', *Social and Economic Studies* 3 (1954): 72–81. However, the image of propriety was smudged by a Jamaican-born crown lawyer's allegations of bribe-taking and insider trading against the colony's Attorney General who had presented the case for undertaking this deal in London. The evidence remained hearsay. Making a claim he could not prove consequently ruined the Jamaican's public career. F.L. Casserly, 'The Grey-Hocking Bribery Affair (1893–1894)', 2 parts, *Jamaican Historical Society Bulletin* 2:1 (1957): 4–7, and 2:2 (1957): 23–6.

43. Olivier, *Jamaica*, 248.

44. NLJ Ms 1612a, F.L. Casserly, 'Jamaica Railway Fiasco, 1890–1900', nd. [1950s]; for an American appraisal of the line's operations just before it was taken over, Ms. 1612, 31 May 1898, Jackson Smith to James P. McDonald. American managers viewed the railway as heavily over-staffed, accustomed to working Jamaican government hours – 8:30 to 5:00 p.m., five days a week – and employing a time-consuming and useless bookkeeping system. There therefore appeared to be considerable scope for wringing further economies out of the existing network.

45. Algernon S. Aspinall, *The Pocket Guide to the West Indies* (London: Edward Stanford, 1907), 110.

46. These technical constraints are outlined in E.M. Bland, *Report of the Jamaican Government Railway* (Kingston: [Government Printer], 1937), 1, 4, 7. Admiring the views, Pullen-Burry, *Jamaica as it is*, 153–4.

47. F.L. Casserly, 'Crown Colony Crisis: The Henning-Gideon Correspondence', *Jamaican Historical Review* 3 (1957): 40, 43. The £88,000 figure at 3½ per cent is

from 16 December 1899, C.P. Lucas to Secretary of the Treasury, a copy of which is in JA 1B/5/76/93, 'The Government Railway and Winding up of Railway Company'. In the event, resolving a protracted four-cornered legal dispute in Jamaica between the Central Trust Company of New York, the bondholders, the Colonial Bank and the Jamaican government prior to the colony's securing this loan, meant that it was only processed after Britain became embroiled in the Boer War. Because of increased wartime public borrowing the British Treasury then added a further ¼ per cent to the rate for the Jamaican loan. 'Judgement in the Railway Litigation', *Daily Gleaner* (6 February 1900); 1B/5/76/93, 6 January 1900, Francis Howatt, (Treasury), to Under Secretary of State, Colonial Office. This raised the cost to Jamaica of bailing out the other bondholders in the West India Improvement Company still higher.

48. The line from Porus to Montego Bay was 64 miles long. The one from Bog Walk to Port Antonio 54¾ miles. JA 4/97/1, Gunter, 'Centenary History of the Jamaica Government Railway', 16; NLJ Ms. 1612a, Casserly, 'Jamaica Railway Fiasco'.

49. Olivier, *Jamaica*, 250.

50. In one instance, at least, the growing interest by New York and Boston investors in Jamaica did help persuade the bank of Nova Scotia's general manager to establish their first West Indian branch in Kingston in 1889. Earlier in the 1880s he had turned down suggestions that the Bank establish a Kingston branch and, in the event, the commercial loan business remained poor. Quigley, 'Bank of Nova Scotia', 808–10.

51. W. Bancroft Espeut, *The Advantages to Result from 'Railway Extension' in Jamaica* (Institute of Jamaica, Popular Lectures, 4th ser. Kingston: the Institute, 1887), 8–9. The example of Trinidad was cited in a contemporary discussion of centralized estates, NLJ Ms 307, D.S. Gideon Papers, no. 5, item C. 3 August 1899, Proposal on Jamaican Sugar Industry. I am grateful to Jacob Moore for this reference. Emphasizing Jamaican planters' persistent ambivalence about such factories, R.W. Beachey, *The British West Indies Sugar Industry in the Late 19th Century* (Oxford: Blackwell, 1957), 83–6.

52. Mary F. Bradford, *Side Trips in Jamaica* (Boston, Mass: Sherwood, [1900], 3rd ed 1902), 29. This guidebook described the cruises offered by the United Fruit Company. Its author would be particularly prone to argue that 'the patronage of foreign companies' had a positive impact.

53. Satchell and Sampson, 'Rise and fall of railways in Jamaica', 11–12, see the extensions to the railway playing a major role in agricultural development in Jamaica between 1890 and 1930. Olivier, *Jamaica*, 252–3, cites the investment by the Colonial government in local roads during the late 1890s which also provided routes for the interior settlements to get their crops to market.

54. NLJ StC.272, 1894, Plan of Proposed enlargement of District Prison, Spanish Town, Surveyor, W. Ivan Harrison. For subsequent additions, see JA 1B/16, Public

Works Department, G21/14, 1 February 1885, St Catherine District Prison, Plan
and Section of extension of existing range of cells; G21/24, May 1885, District
Prison, Spanish Town, Block Plan; G23/48, 19 April 1892, District Prison,
Residence for Dispenser and Matron, (Plan, Elevation and Section); G23/35, July
1896, Distinct Prison, [Details of] Hospital for Males; H19/73, 9 October 1896,
District Prison, Type of Entrance Gate; F14/21, May 1897, District Prison, Plan,
Residence Chief Warden; G23/32, April 1898, District Prison, Details, Iron gate
and windows for stores. The series of dated plans continues up to the First World
War, while there are many more undated plans of this period showing further
alterations and additions to the prison.

55. Frank Fonda Taylor, *To Hell with Paradise: A History of the Jamaican Tourist
Industry* (Pittsburgh, Penn: University of Pittsburgh Press, 1993), 75–9, also Karen
Booth, 'When Jamaica Welcomed the World: The Great Exhibition of 1891',
Jamaica Journal 18:3 (1985): 42–3, 47–9.

56. Richard Cobb, *French and Germans, Germans and French: A Personal
Interpretation of France under Two Occupations, 1914–1918, 1940–1944* (Hanover,
NH: University Press of New England, 1983), 123, commenting on German
troops on leave in Paris.

57. Bradford. *Side Trips in Jamaica*, 37. This summary is from Alfred Leader, *Through
Jamaica with a Kodak* (Bristol: John Wright & Co, 1907), 191–2. It omits the
'tablets' at the Cathedral included in Bradford's original text.

58. The signatures and addresses in one surviving visitor's book from the old King's
House show a high proportion of visitors from Kingston, but also some from
other parishes. JA 1B/34/1/163, Old King's House Visitor's Book, 1879–80. This
volume was kept because it includes the signature of a visiting English Prince. A
royal visit would provide a social magnet in its own right, but visitors with
addresses elsewhere in Jamaica continued to come to Spanish Town over the
whole Christmas season the volume spans.

59. *World's Fair: Jamaica at Chicago* (New York: Pell, 1893), 42.

60. Edgar Mayhew Bacon and Eugene Murray Aaron, *The new Jamaica: describing the
island, explaining its conditions of life and growth and discovering its mercantile
relations and potential importance* (New York: Walbridge & Co, 1890), 89;
Bradford, *Side Trips in Jamaica*, 47.

61. RHL Ms W.I.s.22, Crosbie-Smith, *History of the Jamaica Constabulary*, the
accompanying photographs include a 1909 group of the Jamaica Constabulary's
detectives sitting on the porch of the Rio Cobre Hotel after a meal; Smith, *Travels
at Home and Abroad* 1, 47–8. This was in 1902.

62. Rampini, *Letters from Jamaica*, 45; Feurtado, *Forty-Five Years' Reminiscence*, 37; JA
7/12/198, f. 1, 31 October 1959, Massias.

63. Jack London and his wife undertook a pony-trekking tour of this sort. Ella
Wheeler Wilcox, *Sailing Sunny Seas: A Story of Travel* (Chicago, Ill: W.B. Conkey

Company, 1909), 40–41; UWI Mona, A.E.C[lark?], Three Days in Jamaica, (1906).

64. Smith, *Travels at Home and Abroad* 1, 48; James Johnston, *Jamaica: The New Riviera* (Brown's Town: for the author, 1903), 31; *is,* 73; Bradford, *Side Trips in Jamaica*, 40.

65. Smith, *Travels at Home and Abroad* 1, 47; Johnson, *Jamaica: The New Riviera*, 51.

66. 'History' was formally included in the local syllabus in 1893, Turner, 'Socialisation Intent', 69–70, and discussed in John Aarons, 'The Making of Cultural Policy in Colonial and Post-Colonial Jamaica', read to the History Department's Faculty/Graduate Seminar, University of the West Indies, Mona, 5 December 1997. The Rodney-as-hero phrase, Smith, *Travels at Home and Abroad* 1, 47. Elaborate explanations were themselves prone to misconceptions; another tourist's snapshot of the Rodney Memorial is miscaptioned as the 'Draden Monument', suggesting jumbled recollections. CLM F-512.3, J.A. Savage, 'A Winter Cruise to The West Indies', (1908), 17.

67. 'Rodney', 'Spanish Town's Ancient Glory', *Daily Gleaner* (26 June 1906). The editorial comment on this letter 'familiar suggestions put forward again' suggests why little came of these observations. I am grateful to Shakeira Maxwell for bringing this reference to my attention.

68. The room descriptions are cited on a plan of the building, made by the Public Works Office, Kingston. 6 March 1884. I consulted a copy in the JNHT basement plan chests. The visitor's notes, CLM F-512.3, Savage, 'Winter Cruise', 17. One locally published guidebook did urge visitors to 'get someone to take you through the building'. Johnston, *Jamaica: The New Riviera*, 31.

69. Johnston, *Jamaica: The New Riviera*, 31. This claim was certainly far more positive than a brisk dismissal offered in 1874, which asserted that 'with the exception of a few monuments' this 'ungainly-looking brick church' was 'not worth seeing'. Scott, *To Jamaica and Back*, 246.

70. Bradford, *Side Trips in Jamaica*, 45.

71. Henderson, *Jamaica*, 164. Unless they had the good fortune to encounter the rector or verger, who might invite them to climb the Cathedral tower, from which they could enjoy a splendid view of not only the town but the 'magnificent new prison and hospital'. "Master Tommy" [Thomas Carpenter Smith], 'Three Weeks in Jamaica', *Jamaican Historical Society Bulletin* 1:15 (1956): 189; Pullen-Burry, *Jamaica as it is*, 73,

72. Johnston, *Jamaica: The New Riviera*, 31.

73. Leader, *Through Jamaica with a Kodak*, 161.

74. Smith, *Travels at Home and Abroad* 1, 45.

75. Johnston, *Jamaica: The New Riviera*, 32.

76. Bradford, *Side Trips in Jamaica*, 46.

77. For a photographic record of such an itinerary, NGJ Matalon Collection, 'Album of Photographs', (1919).

78. Mrs Peter Marshall, 'Ye Ancient Capital of Jamaica', *Jamaica Standard* (30 May 1938): 8-9.

79. JA 1B/5/77/981, 'Tourist Trade Development Board, Erection of *Notice Boards* and Sign Posts'.

80. JA 4/90/37, 'A Trip to Jamaica July-August, 1905', 8 August 1905. As a booster for the island explained, after the Kingston fires of 1780, 1843, 1862, and 1882 'it is not to be wondered that the city . . . presents few features of architectural interest and contains few buildings of magnificent proportions'. *World's Fair: Jamaica at Chicago*, 9.

81. Harry A. Franck, *Roaming Through the West Indies* (New York: Century, 1921), 404; NLJ Ms 261, E.V. Lucas, 'Impressions of Jamaica', nd. [*c.* 1927], 4.

82. Chicago Historical Society, Morton, 'On the Spanish Main', 27. This was in 1912.

83. de Montuelé, *A Voyage*, 39, 22 March 1817; NLS, Acc. 5297 (1), A Trip to Jamaica, 1924, 1 February 1924.

84. Judah, *Old Saint Jago*, 23.

85. Rampini, *Letters from Jamaica*, 46.

86. Hakewill, *Picturesque Tour*, 'Bridge Over Rio Cobre at Spanish Town'; NLJ Ms 112, Yates, Journal, 1. f. 179, 17 December 1841.

87. NLJ 31, W.G. Freeman, 'Pickwick in Jamaica', f. 33; Bigelow, *Jamaica in 1850*, 31, also invoking 'Spanish' buildings, Bridges, *Annals of Jamaica* 1, 24. This last was published in 1828.

88. Marshall, 'Ancient Capital of Jamaica', 8–9; phrase from Franck, *Roaming Through the West Indies*, 415.

89. JA 7/32/305. 31 July 1914, Canon S. Purcell Hendricks to Archdeacon Simms, also 7/32/308, September 1914, Acting Colonial Secretary to Hendricks.

90. Algernon E. Aspinall, *A Wayfarer in the West Indies*, (London: Methuen, 1928), 221.

91. NLS Acc. 5297 (1), A Trip to Jamaica, 25 February 1924.

92. *A Happy Month in Jamaica* ([Boston, Mass.]: United Fruit Company, [*c.* 1902]), cited in *Duperly: An Exhibition of the Works of Adolphe Duperly . . .* (Kingston: National Gallery of Jamaica, 2001), 39; Pullen-Burry, *Jamaica as it is*, 7, advised staying for six weeks; Bradford, *Side Trips in Jamaica*, 17; UWI, Mona, A.E.C[lark?], 'Three Days in Jamaica', (1906); ship night, Edmund S. Whitman, *Those Wild West Indies* (New York: Sheridan House, 1938), 255–6.

93. William McFee, *The Gates of the Caribbean: The Story of a Great White Fleet Caribbean Cruise* ([Boston, Mass.]: United Fruit Steamship Service, 1922), 8–11.

94. Aspinall, *Wayfarer in the West Indies*, 217, the first 'American' hotel being the United Fruit Company's Myrtle Bank in Kingston; NLJ Ms 261, Lucas, 'Impressions of Jamaica', 4.

95. JA 1B/5/77/981, number 8, 29 February 1936, N.B. Livingston to Colonial Secretary, C.O. Woolley.

96. A 1937 guidebook recommended lunching in Kingston prior to driving out to Spanish Town, Eleanor Early, *Ports of the Sun: A Guide to the Caribbean, Bermuda, Nassau, Havana and Panama* (Boston, Mass: Houghton Mifflin, 1937), 191.
97. JA 1B/5/77/123, 'Visit to St Catherine's by the Governor', 17 April 1935.
98. 12 May 1937, *Programmes of Celebrations in Spanish Town on the occasion of The Coronation of Their Majesties King George VI and Queen Elizabeth* (np: [1937]), copy at JA 7/32/28.
99. Bacon and Aaron, *The New Jamaica*, 87.
100. Judah, *Old Saint Jago*, 29. The story is repeated in Black, *Spanish Town*, 24.
101. Feurtado, *Forty-Five Years' Reminiscence*, 39.
102. Barrington Chevannes, 'Garvey Myths among the Jamaican People', in Rupert Lewis and Patrick Bryan, eds., *Garvey: His Work and Impact*, 124.
103. JA 7/13/273, Notes re Jamaican folklore, May Jeffrey-Smith, 'Current Superstitious Beliefs, Rites and Customs in Jamaica: A study in folk lore', [1958], 'More Plant Lore', 4.
104. JA 7/13/273, 'Ghosts and Duppies & Obeah Practices', 'Ribba Mumma cont:d', 1–3.
105. Clinton Black, *Tales of Old Jamaica* (Kingston: Longman Caribbean, 1966), 33–8, offers an embroidered and Europeanized retelling of the story.
106. For the other 'gold table' story, this time at '21 Tamarind Tree pond' on the Lyndhurst Road in Lower St Andrew, see JA 7/12/173, f. 3, 15 November 1959, Leonce J. Chavannes, 'Memories, 1901–1959'.
107. Marshall, 'Ancient Capital of Jamaica', 8–9.
108. NLJ Ms 1820, Correspondence of Frank Cundall, 1910–1937, 'W', unfoliated, 13 December 1930, [   ] to Cundall.
109. I am grateful to the late T.O.B. Goldson for the gold-in-the-foundations story. The extent of the Iron Bridge's dilapidation is reported in Steven Panning, 'Observations on the State of the Iron Bridge, Spanish Town', *Jamaican Historical Society Bulletin* 11:5 (2000): 121–5. Subsequent repairs effected with the aid of grants from the World Monuments Fund and the Government of Jamaica have reconstructed the fronts of the piers.
110. JA 7/12/262, [1959], Daisy E. Jeffrey-Smith, 'Jamaican memories'.
111. JA 7/12/262, and 7/12/170, both [1959], Daisy E. Jeffrey-Smith, 'Jamaican memories'; also, transcribing the tunes from some of the period's cries, Astley Clerk, 'Kingston Street Cries *c.* 1927 and something about their Criers', *Jamaica Journal* 18:2 (1985): 11–7.
112. JA 7/12/261, f. 5, [1959], May Jeffrey-Smith, 'Life in Jamaica Over Sixty Years Ago'.
113. JA 7/12/262, f. 1, Daisy E. Jeffrey-Smith, 'Jamaican memories'.
114. Feurtado, *Forty-Five Years' Reminiscence*, 41–2.
115. Underhill, *Life of Phillippo*, 269; Hill, *Jamaican Stage*, 201.
116. Hill, *Jamaican Stage*, 55–6, 123; Bryan, *The Jamaican People*, 197.

117. JA 7/12/261, f. 5, [1959], May Jeffrey-Smith; 7/12/198, f. 2, 31 October 1959, Massias.

118. JA 1B/5/77/58 (1927), 'Records – Duplicate Registration – approval of building for depositing', for arguments why these rooms should not provide an overflow document store for the Island Records Office offered by 'R.G.' [Registrar General?], 25 July 1928.

119. JA 7/12/262, [1959], Daisy E. Jeffrey-Smith, 'I remember'; Feurtado, *Forty-Five Years' Reminiscence*, 32, 5.

120. The phrase, Thomas, *Story of a West Indian Policeman*, 340.

121. JA 7/12/198, 31 October 1959, Massias, 5–6. He was the youngest competitor and won a prize of six shillings.

122. For basic information on these two schools I drew on prospectuses that they each published: *Scheme and By-Laws of Beckford and Smith's School, Jamaica* (Kingston: Government Printing Office, 1915) and *Scheme and By-Laws of Cathedral High School, Spanish Town, Jamaica* (Kingston: Mortimer C. DeSousa, 1921). Copies are in the papers of a former Governor of both institutions, JA 7/28, Canon Jolly Papers, 'Schools and Education in Jamaica', items 320, 324. On the relocation of Beckford and Smith's School, JA 1B/5/77/172, (1929), Beckford & Smith's Old School Buildings – Sale of. The decision to move was taken 22 May 1925. Citing the trustees' minutes, ibid. item 20, 1 December 1944, D.E. Jeffrey Smith, Secretary, Beckford and Smith's School to Secretary Jamaica Schools Commission. The former brick schoolhouse by the Cathedral is still standing. It is now the Anglican church hall.

123. Ruby Hope King, 'The Jamaica Schools Commission and the Development of Secondary Schooling', (1979), rpt. in idem. ed., *Education in the Caribbean*, 99. The merits of this examination regime for class rooms in Jamaica was hardly self-evident. Initially, the American-educated Jesuits who staffed St George's College in Kingston preferred teaching a 'well-rounded liberal arts course' rather than 'preparing students for external examinations', but even there 'the importance of the Cambridge examination would grow with the years and so influence both content and method of teaching' as 'these examinations became the scholastic criteria of worth of a secondary school'. Osborne, *History of the Catholic Church in Jamaica*, 420–1.

124. NLJ Ms 2035, f.6, 1st Autobiography of Norman Washington Manley; Philip Sherlock, *Norman Manley* (London: Macmillan, 1980), 46–55. Here Manley's experience showed the role assigned within the island's late nineteenth-century educational system to the endowed schools in the individual parishes as feeders for the classical grammar school education offered at the re-established Jamaica College, King, 'Jamaican Schools Commission', 94–9.

125. Above, 251.

126. JA 7/32/210, 16 February 1914, Canon Hendricks to Board of Visitors, Beckford

and Smith's School; 7/32/211, 17 February 1914, Hendricks to W. Manley Esq.; 7/32/213, 18 February 1914, Manley to Hendricks. Manley was unable to take up the offer as he was already contracted to teach at Titchfield School in Port Antonio.

127. May Jeffrey-Smith, 'Guiding in Jamaica: The First Fifteen Years', *The Leaflet: The Official Publication of the Girl Guides Association of Jamaica* 19 (1955): 16; JA 7/13/31, May Jeffrey-Smith Papers, nd. [1964] Clare Graham, enclosure in 31 October 1964, Violet [ ] to May Jeffrey-Smith; the figures, 7/13/13, 6 May Jeffrey-Smith, 'A History of Guiding in Jamaica: The First Fifteen Years', (draft).

128. I am grateful to Verene Shepherd for recalling one such visit.

129. JA 7/12/262, [1959], Daisy E. Jeffrey-Smith, 'Jamaican memories'; on traveling by railway, 7/12/264, [1959], May Jeffrey-Smith, 'I remember'.

130. JA 7/12/262, [1959], Daisy E. Jeffrey-Smith, 'Jamaica memories'. As with all generalizations, there were exceptions and some subscription balls were staged in Spanish Town, including one in 1884 when the future King George V visited Jamaica. Thomas, *Story of a West India Policeman*, 69.

131. *Lady Nugent's Journal*, 132–4, December 1802; NLJ Ms 112, Yates, Journal, 1. f. 170, 2 December 1841; Ms 1900, Titford Letterbook, Letter 50, 5 December 1806, having received no tickets to the public balls Titford was obliged to have a dance 'at my house'.

132. Underhill, *Life of Phillippo*, 378. In the Phillippos' case the break was particularly abrupt as 'His eldest son with his family also was obliged to follow'.

133. JA 1B/5/79/375, Release of Marcus Garvey from St Catherine District Prison, 1929. File includes a confidential memo, 13 December 1929, 'I am typing this myself', and two letters, 29 November 1929 and 10 December 1929, Governor R. Edward Stubbs to Chief Justice Sir Fiennes Barrett-Lennard. The letters are published in *Marcus Garvey and Universal Negro Improvement Association Papers*, 362–3; on the proposed procession, Rupert Lewis, *Marcus Garvey: Anti-Colonial Champion* (Trenton, NJ: 1988), 218–9.

134. Nor were they necessarily alone. That year another group from the Jamaica Trades and Labour Union apparently provided an audience for a speech given by a Communist from North America. Post, *Arise Ye Starvelings*, 4. The speaker was Otto Hiuswoud. His speaking engagements included audiences in Kingston, at Green Island in Hanover and 'possibly' Spanish Town.

135. Bryan, *The Jamaican People*, 144.

136. Though its local reputation was dented. In 1906 the Bank of Nova Scota was able to take advantage of its rival's vulnerability and secure the Colonial government's accounts, Quigley, 'Bank of Nova Scotia', 810.

137. Brodber, 'The Second Generation of Freemen in Jamaica', 82. The cuts are described in Turner, 'Socialisation Intent', 74–7.

138. This is a subjective opinion based on my examining registers of land titles from the 1920s held at the Land Titles Office, Kingston. On the social prestige attached

to bungalows at this juncture, Elizabeth Pigou-Dennis, 'The Jamaican Bungalow: Whose Language?' in Monteith and Richards, *Jamaica in Slavery and Freedom*, 185–91.

139. Albinia C. Hutton, *Life in Jamaica: A Series of Sketches* (London: Arthur H. Stockwell, nd. [1926/7]), 6.

140. Roberts, *Population of Jamaica*, 151.

141. Anthony Johnson, *J.A.G. Smith* (Kingston: Kingston Publishers and Jamaica Institute of Political Education, 1991), 63; its ownership by the United Fruit Company, Chalmin, *Making of a Sugar Giant*, 311.

142. JA 1B/5/77/43, (1927), 'Proposed Contour survey of the Irrigable land in St Catherine, 1927–8'. This project followed hard on the heels of an extension of the irrigation network east towards the Ferry River in the early 1920s which mostly directed river water to the United Fruit Company's plantations in that area. The main questions engaging official attention were possible conflicts of interest should a further hydroelectric scheme to power the irrigation scheme's own pumps need to draw on this water. 1B/5/77/5, (1927), 'Report on the Rio Cobre Extension Scheme by Irrigation Adviser', C.F. Stewart Baker; 1B/5/77/59, (1926), 'United Fruit Company in relation to the Ferry River Scheme', and for proposals and costings, PRO CO 137/781/8, May-December 1926.

143. Owen Rutter, *If Crab No Walk: A Traveler in the West Indies* (London: Hutchinson, 1933), 159.

144. In the early 1930s the Caymanas Estate to the east of the town was still planting bananas while the United Fruit Company sought more land too, obtaining a lease to plant bananas on an 11¼ acre plot near to the Gregory Park railway station, the next stop east of Spanish Town on the line to Kingston. The trend continued into 1935, when the United Fruit Company arranged for a new tramway to cross the main Spanish Town-Kingston road to take fruit south to their banana pier. Developments at the Caymanas Estate, Rutter, *If Crab No Walk*, 157–9; the field at Gregory Park, IRO Deeds, n.s. 378, 6 March 1931, ff. 225–9, Colonial Secretary to United Fruit Company; the tramway, Deeds, n.s. 454, ff. 201–204, 22 February 1935, Lease, Parish of St Catherine to United Fruit Company.

145. Hutton, *Life in Jamaica*, 28.

146. Brown, 'King's House Fire, 1925', 153–7.

147. JA 1B/5/79/325, 'Rum Store: Spanish Town, 1926–7'.

148. John M. Lynch, letter 16 April 1929, published *Daily Gleaner* (18 April 1929); 20 April, 1929, idem. to Lady Swettenham, and 26 April 1929, idem. testimonial. PRO CO 137/788/12, item 13.

149. Marquardt, '"Green Havoc",' 49–80; Jenkins, *Bananas*, 42–4, 48–55.

150. From 1931 new techniques in boring deep wells permitted the irrigation of lands around Old Harbour, ten miles to the west of Spanish Town. These virgin fields were planted with bananas and initially yielded well. By the 1940s the Panama

Disease spread there too. NLJ Ms 1954, Box B, SAG Taylor Papers, 'The History of St Catherine', 34.

151. Sealy and Hart, *Jamaica's Banana Industry*, 2, 7, 10; Davies, *Fyffes and the Banana*, 150. The initial supplies of bananas for the British market came from the Canary Islands which grew thinner-skinned bananas. The existing British distribution network was therefore ready to handle *lacatan* bananas when they arrived from Jamaica.

152. JA 1B/5/79/192, 'Railway, Sale of', [25 October 1927], Governor's annotation on cover of file. This was in replying to a query from a Kingston solicitor, H.A. Laselve Simpson, writing 'on behalf of clients having large business and financial interests in Canada and the United States of America', whether 'it is a desire of your government to sell the Jamaica Railway'.

153. Eisner, *Jamaica 1830–1930*, 365, 180–81.

154. Bland, *Report of the Jamaica Government Railway, passim*. A response by the Director of the railway laid even more emphasis on the competition from road haulers. JA 1B/5/77/289, (1926), 1 March 1937, Director, Jamaica Government Railway to Colonial Secretary.

155. JA 1B/5/77/18, (1928), 'Banana lands on the Prison Farm at Spanish Town to be used for experimental purposes'.

156. These options are discussed more fully in Annette Constance Brown, 'The Old King's House, Spanish Town, 1872–1962', MA. thesis, UWI, Mona, (1999). This paragraph benefited from several discussions with Ms Brown as she completed her valuable thesis.

157. Rutter, *If Crab no Walk*, 153.

158. PRO CO 137/788/12, item 16, 2 September 1929, Mary Swettenham to Sir Martin Conway, MP.

159. The phrase, PRO CO 137/788/12, item 9, 25 April 1929, Mary Swettenham to Lord Sandon.

160. NLJ Ms 169, Hubert C. Corlette, 'The King's House in the King's Square, Spanish Town, Jamaica', ([London], Lincoln's Inn, 1932), a draft typescript, to Old King's House Restoration Committee. Further copies are in the UWI Mona Library, West Indies Collection and enclosed in PRO CO 137/796/10, item 7.

161. Thus both for Lady Swettenham's attempt to get a plug for the rebuilding scheme included in a speech of welcome from the Legislative Council to two royal visitors and for a comment by the then Colonial Secretary that it 'will amuse and astonish you (if indeed one can yet be astonished by Lady Swettenham).' JA 1B/5/77/191, (1931), 'Visit to Jamaica of the Prince of Wales and Prince George – Welcoming address', 17 December 1930, Mary Swettenham to da Costa, and 22 December 1930, Colonial Secretary to Governor.

162. JA 1B/5/77/51, (1927), 'Historic Sites and Monuments, Preservation of', annotations on cover, undated, and by 'R.E.S.' [R.E. Stubbs (?), Governor, about 22

August 1927]. The proposal aimed to revive an older project listing Jamaica's historical monuments initiated in 1908.

163. 'Old King's House Frontage New Again!' *Daily Gleaner* (9 March 1938): 13.
164. 'Friends of the Cathedral', nd. (1930s). A copy is in JA 4/31, Canon Jolly, Scrapbooks. I am grateful to Alaric Joseph for alerting me to this collection.
165. JA 1B/5/77/85, (1928), 'Restoration of the Cathedral at Spanish Town, 1928/32'.
166. The superlative, Aspinall, *Wayfarer in the West Indies*, 222.
167. The 'rough labour' phrase, JA 1B/5/77/859, (1935), 'Plans being undertaken for the relief of unemployment in St Catherine', initial 'minutes', 49, item 181, 25 November 1938, [Director, Public Works Department?] to Colonial Secretary.
168. Norman Manley, 5 March 1944, quoted in Edna Manley, *The Diaries*, 14.
169. A. Carliss, 'The Official Attitude Towards the Elected Members of the Jamaican Legislative Council, 1918–1938', *Jamaica Journal* 7:3 (1973): 7. The currency of the 'natives' phrase, Olivier, *Jamaica*, 10–11.
170. Sir Arthur Lewis, the St. Lucian Nobel Prize winner in Economics, quoted in Sherlock and Bennett, *Story of the Jamaican People*, 349.
171. Anthony Kirk-Green, '"Not Quite a Gentleman": The Desk Diaries of the Assistant Private Secretary (Appointments) to the Secretary of State for the Colonies, 1899–1935', *English Historical Review* 117 (2002): 631.
172. JA 1B/5/77/859, (1935), item 46. 18 October 1936, Leo A. Bonello to Governor. On the wider public distrust, Johnson, *J.A.G. Smith*, 58–60.
173. de Lisser, *Twentieth Century Jamaica*, 161, and more forcefully still in John Henderson's 1906 reports of discussions of Jamaica's prospects and politics, *Jamaica*, 103–18.
174. Franck, *Roaming Through the West Indies*, 406–7.
175. UWI Mona, Winifred M. Cousins Papers, 'Freedom in Jamaica', (nd. but reflecting opinions from the mid-1920s); on the action by the elected members of the Legislative Council in 1924 in censoring an expatriate official, Carnegie, *Some Aspects*, 74–5; for those potential white candidates, Governor Sir Samuel Wilson in 1925, quoted in Carliss, 'The Official Attitude', 7.
176. JA 1B/5/77/15, (1935), 'Visit of Governor Edward Denham to St Catherine'. This file also includes material on his successor's visit: 29 August 1939, Governor Richards at a special meeting of the St Catherine parochial board.
177. JA 1B/5/77/859, (1935), item 90A, 23 June 1937, The speech was delivered at a union meeting in Linstead.
178. JA 1B/5/77/859, (1935), item 46, 18 October 1936, Bonello to Governor.
179. Early, *Ports of the Sun*, 196. Nor was she alone in expressing this view, in 1926 the town could appear 'a dreary place in the midst of a sun-baked plain'. Hutton, *Life in Jamaica*, 28.
180. JA 1B/5/77/859, (1935), item 53a, 28 October 1936, T.N. Drake, Inspector i/c St Catherine to Inspector General of Police.

181. JA 1B/5/77/859, (1935), item 71, 11 December 1936, E.A. McNeill, Chair, Parochial Board, St Catherine, to Colonial Secretary.

182. JA 1B/5/77/859, (1935), item 127, 8 May 1938, Resolution moved by Leslie Washington Rose, Divisional Secretary, Jamaica Workers and Tradesmen Union. These claims were repeated a year later, item 227, 16 August 1939, Resolution now moved by Rose as Vice President, Bustamante Industrial Trades Union.

183. PRO CO 137/817/11, item 8, 29 March 1937, Sir Edward Denham, 'Memorandum on Unemployment in Jamaica'. This was sent to the Secretary of State for the Colonies in response to a request for current information from the Governor after a British MP asked questions in Parliament about the situation in Kingston.

184. Olivier, *Jamaica*, 38. Discussing the reform of the government's forestry policy in 1937, Rita Pemberton, 'Protecting Caribbean environments: The development of the forest conservation in Jamaica, 1855–1941', in Fouch *et al.* eds., *Regards sur l'historie de la Caraïbe*, 271–2.

185. Carnegie, *Some Aspects*, 115–16. Carnegie's list of Citizens Associations does not include the Spanish Town Association, ibid. 179. The Secretary for the Spanish Town Association was 'R.A. Peat', presumably Reginald Albert Peat, a local brewer's son, educated at Beckford and Smith's School, who up to 1935 was a member of the Jamaican Civil Service. He then left for Scotland to train as a medical doctor. *Who's Who, Jamaica, British West Indies, 1941–1946* (Kingston: Who's Who (Jamaica), Ltd, 1946), 471, 'Peat, Reginald Albert'. He retained a close interest in Jamaican affairs and after the 1938 riots wrote from Aberdeen to the Colonial Office in London offering a variety of suggestions, PRO CO 137/836/3, 16 February 1939, R.A. Peat to Under Secretary of State, Colonial Office. There is, as yet, no study of these groups or how far their leaders and members provided recruits for the People's National Party. I am grateful to Rupert Lewis for discussing this question with me.

186. JA 1B/5/77/100, (1933), page 3, comment 7, [Governor], 29 September 1933. These views would be confirmed by 40 years of Colonial Office practice in propping up existing social hierarchies rather than listening to urban or educated groups, David Cannadine, *Ornamentalism: How the British Saw their Empire* (New York: Oxford University Press, 2001).

187. *Who's Who and Why in Jamaica* 2. *1939–1940*, 135–6, Captain Henry Wilfred Scott McGrath, custos, a cattle breeder at Charlemount and ibid. 138, Eustice Augustus McNeill, Legislative Council Member, a large scale banana grower at Troja on the northern side of the former parish of St Thomas in the Vale. In 1930 McNeill had run for election with Marcus Garvey's support – but had been defeated.

188. JA 1B/5/77/15, (1935), 'Visit of Governor Edward Denham to St Catherine', this file includes not only full transcripts of the custos's speech and the Governor's reply, tactfully noting 'laughter' after His Excellency's witticisms, but also a preliminary draft of the custos's speech and the note-taking preliminaries for the

official answers. Townspeople's worries about patients wandering from the leper hospital proved a persistent issue, 1B/5/77/100, (1933), 'Lepers visiting the business places, etc, Spanish Town', item 1, 1 September 1933, R.A. Peat, Spanish Town Citizens' Association to Acting Colonial Secretary, also ibid. item 10, 10 November 1933, same to same, and item 13, 23 April 1937, memorandum of a visit by the parish's Legislative Council Member to the Colonial Secretary and associated comments.

189. Itinerary from JA 1B/5/77/15, (1935), 'Visit of Governor Edward Denham to St Catherine', 2 April 1935,

190. 20 December 1934, Leslie Washington [Rose], President, Spanish Town Division, UNIA to Governor, in JA 1B/5/77/88, (1935), 'Invitation to Governor Denham to visit Spanish Town Slum Areas'.

191. Spanish Town UNIA, resolutions, 2 January 1935 and 23 April 1935, also cover sheet, nd. [1935], all in JA 1B/5/77/88, (1935).

192. On both the Land Settlement Law and the Kellets scheme in Clarendon Parish, Johnson, *J.A.G. Smith*, 113–15, 192–3; and, more generally, Marleen A. Bartley, 'Land Settlement in Jamaica, 1923–1949', in Monteith and Richards, *Jamaica in Slavery and Freedom*, 324–39, along with the contemporary comments offered in Olivier, *Jamaica*, 286-89, and JA 1B/5/77/5, (1938), Land Association in Jamaica, Memorandum by the Jamaica Imperial Association and, reporting on a 1940 scheme in St Mary, James Wright, 'An Experiment in Land Settlement at Lucky Hill, Jamaica', *Caribbean Quarterly* 1:2 (1949): 29–39. Claus Stolberg is more pessimistic about the practical impact of these projects, 'British Colonial Policy and the Great Depression – the Case of Jamaica', *Journal of Caribbean History* 23 (1989): 150–1, and 'Plantation Economy, Peasantry and the Land Settlement Schemes of the 1930s and 1940s in Jamaica', in idem. and Swithin R. Wilmot, eds., *Plantation Economy, Land Reform and the Peasantry in a Historical Perspective: Jamaica 1838–1980* (Kingston: Friedrich Ebert Stifung, 1992), 43–50. The ups and downs of the British West India Regiment veterans' scheme in St Catherine, Coolshade, can be traced in the Colonial Secretary's Office's files, for example 1B/5/77/80, (1935), 'Ex-BWIR. Soldiers – Land Settlements St Catherine'. Police reports on Howell and the settlement on the Sligoville road are included in, 1B/5/77/283, (1934), 'Information relating to Ras Tafarian followers in St Catherine'. When the camp closed down in 1944 after Howell's arrest and imprisonment it housed some 500 people, 300 adults and 200 children under 14.

193. JA 1B/5/77/859, item 157B, quotation at f. 6. Transcript of questions and answers at a meeting organized by the custos of St Catherine 'of employers and representatives of labour . . . in the Court House, Spanish Town, 8 June, 1938'; ibid. item 161, 11 August 1938, W.J. Bird, Divisional Secretary Bustamante General Workers Union, Spanish Town to C.M. Woolley, Officer Administering Colonial

Government. This was after the death of Governor Denham and before his replacement's arrival.

194. Minutes of Special Meeting, St Catherine Parochial Board, 29 August 1939, copy in JA 1B/5/77/123, (1935), 'Visit to St Catherine's by the Governor'.

195. JA 1B/5/77/293, (1938), vol II. 'Well-Being of the Colony Returns,' item. 10, 22 April 1938, W. Beaumont to Inspector General.

196. On 23 May 1938, two days after dock strikes resumed in Kingston and when crowds in Kingston's Parade were broken up by police supported by British soldiers, sanitary workers in Spanish Town took the lead in going out on strike too, which then escalated into 'a general strike and demonstrations', Post, *Arise ye Starvelings*, 281.

197. JA 1B/5/77/859, (1935), item 147, 13 May 1938, McGrath, custos of St Catherine, to Colonial Secretary.

198. The 2 April 1935, date for the foundation of the union is cited in JA 1B/5/77/859, (1935), initial 'minutes', iv. item 7, 23 April 1935, Report from Inspector General of Police to Colonial Secretary.

199. JA 1B/5/77/859, (1935), item 17, [September], 1936, Rose to Governor.

200. JA 1B/5/77/859, (1935), item 18, 10 September 1936, Acting Inspector General, Jamaica Constabulary to Colonial Secretary.

201. Lawrence Washington Rose was born at Spitzbergen, Walderston, Manchester in 1905. For this and his earlier UNIA experience, *Who's Who Jamaica, 1941–1946*, 'Rose, Lawrence Washington', 510; JA 1B/5/77/859, (1935), the 'principal mover' phrase, initial minutes, iv, item 7, 23 April 1925, Inspector General of Police to Colonial Secretary. The union's first address, ibid. item 1, 2 April 1935, Lawrence Washington Rose, (as Union Corresponding Secretary) to Governor, which gives the same Young Street address as the UNIA branch's correspondence to the Governor earlier in the year (later letters do not include a street address); and item 9, 16 April 1935, same to same, for the resolution and mass meeting format, similarly, item 15, 6 June 1935, same to same. As a Branch of the Jamaica Workers and Tradesmen Union its address for correspondence changed, to 26 Cumberland Street. L.E. Barnett, another important early official was a returning Jamaican resident who had served as Vice-President of the Limon Federation Union in Costa Rica. Post, *Arise Ye Starvelings*, 243. He later became more involved in the activities of the union's Linstead branch,

202. JA 1B/5/77/859, (1935), item 157A, f. 2, 23 June 1938, McGrath, custos of St Catherine, to Chairman, Board of Conciliation, 'Confidential'. Erna Brodber argues that promoting black self-confidence was itself a central element in Garveyism's appeal for Jamaicans, 'Marcus Garvey and the Politicisation of some Afro-Jamaicans in the 1920s and 1930s', *Jamaica Journal* 20:3 (1987): 66–72.

203. JA 1B/5/77/859, (1935), 'minutes', 6v, item 33, 17 October 1936, Acting Inspector General of Police to Colonial Secretary. There is, as yet, no analysis of A.G.S.

Coombs as a pioneering union leader or of the recommendations proposed by the union he led. It was founded in Kingston, 17 May 1936. For summaries of Coombs' dealings with Alexander Bustamante see Post, *Arise Ye Starvelings*, 250–60, also, George E. Eaton, *Alexander Bustamante and Modern Jamaica* (Kingston: Kingston Publishers, 1975), 34–6, and Richard Hart, *Towards Decolonisation: Political, Labour and Economic Developments in Jamaica, 1938–1945* (Kingston: University of the West Indies Press, 1999), *passim*. On Norman Manley's intervention in these disputes in 1939, Sherlock, *Norman Manley*, 105–07.

204. 'Jamaica Workers and Tradesmen Union', *Daily Gleaner* (20 October 1936), reporting a meeting on Sunday 18 October 1936.

205. JA 1B/5/77/859, (1935), item, 157B, ff. 1–2, 8 June 1938, transcript of 'A meeting summoned by the Custos of employers and representatives of labour held in the Court House, Spanish Town'. The questions about Bustamante's current status were posed twice.

206. Post, *Arise ye Starvelings*, 350. This was on 26 June 1938. In November 1937, in an earlier split within the Jamaica Workers and Tradesmen's Union, Rose and the St Catherine Union had sided with Bustamante, ibid. 259.

207. JA 1B/5/77/859, (1935), item 70, 17 December 1936, Colonial Secretary to L.W. Rose.

208. Osborne, *History of the Catholic Church*, 367–71.

209. Other parishes had secured co-operative banks earlier. For the Spanish Town based institutions, see IRO Deeds, n.s. 518, f. 364, 5 April 1939, mortgage to Zachariah Hibbert. The property was near Old Harbour. The loan document was signed in Spanish Town by the Secretary to the Lower St Catherine People's Co-Operative Bank. This is the earliest mortgage by the Bank that I have identified. It was for one year. Many others were for shorter terms. For example, Deeds, n.s. 537, ff. 212–25, for a block of 20 mortgages from early 1940. An early mortgage by the St Catherine Mutual Building Society is enrolled in Deeds, n.s. 563, ff. 309–311, 10 October 1940, to Jeremiah Osgill of Brunswick Street, Spanish Town.

210. JA 1B/5/77/293, (1938), vol. II, 'Well-Being of the Colony', 17 October 1938, L. Beaumont to Inspector General of Police, f. 2.

211. JA 1B/5/77/23, (1942), Poor Relief, St Catherine, vol. 1, Minute, no. 7, 11 February 1942, Secretary, Board of Control to Colonial Secretary. For 'laxity', Minute no. 3, 5 November 1941, Acting Colonial Secretary to Secretary, Board of Control.

212. Editorial, 'Then and Now', *Daily Gleaner* (19 April 1943), reprinted in James G. Allen, *Editorial Opinion in the Contemporary British Commonwealth and Empire* (University of Colorado Studies, series C, Studies in the Social Sciences, 1:4, Boulder, Colo: the University, 1946), 566–8.

213. JA 1B/5/77/83, (1943), House of Assembly and Legislative Council – offers of premises for housing of.

214. Sherlock, *Norman Manley*, 122–39.
215. *House of Representatives*, Minutes, 17 September 1946. See JA 1B/5/77/871, (1935), 'Unemployment, St Catherine, 1944–1948', 3 parts, part 1.

Epilogue

1. Jean Rhys, *Wide Sargasso Sea* (London, 1966, rpt New York: Norton, 1982), 28.
2. For historical introductions to the social and political changes during the last 60-years the 1969 and 1996 editions of David Buisseret, *Historic Jamaica from the Air* are both invaluable, while Patrick Bryan's *Inside Out & Outside In*, provides valuable thumbnail sketch. There are no studies of Spanish Town itself during this period, but changing official attitudes towards urban issues in pre-independence Jamaica can be followed in Colin Clarke's *Kingston, Jamaica: Urban Development and Social Change, 1692–1962*. Recent general histories of Jamaica cover the period. Thus the final two chapters of Samuel J. and Edith Hurwitz, *Jamaica: A Historical Portrait* (London: Pall Mall, 1971), offer a brisk overview of the preceding 30 years. The pre-Independence political narrative can be followed in Trevor Munroe's *Politics of Constitutional Decolonisation,* though this study is not particularly sympathetic for interpreting developments in a town that remained a stronghold of the Jamaica Labour Party. The biographies by Philip Sherlock of *Norman Manley* and by George Eaton of *Alexander Bustamante* are both helpful. The relevant volume of the *British Documents on the End of Empire Series*, (Series B:6), S.R. Ashton and David Killingray, eds., *The West Indies* (London: HMSO for Institute of Commonwealth Studies, 1999), presents a metropolitan view of the West Indies Federation project and of its breakdown. Useful insights on the priorities shaping the island's postwar development-driven economy can be found in Carlton E. Davis, *Jamaica in the World Aluminium Industry, 1938–1988* 2 vols (Kingston: Jamaica Bauxite Institute, 1989, 1995) and Patrick Bryan, *Jamaica: The Aviation Story* (Kingston: Arawak Publications, 2003). On wider social trends Rex Nettleford, ed., *Jamaica in Independence: Essays on the Early Years* (Kingston: Heinemann, 1989), provides Jamaican perspectives. Anthony J. Payne's essays, *Politics in Jamaica* (London, 1988, rev ed Kingston: Ian Randle Publishers, 1994), and a further essay by Brian Meeks, 'Jamaica's Michael Manley (1924–97): Crossing the Contours of Charisma', in Anton L. Allahar, ed., *Caribbean Charisma: Reflections on Leadership, Legitimacy and Populist Politics* (Kingston: Ian Randle Publishers, 2001), 192–211, offer suggestive insights. The republished columns by two newspaper commentators collect contemporaries' views of affairs. Morris Cargill, *Morris Cargill: A Selection of his Writings in the Gleaner, 1952–1985* ed., Deryck Roberts, (Kingston: Tropical Publishers, 1987); idem. *Public Disturbances: a Collection of Writings 1986–1996* ed., David D'Costa (Kingston:

Mill Press, 1998), along with Carl Stone, *The Stone Columns: The Last Year's Work* ed., Rosemarie Stone, (Kingston: Sangster's, 1994).

3. PRO CO 137/790/2, item 6, 7 June 1930, Sir Reginald Stubbs, Governor of Jamaica to Lord Pasfield, Secretary of State for the Colonies.

4. Satchell and Sampson, 'Rise and fall of railways', 10; JA 1B/5/77/680, (1935), 'UNIA Representation and Correspondence, 1943–46', comment sheet, pages 3–4, memo number 15, 24 April 1944 Chairman, Transport (Defense) Board, refusing a request by the UNIA for permission for a member to run a bus between Kingston and Spanish Town, as 'in order to curtail the use of tires and petrol, all duplicating Services have been discontinued'.

5. Amy Oakley, *Behold the West Indies* (New York: Appleton-Century, 1941), 100. In 1944 the members of the Irvine Commission, investigating the options for tertiary education in the West Indies, followed the same route when they drove over to the north side of the island. UWI Mona, R.E. Priestley, 'My West Indian Journey', 1, 4 April 1944.

6. B.W. Thompson, *Black Caribbean* (London: Macdonald, 1946), 257–58; commenting on American servicemen going out with local girls 'in Spanish Town, or May Pen', ibid. 83.

7. JA 1B/5/77/613, (2), Unemployment, St Catherine, 28 August 1941, Labour Advisor to Colonial Secretary. In the event transport proved difficult and the numbers coming from Spanish Town remained low in relation to the town's high unemployment rates. This would not prevent some local landowners and employers from blaming the 'very large number of people [who] obtained work on the United States Air Base at Sandy Gully in Kingston' for the difficulties they found 'in obtaining a sufficient quantity of work men'. 1B/5/77/293, vol 3 'Well-being of Colony', 17 January 1942, Inspector i/c, St Catherine to Inspector General.

8. AKA, Mission Station 'S,' St Joseph – Spanish Town, 21 September 1944, Fr. Gilday, to Bishop.

9. JA 7/109, Donor Miss Violet M. Hill. US Army Air Corps aerial photographic map of Jamaica.

10. JA 1B/5/77/613 (2), 2 October 1941, Labour Adviser to Colonial Secretary and 17 October, 1941, same to same.

11. Thompson, *Black Caribbean*, 67.

12. JA 1B/5/77/122, (1943), 'Roads – Kingston/Spanish Town – Deviation at White Marl', item 65, 15 September 1945, Alexander Bustamante to Acting Colonial Secretary.

13. Jamaica Tourist Trade Development Board and the Tourist Trade Convention Committee, *Survey and Report on the Potentialities of the Tourist Industry of Jamaica, with Recommendations for Post-War Development* (Kingston: Government Printer, 1945), 1, 7.

14. JA 1B/34/6/2, unfoliated, 10 October 1958, Gene McDonald (General Manager, Martin's Tours) to Governor Sir Kenneth Blackburne. These remarkable calculations were undertaken by 'the Statistical Section of our Accounting Department'.
15. In New Bern, North Carolina, another eighteenth-century capital city, where the burnt-out ruins of the colonial-era governor's palace were restored in the 1950s, a *circa* 1990 estimate by the local Convention and Visitors' Bureau for tourists' spending suggested that 'the average impact per night with thirty five people on a bus is about three thousand dollars with food, tours, fuel, shopping and overnight accommodation'. Colin W. Barnett, *The Impact of Historic Preservation on New Bern, North Carolina: From Tryon Palace to the Coor-Cook House* (Winston-Salem, NC: Bandit Books, 1993), 87. This figure is in United States dollars.
16. JA 1B/5/77/293, vol. 3, 'Well-being of Colony', 17 January 1942, Inspector i/c, St Catherine to Inspector General.
17. Smith, *Travels at Home and Abroad* 2, 18, in 1906; also noted in JA 4/90/37, 'A Trip to Jamaica', 8 August 1905; Chicago Historical Society, Sterling Morton, 'On the Spanish Main', 25–26, in 1912, and in Franck, *Roaming Through the West Indies*, 414, in the early 1920s.
18. Marking some of the cultural shifts that this transition required, Theodore Sealy, *Industrialization of Jamaica* (Kingston: Gleaner, 1952).
19. 'Pottery Co. uses local staff with great results', *Sunday Gleaner* (24 February 1963): 19.
20. Davis, *Jamaica in the World Aluminium Industry, I, 1938–1973*, 65–89; the expert, Edna Manley, *The Diaries*, 49, 1 April 1955. W. Stanley Moss, column, *Daily Gleaner* (6 July 1962)
21. Hugh Foot, *A Start in Freedom* (London: Hodder and Stoughton, 1964), 130.
22. 'Modern ceramics plant for Jamaica: Royal Worcester project', *Daily Gleaner* (23 March 1962); invoking the prospective American competitor, 'A Shot in the Arm for Jamaica: British firm shows the way', *Guardian* (9 February 1962). All these clippings are included in NLJ HN 'Pottery'.
23. '4,000-Piece set for Banquet', *Daily Gleaner* (24 May 1962).
24. 'Jamaica's new dinnerware designs by Vera big hit', *Daily Gleaner* (25 June 1964): 3.
25. Vincent Hill, 'Distribution and Potential – Clays in Jamaica', *Jamaica Journal* 42 (1978): 73.
26. I am grateful to Norma Harrack for discussing this point with me.
27. Hugh B. Cave, *Four Paths to Paradise: A Book about Jamaica* (Garden City, NY: Doubleday, 1961), 302.
28. Even a brisk examination of the post-hurricane Damage Reports for Spanish Town compiled by the local tax office shows a disheartening number of buildings written off as a 'total loss' or else sustaining severe damage. JA 1B/80/12/119, Spanish Town Tax Office, Hurricane Damage Reports, 1951. 29 December 1953, [T.O.B. Goldson, ed.,] *Souvenir Brochure of the Spanish Town Methodist Church*

(Kingston: Gleaner Company for Methodist Church, Spanish Town, 1953).

29. I am grateful to Deacon Ivy Scot of the Phillippo Baptist Church for this point.

30. Kingston, Land Titles Office, Liber 821, f. 85, 27 December 1956.

31. *St Joseph's Centenary History*, (unpaginated). The initial post-hurricane report on the Gregory Park church had described it as only suffering 'minor damage', while the church at Port Henderson was 'entirely destroyed'. 'Hurricane Damage to Mission Property', *Catholic Opinion* (26 August 1951): 6.

32. Mona Macmillan, *The Land of Look Behind: A Study of Jamaica* (London: Faber, 1957), 142–3.

33. The prewar antecedents of this factory, and the wartime stalling by the main British supplier of cement to Jamaica are described in Hart, *Towards Decolonisation*, 107–12.

34. On this process of transformation, Concannon, 'Our Architectural Heritage', 23–8.

35. 19 February 1950, *Order of Service held at the Cathedral Church of St Jago de la Vega, Spanish Town, on the occasion of the instilation of H.R.H. the Princess Alice, Countess of Athlone, as Chancellor of the University College of the West Indies* (copy at JA 7/32/10); Sherlock and Nettleford, *University of the West Indies*, 35-7.

36. 'The Royal Visit', *Jamaican Historical Society Bulletin* 1:6 (1953): 67–8; 'Dialect Verse: On the Occasion of Her Majesty's Visit to Spanish Town, 1953', JA 7/13/272, Poems Written by May Jeffrey-Smith.

37. 20 February 1955, *Form of Service . . . The Service will be attended by Her Royal Highness the Princess Margaret*. A ticket uses the phrase 'State Service', copy at JA 7/32/16. This was not the official tercentenary thanksgiving service, which was held in November. Cf. JA 7/32/17, 13 November 1955.

38. Edna Manley, *The Diaries*, 62.

39. Michelle A. Johnson, '"To Dwell Together in Unity": Referendum on West Indian Federation, 1961', in Moore and Wilmot, *Before and After 1865*, 261.

40. I am grateful to Roy Augier for discussing these questions with me.

41. Clinton V. Black, *Our Archives* (Kingston: Government Printer, 1962), 7–9.

42. JA 1B/34/6/1, 12 August 1958, Donald Sangster to Sir Kenneth Blackburne.

43. Brown, 'The Old King's House', found the papers of the King's House Restoration Committee and offers a fuller discussion of this material. For a contemporary summary, JA 1B/34/6/1, 11 September 1957, 'Memorandum on a Proposed National and Historical Museum in Spanish Town'.

44. Sherlock and Nettleford, *University of the West Indies*, 48–51.

45. 'Memorandum on a Proposed National Historical Museum in Spanish Town', 3.

46. Kenneth Blackburne, *Lasting Legacy: A Story of British Colonialism* (London: Johnson Publications, 1976), 160. The Governor's own phrase.

47. 'Memorandum on a Proposed National Historical Museum in Spanish Town', 2.

48. JA 1B/34/6/4, 17 January 1962, Bernard Lewis to Blackburne.

49. Macmillan, *Land of Look Behind*, 143.

50. Cave, *Four Paths to Paradise*, 303. This was published in 1961.

51. Chevannes, 'Garvey Myths', 128.

52. See above, 283.

53. 'Opening of the Arawak Museum at White Marl', *Jamaican Historical Society Bulletin* 4:4 (1965): 63. Discussing the 'dry' original exhibit design – which has since been reorganized. Sharon Chacko, 'Museum Representation of the Taino and Cultural Power in the Columbian Quincentenary', in Monteith and Richards, *Jamaica in Slavery and Freedom*, 194–221.

54. The chronology of local archaeologists' recognition of what was being lost and their efforts to salvage something from the site is sketched in Allsworth-Jones, 'White Marl site summary'. Some excavators published their findings.

55. *Town and Country Planning (Spanish Town) Provisional Development Order, 1964* (Kingston: Government Printer, 1964), 6–7. Conservation areas were only introduced in Britain in 1967.

56. It is often difficult to trace a non-event but a particularly well-documented instance demonstrates the practical effectiveness of such official circulars. In 1993 the priest at Spanish Town's St Joseph's Roman Catholic Church received an official notification of the church complex's protected status. Although the vestry had recently sought quotations from local building contractors for demolishing its 1890s wooden rectory and transforming the 1872 brick church into a church hall, the parish changed its policies abruptly. The old rectory, hitherto written off as unsalvageable, was instead stabilized and reused as a parish library and meeting area; St Joseph's Church would remain as it was and a house just across the street bequeathed to the church a decade before would be refurbished to serve as the rectory. AKA 29 January 1993, Francis D. Shaw, proposal; 22 August 1994, Fr. Kingsley W. Asphall to Archbishop Samuel Carter. Ten years later these buildings are all still standing, though the old rectory is, once again, a rectory, while the donated house holds the parish meetings.

57. JNHT Basement Plan Chests, Development Sketches, include 11 July 1972, photocopy of architectural details, Old King's House and 20 October 1972, Consultant Engineer's ground floor plan, Old King's House.

58. R. Duncan Mathewson, 'The Old King's House Archaeological Project', *Jamaican Historical Society Bulletin* 5:11 (1971): 140–50.

59. The site notes were left with the Institute of Jamaica, but can no longer be traced there. I am grateful to Dr Duncan Mathewson for clarifying where he deposited these records. The excavation's finds are held by the JNHT. The staff of the Archaeology Division at Port Royal assisted my access to their lists and boxes. Some of the most striking items from the excavations were incorporated into a small site exhibition. This material is now held at the Institute of Jamaica. Sevreena Thame, then of the Institute's Museums Division, kindly allowed me to examine the contents of these crates.

60. A photographic survey was undertaken by the Georgian Society of Jamaica in June 1973. *Spanish Town: a photographic record* (Kingston: the Georgian Society of Jamaica, [1973]). I am grateful for Pauline Simmonds, the Society's Honorary Secretary, for a photocopy of this important compilation.

61. 'Cuban Gift School a Movement Against Propaganda', *Daily Gleaner* (22 November 1976).

62. The verdict offered by a newspaper columnist at this juncture that Cuba was 'the symbol for much of the division in this country' highlights the contentiousness of the policies that this 'fraternal gift' exemplified. Malcolm Sharp, 'Fidel si, visit no!', *Daily Gleaner* [1976, undated clipping], JA 4/77/19, Edith Clarke papers, 'the Cuban school'.

63. *Morris Cargill: A Selection*, 184, 5 February 1976.

64. 'Cuban gift school to produce the new Jamaican, based on principle of work and study', *Daily Gleaner* (14 April 1976): 2, 21.

65. 'Opening of St Jago High School Building today', *Daily Gleaner* (28 January 1959): 1. I owe this reference to research undertaken by Georgia Brown. JNHT Research File, Spanish Town Research Project.

66. AKA 22 February 1994, Sister Theresa Lowe Ching to Archbishop Carter.

67. On the purchase of the 30–32 White Church Street plot, AKA St Catherine, Deeds, Certificate of Title, 22 March 1944, Register book, Vol 415, f. 40. This is annotated 'acquired during the pastorate of Rev Fr. Gilday SJ'. The new science classrooms at the Catholic St Catherine's High School were to be ready for occupation by 24 December 1961. Deeds: folder S3, Spanish Town, 6 June 1961, contract between Roman Catholic Archbishop of Jamaica and Leonard L. Chang.

68. Describing the subsequent growth, *Centenary Celebrations . . . St Joseph's Church*, unpaginated and 'History of St Catherine High School', *Student's Handbook, St Catherine High School*.

69. Jean D'Costa, *Sprat Morrison* (Kingston, 1972, 2nd ed Kingston: Longman, 1990), 'Foreword to the Second Edition', (May, 1989).

70. Feurtado, *Forty-Five Years' Reminiscence*, 37–8.

71. Couplet from One World's 1997 Jamaican hit, 'Two White Girls pon a Mini Bus', *Withonereddaizy* (One World Records: 1997). The song was written by Maureen Sheridan. I am grateful to Matthew Smith for locating this track and citation.

72. Describing the approaches used in tracing similar field patterns underlying the expansion of nineteenth-century Leeds, Maurice Beresford, *East End, West End: The Face of Leeds During Urbanisation, 1684–1894* (Thoresby Society 1st ser 60 61, nos 131&132, Leeds: The Society, 1988).

73. Patrick Leigh Fermor, *The Traveller's Tree: A Journey through the Caribbean Islands* (London: John Murray, 1950), 379. The subsequent depiction of the King's House Square provided the finale for Leigh Fermor's description of the whole region as the colonial era was ending. Ibid. 380–382.

74. Positive responses to a very rough poll conducted in Spanish Town in 1994 by an enterprising geography student, just after the *Daily Gleaner's* proposal, are reported in Karen S. Beckford, 'Changing Functions, Structures and Land Use in Urban Spanish Town, Jamaica: Selected Areas', BA thesis, Geography, UWI Mona, (1995), 34–5.

75. Marcus Binney, John Harris and Kit Martin, *Jamaica's Heritage: an untapped resource – a preservation proposal by Tourism Action Plan Limited in collaboration with the Jamaican National Heritage Trust* (Kingston: Mill Press, 1991), 48–51.

76. Some of these issues are discussed at greater length in Robertson, 'Inherited cityscapes: Spanish Town, Jamaica', in Malm, ed., *Building Archaeology in a Global Context,* 89–104.

77. *Feasability Study for Conservation and Restoration of Cultural Heritage in Jamaica* [1986]. I consulted a copy at the JNHT.

78. Proposals offered to a studio at the Caribbean School of Architecture demonstrate the range of possible adaptations and reuses, Salvadore Autorino, 'A Library for Spanish Town', *Axis: Journal of the Caribbean School of Architecture* 3/4 (1999): 10–14.

79. Lawrence Brown, 'Monuments to Freedom, Monuments to Nation: The Politics of Emancipation and Remembrance in the Eastern Caribbean', *Slavery & Abolition* 23 (2002): 93–116.

80. Cf. Edward W. Said, 'Invention, Memory, and Place', *Critical Inquiry* 26 (2000): 175–92, also Rahul Mehrotra, 'Bazaars in Victorian Arcades: Conserving Bombay's Colonial Heritage', in Ismail Serageldin, Ephrim Shulger, Joan Martin-Brown, eds., *Historic Cities and Sacred Sites: Cultural Roots for Urban Futures* (Washington, D.C: World Bank, 2001), 154–63.

Bibliography

—

Manuscript

JAMAICA

Kingston

AFRICAN-CARIBBEAN INSTITUTE OF JAMAICA

Video Vно, Heritage Week, 1985.

CATHOLIC ARCHDIOCESE ARCHIVES

Correspondence: Mission Station 'S', St Joseph – Spanish Town.
Correspondence: Spanish Town, September 1978–
Reply by Reverend J.M. Bartolio, SJ to an Address Presented by the Congregation of
    St Joseph's Church, Spanish-Town, 8 May 1870.
St Catherine, Deeds.
Summary of Documents Contained in Chancery Office, Kingston, Jamaica.

JAMAICA NATIONAL HERITAGE TRUST, HEADQUARTERS HOUSE

Green, Patricia E., *Proposal for the Preparation of a Preservation Scheme Master Plan for
    Spanish Town Historic District, Final Draft* (UNDP/UNESCO/GoJ Project,
    JAM/91/008, typescript, 25 January 1995).
Research File, 'Spanish Town Research Project'.

NATIONAL GALLERY OF JAMAICA

Matalon Collection, 'Album of Photographs', (1919).

NATIONAL LIBRARY OF JAMAICA

HN 'Maces'.
HN 'Pottery'.
Ms 16, Major General Archibald Campbell, 'Memoir Relative to the Island of Jamaica,
    1782'.
Ms 24, Letters from Leslie Alexander to Frank Cundall, 1897.
Ms 31, W.G. Freeman. 'Pickwick in Jamaica'.

Ms 60, 'Jack-Jingle'.

Ms 62a, Jacob A.P.M. Andrade, '[St Catherine] Parochial Handbook'.

Ms 72, Nugent Correspondence.

Ms 91, Leslie Alexander, 'Poems', volume 2, only.

Ms 105 John Taylor, 'Multum in Parvo or Taylor's History of his Life and Travells in America', 3 vols.

Ms 111, 'The Wanderings of a Marine', (1831).

Ms 112, E.R. Wingfield Yates, Journal, 3 vols.

Ms 169, Hubert G. Corlette, 'The King's House in the King's Square, Spanish Town, Jamaica', ([London], Lincoln's Inn, 1932).

Ms 227, J.E. Pietersz, Scrapbook, 1826–1944.

Ms 254, Leslie Alexander, 'List of Plans in the Record Office'.

Ms 261, E.V. Lucas, 'Impressions of Jamaica', nd. (*c.* 1927).

Ms 284, A. Light, 'Sketch for Improving the Condition of our Troops in the West Indies', (1816).

Ms 291, Pietersz Bequest, 2nd. series 'Translations, Seville'.

Ms 307, D.S. Gideon Papers.

Ms 321, Beldam Papers.

Ms 383, Edward D'Oyley to Commissioners of the Admiralty, 1659/60.

Ms 617, 'Plan for the Defense of the West India islands by natives from the East Indies', 1796.

Ms 624, William Taylor to Dundas, 6 July 1798.

Ms 703, Rev Thomas Godden to Rev C. Kitchen, 26 June 1819.

Ms 1579, Papers of Captain David Hamilton, 1744–47.

Ms 1612, Jackson Smith to James P. McDonald, 31 May 1898.

Ms 1612a, F.L. Casserly, 'Jamaica Railway Fiasco, 1890–1900', nd. [1950s].

Ms 1646, Jamaica Papers 1768.

Ms 1681, Captain Robert Rollo Gillespie to Earl Balcarres, 24 September 1796.

Ms 1682, Admiral Parker to Earl Balcarres, 12 December 1799.

Ms 1820, Correspondence of Frank Cundall, 1910–37.

Ms 1839, Draft Railway Bill, 9 March 1867.

Ms 1900, Letterbook of William Jowett Titford, 1802–07, (transcript).

Ms 1954, S.A.G. Taylor Papers, Box B, 'The History of St Catherine'.

Ms 1983, James McFayden, 'Sketch of a short botanical excursion in Jamaica', (transcript).

Ms 2006, Bruce E. Burgoyne, (trans.), 'As they Saw us: Hessian Views of America During the Revolutionary War'.

Ms 2035, 1st Autobiography of Norman Washington Manley, 16 April–30 May 1969.

P/702, Richard Glynn Vivian, 'West Indian Islands: A pictorial record of a voyage, 1868–1869'.

P/699, Quizem, [Robert Hawkins], 'Book of watercolours', [1810–11].

St C 140, 'Plan of 13 acres 3 roods and 37 perches of land . . . occupied as a terminus of the Jamaica Railway Company', surveyor, John M. Smith, (1846).

St C 143, 'Rough Plan of the St Catherine parish lands around Spanish Town showing the names of the persons in possession', surveyor, Thomas Harrison, (1867).

St C 154, 'Lots of Footland in St Jago de la Vega', (1748/9).

TITLES OFFICE

Libers.

UNIVERSITY OF THE WEST INDIES, MONA, MAIN LIBRARY, WEST INDIES AND SPECIAL COLLECTIONS

Osborne, F.J., and S.A.G. Taylor, eds., 'Edward D'Oyley's Journal: part 3'.

Papers relating to the Wilson Family of Bromhead, Yorkshire, *c.* 1694–1768.

A.E.C[lark?], 'Three Days in Jamaica', (1906).

Priestley, R.E., 'West Indian Journey, 1944'.

Wilma Williams [Bailey], 'A note on the Spanish Towns of Jamaica', typescript. (nd).

Winifred M. Cousins Papers, 'Freedom in Jamaica', (nd.).

Spanish Town

ISLAND RECORDS OFFICE

Deeds, old series.

Deeds, new series.

Laws of Jamaica, 1st ser.

JAMAICA ARCHIVES

1A/3/1, Earliest Chancery Record, 1676–8 and 1684.

1A/5/32, Spanish Town Journal, Estate of D.P. Mendes, December 1876 –November 1878.

1A/11/1, Writs of Extents, 1755–1769.

1A/5/2/29, Port Henderson Journal, May 1803–January 1805.

1B/5/3, Council Minutes.

1B/5/5/11, Legislative Council Journals, 1864–65.

1B/5/8/1, Finance Letter Book 2, 21 May 1864–27 April 1865.

1B/5/9/1, Legislative Council Minutes, October 1866–January 1869.

1B/5/15/1–2, Minute Books of the Commissioners for Forts, Fortifications and Public Buildings, 1769–71, 1773–83.

1B/5/18, Dispatches, Jamaica to England, 1725-35 and 1871–73.

1B/5/19/1, Dispatches (Draft) Jamaica to England, 1866–67.

1B/5/75/1, Colonial Secretary's Office Correspondence, General, 1867–69.

1B/5/76/3/7, The Proposed Irrigation Canal from the Rio Cobre.

1B/5/76/93, The Government Railway and Winding up of Railway Company.

1B/5/77/59, (1926), United Fruit Company in relation to the Ferry River Scheme.

1B/5/77/289, (1926), Director Jamaica Government Railway to Colonial Secretary.

1B/5/77/5, (1927), Report on the Rio Cobre Extension Scheme by Irrigation Adviser.

1B/5/77/43, (1927), Proposed Contour survey of the Irrigable land in St Catherine.

1B/5/77/51, (1927), Preservation of Historic Sites and Monuments.

1B/5/77/58, (1927), Records – Duplicate Registration – approval of building for depositing.

1B/5/77/109, (1927), Proposals for the Establishment of a West Indian University.

1B/5/77/18, (1928), Banana lands on the Prison Farm at Spanish Town to be used for experimental purposes.

1B/5/77/85, (1928), Restoration of the Cathedral at Spanish Town.

1B/5/77/172, (1929), Beckford and Smith's Old School Buildings – Sale of.

1B/5/77/191, (1931), Visit to Jamaica of the Prince of Wales and Prince George – Welcoming address.

1B/5/77/100, (1933), Lepers visiting the business places, etc, Spanish Town.

1B/5/77/283, (1934), Information relating to Ras Tafarian followers in St Catherine.

1B/5/77/15, (1935), Visit of Governor Edward Denham to St Catherine.

1B/5/77/80, (1935), Ex-BWIR Soldiers – Land Settlements St Catherine.

1B/5/77/88, (1935), Invitation to Governor Denham to visit Spanish Town Slum Areas.

1B/5/77/680, (1935), UNIA Representation and Correspondence, 1943–46.

1B/5/77/859, (1935), Plans being undertaken for the relief of unemployment in St Catherine.

1B/5/77/871, (1935), Unemployment, St Catherine, 1944–48, 3 parts.

1B/5/77/981, (1935), Tourist Trade Development Board, Erection of Notice Boards . . .

1B/5/77/5, (1938), Land Settlement in Jamaica: Memorandum by the Jamaica Imperial Association.

1B/5/77/293, (1938), Well Being of the Colony Returns.

1B/5/77/23, (1942), Poor Relief, St Catherine.

1B/5/77/83, (1943), House of Assembly and Legislative Council – offers of premises for housing of.

1B/5/77/122, (1943), Roads – Kingston/Spanish Town – Deviation at White Marl.

1B/5/79/41, Colonial Secretariat, Confidential Correspondence, The Hamatic Church, 1926.

1B/5/79/192, Railway, proposed sale of, 1927.

1B/5/79/325, Rum Store: Spanish Town, 1926–27.

1B/5/79/347, Interference with traffic of a UNIA procession in Spanish Town, 1929.

1B/5/79/375, Release of Marcus Garvey from St Catherine District Prison, 1929.

1B/5/81/2, Island Letter Book, 8 May 1827–26 December 1831.

1B/5/83/1, Attorney's Letter Book, J.G. V[idal] for Messers Michell, 21 November 1831–25 April 1838.

1B/5/104/12, Ordinance Survey Maps of Jamaica, (1920), Kingston District, sheets 2 and 3.

1B/8/3, Collector General's Department, Letter Book, April 1900–February 1904.

1B/11/1, Patents.

1B/11/2/1, St Andrew's Plat Book, 1, 1661–1712.

1B/11/2/5–7, St Catherine Plat Books, 1–3, 1661–1711.

1B/11/2/8, Clarendon Plat Book, 1, 1663–1733.

1B/11/8/3/18, St Catherine, Burials, 1848–55.

1B/16, Public Works Department, Plans.

1B/34/1/163, Old King's House Visitors' Book, 1879–1880.

1B/34/6, King's House Restoration Committee.

1B/56/1, Rio Cobre Irrigation Canal, Maps and Plans.

1B/80/12/119, Spanish Town Tax Office, Hurricane Damage Reports, 1951.

2/2/4, St Catherine, Vestry Minutes.

2/2/27, St Catherine, List of Freeholders, 1757–1840.

2/2/28A, St Catherine, Register of Free Persons, 1789–1840.

2/2/45, St Catherine, Accounts Current, 1810–24.

2/6/2, Kingston Vestry Minutes, 1750–52.

4/31, Canon F.G. Jolly Papers.

4/77, Edith Clarke papers.

4/90/37 A Trip to Jamaica, July-August, 1905.

4/97/1, Gunter Papers, Sir Geoffrey Gunter, 'Centenary History of the Jamaica Government Railway', (1945).

5/1/5/1, Jamaican Church Theological College (St Peter's), Minutes of the Committee of the Training Institute, 1871–76.

5/6/1/1, Methodist District Minutes, (Jamaica Synod), 1817–27.

5/6/10, Extracts and Copies of Letters from the Wesleyan Missionary Committee, London.

5/6/13/6, Spanish Town [Methodist] Circuit Accounts, 1829–49.

7/12, 'Jamaica Memories', *Gleaner* Essay Contest, 'Fifty Years Ago', November 1959.

7/13, May Jeffrey-Smith Papers.

7/15/1, 'Summary of and extracts from letters written by Curtis Brett to his son Curtis, 1775–80', (partial transcript).

7/28, Canon F.G. Jolly Papers.

7/32, Ivy Jeffrey-Smith Papers.

7/108, Owen F. Wright Papers.

7/109, US Army Air Corps aerial photographic map of Jamaica (donor Miss Violet M. Hill).

Supreme Court, 1856–1865, Shelf AB, no 1.

T1018, Treasury, General Ledger, 1828–32.

T1000, Treasury, General Ledger, 1859–60.

AUSTRALIA
Adelaide

PUBLIC LIBRARY OF SOUTH AUSTRALIA, ARCHIVES DEPARTMENT
(PHOTOCOPIES, AT UWI, MONA LIBRARY)

SA Archives, R.G. 58, Sir Anthony Musgrave to Sir Henry Ayres.

BRITAIN
Edinburgh

NATIONAL LIBRARY OF SCOTLAND

Acc. 5297 (1), A Trip to Jamaica, 1924.
Ms 3942, Robertson-Macdonald Papers.
Ms 9250, Dunlop Correspondence, 1605–92.
Ms 9253, Dunlop Correspondence, 1761–1816.
Ms 9266, Alexander Graham Dunlop, Journals.
Ms 10925, Airth Mss.
Ms. 17956, 1823–1824, Journal of a visit to Jamaica by [   ] of Loanhead near Ruthven,
Banffshire.

London

BRITISH LIBRARY

Add. Ms 12439, John Lindsay, 'A Few Conjectural considerations upon the creation of
the Humane Race, occasioned by the present British Quixottical rage of setting the
slaves from Africa at liberty, by a inhabitant'.
Add. Ms 18986, Papers Relating to the Navy, 1644–99.
Add. Ms 22676, Miscellaneous Papers relating to Jamaica 1662–1791, (Long Ms).
Add. Ms 33029, Newcastle Papers, 344, Papers relating to the affairs of the American
and West Indian Colonies, 2. 1744–58.
King's Ms 205, General Report of the State of the American Colonies.
King's Ms 213, Journal of an Officer . . . 1764–65.
Sloane Ms. 1394, [Thomas Lynch], 'Description of Jamaica', (c. 1660).
Sloane Ms. 3918, Henry Barham, 'Account of Jamaica', (1722).
Sloane Ms. 3984, Papers relating to Jamaica, 1670–88.

LONDON METROPOLITAN ARCHIVES

Ms. F/LEG/897, Diary of Lt Col Edward H. Legg.

NATIONAL ARCHIVES, PUBLIC RECORD OFFICE

ADM 98/284, Office of the Commissioners of Sick and Wounded Seamen (Sick and
Hurt Board), Out-Letters, Correspondence relating to Prisoners of War.

ADM 101/230, Admiralty, Office of Director General of the Medical Department of the Navy, Log, Septimus Terry, Assistant Surgeon, *HMS Wolverine*, 1 June 1865–22 December 1865.

CO 5, Board of Trade and Secretaries of State, America and West Indies, Original Correspondence.

CO 137, Colonial Office, Jamaica, Original Correspondence.

CO 351/7, Colonial Office, Jamaica, Registers of Correspondence, 1865–67.

HO 50/366, Home Office, Military Correspondence, 1791.

MINT 13/54, Royal Mint, Coinage, Colonial and Foreign, 1868–1897, Currency, Colonial, Jamaican.

PRO 30/48/42, Viscount Cardwell Papers, Jamaica, August to December 1865.

WO 55/1620/6, Ordinance Office and War Office, Miscellaneous Entry Books and Papers, Jamaica Rents, December 1826.

NATIONAL MARITIME MUSEUM, CAIRD LIBRARY

WYN 10/2, W[illiam] B[urrows], 'A journal of every dayes proceedings in the expedition of the Fleet sent into the West Indies under the command of General William Penn', 20 December 1654–4 September 1655.

ROYAL BOTANIC GARDENS, KEW, LIBRARY AND ARCHIVES

Forsyth Correspondence, Foreign Letters.

UNIVERSITY OF LONDON, SCHOOL OF ORIENTAL & AFRICAN STUDIES, ARCHIVES

Wesleyan Methodist Missionary Society Papers Jamaica, Correspondence, Box 47, 1838, – Box 49, 1867.

West Indies, General, Boxes 111, 112, 132, 662, 663.

Oxford

BODLEIAN LIBRARY

Rawlinson A. 175, 'Pepys Papers, 6'.

Rawlinson A. 312, 'Papers . . . chiefly relating to Jamaica'.

Rawlinson A. 232, 'Orders from naval commanders in the West Indies to Joseph Gyde, victualing agent in Jamaica, 1706–1710'.

REGENT'S PARK COLLEGE, ANGUS LIBRARY

Baptist Missionary Society Papers.

Committee Minute Book, A, 1819–23.

Committee Minute Book, B, 1823–27.

H14/2, Letters to Edward Underhill about Jamaica, 1852–1866.

Langton Collection, 6, 'History of Jamaica by Rev John Clarke', (*c.* 1864).

Phillippo, James, autobiography, 'Rough Sketch or an Outline only to be completely revised'.
Sub-Committee Reports, 1878–9.
WI/1, Jamaican Correspondence.
WI/5, James Coultart Correspondence, notebook by Muhammad Kaba Saghanughu.
West Indies Missionary Letters, 1840–46.

Rhodes House Library

Ms Brit Emp s. 23, British and Foreign Anti-Slavery and Aboriginal Protection Society, G. 49, 'Lady Albion's Caribbean University', nd.
Ms W. Ind. s.22, Clive A. Crosbie-Smith, *History of the Jamaica Constabulary*, nd.
Ms W. Ind. s.51, Journal of Thomas Capper, Inspector of Schools, Jamaica, January–July, 1881.
USPG, C/WIN/GUI, Correspondence, Guiana and Mosquito Coast.
USPG, C/WIN/JAM2, Correspondence, Jamaica.

TRINIDAD
St Augustine

University of the West Indies, St Augustine, Westindiana Collection

West India Committee Papers, 16, Minutes, 4 January 1845–July 1851.
West India Committee Papers, 39, Letters and Memoranda, 1866–70.

USA
Ann Arbor, Michigan

William E. Clements Library

7-F-4, George Gauld, 'A General Plan of the Harbours of Port Royal and Kingston, Jamaica . . .', (1772).
F-512.3, J.A. Savage, 'A Winter Cruise to The West Indies', (1908).
Shelbourne Papers, v. 87, John Dalling 'Observations Respecting the Island of Jamaica'.

Boston, Massachusetts

Boston Public Library

Ms Eng.179. Dr Smallwood's Memoranda.

Chicago, Illinois

Chicago Historical Society

Sterling Morton Papers, Box 1, folder '1908–1914', Sterling Morton, 'On the Spanish Main: Account of a Trip from New York City to the West Indies, Panama,

Columbia and Venezuela, January 17 – February 20, 1912'.

La Jolla, California

UNIVERSITY OF CALIFORNIA, SAN DIEGO, MANDERVILLE LIBRARY
Ms 171, Hill Collection, Hugh H. Cline, Diary, 1872–76.
Ms 220, Barnett/Hall Collection.

Pasadena, California

HENRY E. HUNTINGTON LIBRARY
ST 14, Roger Hope Elletson, Letters to and from Jamaica, 1769–76.
STG Box 44 (3), Grenville Correspondence, personal and political.
STG Box 152 (3), J[ohn] Halkett, to Henry Petty-Fitzmaurice, 3rd. Marquis of
Lansdowne.

Richmond, Virginia

LIBRARY OF VIRGINIA
Record Group 3, Governor's Papers: Executive Papers, Francis H. Pierpont, (Accession
#37024).

Printed Primary

A Book of the Continuation of Foreign Passages. London: M.S. for Thomas Jenner, 1657.
*Act of the Legislature of 2nd William IV c. 7, Establishing a College of Physicians and
Surgeons in Jamaica* . . . Spanish Town, Alexander Aikman, 1835.
'A Fellow of the Royal Geographical Society', *Jamaica and its Governor During the Last
Six Years.* London: Edward Stanford, 1871.
'A true relation of the voyage undertaken by Sir Anthony Shirley', in Richard Hakluyt,
The Principal Navigations . . . 12 vols Hakluyt Society, Extra Series, Glasgow: the
University Press, 1903–5.
'An Anglo-Indian', *A Letter to the Colonial Secretary on the Precarious Tenure of the Island
of Jamaica and the other West-Indian Possessions.* London: Effingham Wilson, 1839.
An Inventory of Nonconformist Chapels and Meeting-Houses in Central England. London:
HMSO, 1986.
'Barrington Manuscripts', *Historical Manuscripts Commission 7*, London: HMSO, 1879.
Centenary Celebrations 1872 to 1972: St Joseph's Church, Spanish Town, November 29, 1972.
[Spanish Town: St Joseph's Church], 1972.
'Characteristic traits of the Creolian and African Negroes in this Island', *Columbian
Magazine* 2:4 (April, 1797), 699–704.
'Further observations on the projected Canal from St Thomas in the Vale', *Columbian
Magazine* 2:4 (April, 1797), 747–51.

Georgian Society of Jamaica, *Spanish Town: a photographic record.* [Kingston: the Society, 1973].

Handbook of Jamaica for 1902. Kingston: Government Printing Office, 1902.

Hymns adopted for the Celebration of the Negro's Jubilee. Finsbury: J. Haddon, 1834.

Jamaica Tourist Trade Development Board and the Tourist Trade Convention Committee, *Survey and Report on the Potentialities of the Tourist Industry of Jamaica, with Recommendations for Post-War Development.* Kingston: Government Printer, 1945.

Journals of the Assembly of Jamaica. 14 vols Spanish Town: Alexander Aikman, 1811.

Letters on the Necessity of Establishing a College of Physicians and Surgeons in Jamaica, Addressed to the Editor of the Kingston Chronicle and Originally Published in that Paper, with Additional Notes and Observations. [Kingston: Kingston Chronicle], 1830.

'Letters showing the Rise and Progress of the early Negro Churches of Georgia and the West Indies', *Journal of Negro History* 1 (1916), 69–92.

'New Synagogue, Spanish Town', *Columbian Magazine* 1:3 (September 1796), 256–57.

Papers Relating to the Proposed Irrigation Canal for the Rio Cobre. Kingston: Government Printing Establishment, [1876?].

Programme of Celebrations in Spanish Town on the occasion of The Coronation of Their Majesties King George the VI and Queen Elizabeth. np. [1937].

Regulations of the Legislative Council of Jamaica. Spanish Town: George Henderson, 1867.

Report on the Rio Cobre Irrigation Works, From their First Construction to the Present Time, with the Opinion of the Director of Roads and Surveyor-General as to their Future Prospect. [Kingston: np.], 1876.

'Rodney's Glory', London: J. Pitts, [1819–1844], copy in Bodl. Firth c.12(24).

Scheme and By-Laws of Beckford and Smith's School, Jamaica. Kingston: Government Printing Office, 1915.

Scheme and By-Laws of Cathedral High School, Spanish Town, Jamaica. Kingston: Mortimer C. DeSousa, 1921.

Statutes and Laws of the Island of Jamaica: Revised Edition. Kingston: George Henderson, 1875.

The Covenant of the Anabaptist Church. [Kingston]: 1796.

The First Annual Report of the Jamaica Native Baptist Missionary Society. [Kingston?: np., nd. 1841?].

The Laws of Jamaica: Comprehending All the Acts in Force Passed between the Thirty-Second Year of the Reign of King Charles the Second, and the Thirty-Third Year of the Reign of King George the Third. Spanish Town: Alexander Aikman, 1792.

'The Rio Cobre Bridge', *Columbian Magazine* 2 (May, 1797), 263–64.

'The Royal Visit', *Jamaican Historical Society Bulletin* 1:6 (1953), 67–8.

'The Slave', Pocklington: J. Firth, nd., copy in Bodl. Firth b.25(279).

'The Watery Gods', London: J. Pitts, [1819–1844], copy in Bodl. Firth c.12(24).

'Through European Eyes: Jamaica 200 Years Ago', *Jamaica Journal* 17:4 (1985), 32–42.

Town and Country Planning (Spanish Town) Provisional Development Order, 1964. Kingston: Government Printer, 1964.

Who's Who in Jamaica 1916. Kingston: the Gleaner for Stephen A. Hill, 1916.

Who's Who and Why in Jamaica 2. *1939–1940.* Kingston: np. 1939.

Who's Who, Jamaica, British West Indies, 1941–1946. Kingston: Who's Who (Jamaica), Ltd, 1946.

World's Fair: Jamaica at Chicago. New York: Pell, 1893.

A.B., 'Further observations on the projected Canal from St Thomas in the Vale', *Columbian Magazine* 2 (April, 1797), 747–751.

H.F., of Port Royal, 'To the Printer of this Magazine', *Columbian Magazine* 2:5 (May, 1797), 827–828.

R.H., *The Insurrection in Jamaica.* London: Richard Barrett, 1866.

X.Y., 'Proposal for an Inland Navigation on the South-side Jamaica; and on the fertilising the land for Irrigation', *Columbian Magazine* 2:2 (February, 1797), 570–7.

Alexander, J.E., *Transatlantic Sketches, Comprising Visits to the Most Interesting Scenes in North and South America and the West Indies.* Philadelphia, Penn: Key and Biddle, 1833.

Allen, James G. *Editorial Opinion in the Contemporary British Commonwealth and Empire.* University of Colorado Studies, C. Studies in the Social Sciences, 1:4, Boulder, Colo, the University, 1946.

Ashton, S.R., and David Killingray, eds., *The West Indies.* British Documents on the End of Empire, B:6, London: Stationary Office for Institute of Commonwealth Studies, 1999.

Aspinall, Algernon S., *A Wayfarer in the West Indies.* London: Methuen, 1928.

_____ *The Pocket Guide to the West Indies.* London: Edward Stanford, 1907.

Bacon, Edgar Mayhew and Eugene Murray Aaron, *The new Jamaica: describing the island, explaining its conditions of life and growth and discovering its mercantile relations and potential importance.* New York: Walbridge & Co, 1890.

Barnett, Richard D., and Philip Wright, *The Jews of Jamaica: Tombstone Inscriptions, 1663–1880.* ed., Oron Yoffe, Jerusalem: Ben Zvi Institute, 1997.

Battick, John F., ed., 'Richard Rooth's Sea Journal of the Western Design, 1654–55', *Jamaica Journal* 5:4 (1971), 3–22.

Beeston, William 'A Journal Kept by Col. William Beeston from his first coming to Jamaica', in *Interesting Tracts relating to Jamaica.* St Iago: Lewis, Luna and Jones, 1800, 271–300.

Bell, H.C., D.W. Parker *et al.* eds., *Guide to British West Indian Archive Materials, in London and in the Islands, for the History of the United States.* Washington, DC: Carnegie Institution, 1926.

Benghiat, Norma, *Traditional Jamaican Cookery.* London: Penguin, 1985.

Benzoni, Girolamo, *History of the New World,* (1565), ed/trans., W.H. Smyth, Hakluyt Society, 21, London, the Society, 1857.

Bigelow, John, *Jamaica in 1850: or, the effects of sixteen years of freedom on a slave colony*. New York & London: George E. Putnam, 1851.

Birch, Thomas, ed., *A Collection of the State Papers of John Thurloe, Esq: . . .* 7 vols London: Executor of Fletcher Gyles, 1742.

Blackburne, Kenneth, *Lasting Legacy: A Story of British Colonialism*. London: Johnson, 1976.

Bland, E.M., *Report of the Jamaican Government Railway*. Kingston: [Government Printer], 1937.

Bradford, Mary F., *Side Trips in Jamaica*. 1900, 3rd ed., Boston, Mass: Sherwood, 1902.

Browne, Howe Peter, 2nd Marquess of Sligo, *A Letter to the Marquess of Normanby Relative to the Present State of Jamaica and the Measures which are rendered necessary by the refusal of the House of Assembly to Transact Business*. London: John Andrews, 1839.

Buisseret, David, ed./trans., 'A Frenchman looks at Jamaica in 1706', *Jamaica Journal* 2:3 (1968), 6–9.

Cadbury, Henry J., 'Conditions in Jamaica in 1687', *Jamaican Historical Review* 3 (1957), 52–7.

Campbell, John Douglas Sutherland, Marquis of Lorne (later 9th Duke of Argyle), *A Trip to the Tropics and Home through America*. London: Hurst and Blackett, 1867.

Campbell, R.J., 'Education in Jamaica: moral sense needs purifying', *The Church Family Newspaper* (9 January – 26 March 1920).

Candler, John, *West Indies Extracts from the Journal of John Candler whilst travelling in Jamaica*. London: Harvey and Darton, 1840.

Cargill, Morris, *Morris Cargill: A Selection of his Writings in the Gleaner 1952–1985*. ed. Deryck Roberts, Kingston: Tropical Publishers, 1987.

_____ *Public Disturbances: a collection of writings 1986–1996*. ed., David D'Costa, Kingston: Mill Press, 1998.

Casserly, F.L., 'Crown Colony Crisis: The Henning-Gideon Correspondence', *Jamaican Historical Review* 3 (1957), 39–78.

Cave, Hugh B., *Four Paths to Paradise: A Book about Jamaica*. Garden City, NY: Doubleday, 1961.

Clarke, John, *Memorials of the Baptist Missionaries in Jamaica*. London and Kingston: Yates & Alexander and McCartney & Wood, 1869.

Clerk, Astley, 'Kingston Street Cries c. 1927 and something about their Criers', *Jamaica Journal* 18:2 (1985), 11–17.

Clodd, Edward, *Grant Allen: A Memoir*. London: Grant Richards, 1900.

Coke, Thomas, *Extracts from the Journals of the Rev Dr Coke's Five Visits to America*. London: G. Paramore, 1793.

Colon de Portugal y Castro, Don Pedro, Duke of Veragua and La Vega, *The Columbus Petition Document . . . for the Island of Jamaica, 1672*. trans., Jeremy Lawrence, Kingston: Mill Press, 1992.

Cundall, Frank, ed., 'What a French Traveller in Jamaica saw in 1765', *Jamaica Times* (1 April 1922): 2–3.

Cundall, Frank and Joseph Pietersz, ed/trans., *Jamaica under the Spaniards*. Kingston: Institute of Jamaica, 1919.

Currie, Sir James, and R.R. Sedgwick, *West Indian University, Resolution of the First West Indian Conference*. np, 1927.

D'Costa, Jean, *Escape to Last Man Peak*. Harlow, Longman, 1975.

_____ *Sprat Morrison*. 1972, 2nd ed Kingston: Longman, 1990.

de Castilla, Julian, 'The English Conquest of Jamaica (1655–1656)', ed/trans., Irene A. Wright, *Camden Miscellany XIII*. Camden Society, 3rd ser 34, London: Royal Historical Society, 1923, v–32.

de la Beche, H.T., *Notes on the Present Condition of the Negroes in Jamaica*. London: T. Cadell, 1825.

de Lisser, H.G., *Twentieth Century Jamaica*. Kingston: Jamaica Times, 1913.

de Segura, Fr Andrés, *An Early Florida Adventure Story*. ed/trans., John H. Hann, Gainesville, Fla: University Press of Florida, 2000.

[D'Oyley, Edward], *A Brief Relation of a Victory, Obtained by the Forces under the Command of Gen. Edward D'Oyley, Commander in chief of his Highness's FORCES in the Island of JAMAICA against the Forces of the King of SPAIN, Commanded by Don Christopher Arnoldo Sasi, Commander in Chief of the Spanish Forces there*. Edinburgh: Christopher Higgins, 1659.

Early, Eleanor, *Ports of the Sun: A Guide to the Caribbean, Bermuda, Nassau, Havana and Panama*. Boston, Mass: Houghton Mifflin, 1937.

Espeut, W. Bancroft, *The Advantages to Result from 'Railway Extension' in Jamaica*. Institute of Jamaica, Popular Lectures, 4th ser, Kingston: the Institute, 1887.

Fermor, Patrick Leigh, *The Traveller's Tree: A Journey through the Caribbean Islands*. London: John Murray, 1950.

Feurtado, Walter Augustus, *A Forty-Five Years' Reminiscence of the Characteristics and Characters of Spanish Town*. Kingston: W. Alexander Feurtado, 1890.

Firth, Charles H., ed., *Naval Songs and Ballads*. Navy Records Society, 33, London: the Society, 1908.

_____ *The Narrative of General Venables*. Camden Society, n.s. 40, London: Longmans for Royal Historical Society, 1900.

Foot, Hugh, *A Start in Freedom*. London: Hodder and Stoughton, 1964.

Foulks, Theodore, *Eighteen Months in Jamaica with Recollections of the Late Rebellion*. London: Whittaker, Treacher and Arnott, 1833.

Franck, Harry A., *Roaming Through the West Indies*. New York: Century, 1921.

Gage, Thomas, *Thomas Gage's Travels in the New World*. ed., J. Eric S. Thompson, Norman, Okl: University of Oklahoma Press, 1958, 2nd ed. 1969.

Gardner, William James, *A History of Jamaica*. London: Elliot Stock, 1873.

Garvey, Marcus, *The Marcus Garvey and Universal Negro Improvement Association*

Papers. eds., Robert A. Hill *et al.* Berkeley, Cal: University of California Press, 1983–, 7 *November 1927–August 1940*.

Gosse, Philip Henry, *A Naturalist's Sojourn in Jamaica*. London: Longman, 1851.

Gurney, Joseph John, *A Winter in the West Indies: Described in Familiar Letters to Henry Clay of Kentucky*. London: John Murray, 1840.

_____ *Reconciliation Respectfully Recommended to all Parties in the Colony of Jamaica Addressed to the Planters*. London and Kingston: George Eightman and Cathcart & Sherlock, 1840.

Hakewill, James, *A Picturesque Tour of the Island of Jamaica, from Drawings made in the Years 1820 and 1821*. London: Hurst & Robinson and E. Lloyd, 1825.

Harlow, Vincent T., ed., 'The Voyages of Captain William Jackson (1642–1645)', *Camden Miscellany XIII*. Camden Society, 3rd ser 34, London: the Society, 1924.

H[eeson], F[rancis], 'To the Reader', *The Laws of Jamaica, Passed by the Assembly And Confirmed by His Majesty in Council, February 23 1683*. London: H. Hills for Charles Harper, 1683.

Henderson, John, *Jamaica*. London: Black, 1906.

Higman, B.W., ed., *The Jamaican Censuses of 1844 and 1861*. Kingston: Social History Project, History Department, UWI, Mona, 1980.

Houstoun, James, *The Works of James Houstoun, M.D.* London: S. Bladon, 1753.

Hutton, Albinia C., *Life in Jamaica: A Series of Sketches*. London: Arthur H. Stockwell, nd. [1926/7].

Johnston, James, *Jamaica: The New Riviera*. Brown's Town: for the author, 1903.

Jeffrey-Smith, May, 'Guiding in Jamaica: The First Fifteen Years', *The Leaflet: Official Publication of the Girl Guides Association of Jamaica* 19 (1955), 16–19.

J[udah], G.F., *Old Saint Jago*. Kingston: W.A. Feurtado's Sons, 1896.

Kelly, James, *Jamaica in 1831: Being a Narrative of Seventeen Years' Residence in that Island*. Belfast: James Wilson, 1838.

Krise, Thomas W., ed., *Caribbeana: An Anthology of English Literature of the West Indies, 1657–1777*. Chicago, Ill: University of Chicago Press, 1999.

Leader, Alfred, *Through Jamaica with a Kodak*. Bristol: John Wright & Co, 1907.

Le Guin, Ursula K., *Tales from Earthsea*. New York: Harcourt, 2001.

Leslie, Charles, *A New History of Jamaica from the Earliest Accounts to the Taking of Porto Bello by Vice Admiral Vernon In Thirteen Letters from a Gentleman to a Friend*. 2nd ed. London: J. Hodges, 1740.

Lewis, Matthew Gregory, *Journal of a West India Proprietor, Kept During a Residence in the Island of Jamaica*. London: John Murray, 1834.

_____ *The Monk*. ed., Howard Anderson, Oxford: Oxford University Press, 1973.

Lindsay, John, 'An Examination of the Hypothetical Doctrine of Water-Spouts in Opposition to the ingenious Speculation of Dr B. Franklin of Philadelphia', *Gentleman's Magazine* 51 (1781), 559–60. (with diagram), 615–16.

_____ 'Continuation of Dr Lindsay's Ingenious and original Hypothesis on Waterspouts', *Gentleman's Magazine* 53 (1783), 1025–28.

_____ 'Sermon for Annual Fast for Earthquake, 1760', *Columbian Magazine* 2 (1797), 497–506.

Long, Edward, *History of Jamaica*. 3 vols. London: Lowndes, 1774.

Macmillan, Mona C.M., *The Land of Look Behind: A Study of Jamaica*. London: Faber, 1957.

Macmillan, William, *Warning from the West Indies: A Tract for Africa and the Empire*. London: Faber, 1936.

M'Mahan, Benjamin, *Jamaica Plantership*. London: E. Wilson, 1839.

Manley, Edna, *The Diaries*. ed., Rachel Manley, Kingston: Heinemann Caribbean, 1989.

Marshall, Mrs Peter, 'Ye Ancient Capital of Jamaica', *Jamaica Standard* (30 May 1938), 8–9.

McFee, William, *Gates of the Caribbean: The Story of a Great White Fleet Caribbean Cruise*. [Boston, Mass]: United Fruit Steamship Service, 1922.

Milner, Thomas Hughes, *The Present and Future State of Jamaica Considered*. London: H. Hooper, 1839.

Montuelé, de Édouard, *A Voyage to North America, the West Indies and the Mediterranean*. New Voyages and Travels, 3rd ser, 9:2, London: Sir Richard Phillips, 1821.

[Morris, William], 'Twilight in Jamaica', *Douglas Library Notes* 14:2 (1965), 2–12.

Nugent, Maria, *Lady Nugent's Journal of Her Residence in Jamaica from 1801 to 1805*. ed., Philip Wright, new edition, Kingston: University of the West Indies Press, 2002.

Oakley, Amy, *Behold the West Indies*. New York: Appleton-Century, 1941.

Ogilby, John, *America: Being the Latest and Most Accurate Description of the New World*. London: by the author, 1671.

Olivier, Sydney Haldane, Lord Olivier, *Jamaica: The Blessed Island*. London: Faber, 1936.

[Osborne, Francis J., ed.], 'A Spanish Account of the Attack by Christopher Newport on Jamaica in January, 1603', *Jamaican Historical Society Bulletin* 3:12 (1963), 188-90.

Phillippo, James Cecil, *Jamaica: Its Government and its People*. Kingston: R. Jordon, 1883.

Phillippo, James M., *Jamaica: Its Past and Present State*. London: John Snow, 1843.

_____ *Speech of the Rev J.M. Phillippo delivered at the Baptist Chapel, Spanish Town . . . 1839*. Kingston: np. 1839.

[Phillippo, James M.?], *Report of the Schools composed of the Negro and Free Population of Spanish Town, Jamaica, for the year ending May, 1831*. Leicester: R. Tebbutt, 1831.

Pietersz, Joseph, 'Spanish Documents Relating to Jamaica', *Jamaican Historical Review* 1 (1945), 100–15.

_____ and H.P. Jacobs, trans., S.A.G. Taylor, intro., 'Two Spanish Documents of 1656', *Jamaican Historical Review* 2 (1948), 11–35.

Pinckard, George, *Notes on the West Indies . . . with additional letters from Martinique, Jamaica and St Domingo*. 2 vols 1806, 2nd expanded, ed., London: Baldwin, Craddock & Joy, 1816.

Pitcairn, John, 'A Plan of St Jago de la Vega in the Island of Jamaica', London: W. Hinton, 3 January 1786.

Plowden, Alfred Chichele, *Grain or Chaff? The Autobiography of a Police Magistrate*. London: Thomas Nelson, [1908].

Pringle, Alexander, *Prayers for the Revival of Religion in all the Protestant Churches*. Edinburgh: Schaw and Pillans, 1796.

Pullen-Burry, R., *Jamaica as it is*, 1903, London: Fisher Unwin, 1903.

Rampini, Charles Joseph Galliari, *Letters from Jamaica: The Land of Streams and Woods*. Edinburgh: Edmonston and Douglas, 1873.

Renny, Robert, *An History of Jamaica*. London: J. Cawthorn, 1807.

Rhys, Jean, *Wide Sargasso Sea*. London, 1966, reprint New York: Norton, 1982.

'Rodney', 'Spanish Town's Ancient Glory', *Daily Gleaner* (26 June 1906).

Rodney, George Brydges, Lord Rodney, *Letter-Books and Order-Book of George, Lord Rodney, Admiral of the White Squadron 1780–1782*. 2 vols Publications of the Naval Historical History Society, 12, 13, New York: New York Historical Society for Naval History Society, 1932.

Rogers, Francis, 'The Diary of Francis Rogers', in Bruce S. Ingram, ed., *Three Sea Journals of Stuart Times*. London: Constable, 1936, 143–230.

Roby, John, *The History of the Parish of St James, in Jamaica, to the Year 1740 . . .* Kingston: R.J. De Cordova, 1849.

_____ *Monuments of the Cathedral-Church and Parish of St Catherine*. Montego Bay: Alex: Holmes, 1831.

Rutter, Owen, *If Crab No Walk: A Traveller in the West Indies*. London: Hutchinson, 1933.

Samuel, Peter, *The Wesleyan-Methodist Missions, in Jamaica and Honduras, Delineated*. London: Partridge & Oakey, 1850.

Scott, Michael, *Tom Cringle's Log*. 1833, Everyman edition, London: Dent, 1915.

Scott, Sir Sibbald David, Bart., *To Jamaica and Back*. London: Chapman & Hall, 1876.

Sealy, Theodore, *Industrialization of Jamaica*. Kingston: Gleaner, 1952.

[Senior, Bernard Martin], 'A retired military officer', *Jamaica, as it was, as it is and as it may be: Comprising Interesting Topics for Absent Proprietors, Merchants &c and Valuable Hints to persons intending to emigrate to the Island*. London: T. Hurst, 1835.

Seton-Karr, Walter Scott, *Grant of Rothiemurchus: A Memoir of the Services of Sir John Peter Grant, G.C.M.G., K.C.B.* London: John Murray, 1899.

Sloane, Sir Hans, *A Voyage to the Islands of Madeira, Barbados, Nieves, S. Christopher and Jamaica . . .* 2 vols London: B.M. for author, 1707, 1725.

Smith, E. Quincy, *Travels at Home and Abroad*. 2 vols New York: Neale, 1911.

[Smith, Thomas Carpenter], 'Master Tommy', 'Three Weeks in Jamaica', *Jamaican Historical Society Bulletin* 1:15 (1956), 187–190.

Spedding, James, 'Bill for the Suppression of the Jamaica Constitution, 1839', (1839), reprinted in idem. *Reviews and Discussions: Literary, Political, and Historical, Not Relating to Bacon.* London: Kegan Paul, 1879, 87–120.

[Stewart, John], *An Account of Jamaica and its Inhabitants, by a Gentleman long Resident in the West Indies.* London: Longman, 1808.

Stone, Carl, *The Stone Columns: The Last Year's Work.* ed., Rosemarie Stone, Kingston: Sangster's, 1994.

Stuart, Villiers, *Adventures Amidst the Equatorial Forest and Rivers of South America also in the West Indies and the Wilds of Florida, to which is added 'Jamaica Revisited'.* London: John Murray, 1891.

Sturge, Joseph, and Thomas Harvey, *The West Indies in 1837: Being the Journal of a Visit to Antigua, Montserrat, Dominica, St Lucia, Barbados and Jamaica, Undertaken for the Purpose of Ascertaining the Actual Conditions of the Negro Population of those Islands.* London: Hamilton, Adams & Co, 1838.

Taylor, S.A.G., ed., 'Edward D'Oyley's Journal', 2 parts published (of three) *Jamaican Historical Review* 10 (1973), 33–112; 11 (1978), 62–117.

Thomas, Herbert T., *The Story of a West Indian Policeman: or, Forty-Seven Years in the Jamaican Constabulary.* Kingston: Gleaner, 1927.

[Thompson, Edward, William Smith, William Girod], *Statement of Facts Relative to the Island of Jamaica.* London: Noseworthy and Lewis, 1852.

Thompson, R.W., *Black Caribbean.* London: Macdonald, 1946.

Trollope, Anthony, *An Autobiography.* ed., David Skilton, Harmondsworth: Penguin, 1998.

_____ N. John Hall, ed., *The Letters of Anthony Trollope.* Stanford, Cal: Stanford University Press, 1983.

_____ 'Miss Sarah Jack of Spanish Town, Jamaica', (1860), reprinted in Betty Jane Breyer, ed., *Anthony Trollope: The Complete Short Stories. 3 Tourists and Colonials.* Fort Worth, Tex: Texas: Christian University Press, 1981, 1–25.

_____ *The West Indies and the Spanish Main.* 2nd. ed. London: Chapman & Hall, 1860.

Underhill, Edward Bean, *A Letter Addressed to the Rt. Honourable E. Cardwell, with illustrative documents on the condition of Jamaica, and an explanatory statement.* London: Arthur Miall, nd. [1865].

_____ *Life of James Mursell Phillippo: Missionary in Jamaica.* London: Yates & Alexander, 1881.

_____ *The Tragedy of Morant Bay.* London: Alexander & Shepheard, 1895.

Verrill, H. Hyatt, *In the Wake of the Buccaneers.* New York: Century, 1923.

_____ *Jamaica of Today.* New York: Dodd, Mead & Co., 1931.

_____ *The Book of the West Indies.* New York: Dutton, 1917.

[White? Charles], *An Inquiry Concerning the Trade, Commerce and Policy of Jamaica, Relative to the Scarcity of Money . . . c* 1751, reprint, London: T. Kinnersly and G. Woodfal, 1759.

Whitman, Edmund S., *Those Wild West Indies.* New York: Sheridan House, 1938.

Wilcox, Ella Wheeler, *Sailing Sunny Seas: A Story of Travel*. Chicago, Ill: W.B. Conkey, 1909.

Wilmot, Swithin R., ed., *Adjustments to Emancipation*. Kingston: Social History Project, 1988.

Wood, Betty, *et al.* eds. 'The Letters of Simon Taylor of Jamaica to Chaloner Arcedekne, 1765–1775', *Travel, Trade and Power in the Atlantic, 1765–1884: Camden Miscellany XXXV*. Camden 5th ser 19, Cambridge: Cambridge University Press, 2002, 1–155.

Woolley, E., *The Land of the Free, or, A Brief View of Emancipation in the West Indies*. Cincinnati, Oh: Caleb Clark, 1847.

Wright, Irene A., ed., 'Spanish Narratives of the English Attack on Santo Domingo 1655', *Camden Miscellany XIV*. Camden Society, 3rd ser 37, London: Royal Historical Society, 1926, i–80.

Wright, James, 'An Experiment in Land Settlement at Lucky Hill, Jamaica', *Caribbean Quarterly* 1:2 (1949), 29–39.

Wright, Philip, ed., *Monumental Inscriptions of Jamaica*. London: Society of Genealogists, 1966.

UNPUBLISHED PAPERS AND THESES

Aarons, John, 'The Making of Cultural Policy in Colonial and Post-Colonial Jamaica', read to the History Department's Faculty/Graduate Seminar, University of the West Indies, Mona, 5 December 1997.

Addoun, Yacine Daddi, and Paul Lovejoy, 'The Arabic Manuscript of Muhammad Kaba Saghanughu of Jamaica, *c*. 1823', Second Conference on Caribbean Culture, University of the West Indies, Mona, January 2002.

Bailey, Wilma R., 'Kingston 1692–1843: A Colonial City', PhD thesis, University of the West Indies, Mona, (1974).

Beckford, Karen S., 'Changing Functions, Structures and Land Use in Urban Spanish Town, Jamaica: Selected Areas', BA thesis, Geography, University of the West Indies, Mona, (1995).

Brodber, Erna, 'The Second Generation of Freemen in Jamaica, 1907–1914', PhD thesis, University of the West Indies, Mona, (1984).

Brown, Annette Constance, 'The Old King's House, Spanish Town, 1872–1962', MA thesis, University of the West Indies, Mona, (1999).

Catherall, Gordon A., 'British Baptist Involvement in Jamaica 1783–1865', PhD thesis, Keele University, (1970).

Cousins, Winifred Mary, 'The Emancipation of Slaves in Jamaica and its Repercussions', PhD thesis, University of London, (1927), (transcript, NLJ Ms 168).

Davis, Beverley, 'The Effects of the Removal of the Capital on Spanish Town, 1872–1900', Caribbean Study, University of the West Indies, Mona, (1976).

Dickenson, A. John, 'The Jamaica Railway, 1845 to 1915: An Economic History', MSc thesis, University of the West Indies, Mona, (1969).

Duncker, Sheila, 'The Free Coloureds and their Fight for Civil Rights in Jamaica, 1800–1830', MA thesis, University of London, (1960).

Eaton, Michelle, '"The Shaping of a Town": The Historical Development of Port Maria, 1821–1921', MA thesis, University of the West Indies, Mona, (2003).

Sturtz, Linda, 'Proprietors and Tenants: People of Free Condition, Spanish Town, 1754', Text & Testimony Collective Conference, 'City Life in Caribbean History: Celebrating Bridgetown', University of the West Indies, Cave Hill, (2003).

Woodward, Robyn Patricia, 'The Charles Cotter Collection: A study of ceramic and faunal remains', MA thesis, Texas A&M University, (1988).

Secondary

Duperly: An Exhibition of the Works of Adolphe Duperly . . . Kingston: National Gallery of Jamaica, 2001.

Victorian Church Art. London: HMSO, 1971.

Aarons, G.A., 'Archaeological Sites in the Hellshire Area', *Jamaica Journal* 16:1 (February, 1983), 76–87.

_____ 'Sevilla la Nueva: Microcosm of Spain in Jamaica', 2 parts. '1: The Historic Background', *Jamaica Journal* 16:4 (1983), 37–46 and '2: Unearthing the Past', ibid. 17:7 (1984), 28–37.

Adams, Frederick Upham, *Conquest of the Tropics: The Story of the Creative Enterprise Conducted by the United Fruit Company*. New York: Doubleday, 1914.

Agorsah, E. Kofi, 'Archaeology of Maroon Settlements in Jamaica', in idem. ed., *Maroon Heritage: Archaeological, Ethnographical and Historical Perspectives*. Kingston: The UWI Press, 1994, 163–87.

Allsworth-Jones, Philip, 'Site summary: White Marl', in *The Lee Collection: CD Rom* (in preparation).

Allsworth-Jones, Philip, D. Gray, and S. Walters, 'The Noveh Shalom synagogue site in Spanish Town, Jamaica', in Gunilla Malm, ed., *Towards an Archaeology of Buildings*. Oxford: British Archaeological Reports, International Series, 1186, Oxford: Archaeopress, 2003, 77–88.

Amato, Joseph A,. *Rethinking Home: A Case for Writing Local History*. Berkeley, Cal: University of California Press, 2002.

Andrade, Jacob A.P.M., *A Record of the Jews in Jamaica From the English Conquest to the Present Time*. Kingston: Jamaica Times, 1941.

Andrews, Charles M., 'The Royal Disallowance', *Proceedings of the American Antiquarian Society* 24 (1914), 342–62.

Arbell, Mordechai, *The Portuguese Jews of Jamaica*. Kingston: University of the West Indies Press, 2000.

Armitage, David, 'The Cromwellian Protectorate and the Language of Empire', *Historical Journal* 35 (1992), 531–555.

Augier, Roy, 'Before and After 1865', *New World Quarterly* 2 (1966), 21–40.

Autorino, Salvadore, 'A Library for Spanish Town', *Axis: Journal of the Caribbean School of Architecture* 3/4 (1999), 10–14.

Bailey, Wilma R., 'Social control in the pre-Emancipation society of Kingston, Jamaica', *Boletín de estudios latinamericanos y del Caribe* 24 (1978), 97–110.

_____ 'The geography of fevers in Jamaica', *Jamaican Historical Review* 10 (1973), 23–31.

Barnes, Thomas G., *The Clerk of the Peace in Caroline Somerset*. Department of English Local History, Occasional Papers, 14, Leicester: Leicester University Press, 1961.

Barnett, Colin W., *The Impact of Historic Preservation on New Bern, North Carolina: From Tryon Palace to the Coor-Cook House*. Winston-Salem, NC: Bandit Books, 1993.

Bartley, Marleen A., 'Land Settlement in Jamaica, 1923–1949', in Kathleen E.A. Monteith and Glen Richards, eds., *Jamaica in Slavery and Freedom: History, Heritage and Culture*. Kingston: University of the West Indies Press, 2002, 324–39.

Basdeo, S., and H. Robertson, 'The Nova Scotia-British West Indies Commercial Experiment in the Aftermath of the American Revolution, 1783–1802', *Dalhousie Review* 61:1 (1981), 53–69.

Beacham, Peter, 'Local Building Materials and Methods', in idem. ed., *Devon Building: An Introduction to local traditions*. Exeter: Devon Books, 1990, 3rd. ed. 2001, 13–31, 163–4.

Beachey, R.W., *The British West Indies Sugar Industry in the Late 19th Century*. Oxford: Blackwell, 1957.

Beckford, George, and Michael Witter, *Small Garden . . . Bitter Weed: Struggle and Change in Jamaica*. Kingston: Institute of Social and Economic Research, 1980.

Beckles, Hilary McD., 'The "Hub of the Empire": The Caribbean and Britain in the Seventeenth Century', in Nicholas Canny, ed., *The Origins of Empire: British Overseas Enterprise to the Close of the Seventeenth-Century*. Oxford History of the British Empire, I, Oxford: Oxford University Press, 1998, 218–40.

Bennett, J. Harry, 'William Whaley, Planter of Seventeenth-Century Jamaica', *Agricultural History* 40 (1966), 113–23.

Beresford, Maurice, *East End, West End: The Face of Leeds During Urbanisation, 1684–1894*. Thoresby Society, 1st ser 60, 61, nos 131 & 132, Leeds: The Society, 1988.

Besson, Jean, *Martha Brae's Two Histories: European Expansion and Caribbean Culture-Building in Jamaica*. Chapel Hill/Kingston: University of North Carolina Press/Ian Randle Publishers, 2002.

Bilby, Kenneth M. '"Two Sister Pikni": A Historical Tradition of Dual Ethnogenesis in Eastern Jamaica', *Caribbean Quarterly* 30 (1984),10–25.

Binney, Marcus, John Harris and Kit Martin, *Jamaica's Heritage: an Untapped Resource – a Preservation Proposal by Tourism Action Plan Limited in collaboration with the Jamaican National Heritage Trust*. Kingston: Mill Press, 1991.

Black, Clinton, *Living Names in Jamaica's History.* Kingston: Jamaica Welfare, 1946.
_____ *Our Archives.* Kingston, Government Printer, 1962.
_____ *Spanish Town: The Old Capital.* Spanish Town: St Catherine's Parish Council, 1960, 2nd ed. 1974.
_____ *Tales of Old Jamaica.* Kingston: Longman Caribbean, 1966.
_____ *The History of Jamaica.* London: 1958, 2nd ed. Harlow and Kingston: Longman Caribbean, 1983.
Blain, Douglas, 'Georgian Jamaica: A New Way of Looking at a Unique Heritage', *Georgian Jamaica: Newsletter of the Friends of the Georgian Society of Jamaica* 3:3 (September, 1995), 3.
_____ 'The Frantic Search for Shade', *Georgian Jamaica: Newsletter of the Friends of the Georgian Society of Jamaica* 3:4 (December, 1995), 3–4.
_____ 'Towards a Tropical Georgian Style', *Georgian Jamaica: Newsletter of the Friends of the Georgian Society of Jamaica.* 4:1 (March, 1996), 3–4.
Blouet, Olwyn M., 'Bryan Edwards and the Haitian Revolution', in David P. Geggus. ed., *The Impact of the Haitian Revolution in the Atlantic World.* Columbia, SC: University of South Carolina Press, 2001, 44–57.
_____ 'Thirst for Knowledge: Education in Barbados, 1823–1838', *Journal of the Barbados Museum and Historical Society* 47 (2001), 185–193.
Booth, Karen, 'When Jamaica Welcomed the World: The Great Exhibition of 1891', *Jamaica Journal* 18:3 (1985), 39–51.
Borsay, Peter, *The English Urban Renaissance: Culture and Society in the Provincial Town, 1660–1770.* Oxford: Oxford University Press, 1989.
_____ 'The Restoration Town', in Lionel K.J. Glassey, ed., *The Reigns of Charles II and James VII and II.* New York: St Martin's, 1997, 171–190, 247–248, 278–288.
Bouws, Jan, 'Sir George Grove' in Stanley Sadie, ed., *The New Grove Dictionary of Music and Musicians. 7. Fuchs-Gyuzeleu.* 20 vols Basingstoke: Macmillan, 1980, 752–55.
Bowden, Martyn, 'The Three Centuries of Bridgetown: An Historical Geography', *Journal of the Barbados Museum and Historical Society* 49 (2003), 1–137.
Bragden, Kathleen, Edward Chappell and William Graham, 'A Scant Urbanity: Jamestown in the Seventeenth Century', in Theodore R. Reinhart and Dennis J. Pogue, eds., *The Archaeology of 17th Century Virginia.* Richmond, Va: Archaeological Society of Virginia, 1993, 223–249.
Brathwaite, Edward Kamau, *The Development of Creole Society in Jamaica, 1770–1829.* Oxford, Oxford University Press, 1971.
Bridenbaugh, Carl, *Peter Harrison, First American Architect.* Chapel Hill, NC: University of North Carolina Press, 1949.
_____ *Seat of Empire: The Political Role of Eighteenth-Century Williamsburg.* 1950, new edition Williamsburg, Va: Colonial Williamsburg Foundation, 1958.
_____ and Roberta Bridenbaugh, *No Peace Beyond the Line: The English in the Caribbean, 1624–1690.* New York: Oxford University Press, 1972.

Bridges, George Wilson, *The Annals of Jamaica*. 2 vols London: John Murray, 1827–8.

Briggs, Asa, *Victorian Cities* 1963, 2nd. rev ed. Harmondsworth: Penguin, 1968.

Brock, Michael, *The Great Reform Act*. London: Hutchinson, 1973.

Brodber, Erna, *A Study of Yards in the City of Kingston*. Working Papers, 9, Kingston: Institute of Social and Economic Research, University of the West Indies, Mona, 1975.

_____ 'Marcus Garvey and the Politicisation of some Afro-Jamaicans in the 1920s and 1930s', *Jamaica Journal* 20:3 (1987), 66–72.

_____ *The People of My Jamaican Village, 1817–1948*. Woodside: Blackspace, 1999.

Brown, Annette Constance, 'Old King's House destroyed by fire', *Jamaican Historical Society Bulletin* 11:6 (2000), 153–7.

Brown, Elsa Barkley, 'Womanist Consciousness: Maggie Lena Walker and the Independent Order of Saint Luke', *Signs* 14:3 (1989), 610–33.

Brown, Lawrence, 'Monuments to Freedom, Monuments to Nation: The Politics of Emancipation and Remembrance in the Eastern Caribbean', *Slavery & Abolition* 23 (2002), 93–116.

Brown, Wallace, 'The American Loyalists in Jamaica', *Journal of Caribbean History* 26:2 (1992), 121–46.

Bryan, Patricia, 'The African Aesthetic in Jamaican Intuitive Art', *ACIJ Research Review* 1 (1984), 1–20.

Bryan, Patrick, 'Émigrés, Conflict and Reconciliation: French Émigrés in Nineteenth Century Jamaica', *Jamaica Journal* 7:3 (1973), 13–19.

_____ *Inside Out and Outside In: Factors in the Creation of Contemporary Jamaica*. Grace Kennedy Foundation Lecture, Kingston: the Foundation, 2000.

_____ *Jamaica: The Aviation Story*. Kingston: Arawak Publications, 2003.

_____ 'Spanish Jamaica', *Caribbean Quarterly* 38 (1992), 21–31.

_____ *The Jamaican People 1880–1902: Race, Class and Social Control*. Basingstoke: Macmillan, 1991.

Buckley, Roger Norman, *The British Army in the West Indies: Society and the Military in the Revolutionary Age*. Gainesville, Fla: University Press of Florida, 1998.

_____ 'The Frontier in Jamaican Caricatures', *Yale University Library Gazette* 58 (1984), 152–62.

Buisseret, David, 'Edward D'Oyley 1617–1675', *Jamaica Journal* 5:1 (1971), 6–10.

_____ 'Fresh Light on Spanish Jamaica', *Jamaica Journal* 16:1 (1983), 72–3.

_____ *Historic Architecture of the Caribbean*. London: Heinemann, 1980.

_____ *Historic Jamaica from the Air*. Barbados: 1969, 2nd. rev ed. Kingston: Ian Randle Publishers, 1996.

_____ 'The Iron Bridge of Spanish Town', *Jamaica Journal* 44 (1980), 106–108.

_____ 'The Stonyhill Barracks', *Jamaica Journal* 7:1–2 (1973), 22–24.

_____ and S.A.G. Taylor, 'Juan de Bolas and His Pelinco', *Caribbean Quarterly* 24 (1978), 1–7.

Bullock, H., 'Major Abraham James, 67th. Foot, Military Author and Artist', *Journal of the Society for Army Historical Research* 39 (1961), 42–9.

Burke, Peter, *The Historical Anthropology of Early Modern Italy: Essays on Perception and Communication*. Cambridge: Cambridge University Press, 1987.

Burnard, Trevor, 'E. Pluribus Plures: African Ethnicities in Seventeenth and Eighteenth Century Jamaica', *Jamaican Historical Review* 21 (2001), 8–22, 56–9.

_____ '"Prodigious riches": the Wealth of Jamaica before the American Revolution', *Economic History Review* 2nd ser 54:3 (2001), 506–24.

_____ '"The Countrie Continues Sicklie": White Mortality in Jamaica, 1655–1780', *Social History of Medicine* 12 (1999), 45–72.

_____ '"The Grand Mart of the Island": The Economic Function of Kingston, Jamaica in the Mid-Eighteenth Century', in Monteith and Richards, *Jamaica in Slavery and Freedom*. 225–41.

_____ 'Who Bought Slaves in Early America? Purchases of Slaves from the Royal African Company in Early Jamaica, 1674–1708', *Slavery & Abolition* 17 (1996), 68–92.

Bernard, Trevor and Kenneth Morgan, 'The Dynamics of the Slave Market and Slave Purchasing Patterns in Jamaica, 1655–1788', *William & Mary Quarterly* 3rd ser 58 (2001), 205–28.

Burns, H.S., 'Rio Cobre Canal – Dream That Came True and Made Money', *Daily Gleaner* (2 June 1951), 6.

Bushnell, Amy Turner, 'How to Fight a Pirate: Provincials, Royalists and the Defence of Minor Ports during the Age of Bureaucracy', *Gulf Coast Historical Review* 5 (1990), 18–35.

Butler, Kathleen Mary, *The Economics of Emancipation: Jamaica and Barbados, 1823–1843*. Chapel Hill, NC: University of North Carolina Press, 1995.

Cadbury, H.J., 'Quakers and the Earthquake at Port Royal, 1692', *Jamaican Historical Review* 8 (1971), 19–31.

Cain, P.J., and A.G. Hopkins, *British Imperialism: Innovation and Expansion, 1688–1914*. Harlow: Longman, 1993.

Campbell, Carl, 'Early Post-Emancipation Jamaica: The Historiography of Plantation Culture 1834–1865', in Monteith and Richards, *Jamaica in Slavery and Freedom*, 52–69.

_____ 'Social and Economic Obstacles to the Development of Popular Education in Post-emancipation Jamaica', *Journal of Caribbean History* 1 (1970), 57–88.

_____ 'Teachers and the Training of Teachers in the first Primary Schools', 2 parts, *Torch: Journal of the Ministry of Education, Jamaica* 24 (1975), 51–58, 25 (1976), 64–72.

Campbell, Mavis, *The Maroons of Jamaica 1655–1796: A History of Resistance, Collaboration and Betrayal*. Trenton, NJ: Africa World Press, 1990.

Cannadine, David, *Ornamentalism: How the British Saw their Empire*. New York: Oxford University Press, 2001.

Carey, Bev, *The Maroon Story: The Authentic and Original History of the Maroons in the History of Jamaica, 1490–1880*. Gordon Town: Agouti Press, 1997.

Carliss, A., 'The Official Attitude Towards the Elected Members of the Jamaican Legislative Council, 1918–1938', *Jamaica Journal* 7:3 (1973), 6–10.

Carnegie, James, *Some Aspects of Jamaica's Politics: 1918–1938*. Cultural Heritage Series, 4, Kingston: Institute of Jamaica, 1973.

Carretta, Vincent, 'Who Was Francis Williams?' *Early American Literature* 38:2 (2003), 213–57.

Carson, Cary, Norman F. Barka, William M. Kelso, Garry Wheeler Stone and Dell Upton, 'Impermanent Architecture in the Southern American Colonies', *Winterthur Portfolio* 16 (1981), 135–196.

Casserly, F.L., 'The Grey-Hocking Bribery Affair (1893–1894)', 2 parts, *Jamaican Historical Society Bulletin* 2:1 (1957), 4-7, and 2:2 (1957), 23–6.

Cassidy, Frederic G., 'The Earliest Place Names in Jamaica', *Names* 26 (1988), 151–61.

Castillero-Calvo, Alfred, 'The City in the Hispanic Caribbean, 1492–1650', in Pieter C. Emmer and German Carrera Damas, eds., *New Societies: The Caribbean in the long sixteenth century*. General History of the Caribbean, 2, Basingstoke: Macmillan for UNESCO, 1999, 201–246.

Cateau, Heather, and S.H.H. Carrington, eds., *Capitalism and Slavery Fifty Years Later: Eric Eustice Williams – A Reassessment of the Man and his Work*. New York: Peter Lang, 2000.

Caulfeild, James E.W.S., *One Hundred Years' History of the 2nd Battalion, West India Regiment*. London: Foster Groom, 1899.

Cauna-Ladevie, Jacques de, 'La Diaspora des colons de Saint-Domingue et le monde créole: Le cas de la Jamaïque', *Revue Française d'Historie d'Outre-Mer* 81 (1994), 333–359.

Chalmin, Philippe, *The Making of a Sugar Giant: Tate and Lyle 1859–1989*. Paris, 1983, Eng. trans. London: Harwood, 1990.

Checkland, Sydney, *The Elgins, 1766–1917: a Tale of Aristocrats, Proconsuls and Their Wives*. Aberdeen: Aberdeen University Press, 1988.

Chevannes, Barrington, 'Garvey Myths among the Jamaican People', in Rupert Lewis and Patrick Bryan, eds., *Garvey: His Work and Impact*. Trenton, NJ: Africa World Press, 1991, 123–31.

Clarke, Colin G., *Kingston, Jamaica: Urban Development and Social Change, 1692–1962*. Berkeley, Cal: University of California Press, 1975.

Claypole, William A., 'The Settlement of the Liguanea Plain between 1655 and 1673', *Jamaican Historical Review* 10 (1973), 7–16.

Clifton-Taylor, Alex, *The Pattern of English Buildings*. 1962, 2nd. edn. London: Faber, 1965.

Cobb, Richard, *French and Germans, Germans and French: A Personal Interpretation of France under Two Occupations, 1914–1918, 1940–1944*. Hanover, NH: University Press of New England, 1983.

Cobham, Rhoda, 'Fictions of Gender, Fictions of Race: Retelling Morant Bay in Jamaican Literature', *Small Axe* 8 (2000), 1–30.

Colley, Linda, *Britons: Forging the Nation 1707–1837*. New Haven, Conn: Yale University Press, 1992.

Collett G.W., *et al.* eds., *Jamaica: Its Postal History, Postage Stamps and Postmarks*. London: Stanley Gibbons, 1928.

Colvin, Howard, *Essays in English architectural history*, New Haven, Conn: Yale University Press, 1999,

Concannon, T.A.L., 'Our Architectural Heritage: Houses of the 18th and 19th Century with Special Reference to Spanish Town', *Jamaica Journal* 4 (1970), 23–8.

_____ 'The Great Houses of Jamaica', in Morris Cargill, ed., *Ian Fleming Introduces Jamaica*. London: André Deutsch, 1965, 117–26.

Conway, Stephen, ' "A Joy Unknown for Years Past": The American Wars, Britishness and the Celebration of Rodney's Victory at the Saints', *History* 86 (2001), 180–99.

Corbitt, Duvon C., '*Mercedes* and *Realengos*: a Survey of the Public Land System in Cuba', *Hispanic American Historical Review* 19 (1939), 262–85.

Cossons, Neil, and Barrie Trinder, *The Iron Bridge: Symbol of the Industrial Revolution*. Bradford-on-Avon: Moonraker Press, 1979.

Costas, Aida R. Caro, 'The Organization of Institutional and Social Life', in Arturo Morales Carrión, ed., *Puerto Rico: A Political and Cultural History*. New York: Norton, 1983, 25–40.

Cotter, Charles S., 'Sevilla Nueva: The Story of an Excavation', *Jamaica Journal* 4 (1970), 15–22.

Coutu, Joan, 'Carving Histories: British Sculpture in the West Indies', *Church Monuments* 13 (1997), 77–85.

_____ 'The Rodney Monument in Jamaica and an Empire Coming of Age', *Sculpture Journal* 2 (1998), 46–57.

Craig, Alan K., *Spanish Colonial Silver Coins in the Florida Collection*. Gainesville, Fla: Florida Bureau of Archaeological Research and University Press of Florida, 2000.

Crain, Edward E., *Historic Architecture of the Caribbean Islands*. Gainesville, Fla: University Press of Florida, 1994.

Craton, Michael, 'The Real Sir Charles Price', *Jamaica Journal* 4:4 (1970), 10–14.

Crewe, Duncan, *Yellow Jack and the Worm: British Naval Administration in the West Indies, 1739–1748*. Liverpool Historical Series, 9, Liverpool: Liverpool University Press, 1993.

Crouch, Dora P., Daniel J. Garr and Axel I. Mundigo, *Spanish City Planning in North America*. Cambridge, Mass: MIT Press, 1982.

Crowley, John E. *The Invention of Comfort: Sensibilities and Design in Early Modern Britain and Early America*. Baltimore, Md: Johns Hopkins, 2001.

Cundall, Frank, *Historic Jamaica*. London: West India Committee for Institute of Jamaica, 1915.

_____ *The Governors of Jamaica in the First Half of the Eighteenth Century.* London: West India Committee, 1937.

_____ *The Life of Enos Nuttall: Archbishop of the West Indies.* London: SPCK, 1922.

_____ *The Mico College, Jamaica.* Kingston: Gleaner Company for Directors of the College, 1914.

Curtin, Philip D., *Death by Migration: Europe's Encounter with the Tropical World in the Nineteenth Century.* Cambridge: Cambridge University Press, 1989.

_____ 'The British Sugar Duties and West Indian Prosperity', *Journal of Economic History* 14 (1954), 157–64.

_____ *Two Jamaicas: The Role of Ideas in a Tropical Colony, 1830–1865.* Cambridge, Mass: Harvard University Press, 1955.

daCosta, H.L., 'The Constitutional Experiment in the Twelve Years Before the Morant Bay Rebellion', *Jamaican Historical Society Bulletin* 4:6 (1966), 109–21.

Dalby, Jonathan, *Crime and Punishment in Jamaica, 1756–1856.* Kingston: Social History Project, 2000.

Davies, K.G., *The Royal African Company.* London: Longman, 1957.

Davies, Peter N., *Fyffes and the Banana: Musa Sapientum, A Centenary History 1888–1988.* London: Athlone, 1990.

Davis, Carlton E., *Jamaica in the World Aluminium Industry, 1938–1988.* 2 vols Kingston: Jamaica Bauxite Institute, 1989, 1995.

Davis, Robert Scott, Jr. 'George Liele', in Kenneth Coleman and Charles Stephen Gurr, eds., *Dictionary of Georgia Biography,* 2 vols Athens, Ga: University of Georgia Press, 1983, 2. 620–21.

_____ 'The Other Side of the Coin: Georgia Baptists who fought for the King', *Viewpoints: Georgia Baptist History* 7 (1980), 47–57.

De Barros, Juanita, *Order and Place in a Colonial City: Patterns of Struggle and Resistance in Georgetown, British Guiana, 1889–1924.* Kingston: McGill-Queen's University Press, 2002.

Debien, Gabriel, and Piere Pluchon, 'Un plan d'invasion de la Jamaïque en 1799 et la politique anglo-américaine de Toussaint-Louverture', *Revue de la Société d'histoire de géographie et de géologie* 36 Notes d'Historie Coloniale, no 186, Port-au-Prince, 1978, 3–72.

Downes, Aviston C., 'Sailing from Colonial into National Waters: A History of the Barbados Landship', *Journal of the Barbados Museum and Historical Society* 46 (2000), 93–122.

Duffy, Michael, 'Contested Empires, 1756–1815', in Paul Langford, ed., *The Eighteenth Century, 1688–1815.* Oxford: Oxford University Press, 2002, 213–242.

_____ *Soldiers, Sugar and Seapower: The British Expeditions to the West Indies and the War against Revolutionary France.* Oxford: Clarendon, 1987.

Dunn, Richard S., *Sugar and Slaves: The Rise of the Planter Class in the English West Indies, 1624–1713.* Chapel Hill, NC: University of North Carolina Press, 1972.

Earle, Peter, *The Wreck of the Almiranta: Sir William Phips and the Hispaniola Treasure.* London: Macmillan, 1979.

Eaton, George E., *Alexander Bustamante and Modern Jamaica.* Kingston: Kingston Publishers, 1975.

Ebanks, Roderick, 'Ma Lou and the African-Jamaican Pottery Tradition', *Jamaica Journal* 17:3 (1984), 31–7.

Eisner, Gisela, *Jamaica, 1830–1930: A Study in Economic Growth.* Manchester: Manchester University Press, 1961.

Ellis, J.B., *The Diocese of Jamaica: A Short Account of its History, Growth and Organisation.* London: SPCK, 1913.

Eltis, David, *Economic Growth and the Ending of the Transatlantic Slave Trade.* New York: Oxford University Press, 1987.

Engel, A.J., *From Clergyman to Don: The Rise of the Academic Profession in Nineteenth-Century Oxford.* Oxford: Clarendon, 1983.

Eudell, Demitrius L., *The Political Languages of Emancipation in the British Caribbean and the US South.* Chapel Hill, NC.: University of North Carolina Press, 2002.

Eyre, Alan, *The Botanical Gardens of Jamaica.* London: André Deutsch, 1966.

Faber, Eli, 'The Jews and their Role in Slaves and Slavery', *Jamaican Historical Society Bulletin* 11:2 (1998), 26–9.

Fergus, Howard A., ed., *Eruption: Montserrat Versus Volcano.* Plymouth: University of the West Indies, School of Continuing Studies, Montserrat, 1996.

———— and E.A. Markham, eds., *Hugo versus Montserrat.* Coleraine and Boston, Mass: Linda Lee Books, 1989.

Fonseca, John W., 'The Cathedral of St Jago de la Vega', *Centenary of the Granting of the Royal Letters Patent to the Cathedral of St Jago de la Vega, 1843–1943.* [Spanish Town, nd. *c*. 1943], 12–16.

Francis-Brown, Suzanne, 'Mama Lou', (1983), reprinted in Linda Gambrill, ed., *A Tapestry of Jamaica: The Best of Skywritings.* Oxford: Macmillan Caribbean, 2002, 272.

Freeman, Michael, *Railways and the Victorian Imagination.* New Haven, Con: Yale University Press, 1999.

Friedman, Ellen G., *Spanish Captives in North Africa in the Early Modern Age.* Madison, Wis: University of Wisconsin Press, 1983.

Gartshore, John F., *Outline History of Shortwood College, 1885–1935.* [Kingston: Gleaner, 1935].

Gaspar, David Barry, '"Rigid and Inclement": Origin of the Jamaican Slave Laws of the Seventeenth Century', in Christopher L. Tomlins and Bruce H. Mann, eds., *The Many Legalities of Early Modern America.* Chapel Hill, NC: University of North Carolina Press, 2001, 78–96.

Gayle, Clement, *George Liele: Pioneer Missionary in Jamaica.* Kingston: Jamaica Baptist Union, [1982].

_____ 'George Liele: Jamaica's First Black Preacher', *Jamaican Historical Society Bulletin* 8:9 (1983), 199–204.

Geggus, David Patrick, *Slavery, War and Revolution: The British Occupation of Saint Domingue, 1793–1798*. Oxford: Oxford University Press, 1982.

_____ 'The Enigma of Jamaica in the 1790s: New Light on the Causes of Slave Rebellions', *William & Mary Quarterly* 3rd ser 44 (1987), 274–99.

Gilmore, John, *Glimpses of Our Past: A Social History of the Caribbean in Postcards*. Kingston: Ian Randle Publishers, 1995.

Girouard, Mark, *Victorian Pubs*. New Haven, Conn: Yale University Press, 1984.

Gocking, C.V., 'Early Constitutional History of Jamaica: with special reference to the period 1838–1866', *Caribbean Quarterly* 6 (1960), 114–33.

Goldfield, David, *Region, Race and Cities: Interpreting the Urban South*. Baton Rouge, La: Louisiana State University Press, 1997.

Goldson, Terence O.B., *Warmed Hearts: Stories of Early Methodism and its Heroes and Heroines in Jamaica*. London: Avon Books, 1997.

[Goldson, T.O.B., ed.,] *Souvenir Brochure of the Spanish Town Methodist Church*. Kingston: Gleaner Company for Methodist Church, Spanish Town, 1953.

Gordon, Shirley, 'Schools of the Free', in Brian J. Moore and Swithin R. Wilmot, eds., *Before and After 1865: Education, Politics and Regionalism in the Caribbean in honour of Sir Roy Augier*. Kingston: Ian Randle Publishers, 1998, 1–12, 375–76.

Gosner, Pamela, *Caribbean Baroque: Historic Architecture of the Spanish Antilles*. Pueblo, Colo: Passeggiata Press, 1996.

_____ *Caribbean Georgian: The Great and Small Houses of the West Indies*. Washington, DC: Three Continents, 1982.

Goveia, Elsa V., *A Study on the Historiography of the British West Indies to the End of the Nineteenth Century*. Tacubaya, Mexico: Instituto Panamericano de Geografa e Historia, 1956, reprint Washington, DC: Howard University Press, 1980.

Gragg, Larry, 'The Port Royal Earthquake', *History Today* 50:9 (2000), 28–34.

Greene, Jack P., *Pursuits of Happiness: The Social Development of Early Modern British Colonies and the Formation of American Culture*. Chapel Hill, NC: University of North Carolina Press, 1988.

_____ *Negotiated Authorities: Essays in Colonial Political and Constitutional History*. Charlottesville, Va: University of Virginia Press, 1994.

Guillebaud, C.W., 'The Crown Colonies, 1845–1870', in J. Holland Rose, A.P. Newton and E.A. Benians, eds., *The Growth of the New Empire, 1783–1870*. Cambridge History of the British Empire, 2, Cambridge: Cambridge University Press, 1940, 705–738.

Hackman, W.K., 'William Beckford's Profits from Three Jamaican Offices', *Historical Research* 63 (1990), 107–9.

Hainsworth, Roger, *The Swordsmen in Power: War and Politics under the English Republic 1649–1660*. Stroud: Sutton, 1997.

Hall, Catherine, *Civilising Subjects: Metropole and Colony in the English Imagination 1830–1867*. Cambridge: Polity, 2002.

Hall, Catherine, Keith McClelland and Jane Rendall, *Defining the Victorian Nation: Class, Race, Gender and the Reform Act of 1867*. Cambridge: Cambridge University Press, 2000.

Hall, Douglas, *Free Jamaica 1838–1865: An Economic History*. New Haven, Conn: Yale University Press, 1959.

_____ 'Sir Charles Metcalfe', *Caribbean Quarterly* 3:2 (1953), 90–100.

Hall, N.A.T., 'Public Office and Private Gain: A Note on Administration in Late Eighteenth Century Jamaica', *Caribbean Studies* 12:3 (1972), 5–20.

Handler, Jerome S. and Kenneth M. Bilby, 'On the Early Use and Origin of the Term "Obeah" in Barbados and the Anglophone Caribbean', *Slavery & Abolition* 22:2 (2001), 87–100.

Harriott, Anthony, 'Captured Shadows, Tongue-Tied Witnesses, "Compellants" and the Courts: *Obya* and Social Control', in Monteith and Richards, *Jamaica in Slavery and Freedom*, 115–143.

Harris, H.C., 'The Cape Verde Region (1499 to 1549): the Key to Coconut Cultivation in the Western Hemisphere?', *Turrialba* 27 (1977), 227–31.

Harrison, David, '19 White Church Street', *Jamaican Historical Society Bulletin* 8:7 (1982), 167–78.

Harrison, J.R., 'The Mud Wall in England at the Close of the Vernacular Era', *Transactions of the Ancient Monuments Society* n.s. 28 (1984), 154–74.

Hart, Richard, *Towards Decolonisation: Political, labour and economic developments in Jamaica 1938–1945*. Kingston: University of the West Indies Press, 1999.

Hendricks, S. Purcell, *History of the Cathedral Church of St Jago de la Vega, Spanish Town*. Kingston: Jamaica Times, 1911.

Henretta, James A., *'Salutary Neglect': Colonial Administration under the Duke of Newcastle*. Princeton, NJ: Princeton University Press, 1972.

Herman, Bernard L., 'Slave and Servant Housing in Charleston, 1770–1820', *Historical Archaeology* 33 (1999), 88–101.

Hurwitz, Samuel J., and Edith, *Jamaica: A Historical Portrait*. London: Pall Mall, 1971.

Heuman, Gad, *Between Black and White: Race, Politics, and the Free Coloreds in Jamaica, 1792–1865*. Westport, Conn: Greenwood, 1981.

_____ *'The Killing Time': The Morant Bay Rebellion in Jamaica*. Basingstoke: Macmillan, 1994.

Higgins, Brian T., and Kenneth F. Kipple, 'Cholera in Mid-Nineteenth-Century Jamaica', *Jamaican Historical Review* 17 (1991), 31–47.

Higman, Barry W., *Montpelier, Jamaica: A Plantation Community in Slavery and Freedom 1739–1912*. Kingston: University of the West Indies Press, 1998.

_____ *Slave Population and Economy in Jamaica 1807–1834*. Cambridge: Cambridge University Press, 1976.

_____ "'To Begin the World Again": Responses to Emancipation at Friendship and Greenwich Estate, Jamaica', in Monteith and Richards, eds., *Jamaica in Slavery and Freedom*, 291–306.

Hill, Errol, *The Jamaican Stage, 1655–1900: Profile of a Colonial Theatre*. Amhurst, Mass: University of Massachusetts Press, 1992.

Hill, Richard, *Lights and Shadows of Jamaican History: Being Three Lectures*. Kingston: Ford and Gall, 1859.

Hill, Vincent, 'Distribution and Potential – Clays in Jamaica' *Jamaica Journal* 42 (1978), 64–75.

Hobbs, Colleen A., *Florence Nightingale*. New York: Twayne, 1997.

Holt, Thomas C., '"An Empire over the Mind": Emancipation, Race and Ideology in the British West Indies and the American South', in J. Morgan Kousser and James M. McPherson, eds., *Region, Race and Reconstruction: Essays in Honor of C. Vann Woodward*. New York: Oxford University Press, 1982, 283–313.

_____ *The Problem of Freedom: Race, Labor, and Politics in Jamaica and Britain, 1832–1938*. Baltimore and Kingston: Johns Hopkins University Press and Ian Randle Publishers, 1992.

Horner, Dave, *Shipwreck: A Saga of Sea Tragedy and Sunken Treasure*. Stroud: Sutton, 1999.

Horwood, Tom, 'The Rise and Fall of the Catholic University College, Kensington, 1868-1882', *Journal of Ecclesiastical History* 54 (2003), 302–18.

Hough, Samuel L., *The Italians in the Creation of America: An Exhibition at the John Carter Brown Library*. Providence, RI: John Carter Brown Library, 1980.

Howard, Maurice, *The Early English Country House: Architecture and Politics 1490–1550*. London: George Philip, 1987.

Howard, Richard A., and Dulcie A. Powell, 'The Indian Botanic Garden, Calcutta and the Gardens of the West Indies', *Bulletin of the Botanical Survey of India* 7 (1965), 1–7.

Howard, Robert, *et al.* 'Arawak Findings at White Marl', 2 parts, *Jamaican Historical Society Bulletin* 3:4 (1961), 59–63; ibid. 3:5 (1962), 79–82.

Hudson, Nicholas, '"Britons Never Will be Slaves": National Myth, Conservatism, and the Beginnings of British Antislavery', *Eighteenth-Century Studies* 34 (2001), 559–576.

Hutton, Clinton, 'The Defeat of the Morant Bay Rebellion', *Jamaican Historical Review* 19 (1996), 30–8, 65–6.

Ingram, K.E., *Manuscripts Relating to the Commonwealth Caribbean Countries in US and Canadian Repositories*. Barbados: Caribbean University Press, 1975.

_____ *Manuscript Sources for the History of the West Indies, with Special Reference to Jamaica in the National Library of Jamaica and Supplementary Sources in the West Indies, North America, the United Kingdom and Elsewhere*. Kingston: University of the West Indies Press, 2000.

_____ *Sources for West Indian Studies: A Supplementary Listing with particular reference to manuscript sources*. Zug: Inter-Documentation, 1983.

_____ *Sources of Jamaican History, 1655–1838: A Bibliographical Survey with Particular Reference to Manuscript Sources.* 2 vols Zug: Inter-Documentation, 1976.

_____ *The QC and the Middleman.* Bishop Auckland: Pentland Press, 1997.

James, Winston, *A Fierce Hatred of Injustice: Claude McKay's Jamaica and his Poetry of Rebellion.* Kingston: Ian Randle Publishers, 2001.

Jenkins, Virgina Scott, *Bananas: An American History.* Washington DC: Smithsonian Institution, 2000.

Johnson, Anthony S., *City of Kingston Souvenir: Commemoration of the Bicentennial of the City Charter.* Kingston: ISKAMOL, 2002.

_____ *J.A.G. Smith.* Kingston: Kingston Publishers and Jamaica Institute of Political Education, 1991.

Johnson, Howard, 'Historiography of Jamaica', in B.W. Higman, ed., *Methodology and Historiography of the Caribbean.* General History of the Caribbean, 6, Basingstoke: Macmillan for UNESCO, 1999, 478–530.

_____ 'The British Caribbean from Demobilisation to Constitutional Decolonisation', in Judith M. Brown and W. Roger Louis, eds., *The Twentieth Century.* Oxford History of the British Empire, 4, Oxford: Oxford University Press, 1999, 597–622.

Johnson, Michelle A., '"To Dwell Together in Unity": Referendum on West Indian Federation, 1961', in Moore and Wilmot, *Before and After 1865,* 261–71, 404–06.

Kagan, Richard L., *Urban Images of the Hispanic World, 1493-1793.* New Haven, Conn: Yale University Press, 2000.

King, J.M. 'Walter Augustus Feurtado and His Manuscripts', *Jamaica Journal* 3 (1969), 13–15.

King, Ruby Hope, 'The Jamaica Schools Commission and the Development of Secondary Schooling', (1979), in idem. ed., *Education in the Caribbean: Historical Perspectives. Caribbean Journal of Education* 14:1&2 (1987), 88–108.

Kirk-Green, Anthony, '"Not Quite a Gentleman": The Desk Diaries of the Assistant Private Secretary (Appointments) to the Secretary of State for the Colonies, 1899–1935', *English Historical Review* 117 (2002), 622–33.

Klein, Herbert S., 'The English Slave Trade in Jamaica, 1782–1808', *Economic History Review* 2nd ser 31 (1978), 25–45.

Klingberg, Frank J., 'The Lady Mico Charity Schools in the British West Indies, 1835–1844', *Journal of Negro History* 29 (1939), 291–344.

Knight, Franklin W. and Peggy K. Liss, eds. *Atlantic Port Cities: Economy, Culture, and Society in the Atlantic World, 1650–1850.* Knoxville, Tenn: University of Tennessee Press, 1991.

Knox-Johnson, Robin, *The Columbus Venture.* London: BBC, 1992.

Laithwaite, Michael, 'Totnes houses 1500–1800', in Peter Clark, ed., *The Transformation of English Provincial Towns.* London: Hutchinson, 1984, 62–98.

_____ 'Town Houses up to 1660', in Beacham, *Devon Building,* 95–115, 165.

Langford, Paul, *Englishness Identified: Manners and Character, 1650–1850*. Oxford: Oxford University Press, 2000.

Lazarus-Black, Mindie, 'John Grant's Jamaica: Notes Towards a Reassessment of Courts in the Slave Era', *Journal of Caribbean History* 27 (1993), 144–59.

Lewis, Bernard, *Cultures in Conflict: Christians, Muslims and Jews in the Age of Discovery*. New York: Oxford University Press, 1995.

Lewis, Charles Lee, *Admiral de Grasse and American Independence*. Annapolis, Md: United States Naval Institute, 1945.

Lewis, Lesley, 'English Commemorative Sculpture in Jamaica', *Jamaican Historical Review* 9 (1972), 7–123.

Lewis, Rupert, *Marcus Garvey: Anti-Colonial Champion*. Trenton, NJ: Africa World Press, 1988.

Lieberman, Seymour B., 'The Secret-Jewery in the Spanish New World Colonies, 1500–1820', in R.D. Barnett and W.M. Schwab, eds., *The Sephardi Heritage: Essays on the history and cultural contribution of the Jews of Spain and Portugal 2 The Western Sephardim*. Grendon, Northants: Gibraltar Books, 1989, 474–96.

Loker, Zvi, 'An Eighteenth-Century Plan to Invade Jamaica – Isaac Yeshurun Sasportas – French Patriot or Jewish Radical Idealist', *Transactions of the Jewish Historical Society of England* 28 (1984), 132–44.

Long, Anton V., *Jamaica and the New Order, 1827–1847*. Special Series, 1, Kingston: Institute of Social and Economic Research, UCWI, 1956.

Loundsbury, Carl R., *From Statehouse to Courthouse: An Architectural History of South Carolina's Colonial Capitol and Charleston County Courthouse*. Columbia, SC: University of South Carolina Press, 2001.

Lovett, Richard, *The History of the London Missionary Society, 1795–1895*. 2 vols. London: Henry Frowde, 1899.

Lumsden, Joy, 'A Forgotten Generation: Black Politicians in Jamaica, 1885–1914', in Moore and Wilmot, *Before & After 1865*, 112–122, 387–8.

Lyon, Eugene, *The Search for the Atocha*. New York, 1979, 2nd edn. Port Salerno, Fla: Florida Classics Library, 1989.

Macmillan, Mona C.M., *Sir Henry Barkly: Mediator and Moderator, 1815–1898*. Cape Town: A.A. Balkema, 1970.

Maltby, William S., *The Black Legend in England: The Development of anti-Spanish Sentiment*. Durham, NC: Duke University Press, 1971.

Manucy, Albert, *Sixteenth-Century St Augustine: The People and Their Homes*. Gainesville, Fla: University Press of Florida, 1997.

Manucy, Albert and Ricardo Torres-Reyes, *Puerto Rico and the Forts of Old San Juan*. Riverside, Conn: Chatham Press, 1973.

Marquardt, Steve, '"Green Havoc": Panama Disease, Environmental Change, and Labor Process in the Central American Banana Industry', *American Historical Review* 106 (2001), 49–80.

Marsala, Vincent John, *Sir John Peter Grant, Governor of Jamaica, 1866–1874: An Administrative Study*. Cultural Heritage Series, 3, Kingston: Institute of Jamaica, 1972.

Marshall, H.V. Ormsby, 'Eagle House', *Jamaican Historical Society Bulletin* 3:16 (1964), 260–63.

Marshall, Woodville K., 'Charity for the undeserving? The Carpenter Trust and the Creation of the Parish Land Tenantry in St Philip', *Journal of the Barbados Museum and Historical Society* 49 (2003), 167–91.

_____ '"We be wise in many tings": Blacks' Hopes and Expectations of Emancipation', in F.R. Augier, ed., *The University of the West Indies: 40th Anniversary Lectures*. Kingston: University of the West Indies, 1990, 31–46.

Mathewson, R. Duncan, 'Archaeological Analysis of Material Culture as a Reflection of Sub-Cultural Differentiation in 18th Century Jamaica', *Jamaica Journal* 7:1–2 (1973), 25–29.

_____ 'History from the Earth: Archaeological Excavation at Old King's House', *Jamaica Journal* 6:4 (1972), 3–11.

_____ 'The Old King's House Archaeological Project', *Jamaican Historical Society Bulletin* 5:11 (1971), 140–50.

Mathurin, Lucille, 'Creole Authenticity', *Savacou* 5 (1971), 115–20.

Meeks, Brian, 'Jamaica's Michael Manley (1924–97): Crossing the Contours of Charisma', in Anton L. Allahar, ed., *Caribbean Charisma: Reflections on Leadership, Legitimacy and Populist Politics*. Kingston: Ian Randle Publishers, 2001, 192–211.

Mehrotra, Rahul, 'Bazaars in Victorian Arcades: Conserving Bombay's Colonial Heritage', in Ismail Serageldin, Ephrim Shulger, Joan Martin-Brown, eds., *Historic Cities and Sacred Sites: Cultural Roots for Urban Futures*. Washington, DC: World Bank, 2001, 154–63.

Metcalf, George, *Royal Government and Political Conflict in Jamaica, 1729–1783*. London: Longmans for Royal Commonwealth Society, 1965.

Metcalf, Thomas R., 'Architecture in the British Empire', in *Historiography*. eds., Robin W. Winks and Alaine Low, Oxford History of the British Empire, 5, Oxford: Oxford University Press, 1999, 584–595.

Miller, Henry C., 'Archaeology and Town Planning', in Geoff Egan and R.L. Michael, eds., *Old and New Worlds*. Oxford: Oxbow, 1999, 72–83.

_____ 'The Country House Site: An Archaeological Study of a Seventeenth-Century Domestic Landscape', in Paul A. Shackel and Barbara J. Little, eds., *Historical Archaeology of the Chesapeake*. Washington, DC: Smithsonian Institution, 1994, 65–83.

Milne, Gustav, *The Great Fire of London*. New Barnet: Historical Publications, 1986.

Minter, R.A., *Episcopacy Without Episcopate: The Church of England in Jamaica before 1824*. Upton-upon-Severn: Self Publishing Association, 1990.

Monteith, Kathleen, 'Planting and Processing Techniques on Jamaican Coffee

Plantations during Slavery', in Verene Shepherd, ed., *Working Slavery, Pricing Freedom:Perspectives from the Caribbean, Africa and the African Diaspora*. Kingston: Ian Randle Publishers, 2002, 112–29.

_____ 'Regulation of the Commercial Banking Sector in the British West Indies, 1837–1961', *Journal of Caribbean History* 37:2 (2003), 204–232.

Morgan, Doreen, 'Ma Lou: Profile of a Potter', [Kingston]: Petroleum Corporation of Jamaica, [nd. post 1989].

Morison, S.E., *The Second Voyage of Christopher Columbus from Cadiz to Hispaniola and the Discovery of the Lesser Antilles*. Oxford: Oxford University Press, 1939.

Morrill, John, 'Postlude: Between War and Peace 1651-1660', in John Kenyon and Jane Ohelmeyer, eds., *The Civil Wars: A Military History of England, Scotland and Ireland 1638–1660*. Oxford: Oxford University Press, 1998, 306–28, 342–4.

Morris, R.J., 'Clubs, societies and associations', in F.M.L. Thompson, ed., *Social agencies and institutions*. Cambridge Social History of Britain, 1750–1950, 3, Cambridge: Cambridge University Press, 1990, 395–443.

Morrissey, Carol Mae, '"Ol' Time Tram" and the Tramway Era, 1876–1948', *Jamaica Journal* 16:4 (1983), 12–21.

Morse, Richard M., 'Urban Development', in Leslie Bethell, ed., *Colonial Spanish America*. Cambridge: Cambridge University Press, 1987, 165–202.

Munroe, Trevor, 'The Bustamante Letters 1935', *Jamaica Journal* 8:1 (1974), 2–15.

_____ *The Politics of Constitutional Decolonisation: Jamaica, 1944–62*. Kingston: Institute of Social and Economic Research, University of the West Indies, 1972.

Murray, David, *Odious Commerce: Britain, Spain and the abolition of the Cuban slave trade*. Cambridge: Cambridge University Press, 1980.

Muthesius, Stefan, *The High Victorian Movement in Architecture, 1850–1870*. London: Routledge, 1972.

Nader, Helen, *Liberty in Absolute Spain: The Habsburg Sale of Towns, 1516–1700*. Baltimore, Md: Johns Hopkins University Press, 1990.

Nelson, Lewis, 'Building "Cross-wise": Reconstructing Jamaica's Eighteenth-Century Anglican Churches', *Jamaican Historical Review* 22 (2003), 11–39, 70–76.

Nettleford, Rex, ed., *Jamaica in Independence: Essays on the Early Years*. Kingston: Heinemann, 1989.

Newman, Aubrey N., 'The Sephardim of the Caribbean', in Barnett and Schwab, *The Sephardi Heritage*, 445–73.

Newton, Norman, *Thomas Gage in Spanish America*. London: Faber, 1969.

Oatts, L.B. *Emperor's Chambermaids: The Story of the 14th/20th King's Hussars*. London: Ward Lock, 1973.

Olivier, Sidney Haldane, Lord Olivier, *The Myth of Governor Eyre*. London: Hogarth Press, 1933.

Osborne, F.J., *The History of the Catholic Church in Jamaica*. 2nd. edn. Chicago, Ill: Loyola University Press, 1988.

O'Shaughnessy, Andrew Jackson, *An Empire Divided: The American Revolution and the British Caribbean*. Philadelphia, Penn: University of Pennsylvania Press, 2000.

Outlaw, Alain Charles, *Governor's Land: Archaeology of Early Seventeenth-Century Virginia Settlements*. Charlottesville, Va: University Press of Virginia, 1990.

Pabón, Arlee, '*Por la encendida calle antillana*: Africanisms and Puerto Rican Architecture', *CRM: The Journal of Heritage Stewardship* 1:1 (2003), 14–32.

Padrón, Francisco Morales, *Spanish Jamaica*, trans., Patrick Bryan, Kingston: Ian Randle Publishers, 2003.

Palm, Erwin Walter, 'Plateresque and Renaissance Monuments of the Island of Hispaniola', *Journal of the Society of Architectural Historians* 5 (1946), 1–14.

Panning, Steven, 'Observations on the State of the Iron Bridge, Spanish Town', *Jamaican Historical Society Bulletin* 11:5 (2000), 121–125.

_____ 'Spanish Ruins at Orange Valley', *Jamaican Historical Society Bulletin* 10:12 (1995), 134–136.

Pares, Richard, *Merchants and Planters*. Economic History Review Supplement, 4, Cambridge: for the Economic History Society, 1960.

_____ 'Prisoners of War in the West Indies in the Eighteenth Century', *Journal of the Barbados Museum and Historical Society* 5 (1937), 12–17.

Parraux, André, *The Publication of The Monk: A Literary Event, 1796–1798*. Paris: Didier, 1960.

Parry, J.H., 'American Independence: The View from the West Indies', *Proceedings of the Massachusetts Historical Society* 87 (1974), 14–31.

_____ 'The Patent Officers in the British West Indies', *English Historical Review* 69 (1954), 200–25.

Pawson, Michael, and David Buisseret, *Port Royal, Jamaica*. Oxford, 1974, 2nd edn Kingston: University of the West Indies Press, 2000.

Payne, Anthony J., *Politics in Jamaica*. London, 1988, rev edn. Kingston: Ian Randle Publishers, 1994.

Pemberton, Rita, 'Protecting Caribbean Environments: The Development of the Forest Conservation in Jamaica, 1855–1945', in Serge Mam Lam Fouch, *et al.* eds., *Regards sur l'historie de la Caraïbe, des Guyanes aux Grandes Antilles: Les actes de la 32e Conférence de l'Association des Historiens de la Caraïbe, Cayenne, avril 2000*. Petit-Bourg, Guadeloupe: Ibis Rouge, 2001, 257–73.

Pérez-Mallaína, Pablo E., *Spain's Men of the Sea: Daily Life on the Indies Fleets in the Sixteenth Century*. Baltimore, Md: Johns Hopkins, 1998.

Pérotin-Dumon, Anne, *La Ville aux Îles, la ville dans l'île: Basse-Terre et Pointe-à-Pitre, Guadeloupe, 1650–1820*. Paris: Éditions Karthala, 2000.

Pevesner, Nikolaus, 'Scrape and Anti-scrape', in Jane Fawcett, edn., *The Future of the Past: Attitudes to Conservation, 1174–1974*. London: Thames & Hudson, 1976, 35–53.

Phillips, Carla Rahn, 'The Growth and Composition of Trade in the Iberian empires, 1450–1750', in James D. Tracy, ed., *The Rise of Merchant Empires: Long-Distance Trade in the Early Modern World, 1350–1750*. Cambridge: Cambridge University Press, 1990, 34–101.

Pietersz, Joseph, 'The Last Spanish Governor of Jamaica', *Jamaican Historical Review* 1 (1945), 24–30.

Pigou, Elizabeth, 'A Note on Afro-Jamaican Beliefs and Rituals', *Jamaica Journal* 20:2 (1987), 23–6.

Pigou-Dennis, Elizabeth, 'The Jamaican Bungalow: Whose Language?' in Monteith and Richards, *Jamaica in Slavery and Freedom*, 179–193.

———— 'Traditional Ornament: Fretwork', *Axis: Journal of the Caribbean School of Architecture* 2 (1998), 55.

Pinto, Geoffrey de Sola, and Anghelen Arrington Phillips, *Jamaican Houses a vanishing legacy*. Montego Bay: de Sola Pinto Printers, 1982.

Plant, O.C., 'The Architecture of the Cathedral', *Centenary . . . Royal Letters Patent*, 20–21.

Pocock, J.G.A., *The Machiavellian Moment: Florentine Political Thought and the Atlantic Republican Tradition*. Princeton, NJ: Princeton University Press, 1975.

Porter, Stephen, and Adam White, 'John Colt and the Charterhouse Chapel', *Architectural History* 44 (2001), 228–36.

Post, Ken, *Arise ye Starvelings: The Jamaican Labour Rebellion of 1938 and its Aftermath*. Institute of Social Studies Series on the Development of Societies, 3. The Hague: Nijhoff, 1978.

Potts, E. Daniel, *British Baptist Missionaries in India 1793–1837: The History of Serampore and its Missions*. Cambridge: Cambridge University Press, 1967.

Priddy, Anthony, 'The 17th and 18th Century Settlement Pattern of Port Royal', *Jamaica Journal* 9:2–3 (1975), 8–10, 17.

Quigley, Neil C., 'The Bank of Nova Scotia in the Caribbean, 1889-1940', *Business History Review* 63 (1989), 797–838.

Rashford, John, 'Arawak, Spanish and African Contributions to Jamaica's Settlement Vegetation', *Jamaica Journal* 24:3 (1993), 17–23.

———— 'The Search for Africa's Baobab Tree in Jamaica', *Jamaica Journal* 20:2 (1987), 1–7.

Richards, Glen, 'Friendly Societies and Labor Organisation in the Leeward Islands, 1912–19', in Moore and Wilmot, *Before & After 1865*, 136–149, 390–391.

Rivera-Pagán, Luis R., 'Freedom and Servitude: Indigenous Slavery and the Spanish Conquest of the Caribbean', in Jalil Sued-Badillo, ed., *Autochonous Societies*. General History of the Caribbean, 1, Basingstoke: Macmillan for UNESCO, 2003, 316–362.

Roberts, Franklin A., *The Origin and Development of Methodism in Spanish Town and its Environs, 1791–1841*. William Fish Lecture, Kingston, Methodist Book Centre, 1977.

Roberts, George W., *The Population of Jamaica*. Cambridge: Cambridge University Press, 1957.

Robertson, Glory, 'Death of a Constitution', *Jamaican Historical Society Bulletin* 5 (1972), 175–181.

_____ 'Some Early Jamaican Postcards: their Photographers and Publishers', *Jamaica Journal* 18:1 (1985), 13–22.

Robertson, James, 'Inherited Cityscapes: Spanish Town, Jamaica', in Malm, ed., *Towards an Archaeology of Buildings*, 89–104.

_____ 'Jamaican Architectures before Georgian', *Winterthur Portfolio* 36 (2001), 73-95.

_____ 'Jamaican Archival Resources for Seventeenth and Eighteenth Century Atlantic History', *Slavery & Abolition* 14 (2001), 109–40.

_____ 'Re-inventing the English conquest of Jamaica in the Late Seventeenth Century', *English Historical Review* 117 (2002), 813–39.

_____ '"Stories" and "Histories" in Late Seventeenth-Century Jamaica', in Monteith and Richards, *Jamaica in Slavery and Freedom*, 25–51.

_____ 'Stuart London and the Idea of a Royal Capital City', *Renaissance Studies* 15 (2001), 37–58.

_____ 'The Last Cromwellian Victory: Rio Nuevo, 15–17 June, 1658', *Jamaican Historical Society Bulletin* 11:10 (2002), 285–294.

Robotham, Don, 'Nineteen Thirty Eight', in Kari Levitt and Michael Witter, eds., *The Critical Tradition of Caribbean Political Economy: The Legacy of George Beckford*. Kingston: Ian Randle Publishers, 1996, 119–28.

Rollinson, David, *Railways of the Caribbean*. Basingstoke: Macmillan Caribbean, 2001.

Rothblatt, Sheldon, *The Revolution of the Dons: Cambridge and Society in Victorian England*. New York: Basic Books, 1968.

Russell, Horace O., *The Missionary Outreach of the West Indian Church: Jamaican Baptist Missions to West Africa in the Nineteenth Century*. New York: Peter Lang, 2000.

Ryan, Alan, 'Transformation, 1850-1914', in John Buxton and Penry Williams, eds., *New College, Oxford, 1379–1979*. Oxford: New College, 1979, 72–106.

Ryden, David, '"One of the fertilest, pleasantest Spotts": an Analysis of the Slave Economy in Jamaica's St Andrew Parish', *Slavery & Abolition* 21 (2000), 32–55.

Rykwert, Joseph, *The Palladian Ideal*. New York: Rizzoli, 1999.

Said, Edward W., 'Invention, Memory, and Place', *Critical Inquiry* 26 (2000), 175–92.

St. Pierre, Paul Matthew, 'Grant Allen (24 February 1848-28 October 1899)', in W.H. New, ed., *Canadian Writers, 1890–1920*. Dictionary of Literary Biography, 92, Detroit, Mich: Gale Research, 1990, 3-9.

Samaroo, Brimsley, 'The Caribbean Consequences of the Indian Revolt of 1857', in Fouch, *et al. Regards sur l'historie de la Caraïbe*, 439–54.

Satchell, Veront M., 'Early Use of Steam Power in the Jamaican Sugar Industry, 1768–1810', *Transactions of the Newcomen Society* 67 (1996), 221–31.

_____ 'Steam for Sugar-Cane Milling: The Diffusion of the Boulton and Watt Stationary Steam Engine to the Jamaican Sugar Industry, 1809–1830', in Monteith and Richards, *Jamaica in Slavery and Freedom* 242–58.

Satchell, Veront M., and Cezley Sampson, 'The rise and fall of railways in Jamaica, 1845–1975', *Journal of Transport History* 24 (2003), 1–21.

Schofield, John, 'Urban Housing in England 1400–1600', in David Gaimster and Paul Stamper, eds., *The Age of Transition: The Archaeology of English Culture, 1400–1600*. Oxford: Oxbow, 1997, 127–44.

Schuler, Monica, *'Alas, Alas, Kongo': A Social History of Indentured African Immigration into Jamaica, 1841–1865*. Baltimore, Md: John Hopkins, 1980.

Sealy, Theodore, and Herbert Hart, *Jamaica's Banana Industry: A History of the Banana Industry with particular reference to the part played by The Jamaican Banana Producers Association Ltd*. Clinton V. Black, ed. Kingston: Jamaica Banana Producers Association, 1984.

Senior, Carl H., 'Asiatic Cholera in Jamaica (1850–1855)', *Jamaica Journal* 26:2 (1997), 25–42.

_____ 'German Immigrants to Jamaica, 1834–8', *Journal of Caribbean History* 10 & 11 (1978), 25–53.

Shepherd, Verene, 'The Politics of Migration: Government Policy towards Indians in Jamaica, 1845–1945', in Moore and Wilmot, edn. *Before and After 1865*, 177–89, 394–95.

_____ *Transients to Settlers: The Experience of Indians in Jamaica, 1845–1950*. Leeds: Peepal Tree, 1993.

Sheridan, Richard, 'The Formation of Caribbean Plantation Society, 1689–1748', in P.J. Marshall. ed., *The Eighteenth Century*. Oxford History of the British Empire, 2, Oxford: Oxford University Press, 1998, 394–414.

_____ 'The Jamaican Slave Insurrection Scare of 1776 and the American Revolution', *Journal of Negro History* 61 (1976), 290–308.

Sherlock, Philip, *Norman Manley*. London: Macmillan, 1980.

Sherlock, Philip and Hazel Bennett, *The Story of the Jamaican People*. Kingston: Ian Randle Publishers, 1998.

Sherlock, Philip and Rex Nettleford, *The University of the West Indies: A Caribbean response to the challenge of change*. Basingstoke: Macmillan Caribbean, 1990.

Simmonds, Lorna, 'The Afro-Jamaican and the Internal Marketing System: Kingston, 1780–1834', in Monteith and Richards, eds., *Jamaica in Slavery and Freedom*, 274–90.

Sires, Ronald V., 'Governmental Crisis in Jamaica, 1860–1866', *Jamaican Historical Review* 2:2 (1953), 1–26.

_____ 'The Jamaican Constitution of 1884', *Social and Economic Studies* 3 (1954), 64–81.

Smail, Daniel Lord, 'The Linguistic Cartography of Property and Power in Late Medieval Marseille', in Barbara A. Hanawalt and Michael Kobialka, eds., *Medieval Practices of Space*. Medieval Cultures, 23, Minneapolis, Minn: University of Minnesota Press, 2000, 37–63.

Smith-McCrea, Rosalie, 'Fiction, Personality and Property: A Jamaican Colonial Representation in Miniature', in *In Tribute to David Boxer: Twenty Years at the*

National Gallery of Jamaica, 1975–1995. Kingston: Institute of Jamaica, 1995, 4–9.

Spurdle, Frederick G., *Early West Indian Government: Showing the Progress of Government in Barbados, Jamaica and the Leeward Islands, 1660–1783.* Palmerston North, New Zealand: the author, 1963.

Stanley, Brian, *A History of the Baptist Missionary Society, 1792–1992.* Edinburgh: T&T Clark, 1992.

Steel, M.J., 'A Philosophy of Fear: The World View of the Jamaican Plantocracy in a Comparative Perspective', *Journal of Caribbean History* 27 (1993), 1–20.

Stewart, Robert J., *Religion and Society in Post-Emancipation Jamaica.* Knoxville, Tenn: University of Tennessee Press, 1992.

Stolberg, Claus F., 'British Colonial Policy and the Great Depression – The Case of Jamaica', *Journal of Caribbean History* 23 (1989), 142–60.

_____ 'Plantation Economy, Peasantry and the Land Settlement Schemes of the 1930s and 1940s in Jamaica', in idem. and Swithin R. Wilmot, eds., *Plantation Economy, Land Reform and the Peasantry in a Historical Perspective, Jamaica 1838–1980.* Kingston: Friedrich Ebert Stifung, 1992, 39–68.

Sturtz, Linda L., 'The 1780 Hurricane donation: "Insult offered instead of relief"' *Jamaican Historical Review* 21 (2001), 38-46, 66–9.

Summers, R.F.K., *A History of the South African Museum, 1825- 1975.* Cape Town: A.A. Balkema for the Trustees, 1975.

Taylor, Clare, 'Planter Attitudes to the American and French Revolutions', *National Library of Wales Journal* 21 (1979), 113–130.

_____ 'The Williams Brothers: Welsh Stone Masons in Jamaica', *Jamaican Historical Society Bulletin* 8:1 (1981), 10–12.

Taylor, Frank Fonda, *To Hell with Paradise: A History of the Jamaican Tourist Industry.* Pittsburgh, Penn: University of Pittsburgh Press, 1993.

Taylor, S.A.G., *The Western Design: An Account of Cromwell's Expedition to the Caribbean.* Kingston: Institute of Jamaica and Jamaica Historical Society, 1965.

Thomas, Mary E., 'Jamaica and the US Civil War', *Americas* 24 (1972), 25–32.

Thompson, Edward, *The Life of Charles, Lord Metcalfe.* London: Faber, 1937.

Thornton, A.P., *West India Policy Under the Restoration.* Oxford: Oxford University Press, 1956.

Thornton, John K., 'The African Experiences of the "20. and odd negroes" Arriving in Virginia in 1619', *William & Mary Quarterly* 3rd ser 55 (1998), 421–34.

Thorp, John, 'Town Houses of the Late Seventeenth and Early Eighteenth Centuries,' in Beacham, *Devon Building,* 116–27, 165.

Trevor-Roper, Hugh, *From Counter-Reformation to Glorious Revolution.* London: Secker and Warburg, 1992.

Turner, Mary, 'Religious beliefs', in Franklin W. Knight, ed., *The Slave Societies of the Caribbean.* General History of the Caribbean, 3. Basingstoke: Macmillan for UNESCO, 1997, 287–321.

_____ *Slaves and Missionaries: The Disintegration of Jamaican Slave Society, 1787–1834*. Chicago, Ill: University of Illinois Press, 1982, reprint. Kingston: University of the West Indies Press, 1998.

Turner, Trevor A., 'The Socialisation Intent in Colonial Jamaican Education, 1867–1911', (1977), in Ruby Hope King, ed., *Education in the Caribbean*, 54–87.

Tyndale-Biscoe, J.S., 'Arawak Specimens from some middens of Jamaica', *Jamaican Historical Society Bulletin* 1:10 (1954), 123–27.

Upton, Dell, *Holy Things and Profane: Anglican Parish Churches in Colonial Virginia*. Boston, Mass: Massachusetts Institute of Technology, 1986, reprint. New Haven, Conn: Yale University Press, 1997.

Van Andel, Joan D., *Caribbean Traditional Architecture: The Traditional Architecture of Philipsburg, St Martin (NA)*. Antillen Working Papers, 10, Leiden: Caraibische Afdeling Koninklijl Instituut voor Taal-, Land- en Volkenkunde, 1986.

Verger, Pierre, *Bahia and the West Coast Trade (1549–1851)*. Ibadan: Ibadan University Press, 1964.

Vendryes, Harry, 'Great Fires of Kingston: the Fisher Fire of 1862', *Jamaican Historical Society Bulletin* 3:15 (1961), 26–28.

_____ 'Great Fires of Kingston: the James the Founder Fire of 1843', *Jamaican Historical Society Bulletin* 6:15 (1976), 277–282.

Venning, Timothy, *Cromwellian Foreign Policy*. Basingstoke: Macmillan, 1995.

Walker, Daniel E., 'Colony versus Crown: Raising Black Troops for the British Siege of Havana, 1762', *Journal of Caribbean History* 33 (1999), 74–83.

Walvin, James, *The Life and Times of Henry Clarke of Jamaica, 1828–1907*. London: Frank Cass, 1994.

Ward, J.B., *British West Indian Slavery, 1750–1834: The Process of Amelioration*. Oxford: Oxford University Press, 1988.

Watts, Arthur P., *Une Histoire des Colonies Anglaises aux Antilles (de 1649 à 1660)*. Paris: Presses Universitaires de France, 1924.

Weiss, Joaquin E., *La Arquitectura Colonial Cubana*. 2 vols. Havana: Editorial Letras Cubanas, 1972, reprint. in one volume, Havana and Seville: Instituto Cubano del Libro and Conserjerio de Obras Publicas y Transportes, 1996.

Welch, Pedro L.V., *Slave Society in the City: Bridgetown, Barbados 1680–1834*. Kingston: Ian Randle Publishers, 2003.

Welds, Jacqueline, 'The Bank Secretary Embezzled the Money', *Jamaican Historical Society Bulletin* 5:8 (1970), 110–113.

Whelan, Kevin, 'Towns and Villages', in F.A.H. Aalen, Kevin Whelan and Matthew Stout, eds., *Atlas of the Irish Rural Landscape*. Cork: Cork University Press, 1997, 180–96.

Whiffen, Marcus, *The Public Buildings of Williamsburg, Colonial Capital of Virginia: An Architectural History*. Williamsburg Architectural Studies, 1, Williamsburg, Va: Colonial Williamsburg, 1958.

Whinney, Margaret, *Wren*. London: Thames & Hudson, 1971.

Wilmot, Swithin R., "'A Stake in the Soil": Land and Creole Politics in Free Jamaica, the 1849 Elections', in Alvin O. Thompson, ed., *In the Shadow of the Plantation: Caribbean History and Legacy*. Kingston: Ian Randle Publishers, 2002, 314–33.

_____ 'Baptist Missionaries and Jamaican Politics, 1838–54', in Keith Laurence, ed., *A Selection of Papers Presented at the Twelfth Conference of the Association of Caribbean Historians (1980)*. [St Augustine, Trinidad]: Association of Caribbean Historians, 1986, 45–62.

_____ 'Black Space/Room to Manoeuvre: Land and Politics in Trelawny in the Immediate Post-Emancipation Period', in Stolberg and Wilmot, *Plantation Economy, Land Reform and the Peasantry*, 15–22.

_____ 'Emancipation in Action: Workers and Wage Conflict in Jamaica 1838–40', *Jamaica Journal* 19:3 (1986), 55–62.

_____ *Freedom in Jamaica: Challenges and Opportunities, 1838–1865*. Kingston: Jamaica Information Service, 1997.

_____ 'From Bondage to Political Office: Blacks and Vestry Politics in Two Jamaican Parishes, Kingston and St David, 1831-1865', in Monteith and Richards, *Jamaica in Slavery and Freedom*, 307–23.

_____ 'Politics and Labour Conflicts in Jamaica: 1838–1865', in Levitt and Witter, *The Critical Tradition of Caribbean Political Economy*, 101–117.

_____ 'Politics at the "Grassroots" in Free Jamaica: St James, 1838–1865', in Shepherd, *Working Slavery, Pricing Freedom*, 449–466.

_____ 'Race, Electoral Violence and Constitutional Reform in Jamaica, 1830–54', *Journal of Caribbean History* 17 (1982), 1–13.

_____ 'The Growth of Black Political Activity in Post-Emancipation Jamaica', in Lewis and Bryan, *Garvey*, 39–46.

_____ "'The Old Older Changeth": Vestry Politics in two of Jamaica's Parishes, Portland and Metcalfe, 1838–65', in Moore and Wilmot, *Before and After 1865*, 101–111, 384–87.

_____ 'The Politics of Protest in Free Jamaica – The Kingston John Canoe Riots, 1840 and 1841', *Caribbean Quarterly* 36: 3&4 (1990): 65–75.

_____ 'The Politics of Samuel Clarke: Black Creole Politician in Free Jamaica, 1851–1868', in Verene A. Shepherd and Glen L. Richards, eds., *Questioning Creole: Creolisation Discourse in Caribbean Culture*. Kingston: Ian Randle Publishers, 2002, 227–42.

Will, H.A., 'Problems of Constitutional Reform in Jamaica, Mauritius and Trinidad, 1880-1895', *English Historical Review* 81 (1966), 693–716.

Williams, I.L., 'The Urbanity of Marlborough: a Wiltshire Town in the Seventeenth Century', *Wiltshire Studies: Wiltshire Archaeological and Natural History Magazine* 94 (2001), 139–47.

Winks, Robin W., *Canadian-West Indian Union: A Forty-Year Minuet*. Institute of

Commonwealth Studies, Commonwealth Paper, 11, London: Athlone, 1968.

Woodward, Robyn, '*Sevilla La Nueva* Archaeological Project, 2002', *Archaeology Jamaica* n.s. 14 (2002), 8–9.

Worsley, Giles, *Classical Architecture in Britain: The Heroic Age*. New Haven, Con: Yale University Press, 1995.

Wright, Irene, *Santiago de Cuba and its District (1607–1640)*. Madrid: Felipe Pena Cruz, 1918.

_____ 'The Early History of Jamaica, 1511–1536', *English Historical Review* 36 (1921), 76–95.

_____ 'The Spanish Resistance to the English Occupation of Jamaica, 1655–1660', *Transactions of the Royal Historical Society* 4th ser 13 (1930), 117–147.

Wright, Philip, and Gabriel Debien, 'Les colons de Saint-Domingue passés à la Jamaïque (1792–1835)', *Bulletin de la société d'historie de la Guadeloupe* 26 (1975).

Wright, Richardson, *Revels in Jamaica, 1682–1838*. New York, 1936, reprint Kingston: Bolivar, 1986.

Wynter, Sylvia, *New Seville: Major Facts, Major Questions*. Kingston: Jamaica National Heritage Commission, 1984.

New Seville, Major Dates: 1509–1536 with an aftermath 1537–1655. Kingston: Jamaica National Trust Commission, 1984.

Young, J.G., 'The Founding of Kingston', in W. Adolphe Roberts, ed., *The Capitals of Jamaica*. Kingston: Pioneer Press, 1955, 38–47.

_____ 'Who Planned Kingston?' *Jamaican Historical Review* 1 1946, 144–53.

Zahedieh, Nuala, 'A Frugal, Prudential and Hopeful Trade: Privateering in Jamaica, 1655–89', *Journal of Imperial and Commonwealth History* 18 (1990), 145–68.

_____ 'The Capture of the Blue Dove, 1664: Policy, Profits and Protection in Early English Jamaica', in Roderick A. McDonald, ed., *West Indies Accounts: Essays on the History of the British Caribbean and the Atlantic Economy*. Kingston: University of the West Indies Press, 1996, 29–47.

_____ '"The wickedest city in the world": Port Royal, Commercial Hub of the seventeenth-century Caribbean', in Shepherd, *Working Slavery, Pricing Freedom*. 3–20.

Index
—

crisis in Britain, 190, oust Sir Lionel
Smith, 171, 190; tax policy shelters
plantations, weighs on peasants, 191;
contributions to places of worship,
169, 177; funds geological surveys and
Port Morant lighthouse, 185;
incorporate Jamaica Railway
Company, 186, 190; plan to dis-
establish Anglican church prompt
snap election, 189; retroactive
authorization for sale of property of
Fletcher's charity, 350 n73; rejection of
two education acts in 1856, 388 n 102;
Lady Barkly's archery parties for
Assemblymens' wives, 265; debates on
extending railway, not deliver, 188, 373
n92; ending Spanish Town races a
disincentive for Assemblymen, 194;
policy of 'retrenchment' provokes
stalemate, 193; protest end of sugar
duties by refusing to pass revenue
bills, English government not
concede, 194; Constitutional reform
to de-fang Assembly, 194–5; bill to
absorb British Post Office's charges
unpopular, Anthony Trollope
unimpressed, 197–8; in period of high
unemployment plans for recruiting
further labour, 200; Assemblyman
Gordon executed after Morant Bay,
204; alter Constitution, 205–6;
surrender it, 206–7; recalled to
authorize Commission of Enquiry,
207; clock to Government Audit
Office, Kingston, 217; canons in its
foundations, 263; Beckford and
Smith's School use, 261, 265, 266; not
considered for House of
Representatives in 1944, 288.
Audiencia, 28, 53, 83, 98.
avocados, 394 n30.

Bacon, John, sculptor, Assembly
commissions statue of Admiral
Rodney, 127, 128 (illustration).
Baker, Lorenzo Dow, 247, *see also* United
Fruit Company.
bananas, 240, 247, 256, 271, Spanish
introduce from Canary Islands, 35;
gros michel transplanted from
Martinique, known as *martinick*, 172;
Abyssinian banana at Cinchona, 394
n31; attempts to develop blight-
resistant strains, 272–4.
Banks, 241, failure of Planters' Bank, 188;
restrictions on colonial banks taking
mortgages as security, 384, n52;
Government Savings Bank, 214, 220,
255; Colonial Bank, nearly collapses,
250, 270, and Bank of Nova Scotia
receives Government's accounts, 402
n136; Bank of Nova Scotia's branches
in Spanish Town and elsewhere, 392
n5; Lower St Catherine's People's
Cooperative Bank, 287, 409, n209; St
Catherine Mutual Building Society,
287, 409 n209.
baobob trees, 88.
Baptists, 12, 123, 130, 135–6, 151–2, 161,
170, 179; schools, 154–5, new chapel,
156–8, 178, 363 n141, 157 (illustration),
focal point for celebrations in 1838,
164–6; Native Baptists, 176, 177, 235,
preservation status for Phillippo
Chapel, 305. *see also*, Churches;
Duggan, William; Ebenezer Chapel;
Gibbs, George; Missionaries; Liele,
George; Phillippo, James Munsell.
Barkly, Sir Henry, British Governor,
education acts rejected by Assembly,
388 n102; Lady Barkly's archery
parties, 265.
barracks, in Spanish Town, 76, 84, 113–4,

English Mechanics, Independent United Order of, 242.

English raids on Spanish Jamaica, Sir Anthony Shirley, 1597, 35, 46, 325 n21; Christopher Newport, 1603, 32–34, 35; William Jackson, 1642, 35, 46.

Episcopalians, *see* Anglicans.

Escape to Last Man Peak, by Jean D'Costa, 11.

Ewarton, 198, 246, 253.

Executive Committee, formerly Governor's Council, elevated to a second chamber, 195, members invoke House of Lords, 376 n128; their room in Spanish Town, 217, succeeded by Legislative Council.

Eyre, Edward, British Governor, 204, 210, 288, ominous swearing in, 209, dry dock scheme, 200, 377 n147; uses prison labour and imports when refurnishing King's House on Assembly's grant, 201, 378 n152; will not listen to Baptists' suggestions, 202–3; scaremongering and a new constitution, 205; not vindicated by Commission of Enquiry, 206–7.

Falmouth, Trelawny, 143, 170, 198.

Federation of the West Indies, referendum, 300.

Ferry River, 17, 234, 403 n142.

Feurtado, William Augustus, raconteur, 6; records searcher, 384 n53.

fire, burning of King's House, 11, 272; Kingston burns in 1843 and 1862, 188–9, again in 1907, 238, 256, 272, 384 n52; fire brigades in Kingston, 214, and Spanish Town 222.

Fletcher, George, benefactor, vestry's sale of lands authorised retroactively, 350 n73.

floods, 17, destroy incomplete Rio Cobre dam, 234.

Folk Museum, *see* People's Museum

forts, in Spanish Town, stockades in Parade, 41; Fort Henry to south, 43, 53; report of fort behind the church, 69; in Port Royal, a battery becomes Fort Cromwell, 45, renamed Fort Charles, 53, nearly explodes, 112; Fort Augusta, 112–3, 116, 142, 330 n44.

Franciscans, friary of St John, 25.

free black community, Spanish Town, 85; 91–2, 142, enfranchised, 161.

Free Foresters, Ancient Order of, 242.

free villages, 169-70, 173, *see also*, Sligoville.

Freeman, W.G. author of *Pickwick Jamaica*, 369 n34.

Freemasons, 242, 245, 1754 jollification, 78; in late nineteenth-century politicians' careers, 392 n9.

Fuller, Alexander, 170.

Gage, Thomas, ex-friar, author *English-American*, expert on Spanish West Indies, interpreter, 38, preaches and buried in parish church, 63.

Garvey, Marcus, stories about, 262, in St Catherine District Prison, 262, 270, Governor's fears welcome at end of his sentence, 270; People's Party proposals for a Jamaican University, 233, 388 n114; Rastafarians attribute prophecy to, 303, *see also*, Universal Negro Improvement Association.

geological surveys, 185, an oil expert, 294, hopes for kaolin clay, 294–96.

George V, as Prince visits Jamaica in 1884, 402 n130.

George VI, coronation celebrations in Spanish Town, 261–2.

Georgian Society of Jamaica,

King's House, Spanish Town, 137, 145,
149–150, 162, 197, 198, 203, rebuilt
1711 and further extensions, 71; 1760s,
foundations reused, 72, 1760s, 98–9,
138 (illustrations), 99–100, 109–10;
expectations of hospitality, 112, balls,
124, 110 (illustration); a landmark, 117;
West India Regiment provide guards,
142; refurbishment, as employment
scheme or for Governor's comfort,
201; Paul Bogle and delegation get no
hearing, 203; provokes discussions of
a move to Kingston, 215; houses a
University, 211; some Jamaican visitors
in 1870s, 253; Governor uses after
1907 earthquake destroy's King's
House in Kingston, 274; houses
Cathedral High School for girls, 266;
burns, 1925, 11, 272, 279; Folk
Museum (now People's Museum), 302
archaeology at, xiii, 305, fate of site
notes, 414, n59, continuing potential
for re-use, 314; Emancipation Square,
314.
Kingston, development: founded after
1692 earthquake, 65–6, 336 n3;
intended as seat of government, 66; a
flourishing slave trading centre
encourages disease, 79–80.
Kingston Chronicle, proposals for College
of Physicians and Surgeons, 184.
Kingston Harbour, 56, 171-2, Guavayara,
name for today's Kingston Harbour,
44, 330, n42; Newport anchors in, 33;
Liele baptizes converts, 130; prison
hulks in, 135; steam ferry service, 172;
perhaps a mechanised dry dock, 200,
377 n147; flying boat depot in, 290.
Knowles, Admiral Charles, 337 n11,
British Governor, 215, moves capital
to Kingston, 89–93.

Labouring Class Political Party, brief
identity for St Catherine trade union,
then join Coombs, 286.
Lady Albion's Caribbean University, 230.
land settlement, proposed as social
remedy, 283, Land Settlement Law of
1920, 283; Coolshades scheme in
northern St Catherine, 283, 407 n192,
Twickenham Park as candidate, 283.
Along with Portmore, 284, but
Legislative Council not persuaded,
284.
lavender, 63.
Legg, Lt Col Edward, 187.
Legislative Council, succeeds Executive
Committee, few Jamaican voices, 218.
Leper Hospital, 252, 291, from Kingston
to Hellshire in 1860s, 221, to Spanish
Town in 1890s, 221–2; a local
grievance in 1935, 281–2; Governor
tours, 282; still an issue in 1939, 283;
Marist nuns to run, 287.
Levy, Isaac, future custos, running a rum
shop, 262.
Lewis, Matthew, 'Monk', 144, 178.
Liele, George, evangelist, 130, 134, 136;
invoked, 177.
Liguanea, St Andrew, 17, 56, 303, Spanish
name retained, 44; Sunday market,
336 n2; settlement flattened in
earthquake, 66.
Linstead, St Ann, 198, 243, 393 n13;
market, 199–200, 205, shops, 200,
202; speech by Bustamante, 278.
Literary and Reading Society, 265.
Liverpool, merchants' petition, 90.
Long, Edward, 223, eighteenth-century
historian of Jamaica, 6; house in
town, 5, 317 n15; comments on
Kingston and Spanish Town's roads,
5; *History of Jamaica*, engravings,

152, fund teaching assistant at Baptist
school, 155; Church of Scotland
(Presbyterian), 136; Congregation-
alists, 136; Moravians, 136; Wesleyan
Methodist Missionary Society, 12, 121,
133, 150–1.
Modyford, Sir Thomas, British
Governor, grave slab, 63.
Molesworth, Sir John, Bart, 85.
Moneague, St Ann, 98, 370 n42.
The Monk, by Matthew Lewis, 144.
Montego Bay, St James, 120, 121, 143, 175;
railway extension, 248, arrives, 249;
banana boats and tourists, 254, 256; a
bank of Nova Scotia branch, 392 n5;
air travel and tourists, 290; Charles
Square (now Sam Sharpe Square),
campaign for Federation of the West
Indies, 300.
Morant Bay, St Thomas, also Morante,
32, 297, English retain Spanish name,
44; Port Morant iron lighthouse, 185;
riot, 205; put down as a rebellion,
203–4, 205, 379 n168.
Morris, William, Canadian legislator,
107, 168.
Mount Diablo, 17, may retain a Spanish-
era name, 44.
Mowatt, Andrew Duffus, 243, 393 n13.
Mulberry Gardens, Monk Street, tourists
visit in 1870s, 257, purchased for
parish Alms House, 257, dropped
from tourist itinerary, 257, early cycle
races held there, 266.
Musgrave, Sir Anthony, 219.
Newcastle, St Andrew, 141, 256.
New Seville, Spaniards' first capital in
Jamaica, 4; parallels with Santiago de
Cuba, 23; hopes for gold, find none,
18; claims that Spanish Town
healthier, 23; residents vote to leave,

23; French raiders destroy remaining
houses, 22, 32; aqueduct and ruins
remain, 51; granted to Hemmings
family, 53; proposed as World
Heritage site, 313–4.
Nightingale, Florence, 223.
Nugent, Sir George, British Governor, at
Port Henderson resort, 172, 368 n20;
street named for, 160.
obeah, 132–3, 356 n42.
Ocho Rios, St Ann, 256, 290, 311.
Odd Fellows, Independent Order of,
242, Grand United Order of, 242.
Oristán, 22, 323 n16.
Our Lady of Belén, Spanish hermitage,
becomes a sheep pen, 43.
Our Lady of Mercy, Dominican friars'
church, 24, 28 (illustration), 62.
Panama Disease, 279, 280, 281, kills *gros
michel* bananas, 272, attempts to find
resistant types, 272–4; lingers in soil,
290.
Passage Fort, English land at, 38; new
fort built, 43; market held near, 58;
butchering cattle, 58; Royal African
Company's barracoon there, 80;
rebuilt after earthquake, naval storehouse, 77; storm in 1722 wipes out,
340 n53, Portmore estate near, 284.
Peart, Reginald Albert, 406 n185.
People's Museum, 302, 308, 312.
People's National Party, victory in 1972
election, 305.
People's Party, celebrations at Garvey's
release a potential election boost, 270,
platform recommends a Jamaican
University, 233.
Perkins, Thomas, 115–6.
Perkins, William, 116, 350 n80.
Phillipo, Dr James, moves to Kingston,
269, 402 n 132; pamphleteering, 238.

Taino settlements, New Seville sited near one too, 21; White Marl, largest identified on island, 21; Taino settlement probably not underlying Spanish Town, 22, though burial mounds may well, 5; Henderson Hill site, perhaps post-Columbus, 325–6, n21; Maroons' possible continuity, 331 n50, *see also*, White Marl.

tamarinds, avenue of, 34, 257, 262, 297; surround a pond where a Gold Table lurks, 263.

Teach, Edward, 'Blackbeard', his mother, 77.

tourism, information signs for tourists, 256, scheduled drives, 261; Great Depression shrinks numbers, 278; arriving by air, 290, 292; Island Motor Highways proposal, an unsurpassed attraction, 292; numbers visiting Kingston shrinking, 305.

tourists, 240, itinerary for, 252–261, visits contract to 'ship night', 259; air travel, flying boats into Kingston, 290; hopeful estimates for numbers traversing Spanish Town, 293; expect historic architecture to look pretty, 302–3.

trade union, founded in Spanish Town, 13, spreads across parish, 283, protest unemployment, 280, articulates issues, 283, in 1938 affiliates with Bustamante Industrial Trade Union, 283 see also, Universal Negro Improvement Association.

Trinidad, 142, 191, 251, 396 n51, model for Crown Colony, 207; Imperial School of Tropical Agriculture and Panama Disease, 272, *see also* Port of Spain.

Trelawny parish, 301, *see also* Falmouth, Martha Brae.

Trinity Chapel (Anglican), 169, 176–7, 183.

Trollope, Anthony, novelist and Post Office bureaucrat, visits and unimpressed, 5, 196–8, 210, 215, 219, 237–8, 373, n92; scheme for Kingston to replace Virgin Islands as a terminus, 377 n147; 'going a-Trolloping', 215.

Twickenham Park Estate, 248, 283, 294, 294–7, 306.

Underhill, Edward Bean, Baptist minister, 'Underhill Surveys', 201–2, 378 n153.

United Fruit Company, 247, Jamaican foremen's expertise, 247–8; Twickenham Park Estate, 248; banana boats and tourism, 252–3, 261, 'Great White Fleet', 259, 260; Titchfield Hotel, Port Antonio, 253; plantation at Great Salt Ponds, 256; sugar factory at Bernard Lodge, 271; lease land at Gregory Park, 403 n144; responses to Panama Disease, 272; wants to sell Twickenham Park – a land settlement, 283, sell to Government, 294.

United Nations Educational, Scientific and Cultural Organization, (UNESCO), 1, 289, Spanish Town remains a candidate for World Heritage status, 313–4.

Universal Negro Improvement Association, (UNIA), 262, in Spanish Town, 13.

University of the West Indies (initially, University College of the West Indies), 227; pageantry installing first Chancellor at Cathedral, 299–300; new chapel, 301.

Up Park Camp, near Kingston, 139–140.

Venables, Robert, leads initial invasion, then leaves, 47.

Veracruz, 19.

Vere parish, 56, 251, its school, 339, n42; land offered for a Baptist training college, 184.

Vernam Field, Clarendon, Fort Simonds, US wartime base, 290, road to from Kingston, 292.

Vickars, Edward, Assenblyman, 168-9, 367 n9, 193.

Victoria, 164, 165, 167, 168, 174, 175, 204, 206, should Jamaica's slaves be freed on her Coronation day, 163, 365 n162; her emancipation proclamation, 163; royal assent to bill for new Jamaican government, 207.

Wag Water, river, name from Taino Guiguata, alternatively from Agua Alta, 44, 330 n41, *see also* Junction Road.

Warren, Thomas, Anglican clergyman, 131, 356 n34.

West India Committee, London, 275.

West India Improvement Company, 249, 395 n44, 250-1.

West India Regiment, 141, 142; standards in Cathedral, 255-6.

West Indies Chemical Works, 243.

Western Design, Cromwell's West Indian adventure, 36.

Westmorland parish, 144.

Whigs, British political party, 159, 160, 163; Jamaican political stubbornness leads to Prime Minister's offering resignation, 190; call Jamaica Assembly's bluff, 194.

White Marl, major Taino site, 21, 414 n54; excavations in 1890s, 304, still sliced through by 1940s road schemes, 304; site donated to Jamaica

National Trust Commission, 304; a museum constructed, 304, school trips, 308.

Wide Sargasso Sea, Jean Rhys, 289.

Wilberforce, William, British abolitionist, 134, 135.

William IV, 162, visits Spanish Town as Royal Naval lieutenant, 160, Queen Adelaide commemorated too, 160; signs Reform Bill and Abolition Act, 160; slaves know forthcoming, 161.

Williams, Francis, 74-5 (illustration), 344 n104.

Williamson, Lady Anne, monument for, husband Sir Arthur, Lieutenant Governor, 147.

Woodside, St Mary, 7.

women, a notorious strumpet, 78; residents' names used describing streets, 60, 118; servants, 174-5, 199, 378 n154; landladies, 60-1, 199, 237; seamstresses, 201, 202; vendors' 'Washerwoman Starch', 264; Lady Barkly's archery parties for Assemblymens' wives, 265; Cathedral High School, 267-8; social life for turn of twentieth-century elite women, 264, tennis, 265, an 'upper ten', 269; Order of Good Samaritans and Daughters of Samaria, 242; Girl Guide troops, 268; Lady Mary Swettenham, and committee for restoration of old King's House, 274-5; US troops date, 290; to decorate Island Worcester Company's porcelain, 295.

Yallas, Spanish name retained, 44; an old Spanish tavern, 51.

yellow fever, 81, 140-141, 213, in Spanish Town in 1955, 298.

Ysassi, Cristóbal de, *see* de Ysassi.